Volkswagen Automotive Repair Manual

by J H Haynes
Member of the Guild of Motoring Writers
and K F Kinchin

Models covered
UK: All VW Passat models with petrol engines
1296, 1471 & 1588 cc
USA: All VW Dasher models with gasoline engines
89.7 cu in (1.5 liter) & 97 cu in (1.6 liter)
Does not cover Diesel engined models
Does not cover 'new' Passat introduced September 1981

ISBN 0 85696 590 1 (Hardback)
ISBN 0 85696 962 1 (Paperback)

Printed in England *(238 - 4N3)*

ABCDE
FGHIJ
KLMNO
P

Haynes Publishing Group
Sparkford Nr Yeovil
Somerset BA22 7JJ England

Haynes Publications, Inc
861 Lawrence Drive
Newbury Park
California 91320 USA

Acknowledgements

Special thanks are due to the VW/Audi organisation for their assistance with technical information and the supply of certain illustrations; to Castrol Limited who provided lubrication details, and to the Champion Sparking Plug Company who supplied the illustrations showing the various spark plug conditions.

Mr Jack Hatcher of Dunnicks Mead Motors, Wedmore, Somerset provided invaluable help, he allowed us to examine and photograph several cars on his premises. We are indebted to him for his kind assistance.

About this manual

Its aim

The aim of this manual is to help you get the best value from your vehicle. It can do so in several ways. It can help you decide what work must be done (even should you choose to get it done by a garage), provide information on routine maintenance and servicing, and give a logical course of action and diagnosis when random faults occur. However, it is hoped that you will use the manual by tackling the work yourself. On simpler jobs it may even be quicker than booking the car into a garage and going there twice, to leave and collect it. Perhaps most important, a lot of money can be saved by avoiding the costs a garage must charge to cover its labour and overheads.

The manual has drawings and descriptions to show the function of the various components so that their layout can be understood. Then the tasks are described and photographed in a step-by-step sequence so that even a novice can do the work.

Its arrangement

The manual is divided into fourteen Chapters, each covering a logical sub-division of the vehicle. The Chapters are each divided into Sections, numbered with single figures, eg 5; and the Sections into paragraphs (or sub-sections), with decimal numbers following on from the Section they are in, eg 5.1, 5.2, 5.3 etc.

It is freely illustrated, especially in those parts where there is a detailed sequence of operations to be carried out. There are two forms of illustration: figures and photographs. The figures are numbered in sequence with decimal numbers, according to their position in the Chapter - eg Fig. 6.4 is the fourth drawing/illustration in Chapter 6. Photographs carry the same number (either individually or in related groups) as the Section or sub-section to which they relate.

There is an alphabetical index at the back of the manual as well as a contents list at the front. Each Chapter is also preceded by its own individual contents list.

References to the 'left' or 'right' of the vehicle are in the sense of a person in the driver's seat facing forwards.

Unless otherwise stated, nuts and bolts are removed by turning anti-clockwise, and tightened by turning clockwise.

Vehicle manufacturers continually make changes to specifications and recommendations, and these, when notified, are incorporated into our manuals at the earliest opportunity.

Whilst every care is taken to ensure that the information in this manual is correct, no liability can be accepted by the authors or publishers for loss, damage or injury caused by any errors in, or omissions from, the information given.

Introduction to the VW Passat and Dasher

The VW Passat was introduced to the UK market in 1973, whilst its North American equivalent the Dasher appeared in the USA for the 1974 model year. The vehicles have a strong family resemblance to the Audi 80 and Audi Fox respectively, though many features are completely different.

The Passat/Dasher differs from other front wheel drive VWs in having the engine orientated in the 'north-south' axis rather than 'east-west'. The engine is inclined to one side in order to keep the bonnet line low. The transmission is located behind the engine.

Three engine sizes have been used for the range in the UK of which only the largest two have crossed the Atlantic. Fuel injection was fitted to USA models at a relatively early stage, because of the stringent emission control regulations.

The Passat was superseded by the New Passat, introduced for the 1982 model year. There is no doubt, however, that we shall be seeing the 'old' models around for many years to come, such is the strength and reliability of these vehicles.

Contents

Volkswagen Passat LS- 1975 model (UK)

Volkswagen Passat 1300 2 door (basic) - 1974 model (UK)
Inset: Volkswagen Dasher. This is the North American version of the same model

Buying spare parts and vehicle identification numbers

Buying spare parts

Spare parts are available from many sources, for example: VW/Audi garages, other garages and accessory shops, and motor factors. Our advice regarding spare part sources is as follows:

Officially appointed VW/Audi garages - This is the best source of parts which are peculiar to your vehicle and are otherwise not generally available (eg; complete cylinder heads, internal gearbox components, badges, interior trim etc). It is also the only place at which you should buy parts if your car is still under warranty - non-VW/Audi components may invalidate the warranty. To be sure of obtaining the correct parts it will always be necessary to give the storeman your car's engine and chassis number, and if possible, to take the 'old' part along for positive identification. Remember that many parts are available on a factory exchange scheme - any parts returned should always be clean! It obviously makes good sense to go straight to the specialists on your car for this type of part for they are best equipped to supply you.

Other garages and accessory shops - These are often very good places to buy materials and components needed for the maintenance of your car (eg; oil filters, spark plugs, bulbs, fan belts, oils and greases, touch-up paint, filler paste etc). They also sell general accessories, usually have convenient opening hours, charge lower prices and can often be found not far from home.

Motor factors - Good factors will stock all of the more important components which wear out relatively quickly (eg; clutch components, pistons, valves, exhaust system, brake cylinders/pipes/hoses/seals/shoes and pads etc). Motor factors will often provide new or reconditioned components on a part exchange basis - this can save a considerable amount of money.

Vehicle identification numbers

It is most important to identify the vehicle accurately when ordering spares or asking for information. The *vehicle identification plate* is in the engine compartment by the right-hand bonnet hinge (photo). This is the car's 'birth certificate'. Just behind the washer reservoir in the centre of the engine compartment rear wall the *chassis number plate* is fixed under the fresh air inlet.

The *engine number* is stamped on the cylinder block just above the fuel pump/distributor, and the *transmission code* is stamped on the top of the bellhousing.

These numbers should be identified and recorded by the owner, they are required when ordering spares, going through the customs, and regrettably, by the police, if the vehicle is stolen.

When ordering spares remember that VW/Audi output is such that inevitably spares vary, are duplicated, and are held on a usage basis. If the storeman does not have the correct identification, he cannot produce the correct item. It is a good idea to take the old part if possible to compare it with a new one. The storeman has many customers to satisfy, so be accurate and patient. In some cases, particularly in the brake system, more than one manufacturer supplies an assembly (eg; both Teves and Girling supply front calipers. The assemblies are interchangeable but the integral parts are not, although both use the same brake pads. This is only one of the pitfalls in the buying of spares, so be careful to make an ally of the storeman. When fitting accessories it is best to fit VW/Audi recommended ones. They are designed specifically for the vehicle.

The vehicle's identification plate located on the right-hand side of the engine compartment just below the bonnet hinge

The engine number on the cylinder block just above the distributor

Safety first!

Regardless of how enthusiastic you may be about getting on with the job at hand, take the time to ensure that your safety is not jeopardized. A moment's lack of attention can result in an accident, as can failure to observe certain simple safety precautions. The possibility of an accident will always exist, and the following points should not be considered a comprehensive list of all dangers. Rather, they are intended to make you aware of the risks and to encourage a safety conscious approach to all work you carry out on your vehicle.

Essential DOs and DON'Ts

DON'T rely on a jack when working under the vehicle. Always use approved jackstands to support the weight of the vehicle and place them under the recommended lift or support points.
DON'T attempt to loosen extremely tight fasteners (i.e. wheel lug nuts) while the vehicle is on a jack – it may fall.
DON'T start the engine without first making sure that the transmission is in Neutral (or Park where applicable) and the parking brake is set.
DON'T remove the radiator cap from a hot cooling system – let it cool or cover it with a cloth and release the pressure gradually.
DON'T attempt to drain the engine oil until you are sure it has cooled to the point that it will not burn you.
DON'T touch any part of the engine or exhaust system until it has cooled sufficiently to avoid burns.
DON'T siphon toxic liquids such as gasoline, antifreeze and brake fluid by mouth, or allow them to remain on your skin.
DON'T inhale brake lining dust – it is potentially hazardous (see *Asbestos* below)
DON'T allow spilled oil or grease to remain on the floor – wipe it up before someone slips on it.
DON'T use loose fitting wrenches or other tools which may slip and cause injury.
DON'T push on wrenches when loosening or tightening nuts or bolts. Always try to pull the wrench toward you. If the situation calls for pushing the wrench away, push with an open hand to avoid scraped knuckles if the wrench should slip.
DON'T attempt to lift a heavy component alone – get someone to help you.
DON'T rush or take unsafe shortcuts to finish a job.
DON'T allow children or animals in or around the vehicle while you are working on it.
DO wear eye protection when using power tools such as a drill, sander, bench grinder, etc. and when working under a vehicle.
DO keep loose clothing and long hair well out of the way of moving parts.
DO make sure that any hoist used has a safe working load rating adequate for the job.
DO get someone to check on you periodically when working alone on a vehicle.
DO carry out work in a logical sequence and make sure that everything is correctly assembled and tightened.
DO keep chemicals and fluids tightly capped and out of the reach of children and pets.
DO remember that your vehicle's safety affects that of yourself and others. If in doubt on any point, get professional advice.

Asbestos

Certain friction, insulating, sealing, and other products – such as brake linings, brake bands, clutch linings, torque converters, gaskets, etc. – contain asbestos. *Extreme care must be taken to avoid inhalation of dust from such products since it is hazardous to health.* If in doubt, assume that they *do* contain asbestos.

Fire

Remember at all times that gasoline is highly flammable. Never smoke or have any kind of open flame around when working on a vehicle. But the risk does not end there. A spark caused by an electrical short circuit, by two metal surfaces contacting each other, or even by static electricity built up in your body under certain conditions, can ignite gasoline vapors, which in a confined space are highly explosive. Do not, under any circumstances, use gasoline for cleaning parts. Use an approved safety solvent.

Always disconnect the battery ground (–) cable *at the battery* before working on any part of the fuel system or electrical system. Never risk spilling fuel on a hot engine or exhaust component.

It is strongly recommended that a fire extinguisher suitable for use on fuel and electrical fires be kept handy in the garage or workshop at all times. Never try to extinguish a fuel or electrical fire with water.

Torch (flashlight in the US)

Any reference to a "torch" appearing in this manual should always be taken to mean a hand-held, battery-operated electric light or flashlight. It DOES NOT mean a welding or propane torch or blowtorch.

Fumes

Certain fumes are highly toxic and can quickly cause unconsciousness and even death if inhaled to any extent. Gasoline vapor falls into this category, as do the vapors from some cleaning solvents. Any draining or pouring of such volatile fluids should be done in a well ventilated area.

When using cleaning fluids and solvents, read the instructions on the container carefully. Never use materials from unmarked containers.

Never run the engine in an enclosed space, such as a garage. Exhaust fumes contain carbon monoxide, which is extremely poisonous. If you need to run the engine, always do so in the open air, or at least have the rear of the vehicle outside the work area.

If you are fortunate enough to have the use of an inspection pit, never drain or pour gasoline and never run the engine while the vehicle is over the pit. The fumes, being heavier than air, will concentrate in the pit with possibly lethal results.

The battery

Never create a spark or allow a bare light bulb near a battery. They normally give off a certain amount of hydrogen gas, which is highly explosive.

Always disconnect the battery ground (–) cable *at the battery* before working on the fuel or electrical systems.

If possible, loosen the filler caps or cover when charging the battery from an external source (this does not apply to sealed or maintenance-free batteries). Do not charge at an excessive rate or the battery may burst.

Take care when adding water to a non maintenance-free battery and when carrying a battery. The electrolyte, even when diluted, is very corrosive and should not be allowed to contact clothing or skin.

Always wear eye protection when cleaning the battery to prevent the caustic deposits from entering your eyes.

Mains electricity (household current in the US)

When using an electric power tool, inspection light, etc., which operates on household current, always make sure that the tool is correctly connected to its plug and that, where necessary, it is properly grounded. Do not use such items in damp conditions and, again, do not create a spark or apply excessive heat in the vicinity of fuel or fuel vapor.

Secondary ignition system voltage

A severe electric shock can result from touching certain parts of the ignition system (such as the spark plug wires) when the engine is running or being cranked, particularly if components are damp or the insulation is defective. In the case of an electronic ignition system, the secondary system voltage is much higher and could prove fatal.

Routine maintenance

Maintenance is essential for reasons of safety and reliability, and will help to maintain the value of the vehicle. The service intervals and tasks are essentially those recommended by the manufacturer. Where a vehicle operates under adverse conditions - eg in extremely hot or cold climates, or mainly short journeys - consideration should be given to shortening the intervals between services. Where a low annual mileage is covered, servicing should be done at the time intervals stated, since lubricants and other vehicle components deteriorate with age as well as with use.

Every 250 miles (400 km), weekly, or before a long run

Check engine oil level and top up if necessary (photo)
Check coolant level and top up if necessary
Check brake fluid level (photo). Top up if necessary and investigate any sudden fall in level
Check windscreen washer fluid level and top up if necessary (photo)
Check the battery electrolyte level and top up if necessary
Inspect engine compartment for oil or coolant leaks, loose nuts and bolts, slack or frayed drivebelts, etc
Check tyre pressures, inspect tread and sidewalls
Check operation of lights, horn, direction indicators etc

Every 5000 miles (7500 km) or six months, whichever comes first

Drain engine oil when hot and refill with fresh oil
Check spark plugs, clean and reset gap if necessary
Check contact breaker points (if applicable), clean and reset gap if necessary
Lubricate door hinges, locks and catches and bonnet lock (photo)

Filling the engine with oil through the valve cover

Topping-up the gearbox

The gearbox drain plug

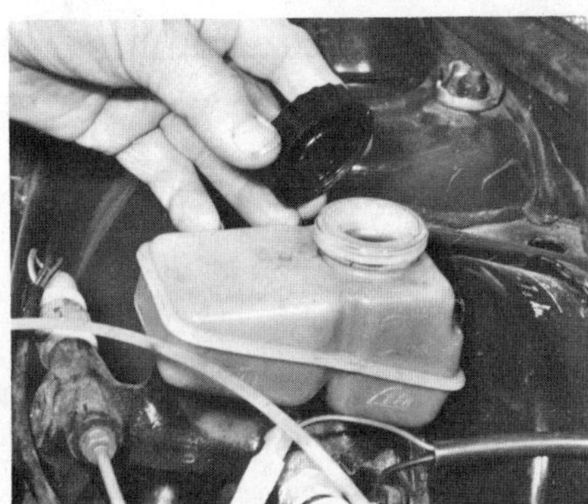
The brake master cylinder fluid reservoir

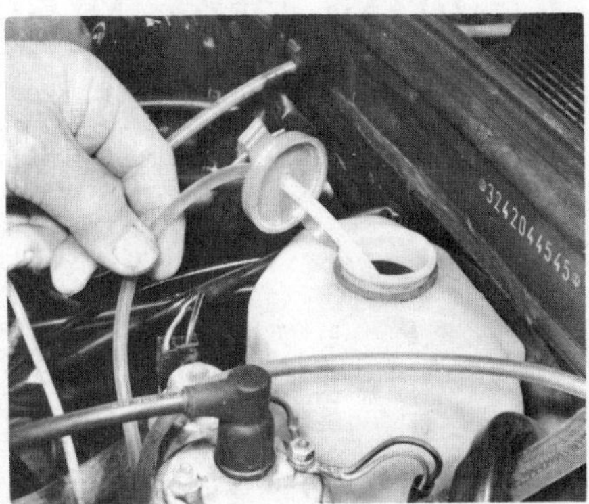
The windscreen washer tank

Oil the door hinges with general purpose oil

Every 10 000 miles (15 000 km) or twelve months, whichever comes first

In addition to, or instead of, the items specified above

Renew engine oil filter
Adjust or renew alternator drivebelt (and air pump and air conditioning drivebelts if so equipped)
Check clutch free play, adjust if necessary
Check coolant antifreeze concentration, replenish if necessary
Renew spark plugs and (if applicable) contact breaker points
Check condition of distributor cap, rotor arm and HT leads
Check ignition timing
Check condition of air cleaner element
Check idle speed and exhaust CO level, adjust if necessary
Check thickness of brake pads and shoes, renew if necessary
Adjust rear brake shoes and/or handbrake (as applicable)
Check condition of hydraulic pipes and hoses, renew as necessary
Check condition and security of exhaust system
Check steering and suspension joints for excessive movement and damage to dust boots
Check driveshaft joint boots for damage
Check manual gearbox or automatic transmission oil level, top up if necessary (photo)
Check final drive oil level (automatic transmission models) and top up if necessary
Check headlight beam alignment
Check steering rack adjustment, correct if necessary
Check operation of emission control systems (as applicable)

Every 20 000 miles (30 000 km) or two years, whichever comes first

In addition to, or instead of, the items specified above

Check/adjust valve clearances
Renew fuel line filter (if so equipped)
Renew air cleaner element
Renew EGR filter and air pump filter (emission controlled models, as applicable)
Drain cooling system, flush and refill with new coolant

Every 30 000 miles (45 000 km) or three years, whichever comes first

In addition to, or instead of, the items specified above

Renew brake hydraulic fluid
Drain manual gearbox oil (photo) or automatic transmission fluid, refill with fresh oil or fluid
Drain final drive and refill with fresh oil (automatic transmission models)

Recommended lubricants and fluids

Engine (1)	Castrol GTX
Gearbox (2):	
Manual	Castrol Hypoy Light (80 EP)
Automatic	Castrol TQ Dexron ®
Final drive (automatic models only)	Castrol Hypoy B (90 EP)
Rack and pinion unit	Obtain special lubricant from VW/Audi agent
Rear wheel bearings (3)	Castrol LM Grease
Parking brake compensator	Castrol LM Grease
Clutch cable	Castrol LM Grease
Hinges, locks, pivots, distributor etc	Castrol GTX
Brake fluid (4)	Castrol Girling Universal Brake and Clutch Fluid

Note: the above are general recommendations. Lubrication requirements vary from territory-to-territory and also depend on vehicle usage. Consult the operators handbook supplied with your car

Chapter 1 Engine

For modifications, and information applicable to later models, see Supplement at end of manual

Contents

Specifications

Engine (1297 cc/79 cu in) - general

Code	ZA	ZF
Output watts/rpm	40/5500	44/5800
Output HP (DIN)/rpm	55/5500	60/5800
Compression ratio	8.5 : 1	8.5 : 1
Torque:		
Nm/rpm	94/2500	93/3500
lbs ft/rpm	68/2500	67/3500
Bore:		
mm	75	75
in.	2.9528	2.9528
Stroke:		
mm	73.4	73.4
in.	2.89	2.89
Weight (no oil)	107 kg (235 lbs)	107 kg (235 lbs)
Oil capacity:		
Litres	3.5	3.5
US pints	7.4	7.4
Imp pints	6.2	6.2
Firing order (No. 1 cylinder at timing belt end)	1 - 3 - 4 - 2	1 - 3 - 4 - 2
Valve timing at 1 mm valve stroke:		
Inlet opens before TDC	9°	9°
Inlet closes after BDC	29°	41°
Exhaust opens before BDC	45°	49°
Exhaust closes after TDC	3°	1°
Fuel requirement RON	91	91

Valve clearance (all 1297 cc engines):	mm	ins.
Inlet:		
Hot	0.20 - 0.30	0.008 - 0.012
Cold	0.15 - 0.25	0.006 - 0.010
Exhaust:		
Hot	0.40 - 0.50	0.016 - 0.020
Cold	0.35 - 0.45	0.014 - 0.018

Engine (1471 cc/89.7 cu in) - general

Code	ZB	ZC	ZD ZE*	XW XV*	XY XZ*
Output watts/rpm	55/5800	63/5800	55/6000		
Output HP (DIN) rpm	75/5800	85/5800	75/6000	78/5800	78/5800
Output HP (SAE)/rpm	—	—	—	75/6000	75/6000
Compression ratio	9.7 : 1	9.7 : 1	8.0 : 1	8.2 : 1	8.2 : 1
Torque:					
Nm (DIN)/rpm	116/3500	123/4000	112/4000	11.8/4000	11.8/4000
lbs ft (DIN)/rpm	84/3500	89/4000	81/4000	85.5/4000	85.5/4000
lbs ft (SAE)/rpm				94/4000	94/4000
Bore:					
mm	76.5	76.5	76.5	76.5	76.5
in.	3.01	3.01	3.01	3.01	3.01
Stroke:					
mm	80	80	80	80	80
in.	3.15	3.15	3.15	3.15	3.15
Weight (no oil):					
kg	111	113	113	113 †	113 †
lbs	242	246	246	246	246
Oil capacity:					
Litres	3.5	3.5	3.5	3.5	3.5
US pints	7.4	7.4	7.4	7.4	7.4
Imp. pints	6.2	6.2	6.2	6.2	6.2
Firing order (No. 1 at timing belt end)	1 - 3 - 4 - 2	1 - 3 - 4 - 2	1 - 3 - 4 - 2	1 - 3 - 4 - 2	1 - 3 - 4 - 2
Fuel requirement (RON)	98	98	91	—	—
Valve timing at 1 mm valve stroke (zero tappet clearance): **					
Inlet opens before TDC	9°	9°	9°	7°	7°
Inlet closes after BDC	41°	41°	41°	43°	43°
Exhaust opens before BDC	49°	49°	49°	47°	47°
Exhaust closes after TDC	1°	1°	1°	3°	3°

** Used with automatic transmission*
† Does not include reburn equipment or air-conditioner
*** Correct at time of publication, but may vary. Consult agent if in doubt.*

Valve clearance (1471 cc engines):	mm	ins.
Inlet:		
Hot	0.20 to 0.30	0.008 to 0.012
Cold	0.15 to 0.25	0.006 to 0.010
Exhaust:		
Hot	0.40 to 0.50	0.016 to 0.020
Cold	0.35 to 0.45	0.014 to 0.018

Lubrication (all engines)

Pump ... Gear type driven by distributor shaft off intermediate shaft

Pressure:
- lbs/sq. in. ... Maximum 100; Minimum 14 at 80°C (176°F)
- kg/sq. cm ... Maximum 7; Minimum 1

Oil filter ... Full-flow

Oil capacity:	Imp. pints	US pints	Litres
With filter change	6.2	7.4	3.5
Without filter change	5.3	6.4	3.0

Pistons (all engines)

Type ... Aluminium alloy with steel inserts
Rings ... 2 pressure; 1 scraper
Piston pins ... Fully floating, secured with circlips

Limits and fits (all engines)

Pistons and cylinder bores: ... See text Chapter 1, Section 13 for selective assembly code and different shapes of piston

Maximum wear on piston diameter ... 0.0016 in. (0.04 mm) from code size, checked at 5/8 in. (16 mm) from bottom skirt edge 90° to piston pin bore

Clearance piston/cylinder (max.) ... 0.0028 in. (0.07)

Clearance piston/cylinder standard (new) ... 0.0012 in. (0.03 mm)

Piston rings:	in.	mm
Groove clearance, all rings (max.)	0.0059	0.15
Ring thickness:		
Top pressure	0.0787	2
Middle pressure	0.0984	2.5
Scraper	0.1575	4

	in.	mm
Piston ring gap (new):		
Top ring	0.012 to 0.018	0.3 to 0.45
Middle ring	0.012 to 0.018	0.3 to 0.45
Scraper ring	0.009 to 0.016	0.25 to 0.40
Piston ring gap (maximum)	0.0394	1
Connecting rods:	in.	mm
Axial play of big-end bearing	0.001	0.25
Crankshaft:	in.	mm
Endfloat measured at No. 3 main bearing:		
New	0.0028 to 0.0067	0.07 to 0.17
Max.	0.0098	0.25
Main bearing sizes:	in.	mm
Crankshaft journal:		
Original size (new)	2.126	54.00
1st regrind	2.116	53.75
2ndregrind	2.106	53.50
3rd regrind	2.096	53.25
Tolerance allowed	−0.0016 to −0.0024	−0.04 to −0.06
Maximum clearance main journal to main shell bearing	0.0047	0.12
Maximum ovality of main bearing journal	0.0012	0.03
Big-end bearings:	in.	mm
Crankshaft journal:		
Original size (new)	1.811	46
1st regrind	1.801	45.75
2nd regrind	1.791	45.50
3rd regrind	1.781	45.25
Tolerance allowed	−0.0016 to −0.0024	−0.04 to −0.06
Maximum clearance, journal to big-end shell	0.0047	0.12
Maximum ovality of connecting rod journal	0.0012	0.03
Camshaft:	in.	mm
Axial play:		
New	0.002 to 0.005	0.048 to 0.12
Wear limit	0.006	0.15
Radial play	0.0015 to 0.0024	0.04 to 0.06
Valve guides:	in.	mm
Maximum rock at end of NEW valve stem, - valve fully inserted:		
Exhaust	0.032	0.8
Inlet	0.016	0.4
Valves:	in.	mm
Inlet:		
Head diameter	1.338	34.0
Stem diameter	0.314	7.97
Seat width	0.078	2.0
Seat angle	45° (upper correction angle 60°)	
Exhaust:		
Head diameter	1.221	31
Stem diameter	0.078	7.97
Seat width	0.094	2.4
Seat angle	45° (upper correction angle 60°)	
Valve springs:	in.	mm
Outer - length at load 100 lbs (47 kg)	0.916	22.8
Inner - length at load 48 lbs (22 kg)	0.719	18.3

Torque wrench settings

	size (mm)	lbs ft	kg m
Cylinder head bolts (engine cold):			
Stage 1	12 (splined socket) or 10 (hex socket)	29	4
Stage 2		44	6
Stage 3		55	7.5
Stage 4 (splined bolts only)		Further ¼ turn	
Camshaft bearing caps	8	14.5	2
Camshaft sprocket screws	12	58	8
Valve cover (cylinder head cover)	6	6	0.8
Heater flange to cylinder head	6	7	1
Coolant adapter to cylinder head	6	7	1
Spark plugs	14	28	3
Timing belt guard	—	6	0.8
Water pump to cylinder block	8	7	1

Fuel pump to cylinder block ...	8	14	2
Distributor clamp to cylinder block ...	8	14	2
Alternator bracket to cylinder block ...	8	22	3
Alternator to bracket ...	8	14	2
Alternator belt tension adjuster clamp (both ends) ...	8	14	2
Coolant drain plug ...	10	25	3
Water pump impellor housing to case ...	6	7	1
Water pump pulley hub ...	8	14	2
Exhaust manifold to cylinder head ...	8	18	2.5
Inlet manifold to cylinder head ...	8	18	2.5
Carburetor to inlet manifold ...	8	14.4	2
Exhaust manifold guard ...	8	14.4	2
Inlet manifold support bar ...	8	14.4	2
Oil pump to engine block ...	8	14.4	2
Oil pump cover to pump ...	6	7.2	1
Sump (oil pan) drain plug ...	14	18	2.5
Sump (oil pan) to block - socket head bolts ...	6	6	0.8
Sump (oil pan) to block - hexagon head bolts ...	—	14	2.0
Oil filter to holder ...	Special	20	3
Oil filter holder to block ...	8	14.4	2
Oil pressure switch ...	—	8.6	1.2
Crankshaft main bearing caps ...	10	47	6.5
Crankshaft big-end bearing caps ...	9	32	4.5
Intermediate shaft guide ...	8	18	2.5
Flange to block ...	6	7.2	1
Sprocket to intermediate shaft ...	12	58	8
Flywheel to crankshaft ...	10	45	6.5
Clutch to flywheel ...	8	18	2.5
Timing pulley to crankshaft ...	12	58	8
Vee belt pulley to timing pulley ...	8	18	2.5
Timing belt tensioner pulley ...	10	32.5	4.5
Engine to transmission ...	12	40	5.5
Engine mounting to cylinder block ...	10	32	4.5
Torque converter to driveplate ...	—	22	3

1 General description

1 A four cylinder, in line, four stroke, water cooled engine, having an overhead camshaft is installed over the front suspension. It is set at an angle of 20° to the vertical to reduce overall height. The one piece cylinder block and crankcase is made from cast iron. The cylinder head is made of light alloy and the oil sump a sheet metal pressing. Timing drive is by a cogged belt which is driven by the crankshaft pulley and operates the overhead camshaft and an intermediate shaft which in turn drives the fuel pump, oil pump and distributor. The belt is adjusted for tension by an idler pulley mounted on an eccentric cam. The water pump and the alternator are driven by a V-belt operated by a pulley bolted to the crankshaft timing belt pulley.

2 To save space length-wise, the radiator has been mounted at the side of the engine and is cooled by an electrically driven fan controlled by a thermostat type switch in the bottom radiator tank. The inlet manifold has a water jacket supplied with hot coolant from the coolant pump.

3 Lubrication is by a gear pump. The oil is drawn from the sump through a strainer and delivered to a filter from whence it is destributed to the various bearings. The maximum oil pressure is 100 lbs/square inch (7.0 kg/sq cm) at 500 rpm, and the minimum 14 lbs/square inch (1 kg per sq cm) at idling speed at 80° C (176° F).

4 The engine comes in two sizes, 1296 cc and 1471 cc. To obtain these dimensions without too much duplication, the cylinder bore is 75 mm for the 1296 cc increased to 76.5 mm for the 1471 cc. To match these the stroke of the 1296 cc engine is 73.4 mm and the 1471 cc engine 80 mm. Thus it will be seen that the original cylinder block has been bored out to a larger dimension and a crankshaft with a 3.3 mm longer throw installed in the 1500 version.

There are other differences; mainly the clutch and a few other minor details. The engine discussed in the text of this Chapter (the one we took to bits) is a 1296 cc engine, where the larger engine differs is pointed out in the Specification Section of this Chapter and in the text.

5 Engine code letters are confusing. ZA and ZF are the 1297 cc engines. The ZA engine has an output of 55 BHP at 5500 rpm. The ZF is quoted at 60 BHP at 5800 rpm and is the one normally quoted in all the technical advertisments. The shape of the camshaft differs giving different valve opening times.

ZB and ZC are 1471 cc engines with a compression ratio of 9.7 : 1 requiring fuel at 98 RON. ZC has a quoted output of 85 BHP, ZB of 75 BHP.

The North American version was fitted at first with the ZD (or ZE for automatic gearbox) with a lower compression ratio of 8.0 : 1 for its 1471 ccs. This was changed in 1974 to different codings XW and XV (manual and automatic) for USA, and XY, XZ (manual and automatic) special to California. The output is quoted as 75 BHP at 6000 rpm and the lower compression ratio allows the use of fuel at 91 RON. The main alterations to the XY etc range are in ignition timing and details to allow the fitting of EGR and Afterburn to meet the exhaust gas regulations.

2 Repairs possible with the engine in the car

1 All the minor units, water pump, fuel pump, distributor, radiator and timing belt may be removed and replaced without removing the engine. The exception is the oil pump and even this may be serviced with the engine in-situ if the subframe is lowered so that the sump may be removed.

2 The cylinder head may be removed for normal decarbonizing and the valves and valve gear serviced. The removal and replacement of the cogged timing drivebelt is a matter of minutes, as is the replacement of the alternator/water pump drive V-belt. Removal and overhaul of sub-assemblies is discussed later. The procedure is the same whether the engine is in or out of the car.

3 The clutch may be inspected and if necessary replaced with the engine in the frame by removing the gearbox, (see Chapter 6) which is not a difficult or lengthy task.

4 By using VW/Audi special tools 10-222 and 10-207, or very simply making your own, about which more is said later in this Section, the engine may be supported in the car and the subframe removed. It is then possible if you have a metric sized Allen key 6 mm size and at least 11 in (279 mm) long, to remove the sump and service the oil pump. The connecting rod caps may be removed and the pistons and connecting rods removed through the top of the block if the head is dismantled.

Removal of the subframe is discussed in detail in Chapter 12.

5 VW/Audi tool 10-222 consists of a beam which is placed across the opening of the engine compartment supported on either side by brackets which lodge on the wings. The brackets sit in the channels of the wing. A centre lifting jack is then connected by VW/Audi tool 10-207 which is a simple chain sling to the lifting lugs of the engine (one in the

alternator support bracket and the other at the rear of the block just above the distributor.

A suitable arrangement can be made from a wooden beam, using a small hydraulic or screw jack as a lifting device.

The engine weighs roughly 250 lbs (113.5 kg) so you can test your improvised beam by getting a really heavy man to stand on it while it is on the floor (or by an ordinary sized man jumping on it).

6 The problem with the oil pan (sump) bolts is that they are socked head bolts requiring an Allen key suitable for 6 mm sockets. Due to the depth of the oil pan it is not possible to turn the Allen key unless the tommy bar portion is clear of the bottom of the sump. This applies only to half of them. They are not screwed up very tight (6 lb/ft (10.82 kg/m) and so it should be easy enough to improvise a suitable key with a piece of round bar and a file using the 6 mm key as a pattern.

7 It is indeed a change from the VW Beetle to be able to repair the engine in-situ and without kneeling down. If you do not have a hoist it is still possible to do major overhauls but the authors consider that the removal of the engine is so easy that the engine should be taken out if extensive overhaul is contemplated.

8 Two final things about working with the engine in the car. The hood (bonnet) is secured by four bolts. Mark the hinge positions and then remove the nuts and ease the bonnet away. It can then be stored in a safe place, giving you much more room and light to work. The removal/replacement takes about five minutes. The other thing (for Beetle people) is that this engine is full of expensive antifreeze. Be careful what you undo, especially the inlet manifold.

3 Engine - removal and replacement (manual transmission)

1 Unless the car is fitted with an air-conditioner it is possible to remove the engine from the top through the bonnet opening using a hoist capable of lifting 250 lbs (113.5 kg). If the vehicle has an air-conditioner then the engine and subframe must be removed from below. There may be other occasions when this is desirable and the procedure for this operation is discussed in Section 6. Please read the whole of this Section, particularly paragraph 27 before you start work.

The engine and gearbox must be separated if the engine is to come out of the top. Once the engine is out the gearbox may be removed either from underneath or through the bonnet opening.

Apart from a hoist, a suitable sling and a jack (mobile or static), no special tools are required, but the car should be over a pit or on a ramp so that access may be had to work underneath it, once work has started. If a static hoist is used there must be room to push the car away once the engine is lifted clear so that the engine may be lowered to the ground.

2 Mark the position of the bonnet hinges with a pencil and remove the bonnet. Two people will be required for this task. Move the car away from the work area.

3 Drain the coolant by removing the bottom hose of the radiator and the plug screw (photo) from the cylinder block.

Since this coolant is expensive VW/Audi antifreeze arrange to drain it into a container so that it may be used again.

4 The engine oil drain plug is at the back of the sump (photo). Arrange a container with a capacity of 1 gallon (5 litres) and remove the drain plug. Catch the oil in the container. It will take some time to drain. Replace the plug and move the car back to the work place. If you do this you will not have to lie/sit/kneel in a puddle of oil/antifreeze.

5 Undo the five clips and remove the air cleaner cover. Remove the paper element, then undo the nut which you can now see, then undo the clips that hold on the warm air and fresh air hoses, remove the hoses and then lift off the air cleaner housing. Clean it out thoroughly, blow low pressure compressed air (foot pump) through the element, and set the cleaner on one side ready to go back on the engine.

6 Remove the earth strap from the battery. If the battery has been in the car for a year or more now is a good time to take it out of the car and have it serviced (Chapter 10).

7 If the metal round the battery carrier is rusty or sulphated clean it off and paint it with anti-corrosion paint.

8 Remove the securing clip from the throttle cable and remove the cable from the lever. Undo the upper nut of the clutch cable where the outer cable terminates in the engine mounting and unhook the inner cable plastic end piece from the clutch operating lever (photo). Tie the clutch cable to the cap of the radiator overflow tank or some convenient place.

9 At this stage stop and get your note book. From now on note each wire or hose, put a tag on it to identify it and note where it came from.

10 Disconnect the LT wire from terminal 1 of the coil to the distributor at the coil. Remove the cap from the distributor, the leads from the plugs (tag these leads 1. 2. 3. 4. starting with No 1 at the front), and remove the HT lead from the centre of the coil. Put the distributor cap and rotor arm in a safe place after you have cleaned them.

11 Remove the wires from the oil pressure switch at the back of the block. They are push on tags. Repeat the process for the temperature sender unit. This is in the 'Tee' of the coolant outlet at the back of the cylinder block.

12 Disconnect the multipin plug from the alternator, move the clip first and then disengage the wire from the clip on the radiator cowl.

13 There is a plastic valve for the heater hoses, disconnect the control wire from the valve. Leave the hoses connected to the valve but undo each one at the other end and remove it from, in turn, the water pump, the heater and the inlet manifold. Slip the hose out of the clip which supports the valve and remove the assembly complete. Doing it this way makes assembly much easier as the hoses are set at the correct angles.

14 Disconnect the radiator hose from the bottom of the radiator leaving it on the water pump. Disconnect the top hose from the radiator and engine and remove it. Remove the hose to the overflow tank.

Follow the wire from the fan motor to the plastic plug and disconnect the plastic plug. At the bottom of the radiator is a thermo-switch screwed into the bottom tank. The connections to this are two push on tags inside a rubber sleeve. Remove the tags and put the wire to one side.

15 One of the more unfortunate fittings to the vehicle is the radiator cowling. It is made of hardboard and does not fit very well. It is secured by a rubber strap at the top and by screws at the sides and base. These must be removed and the cowling eased out of the way. It may be necessary to undo the three screws holding the relay/fuse console and move it slightly to facilitate dismantling the radiator.

16 The radiator is held by a strap at the top to the front of the engine compartment. On the side opposite to the engine is a nut and stud halfway down the radiator and underneath the radiator a stud protrudes through the casing supporting the radiator on a rubber block. Undo these fastenings and the radiator complete with fan may be lifted out. Be careful with the nut from the side fastening. If you drop it there is a possibility that it will fall through a hole just below into the bodyframe, as we did, and then you will have to fish for it with a piece of wire (as we did).

17 Now go round to the other side of the engine. Remove the wire tag connector from the carburettor electro-magnetic valve. Now remove the valve, it sticks out, and may catch and fracture as the engine is lifted out.

Undo the four nuts from the exhaust pipe flange and lower it from the manifold. Undo the clip holding the exhaust pipes to the gearbox.

18 At the front of the engine is a so called engine bearer. It does not take any weight but is there to stop excessive vibration. One part is secured by two bolts to the frame and the other, with the rubber stop to the block. Note how they are positioned and remove them (photo).

19 Undo the clip on the fuel pump hose and remove the hose from the fuel pump. Have a clip or a plug ready to seal the hose and put a cloth under the pump to catch any spillage.

20 Now get underneath the vehicle and disconnect the wires from the starter solenoid. Note where they fit. The starter must now be removed. The inner bearing is in the clutch bell housing. Remove the three nuts holding the starter to the engine and socket head bolt holding the starter mounting plate to the block. Next remove the flywheel guard plate from beneath the gearbox.

21 Arrange a suitable support for the gearbox at this stage, remove the lower transmission/engine bolts and firmly support the gearbox but do not push it upward.

22 From the top remove the nuts from the engine bearer studs. Sling the engine using the lugs on the alternator bracket and at the rear of the block. We found it easier to use shackles on these lugs as the holes are quite cramped.

23 Have a final check round to see that everything is disconnected and then lift gently with the hoist until the sling is just taking the weight. Undo the remaining transmission bolts a few turns and then raise the hoist until the gearbox casing *just* touches the steering cross-tube. Now remove the upper transmission/engine bolts complete (photo). One of them carries a support clip. Note which one so that it isnt forgotten on assembly. Follow the gearbox up with its supporting arrangement.

24 The engine and gearbox are still held together by short dowels in the joint flange and by the gearbox mainshaft in the flywheel bearing. There is also a connector plate between the two units.

Lever the engine away from the gearbox keeping it level and making sure no strain goes on the flywheel needle bearing until the gearbox mainshaft is clear of the bearing and the dowels are free from the housing. There isnt much room so keep a good hold on the engine.

25 Lift the engine steadily at the same time turning it so that the timing belt cover moves into the space left by removing the radiator. It will be seen from the photograph how little room is available. At an early stage in the lifting remove the connecting plate. Either push the car from under the engine or if you have a mobile crane move the crane away.

26 Lower the engine to the ground and move it away to a suitable area for cleaning.

27 Replacement is the reverse procedure but it isn't quite as simple as that. Sling the engine as nearly as possible at the same angle. Lift the engine over the engine compartment and then fit the connecting plate in place over the dowels. Grease the joint face to stick the plate in position as the engine is lowered. **If the clutch has been removed during the overhaul and not centred correctly the next operation will be to take the engine out again and centre the clutch correctly because the end of the gearbox mainshaft will not enter the flywheel bearing and trying to force it will cause expensive damage.**

However, assuming that the clutch is correctly assembled, continue to lower the engine turning it at the same time (photo), until it is level and in line with the gearbox. If the sling angle isnt quite right it may be necessary to move the gearbox a little but do not lower it too much or the engine bearers will foul the mounting studs eventually. Use the dowels and bolt holes as a guide and gently ease the flywheel bearing over the mainshaft and the dowels into the bellhousing. It may be that the shaft will enter and go so far easily, and then stick. This is probably because the splines on the shaft are not aligned with those in the clutch driven plate. Using a spanner on the crankshaft pulley nut turn the shaft a little and they will enter and the engagement may be completed.

28 Install the upper transmission/engine bolts and tighten them gently. Do not forget the heater tube support. Keep the weight on the sling and remove the support from the gearbox. Install the lower transmision/engine bolts and tighten them gently. Next lower the engine so that the engines bearers fit over the studs. This may again be tricky but the studs may be moved about to enter the holes by inserting a rod in the rubber just below the stud. Be careful again not to force things or you may strip the thread on the bearer stud.

Once this is done fit the nuts and tighten the engine/transmission bolts and engine bearer bolts to the specified torque. Next refit the front bearer.

29 Refit the starter and the exhaust pipe. Install the radiator and connect up all the wires and hoses. Do not forget to adjust the free-play of the clutch (Chapter 5). It should be 0.6 in (15 mm) at the pedal.

30 When the engine is running check the ignition timing and dwell angle.

4 Engine - removal and replacement (automatic transmission)

1 The procedure is exactly as for the manual transmission as described in Section 3, as far as paragraph 22. At this stage the engine is stripped ready to be parted from the transmission and lifted out. The sling is in position ready to lift.

2 Working through the starter hole turn the engine until the three torque converter/drive shell connecting bolts each become visible. Remove each one in turn holding the starter ring steady with a screw-driver (photo).

The torque converter will now be free from the flywheel. Pull the vacuum hose through the ring clamp on the back of the cylinder head.

3 Support the transmission and remove the transmission/engine bolts. Now take the weight off the engine bearers and remove the left and right engine mountings. The engine may now be lifted up straight once it is levered away from the transmission.

4 Be careful that the torque converter does not fall out spilling ATF. Bolt a piece of angle-iron across the bellhousing using the engine/transmission bolt holes.

5 Installation is the reverse. Remove the strap holding the torque converter and lower the engine into place and bolt it to the transmission. Install the engine mountings and tighten them to the correct torque. Remove the lifting tackle and transmission support. Reconnect the vacuum tube and finally re-install the three torque converter/drive shell connecting bolts, torquing them to the correct amount (22 lbs/ft - 3 kg/m).

6 Reconnect as for the manual gearbox but remember when checking the timing that this is different (Chapter 4 and Chapter 7).

5 Engine (with air-conditioner) - removal and replacement

1 On vehicles equipped with air conditioning, the engine can be removed after the air conditioning components have been detached and moved aside as described later in this Section. *On no account disconnect any hose or pipe which is part of the refrigerant circuit.*

2 The refrigerant used is Freon 12 which is odourless, non-poisonous, non-inflammable and non-corrosive. Leaks are not dangerous provided the refrigerant does not come into contact with a naked flame, in which case a poisonous gas is created. Fluid contact with eyes or skin should be avoided.

3 Remove the radiator grille and release the clamp for the air conditioner hoses.

4 Unbolt the condenser and move it aside as far as the flexible connecting hoses will allow.

5 Remove the horn.

6 Unbolt the compressor with mounting bracket and move it aside within the limits of its connecting hoses.

6 Engine and transmission - removal and replacement from below

Manual transmission

1 Read through this Section completely before commencing work. Unless the owner has sufficient lifting tackle and a large enough workshop the task is beyond his capabilities. It should not be attempted unless the vehicle has been damaged preventing the simpler removal.

2 Refer to Section 3 and carry out the work involved in paragraphs 3, 6, 7, 8, 9, 10, 11, 12, 13, 14, 15, 16, 17, 18, 19.

3 Disconnect the starter leads. Unscrew and remove the speedometer cable drive from the top of the gearbox. Disconnect the clutch cable and remove it.

4 Remove the clips holding the exhaust pipe and silencers to the body and remove the complete system.

5 Jack-up the front of the car and remove the front wheels. Remove the outer end of the steering tie-rods from the steering knuckles (see Chapter 12). The car should be very firmly supported at this stage. Now remove the front brake calipers from both sides and tie them back to the body. The alternative is to disconnect the front brake hoses with the consequent work of bleeding the brakes on reassembly.

6 Remove the plastic cap from the top of the MacPherson struts and the two holding nuts on both sides so that the top of the struts may be lowered with the subframe (Chapter 12).

7 Remove the wire and square headed nut and disconnect the gearshift rod (Chapter 6). Support the transmission and remove the two nuts holding the support bracket at the rear of the transmission (see Chapter 6).

8 Sling the engine and take the weight on the hoist but do not lift. Remove the four bolts holding the subframe to the body/chassis. Before lowering measure the height of the subframe from the ground.

9 Lower the hoist supporting the engine and the gearbox support, disconnecting the back-up switch wiring from the back of the gearbox as soon as you can, until the engine and transmission are on whatever support has been arranged at ground level. Guide the MacPherson struts down with the engine. It is suggested that a simple platform such as shown in the sketch mounted on rollers will suffice, but doubtless there are better ways.

10 Once the engine and transmission are firmly on the support. There remains the problem of raising the body to permit the withdrawal of the assembly. As the MacPherson struts have decended with engine and subframe the clearance required is considerable. We found it necessary to lift the front of the car until the underside of the bumper was 36 in (914 mm) from the ground. How this is done depends upon the tools available. If the engine/transmission is on a mobile platform then it should be possible to sling the front of the body, we removed the grille and arranged the sling as shown in the photograph, and hoisted the front of the car, moving the engine back slightly, with the same hoist used to lower the engine without moving its location, providing that it has sufficient 'headroom'.

11 The engine and transmission may now be drawn forward to enable

3.3 The pencil is pointing to the cylinder block drain plug by the starter

3.4 From underneath looking at the sump from the back, 'A' is the drain plug

3.8 'A' by the carburettor is the control cable 'B' by the alternator is the clutch cable mounting

3.18 The front mounting which connects the engine to the front crossframe

3.23 One of the transmission/engine bolts partially undone

3.25 The engine slung correctly on its way up. It will be seen that there is very little room to turn it.

3.27 Refitting engine means the clutch will approach the gearbox main drive shaft at this angle.

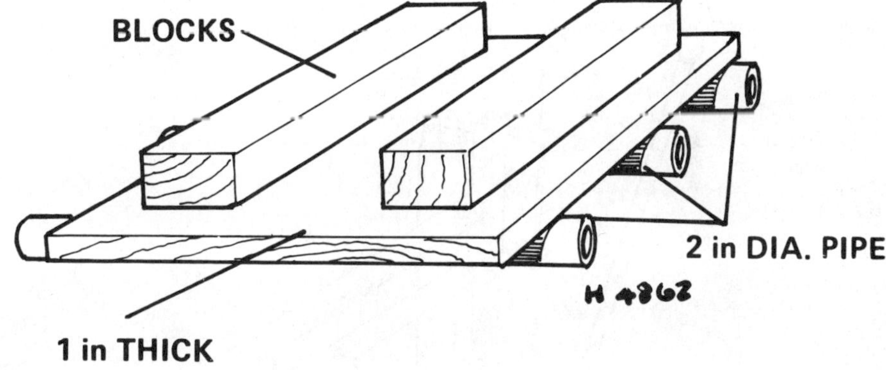

Fig. 1.1 Simple layout for engine handling platform

remains the problem of raising the body to permit the withdrawal of the assembly. As the MacPherson struts have decended with engine and subframe the clearance required is considerable. We found it necessary to lift the front of the car until the underside of the bumper was 36 in (914 mm) from the ground. How this is done depends upon the tools available. If the engine/transmission is on a mobile platform then it should be possible to sling the front of the body, we removed the grille and arranged the sling as shown in the photograph, and hoisted the front of the car, moving the engine back slightly, with the same hoist used to lower the engine without moving its location, providing that it has sufficient 'headroom'.

11 The engine and transmission may now be drawn forward to enable them to be separated and for work to proceed.

12 However, the body still has a number of things dangling from the front end. The compressor and condenser, plus the brake calipers. Check round that these are safe, and if not increase the lashings.

13 Assembly in this case is not quite the same problem as removal. There are several ways to which it may be done. If you can borrow a jack similar to the one shown in the diagram and make a fitting to hold the subframe with all the assemblies on it level and secure then the job becomes much more simple. The complete assembly is then wheeled under the car, the car lowered down and the engine assembly raised and guided into place. Once the MacPherson struts are in position fastened to the bodyframe the car wheels may be replaced temporarily and the car weight removed from the hoist. The hoist may be used to take the weight of the engine while the trolley jack is removed and the subframe bolted to the car frame. It will be necessary to support the transmission at this stage.

Alternatively, the hoist may be left in position and a device such as described in Section 2 paragraph 6 used to take the weight of the engine while the subframe bolts are inserted.

14 It may not be possible to obtain a suitable trolley jack, and assuming this we put the engine back without using a special fitting. We did use a mobile floor jack but even that could be substituted. The method took about 1 hour since we hadn't done it before and needed three people for about ten minutes of that hour. For the remainder of the time two people are necessary.

15 The photograph shows the car minus engine assembly supported on normal stands. The next photograph shows the subframe and MacPherson struts with the hubs and driveshafts. On to this must be lowered the engine and transmission. We found this difficult because the load is out of balance and fits over one bearer stud first. It then distorts the rubber mounting as weight goes on it with further lowering. However, by putting a screwdriver under the stud in the other mounting so that the rubber block may be distorted it was possible to bring the stud into line and guide it through the engine mounting (photo). We then assembled the mounting nuts and torqued to specification. A trial lift was then tried and it was found necessary to reconnect the driveshafts and lash the back part of the subframe to the transmission so that the entire unit moved up as a rigid load. The tops of the MacPherson struts are of course movable.

16 The engine is then moved under the vehicle. As will be seen we used the floor crane as a transporter by resting the subframe on the legs of the crane (photo), but we think it is better to use a trolley. When the engine is approximately in the correct place under the car it should be raised and the subframe located on blocks at, as near as possible, the height measured in paragraph 8 of this Section (photo). The transmission must also be supported.

17 The hoist should now be attached to the car body and the stands removed. The car must now be lowered down over the engine assembly. This is where three people are needed. One must work the hoist, the other two guide the body down so that the suspension struts locate in their sockets and the body does not foul the carburettor, the timing belt cover, or any of the detached parts such as the brake caliper or the compressor. Reconnect the back-up switch wiring to the gearbox as soon as possible.

18 Once the suspension struts are located in their sockets install the nuts and fittings on the top of them and tighten the nuts.

19 The next problem is to take the weight of the engine off the subframe so that the subframe supports may be moved and the frame jockeyed until the bolts holding it to the vehicle body may be installed. Depending upon how the subframe is supported it may be possible to insert a small jack under the engine and with suitable packing take the weight so that the blocks may be moved from under the subframe

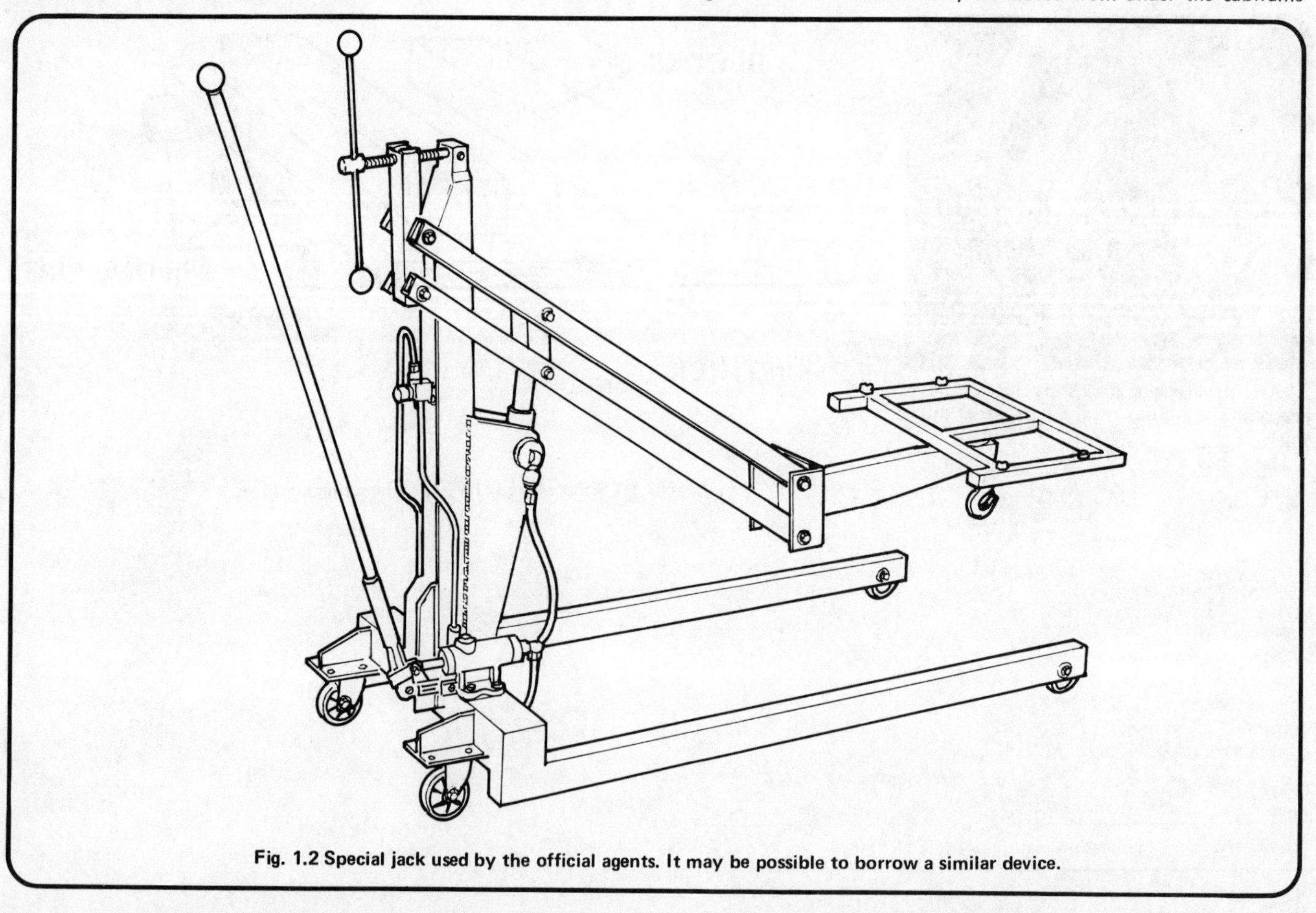

Fig. 1.2 Special jack used by the official agents. It may be possible to borrow a similar device.

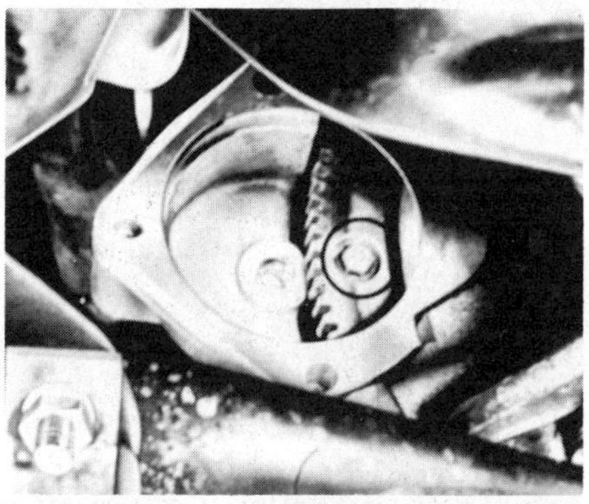
4.2 The torque converter bolts viewed through the hole which houses the starter

6.15a A view of the car (engine removed), showing engine stands and plank supporting the body

6.15b The subframe assembly ready for fitting the engine

6.15c Lowering the engine on to the subframe

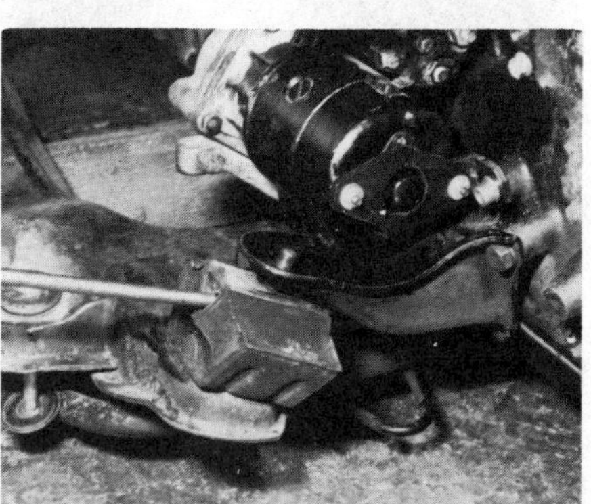
6.15d Levering the rubber mounting with a screwdriver to fit the mounting bolt into the mounting plate

6.16a The engine and subframe moved under the vehicle

select all gears, then finally tighten the square headed bolt and wire it in place. Re-install the exhaust system. If applicable, replace the compressor and condenser. Refit the radiator and cowling and the front engine bearer.

22 Connect up the fuel system hoses and the accelerator cable. Refit the water hoses to the radiator, car heater, inlet manifold and overflow tank and refill the system with antifreeze. Reconnect the heater valve cable.

23 Reconnect the wiring to the radiator thermal switch, plug in the fan motor and the alternator. Refit the wires to the carburettor thermal cut off switch, the oil pressure switch and the temperature sender unit.

24 Reconnect the ignition system wiring and replace the distributor rotor and cap. It will be necessary to crawl underneath to reconnect the starter motor.

25 Re-install the clutch cable and adjust the free-play to 15 mm at the pedal (0.6 in.). Refit the speedometer drive.

26 Refit the air cleaner and then install the battery. Fill the engine with the right amount of oil.

27 Check round that no wires or hoses are not connected, make sure the gearbox is in neutral and then start the engine.

28 Check the timing and then refit the bonnet.

Automatic transmission

29 The operations are very similar to those just described for engines with manual transmission, but the following additional operations will be required.

30 Disconnect the hose from the vacuum modulator on the transmission.

31 Extract the circlip and disconnect the speed selector cable from the arm on the transmission.

32 Disconnect the leads from the kickdown switch.

7 Engine overhaul - general preparation

1 The engine, separated from the transmission is on the workshop floor, the oil drained from it and all coolant removed. This is sometimes a fallacy for water and oil seem to lodge in the block and come out in small but trying quantities right throughout dismantling so be prepared to deal with them.

2 Clean the engine down externally using paraffin, or some propriety compound such as 'Gunk', wiping it clean and dry.

3 Cover the work surface with clean paper and provide a suitable number of small receptacles to contain small parts.

4 A paraffin bath will be needed, a stiff brush and a quantity of clean, non-fluffy rag. Sufficient space must be available to lay the engine components out in an ordenly manner as they are dismantled.

5 When dismantling the cylinder head it is essential that valves, tappet discs, tappet buckets and valve springs should be reassembled to the same place from whence they came so some method of storing them together, labelled with the origin eg; No 1 exhaust, is thought out **before** dismantling.

6 A set of metric spanners, flat open end, ring and socket are desirable and a number of metric size Allen hexagonal keys are required to fit socket head bolts 6 mm, 8 mm and 10mm metric bolts. Alternatively, it is possible to buy special tools to fit the sump and cylinder head bolt long socket screwdriver which will fit a torque wrench and make removal and replacement of the cylinder head very much easier. Official agents use quite a lot of special spanners and fixtures, which are mounted on special boards. These are pointed out and explained as the text proceeds. We did not use any special tools.

7 Once the engine is clean set it on the bench and support it firmly with the cylinder block in a vertical position. It is worth taking some care about this for some of the bolts are very tight and unless the engine is firm it may fall over as you struggle. It weighs 250 lbs (113.5 kg) fully dressed so you need a strong bench too.

8 Engine overhaul - Phase I: removal of parts bolted to the exterior of the head and block

1 Take off the camshaft cover, noting where the packing pieces fit under the bolts, and then remove the cover from the timing belt. Note where the two tee-headed bolts go and put them back in the cover.

6.16b The subframe raised on blocks

6.19 Lowering the body and taking the weight off the subframe with a floor jack

8.2 The centre-punch mark 'A' on the gear tooth of the intermediate shaft pulley must line up with the 'V' notch in the 'V' belt pulley on the crankshaft. This sets the relationship between the crankshaft, pistons and the distributor. It is essential that these relationships are correct — Take care!

8.3a Centre-punch mark on camshaft sprocket 'A' must be in line with shoulder of head. This lines up valves with pistons

8.3b The cams of No. 1 cylinder both in the valve closed position

8.3c The window in the cylinder block over the flywheel

8.3d Note the position of the rotor arm. It should point to the No. 1 cylinder mark on the rim of the distrubutor body

9.2 The camshaft bearing caps are numbered. This one is No. 4. Note which way round it goes before removing it

9.3 The tappet bucket with the disc lifted up

9.15a The valve spring

9.15b The valve, springs, cap and collets ready for assembly

2 It is now possible to save a lot of trouble when assembling the engine by studying the timing marks. On the intermediate pulley for the timing belt one tooth has a centre-punch mark. Turn the engine until this mates with a notch on the V-belt pulley bolted to the crankshaft drive pulley (photo). The easiest way to turn the engine is to remove the plugs and turn it with a socket spanner on the crankshaft pulley nut.
3 When these match look at the drivebelt sprocket on the camshaft. One tooth of this has a centre-punch mark. This should be level with the camshaft cover flange (photo). Having turned the engine until these marks agree now look at the cams for No 1 cylinder, the one nearest the timing belt. They will both be in the 'valve closed' position (photo). Now look through the window in the cylinder block (photo) where the timing marks show on the periphery of the flywheel and note the reading. Check where the rotor arm points on the distributor, it should point to No 1 plug lead and a mark on the edge of the rim of the base of the distributor (photo). The distributor body is held in position by a bolt and clamp. Using a centre-punch move the distributor body and the cylinder block in such a way that the marks are adjacent and may be used to set the distributor body at the right position on reassembly of the engine.
4 Remove the clamp, and holding the crankshaft to prevent it turning, lift the distributor body slowly out of the cylinder block. This will cause the distributor shaft to rotate slightly as its skew drive gear moves over the one on the intermeidate shaft. Do not allow the distributor body to rotate. Note the amount it has rotated and replace the distributor. The rotor should rotate to the mark on the rim for No 1 cylinder. When you are satisfied that you understand the method of resetting the timing remove the distributor. If you look down the hole left in the cylinder block you will see the top of the oil pump driveshaft. This has a slot in it. Note the angle of the slot carefully so that it can be set for easy reassembly. It is quite easy to reach and turn with a finger or a screwdriver. It should be parallel to the crankshaft.
5 Remove the oil filter, be careful there is still oil inside it, and then remove the bracket holding it to the block. This requires an Allen key, the same key being used for the fuel pump which is next to the filter. Set the pump aside for overhaul (Chapter 3). Remove the oil pressure transmitter unit.
6 Slacken the bolts holding the alternator strap to the alternator and the block and then slacken the socket headed bolt which acts as a hinge pin for the alternator tensioning system. If you cannot slacken this bolt do not shear off the serrations in the bolt socket but undo the two bolts holding the alternator bracket to the block, remove the tensioning strap and ease the V-belt off the pulley taking the alternator away. The socket head bolt head may now be held in a vise and the bracket with alternator turned to loosen it.

However, if you can slacken the bolt then remove the tensioning strap, move the alternator to slacken the V-belt and remove the V-belt. Then take the long hinge bolt right out and remove the alternator. Remove the V-belt, inspect if for wear cracks or fraying and replace with a new one if necessary.
7 Undo the clip holding the water hose to the flange on the side of the cylinder block and ease the hose clear. Remove the four bolts holding the water pump to the cylinder block (2 long, 2 short) and lever the pump away from the block. It may have stuck but be gentle and do not push wedges in between machined surfaces. Note where the O-ring fits. Set the water pump with hoses and pulley on one side for overhaul (Chapter 2).
8 Before removing the timing drivebelt check it for correct tension. If held between the finger and thumb halfway between the intermediate shaft and the camshaft it should be possible to twist it through 90°. If it is too slack, adjust it by slackening the bolt holding the eccentric cam on the tensioner wheel. If you are satisfied it can be adjusted to the correct tension remove it and examine it for wear. Now is the time to order a new one if necessary, not when the engine is almost assembled. Remove the crankshaft pulley by taking out the centre bolt and drawing off the two pulleys together. Do not separate them unless necessary, and if you do the angular relationship between the pulley keyway and the timing notch on the V-belt pulley must be maintained on reassembly. Remove the centre bolt from the camshaft driving sprocket and pull it off the camshaft. Do not lose the Woodruff key.
9 Remove the exhaust manifold first. There is a small bracket connecting the two manifolds, remove this and then undo the nuts from the studs holding the exhaust manifold to the block. Remove the manifold to one side. The inlet manifold and carburettor may be removed together. There are 8 socket head bolts, four short and four long. Note where each kind goes. Set the carburettor and manifold aside for examination (Chapter 3).

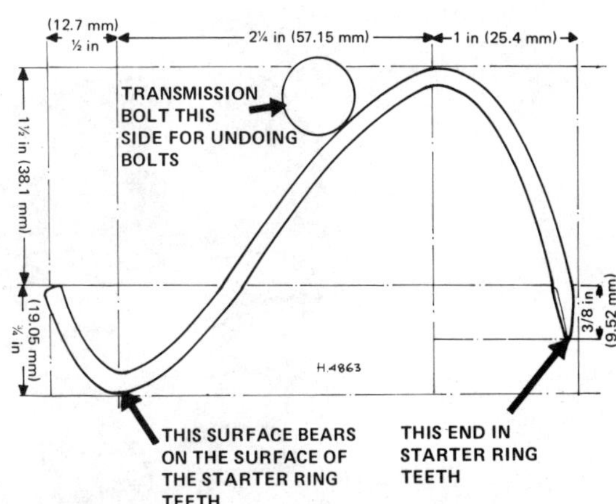

Fig. 1.3 Home-made tool to hold the starter ring still, while undoing the clutch and flywheel bolts

10 The clutch may now be removed. There are six bolts to be removed but once again the question of assembly must be considered before taking the clutch apart. If the clutch plate, the one between the flywheel and the pressure plate is not centralized correctly then assembly of the engine to the transmission is not possible. The ideal tool for doing this is the gearbox mainshaft but you are hardly likely to have a spare one of those. If a piece of rod the same diameter as the end of the mainshaft is available, or a wooden spigot turned down to size, this can be wrapped with insulation tape to fit the serrations of the clutch plate. If you can make the tool before dismantling the clutch so much the better. Unless it is proposed to take the crankshaft out of the main bearings and the clutch has shown no signs of wear then it is best left in position. However, if it must be removed the six bolts must be undone. Make centre-punch marks on the pressure plate and the flywheel to ensure they go together in the same way.
11 The question of holding the clutch and flywheel while undoing the bolts may cause problems. This can be overcome by bending a piece of 1/8 in x ½ in plate about 6 in long (3.175 mm x 12.7 mm x 152.5 mm) into the shape shown in the diagram Fig. 1.3. This may be wedged under a transmission bolt as shown with the one end engaged in the starter ring. The harder you twist the stronger the resistance to turning and to tighten turn the fixture round to the other side of the transmission bolt.

Undo the bolts one or two threads at a time slackening off the diaphragm plate springs until the bolts may be removed and the pressure plate and clutch plate set aside for inspection (Chapter 5).
12 Using the same clamping devise to prevent turning remove the six bolts holding the flywheel and remove it from the shaft. Due to the spacing of the bolt holes and the dowel it will go back only one way so there is no need to mark it.

9 Engine overhaul - Phase II: cylinder head removal and overhaul

1 The engine supports should be checked and re-aligned if necessary. It is best to carry right through with the overhaul of the cylinder head as it is dismantled.
2 Refer to Fig. 1.4. Remove the camshaft bearing caps. These have to go back the same way round in the same place. They are numbered (photo) but put a centre-punch mark on the side nearest the front of the head (where the sprocket was). No 1 is the one with a small oil seal on it.

Remove bearing caps 5, 1 and 3 in that order. Now undo the nuts holding 2 and 4 in a diagonal pattern and the camshaft will lift them up as the pressure of the valve springs is exerted. When they are free lift the caps off and the camshaft may be lifted out as well. The oil seal on the front end will come with it.
3 The tappet buckets are now exposed and may be lifted out. Take each one out in turn, prise the little disc out of the bucket by inserting a small screwdriver either side and lift the disc away. On the reverse the disc is engraved with a size (eg; 3.75). This is its thickness number. Note the number and then clean the disc and replace it number side down.

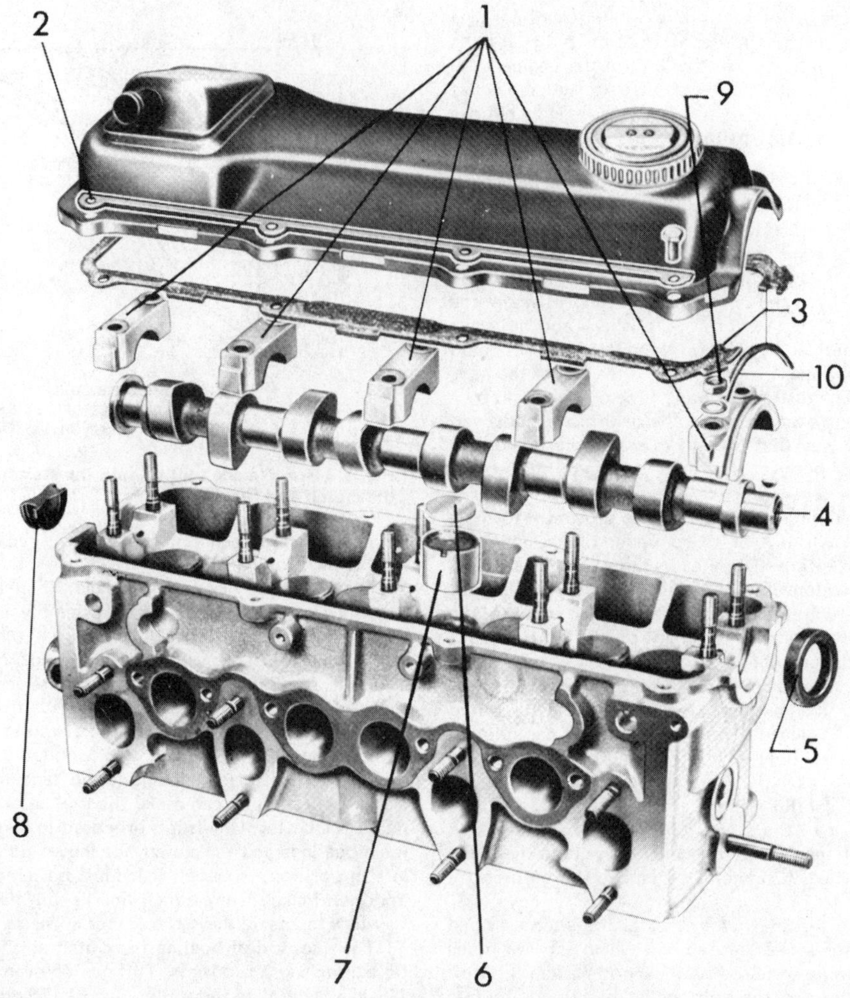

Fig. 1.4 Cylinder head and camshaft

1 *Bearing caps 2. 3. 4. 5*
2 *Valve cover*
3 *Valve cover packing strips*
4 *Camshaft*
5 *Seal*
6 *Tappet disc*
7 *Tappet bucket*
8 *Plug*
9 *No 1 bearing cup*
10 *Oil seal*

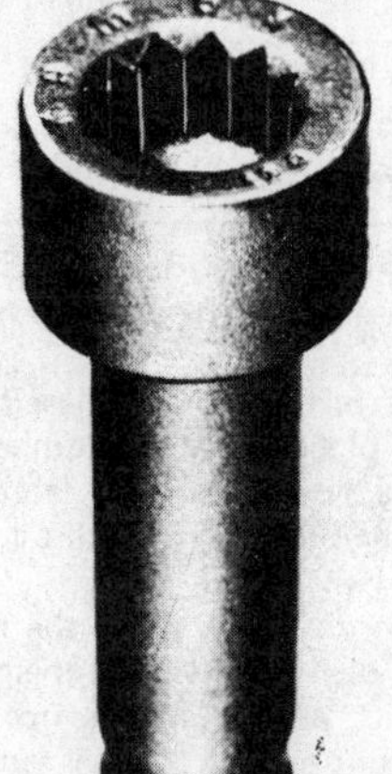

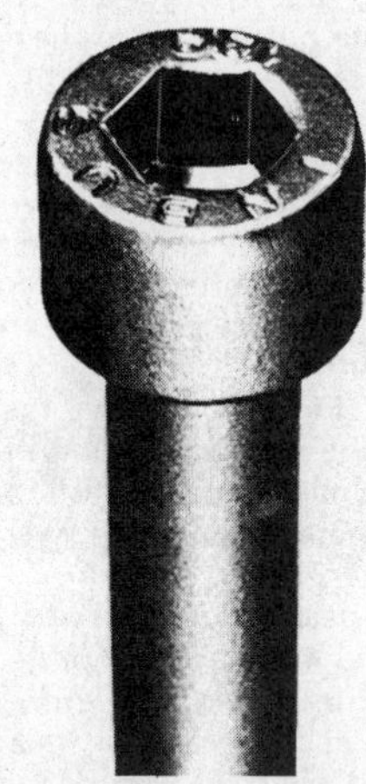

Fig. 1.5 Splined socket cylinder head bolts (left) must always be used. Hexagon socket type (right) should be discarded

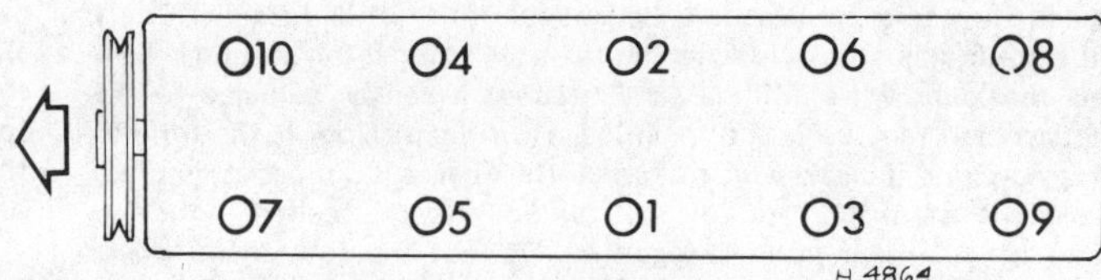

Fig. 1.6 Tightening and loosening sequence for cylinder head bolts

There are eight of these and they must not be mixed. On assembly they must go back into the bore from which they came. This problem exists also for the valves so a container for each valve assembly and tappet is indicated. Label them 1 to 8, 1 and 2 will be No 1 cylinder exhaust and inlet respectively. No 3 will be No 2 cylinder exhaust and No 4 its inlet valve. No 5 will be the inlet valve for No 3 cylinder and No 6 its exhaust valve. No 7 will be the inlet valve for No 4 cylinder and No 8 its exhaust valve. Note down the thickness of all the tappet clearance discs from No 1 valve to No 8 valve and keep it for use on reassembly.

4 Slacken the cylinder head bolts in the sequence shown in Fig. 1.6. Use a well-fitting splined tool or Allen key, as appropriate. If hexagon socket type bolts are found at dismantling, obtain splined socket bolts for use on reassembly (Fig. 1.5). Always use the correct splined tool on these bolts, do not attempt to improvise.

5 When all ten bolts have been removed lift the head from the cylinder block. It may need a little tapping to loosen it but **do not** try to prise it loose by hammering in wedges. The one we took off was not stuck hard. Lift off the gasket and cover the top of the cylinder block with a clean cloth.

6 Take the cylinder head away from the clean area and with a wire brush, blunt screwdriver and steel wool clean off all the carbon from inside the cylinder head combustion chambers, valve faces and exhaust ports. When the head is clean and shining wash your hands and take it back to the work area. Remove the sparking plugs for servicing (Chapter 4).

7 The valves are not easy to get out unless a suitable extractor is available. Because the cotters and spring caps are set so far down in the head a long claw is necessary on the extractor, and it must be split sufficiently to enable the collets to be removed and inserted. If such a tool is not to hand then find a piece of steel tube about 1 inch (25.4 mm) inside diameter which will fit over the valve stem and press down the spring cover (see Fig. 1.7). The length will depend on the size of the extractor so fit the extractor over the head fully extended, measure the distance between the claw and the valve spring seat and cut the tube to a suitable length.

8 The next step is to cut two windows of suitable size, say one inch (25.4 mm) long and 5/8 in. (15.9 mm) wide in opposite sides of the tube. The tube may then be used with the compressor to extract the collets from each valve stem in turn and the valve, springs, collets and seats may joint the tappet in the appropriate receptacle, keeping them strictly together for replacement in the same valve guide from which they were taken.

9 The valve springs may easily be checked. It is unlikely that you have a calibrated valve spring compressor, so arrange the spring on the top of a vice with the upper seat in position. Pass a piece of stout wire through

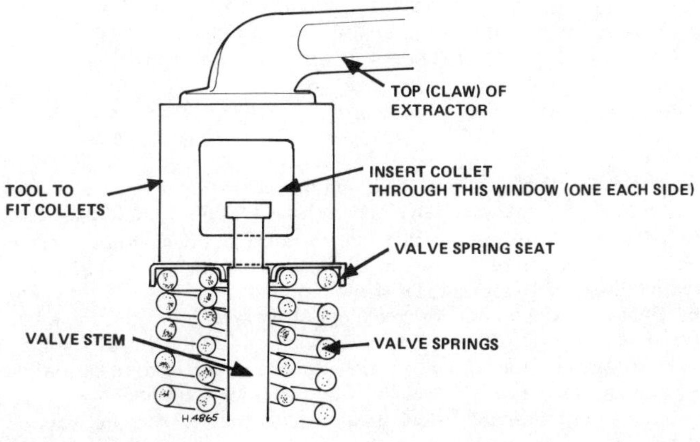

Fig. 1.7 Improvised tool used to remove and refit collets to valve stems

the seat and the spring, tie a big knot in the end above the seat so that it will not pull through the hole and hang 100 lbs (45.4 kg) on the other end (for the outer spring). The measurement of the length of the spring under this load should be 0.916 inches (23.266 mm). If it is less than 0.900 inches (22.86 mm) then it needs replacing. Check all the outer springs first and then repeat for the inners 48 lbs (21.8 kg) and a limit of 0.17 inches (17.78 mm).

10 The valves should be cleaned and checked for signs of wear or burring. Where this has occurred the inlet valves may be reground on a machine at the agents, but exhaust valves must not be reground in the machine but ground in by hand. Dimensions are shown on Fig. 1.8.

There is also the question of wear in the valve guides. This may be detected by fitting a new valve in the guide and checking the amount that the rim of the valve will move sideways, when the top of the valve stem is flush with the top of valve guide. The rock limit for the inlet valve guide is 0.016 ins (0.4 mm) and 0.032 ins (0.8 mm) for the exhaust valve. This can be measured with feeler gauges if you use a clamp as a datum but it must be with a new valve. If the rock is at this limit with your own valve, or less than this then there is nothing to worry about. If the rock exceeds the limit with a new valve then this will probably mean a new cylinder head so consult an agent before going any further.

11 Do not labour away too long grinding in the valves. If the valve seat and valve are not satisfactory after fifteen minutes hard work then you will probably do more harm than good by going on. Make sure both surfaces are clean, smear the grinding paste onto the valve evenly and using a suction type cup work the valve with an oscillating motion, lifting the valve away from the seat occasionally to stop ridging. Clean the seat and valve frequently and carry on until there is an even band, grey in colour on both seat and valve (about 1/16 in/1.58 mm wide). Wipe off all the paste and leave well alone.

12 The surface of the head must be checked with a straight-edge and feeler gauge. Lay the straight-edge along the centre of the machined face of the head. Make sure there are no ridges at the extreme ends and measure the clearance with feelers between each combustion chamber head. This is the area where the narrowest part of the cylinder head gasket comes - and where the gasket is most likely to fail. If the straight-edge is firmly in place and feelers in excess of 0.004 in (0.1 mm) can be put between the head and the straight-edge then the head should be taken to the agent for servicing or, more probably, a new one.

13 Finally, there is the question of valve stem seals. It is best to replace them if there is any appreciable amount of oil carbon (the soft greasy sort) on the valve head (not the valve face) for this means oil has been finding its way down the guides. If there is no such carbon then leave well alone, but if it is necessary to replace the seal there may be snags. Pulling off the old seal is simple with pliers. With a packet of new oil seals is a small plastic sleeve. This is fitted over the valve stem and lubricated and then the seal should be pushed on over the plastic sleeve until it seats on the guide. This must be done with a special tool VW 10 204 which fits snugly round the outside of the seal and pushes it on squarely. If the seal is assembled without the plastic sleeve the seal will be damaged and oil consumption will become excessive. If you cannot put them on properly then ask the agent to do it for you.

14 The camshaft should be tested if possible for 'run-out' by mounting it between centres in a lathe and checking the bearing surfaces with a dial gauge. Examine the cam lobes for wear and burns. Small blemishes may be removed with a fine oil stone but do not attempt to remove grooves or ridges. If it is necessary to replace the camshaft be careful that you get the right one, there are several kinds which will fit but give entirely the wrong valve timing. Refit the camshaft and its bearings without the valves in the head and check the endplay. The limit for this is 0.005 in (0.015 mm). Radial play must be negligable 0.0015 to 0.0024 in (0.04 to 0.06 mm). The limits are tight in all cases, and measurement is difficult, but fortunately the camshaft bearings do not seem to wear and, the valves keep the shaft in the upper half of the bearing.

15 When all the parts, head, valves, seats, springs, guides, seals and camshaft have been pronounced satisfactory (photo) then assembly of the head may commence. Insert the valve in the correct guide (photo), fit the inner seat, valve springs and outer seat (photo), assemble the valve spring compressor and possibly the small tube and compress the valve spring until the collets may be assembled to the valve stem (photo). If your fingers are too big, as mine are, put a blob of grease on the collet and pick it up with a small screwdriver, then insert it into the slot on the valve stem, assemble the second collet and holding them

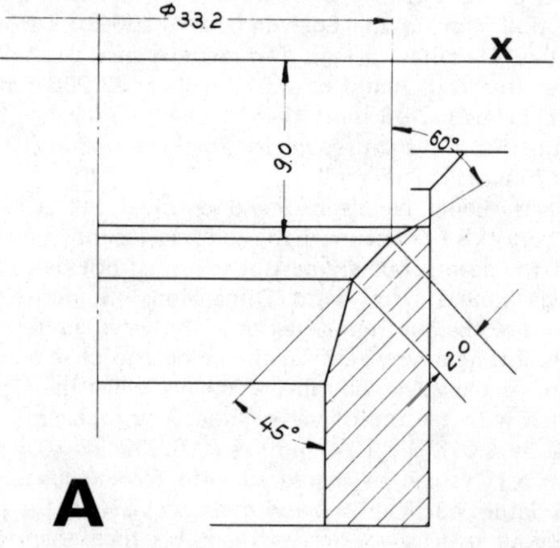

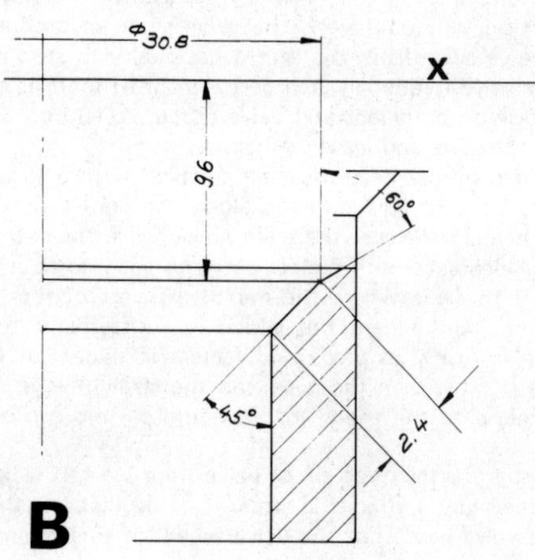

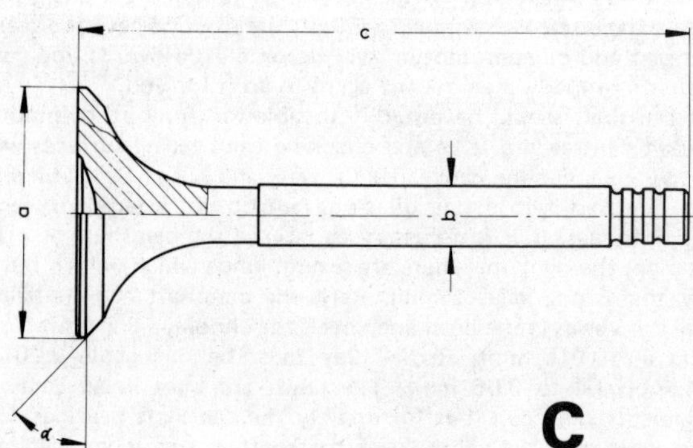

Fig. 1.8 Dimensions - valves and valve seats

Note: the valves are inset into the cylinder head 'X' is head face. Exhaust valves cannot be serviced they must be renewed.

A Inlet valve seat. Dimensions in millimetres and degrees
B = diameter
C Inlet valve. a = 1.338 in (34 mm); b = 0.314 in (8 mm); c = 3.866 in (99 mm), d = 45o

carefully together in place ease off the compressor until the spring seats the collets home. Remove the compressor, put a rag over the valve stem and compress the spring by pushing down on the valve stem. Let the valve close sharply. This is to ensure that the collets are seated correctly. If they are they will not come out, if they are not then they will and you will find them in the rag. If you did not have a rag you may never find them again, for if they do come out they fly a considerable distance if allowed so to do. Repeat until all eight valves are in position in the cylinder head.

16 Replace the tappets in the bores from which they came (photo) and install the camshaft. Fit a new oil seal at the sprocket end, lubricate the bearings, set the shaft in position and install bearing caps (photo). Nos 2 and 4 tightening the nuts in a diagonal pattern until the shaft is in place. Now install the other bearing caps making sure they are the right way round (centre-punch marks toward the drive pulley) and torque the caps down using a diagonal pattern to the specified torque. Install a new plug at the opposite end to the sprocket. The head is now ready for assembly except that valve clearances have not been adjusted.

10 Engine overhaul - adjustment of valve clearances

1 A special section is devoted to this task to make reference in other parts of the book more simple.

2 Briefly the adjustment consists of measuring the clearance, calculating the error and replacing the disc with one of the correct thickness. The 26 different thicknesses of tappet clearance disc progress from 3.00 mm to 4.25 mm in stages of 0.05 of a milli metre which seems to indicate that the first thoughts of a sensible man contemplating adjustment of tappet clearance will be to buy a set of feeler gauges graduated in metric measure. Otherwise a lot of calculation will be necessary and a set of conversion tables to transpose 0.05 mm steps into thousandths of an inch. However, it is not too difficult referring to the table at the foot of this section the thinnest disc is 3.00 mm (0.1181 inches). The thickness progresses at the rate of 0.05 mm (0.001969 inches) and since feeler gauges measure only to the nearest thousandth 0.001969 inches may be taken for practical purposes as 0.002 inches. By calculating 25 size increases at this rate the thickest disc 4.25 mm becomes 0.1681 inches where as its true value is 0.1673 and the error over the total range is 0.0008 inches which is acceptable.

3 If routine adjustment is to be done with the engine in the car first remove the air cleaner and then the valve cover (cylinder cover). The procedure is the same except that during an engine overhaul the adjustment discs will already have been removed and cleaned. Further, the size etched on the back of the disc will be known.

4 Remove the number plate and the plugs if the car is in the engine and with a socket on the crankshaft pulley nut turn the engine. **Do not** turn the camshaft pulley or the belt will be strained. Continue to turn until the two cams above No. 1 cylinder point away from their respective tappets (ie; both valves are closed). Using feeler gauges measure the clearance between the cam and the tappet (photo). Compare this with the stated clearance.

	Hot	Cold
Inlet valve	*0.20 to 0.30 mm (0.008 to 0.012 in)*	*0.15 to 0.25 mm (0.006 to 0.010 in)*
Exhaust valve	*0.40 to 0.50 mm (0.016 - 0.020 in)*	*0.35 to 0.45 mm (0.014 to 0.018 in)*

5 If the clearance is within the limits then no action is required but let us suppose that the inlet valve had clearance 0.05 mm (0.002 in) cold. It is therefore 0.10 mm outside the tolerance and dangerously near to burning the valve. To bring it to the correct measurement (0.20 mm) a tappet disc of 0.15 mm smaller size is required.

6 Repeat this operation for the exuaust valve and turn the crankshaft (or if the head is off the block, camshaft) until the valves for No 3 cylinder are in the firing position (both closed) and measure the clearances. Repeat for No 4 cylinder and then No 2 cylinder.

If the clearances are below the limit then thinner discs are required, if the clearances are too large then thicker discs are needed. Calculate the differences between the actual clearance and the middle of the tolerance of the required clearance: ie; if the required clearance is 0.15 to 0.25 mm the recommended clearance is 0.20 mm ± 0.005 mm, and divide the difference by 0.05 mm (or 0.002 inches if you are working in

9.15c Fit the springs and cap

9.15d Fit the compressor and assemble the collets

9.16a The tappet bucket and disc ready for assembly

9.16b Fit the camshaft ...

9.16c ... and the bearing caps

10.4 Measuring the clearance between the cam and the tappet

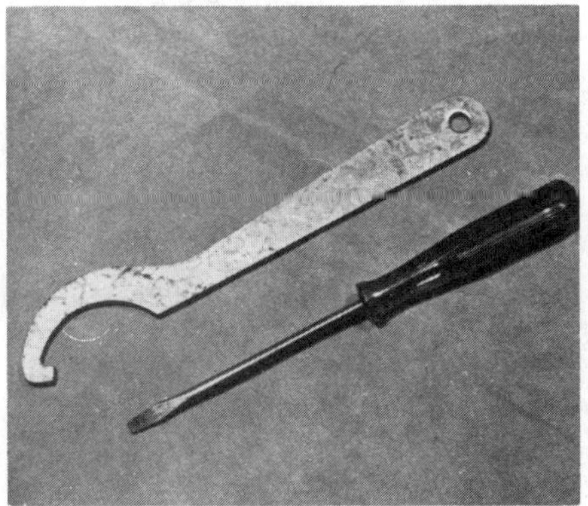

10.7a Ideally use VW/Audi tools 10.209 and 10.208 but the 'C' spanner and screwdriver shown do the job adequately

10.7b Press the tappet bucket rim down against the spring and lever the disc away

11.3a The two bolts holding the intermediate shaft (A)

11.3b Removing the intermediate shaft

11.6 On top of the piston is an arrow

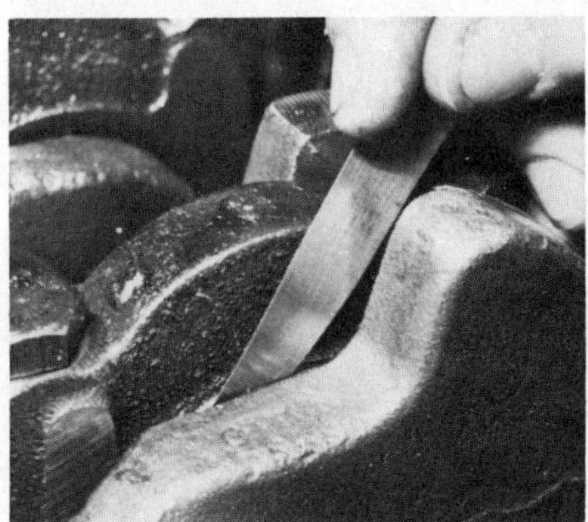

11.7 Measuring the endfloat of the crankshaft at No. 3 bearing

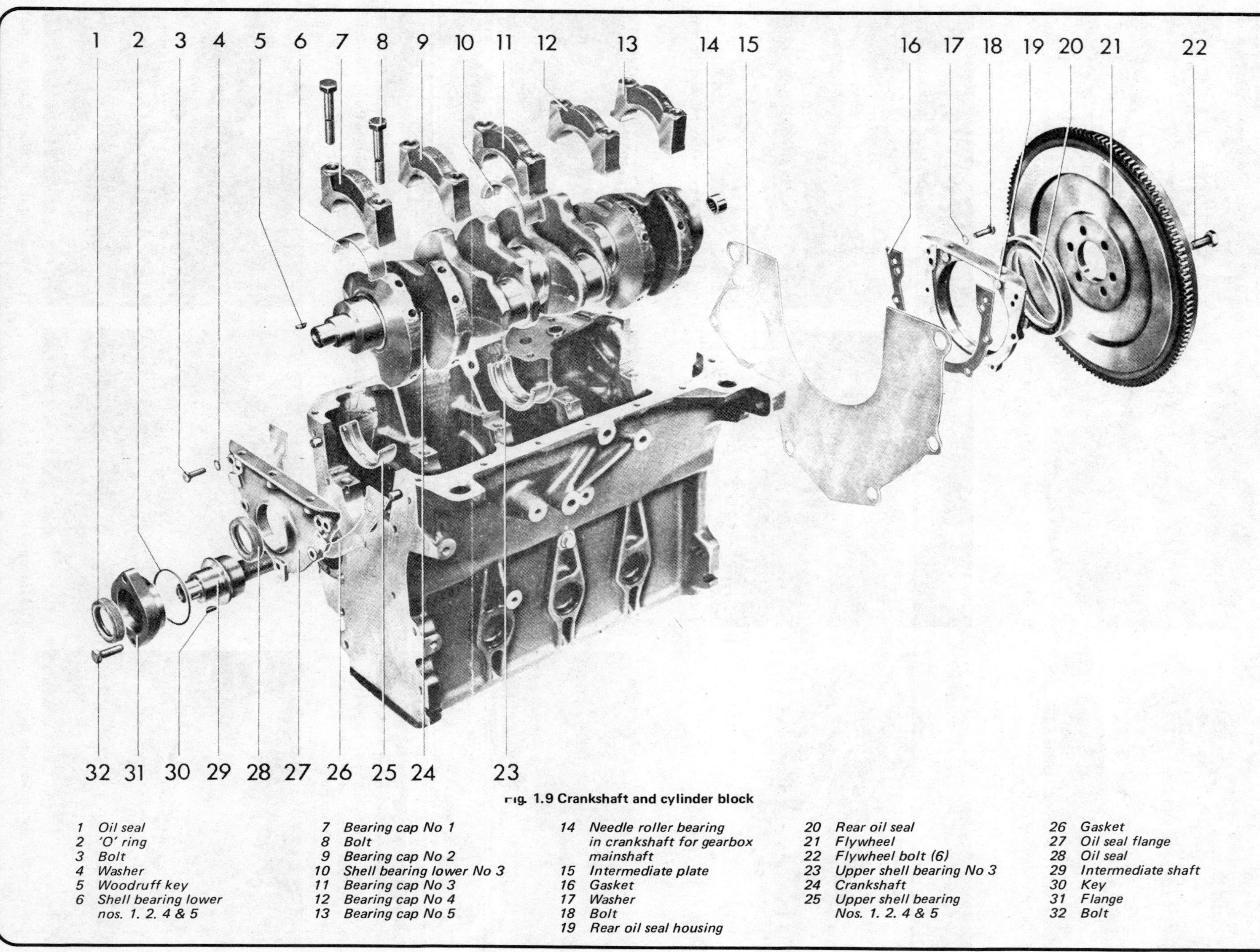

Fig. 1.9 Crankshaft and cylinder block

1 Oil seal
2 'O' ring
3 Bolt
4 Washer
5 Woodruff key
6 Shell bearing lower nos. 1. 2. 4 & 5
7 Bearing cap No 1
8 Bolt
9 Bearing cap No 2
10 Shell bearing lower No 3
11 Bearing cap No 3
12 Bearing cap No 4
13 Bearing cap No 5
14 Needle roller bearing in crankshaft for gearbox mainshaft
15 Intermediate plate
16 Gasket
17 Washer
18 Bolt
19 Rear oil seal housing
20 Rear oil seal
21 Flywheel
22 Flywheel bolt (6)
23 Upper shell bearing No 3
24 Crankshaft
25 Upper shell bearing Nos. 1. 2. 4 & 5
26 Gasket
27 Oil seal flange
28 Oil seal
29 Intermediate shaft
30 Key
31 Flange
32 Bolt

Imperial measure). This will give you the number of steps to go down or up the table of thicknesses to obtain the correct disc thickness.

7 If you know the size (etched on the back of the disc) then the actual part number required can be worked out right away. If you do not then the disc must be removed to find out. Ideally VW/Audi tools 10.209 and 10.208 should be used but we managed quite well with the tools shown in the photograph. They were a small electricians screwdriver and, oddly enough, a 'C' spanner which was just the right size to push the tappet down without pushing the tappet disc (ie; push the rim down). With the cam turned to give maximum clearance the tappet is pushed down with VW/Audi 10.209 or its counterpart against the valve springs while the tappet disc is levered out and removed by the VW/Audi 10208 or a screwdriver. Be careful, if the spanner slips when the disc is halfway out the disc will fly out sharply.

Once all the disc sizes are known a table may be constructed and the sizes of the new discs required may be calculated. Going back to the example in paragraph 5; if the disc in No 1 cylinder inlet valve tappet was etched with size 3.75 the required disc is 0.15 mm thinner ie; 3.60 and you will need disc part No 056 109567.

8 As it is unlikely that you will have the spares it will be necessary to wait until they have been obtained until the tappets can be adjusted. If the adjustment was done cold then it must be checked again when the engine is hot, and if the cylinder head has been overhauled it should be checked again, hot, after 500 km (300 miles). The recommended mileage for checking is at 1000 km (600 miles) from new and then every 30,000 km (20,000 miles). Hot is defined as engine operating temperature 176°F (80°C). It would seem a good idea to keep the piece of paper with the sizes of tappet discs fitted in a safe place.

9 The table of disc sizes is below.

Part No.	Thickness (mm)	Part No.	Thickness (mm)
056 109 555	*3.00*	*056 109 568*	*3.65*
056 109 556	*3.05*	*056 109 569*	*3.70*
056 109 557	*3.10*	*056 109 570*	*3.75*
056 109 558	*3.15*	*056 109 571*	*3.80*
056 109 559	*3.20*	*056 109 572*	*3.85*
056 109 560	*3.25*	*056 109 573*	*3.90*
056 109 561	*3.30*	*056 109 574*	*3.95*
056 109 562	*3.35*	*056 109 575*	*4.00*
056 109 563	*3.40*	*056 109 576*	*4.05*
056 109 564	*3.45*	*056 109 577*	*4.10*
056 109 565	*3.50*	*056 109 578*	*4.15*
056 109 566	*3.55*	*056 109 579*	*4.20*
056 109 567	*3.60*	*056 109 580*	*4.25*

10 Once the correct clearances have been achieved the cylinder head may be put on one side until required for reassembly. Replace the spark plugs loosely. If the engine is in the car the valve cover should be replaced and the air cleaner reassembled.

11 Engine overhaul - Phase III crankshaft, pistons and connecting rods - removal

1 Turn the engine on its side and remove the sump (oil pan). There may be more oil to run out so be ready to catch it. The oil pump complete with strainer may now be removed after undoing the two socket headed bolts. Lay it on one side for inspection and overhaul.

2 At the flywheel end remove the six bolts holding the oil seal flange and the gasket to the cylinder block and take off the flange.

3 Remove the intermediate pulley and then undo the two bolts holding the intermediate shaft oil seal flange after which the intermediate shaft may be drawn out (photos).

4 Undo the five bolts holding the oil seal flange to the front of the block and remove the flange and seal.

5 Refer to Fig. 1.9. It is important that all the bearing caps are replaced in exactly the way they are fitted before dismantling. This applies also to the shell bearings and pistons. Using a centre-punch mark the connecting rod bearing caps on the edge nearest the front (timing wheel end) using one dot for number 1, two for number 2, and so on.

6 Undo the nuts or bolts from No 1 connecting rod bearing and remove the bearing cap. It would appear that some connecting rods have bolts which fit from the top with nuts holding the caps whereas others have bolts fitting through the caps into the rods. Whichever are fitted VW recommend that they be replaced by new ones on overhaul, so add them to the order list. Gently push the connecting rod and piston out of the block through the top. Do not force it, if there is difficulty then draw the piston back and you will probably find a ridge of carbon at the top of the bore. Remove this with a scraper and if there is a metal ridge reduce this as well but do not score the bore. The piston and connecting rod will now come out. On the top of the piston there is an arrow which should point towards the front of the engine (photo). Replace the connecting rod bearing cap the right way round and mark the connecting rod and bearing cap with a centre punch so that they may be easily assembled correctly. All this takes time but the effect on assembly more than saves any time spent now on marking parts. Set the connecting rod and piston on one side labelled No 1 and proceed to remove 2, 3, and 4 labelling them likewise.

7 Now examine the main bearing caps. It will be seen that the caps are numbered one to five and that the number is on the side of the engine opposite the oil pump housing. Identify these numbers. If any are obscured then mark the caps as in the same way as the connecting rod caps. Before removing the caps push the crankshaft to the rear and measure the endfloat at No. 3 main bearing (photo). It should not be more than 0.010 in (0.25 mm) (See also Section 20, paragraph 3).

Remove the bearing caps retaining nuts, remove the bearing caps and lift out the crankshaft. If the main bearings are not being renewed make sure the shells are identified so that they go back into the same housing the same way round. The engine is now completely dismantled. Clean the carbon off the pistons and tidy up all round. It is now time to start measuring and sorting out what needs to be done to bring the engine back to standard.

Fig. 1.10 Measurement of bearing clearances using plastigauge strip

A The plastigauge packet (a) packaging (b) scale mm and ins. (c) the plastigauge 'wire'
B The guage 'wire' should be set along the journal as shown at 'a'

12 Measurement of crankshaft journals and shell bearings

1 There are two ways of doing this. If you can get the appropriate 'Plastigauge' packets (PR1 red) which has a range of 0.050 to 0.150 mm (0.002 to 0.006 in.) then the bearings can be checked this way. As each bearing should be checked for ovality two strips will be needed for each journal, a total of 16 strips. There are two other grades PG1 green 0.025 to 0.075 mm (0.010 to 0.030 in) and PB1 blue 0.100 to 0.230 mm (0.004 to 0.009 in). Since the maximum radial clearance for both main and big-end bearings is 0.12 mm (0.005 in) the red packet is the one to use. If 'Plastigauge' is not available, then use micrometers internal and external to measure the journals and bearings subtracting the journal size from the bearing size to get the radial clearance.

2 Refer to Fig. 1.10. To use 'Plastigauge' strip along the journal, replace the bearing cap and tighten the nuts to 47 ft lb (6.5 mkg) for the main journal or 32 lb ft (4.5 mkg) for the connecting rod. Take care that the shaft or connecting rod does not rotate while doing this or the 'Plastigauge' will be scrapped.

Undo the bearing cap and remove the strip. Measure the width at both ends. This will show whether there is taper or not. If there is no taper and the radial play is less than 0.12 mm then the journal and bearing are servicable at that point. Now repeat the test with the crankshaft rotated 90°. Any difference in reading will indicate ovality. The maximum ovality is 0.03 mm (0.0012 in). It will be noted that the dimensions given here in inches vary a little from the Specification figures. The Specification is given to four places of decimals, these are confined mainly to the nearest one thousandth.

3 If the bearings do not come within the tolerance allowed then the shaft must be measured with a micrometer. Consult the Specification for sizes. Briefly, the standard size is:

Main bearing journal	*54 mm (−0.04 to −0.06 mm)*
	2.126 in (−0.001 to −0.0015 in)
Big-end bearing journal	*45 mm (−0.04 to −0.06 mm)*
	1.811 in (−0.001 to −0.0015 in)

The ovality must also be considered. By much the best thing to do is to consult your VW agent or a reputable engineering company who specialize in regrind operations and take their advice. In the event that the shaft must be reground the workshop doing the work should be asked to fit the bearings.

It is early days to expect undersize II and III to be arriving but these represent further standard regrind sizes for which shell bearings are available. The dimensions are given in the Specifications.

4 If you do not use 'Plastigauge' and measure the journals and bearings with a micrometer there are a number of things to consider. Are the micrometer correctly zeroed, and are you experienced in measuring with a precision instrument? Do not accept a marginal decision but get it checked. The grinding of shafts is an expensive business.

5 When you are satisfied that the main and big-end bearings are servicable remove the shaft and clean it very carefully. Clean out the oilways and be sure no bits of rag get into them. Set the crankshaft aside and proceed to examine the state of the pistons and bores.

13 Measurement of the cylinder bores and pistons

1 If you look just above the alternator/water pump area of the cylinder block you will find a three figure number. It will be between 501 and 753 but more likely either 501, 502 or 503 for 1300 cc engines capacity or 651, 652 or 653 for 1500 cc engines. This is the code letter for the cylinder bore. As selective assembly is done the acceptable dimension of a new cylinder bore is increased from 75.01 to 75.02 to 75.03 mm for the 1300 cc vehicle and 76.51 to 76.52 to 76.53 mm for the 1500 cc vehicle. This code is most important for it states the cylinder dimension at which the engine started life. There are sizes of pistons to match and generally the clearance of the piston in the bore should be 0.03 mm on installation and with a wear limit of 0.07 mm (0.003 in).

If the table of sizes at paragraph 3 is studied it will be seen that if the piston from code 678 is fitted to a cylinder bore to code 676 the clearance is reduced to 0.0004 in (0.01 mm) although both codes are in the 1st oversize category. It is therefore most important to understand the size table, or consult someone who does for fitting the piston quoted would cause engine seizure.

2 The wear on the cylinder bores is uneven. Maximum wear may be expected on the diameter at 90° to the piston pin. There is no short cut to measuring the bore. It must be done with an internal micrometer. Measure the diameter, parallel to the piston pin and at right-angles to the pin, at 10 mm (0.04 in) from the top of the bore, midway, and 10 mm (0.04 in) from the bottom of the bore. This will give six readings and if any of them vary more than 0.04 mm (0.0016 in) from the bore diameter given by the honing code them the block must be machined and new pistons fitted. Should the difference be much more than 0.04 mm then the lubrication system is suspect. Scores due to broken rings or other misfortunes are even worse and the block should be taken to the agent should these be present for his advice.

Ovality must not be more than 0.03 mm (0.0011 in), measurement in excess of this also requires machining.

3 Table of cylinder bore and piston sizes.

Engine	Hone state	Code No.	Cylinder diameter mm.	in.	Piston diameter mm	in.
	Basic	*501*	*75.01*	*2.9531*	*74.98*	*2.9520*
	Basic	*502*	*75.02*	*2.9535*	*74.99*	*2.9524*
	Basic	*503*	*75.03*	*2.9539*	*75.00*	*2.9528*
	1st O/s	*526*	*75.26*	*2.9630*	*75.23*	*2.9618*
	1st O/s	*527*	*75.27*	*2.9634*	*75.24*	*2.9622*
	1st O/s	*528*	*75.28*	*2.9638*	*75.25*	*2.9626*
1300 cc	*2nd O/s*	*551*	*75.51*	*2.9728*	*75.48*	*2.9716*
	2nd O/s	*552*	*75.52*	*2.9732*	*75.49*	*2.9720*
	2nd O/s	*553*	*75.53*	*2.9736*	*75.50*	*2.9724*
	3rd O/s	*601*	*76.01*	*2.9925*	*75.98*	*2.9913*
	3rd O/s	*602*	*76.02*	*2.9929*	*75.99*	*2.9917*
	3rd O/s	*603*	*76.03*	*2.9933*	*76.00*	*2.9921*
	Basic	*651*	*76.51*	*3.0122*	*76.48*	*3.0110*
	Basic	*652*	*76.52*	*3.0126*	*76.49*	*3.0114*
	Basic	*653*	*76.53*	*3.0130*	*76.50*	*3.0118*
	1st O/s	*676*	*76.76*	*3.0220*	*76.73*	*3.0209*
	1st O/s	*677*	*76.77*	*3.0224*	*76.74*	*3.0213*
	1st O/s	*678*	*76.78*	*3.0228*	*76.75*	*3.0217*
1500 cc	*2nd O/s*	*701*	*77.01*	*3.0319*	*76.98*	*3.0307*
	2nd O/s	*702*	*77.02*	*3.0323*	*76.99*	*3.0311*
	2nd O/s	*703*	*77.03*	*3.0327*	*77.00*	*3.0315*
	3rd O/s	*751*	*77.51*	*3.0516*	*77.48*	*3.0504*
	3rd O/s	*752*	*77.52*	*3.0520*	*77.49*	*3.0508*
	3rd O/s	*753*	*77.53*	*3.0524*	*77.50*	*3.0512*

4 It is no use considering the pistons until the cylinder bore problem has been settled, but once that has been done the required piston size may be read from the table in paragraph 3. If the bore has not worn enough to warrant rework the next thing is to see whether the pistons are in limit. On the piston crown are two pieces of information. An arrow which points, when the engine is assembled to the front of the engine and the piston nominal diameter in millimetres. The piston diameter should be measured 16 mm (5/8 in) from the bottom edge of the piston at right-angles to the piston pin. If the measured diameter varies from the nominal diameter by more than 0.04 mm (0.0016 in) then the piston should be replaced. If the bores show no wear and the pistons are in limit then they may be put back in the engine. If only the pistons are worn then new pistons to fit the bores may be fitted but care must be taken to see that the difference in weight between any of the pistons in one engine does not exceed 17 grams.

5 There are more measurements to be taken concerning the rings. These are dealt with in Section 14.

6 When buying new pistons care should be taken not only to obtain the correct weight and diameter but also the correct shape. There are three different shapes of piston. Two are concave on top but with different depths of 'dish', the third one has a flat top. The 1300 cc engine has concave pistons with depth of 'dish' 4.5 mm (0.177 in), the 1500 cc engines ZB and ZC having compression ratio 9.7 have flat top pistons, and the remainder of the 1500 cc range have pistons with 'dish' 6.0 mm (0.236 in) deep.

7 To summarize this Section:

a) The maximum wear allowable in the bore is 0.04 mm (0.0016 in) from the code size. Wear above this means machining and new pistons. Ovality over 0.03 mm (0.0011 in) also requires this treatment.

b) The maximum wear on the piston is 0.04 (0.0016 in) from code size. Wear above this means new pistons but not necessarily reboring. Remember the weight limit.

c) If both are within the limits then they may be reassembled after the rings have been serviced.

14 Measurement and servicing of piston pins and piston rings

1 As yet the pistons have not been removed from the connecting rods. If the piston has passed inspection so far then it must be removed from the connecting rod, the piston pin checked and the rings removed, checked and possibly replaced. It is suggested that each piston is removed serviced and replaced in turn, this avoids confusion.

2 If the piston failed its inspection then remove the piston pin and fit a new piston assembly with new rings as supplied from the VW store.

3 From the outset it must be clear that rings come in sets, if you break one then the minimum purchase is three, so be careful.

4 To remove the piston pin first remove the circlips from each end and then push the pin out. If it is tight, then raise the temperature of the piston to 60°C (140°F), hold it by a light bulb, and the pin will come out easily. Check the play in the connecting rod bush, if the pin seems loose the running clearance limits are 0.011 to 0.025 mm (0.0004 to 0.0009 in) which means if you can rock it at all then either the bush or the pin are worn. New bushes can be obtained and pressed in to the connecting rod if necessary but they must then be reamed to size to fit the pin. It is felt that this job should be left to the agent, not because it is difficult but because it requires an expensive reamer. However this is rarely necessary.

5 It is almost certain that the rings will require attention. There are three, the top two are compression rings, the lowest one is the oil scraper ring. The compression rings will probably be free in the grooves but the scraper ring may be seized in the groove. This presents a problem, soak the ring in paraffin or some suitable solvent and ease it gently until it will rotate round the piston. The rings must now be removed from the piston. This is done only with care. There are special tools which are called piston ring pliers which can be bought and will break rings just as easily as any other tool if not used carefully, but do make the job simpler if used with care. Once the rings are eased out of the grooves and off the piston make sure that the top compression ring is marked so that it can go back into the top groove the right way up. The middle ring has 'TOP' marked on it as does the scraper ring. Gently remove all carbon from the rings and grooves. Now insert the rings in its groove and roll it round the piston to see that the groove is clear (photo).

6 Clean the cylinder bore and using the piston as a fixture push the ring down the bore until it is 15 mm (5/8 in) from the top. Now measure the gap with a feeler gauge (photo). This should be not more than 1.0 mm (0.039 in) for compression and scraper rings.

7 Refit the rings to the piston spacing the gaps at 120 degree intervals and making sure the top is the right way up. With a feeler gauge measure the clearance between the ring and the piston groove (photo). This must not exceed 0.15 mm (0.006 in).

8 If new rings are to be fitted the gap must be measured in the cylinder and adjusted if necessary with a fine file to the limits shown in the Specification. The bores must be deglazed using abrasive paper, or a glaze busting tool held in an electric drill, in order to assist the bedding-in of the new rings.

9 If the rings are correct then refit the piston to the connecting rod, making sure the arrow on the piston points to the front, (you marked the bearing cap), refit the circlips and proceed to check the rings on the other three pistons.

10 The later vehicles use a different scraper ring. It can be recognized by a spiral spring in the ring and across the gap. This is where things become difficult. Two types of piston are used in production (MAHLE and KS) and there are different diameters for the oil scraper grooves. If you find your vehicle has these rings it would be best to go to the agent and ask how to refit them according to the latest instructions. The modification is to overcome excessive oil consumption, so if you have this problem and the old pattern rings a visit to the agent is also required, for this may be cure for your trouble.

14.5 Checking the ring/groove for burrs

14.6 Insert the ring in the bore and check the gap with a feeler gauge

14.7 Checking the ring/groove clearance

15.2 Examine the cover of the oil pump for scoring

15.3 Checking the backlash of the oil pump gears

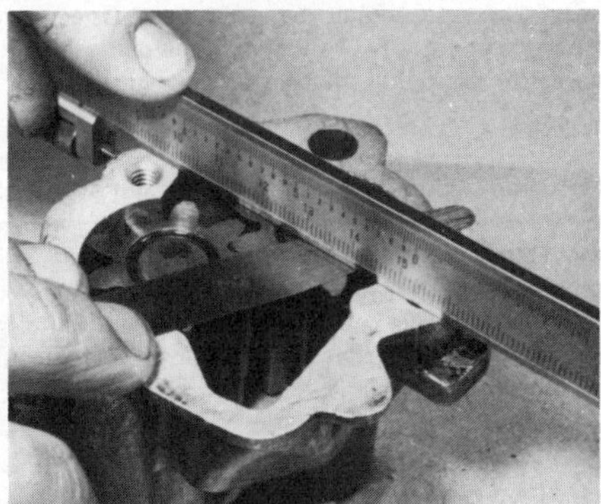

15.4 Checking endfloat of the oil pump gears

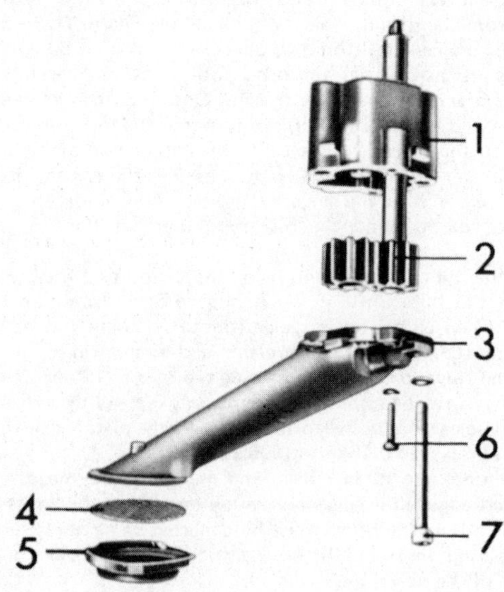

Fig. 1.11 Oil pump - exploded view

1 Body
2 Gears
3 Cover
4 Strainer
5 Cap
6 Bolt (2)
7 Bolt (2)

15 Oil pump - inspection and overhaul

1 Refer to Fig. 1.11. The strainer gauze may be removed when the cap is levered off with a screwdriver. Clean the gauze, replace it and refit the cap.

2 Remove the two small bolts and take the cover away from the body. Examine the face of the cover (photo). As will be seen in the photograph the gears have marked the cover. If the depth of this marking is significant then the face of the cover must be machined flat again.

3 Remove the gears and wash the body and gears in clean paraffin. Dry them and reassemble the gears, lubricating them with clean engine oil. Measure the backlash between the gears with a feeler gauge (photo). This should be 0.05 to 0.20 mm (0.002 to 0.008 in).

4 Now place a straight-edge over the pump body along the line joining the centres of the two gears and measure with a feeler gauge the axial clearance between the gears and the straight-edge (photo). This must not be more than 0.15 mm (0.006 in).

5 If all is well check that the shaft is not slack in its bearings, and reassemble the pump for fitting to the engine.

6 If there is any doubt about the pump it is recommended strongly that a replacement be obtained. Once wear starts in a pump it progresses rapidly. In view of the damage that may follow a loss of oil pressure skimping the oil pump repair is a false economy.

16 Intermediate shaft - inspection and overhaul

1 Check the fit of the intermediate shaft in its bearings. Examine the surface of the fuel pump drive cam and check the teeth of the distributor drive gear for scuffing or chipping (photo).

2 It is unlikely that serious damage has occurred but if in doubt take it along to the official agent for advice.

17 Flywheel - inspection and overhaul

1 If the face of the flywheel is scored or pitted due to a slipping clutch it may be necessary to have it machined. Overheating can cause surface cracking. Any such cracks mean that the flywheel must be replaced. It is difficult to define limits for such defects. Should there be doubt consult an experienced automotive mechanic.

2 On rare occasions the starter ring may be damaged. The solenoid type starter does not switch on full power until the teeth are in mesh so the type of wear associated with an inertia starter is absent. If necessary the ring may be removed from the flywheel by drilling a hole between two teeth and splitting the ring with a chisel. A new ring should be heated to 500°F (250°C), pushed into place, and allowed to cool slowly. However, unless you have experience in this type of work and means of measuring the temperature accurately then the job is best left to experts. If the ring is shrunk on in the wrong place it must be removed by splitting and yet another fitted.

3 It is possible to remove the flywheel with the engine still in the vehicle if the gearbox and clutch are taken out from underneath.

18 Engine overhaul - assembly, general instructions

If the work has been carried out carefully all of the components of the engine have been overhauled, or new ones obtained, and the engine is ready for assembly. This is the most pleasant part of the job.

Clear away any dirty rags, old parts, dirty paraffin and with clean hands and clean overalls, lay out the clean tools on a clean bench.

Plenty of clean non-fluffy rag will be needed, an oil can full of clean engine oil and a set of engine overhaul gaskets. This is a standard pack. Undo the pack and identify each of its contents.

A further tool is required. This is a torque wrench capable of measuring up to 60 lb ft (8.5 kg m). It will also be necessary to have an extension bar and socket spanners for metric sizes (mm) 6, 8, 10, 12 and 14.

From now on nuts and bolts must be tightened to specified torques. These are not quoted in the text but are listed in the Specification. Use the open end or ring spanners to do up the nuts and bolts but use the torque wrench to tighten the last bit.

We have tried to divide the job so far into tasks without being dogmatic. The assembly problem will follow the same pattern and we suggest you complete the tasks without interruption. Put the crankshaft in place and fit all the main bearings and then think about the next job. This way you will not forget things. Finally, take your time, if you are not sure then go over it again.

19 Crankshaft oil seals - removal and replacement

1 This task has been left until the assembly of the engine is ready to commence because the seals are easily damaged and once placed in the flanges should be assembled to the engine.

2 The rear (flywheel) oil seal is contained in an aluminium frame (photo). Ease out the old seal, clean the housing and press in the new seal. Official agents have two special tools to do this 10.205 and 10.220, so it is evident that the seating of this seal needs care. In August 1974 a modification to the crankshaft changed the diameter of the flange to which the flywheel in fitted from 82 mm to 85 mm. The inner diameter of the oil seal has been altered to suit. The outer diameter remains the same. Tools VW/Audi 10.205 and 10.220 are no longer of use to remove and fit the new seal and tool 2003 must be used. This seems all the more reason why the flange should be removed before refitting the oil seal. Ease it in very gently and press it in the last bit either with a plate in a large vice or a mandrel press. Alternatively use the flywheel bolts and make up a suitable disc. **Do not** hammer it in, if the lips of the seal are damaged oil will seep through to the clutch eventually and you will be in the repair business again.

3 The front seal is also delicate, although if this one does not work at the worst you will only lose oil. Ease the seal out of the flange, clean the flange and press the seal into position. VW/Audi say this seal may be replaced with the engine in position in the car and so it may if you have VW/Audi tools 10.219 and 10.203 to remove and replace it and you have practiced the job with the engine out of the chassis. We did not think this was a job for the DIY owner. Tool 10 219 is a piece of steel rod shaped to extract the seal. 10 203 is a collar placed over the crankshaft in place of the pulley and pushes the seal into position when the pulley nut is tightened. A modification introduced in August 1974 requires this seal to be pressed in until it is 2 mm (0.08 in) below the outer face of the flange. Tool 10 219 is no use for removing this seal and tool 10

203 must be modified to allow the tool to enter the flange to a depth of 2 mm (0.08 in). If the rear and front seals are to be replaced with the engine in position we believe that it is better to remove the oil seal flanges, replace the seals and fit new gaskets using a sealing compound such as Golden Hermatite. This will permit proper examination of the shaft for scoring or wear (photos).

20 Engine overhaul - Phase IV assembly of connecting rods, pistons and crankshaft to the cylinder block

1 Place the cylinder block upside down on the bench. Wipe carefully the main journal seatings and fit the main bearing top halves into place. Nos 1, 2, 4 and 5 are plain shells with grooves in them No 3 has small flanges (photo). If the old bearings are being refitted it is essential that they go back in the same housing the same way round. Lightly oil the shells (photo) and lift in the crankshaft (photo).

2 Fit the lower shells to the bearing caps and install them over the studs (photo). These are plain shells. Once again if the old ones are being used they must go back in the same place the same way round. This applies anyway to the bearing caps. They are numbered, one goes next to the timing gears and the numbers are on the side opposite to the oil pump.

3 Tighten the bearing cap nuts to 12 ft lb (1.8 kg m) and then tap the shaft to the rear to seat the bearings. Now using a diagonal pattern torque the cap nuts to 47 lb ft (6.5 kg m) (photo). Lever the shaft to the rear as far as it will go and check the clearance between No 3 main bearing and the crankshaft with a feeler gauge to determine crankshaft endfloat (photo). It should be between 0.07 to 0.17 mm (0.0028 to 0.0067 in) for new bearings and not more than 0.25 mm (0.010 in) maximum. If the maximum is exceeded then No 3 bearing must be replaced by a new one.

4 Lubricate the rear of the crankshaft and using a new gasket install the rear oil seal and flange (photo 19.3a). Tighten the six bolts to the correct torque 7 ft lb (1 kg m).

5 Lubricate the front of the shaft and install the front oil seal and flange and tighten the bolts (photo 19.3b).

6 Install the intermediate shaft. A new O-ring must be fitted to the oil seal flange and a new oil seal inside the flange. Tighten the two bolts holding the flange to the cylinder block.

7 Lay the block on one side. Fit a ring compressor to No 1 piston (see next paragraph) and insert the connecting rod (minus bearing cap) and piston into No 1 cylinder (photo). Check that the arrow on the piston points to the front of the block and gradually ease the piston and rings into the block removing the ring compressor as the rings go into the bore. When all the rings are safely in, pull the big-end bearing to one side of the crankshaft, check that the shell bearing is seated correctly in the connecting rod, lubricate the shell, and fit the connecting rod to the crankshaft journal. Check that the other half of the shell bearing is seated in the bearing cap, lubricate the bearing and fit the cap to the connecting rod (photo). Check that all the markings (installed on dismantling) agree and having fitted **new** bolts or nuts (see Section 11, paragraph 6), torque the nuts to the correct torque of 32 lb ft (4.5 kg m). Repeat the process for pistons 2, 3 and 4.

8 The use of a ring compressor is strongly recommended. It is cheap enough to buy, but if you cannot get one then make one. A piece of 1/16 in (1.58 mm) thick sheet metal about 2 in (50.8 mm) wide wrapped round the piston to compress the rings into the grooves is all that is required. It may be held in position with a large Jubilee clip or some similar device. This way the rings go in safely. It is very difficult to coax the rings in one at a time and a broken ring will not only hold up the job for even a week, but a new set of rings must be bought. That will cost more than a ring compressor.

9 Once all the big-end bearings are installed check the axial play of each bearing. Push the connecting rod against the crankshaft web and measure the gap on the other side with a feeler gauge. It should not be more than 0.40 mm (0.015 in). If it is then consult the agent. Either the bearings are faulty or there has been a possible fault introduced when regrinding the journal. Turn the cylinder block back onto the face to which the cylinder head fits.

16.1 Examine the intermediate shaft gear and bearing for wear and damage

19.2 The rear oil seal in its mounting

19.3a The rear oil seal in its casing installed over the crankshaft flange

19.3b The front oil seal in its housing installed over the crankshaft

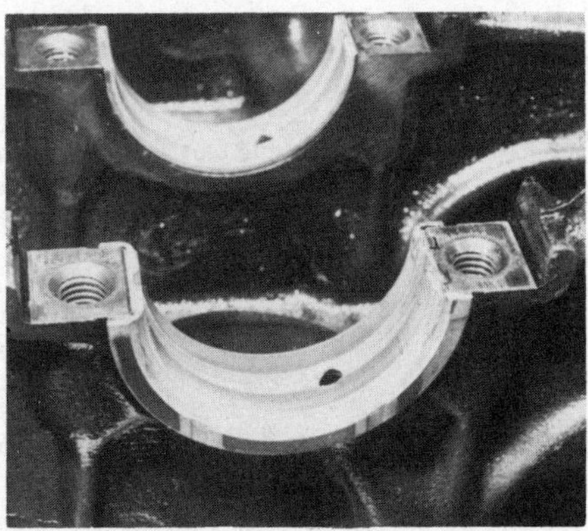
20.1a Fit the upper bearing shells to the block. This is No. 3 with the flanges

20.1b Lightly oil the bearing shell and ...

10 Replace the oil pump. There are two bolts torque to the correct valve (photo).
11 Clean round the machined face to which the oil pan (sump) is fitted, smear it with jointing compound, fit a new gasket and install the oil pan (photo). Tighten down steadily to the required torque. This could be difficult if you do not have the special tools but pull the bolts down evenly to 7 lb ft (1 kg m). The later models have a cast sump, this needs more care when pulling down than the early pressed steel version.
12 Install the timing belt pulley on the intermediate shaft (photo).
13 Install the double pulley (timing belt and V-belt) pulley onto the crankshaft. Do not forget the keys and torque the holding bolts to the correct amount. Turn the engine the right way up and support it securely with blocks, under the oil pan.

21 Engine overhaul - Phase V assembly of cylinder head, timing belt and distributor

1 Clean the top face of the cylinder block. Make a final inspection of the bores and lubricate them. Turn the engine two or three revolutions to distribute the oil round the pistons.
2 If you look at the edge of the block between No 3 and 4 cylinders on the side above the distributor, the engine number is stamped on an inclined surface. Using this as a datum, install a **new** cylinder head gasket so that the word 'OBEN' engraved on the gasket is over this datum point and on the top side of the gasket (photo).
3 The cylinder head was overhauled in Phase II, Section 9 and the camshaft assembled with the correct clearances for the valves in Section 10. Refer to Fig. 1.4, replace the head on the block (photo) and refit No 7 and 8 holding down bolts. **Do not** use jointing compound. Check that the gasket is seating correctly and fit the remainder of the holding down bolts. Now following the sequence in Fig. 1.6 tighten up the bolts until the head is firmly held. Now using the torque wrench (see Fig. 1.12), tighten the bolts in the same sequence in the stages and to the torque wrench settings given in the Specifications.
4 Fit the pulley to the camshaft and torque to Specification.
5 Turn the camshaft pulley so that both cams for No 1 cylinder are in the open position and the dot on the camshaft gear tooth is in line with the valve cover (photo 8.3a). The photo shows it in line with the edge of the head, allow for the thickness of the cover flange and gasket.
6 Rotate the crankshaft pulley and the intermediate shaft pulley until the dot on the intermediate shaft pulley and the mark on the V-belt pulley coincide (photo 8.2). Install the timing belt tensioner loosely

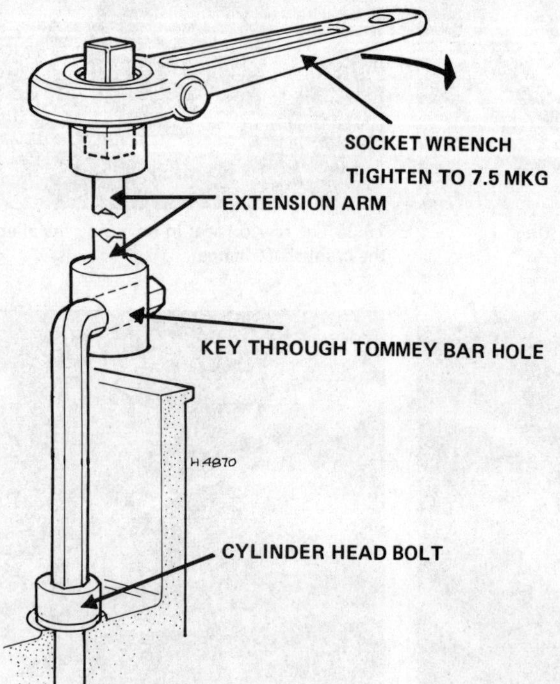

Fig. 1.12 Method of tightening cylinder head bolts if correct tools are not available (early type bolts only)

and then the timing belt. Making sure the marks are still in place put a spanner on the adjuster and tighten the belt until it will twist only 90 degrees when held between the finger and thumb halfway between the camshaft pulley and the intermediate shaft pulley. Tighten the eccentric adjuster fixing nut to 32 lb ft (4.5 kg m). Re-check the timing marks, repeat the operation if they do not agree with Specification (ie; one shaft has moved).
7 Refer back to Section 8, Phase I, paragraph 2, and read paragraphs 2, 3 and 4. The timing marks are all set ready to install the distributor so install it (photo). If you have lost the place turn to Chapter 4. Tighten the clamp. Make sure the distributor shaft is in mesh with the oil pump shaft: the distributor will not seat correctly if it is not. The points should be set correctly, see Chapter 4.

22 Engine overhaul - Phase VI completion of engine assembly

1 The remainder of the assembly consists of bolting on the various components to the exterior of the engine.
2 Install the oil pressure sender switch. Torque to the correct amount. Using a new gasket and jointing compound refit the oil filter flange to the cylinder block (photo 21.7). Do not fit the filter yet. Assemble the distance piece and the fuel pump to the block (photo, Chapter 3, 4.4). Use a new flange ring. If a new pump is to be fitted it may be different from the old one and will require different holding bolts (8 x 30 mm instead of 8 x 22 mm). Refer to Chapter 3 for details. Make sure the lever is correctly seated on the cam. Now install the **new** oil filter (photo) - hand tight only.
3 Refit the water pump using a new O-ring. Refit the water pump pulley to the water pump coupling. Refit the water hose from the pump to the flange on the cylinder block. The flange should not have been dismantled but if for some reason it has then a new gasket will be needed and jointing compound.
4 If the alternator bracket was removed refit it and then refit the alternator. Install the V-belt and adjust the tension (Chapter 10).
5 Wipe the face of the block and fit a new inlet manifold gasket. Position the four exhaust manifold gaskets at the same time. Carefully fit the inlet manifold (photo) and tighten it squarely there are eight socket head screws, four short and four long. Tighten these to the correct torque. Install the carburettor if not already fitted and the fuel hose from the carburettor to the fuel pump.
6 Fit the exhaust manifold over the studs, fit the washers and nuts and tighten the nuts to the correct torque. (photo)
7 Check that the coolant drain plug is in place and correctly tightened (photo 3.3).
8 Fit the small oil seal to No 1 camshaft bearing cap and check that the plug is in place at the end of the cylinder head. Fit a new gasket to the valve cover and bolt it to the cylinder head. Do not forget the packing pieces. Tighten down methodically to 6 lb ft (1 kg m).
9 Refit the timing belt guard. Rotate the engine and check that the belts do not foul it, adjust if necessary.
10 Fit the spark plugs to the correct torque. They should have been serviced and refitted finger-tight before the head was assembled (Section 10, paragraph 10).
11 Clean the flywheel flange, replace the flywheel over the dowel and fit the flywheel bolts. Fit the clamp shown in Section 8, paragraphs 11, and tighten the bolts to the correct torque. The bolts must then be locked with 'LOCTITE 270' or 'OMNIFIT 150 GREEN M' (photo).
12 When the flywheel is in position find the punch mark you made for the clutch, line up the one on the clutch and assemble the clutch disc and pressure plate. Overhaul of these is discussed in Chapter 5. The long hub of the disc is toward the pressure plate. Enter the bolts and turn them a thread or two. Before the pressure plate locates the clutch disc on the flywheel, using the tool you made in Section 8, paragraph 10, or a spare mainshaft centre the driveplate very carefully. This is again emphasised for if the clutch is not centralized correctly the engine cannot be assembled to the transmission.
13 Tighten the clutch bolts a few turns at a time in a diagonal pattern to pull the spring up squarely. Tighten to Specification.
14 Fit the rotor arm to the distributor and then the cap and leads and connect the leads to the plugs. The engine is now ready to go back into the vehicle.
15 If the transmission was removed with the engine then fit the intermediate plate and then refit the gearbox to the engine (5 bolts).

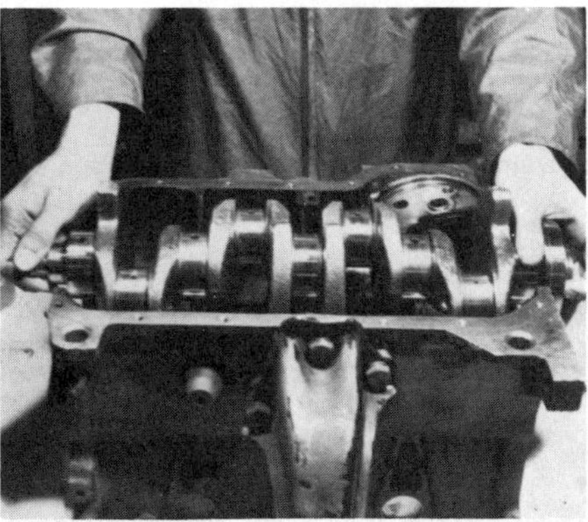
20.1c ... lower the crankshaft into the bearings

20.2 Fit the lower main bearing caps and ...

20.3 ... tighten the nuts to the correct torque

20.7a Fit a ring compressor to the piston and install the piston and connecting rod

20.7b Fit the bearing cap to the connecting rod

20.10 Install the oil pump

20.11 Fit the sump and tighten the bolts

20.12 Install the 'V' belt pulleys

21.2 Clean the head and fit a new cylinder head gasket

21.3 Replace the cylinder head

21.7 Refit the distributor – remember the centre punch marks and refit the oil filter flange to the block

22.2 Install a NEW oil filter

Refit the starter. It is now possible to check the timing mark on the flywheel through the window in the bellhousing as a further check to ignition setting (Chapter 4).

16 The engine and transmission are now ready for assembly to the subframe, carry on from Section 6, paragraph 15.

17 If the engine is to go in from above turn to Section 3, paragraph 27.

22.5 Fit the inlet manifold to the block

22.6 Fit the exhaust manifold to the block

22.8 Fit the oil seal 'A' to No. 1 camshaft bearing cap

23 Fault diagnosis - Engine

Note: When investigating faults do not be tempted into making snap decisions. Start from the beginning of the check procedure and follow it through. There may be more than one fault

Symptom	Reason/s	Remedy
Engine will not turn over when the starter switch is operated	Flat battery Bad battery connections Bad connections at solenoid switch and/ or starter motor	Check that battery is fully charged and that all connections are clean and tight
	Starter motor jammed Solenoid defective Starter motor defective	Remove starter and check (Chapter 10)
Engine turns over normally but will not fire	No spark at plugs No fuel reaching engine Too much fuel reaching engine (flooding)	Check ignition (Chapter 4) Check fuel system (Chapter 3) Check fuel system (Chapter 3)
Engine runs unevenly and misfires or lack of power	Ignition fault	Check ignition, plug leads faulty or loose (Chapter 4)
	Fuel system fault Valve clearances wrong Engine badly worn	Dirt in carburettor, faulty fuel pump (Chapter 3) Check valve clearances Overhaul engine
Excessive oil consumption or smoky exhaust	Wear in engine cylinders Wear in valve stems	Overhaul engine
Oil on engine and garage floor	Leaking gaskets/seals	Locate leak and fit new seal or gasket
Excessive mechanical noise	Wrong tappet setting Worn bearings Piston slap when cold (disappear when hot)	Adjust tappet clearance Overhaul engine Pistons/bores approaching rebore stage
Engine vibrates excessively	Side or front engine bearers require adjustment Ignition not adjusted correctly. Plugs dirty	Refit or replace Check ignition (Chapter 4)
Engine runs on when ignition switched off	Carburettor electro magnetic valve faulty	Check valve (Chapter 3)

Chapter 2 Cooling, heating and exhaust systems

For modifications, and information applicable to later models, see Supplement at end of manual

Contents

Specifications

Cooling system

Type	Pressurized with coolant pump, fan and radiator.
Pump	Centrifugal, belt driven.
Fan	Electrically driven by an integral motor thermostatically controlled by coolant temperature.
Radiator	Honey comb vertical flow.
Radiator cap valve	Opens at 13 to 15 psi (0.9 to 1.15 kg/sq cm)
Coolant capacity:	
With overflow tank	7 litres, 11.4 Imp. pints, 13.8 US pints
Without overflow tank	6 litres, 10.5 Imp. pints, 12.6 US pints
Thermostat:	
Begins to open	80°C (176°F)
Fully open	90°C (194°F)
Stroke when fully open	7 mm (0.27 in)
Radiator fan thermo switch:	
Opens at	90° to 95°C (194 - 203°F)
Closes at	85° to 90°C (185 - 194°F)
Antifreeze	NW G.10 (Ethylene Glycol) see Section 2

Heating system

Type	Fresh air blower assisted
Heating agent	Heat-exchanger using engine coolant.

Torque wrench settings

Included in the text, where necessary.

1 Cooling system - general description

1 The cooling system is conventional, using a centrifugal pump driven from the crankshaft pulley by a V-belt and a thermostatically controlled radiator. The radiator is a normal vertical flow honeycomb with a header and bottom tank. It is cooled by a fan drawing air through a grille and cowling into the honeycomb (see Fig. 2.1). The fan is activated by a thermo-switch screwed into the bottom tank. When the ignition switch is closed the fan circuit becomes live but is completed only when the coolant temperature reaches 90°C (194°F) and the thermo switch closes. The fan then operates until the temperature of the coolant falls below 90°C. This arrangement allows the radiator to be placed by the side of the engine thus shortening the engine compartment. It also means that the fan will run at fast speed while the engine is on tick-over in a traffic jam, preventing overheating.

2 Refer to Fig. 2.2. Coolant is forced into the cylinder block through the pump outlet and under the combined action of the thermo-siphon effect and pump pressure rises to the top of the block through the water jacket and emerges from the block either at the flange halfway along the block (photo), or at the small flange or tee-piece at the back of the block. The small flange circuit is a heater circuit which will be dealt with later. The main coolant circuit has two paths from the top flange, either back to the pump via a large hose, or to the top of the radiator via the other hose from the top flange. Which path is taken depends on the temperature of the coolant.

3 Situated in the inlet of the pump is a bellows type thermostatic valve which will permit coolant to enter the pump direct from the top of the cylinder block when the engine is cold and, as the temperature of the coolant rises to 80°C (176°F), gradually closes off the inlet from the top of the cylinder block and opens the inlet from the base of the radiator. The coolant now takes the second path which includes the radiator. The thermostat valve is fully open at 90°C (194°F) and at this point the cooling fan begins to operate. Thus the engine warms quickly.

Fig. 2.1 Radiator and fan - exploded view

1 Fan and cowling
2 Radiator
3 Side fixing bolt
4 Thermo-switch
5 Bottom fixing bolt
6 Top strap
7 Radiator cap

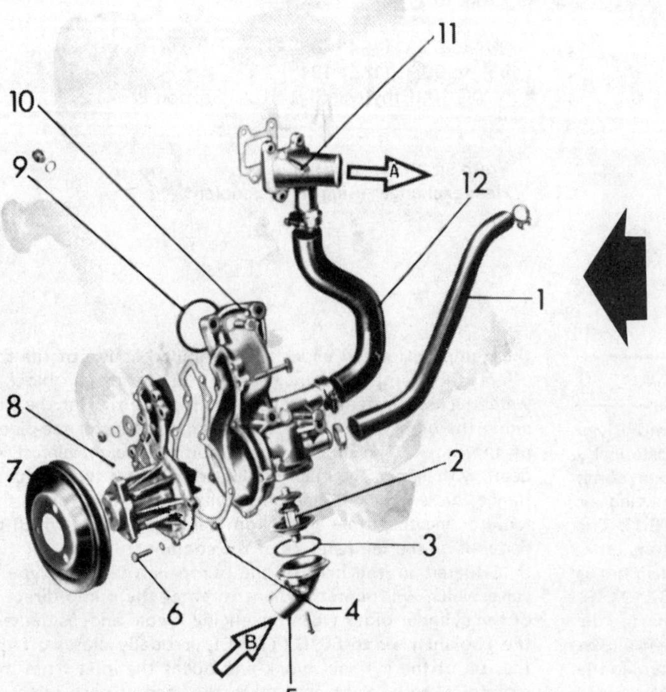

Fig. 2.2 Water pump and hoses - exploded view

1 Return hose from heater valve
2 Thermostat
3 'O' ring
4 Gasket
5 Thermostat housing
6 Bolt
7 Water pump pulley
8 Pump impeller housing
9 'O' ring
10 Pump body
11 Outlet from cylinder block
12 Return hose (cut-out when thermostat opens)

Arrows: A to radiator header tank
B from radiator bottom tank

4 The tee-piece outlet at the back of the engine block supplies hot coolant in two directions. The third arm of the 'Tee' contains the coolant temperature sender which is screwed in, and connected to the temperature gauge by an electric circuit.

The sideways outlet from the tee-piece takes warm coolant through a hose to the warming element of the automatic choke on the carburettor and thence via another hose to the hot coolant jacket of the inlet manifold. From the inlet manifold the coolant returns to the pump via the heater valve junction piece (photo).

The hose leading from the stem of the tee-piece outlet goes direct to the heat exchanger for the car interior warming system. This is actually a small radiator. The outlet from the heat exchanger is connected by a hose to the back of the heater valve. When the heater valve is opened the coolant flows through the heat-exchanger and back to the pump via the same hose as that from the inlet manifold. Thus it is that the hot coolant is used to increase the efficiency of carburation and to warm the interior of the car.

2 Composition of coolant (antifreeze)

1 When the car is supplied new the cooling system is filled with a mixture of soft water and V.W.G.10. The VW antifreeze fluid which has an Ethylene Glycol base gives protection against corrosion and lime deposit. It also has a boiling point considerably higher than water.
2 The solution should be replaced every two years, or before if contaminated in some way. If topping-up is necessary a solution of the same percentage composition should be used.
3 Vehicles having a header tank and expansion chamber or tank need 13.8 US pints (11.4 Imperial pints, 7 litres) to fill the system. Those without expansion tanks slightly less (12.6 US pints, 10.5 Imperial pints, 6 litres).
4 The following table gives the composition for safe working to -25^oC (-13^oF), a 40%/60%solution, and to -35^oC (-30^oF) a 50%/50% solution.

Protection to		Radiator with expansion tank G.10			Water		
C^o	F^o	*Pints US*	*Pints Imp.*	*Litres*	*Pints US*	*Pints Imp.*	*Litres*
−25	*−13*	*5.5*	*4.6*	*2.6*	*8.3*	*6.8*	*3.9*
−35	*−30*	*6.9*	*5.7*	*3.25*	*6.9*	*5.7*	*3.25*

Protection to		Radiator without expansion tank G.10			Water		
C^o	F^o	*Pints US*	*Pints Imp.*	*Litres*	*Pints US*	*Pints Imp.*	*Litres*
−25	*−13*	*5.0*	*4.2*	*2.4*	*7.6*	*6.3*	*3.6*
−35	*−30*	*6.3*	*5.25*	*3.0*	*6.3*	*5.25*	*3.0*

3 Draining, flushing and refilling the system

1 It should be necessary to drain and refill the system only on repair or at two year intervals.
2 If the system is very dirty and the engine has a tendency to overheat the system should be disconnected and the components flushed out separately, running clean water through them in the reverse direction to normal flow. This will only be necessary when the coolant has become contaminated and should be done during the repair period. Attempting to flush the system in the reverse direction while it is connected usually results in the sludge moving from one part to another but not emerging from the engine.
3 To drain the engine, first remove the radiator cap and the overflow tank cap (photo). Set the heater control valve to open, turn it to the right as far as it will go, and remove the lower radiator hose. Catch the coolant in a bowl (15 US pints, 12 Imperial pints, 6 litres). When the coolant has ceased to flow, remove the drain plug from the cylinder block (photo 3.3, Chapter 1). Catch the remainder of the coolant. When no more coolant runs out replace the drain plug and reconnect the hose.
4 Refill the system with the correct mixture of G.10 and soft water (rain water if possible) to the mark in the radiator filler, or, if an overflow tank is fitted, until the radiator is brim full, then fit the radiator cap. Pour coolant into the overflow tank until it is half-full and refit its cap. Run the engine until warm and then stop the engine. With a piece of cloth over the filler cap release the pressure by undoing the cap. Use a rag or the steam may cause a scald. Check the coolant level and add coolant if necessary.
5 The running until warm is necessary, to make sure that the air bubbles are removed from the system. If the system is filled to the right level at running temperature it will appear to need topping-up when cold, because the two gallons of liquid have contracted about 15 cubic inches. Resist the need to do this and check the level again when the engine is hot.

4 Coolant hoses - maintenance and emergency repairs

1 Probably the most neglected part of a car is the coolant hose and yet negligent owners always seem surprised when a hose bursts, or collapses.
2 Hoses age and become hard, crack, split and decay generally over a period of time. They are subject to high temperatures and up to 15 psi (1.1 kg/s. cm) pressure during normal running. Their worst enemy is oil, which, if spilt on hose should be wiped off straight away. Hoses will chafe if not correctly supported, and then pin-hole punctures will release a stream of hot coolant.
3 Examine the hoses when checking oil and battery levels. Check the tightness of clips every three months, or after a long fast run. If the clips are digging in to the hose too deeply move the clip, or if this is not practical, replace the hose. If a hose is becoming stiff, shows signs of cracks developing, then renew it right away. When a hose bursts the hose must be renewed and the antifreeze — which is expensive.
4 If a hose does burst, stop the engine as soon as possible. Open the bonnet (hood) cautiously, there may be a jet of hot coolant spraying

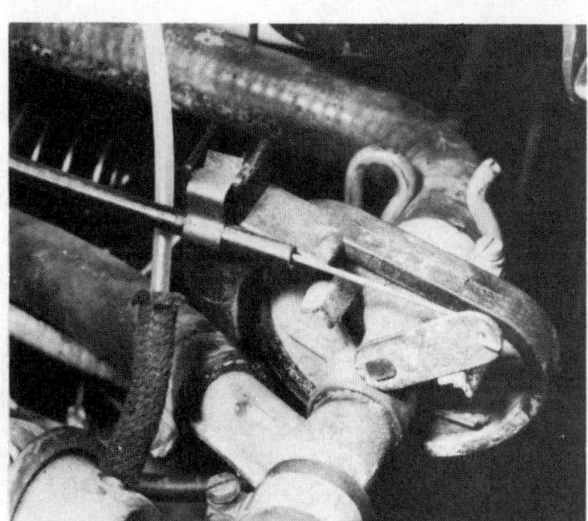
1.3 The heater valve in the engine compartment

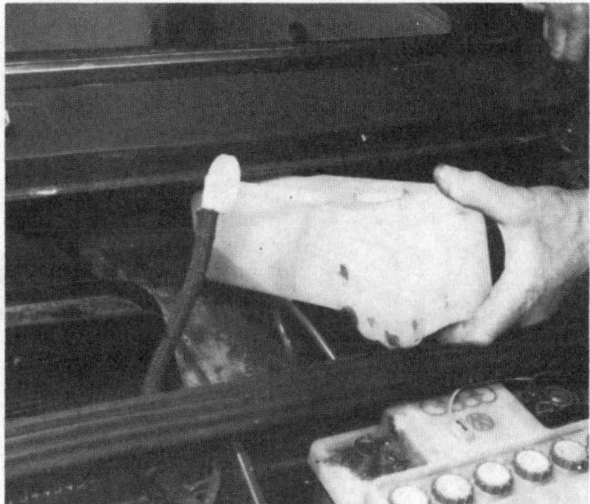
3.3 Removing the overflow tank

5.3 Removing the radiator top hose from the cylinder block

freely. As soon as possible drop a substantial cloth over the actual puncture. Put another cloth over the radiator cap and turn it to release the pressure. The jet spray will subside and the fault may be located. If the problem is with the smaller hoses it may be possible to short circuit the burst. The hose from the tee-piece to the auto-choke could be connected direct to the heater valve and with the heater valve closed the heater, auto-choke and inlet manifold can be cut from the coolant circuit without difficulty and the engine run cautiously. If one of the larger hoses has fractured surgical plaster or even insulation tape may be used as a temporary repair. A more substantial temporary repair may be made by cutting the hose right through and inserting a short length of metal or similar tubing with two jubilee clips. This will hold well until the correct new part can be fitted.

5 **Never** pour cold water into a hot engine while it is not running, that is the easiest way to crack the cylinder head. If sufficient coolant remains to circulate then cold coolany may be added to **hot coolant**, but **not** to hot metal.

6 Finally, if a burst does happen the cause must be located before proceeding. It may be neglect or old age, in which case no further action, other than renewal, is necessary, but if a new hose bursts then the cause must be located right away.

5 Radiator - fault diagnosis, removal, overhaul and replacement

1 The only reason for removing a radiator is to replace it with a new one or to repair a leak. If the radiator requires continual addition of coolant and no leak can be located, either on the radiator or in the coolant pipes, then suspect the radiator pressure cap. A simple way to check this on vehicles without an expansion tank, is to fasten a plastic bottle to the end of the overflow pipe, fill the radiator to the correct level and carry on motoring. If, after ten miles, there is coolant in the plastic bottle, then the pressure cap is faulty and it should be replaced. However, if it is faulty and replaced, look out for trouble. The system is back under pressure and leaks may appear quite suddenly.

2 If the pressure cap is in good order and coolant still disappears without leaking to the outside, then the problem is really expensive; it may be a blown cylinder head gasket or even a cracked block or cylinder head. However, at this point advice from the agent must be sought.

3 If the radiator core or one of the tanks is leaking then two courses are open. One of the several radiator leak cure compounds may be used according to the instructions, and they do sometimes produce startling cures. (But at their best they only delay the inevitable).

The other course is to remove the radiator and either repair the leak or fit a new radiator. Undo the bottom hose and drain off the coolant, then disconnect the top hose. Disconnect the battery earth strap.

4 Undo the top piece of the cowling from the grille to the radiator and then remove the self-tapping screws holding the remainder of the hardboard cowling to the frame.

5 Undo the top strap of the radiator which holds it to the front of the body. Slacken off the nut which clamps the bolt into the U-piece halfway up the radiator on the side opposite the engine, and finally remove the nut from the stud through the lower support.

6 Disconnect the leads from the temperature switch for the fan motor in the bottom tank of the radiator and disconnect the plug in the fan motor supply lead. Follow the lead from the fan motor to find this plug. Loosen the screws holding the relay console so that it may be moved if necessary.

7 The radiator complete with fan may now be eased out of the engine compartment (photos). The fan and motor may now be removed by undoing the three nuts holding the fan in position and sliding the fan bracket away from the radiator cowling.

8 If the radiator is leaking replace it with a reconditioned assembly. Attempts to repair it by soldering are a waste of time unless you are an expert in this line. If the radiator is repaired, either by the owner or by a garage, then it should be pressure tested to at least 20 lbs/sq. inch (1.41 kg/s. cm). To do this seal one outlet with a suitable plug and pump air in to the radiator at 20 lbs/sq. inch (1.41 kg/sq. cm) through the other. The radiator should be immersed in a bath of water at 90°C (194°F). Leave it for fifteen minutes and bring the pressure up to 20 lbs/sq. inch (1.41 kg/sq. cm) again. Watch for bubbles indicating leaks.

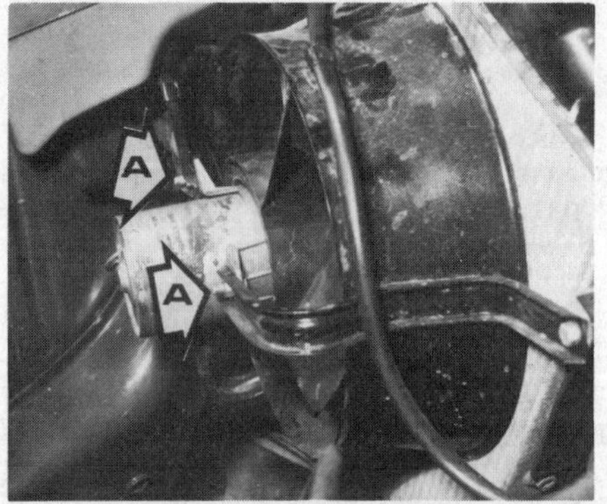

5.7a The fan and radiator. Undo the nuts at 'A' and slide the fan assembly out

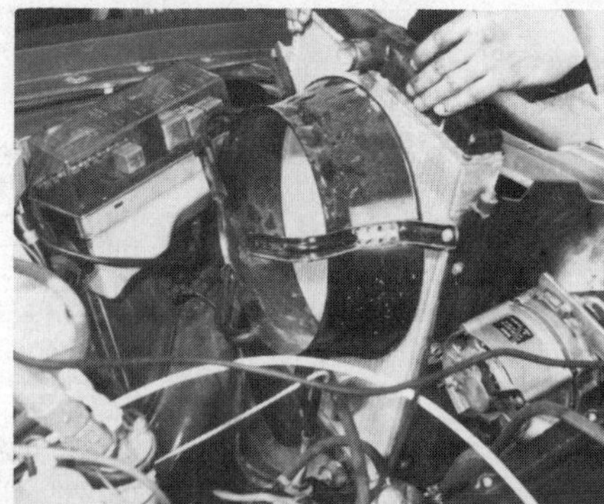
5.7b Removing the radiator

6.4a The fan motor housing. The bearing has come out of the cage - this is not the way to do it

6.4b Fan motor brush gear. Be careful of the thin washers

6.4c Fan motor armature. Note the suppressor

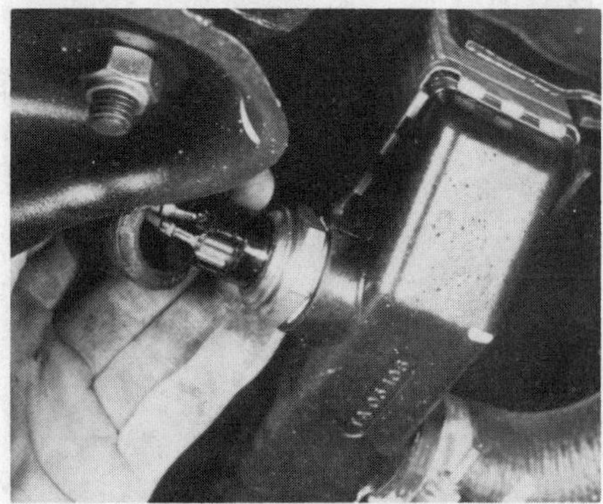
6.6 Removing the thermo-switch from the radiator bottom tank. Picture taken from under the car

If the radiator is not pressure tested it should be watched very carefully for several weeks after re-installation for leaks.

9 Replacement is the reverse of removal. Fit the radiator into position and tighten the holding bolts. Reconnect the fan motor on/off switch and plug in the supply to the fan motor. Reconnect hoses and then refit the cowling. Refill the system with the correct coolant. Tighten the screws holding the relay console. Reconnect the battery earth strap. After running the engine check for leaks at hose clips.

6 Fan and thermo-switch - testing and replacement

1 The fan and cowling may be removed from the radiator or more easily the fan can be removed from the cowling and eased out through the struts. Disconnect the battery earth strap before commencing work, undo the plug connecting the fan to the electric wiring harness, remove the three nuts holding the fan in position and remove motor and assembly together.

2 The fan blades are removed from the motor by undoing the bolt in the centre of the fan hub and levering the plastic blade assembly off the motor shaft.

3 The motor is dismantled by undoing the through bolts and pulling off the end caps, but there is no point in doing this as spares are not available, the unit is replaced in one piece.

4 To satisfy the curious we removed the through bolts. Pulling off the end cap was difficult and unfortunately the bearing came off with the shaft (photo). This presented difficulties on reassembly as the cage for the spherical part of the shaft may only be installed when the bearing has been removed from the housing. The shaft and bearing may then be re-installed. The commutator and brush gear may be cleaned and then reassembled (photo). Be careful of the two thin washers at the end of the commutator. If one of these is damaged replacements are not available. It is recommended that this unit be renewed if faulty.

5 The fan motor either works or it does not. Supply 12 volts to the plug momentarily. If the motor runs it is satisfactory. **Do not** allow it to run for more than a few seconds with the fan removed.

6 The thermo-switch is located in the bottom tank of the radiator. It is covered with a rubber sleeve. Remove the sleeve and disconnect the wires (photo). The switch may be tested by connecting a simple bulb circuit or an ohmmeter across the tags of the switch and observing the point at which the switch closes. The temperature of the coolant in the header tank may then be checked. This will be in excess of the specified 90°C (194°F) but will give a good idea of the temperature in the lower tank.

If the fan does not work shortly after the thermostat has opened and the engine has reached normal running temperature then stop the engine right away. Pull off the leads from the thermo-switch and with a suitable instrument, check whether the switch has closed or not. If it has, then check the fan circuit and do not proceed until this has been sorted out or the engine will overheat. If the switch has not closed, and you are sure the coolant temperature is in excess of 90°C (194°F) then the switch is faulty and must be renewed. To get you home connect the two switch leads together (short out the switch). The fan will then run when the ignition is switched on.

7 Removal of the thermo-switch involves draining the radiator. Once the bottom tank is empty (there is no need to take out the plug from the cylinder block), using a socket spanner remove the thermo-switch. It may be tested then in a beaker of water in the same way as the thermostat (Section 8), but using a meter to determine the opening point. However, more practically, the switch either works or it does not. If it does not fit a new one.

7 Coolant pump - removal, overhaul and replacement

1 The alternator must first be removed before the coolant pump may be taken off the block.

2 Drain the coolant from the circuit by removing the bottom hose from the radiator. Slacken the bolt holding the alternator hinge to the block and slacken the tie strap at the top of the alternator. Push the alternator towards the block and remove the V-belt. Remove the timing

7.3 The water pump ready for removal. It may be removed while the engine is still in the car

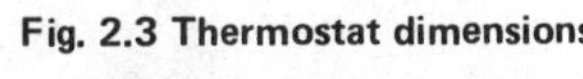

Fig. 2.3 Thermostat dimensions

(a) 31 mm at 80°C (closed)/ 1.22 in at 176°F
(b) 37 mm at 94°C (open)/ 1.46 in at 194°F

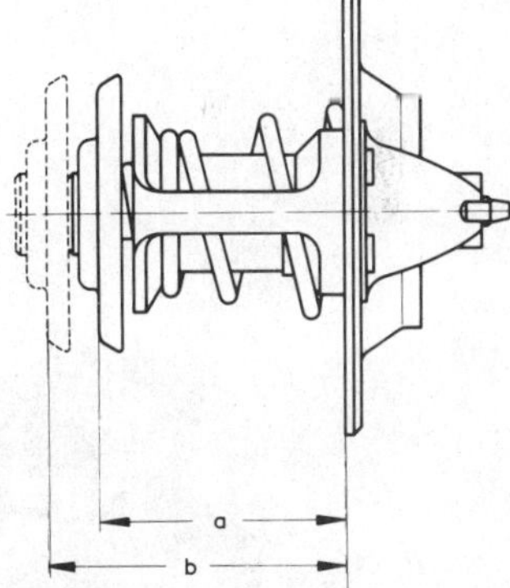

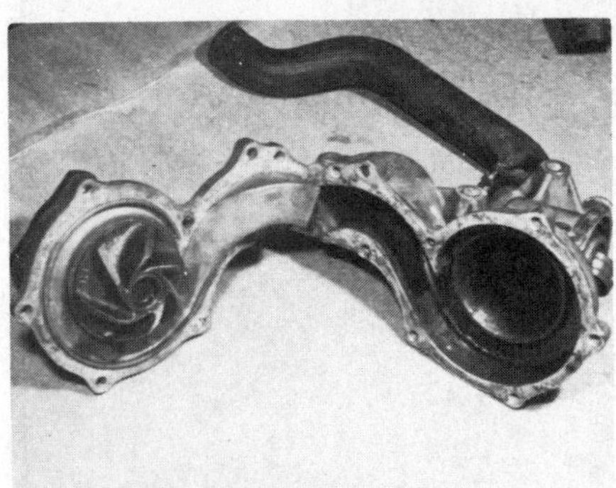

7.4a Water pump split

7.4b Thermostat housing disconnected

7.4c Thermostat removal

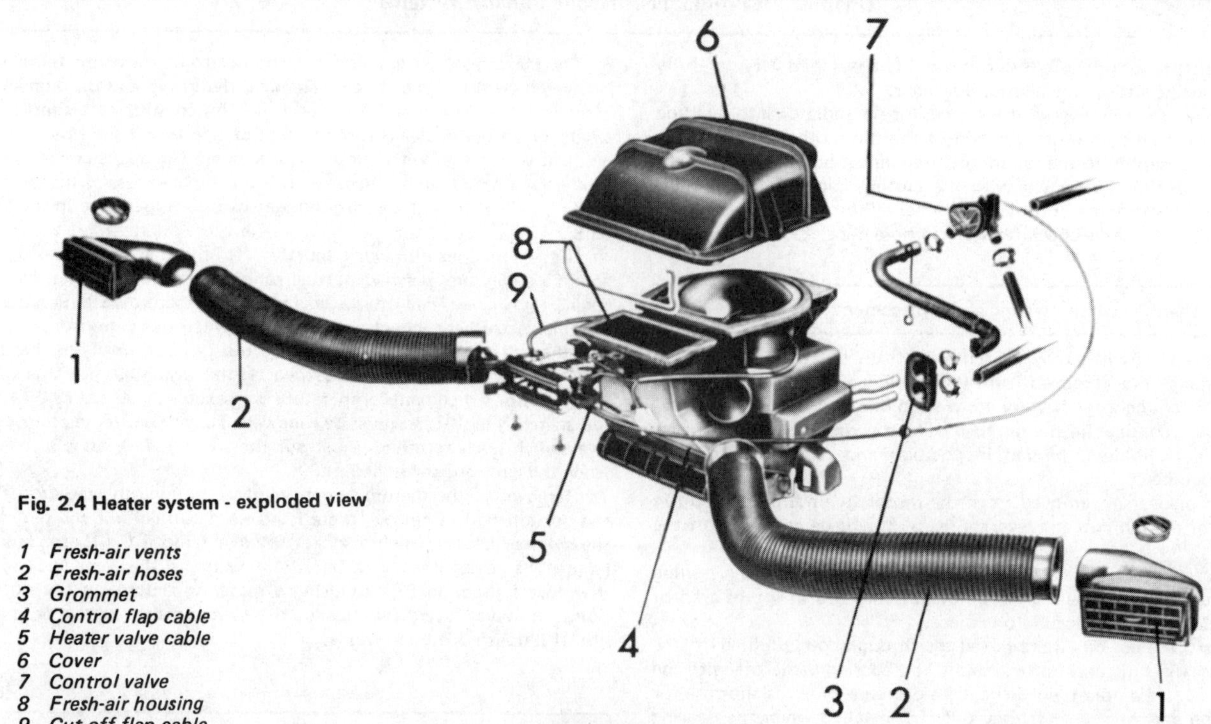

Fig. 2.4 Heater system - exploded view

1 Fresh-air vents
2 Fresh-air hoses
3 Grommet
4 Control flap cable
5 Heater valve cable
6 Cover
7 Control valve
8 Fresh-air housing
9 Cut-off flap cable

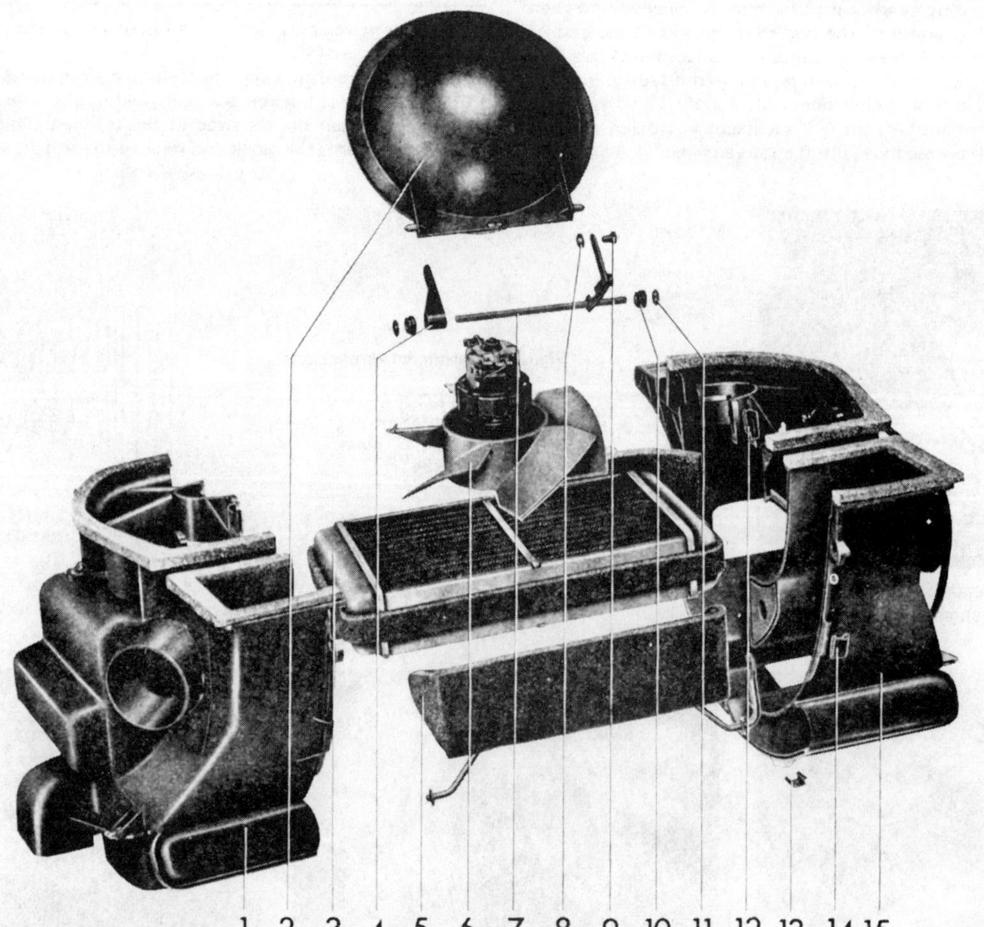

Fig. 2.5 Heater unit - heat exchanger and blower unit

1 Housing (left)
2 Cut-off flap
3 Heater exchanger
4 Lever
5 Control flap
6 Blower
7 Hinge pin
8 Circlip
9 Pin
10 Bushing
11 Clip
12 Clip
13 Clip
14 Clip
15 Housing right

drivebelt guard, disconnect the alternator plug and remove the alternator.

3 Disconnect the three coolant hoses from the pump then remove the four bolts holding the pump to the cylinder block (photo). The pump will probably be stuck to the block but will come off if tapped gently. Remove the O-ring with the pump.

4 Remove the pulley and then take out the eight bolts which secure the bearing housing and impeller to water pump housing. The two halves may now be separated (photo). **Do not** drive a wedge in to break the joint. Clean off the old gasket. Remove the two bolts holding the thermostat housing and remove the housing with the thermostat (photo). Set the thermostat aside for testing if suspect (photo).

5 Examine the thermostat valve seatings in the housing and remove any sludge or scale.

6 The impeller housing and impeller complete with bearing are serviced as one part, so that if the coolant is leaking through the bearing or the impeller is damaged the housing must be replaced with a complete new assembly.

7 Fit a new gasket using a waterproof jointing compound such as Golden Hermatite. Set the halves together and tighten the bolts to 7.2 lb ft (1 kg m). Reassemble the thermostat and housing using a new O-ring. Refit the pulley and tighten to 7.2 lb ft (1 kg m). Again using a new O-ring fit the pump to the block and tighten to 14.4 lb ft (2 kg m). Replace the alternator and fit the drivebelt guard. Refit the V-belt and tension it correctly. Reconnect the hoses and tighten the clips. Refill the cooling system.

8 Thermostat - removal, testing and replacement

1 It is not necessary to remove the water pump to service the thermostat. Drain the system and then remove the two bolts holding the thermostat housing to the water pump body.

2 Bend back the hose and the thermostat may be removed.

3 To check the thermostat refer to Fig. 2.3. Measure the distance 'X' at room temperature. Immerse the thermostat in a pan of water and heat the water, measuring the temperature. Hang the thermostat in such a way that it does not touch the sides or bottom of the pan and is completely immersed in the water. At about 80°C (176°F) the thermostat should have commenced to open at 94°C (194°F). The dimension 'X' should have increased from 31 mm to 38 mm (1.22 to 1.5 in.) an increase of at least 7 mm (0.27 in.). If this dimension is not reached, a new thermostat is needed.

4 When refitting clean the valve seatings in the pump housing and fit a new O-ring.

9 Heating system - general description

1 The system consists of an heat-exchanger, blower motor and fan, a control box behind the dashboard, a control valve in the engine compartment and an extensive ducting system. Refer to Fig. 2.4 and Fig. 2.5.

2 Coolant is fed to the heat-exchanger from the Tee-piece at the back of the cylinder block. It does not circulate until the valve in the engine compartment is opened by rotating the knob on the fascia board. This operates a bowden cable which rotates a lever on the valve. Coolant is then drawn through the heat-exchanger and back to the water pump. The temperature of the coolant is in excess of 90°C when it leaves the cylinder block. The quantity of coolant circulating depends upon how much the valve is opened, so that the heat available to the car interior is governed this way.

3 The heater cover sits in the engine compartment behind the battery (photo). Under the cover, operated by a bowden cable from the control box, is a circular dished flap. This controls the amount of air admitted to the system, and can close the system completely if so wished. Directly under the flap is the fan motor and fan. The flap control also operates the switch for the blower motor. When the flap is fully open the last two notches of movement of the control lever close contacts which, in turn, operate the blower at low and high speed.

4 The air is pushed through the heat exchanger into the fresh-air housing and directed by an adjustable cut-off flap. This is operated by

10.3 The cover for the heater flap valve is next to the overflow tank

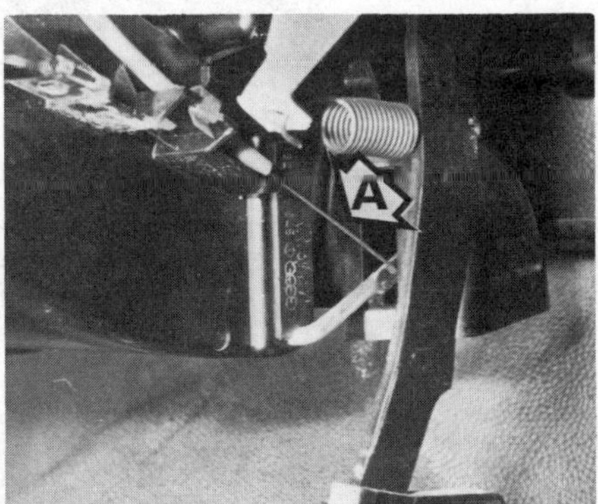

11.4 The bowden wire (A) to the control flap of the heater

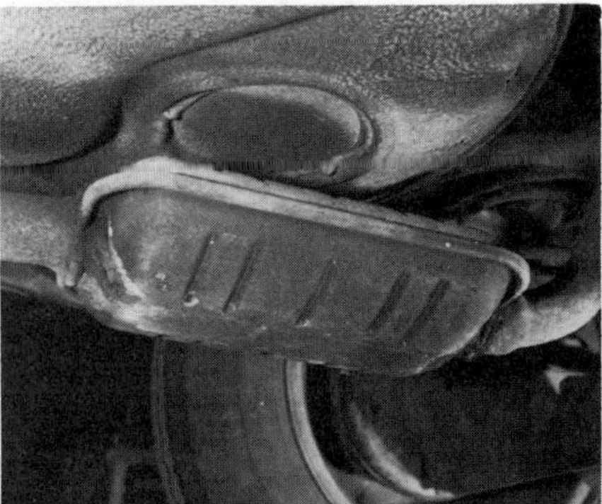

12.1a The rearmost silencer, sometimes called the resonator

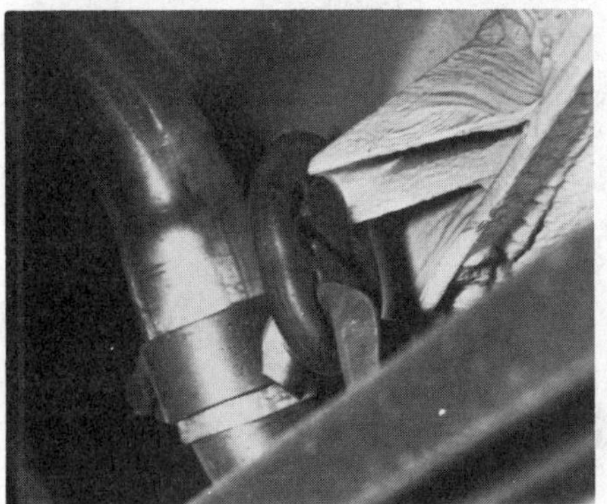

12.1b Pipe leaving the silencer. Note the clip

12.3a Exhaust pipe supported by hanger and clip

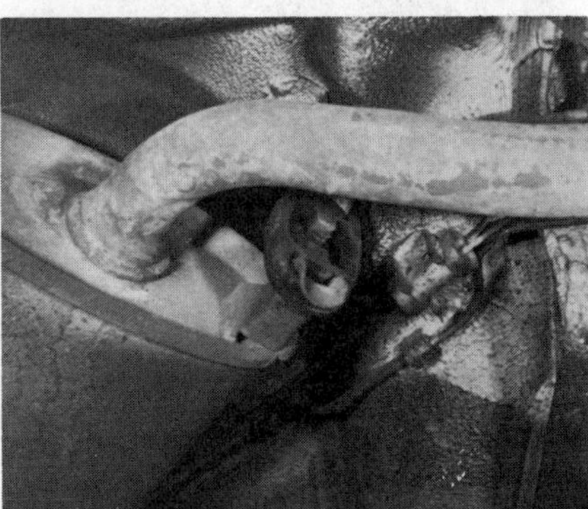

12.3b One end of a muffler ...

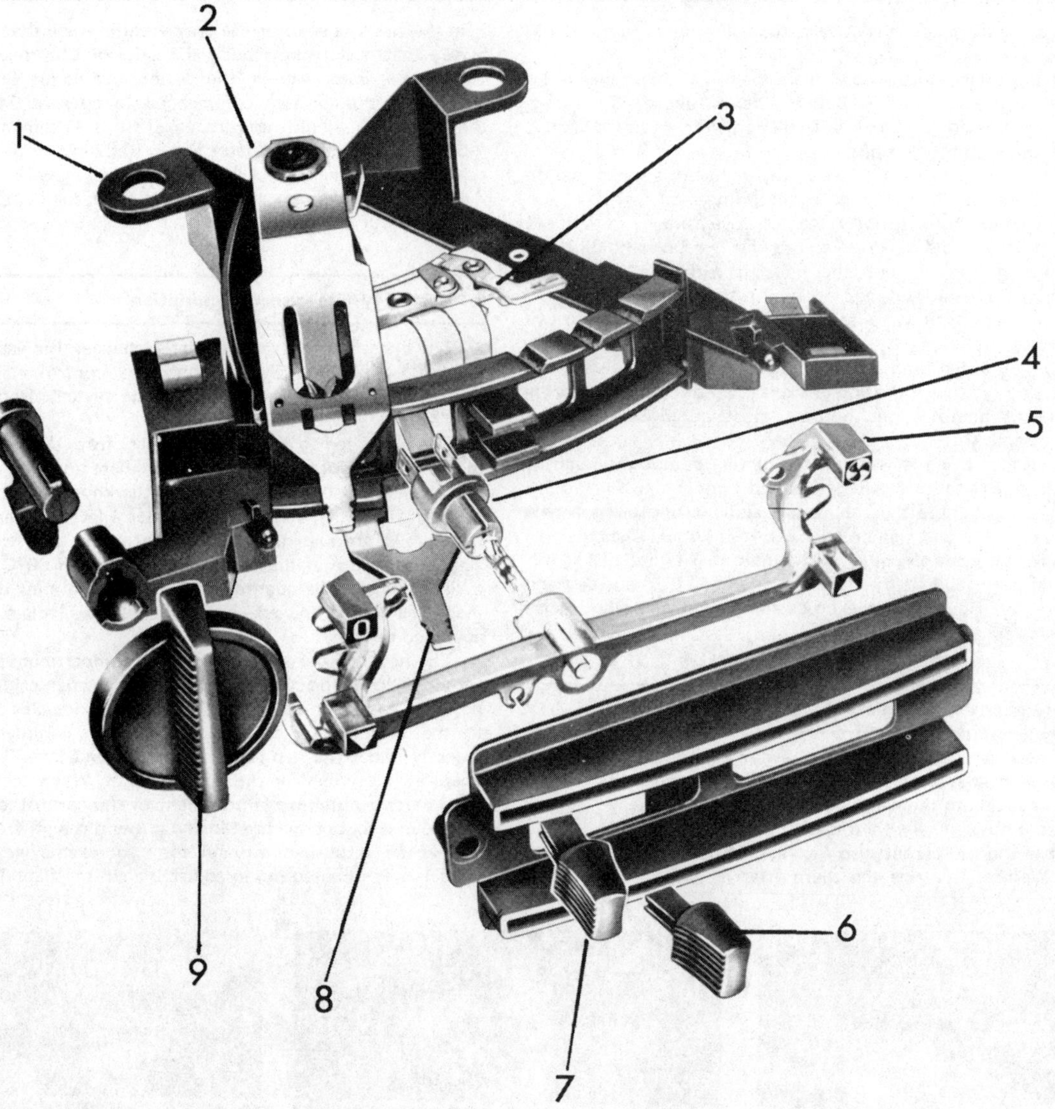

Fig. 2.6 Control for heater unit - exploded view

1 *Bracket bolted to body*
2 *Air cut-off lever*
3 *Electric contacts to activate blower motor*
4 *Bulb and holder*
5 *Prism (LS models)*
6 *Direction control knob*
7 *Volume control and blower motor knob*
8 *Direction (flap) lever*
9 *Heater valve control knob*

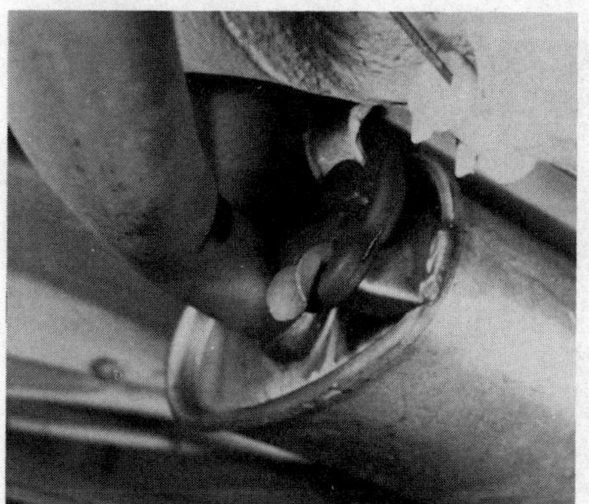

12.3c ... looked at from a different angle

12.3d Another silencer fixing

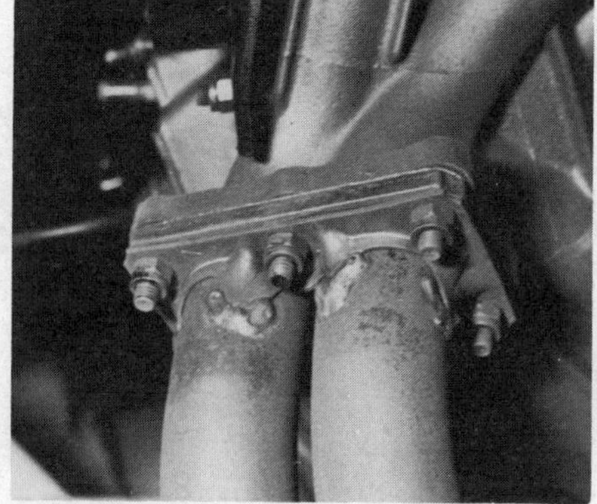

12.3e On some vehicles there is a twin exhaust from the manifold

the lower lever of the control box via a bowden cable, and channels the hot air into ducting leading either to the windscreen and front windows or the footwell as decided by the driver.

10 Heating system controls - removal and replacement

1 The control unit is located in the centre of the dashboard. Refer to Fig. 2.6. Access to it is from below after the glovebox and the centre cover under the instrument panel have been removed. The whole of the covering may be easily removed by undoing the crosshead screws, remove the centre one first and then the others as required. We found this job much easier if the front seats are removed, a job which takes very little time (see Chapter 13). Remove the battery earth strap.

2 Having removed the panelling from under the dashboard, pull off the plastic knobs on the end of the control levers and remove the heater control knob (the one which opens the valve) by prising it away from the dashboard. On 'L' models there is a prism behind the trim plate which diffuses light from the bulb held in the centre of it. The prism is pressed onto the trim plate and can be left in position. Two screws hold the frame of the control box to the body of the car. Remove these and the control box may be lowered sufficiently to get at the terminal ends of the bowden cables.

3 There are three cables, two from the flaps are 550 mm (21.6 in.) long, the third is to the heater valve and is 1225 mm (48.2 in.) long. It is best to replace both inner and outer if the cable is faulty. They are supplied this way with the ends ready to fit the anchorages. Buy some of the clips for clamping the outer cable, the existing ones never seem to fit a new cable.

4 Study the runs of the cables and fit the new one in the same path. Fix the outer ends first, fasten the inner cable and clamp the outer in the same position as the old cables were fastened. The control flap lever is inside the car at the bottom and on the right of the housing. It may be seen after the cover under the fascia is removed (photo). The lever for the cut-off flap is easy enough to locate but it will be necessary to remove the cover from the cut-off flap to make sure it is closed. There are two plastic plugs, one either side of the cover, which must be pulled out. Remove these and the cover may be lifted off.

5 With the outer end fixed and the cables run to the control box the next job is to fix the inner and outer cables so that the movement of the levers and knob produce the desired result.

6 The cable for the heater valve is adjusted as follows. Turn the lever on the valve as far as it will go to the cable anchor. The control knob on the dashboard must be fitted in such a way that the pointer on the knob is vertical. This is done by moving the outer cable. At this position clamp the outer cable in position.

7 When fitting the control for the cut-off flap fix the inner and outer cables in such a way that the lever will not move fully against the left stop when the flap is fully closed. A gap of 2 mm (0.07 in.) between the lever and stop is ideal.

8 For the control flap first fasten the inner cable to the lever and move the lever to the left. Hold it there and push the outer cable as far as it will go to the right. Clamp it in this position.

9 Reassemble the control box to the car, refit the covers and reconnect the battery.

11 Heating system components - removal and replacement

1 How much you remove depends on the fault to be cured. Proceed as follows.

2 Undo the control box as described in paragraph 11 to the point where it is to be detached from the car. Leave the two screws in position.

3 From inside the engine compartment, remove the screen-washer and the ignition coil. Undo the clips and take the hoses off the heat exchanger. Clip the hoses to prevent loss of coolant and catch the contents of the heat-exchanger.

4 Back in the car, remove the screws holding the control box and slide the connection off the fresh-air blower contacts. Remove the bowden cable from the heat control knob. Pull the fresh-air hoses (the big ones) off the housing, now look upwards under the dashboard. There is a clip holding the housing in place. Lever this off with a screwdriver and pull the housing downwards. If the car has done a lot of mileage there will be a lot of dust as the housing is removed.

5 The two halves of the fresh-air housing are held together by clips. When these are removed the housing may be split and the blower and heat-exchanger removed for repair.

6 Assembly is the reverse of dismantling. Put the heat-exchanger, right way up, in the right-hand half of the housing. Now fit the blower in the right-hand half of the housing, making sure the connections are facing the wiring harness. The motor must be held firmly so that there is no axial play. Fit the left housing onto the right housing and clip them together. Refit the cut-off flap and re-install the unit in the car.

12 Exhaust system - description, removal and replacement

1 The normal exhaust system consists of two separate silencers joined together by a short length of pipe. The rear silencer is sometimes described as the resonator (photos). On some versions (USA) a third silencer is fitted.

2 The normal expectation of life is less than 30,000 miles, and very much less if salt spray used for snow melting is allowed to remain on the metal.

3 The system is held to the vehicle by clips which are obvious as the system is traced. The photos show a variety of these fixings. The exhaust is jointed at the entrance to some of the silencers. On later models a twin exhaust system is led away from the manifold (photo).

4 In the authors experience once the exhaust system begins to leak it is best to renew the whole system, rather than replace it piece-meal. It is also worth considering whether to fit a stainless steel version. They are more expensive but they last a lot longer and may well be cheaper in the long run.

5 The more complicated arrangement of exhaust for E.G.R. and afterburning is discussed in Chapter 3.

6 When installing pipes and silencers there must be at least 3/8 in. (10 mm) between the exhaust pipe and the floor at all points.

Fault diagnosis overleaf

13 Fault diagnosis - cooling system

Note: Check that the coolant level is correct and that the slide in the radiator grille is in the open position in summer and closed in the winter. Check that the radiator is not obstructed by flies, leaves or other debris.

Symptom	Reason	Remedy
Engine apparently cool gauge registers in the red sector or Engine overheating gauge does not register in the red sector	1 Engine temperature sensor or wiring defective 2 Voltage stabilizer faulty 3 Temperature gauge defective	1 Replace sensor check wiring and ground connections (Chapter 11). 2 Check stabilizer (Chapter 11). 3 Replace gauge.
Engine and radiator overheating, gauge shows red. Fan operating	1 Coolant level too low 2 Water pump belt slipping or broken	1 Check for leaks Check radiator cap valve. 2 Adjust or replace.
Engine overheats very quickly. Bottom tank of radiator cool	Thermostat not opening, water not circulating through radiator	Replace thermostat
Engine cool, gauge not in red despite hard driving	Normal operation but if very cool then thermostat stuck open	Replace thermostat
Engine overheating, pump and fan working gauge in red	Brakes binding Ignition retarded Mixture incorrect Cylinder head gasket blown	Adjust (Chapter 9). Check and adjust (Chapter 4). Adjust (Chapter 3). Replace (Chapter 1)
Engine overheating gauge red, fan not working.	1 Thermo switch not working 2 Fuse blown 3 Relay defective	1 Bridge terminals. Fan should run. 2 Check fuse and replace if necessary. Trace fault. 3 Remove relay, bridge terminals '30' and '87'. If fan runs replace relay.
Engine overheating all systems working correctly	Wrong grade of fuel	Use correct grade RON. See operating handbook.

Chapter 3

Carburation; fuel and emission control systems

For modifications, and information applicable to later models, see Supplement at end of manual

Contents

Specifications

	Litres	US Gallons	Imperial Gallons
Fuel tank capacity			
Variant	50	13¼	11
Sedan	46	12¼	10

Air cleaner ... ... Circular paper element

Fuel pump

Type ... ... Mechanically operated diaphragm type operated by a cam on the intermediate shaft

Delivery pressure:

- Minimum ... ... 2.56 lb/sq. in. 0.18 kg/cm^2
- Maximum ... ... 3.55 lb/sq. in. 0.25 kg/cm^2

Carburettor

Single barrel ... ... Solex PDSIT 35

Double barrel ... ... Solex 32/35 TDID with mechanically operated second stage actuated by stage 1
Solex 32/35 DIDTA identical with TDID except that the second stage is vacuum operated independantly of stage 1

Carburettor specification

Because there are so many specifications already and that there will certainly be more, three specifications only are given. These are typical, but consult the VW dealer as to the exact specification of the carburettor fitted to your engine. THIS IS IMPORTANT as the wrong jets will break the emission regulations as well as effecting the car's performance.

	1300 cc 'ZA' Engine	1500 cc 'ZC' Engine	1500 cc 'XW' Engine
Carburettor type	Single barrel (stage)	Twin barrel (stage)	Twin barrel (stage)
Carburettor - designation	Solex 35 PDSIT	Solex 32/35 TDID	Solex 32/35 DIDTA
Venturi (mm)	27	24/27	24/27
Main jet	X 140	X 117.5/X 140	
Air correction jet	100	140/140	150/140
Pilot jet *	52.5	45	52.5/50
Pilot air jet **	150	180	180
Auxiliary fuel jet	—	60	45.5
Auxiliary air jet	—	130	110

Injection capacity cm^3 per stroke (slow)	0.55 - 0.85	0.75 - 1.05	0.75 - 1.05
Float needle valve diameter (mm) ...	1.5	1.75	1.75
Float needle valve washer thickness (mm)	1.0	0.5	2
Enrichment system (with/without ball)	80/60 with	57.5/75 with	57.5/80 without
Throttle valve gap (mm)	0.6 to 0.7	0.6 to 0.7	0.75 to 0.85
Choke valve gap (mm)	4.05 to 4.35	3.55 to 3.85	3.35 to 3.65
Float weight grams	7.3	7.3	7.3
Octane requirement (RON)	91	98	91
Idling speed (rpm)	900 - 1000	900 - 1000	850 - 1000
C.O. value volume (%)	1.3 - 1.7	1.3 - 1.7	0.4 - 1.6

** Sometimes known as idle jet*
*** Sometimes known as idle air jet*

1 General description

1 Fuel is drawn from a tank situated under the luggage compartment, by a mechanically operated diaphragm pump, bolted to the left side of the engine and driven by a cam on the intermediate shaft.

2 This supplies fuel to a Solex downdraught type carburettor. For the 1300 cc and 1500 cc (75 HP) a single barrel carburettor is used, but for the 1500 cc (85 HP) and vehicles for America, a double barrelled carburettor is fitted. Both types are equipped with idle air control and an automatic choke, In each case the automatic choke and the inlet manifold are heated by circulating the engine coolant through a jacket, situated round the choke control and manifold.

The carburettors are basically alike. The second stage or barrel is operated mechanically for the 1500 cc (85 HP) but by a vacuum capsule in the case of the vehicles for America. Each type is set at the factory with the correct jets and adjustments to conform with the emission regulations of the country for which the vehicle is intended, and these settings **must not** be altered.

3 A paper element, circular air cleaner, is fitted to the air intake of the carburettor. Thermal intake control is incorporated to the air cleaner fitted to the vehicles for America.

4 Exhaust gas recirculation (EGR) is fitted to all vehicles exported to the USA and those destined for California have afterburn as well. These systems and the modification they cause to the air cleaner and exhaust systems are discussed later in the Chapter.

5 Numerous modifications of jet sizes and adjustments have been made to suit the different types of engine. A selection of these is given in the Specifications but in the interests of accuracy no attempt has been made to provide extensive, and sometimes out of date, information on this subject. It is best to consult the agent for the latest data. We have four different sets for the 1300 cc and thirteen for the 1500 cc engine to-date, so you will see what we mean.

6 A modified fuel pump has been issued. This is supplied as a replacement for the old type and requires a new flange and securing screws. Detail is in the fuel pump section.

7 On later models a filter is fitted in the fuel line in the engine compartment (photo).

2 Fuel tank - evaporative control system (emission controlled models only)

The fuel tank is fitted with an evaporative control system. This consists of a small expansion tank which is part of the main tank, a charcoal filter usually fitted to the left side of the engine compartment, and hoses connecting the expansion tank to the filter and the filter to the air cleaner. Fumes from the tank are thus prevented from entering the atmosphere direct and are consumed either in the filter when the vehicle is stationary, or, when the engine is running, drawn into the engine and burned.

Apart from checking the hoses periodically no repair is required for this system. The activated carbon filter should be renewed every 50,000 miles.

3 Fuel tank - removal, overhaul and replacement

1 Remove the floor-covering of the luggage compartment and a circular plate about six inches diameter will be seen. Remove the screws holding this and fuel gauge sender unit will be seen with the vent pipe in the same group (photo).

2 Disconnect the battery earth strap, no sparks are needed for this operation!

3 Clip the fuel hose and pull it off the pipe going into the tank. Remove the brown lead from the fuel gauge sender unit, this is the earth strap and then the other lead, which is the one to the gauge unit.

4 Remove the tank breather hose (emission control vehicles only).

5 Remove the strap holding the tank and lift out the tank.

6 Unless you are a skilled artisan well versed in petrol tank repair **do not** attempt to repair or derust the tank yourself at home. If you are skilled then no instruction is required, but for the D-I-Y owner driver, this is a job which must be left to the experts with the proper equipment. Derusting requires a special fluid and very careful handling.

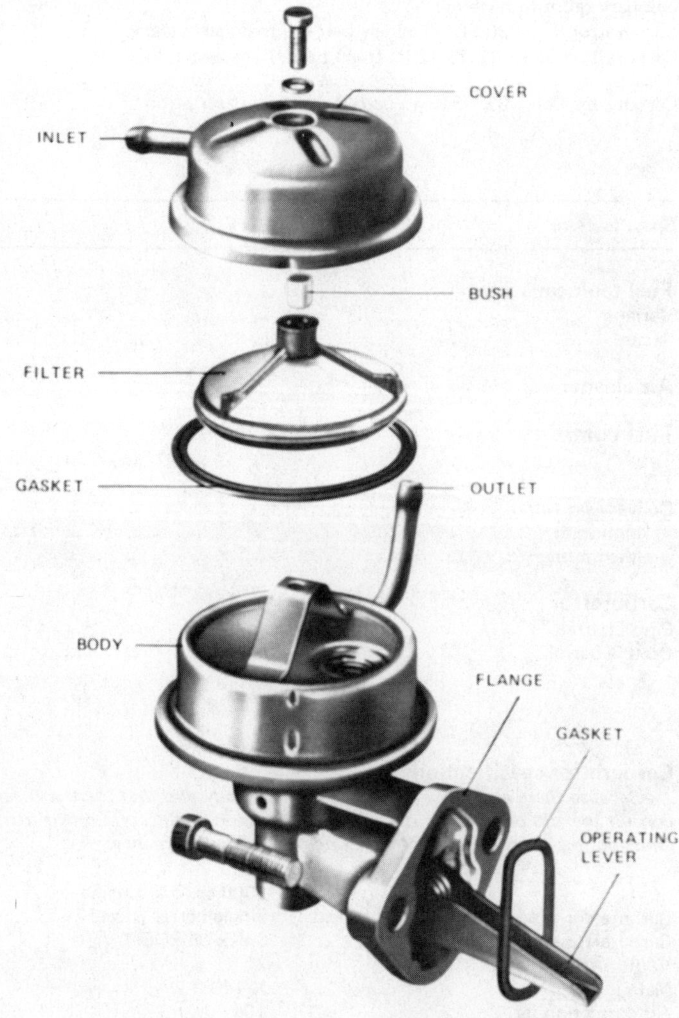

Fig. 3.1 Fuel pump - exploded view

After derusting the tank must be treated straightaway with an anti-rust solution. Both solutions are expensive and are difficult to store.

7 Repairing leaks in petrol tanks is also a dangerous task. It is doubtful whether the insurance company would honour a claim by your widow, and the explosion usually wrecks the workshop also — you have been warned! The repair should be left to people with the proper equipment for clearing all the vapour from the tank. The repair also needs treatment against corrosion, and the tank should be pressure tested before re-installation.

8 Re-installation is the reverse of removal. Always use a new clip on the vent and the breather hoses.

4 Fuel pump - testing, removal, repair and replacement

1 Refer to Fig. 3.1. Although it rarely goes wrong the fuel pump can be the unsuspected reason for poor starting and irregular running. If the filter is choked, the diaphragm damaged or the valves leaking, the pump may deliver enough petrol to keep the engine running, but not enough for a cold start or running under heavy load. It is easy to test the pump and to clean or replace the filter, but beyond that no repair may be done as the unit is sealed on manufacture and must be renewed if faulty (photo).

2 Undo the small screw on the top cover and lift off the cover and filter, inspect the filter and clean it if necessary. Replace the filter and cover using a new sealing ring if necessary.

3 To test the quantity output of the pump first run the engine for a few minutes until the carburettor is full. Switch off and remove the hose from the carburettor intake. Be careful not to spill any fuel and arrange to catch the fuel in a measuring glass or similar container. There is plenty of hose so that the container may be held well away from the engine.

Now get a helper to start the engine and run it at a fast tick-over for 30 seconds. There will be enough petrol in the carburettor bowl for this. Stop the engine and measure the amount of petrol in the container. There should be at least 200 ccs (½ US pint). There is not much point in pressure testing the pump for it cannot be repaired, but if it is wished to confirm the quantity test it is possible to fit a Tee-piece in the supply hose to the carburettor and fit a pressure gauge. The pressure at 3,500 rpm should be between 2.5 and 3.5 lbs per sq. in. (0.2 to 0.25 kg/s. cm). Outside these limits the pump should be renewed.

4 To remove the pump, clip the hoses and remove them, then remove the two socket headed bolts holding the pump and insulating flange to the block (photo). The right-hand one may be difficult as it is near to the oil filter and the filter may have to be removed to get at it if you do not have a suitable key.

5 Replacement pumps may be a new pattern with a heat insulating flange of different thickness from the old pump. The new type pump measures 1.8 inches (47 mm) from the tip of the operating lever to the body flange, the old one is 5 mm (0.2 in.) shorter. The insulating flange is thicker for the new pump and longer screws, 8 mm x 30 instead of 8 mm x 22, are required. The new pump is said to give better hot starting.

6 When replacing the pump always secure the hoses to the pump with clips. It is best to fit the hose to the inlet side first and then turn the engine (not run it, turn it), to check that the pump is working. Catch the ejected fuel in a rag. Then connect the output hose. Tighten the holding bolts to 14 ft lbs (2 kg m).

7 When replacing the filter a repair kit part no. 111 198 555B is available.

5 Air cleaner - servicing

1 The air cleaner filter should be removed and cleaned every 9000 miles (15000 km) under normal conditions. In very dusty atmospheres or if the car is used in a hot sandy place, it would be wise to examine the filter once a week until the amount of sand being collected is determined and thereafter set your own maintenance interval. If the paper element is choked then the supply of air to the engine is constricted and the mixture will be wrong. If it is perforated then sand and grit will enter the engine and wear will accelerate greatly. It is a wise policy to inspect the air-cleaner regularly.

1.7 The filter in the engine compartment

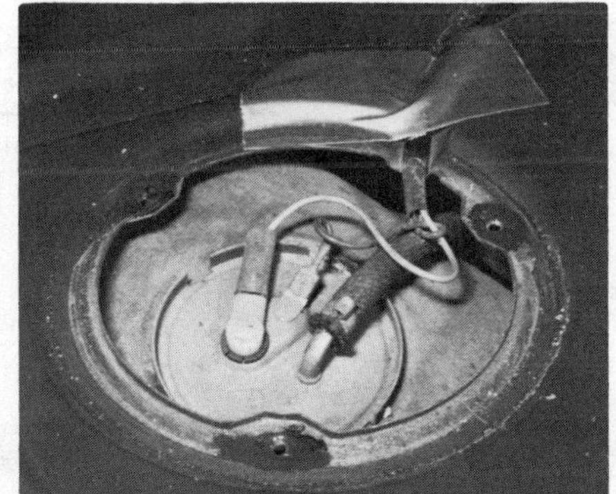

3.1 The fuel gauge sender unit in the top of the tank. Always use a new clip, on the vent pipe.

4.1 Top cover and filter removed for cleaning

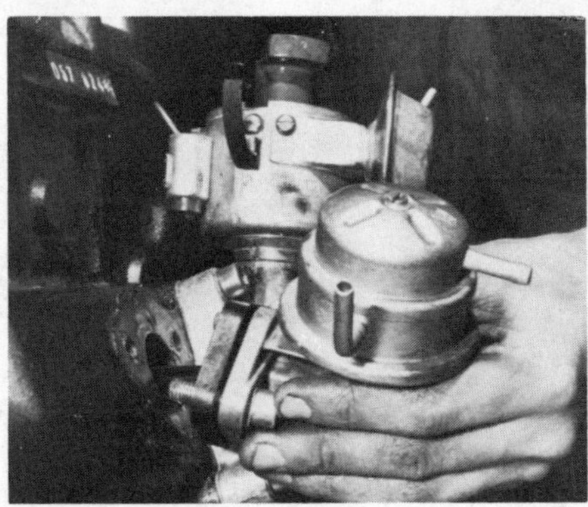

4.4 Removing the fuel pump

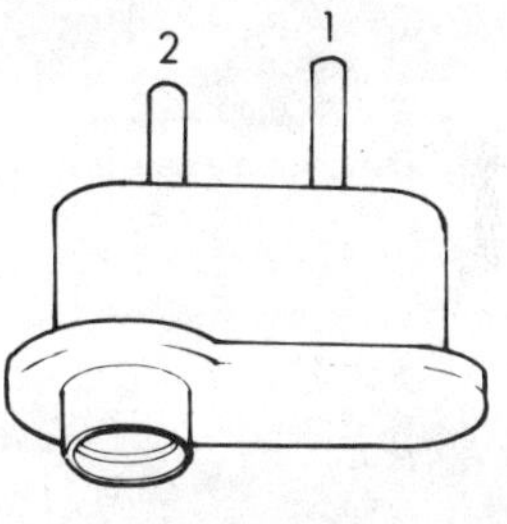

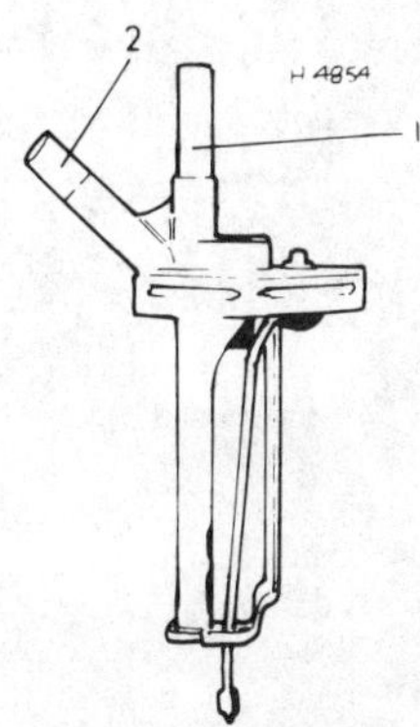

Fig. 3.2 Control valves for thermal intake control

Upper: USA models, in the air cleaner
Lower: California models, in the inlet manifold

1 Hose to vacuum unit in air intake
2 Hose to carburettor

2 Access is simple. There are five clips holding the cover to the body. Undo these and lift off the cover (photo). Inside is the paper element, the locating screw, and the entry part to the carburettor. Cover the entry port to stop dust going down, lift out the element and set it to one side and wipe the inside of the cleaner with a clean rag damped with light oil until all the dust has been removed. Set the element on a sheet of newspaper, away from the vehicle and tap it gently until all the dust has been removed. If access to a compressed air jet is available finish cleaning it with this, but do not use air at more than 5 lbs per sq. in. (0.35 kg/s. cm).

3 Re-install the element, remove the cover from the entry port and refit the top cover to the body.

4 If it is necessary to remove the cleaner from the carburettor, pull off the vent hose from the cylinder head cover, then remove the air cleaner cover, leave the element in place and undo the nut from the locating screw. Undo and remove the air intake hose. On some models the air-cleaner may be now lifted clear. On models with thermal intake control further work is to be done.

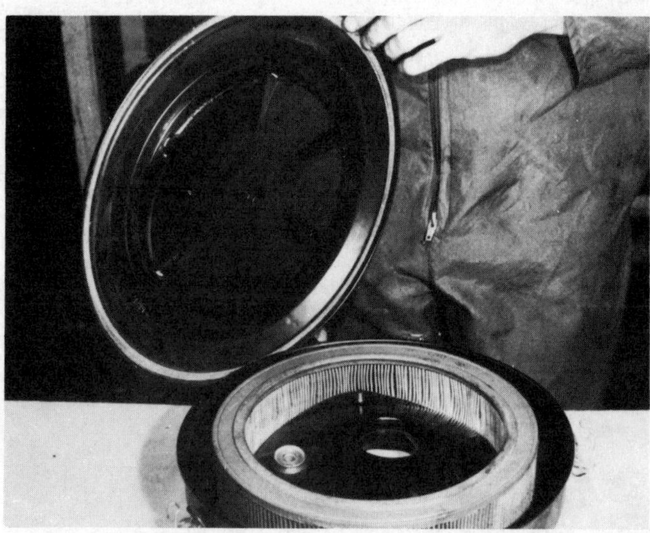

5.2 Air cleaner dismantled away from the car

6 Air cleaner - thermal intake control (emission controlled vehicles only)

1 This is fitted to vehicles destined for North America and Countries where the laws on emission content are strict.

2 The term Thermal Intake Control means in plain language that some effort is being made to pre-heat air going into the carburettor and some method is being used to control the amount of pre-heating. There are two such devices, one for vehicles to the USA generally, but not California. The other is for vehicles for California.

3 The first is the temperature control valve in the air cleaner. A double valve is fitted inside the lower half of the air cleaner (Fig. 3.2). It has two hose connectors protruding through the base of the cleaner. The brass one is connected by hose to the vacuum unit in the air intake, the plastic one by hose to the carburettor. In the elbow of the fresh-air hose from the grille to the cleaner is the vacuum unit and the air control flap. This unit decides whether the intake air is drawn from the radiator grille or warmer air is drawn in from the region of the exhaust manifold. The branch to the exhaust manifold is under the air cleaner and the flap regulates the amount of air from either source.

4 For the California model the temperature control valve in the air-cleaner is discontinued and a valve is inserted in the intake manifold (Fig. 3.2). The hoses to the carburettor and vacuum unit are marked in the diagram. This valve may be removed by undoing two cheese-head screws and lifting the valve away. Always replace with a new gasket.

5 The vacuum unit and flap may be removed by pressing down the spring and lifting the unit away.

6 The vacuum diaphragm unit may be disengaged from the flap by pressing down the diaphragm plunger and removing the flap.

7 Testing of both systems is a simple matter. With the engine at idle speed and cold, remove the hose from the vacuum unit. If the system is working then the flap which should have been admitting warm air to the engine will close and cold air will flow. If the flap does not move then either the valve or the vacuum unit is at fault, or there is a leak in the vacuum lines. Unfortunately neither unit may be repaired, so one or both of them must be renewed.

7 Inlet manifold - general

1 The inlet manifold is heated by a jacket through which the engine coolant is passed. This is fed to the manifold from the auto-choke water

8.a.2(a) Carburettor viewed from right-hand side of the car

1 Automatic choke
2 Inlet hose
3 Accelerator pump
4 Mixture control screw (sealed)
5 Idle speed adjusting screw
6 Magnetic cut off valve
7 Throttle lever
8 Vacuum connection to distributor

8.a.2(b) Carburettor viewed from left-hand side of car

1 Plug for mixture system
2 Basic idle speed throttle stop screw
3 Automatic choke relay rod
4 Throttle return spring
5 Screw securing venturi in body

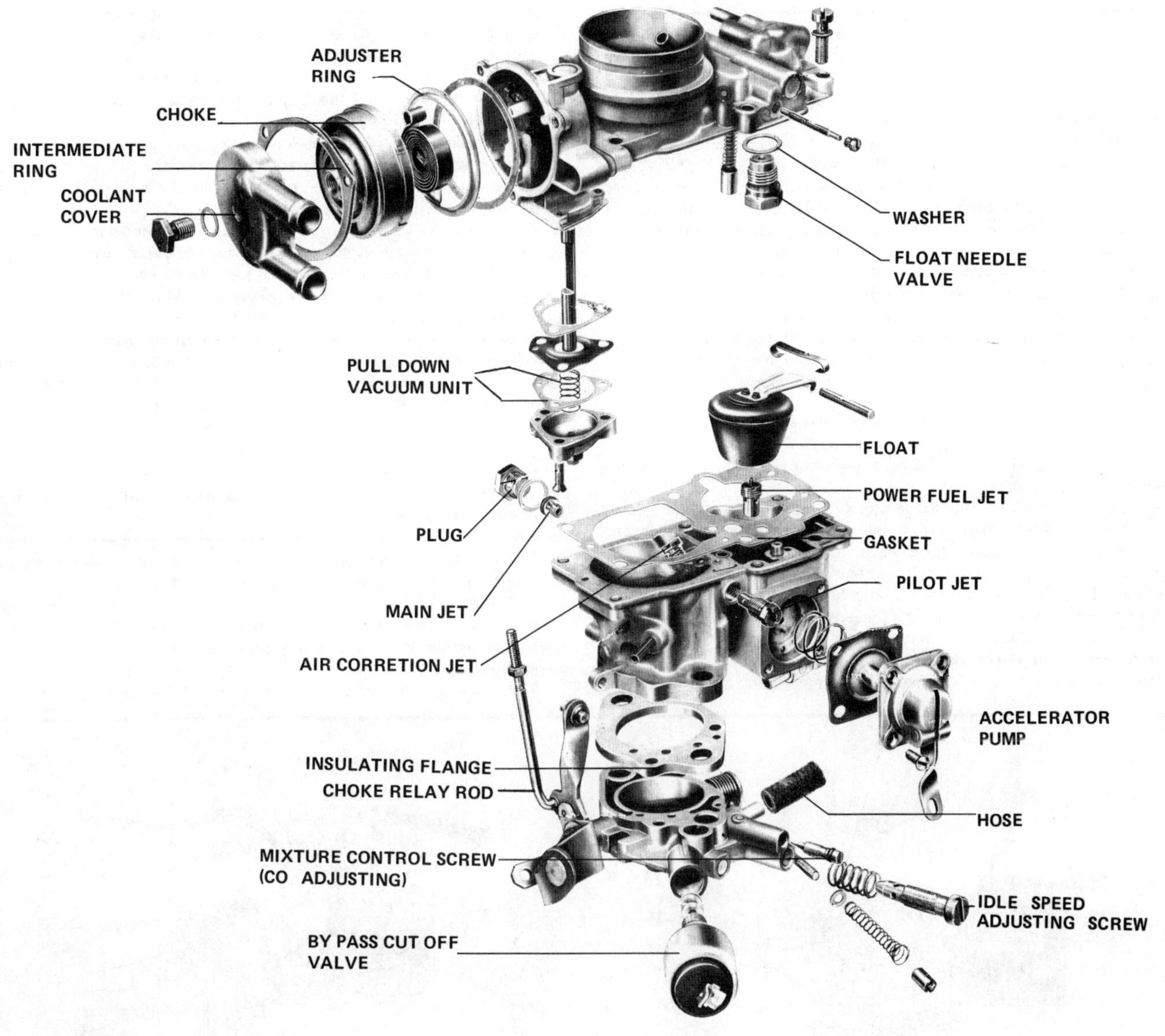

Fig. 3.3 Solex PDSIT 35 single stage carburettor – exploded view

jacket and returned to the heater control valve junction piece. Make sure the hoses are in good condition.

2 When replacing to the cylinder head, tighten the bolts in a diagonal sequence to 18 lbs ft (2.5 kg m).

8A Carburettor Solex 35 PDSIT (single barrel) - general description

1 The carburettor consists of three main components (refer to Fig. 3.3).

a) The throttle body
b) The carburettor body
c) The top half of the carburettor

2 The throttle is the butterfly valve which controls the amount of fuel and air entering the inlet manifold. It is mounted in the throttle body into which the idle mixture screw (C.O. adjustment), the idle speed adjustment screw and the cut-off valve are screwed from the outside. It is isolated from the carburettor body by an insulating flange (photo).

3 The carburettor body consists of the float chamber and the mixture chamber. The venturi tube is a push fit into the mixture chamber, secured by a mounting screw. The mixture tube is part of the casting reaching into the mixture chamber and discharging into the venturi. It is supplied with fuel from the float chamber via the main jet and the idle jet and the air-correction jet all of which feed into the mixture tube so that emulsified fuel is injected into the warm air stream passing into the venturi.

4 The top half of the carburettor holds the fuel inlet from the fuel pump, the needle valve operated by the float in the float chamber and the choke tube and choke. The automatic choke mechanism and its water jacket are mounted in this unit.

5 A pump operated by the accelerator linkage is fixed to the side of the carburettor body. This draws fuel from the float chamber and injects it into the mixture tube via drillings in the top half of the carburettor and an injection tube when the accelerator is depressed suddenly. The amount injected is adjustable, by altering the pump stroke. A ball type non-return valve prevents the fuel flowing back into the float chamber and a valve in the pump outlet stops air entering the pump during the intake stroke.

6 An automatic choke is fitted to the top half of the carburettor (see Fig. 3.3). This is a device to control the composition of the fuel/air mixture when starting from cold, a great advance on the hand-operated choke. The choke shaft is kept in the closed position by a bi-metal spring. When the engine is cold the choke is shut. The bi-metallic clock type spring is located in a housing on the end of the carburettor which is surrounded by a water jacket through which coolant from the cylinder head is circulated. As the coolant temperature rises the tension on the spring decreases until finally the choke flap is fully open. As the engine cools the tension increases and the choke flap is again closed. This is accomplished by a system of levers. The choke flap is also subject to pressure causing it to open by reason of the fact that it is mounted off centre, thus as it opens slightly the passage of air causes pressure on the flap, and the larger segment swings, opening the choke momentarily.

7 This produces the four rules for starting the engine:

a) Below 10°C (50°F) depress the accelerator SLOWLY twice and release it. Then switch on and start the engine but DO NOT touch the accelerator pedal.
b) Above 10°C (5°F) but cold, depress only once and then start.
c) Engine warm — Depress the pedal SLOWLY while turning the starter and release the pedal as soon as the engine fires.
d) Engine hot — Depress the pedal THEN with the pedal on the floor operate the starter.

It all sounds very complicated but a little thought will show that the choke has been set automatically and all that is being done is to inject petrol via the accelerator pump into a cold engine or to open the throttle with a hot engine when the choke is already open.

8B Carburettor Solex 35 PDSIT (single barrel) - idle, transition and auxiliary mixture systems

1 The idle system provides enough fuel for only part of that required to stabilize the mixture at idle speed. (Refer to Fig. 3.4).

2 This part of the fuel, taken from the recess behind the main jet, is metered by the idle jet and emulsified by air from the idle air jet. It meets the remainder of the fuel required in the drilling in front of the cut-off valve.

3 The remainder of the fuel required for the idle speed is drawn from

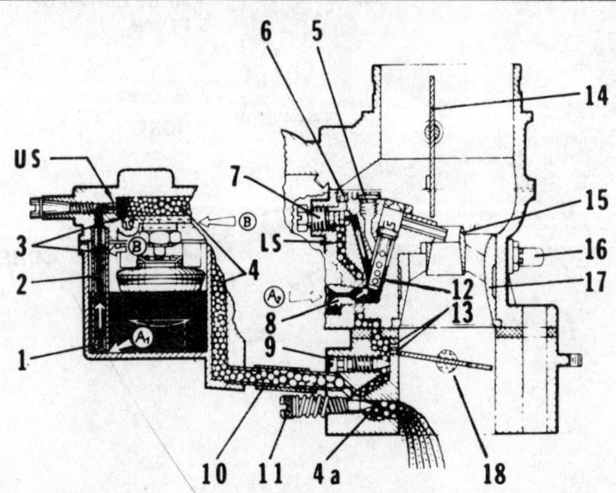

Fig. 3.4 Idle and air mixture control on the Solex 35 PDSIT carburettor

1 Additional fuel jet
2 Riser
3 Air bores for air mixture
4 Air mixture bore
5 Air correction jet
6 Idle air jet
7 Idle fuel jet
8 Main jet
9 Mixture control screw
10 Connecting tube
11 Idle speed adjusting screw
12 Mixture tube
13 Bypass bores
14 Choke
15 Outlet and atmoizer
16 Vacuum connection
17 Venturi
18 Throttle
A Fuel
B Air
LS Idle control system
US Air mixture control system

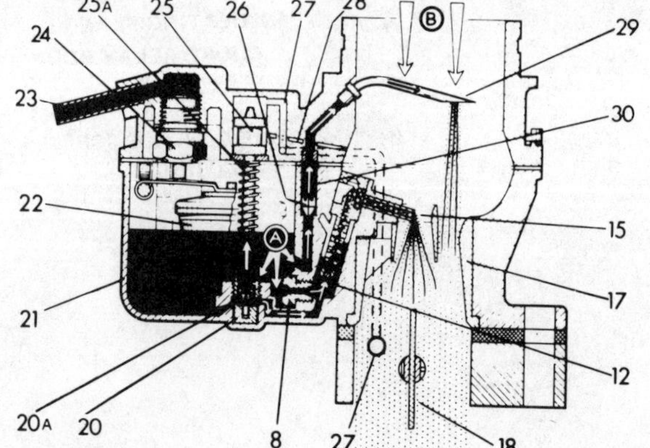

Fig. 3.5 Partial and full load enrichment on the Solex 35 PDSIT carburettor

20 Enrichment valve
20a Enrichment valve spring
21 Float chamber
22 Float
23 Fuel inlet
24 Float needle valve
25 Vacuum piston, operating rod and spring
26 Needle valve
27 Vacuum bore
28 Ventilation bore
29 Enrichment tube
30 Rise
A Fuel
B Air

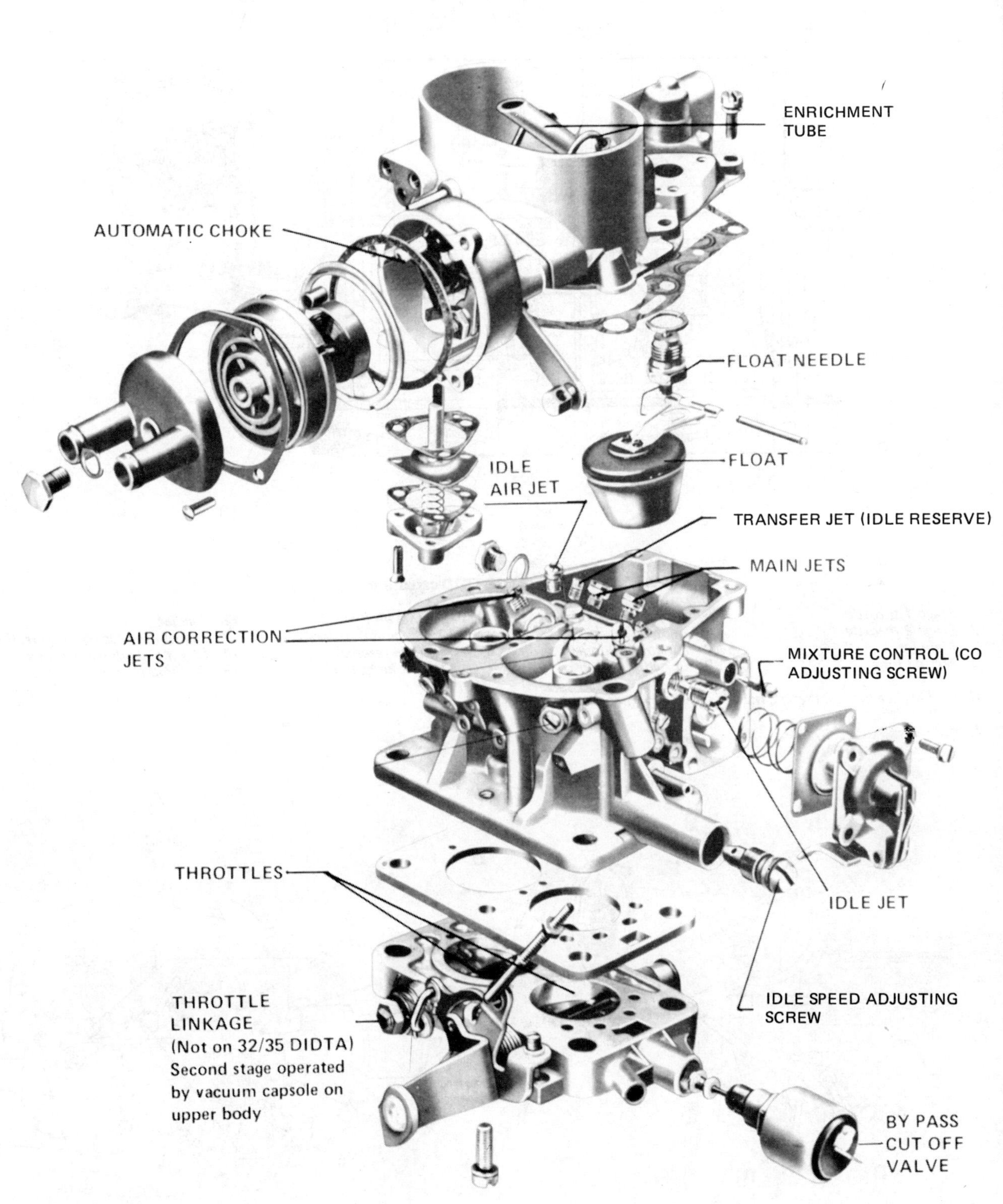

Fig. 3.6 Solex 32/35 TDID twin barrel carburettor - exploded view

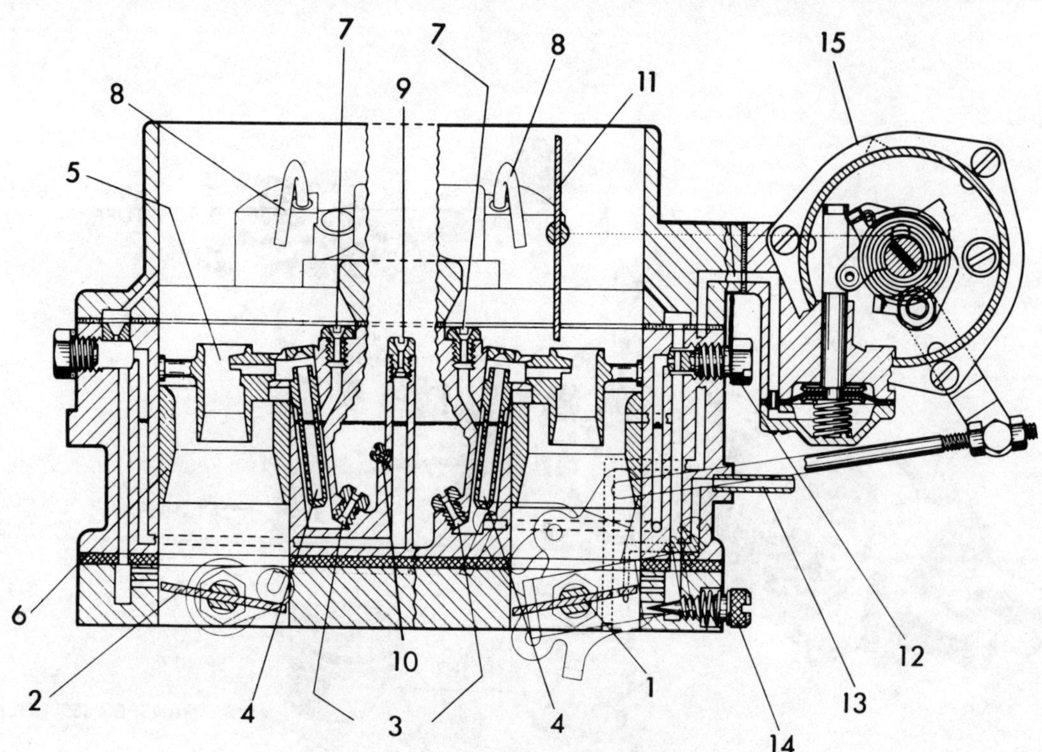

Fig. 3.7 Sectional view of 32 TDID carburettor

1 Stage 1 throttle
2 Stage 2 throttle
3 Main jet
4 Mixing tube
5 Outlet arm atonizer
6 Venturi
7 Air correction jet
8 Enrichment tube
9 Idle air jet
10 Stage 2 transfer jet (idle reserve)
11 Choke butterfly
12 Idle jet
13 Distributor vacuum connection
14 Idle speed adjusting screw
15 Automatic choke

Note: This is a typical layout, models vary from time-to-time

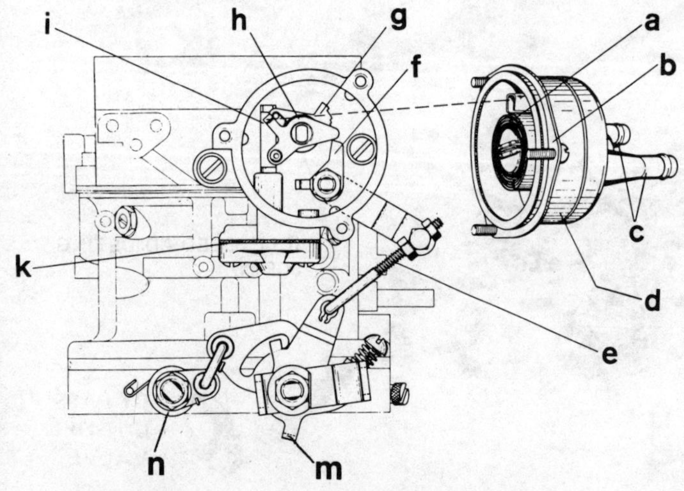

Fig. 3.8 Automatic choke of 32 TDID carburettor

a Bi-metallic spring
b Retaining ring
c Water connections
d Choke cover
e Connecting rod
f Stop lever
g Stepped washer (cam)
h Follower
i Diaphragm rod
k Diaphragm
m Stage 1 throttle lever
n Stage 2 throttle lever

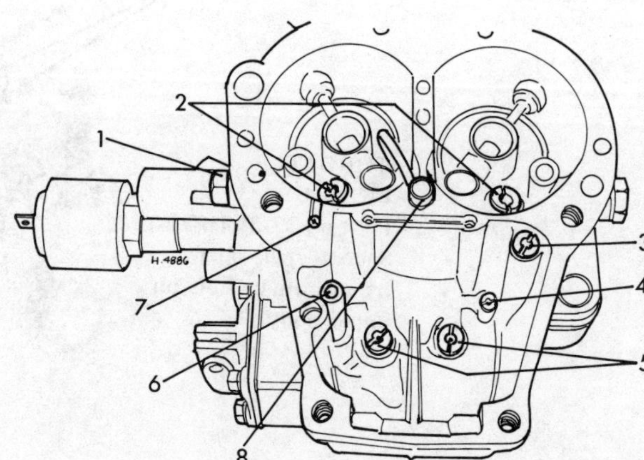

Fig. 3.9 Float chamber and venturi Solex 32/35 DIDTA

1 Idle air jet
2 Air connection jets
3 Idle jet reserve
4 Idle air jet
5 Main jets
6 Pump non-return valve
7 Auxiliary air jet
8 Injection tube

the auxiliary mixture system. This is taken from the float chamber via a riser tube and is metered by the auxiliary mixture jet. Air is drawn from the mixture chamber and the fuel/air mixture flows through a drilling which is controlled by the idle speed screw. This mixture joins the idle emulsion mixture at the front of the cut-off valve and goes to the mixture chamber to make the final idle mixture. This enters the throat of the carburettor via a drilling below the throttle flap. Air for this mixture is provided by setting the gap between the throttle flap and the bore. This is critical and is discussed later.

4 The idle speed may be adjusted by turning the idle speed control screw. Screw in to reduce speed and out to increase speed. This does not alter the fuel/air ratio so that an incorrect adjustment does not alter the carbon monoxide content of the exhaust gases. In this way the carburettor may be set correctly and sealed at the factory, yet the owner can alter the idle speed to suit his wishes, without breaking the law.

5 An electro-magnetic cut-off valve operates when the ignition is switched off, blocking the flow of basic and auxiliary idle mixtures and preventing the engine from running on when hot.

8C Carburettor Solex 35 PDSIT (single barrel) - main jet system

As already described the outlet arm draws fuel from the float chamber via the mixture tube and main jet. A drilling connects the air correction jet, which delivers air from the main air inlet, to the outside of the mixture tube. This has a number of small drillings in it and through these the air is sucked into the fuel stream delivering an emulsion to the outlet arm and thence to the venturi as the engine sucks more and more air through the carburettor. Thus the fuel/air ratio is corrected throughout the speed range. A small hole in the upper part of the outlet arm prevents siphon effect.

8D Carburettor Solex PDSIT (single barrel) - enrichment systems

There are two enrichment systems to provide more fuel to the engine first at increasing speed and then at full speed. The partial system consists of a valve operated by a piston and closed by a spring. The piston is operated by the partial vacuum in the induction manifold, opening the enrichment valve as the vacuum increases, and the spring closes the valve as the engine speed and partial vacuum decreases. At full throttle fuel is drawn through yet another drilling. The fuel at partial enrichment flows into the reserve below the mixture tube, the full throttle enrichment is delivered to the upper part of the inlet by a tube projecting into the inlet above the outlet arm. Both of these systems are preset and cannot be adjusted. Fig. 3.5 refers.

9 Carburettor Solex 32/35 TDID (twin barrel) - general description

1 This is a larger, two stage carburettor fitted to the 1500 cc 85 HP engine and some of the earlier models delivered to USA.

2 The 1st stage is identical to the 35 PDSIT already described, which takes care of the starting and idling arrangements and initial acceleration. When the throttle of stage one is approximately 2/3 open a linkage between the two throttle spindles causes the second stage throttle flap to commence to rotate. Matters are so arranged that the throttle spindles rotate in opposite directions for opening and closing.

3 The major advantages of this carburettor, is that both carburettors share the same auxiliary system, but there is no problem of synchronization. The first stage starts idles and sets the engine on the way, then when more power is required the second stage supplies the fuel for that.

4 The physical layout is shown in Fig. 3.6. A typical cross section is shown in Fig. 3.7 and the layout of the automatic choke in Fig. 3.8.

5 As stated the 1st stage is identical with the PDSIT 35, however the contours of the float chamber are different (see Fig. 3.9). Two main jets and two air correction jets. The emulsion tubes and enrichment systems are duplicated, with an inlet in each bore and an enrichment tube over each bore. There is only one choke butterfly valve over the 1st stage, but the automatic choke can alter the point at which stage 2 operates. This is obvious if you study Fig. 3.8.

6 The mouth of the air-cleaner is modified to suit the throat of the carburettor but otherwise the air cleaner is identical.

7 The adjustment of the second stage throttle is not expected to be disturbed, but if for some reason it has been, then slacken off the locknut on the stop screw, move the stop screw so that the throttle valve closes, then screw it in half a turn and lock it in this position. This stop screw is on the opposite side of the carburettor to the throttle lever.

10 Carburettor Solex 32/35 DIDTA (twin barrel) - general description

1 This carburettor is identical with the 32/35 TDID except in jet sizes and, most importantly, the operation of the second stage. In this carburettor the mechanical linkage is not the controlling medium but a small vacuum capsule attached to the upper carburettor by two screws. This part of the carburettor should not be dismantled. The vehicles to which this carburettor is fitted are subject to strict emission laws and should be serviced only by workshops with the correct meters and equipment to adjust the mixtures correctly.

11 Carburettors (single and twin barrel) - adjustments (general)

1 Apart from the adjustment of the throttle in the second stage already described in Section 9, paragraph 7, adjustments are all confined to the first stage of the carburettor. Adjustments are common to all three types. Details of adjustment procedures will be found elsewhere in this Chapter.

2 The adjustments, all of which can be done with the carburettor in-situ are seven in number. Before checking the idle speed be sure that the ignition timing is correct and the contact breaker dwell angle is correct.

3 Before making adjustments set the vehicle on a level base, run the engine for a few minutes, switch off, and check methodically.

12 Magnetic bypass air cut-off valve - general

1 Unfortunately the engine has a tendency to run-on after the ignition has been switched off. In order to stop this a valve is fitted to stop positively the flow of fuel to the carburettor when the ignition is switched off. This valve is screwed into the throttle body of both types of carburettor (photo). The valve consists of two parts, the solenoid in the cylindrical casing operated by switching on and off the ignition and the spindle which is moved by the solenoid moving the valve body (photo).

2 The operation of the valve may be tested by removing the valve from the carburettor, making sure the body of the valve is earthed (grounded) and switching on and off the ignition. The pin should move about 3 mm (0.12 in.).

3 The original valve fitted was used on the air-cooled engine, and sometimes did not function because of the residual voltage generated by the fresh-air fan running when the ignition was switched off. A new valve, part no. 056 129 412 with a higher operating voltage has been introduced. It is identified by a star on the hexagon.

13 Float chamber - checking fuel level (single barrel carburettor)

1 This level is most important as too high a level will cause flooding and difficult starting while too low a level will cause fuel starvation. Since the level is set correctly at the factory it is difficult to see how this should happen but a punctured float will cause too high a level since the float will not close the needle valve, or a faulty needle valve may cause flooding or fuel starvation.

2 Set the car on a level road, this is important, and run the engine for a few moments. Shut off and remove the air cleaner. Now remove the top of the carburettor by removing the securing screws. Remove the lever from the automatic choke (photo). **Do not** disturb the adjusting nuts. This may be a little difficult as the partial enrichment valve stops the head moving to clear the left-hand end (photo), but a little careful juggling will get it clear.

3 Use a depth gauge and measure the depth of the surface of the fuel from the top surface of the float chamber (photo). Do not do this close to the chamber wall or the float or capilliary attraction will distort the reading. It should be 14 mm $\pm$ 1 mm (0.551 in. $\pm$ 0.004 in.).

4 If the measurement varies considerably then remove the float and immerse it in hot water. If it is punctured there will be a string of bubbles emerging from it. A punctured float must be replaced by a new

one. If this does not find the fault then get someone with an accurate balance to weigh the float. It should weigh 7.3 grams. If the float is alright then check the needle valve. If the valve is held closed it should not be possible to blow through the inlet union. If you can the valve needs to be renewed.

5 If the error in depth level is small and the float and valve seem correct, it is possible to correct the measurement by fitting a different washer under the needle valve, a thicker one will lower the level, a thinner one will raise it (photo). Consult the official agent as to the thicknesses he can supply. **Do not** try to correct the level by bending the float hinge.

6 Reassemble the carburettor and have the C.O. valve checked as soon as possible.

14 Float chamber - checking fuel level (twin barrel carburettor)

1 This is one job that cannot be done without a special gauge.

2 The float and needle valve may be checked as with the PDSIT 35 float weight 7.3 grams, thickness of needle valve washer 2 mm, but no measurement is given for the height of the fuel in the float chamber. Instead, the carburettor cover, removed from the body, should be placed upside down on a 45° to the horizontal base. Tool VW/Audi 20. 100 should be placed over the machined face of the cover and the upper edge of the float collar should align itself with the tips of the gauge. Adjustment is by bending the tongue of the float hinge. This job is not within the scope of the owner driver, and should be left to the official dealer.

15 Automatic choke - general description and adjustment

1 The automatic choke is fitted to both types of carburettor.

2 The mechanism consists of two parts, the thermal section which opens or closes the choke according to the temperature of the engine coolant and the vacuum pull-down unit which acts in conjunction with the thermal unit. Refer to Fig. 3.3.

3 The main control is the thermal unit consisting of the adjuster ring, bi-metallic spring, choke and coolant cover. If the cover is removed (photo) the spring is exposed (photo), and if this is lifted away the operating lever is visible (photo).

4 The pull down (vacuum) unit is operated by a diaphragm and rod activated by the vacuum in the throttle of the carburettor and connected by a drilling which opens opposite the throttle valve.

5 Thus the movement of the choke butterfly valve is closely controlled to admit air to the carburettor as required during the starting and warming up period. When the engine is at normal operating temperature the choke is open.

6 To set the automatic choke adjust the mechanism until all three marks on the cover, intermediate ring and holding ring are in line (photo). This is done by slackening off the screws and moving the intermediate ring until the marks are in line and then tightening the screws.

7 On the twin barrel carburettor of later units the marks have been modified to notches (photo).

8 Yet another modification has been introduced in the automatic choke for the 35 PDSIT and 32/35 DIDTA carburettors. An electric heating element is installed in the coolant chamber of the automatic choke. These types may be identified by a wire which comes from the choke between the two hoses. The heater is controlled by a switch which is inserted in the warming-up circuit (the coolant circuit to the choke). This switch has a tube to which the hoses are clamped and a two pin connector. It operates between 10 and 15°C (50 and 59°F) to activate the heater.

On the automatic gearbox model a double switch is fitted. The switch described is reinforced by another one, called the thermo-pneumatic switch which governs the ignition retard vacuum mechanism.

Neither of these devices affect the setting of the automatic choke, as described in Section 16.

12.1 The magnetic bypass air cut-off valve removed from the throttle body

13.2a The automatic choke operating lever is marked 'A'. To disconnect it remove the pin and push it out. DO NOT disturb the adjusting nuts 'B'

13.2b Removing the carburettor cover. Partial enrichment piston may be seen between cover and body. Be careful not to damage this

13.3 Measuring the fuel level with a depth gauge

13.5 The carburettor cover upside down. 'A' is the needle valve 'B' is the partial enrichment valve

15.3a Removing the automatic choke cover

16 Choke valve - setting adjustment

1 The setting of the choke valve gap is critical. If it is not properly adjusted the automatic device is useless and the engine will not start easily or run properly.
2 The carburettor should be removed from the engine and held firmly in a vice.
3 Remove the automatic choke cover and intermediate ring. Press down the pull down rod to its stop with a screwdriver and measure the gap between the valve and the bore. Use a twist drill shank. Earlier models for the single barrel carburettor should be 4.05 to 4.75 mm (0.16 to 0.17 in.), no. 19 drill, later models 4.45 mm to 4.75 mm (0.175 to 0.182 in.), no. 16 drill. For the twin barrel carburettors, manual transmission, should be 3.85 to 4.15 mm (0.152 to 0.163 in.), no. 20 drill, automatic transmission as for manual *but* for USA models 3.05 to 3.35 mm (0.12 to 0.13 in.), no. 30 drill (photo).
4 Adjustment is by turning the vacuum unit control screw (photo).

17 Throttle valve - setting the gap

1 On both types of carburettor the important setting is on the throttle on no. 1 barrel. The setting of the throttle on no. 2 barrel is described in Section 9, paragraph 7 of this Chapter.
2 The carburettor must be removed from the vehicle to set stage 1.
3 It is not necessary to dismantle the carburettor as the throttle valve can be checked from below. Again a twist drill may be used to check the gap. For the manual two stage and the single barrel the gap should be 0.60 to 0.70 mm (0.024 to 0.028 in.), use a no. 73 drill, for the automatic gearbox, two stage use a no. 68 drill, (0.8 mm - 0.03 in.).
4 These figures should be checked against your carburettor part number. **Refer to Chapter 14 for a revised adjustment procedure.**

18 Accelerator pump - checking input per stroke

1 If this is to be done then it must be done accurately. The special tools required are VW/Audi 119 or a modified form of it for USA vehicles but briefly they consist of a tube suitably bent so that it can be connected to the injection tube with a rubber connection and led out through the mouth of the carburettor to a measuring glass. Secure the choke valve in the open position. Pump the accelerator until fuel comes out of the tube and then catch the fuel ejected by ten strokes of the accelerator. The rate per stroke should be, slow operation, 0.5 to 0.8 ccs for the 1300 cc engine, and the amount varies for the 1500 cc

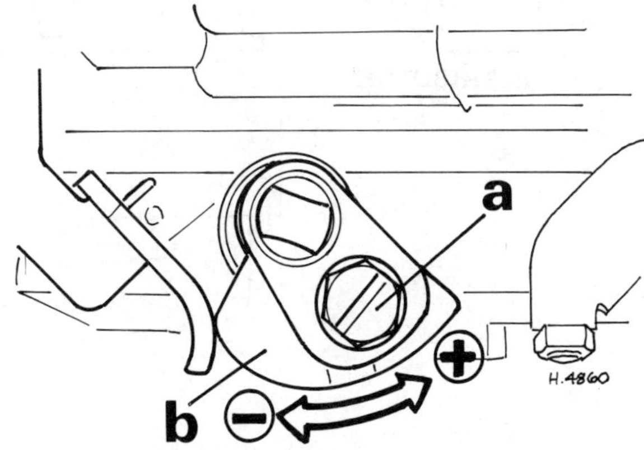

Fig. 3.10 The adjustment for the 1st stage throttle accelerator pump delivery on the double barreled carburettor

(a) Set screw *(b) Curved disc*

15.3b The bi-metallic spring

15.3c The automatic choke operating lever

15.6 The marks on the automatic choke. PDSIT 35

15.7 The marks on the automatic choke. Twin barrel carburettor, 1 Choke cover, 2 Adjusting ring, 3 Carburettor body

16.3 Using a twist drill to set the choke valve gap

16.4 The vacuum unit control screw (A) is directly below the automatic choke body

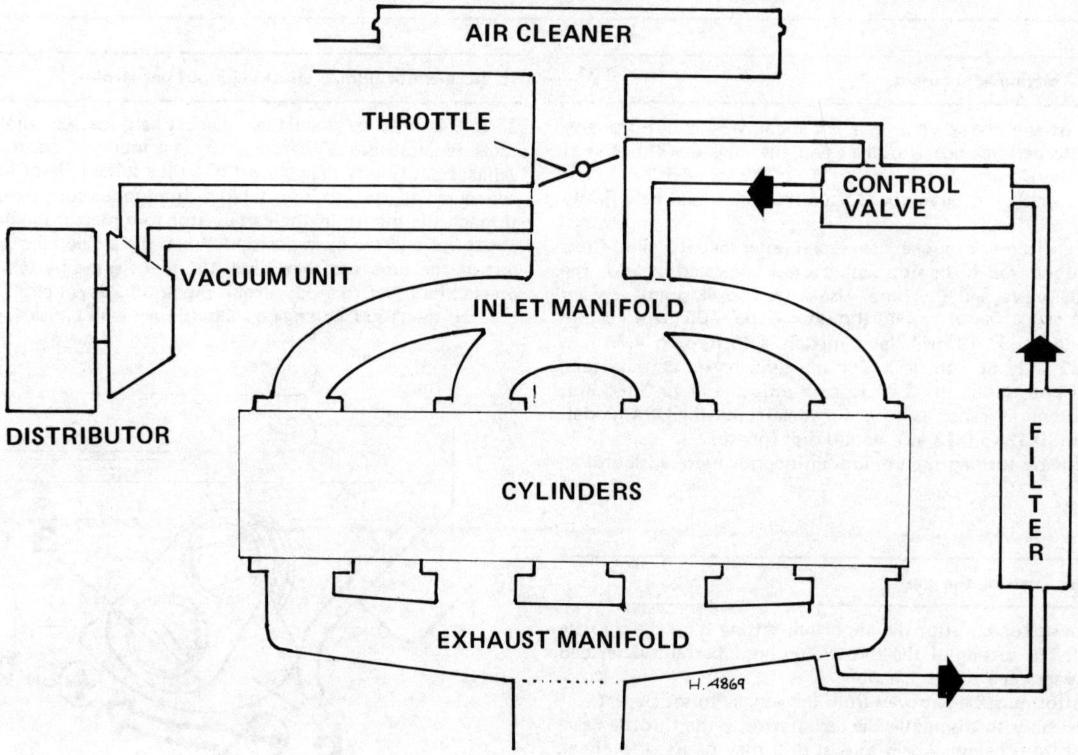

AIR CLEANER
THROTTLE
CONTROL VALVE
VACUUM UNIT
INLET MANIFOLD
DISTRIBUTOR
F I L T E R
CYLINDERS
EXHAUST MANIFOLD
H.4869

Fig. 3.11 Diagramatic layout of Exhaust Gas Recirculation system

THROTTLE
CONTROL VALVE
INJECTORS TO EXHAUST VALVE PORTS
TO INTAKE MANIFOLD
ANTI BACKFIRE VALVE
BELT DRIVEN COMPRESSOR
H.4867
AIR FILTER
AIR PRESSURE REGULATOR VALVE

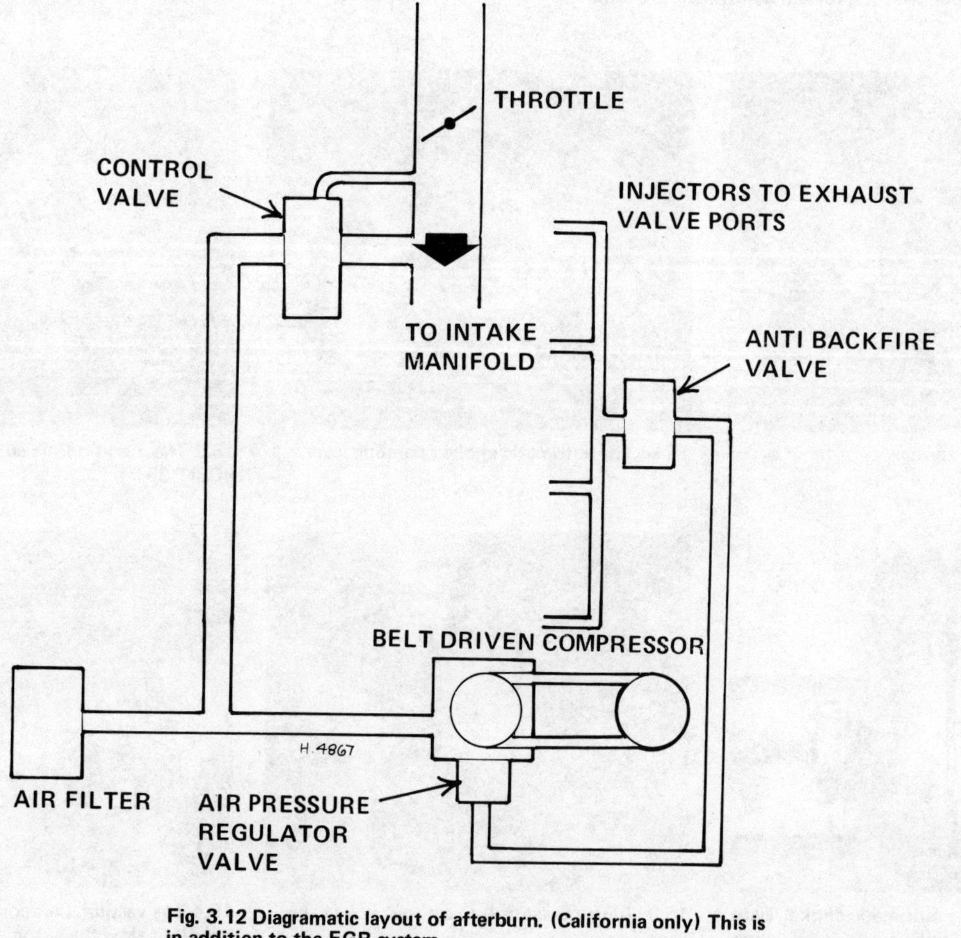

Fig. 3.12 Diagramatic layout of afterburn. (California only) This is in addition to the EGR system

engine but is generally 1.0 ccs. Check the exact figure with your official agent.

2 Adjustment on the PDSIT 35 carburettor is by turning the nut on the pump rod.

3 For the double barrel carburettor the angle lever must be adjusted. The diagram 3.10 is self-explanatory.

19 Checking the carbon monoxide (C.O.) content of the exhaust

1 This operation is confined to vehicles subject to emission laws and we strongly recommend that it be left to the official agent. However, if the necessary meter is available then the following may be of use.

2 First of all, check that the valve clearances are correct, the dwell angle is correct, the ignition timing is correct and there are no leaks in the exhaust system.

3 Run the engine until it is at normal operating temperature.

4 For vehicles without an air pump adjust the idle speed with the auxiliary mixture control screw to 1000 rpm and adjust the C.O. content to 1% volume.

5 For engines with an air pump disconnect the hose or the pump and clip it so that no air can enter. Adjust the C.O. content to 1.5% of volume, reconnect the hose and check that the C.O. content is below 1%.

6 It is strongly recommended that the vehicle is checked by the official dealer after this has been done.

20 Carburettor - cleaning

1 The various ways of adjusting the carburettor have been discussed in the foregoing Sections. The simple task of cleaning the carburettor is almost a relief. Dismantle the unit into its three main parts. Wash them carefully in clean fuel.

2 Jets may be cleaned by removing them from the body and blowing through them with compressed air. If this does not remove the obstruction then buy another jet, **do not** try to clean it with wire, hairpins, or such like. They are machined to fine limits and such treatment will ruin them.

3 It is permissable to clear drillings and airways in this manner but be careful, do not enlarge them and do not push all the foreign matter into the bends.

4 Always fit a new gasket after cleaning the carburettor.

21 Emission control - general

Pollution of the atmosphere is one of the special problems of our age and unfortunately the motor vehicle is a major offender. Fuel and air are drawn into the engine but if the fuel is not correctly burned then what comes out of the exhaust pipe may cause serious problems. These depend on the volume of traffic and the climatic conditions and are aggravated by geographical contours. Where the traffic is light and strong winds blow the fumes away the problem is negligible but where heavy commuter traffic running in an area surrounded by hills or tall buildings pertains the problem escalates to a point where it is dangerous to human life. Thus regulations vary, but obviously the elimination of these noxious fumes is important.

The incomplete burning of petrol results in the emission of carbon monoxide, which is poisonous, nitrous oxides and hydrocarbons, which may form a toxic 'fog' which is most distressing if breathed and can affect eyesight.

In the USA these problems are dealt with in two stages. Overall the regulations demand that exhaust gases be recycled so that nitrides are reduced to an acceptable minimum. This is done by exhaust gas recirculation. In California further measures are demanded to burn completely the C.O. and hydrocarbon content. This is done by injecting air into the exhaust system just behind the exhaust valves so that the C.O. becomes CO_2 by further combustion in the exhaust system. This is known as afterburn.

22 Emission control - exhaust gas recirculation (EGR)

1 Refer to Fig. 3.11. The principle of the system is to extract a portion of the hot burnt gas from the exhaust manifold and to inject it into the inlet manifold where it mixes with the fuel and air and enters the cylinders again. The result is to lower the flame peaks during combustion and so to lower the production of the oxides of nitrogen which are a small but important part of pollution. The exhaust gas passes through a filter which removes any carbon particles and then through a valve which is operated by the depression in the choke of the carburettor. Distributors fitted to engines bound for USA having this system have a hose from the intake to the vacuum unit of the distributor. Those going to California have a second hose from the carburettor venturi to the vacuum unit. The drillings in the exhaust manifold vary in size, for manual transmission 4.00 mm, for automatic transmission 7.0 mm.

The injection of exhaust gases is thus controlled according to the load on the engine and as the maximum input of fuel occurs the maximum EGR occurs, the ignition timing being varied slightly to suit.

2 The filter must be replaced every 20,000 miles.

3 The recirculation valve should be checked every 10,000 miles. Pull off the hose from the filter to the control valve at the control valve end. With the engine idling it should be possible to feel air being drawn in at the filter hose connection. If this is not so the valve must be replaced.

4 The filter is bolted to the exhaust manifold, the valve to the inlet manifold

23 Emission control - afterburn

1 This system is fitted only to vehicles for California. It is in addition to EGR. Its purpose is to lower the emission of carbon monoxide and hydrocarbons. Refer to Fig. 3.12.

2 An air pump belt-driven by the engine, sucks air through a filter and delivers it to the cylinder head by means of a pipe manifold so that the air is injected just behind the exhaust valve port into each cylinder. Inserted between the pump and the manifold is a non-return valve called the anti-backfire valve which prevents the gases blowing back into the pump, if a backfire occurs in the exhaust system.

3 When the driver lifts his foot from the accelerator suddenly the throttle closes and the mixture becomes over-rich. This can cause banging in the exhaust. To prevent this a branch pipe from the air filter supplies air via a control valve to the inlet manifold. The valve is vacuum operated by a line from the inlet manifold.

4 The filter should be replaced every 20,000 miles. Every 10,000 miles the belt tension should be checked and adjusted if necessary and the hoses examined for leaks and chafing.

5 If banging does occur in the exhaust system it must be cured right away as otherwise damage to the silencers will occur. Banging of this sort, is usually caused by a defective air control valve, or a leak in the hose system, but it may be an engine defect. We suggest the car should be taken to the dealer right away and checked on the computor.

6 The anti-backfire valve is screwed to the air injection manifold. To remove it the manifold must be removed from the cylinder head. It is just below the spark plugs.

7 The filter and the control valve are on the right-hand side of the engine compartment. If the wing nut on the bottom of the filter housing is removed the cover and the filter may be removed.

Fault diagnosis overleaf

24 Fault diagnosis - carburation; fuel and emission control systems

Symptom	Probable reason	Remedy
1 No fuel at carburettor	1 Tank empty 2 Fuel pump filter clogged 3 Faulty fuel pump	Fill tank! Clean filter. Replace pump with a new one.
2 Engine will not start	1 Choke valve stuck or throttle stuck 2 Auto choke not working 3 Carburettor flooding	Dismantle and correct. Dismantle and correct. Punctured float or needle valve faulty. Replace.
3 Engine idle or hunts, or stalls	1 Leak in brake servo hose 2 Leak in EGR hose 3 Air leaks round inlet manifold 4 Jets blocked	Replace. Replace. Replace gasket. Clean.
4 Engine will not stop when ignition switched off	Electro-magnetic cut-off valve not working	1 Check wiring. 2 If wiring correct, replace valve.
5 Backfire in exhaust, vehicles fitted with afterburn	Faulty air control valve or leaking hoses	Tighten hoses, if this does not cure then replace valve.
6 'Flat spots' engine will not accelerate from idle evenly	Accelerator pump not working properly Partial or full load enrichment systems choked Fuel pump faulty	Test and adjust. Clean and adjust. Check delivery and replace if necessary.
7 Black smoke from exhaust, engine rough at low speeds. Plugs fouled	Too much fuel	Check pump output. Check needle valve. Check fuel level in float chamber.
8 Engine accelerates but lacks power at speed	Enrichment system not working Dirt in tank or pipe lines	Dismantle and clean. Flush and clean filters.
9 Miles per gallon too low	Wrong jets fitted Float punctured Leaks in fuel hose or petrol tank Automatic choke incorrect Brakes binding Ignition incorrectly set Engine overheating	Check and fit correct jets. Test and replace. Remove and service. Test and adjust. Adjust brakes (Chapter 9). Check and adjust (Chapter 4). Check cooling system (Chapter 2).

Chapter 4 Ignition system

For modifications, and information applicable to later models, see Supplement at end of manual

Contents

Specifications

Distributor

Type	Bosch 1FU4
Condenser	0.22 mfd
Controls	Centrifugal and vacuum
Contact breaker points gap	0.012 to 0.016 in. (0.3 to 0.4 mm)
Dwell angle	42° to 58°

Ignition timing (up to 1974 models)

Engine codes ZA, ZF, ZB, FF, ZC, XX	30° BTDC at 3000 rpm, vacuum hose disconnected

Ignition timing (1975 models)

Engine codes ZA, ZF, YJ, FF, ZC (manual)	9° BTDC at 900 to 1000 rpm, vacuum hose disconnected
Engine codes YJ, ZC (automatic)	0° (TDC) at 900 to 1000 rpm, vacuum hose connected
Engine code XX	9° BTDC at 1050 to 1200 rpm, vacuum hose disconnected

Ignition timing (later models)

Refer to Chapter 14

Coil

12V Bosch KW with a separate resistor in circuit

Firing order

1 - 3 - 4 - 2 (No. 1 cylinder at timing belt end)

Spark plugs

Type:	Engine Code	Bosch	Beru	Champion
All 1300 cc models & USA 1500 cc models	ZA, ZF, XW, XV, XZ, XY	W 175 T30	175/14/3A	N 8 y
1500 cc (75 HP) models - not USA	ZB	W 200 T 30	200/14/3A1	N 8 y
1500 cc (85 HP) models	ZC	W 225 T 30	225/14/3A	N 7 y

Plug thread size	14 mm metric thread
Spark plug gap	0.6 mm to 0.8 mm (0.024 to 0.031 in.)

Torque wrench setting

	lb ft	kg m
Spark plugs	22	3

1 General description

1 The ignition system is conventional. A 12 volt, negative earth supply goes from the battery to terminal '15' on the coil, via the ignition switch on the steering column and a ballast resistor. Removal and replacement of the ignition switch is dealt with in Chapter 11, Section 18. From terminal '1' of the coil the supply goes to the distributor points and, when they are closed, to earth. A small condenser is connected across the points to minimize sparking.

2 The resistor is so arranged that when starting the engine the value of the resistor is small and nearly all the full 12 volts is applied to the coil.

1.7 The window in the flywheel casing

2.2 Undoing the screw that secures the fixed point

2.5 Checking the points gap with a feeler gauge

As the current flows the resistor heats up and increases its resistance lowering the voltage applied to the coil. The coil is rated to work at 12v for comparatively short periods and if the resistor is short circuited the coil will overheat.

3 The high tension winding is connected to the low tension winding inside the coil case and the other end is connected to the central terminal on the top of the coil casing. From here, via well insulated cable, the circuit goes to the centre of the distributor cap and from there via a small carbon bush inside the cap to the rotor arm.

This rotates causing a spark to jump across each rotor/segment gap in turn so that high voltage is led to the plugs where if all is correctly arranged a spark appears across the plug gap at the most propitious moment.

4 Because the engine requires only one spark per cylinder for every two revolutions of the crankshaft the distributor rotates at half the speed of the crankshaft. Refer to Fig. 4.1 where it will be seen that the distributor shaft is the centre of the mechanism with a helical gear driven by the intermediate shaft at the bottom and the rotor arm. In fact the shaft is in two parts joined by the governor mechanism. The vacuum advance and retard mechanisms are discussed in Section 7, of this Chapter.

5 The central electrode of the spark plug is the one which gets hottest. Spark emission theory states that electron flow is from the hotter electrode to the cooler one. It is important therefore to keep the polarity correct. Connecting the LT winding of the coil incorrectly will cause all sorts of troubles and make starting difficult.

6 The heat path of the spark plugs has been carefully designed. Use only the recommended types or again performance will be badly affected.

7 With strict emission laws and the ever increasing cost of fuel it is most important that ignition timing should be exact and correct. It is now the accepted practice to set the distributor points gap by measuring the dwell angle. This requires a special meter and a tacho-meter. The gap can be set with feeler gauges in an emergency but this is not really accurate enough.

The window in the flywheel casing (photo) shows the timing mark to be set for optimum performance. This is good enough to get the engine running (see Chapter 1, Section 21) but the final adjustment needs a stroboscopic light and a tachometer. These jobs are described later in this Chapter.

2 Contact breaker points - removal, replacement and adjustment

1 The contact breaker points require attention every 6,000 miles. Depending upon how badly they are pitted or burned they may be cleaned and peaks removed with a fine oil stone. Do not try to remove craters. Points are cheap enough, it is difficult to set them accurately if they are worn.

2 To remove the points first take off the distributor cap and remove the rotor arm and seal. Two small leads are visible with spade terminals. Lift the spring away from them and pull the spring plus moving point up out of the distributor body. The fixed point is held to the mounting plate by a single screw. Undo this (photo) and the fixed point may be removed.

3 Examination of the points may be instructive. Normal wear gives pitting and small high points with light coloured surfaces. If the surface is grey then either the contact breaker spring is weak or the gap was too small. Yellow or black surfaces indicate over lubrication. A blue surface means that either the coil or condenser is defective.

4 This is a good moment to check side-play in the distributor shaft. If there is significant wear it will not be possible to set the points accurately, with feeler gauges, nor is it possible to obtain spares to remedy the problem. A dealer using a dwell meter may achieve a setting within tolerence but that is only putting off the evil day: a replacement distributor is the answer. There is no reason to buy new points if you need a new distributor.

5 If the shaft and bearings are in good order replace the clean or new points in the reverse order to dismantling. Make sure that the spade terminals are not short circuiting on the distributor body. Tighten the screw holding the fixed point so that it is just possible to move the point sideways. Turn the engine until the heel of the moving point rests on the highest point of the lobe of the cam on the shaft. The spring is now compressed to the maximum. Move the fixed point away from the moving point until a gap appears between them. Insert a 0.35 mm (0.014 in) feeler gauge between the points and close them with the screwdriver

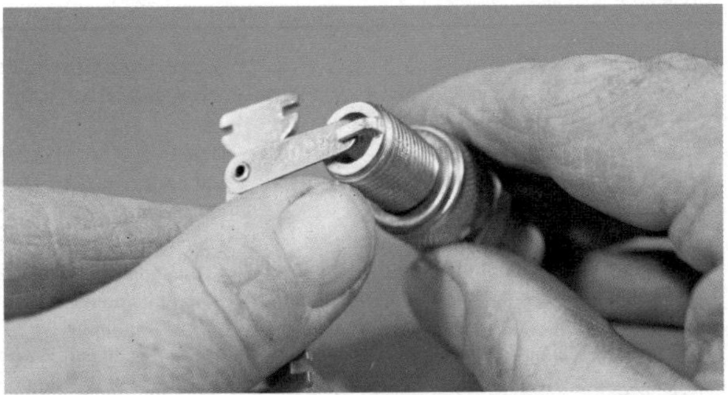

Measuring plug gap. A feeler gauge of the correct size (see ignition system specifications) should have a slight 'drag' when slid between the electrodes. Adjust gap if necessary

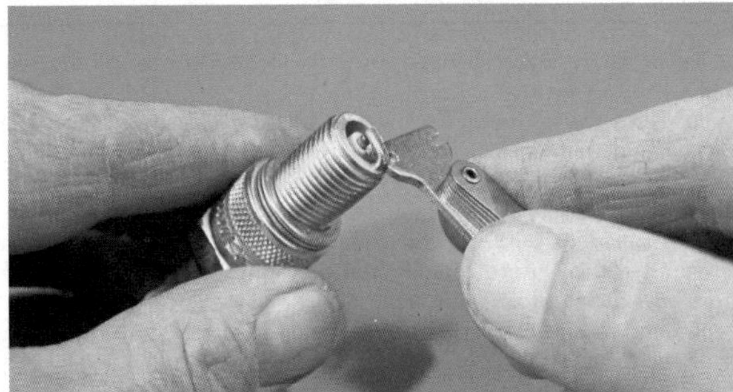

Adjusting plug gap. The plug gap is adjusted by bending the earth electrode inwards, or outwards, as necessary until the correct clearance is obtained. Note the use of the correct tool

Normal. Grey-brown deposits, lightly coated core nose. Gap increasing by around 0.001 in (0.025 mm) per 1000 miles (1600 km). Plugs ideally suited to engine, and engine in good condition

Carbon fouling. Dry, black, sooty deposits. Will cause weak spark and eventually misfire. Fault: over-rich fuel mixture. Check: carburettor mixture settings, float level and jet sizes; choke operation and cleanliness of air filter. Plugs can be re-used after cleaning

Oil fouling. Wet, oily deposits. Will cause weak spark and eventually misfire. Fault: worn bores/piston rings or valve guides; sometimes occurs (temporarily) during running-in period. Plugs can be re-used after thorough cleaning

Overheating. Electrodes have glazed appearance, core nose very white – few deposits. Fault: plug overheating. Check: plug value, ignition timing, fuel octane rating (too low) and fuel mixture (too weak). Discard plugs and cure fault immediately

Electrode damage. Electrodes burned away; core nose has burned, glazed appearance. Fault: pre-ignition. Check: as for 'Overheating' but may be more severe. Discard plugs and remedy fault before piston or valve damage occurs

Split core nose (may appear initially as a crack). Damage is self-evident, but cracks will only show after cleaning. Fault: pre-ignition or wrong gap-setting technique. Check: ignition timing, cooling system, fuel octane rating (too low) and fuel mixture (too weak). Discard plugs, rectify fault immediately

until the feeler gauge is *just* gripped (photo). Tighten the holding screw and recheck the gap again.

6 When using a dwell meter follow the instructions given with the meter concerning connection and timming. It is usual to connect one lead to No 1 terminal on the coil and the other to earth.

7 Run the engine up to 1000 rpm. Read the value of the dwell angle. Now increase speed to 2000 rpm and read the dwell angle again. If the reading has altered by more than 1° the distributor shaft bearings are worn and a new distributor is required.

8 The readings should be compared with the specified figures, given at the start of the Chapter.

9 If they vary then the points gap is incorrect. To adjust slacken the fixed point holding screw and run the engine on the starter. It will not fire as the HT circuit is not connected. Move the fixed point until the correct angle is read on the meter. Tighten the screw, refit the rotor and cap and recheck the dwell angle as in paragraph 7.

3 Distributor - removal and installation

1 This has already been dealt with in Chapter 1, Section 21 but you may want to remove the distributor with the engine in the car.

2 Remove the valve cover and disconnect the battery earth strap.

3 Now bring No 1 cylinder to the firing point. The TDC mark on the flywheel (not the timing mark) must line up with the mark on the window see photo 1.7. Since the crankshaft revolves twice to the distributors once you may be on the wrong revolution. Look at the cams on the camshaft for No 1 cylinder. Both cams must be pointing upwards, valves closed. If they are not turn the engine one revolution. Remove the cap from the distributor.

4 Disconnect the LT lead from the distributor. Check that the rotor arm points to the mark for No 1 cylinder on the rim of the distributor housing. This is a shallow groove. It can be seen in photo 2.2 just by the screwdriver.

5 Pull off the vacuum hoses. Now undo the clamp bolt and draw the distributor up and out. The shaft will turn a little as the gear is drawn away from the intermediate shaft. Note how much. If you are putting the same distributor back it is a good idea to centre-punch the casing and the block so that you get it back correctly.

6 Do not allow the crankshaft to rotate until you are ready to re-install the distributor. Check the position of the oil pump drive before reassembly by looking down the bore for the distributor shaft. The slot in it should be parallel to the crankshaft.

7 Reassembly is the reverse of removal. Make sure the distributor is properly seated with the tongue on the end of the shaft firmly in the groove of the oil pump drive.

4 Distributor - overhaul

1 Refer to Fig. 4.1. Before starting to take the distributor apart check with the official agent what spares can be supplied.

2 The cap may have cracked, or chipped, or the small carbon bush be faulty. Fine cracks will be visible and 'tracking' lines may also be found. When the cap is cleaned carefully, inside and out, what seem to be pencil lines are actually fine cracks harbouring carbon and are fine electricity conductors. All this means a new cap is necessary.

3 The rotor arm must not be cracked or chipped and the spring should be intact. The rotor arm segment has a resistance to suppress radio interference, this measured between the centre and the tip is up to 10,000 ohms.

4 The vacuum unit is not removed and replaced easily, as this involves removing the mounting plate of the contact breaker and dismantling the centrifugal advance and retard mechanism. Unless the owner has had considerable instruction in these matters the job is best left to the expert.

5 The condenser can be removed easily and tested, or tested in position. A separate section on this is included in this Chapter.

6 As stated before wear in the bearings or shaft replacement is not possible as spares are not available. If the teeth on the drive-gear are damaged this will also mean a replacement distributor.

5 Ignition - timing (Static method)

1 This may be done in an emergency with a test lamp.

2 Set the engine so that the TDC mark shows in the window over the flywheel. Remove the distributor cap. Check that the rotor arm points to the No 1 cylinder mark.

3 Connect a 12v test lamp across the No 1 terminal of the coil and earth. Slacken the clamp nut on the distributor, switch on the ignition, and rotate the distributor body gently until the light goes off. At this position the points are closed and the lamp is shorted out. Reverse the direction of rotation of the body until the lamp *just* comes on. Tighten the clamp nut and reassemble the distributor. Have the timing checked dynamically as soon as possible.

6 Ignition timing (Dynamic method)

1 A much better method of setting the timing point is by using a stroboscopic lamp and a tachometer.

2 Refer to the Specification as to speed, flywheel markings and connection of hoses for your model.

3 The stroboscopic light should be connected to No 1 spark plug. The instructions with the lamp explain how to do this. Usually a special connector is supplied, to which No 1 plug lead is connected and a lead from the connector goes to No 1 plug. The lamp is tapped into the connector and the other lead from the lamp to the battery positive (+) terminal.

4 The engine should be at normal operating temperature. Run the engine up to the specified speed and check the hose position. Flash the lamp onto the window on the bellhousing (photo 1.7) and read the timing mark illuminated. Compare with the Specification. If adjustment is required loosen the distributor clamp and rotate the distributor body, clockwise to advance the timing, anticlockwise to retard it. Tighten the clamp and reconnect the hoses if necessary.

7 Vacuum spark control - testing

Connect a stroboscopic lamp to the ignition system and run the engine, as in Section 6. If the test was done with the hose off then set the system up with the hose in the off position and then read the mark in the window. Now reconnect the hose and the timing mark should move. If the test was done the other way with the hose on then remove it and the timing mark should move. If it does not then the vacuum unit is faulty and must be renewed.

8 Centrifugal spark control - testing

Remove the distributor cap and rotor then grasp the shaft at the top and turn it a few degrees. It should turn easily and then stop. Do not force it, release it and it should return easily to the original position. If it does not then the springs are stretched or the mechanism is clogged. It would be as well to have it checked by the agent with his special tester. To clean the centrifugal governor it is necessary to remove the contact breaker and mounting plate. We do not recommend this as the governor should be set to exact readings if the emission control is to remain effective.

9 Ignition coil - testing

1 It is as well to remember that the test voltage output of the coil is in the region of 18,000 volts. To test it accurately a special tester is needed. However, a coil is either all right or all wrong, there are no repairs possible, and there are three simple tests which will determine its condition.

2 Remove the wiring from the top of the coil and clean it carefully. Look for tracking marks and cracks. Check the servicability of the wires and connections and replace them if necessary. Refit the LT wires to the coil and the HT lead to the centre terminal of the coil but remove it from the middle of the distributor. Hold the distributor end of the lead about 3/8 in (10 mm) from the cylinder block and get a helper to switch on the ignition and operate the starter. A spark should jump from the lead to the block. You will jump too if you haven't taken the precaution of holding the lead with insulated pliers or wearing a rubber glove. If there is a big fat spark then the coil is working satisfactory. If no spark emerges then the LT circuit must be tested.

3 Connect a voltmeter between terminal '15' on the coil and earth. With the ignition switched on the reading should be minimum of 9 volts. Less than this, or zero, means that there is a faulty ballast resistor, ignition switch or faulty wiring. If this test registers a minimum of 9 volts then check the continuity of the remainder of the circuit. Connect the voltmeter between terminal one and earth. Remove the distributor cap and rotor. Turn the engine so that the points are closed. Switch on the ignition. There should be no voltage between terminal '1' and earth. Open the points with a piece of wood. There should now be a reading on the voltmeter. Finally check that the lead from the coil to the distributor is not shorting to earth when the points are open. If the lead is in order and there are no volts when the points are opened then the LT system of the coil is faulty and it should be removed for expert testing by the agent or a reputable Auto. Electric specialist.
4 Even though the coil responds to all these tests it may still be the fault in the system. It can develop faults as it warms up. If you have persistant ignition trouble when the engine is warm after an excellent cold start suspect the coil and have it tested by the VW agent.

10 Condenser - testing

1 If the contact breaker points are badly burned or pitted the fault is probably with the condenser. This small unit will also cause problems with the HT circuit for it helps the rapid decay of the magnetic field in the coil and if it is defective the operating voltage of the HT circuit will be much reduced.
2 There are two faults that can affect it. A short circuit, either in its construction or lead will render it inoperative, as will an open circuit.
3 Disconnect cable '1' from the coil and connect a test lamp in series with cable '1' and cable '15' of the coil (in other words put the lamp in place of the coil). Switch on the ignition. If there is a short circuit then the lamp **will not** light, and the condenser must be replaced.
4 Open circuits are very rare. If the short circuit test shows that the condenser is in good condition and extensive pitting of the points has happened then remove the condenser and take it to someone who can measure its insulation resistance and capacitance. If this is not possible then replace it straight away.

11 Spark plugs and HT leads - general

1 Spark plugs should be removed, cleaned and the gaps reset every 12,000 miles or more often if the engine shows signs of burning oil. The best policy is to have two sets of plugs and have a clean set ready to fit when necessary. The dirty ones may then be taken to a garage to be cleaned in the shot blast machine, reset and tested under pressure. In this way the carbon is removed from the plug. Trying to clean it with a wire brush only pushes carbon up inside the plug. **Never** try to clean plugs with solvent.
2 The plug gap is set by bending the outer electrode. Do not attempt to move the centre electrode or you will break the insulator. If you are setting the gap with feelers measuring inches aim at 0.028 in.
3 It is essential to use only the recommended grade of plug. Three choices are given in the Specification but other makers produce equally good plugs. There is a comparison table concerning grades in most garages.
4 When refitting plugs mark sure the washer is not flattened or the plug will be damaged by leaking gases. Be careful not to cross the threads or expensive repairs to the cylinder head may be necessary besides all the bother of taking it off.
5 HT leads are special high resistance cable to deal with suppression of radio interference. If they are frayed or soaked in oil then replace them. **Do not** use insulating tape on HT systems and make sure the terminals are securely crimped on the cable. The resistance of a lead should be between 5,000 and 10,000 ohms.
6 The condition of the plugs gives an interesting comment on the state of the engine. A study of Fig. 4.2 will show why.

12 Fault diagnosis - ignition system

1 This Section is divided into two parts, non-start problems and running problems.
2 Ignition faults can be most exasperating. Read the whole Section and then work quietly through it, check everything and if you cannot find the answer go to the expert. He has instruments specially designed for finding faults. If you explain how you have checked methodically it may help him, if you have been pulling wires off in the hope of curing the fault quickly it may take him a long while to put things right and he may never find out which the original fault was that caused all the trouble.

Engine will not start

1 If the car will not start check first that the engine is not covered with moisture from mist, rain or other sources. If it is then dry inside the distributor cap, dry all leads and covers and generally clean up. A cold engine will not start if it is damp and you will only run the battery down.
2 If the engine is dry then remove one of the plug leads and turn back the insulation. Hold the lead near the block about 3/8 in (9.525 mm) away from it, and get someone to spin the engine with the starter. If there is a fat spark then the ignition is working alright but the timing may have slipped. This will be one of two things on this engine, the clamp holding the distributor has come loose or the timing belt is loose. The latter will make itself known by the noise it makes fouling the guard.
3 To check the distributor timing refer to Section 5. Briefly turn the engine so that the TDC mark on the flywheel shows in the window over the flywheel and see that the rotor arm points to No 1 cylinder firing mark on the distributor body. If it does not then turn the crankshaft through 360° and check again. If the result was correct on either occasion then the timing has not slipped and the fault is not in the ignition circuit.
4 If there **is not** a fat spark when testing as at the start of paragraph 2 then the fault is with the ignition circuit. However, check with another plug lead before doing anything else.
5 There is a tendency to test haphazardly but it is better to stick to a routine even if it takes a little longer. This way you will find the faults and cure them. There may be more than one. Begin by checking the LT circuit in the following order:

(i) *Are the points opening and closing correctly? Are they clean?*
(ii) *Switch on the ignition and check the voltage at terminal '15' on the coil. It should be at least 9 volts. If it is less check the wiring, switch and ballast resistor.*
(iii) *Check the voltage at terminal '1' on the coil. Points closed there should be no volts. points open there should be a reading. Check the LT lead from the distributor to the coil for short circuit to earth (points open). If the lead is correct and there are no volts with the points open then the coil is faulty.*
(iv) *Ignition switched on check the voltage across the points. Points closed - no volts; points open the meter should read, if it does not the condenser is faulty.*

6 Now proceed to test the HT circuit

(i) *Pull the HT lead from the centre of the distributor, hold it close to the cylinder block, switch on the engine and spin it with the starter. No spark - faulty HT winding in the coil. Switch off the ignition and proceed to test the coil (Section 9).*
(ii) *Check the condition of the rotor and distributor cap (Section 4).*
(iii) *Check the centrifugal automatic advance and retard (Section 8).*
(iv) *Remove the plugs and service them. Oily plugs mean worn cylinders; wet plugs, flooding in the carburettor.*

Fault diagnosis overleaf

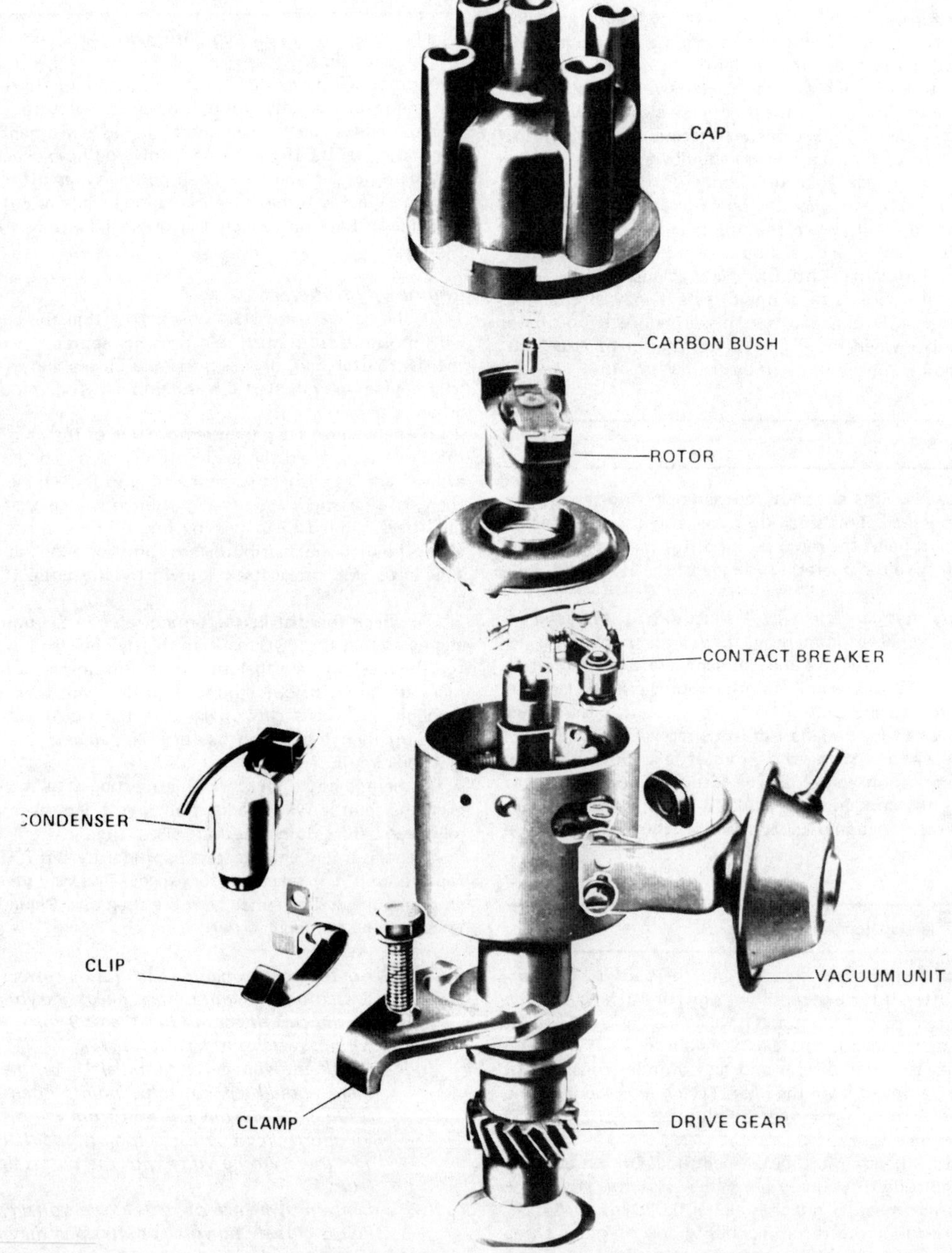

Fig. 4.1 Distributor - exploded view

12 Fault diagnosis - ignition system

Symptom	Probable cause	Remedy
Engine sluggish	CB points not set correctly	Check and set.
	Plug gaps incorrect	Check and set.
	Ignition timing incorrect	Check and adjust.
	Wrong fuel used	Check octane rating of fuel.
Engine misfires, cuts out at low revolutions	CB points gap too large	Reset.
	Distributor shaft and bearings worn	Fit new distributor.
Engine misfires at high revolutions	CB gap too small	Reset.
	Distributor shaft and bearings worn	Fit new distributor.

Chapter 5 Clutch

For modifications, and information applicable to later models, see Supplement at end of manual

Contents

Specifications

Type	Single plate, dry, diaphragm spring	
Operation mechanism	Cable	
Driven plate diameter		
1500 cc engine	7.48 in. (190 mm)	
1300 cc engine	7.09 in. (180 mm)	
Diaphragm spring pressure	900 lbs ± 65 lbs (410 kg ± 30 kg)	
Driven plate		
Thickness	0.30 in. (7.8 mm)	
Maximum out of true	0.02 in. (0.5 mm)	
Free-travel at clutch pedal	5/8 in. (15 mm)	
Torque wrench settings	**lb ft**	**kg m**
Pressure plate to flywheel	18	2.5
Engine to transmission	40	3.3
Clutch release lever	17	2.3
Cable to bracket	2	1.7

1 General description

1 The diaphragm spring dry plate clutch is common to all models with manual transmission. The driven plate for the 1500 cc models is 10 mm (0.4 in.) larger in diameter than that fitted to the 1300 cc models, otherwise detail is the same. When ordering spares check with the dealer that they are the correct ones for your vehicle.
2 The clutch cable is in the engine compartment and is easily accessible for adjustment.
3 The transmission must be removed to get at the clutch - see Chapter 6. This is done from under the vehicle so that a pit or some kind of ramp is necessary. The clutch release mechanism is in the bellhousing of the gearbox and comes away with that item when the transmission is removed.
4 Maintenance is limited to adjusting the free travel of the clutch pedal to 5/8 in. (15 mm), a job which takes less than half an hour.

2 Clutch pedal - adjustment of free-travel

1 The clutch pedal is held in position by a small spring (photo). In some models this spring is on the other side of the pivot shaft (as shown in Fig. 5.1). If the clutch pedal is depressed by hand it will be found to move freely for a short distance and then to encounter steady resistance. This measurement is known as the free-travel. It is most important that this should be correctly adjusted for if there is no free-travel the release bearing will be in contact with the diaphragm fingers continuously: causing wear and eventually clutch slip. Free-travel can be measured by holding a rule against the pedal with one end of the rule on the car floor and then depressing the pedal until resistance is felt.
2 As the lining and the withdrawal mechanism wear a little the free-travel will decrease. This can be rectified by adjusting the anchorage of the outer cable at the end nearest the clutch operating lever. This is marked on Fig. 5.1 and also shown in the photo. Undo the lower nut and screw the upper nut upwards to increase free-travel or downwards to reduce free-travel.

3 Clutch cable - removal and replacement

1 It will be necessary to remove the centre panel and the panel over the pedals from under the fascia board to get at the inner end of the clutch cable.
2 Undo the two adjusting nuts on the anchorage of the clutch cable in

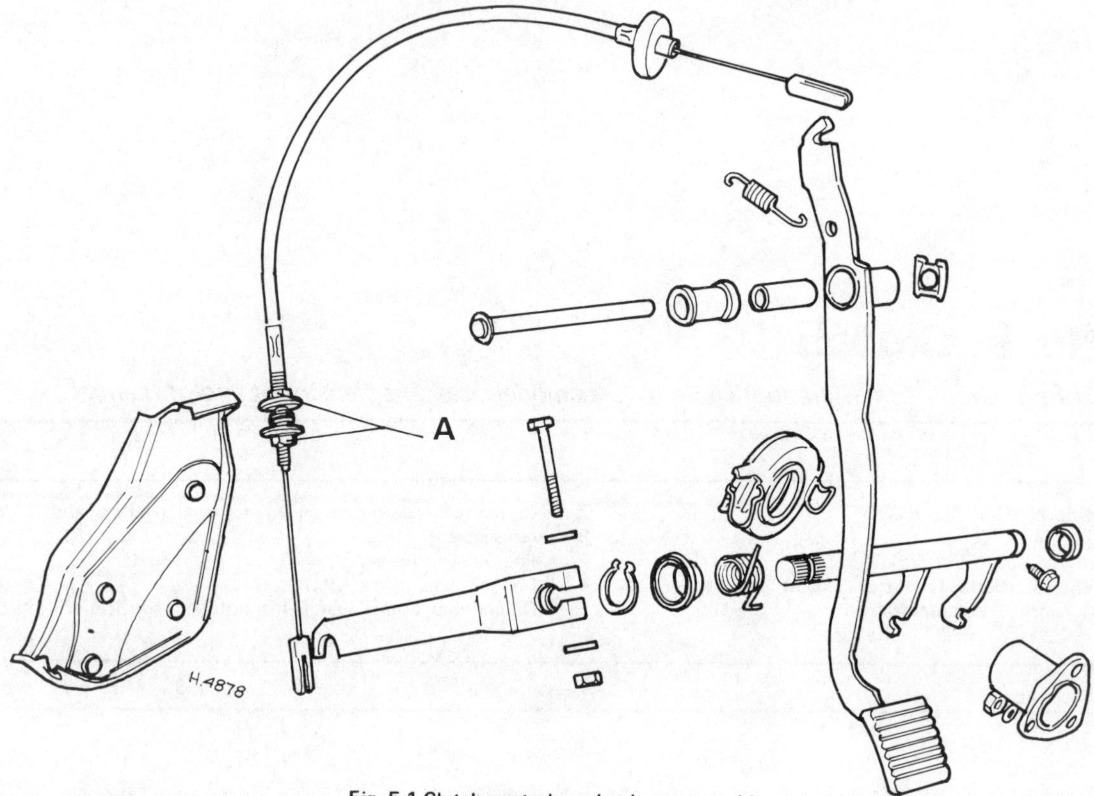

A

H.4878

Fig. 5.1 Clutch control mechanism - general layout

'A' is the adjustment point

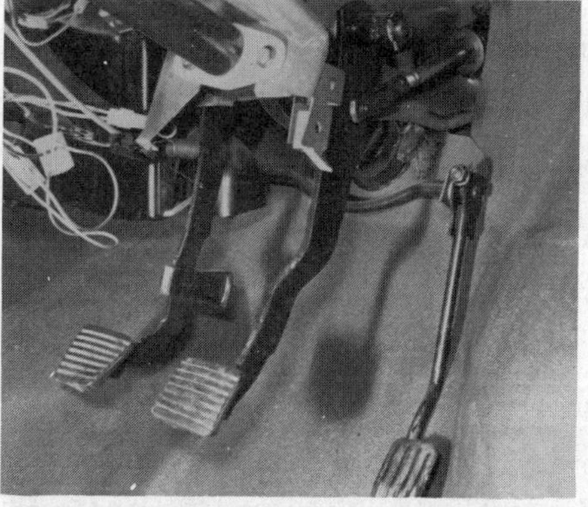

2.1 The clutch pedal is on the left. This shows a R.H.D. vehicle, the covers under the fascia board have been removed

2.2 The clutch cable anchorage in the engine compartment. One adjusting nut (A) is marked, the other is underneath the anchorage. The clutch operating lever and connection is marked 'B'

5.2 The clutch bolted to the flywheel. Make centre-punch marks at 'A'

5.4 The pencil points to the diaphragm spring fingers which must be checked for wear

5.5 Checking the pressure plate surface for distortion

5.7 The pencil points to the rivet head which should be at least 0.025 inches (0.63 mm) below the friction surface

the engine compartment and slide the cable out of the anchorage. Unhook the white plastic end pieces of the cable from the clutch operating lever and the clutch pedal.
3 Pull the rubber grommet away from the bulkhead into the engine compartment and extract the cable.
4 Replacement is the reverse of removal.
5 Adjust the pedal free-travel.

4 Clutch pedal - removal, overhaul and replacement

1 Remove the cable as in Section 3, but do not pull the cable through into the engine compartment, just unhook it from the pedal.
2 Refer to Fig. 5.1. Remove the pedal return spring and then the locking clip from the end of the shaft. Tap out the shaft and bushes. The bush can be pressed out of the pedal lever and renewed if required. This job should not be necessary unless the car is much used. To check this merely test how much the pedal can be twisted. Excessive wear will allow a small amount of twist. It is worthwhile looking at it though when replacing the cable.
3 Replacement is the reverse of removal. When installing the bushes smear them lightly with brake cylinder paste.
4 Adjust the pedal free-travel.

5 Clutch - removal, overhaul and replacement

1 Remove the transmission as described in Chapter 6. Please also read Chapter 1, Section 8, paragraph 10 and Chapter 1, Section 22, paragraph 13.
2 We have already said that there needs to be adequate space to operate under the car. The clutch and flywheel will be observable (photo). Using a centre-punch mark the position of the clutch on the flywheel. Undo the bolts holding the clutch to the flywheel. Slacken them off a little at a time in a diagonal fashion, there is a lot of pressure on this plate. As soon as the bolts are free remove them and lift the clutch away from the flywheel with the driven plate. Note that the longer side of the driven plate faces the gearbox, if you try to put it back the other way round then the clutch holding bolts will have to be undone again, as it will prevent correct assembly.
3 The flywheel will now be visible. If this is badly scored, cracked or distorted this may also be removed for servicing (see Chapter 1), without removing the engine from the vehicle. If the clutch is contaminated with oil the seal may be replaced behind the flywheel (see Chapter 1).
4 Before cleaning the clutch lay the diaphragm plate on a clean surface, pressure plate surface down and examine the ends of the diaphragm spring fingers for scoring (photo). This is where the release bearing pushes the spring and the two surfaces engage at speed. Scoring up to 0.011 in. (0.3 mm) is permissible according to the specification but how you measure the depth is a good question. However, heavy scoring means a new diaphragm, putting the old one back will only ruin a new release bearing. If in doubt, consult the agent.
5 Wipe the clutch clean and turn it over. Place a 12 inch rule or straight-edge across both faces of the pressure plate and using a feeler gauge check the surface for distortion (photo). Inward taper of 0.011 in. (0.3 mm) is permissible, beyond this either machining or a new diaphragm are needed - consult the agent. Excessive scoring, burn marks or cracks due to overheating, will also mean a new clutch.
6 The diaphragm fingers are rivetted to the casing. Check the condition of these rivets. Any scoring, or loose rivets mean that the diaphragm must go for servicing or replacement.
7 Now turn to the clutch disc. Fit it on the gearbox mainshaft splines and check that it slides freely without excessive play. Examine the springs in the centre for cracks or signs of overheating, and the metal between the springs for cracks. The centre hub has been known to break away from the rest of the plate. The depth of lining proud of the rivet head (photo) should not be less than 0.025 in. (0.6 mm). If it is the plate is near the end of its life and needs replacement.
8 The surface of the disc should be smooth, if grooved or pitted the disc should be replaced. If it is smooth, shiny and black then oil is entering the clutch. This problem is discussed later but a disc contaminated with oil should be renewed.
9 Finally, check that the disc is running true. Mount it between lathe-centres and measure the run-out accurately if you can. At 6.8 in. (179 mm) diameter the run-out should not exceed 0.015 in. (0.4 mm).
10 When you are satisfied that all the parts are in good order, reassemble the clutch. Do not be mean about renewing suspect components or you will have the job to do all over again. Once a clutch begins to wear the wear accelerates rapidly. Make sure everything is clean, including your hands. Sandpaper the friction surfaces of the flywheel and pressure plate lightly if you are fitting a new disc to break the glaze on the friction surfaces and give the disc a better chance of bedding down quickly. Clean the metal surfaces with trichlorethylene.

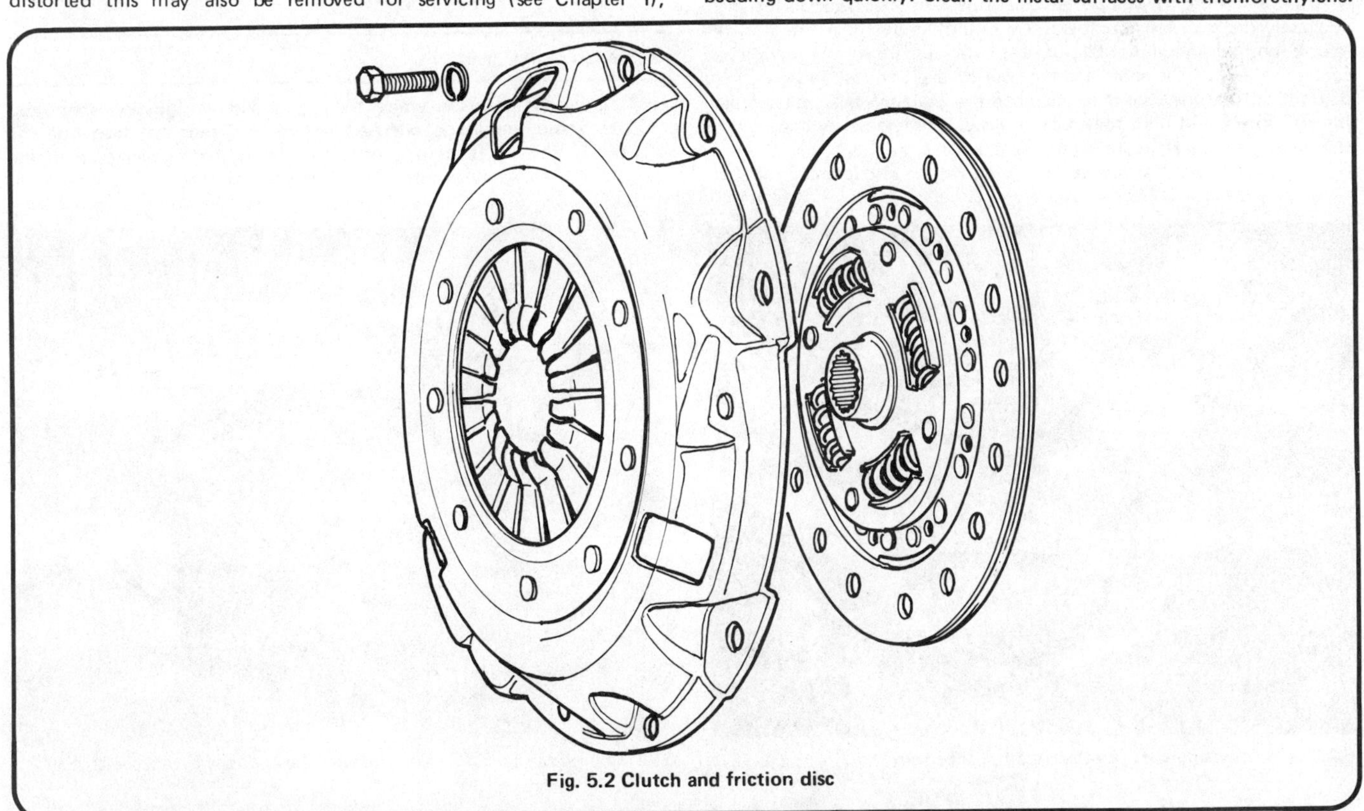

Fig. 5.2 Clutch and friction disc

11 Make sure the clutch disc is the right way round and the centre punch marks on the pressure plate and flywheel line up, insert the bolts and tighten them hand-tight. In Chapter 1, Section 8, paragraph 10 and Section 22, paragraph 13, we have talked about centralizing the clutch. Read this again: if you do not get it right the gearbox cannot be fitted to the engine. We have also stated this in Section 5, of this Chapter. So centralize the clutch **and** the clutch disc and then tighten the bolts in a diagonal fashion to the specified torque.

12 Refit the transmission to the engine (Chapter 6) and adjust the clutch pedal free-travel.

6 Clutch withdrawal mechanism - removal, overhaul and replacement

1 Once again the transmission must be removed (Chapter 6). This job should always be done whenever the transmission is removed.

2 Refer to Fig. 5.1. The release mechanism consists of the release bearing held on the release bearing guide, actuated by the shaft forks, and secured by two clips. The shaft runs in bearings in the bellhousing (photo) and is turned by the clutch operating lever which is outside the bellhousing. The release bearing is kept from contact with the diaphragm fingers by a coil spring (photo).

3 When you make a racing start from the traffic lights the release bearing is stationary and the flywheel doing several thousand revolutions per minute. The pressure on the diaphragm is 900 lbs (400 kg). As you let in the clutch the clutch and the release bearing accelerate in a spectacular fashion. When the clutch is fully released the release bearing retires from the battle and sits still. That is unless you drive along with your foot on the clutch pedal removing all the free-travel. In this case the release bearing bears on the diaphragm fingers all the while and you will soon need a new release bearing. When you declutch at high speed the bearing has maximum load. It has to accelerate suddenly and push hard at the same time. If it disintegrates, the car cannot be driven.

4 To remove the release bearing pull off the two clips and slide it off the release bearing guide. It will make a lot of noise before it breaks up, so if it starts to become noisy it must be renewed at once. Do not attempt to clean it out, it is a sealed bearing. When replacing smear the forks and the bearing guide with a little lithium grease.

5 The release bearing shaft also has a heavy load and should be checked for wear. Before it can be removed the clutch operating lever must be taken off. It is important that this lever goes back on the shaft at exactly the same angle as it was removed otherwise adjustment of the release mechanism will not be possible. Using a sharp scriber mark a line across the end of the shaft and the lever so that accurate lining up may be done. If you lose the marking when the shaft has been reassembled the coil spring will hold the shaft in place. The release lever should be clamped to the shaft, as shown in Fig. 5.3.

6 Having removed the release lever, remove the circlip from the shaft and remove the shouldered bolt from the inside bearing. It is now possible to slide the shaft to the right and push the bearing bush out of the bellhousing. This allows enough play for the shaft to be removed.

7 Check the bearing bushes for undue wear and replace if necessary. If serious wear has taken place on the shaft replace that too.

8 Replacement is the reverse of removal. Remember this shaft is hidden when assembled so lubricate it with lithium grease which will stay put even when things get hot. Ordinary grease or oil will dry up right away.

9 Refit the release bearing, clips the right way up, refit the clutch operating lever. Outside the casing, on the release shaft, between the operating lever and the casing there may be a rubber bush. If there is, it should be replaced on reassembly and a new circlip fitted. The distance which the rubber bush is compressed into between the circlip and the casing should be 0.7 in. (18 mm). If there was not a rubber bush before, do not fit one. Reassemble the transmission to the vehicle.

10 Adjust the clutch free-travel.

7 Oil contamination - source location and rectification

1 If the clutch is contaminated with oil there is no point in replacing it until the source of the contamination has been located and the fault rectified. Assembling a new clutch without this action will only result in a second clutch overhaul.

2 The oil can have come from two sources only, the engine or the transmission. If it is coming from the final-drive casing then the oil seal behind the guide sleeve for the release bearing has collapsed. Oil in some quantity will be seen on the guide sleeve. Take off the screws holding the guide sleeve and remove the guide sleeve to make sure. Unfortunately, this seal cannot be easily removed without damaging the shaft. If the shaft or the casing bore are scored the repair will be extensive and expensive.

3 To do this job properly the transmission must be drained of oil and the final drive housing split from the gear carrier. This is described in Chapter 6, as is the fitting of a new seal. It is a big job but it must be done.

4 If oil is entering from the engine then after removing the flywheel the oil seal may be removed with its flange and a new one fitted. This is described in Chapter 1.

8 Clutch faults - general

1 The various points at which the engine and transmission are bolted to the frame should be checked before beginning to dismantle the clutch. If any of them are loose, or the rubber perished, then the vehicle will shake when moving off and the fault will be diagnosed as

6.2 The bellhousing showing the release mechanism

6.2b The release bearing. Note the way the clips are fitted, see arrow 'A'

Fig. 5.3 Clutch operating arm - install the arm at the angle shown

clutch judder which is incorrect. When describing clutch faults the following terms are used.

2 'Judder' or 'grabbing' is a term used to describe the situation that occurs that when the clutch is engaged the vehicle vibrates excessively and moves off in jerks.

3 'Dragging' or 'clutch spin' means that the clutch will not disengage and the gears cannot be selected.

4 'Clutch slip' means that the engine is driving the flywheel faster than the flywheel is driving the pressure plate. The physical symptom is that the engine accelerates but the vehicle does not, particularly on heavy load or when climbing steep hills. To confirm this diagnosis stand the vehicle on level ground, put the handbrake hard on, and start the engine. You will need a little help for the next bit. Disengage the clutch, engage top gear, accelerate the engine slightly and with the footbrake hard on, engage the clutch. The engine should stall. If it does not the clutch is slipping. If the engine stalls at low engine revolutions, try again with a slightly higher engine speed. This test is best done after the vehicle has been running for an hour. Be gentle and if the clutch does slip, stop the test at once.

9 Fault diagnosis - clutch

Symptom	Probable cause	Remedy
1 Clutch slipping	Oil on linings	Dismantle and replace lining. Repair oil seals.
	Free-travel on clutch pedal incorrect	Adjust free-travel.
	Cable damaged in sheath and sticking	Replace cable.
2 Clutch judder	Engine or transmission mountings loose	Tighten nuts and bolts.
	Diaphragm plate distorted or fractured	Replace (Section 5).
3 Clutch spin	Pedal free-travel too large	Adjust.
	Release bearing or shaft faulty	Dismantle and replace.
	Main driveshaft splines damaged or rusty	Dismantle, and clean splines. Lubricate with lithium grease.
	Friction plate distorted or broken	Replace friction plate.
	Pilot bearing in flywheel damaged	Dismantle and replace.
	Excessive clutch dust on driveplate	Dismantle and clean.
4 Clutch noisy	Pilot bearing worn	Replace.
	Diaphragm fingers loose or damaged	New clutch required.
	Release bearing defective	Replace.
	Splines worn, driven plate fouling the driveplate or pressure plate	Replace driveplate and/or driven plate.

Chapter 6 Manual gearbox and final drive

For modifications, and information applicable to later models, see Supplement at end of manual

Contents

Specifications

	1300 cc (55/60 HP) ZA or ZF engine	1500 cc (75 HP) ZB, ZD, ZE, XW or XZ engine	1500 cc (85 HP) ZC engine
Gearbox type *	ZT	ZS	ZU
Ratios			
1st gear	3.454 (11:38)	3.454 (11:38)	3.454 (11:38)
2nd gear	2.055 (18:37)	2.055 (18:37)	2.055 (18:37)
3rd gear	1.37 (27:37)	1.37 (27:37)	1.37 (27:37)
4th gear	0.968 (32:31)	0.968 (32:31)	0.939 (33:31)
Reverse	3.166 (12:38)	3.166 (12:38)	3.166 (12:38)
Final drive ratio **	4.555 (9:41)	4.111 (9:37)	4.111 (9:37)
Speedo drive ratio	0.5714 (21:12)	0.5714 (21:12)	0.5714 (21:12)

Oil capacity
Initial filling ... 2 litres, 3.5 Imperial pints, 4.4 US pints
Oil change ... 1.6 litres, 2.8 Imperial pints, 3.4 US pints

Oil specification ... Hypoid SAE 80 MIL-L-2105

Synchromesh ... Baulk ring on all forward gears

Torque wrench settings
Torque wrench settings are included in the text.

* *The gearbox type code letters will be found stamped on top of bellhousing with serial number.*
** *These figures are subject to variation on different models and years. Check with the official agent before buying spares.*

1 General description

1 Four types of manual gearboxes are fitted, according to the model of car. The 1300 cc model with both ZA or ZF engine (55 to 60 bhp) are fitted with a ZT type gearbox. The 1500 cc models with either the ZB, ZD or ZE engines (75 bhp) are fitted with the ZS type box. The 1500 cc 85 bhp ZC engine has the ZU type box. All these boxes are of identical construction and vary only in the gear ratios fitted. These are shown in the Specifications.

The American version is fitted with the 1500 cc engine either ZD or ZE, converted to XW or XZ (US general or US California) and has the ZS type box.

Yet a further complication is the more powerful ZC engine which gives 85 bhp and has again a different type of gearbox somewhat strengthened and with different ratios.

2 The construction and operation of all types are identical but obviously the part numbers of the gears, bearings and shafts must vary so be careful if you need to order spares and state very clearly to the storeman the chassis and engine numbers of your vehicle. (See 'Buying spare parts') or you may not get the right result.

3 Each type of box has four forward speeds and one reverse speed.

4 The speedometer drive is taken by a skew gear from the final drive mounted on the left-hand drive flange shaft. The speedo drive is mounted in a bearing in the final drive casing. It is removed by unscrewing the bearing housing from the outside.
5 The reverse light (back-up light) switch is screwed into the end of the gearshift housing and operated by the gearshift linkage.
6 Two types of gearshift mechanism have been fitted. The detail is given in Sections 12 and 13.

2 Layout of manual gearbox

1 The gearbox is a conventional type bolted to the back of the engine. It has two shafts. The mainshaft, housed at the front end in a needle bearing in the engine flywheel, passes through the clutch and clutch engagement mechanism and over the top of the differential into the transmission casing where it carries a gear train.

This gear train meshes with another on the pinion shaft which is situated vertically below it. On the front end of the pinion shaft a helical bevel gear which is an integral part of the shaft, engages the crownwheel of the differential.
2 The differential is housed between the transmission gear casing and the clutch in taper roller bearings carried on cover plates through which the drive flanges pass. The driveshafts carrying the drive to the wheels are connected to them by constant velocity joints.
3 Gear-changing is effected by a change rod which operates the forks from the rear end of the gearbox, where it is connected to the gear-change lever by a linkage and gearshift rod.
4 The system is divided nearly into three main casings each holding a functioning unit. The bellhousing carries the clutch withdrawal gear and the differential final drive. This is bolted at the front end, to the rear of the engine.

Bolted to the back of this is the gear carrier casing which contains the gear trains of the main and pinion shafts.

The third casing, known as the gearshift housing contains the mechanism for operating the shift rods and forks which move the gear trains to engage the gears as required.
5 All four forward gears have synchroniser hubs, those for 1/2nd gear on the pinion shaft and the hub for 3/4 gear on the main driveshaft.

3 Gearbox - removal and replacement (engine in vehicle)

This is much more easily done with the vehicle over a pit or on a hoist. If this is not possible then the vehicle must be lifted on vehicle ramps.
1 Disconnect battery earth strap.
2 Remove the nuts holding the exhaust pipe to the manifold and then undo the clip holding the exhaust pipe to the gearbox.
3 Undo the wire holding the square-headed bolt which clamps the connecting link to the gearchange shaft and holding the shaft steady remove the bolt (photo). Still holding the shaft, prise the stirrup off the shaft. Be careful not to scratch or score the shaft as it goes through an oil seal into the box and if marked may start an oil leak. Later models have a much modified rear support and gearshift arrangement. The rubber mounting shown in photo 3.3a is replaced by a bracket and a left side mounting (photo 3.3b).
4 Working from above, remove the clutch cable from the clutch pedal by pulling off the plastic holder then ease the nuts which hold the clutch cable ferrule to the bracket and draw the cable away from the bracket. Tie the cable up out of the way.
5 Using a screwdriver as a tommy-bar, undo the nut holding the speedo-drive (photo) and remove the speedo-drive cable. Tie it up out of the way.
6 Undo the socket head bolts holding the driveshafts to the final drive flanges and ease the flanges from the box (photo).
7 Disconnect the reversing (back-up) light switch cable. You may have to wait until the back of the box is lowered to get at it but do it as soon as you can or it will be in the way (photo).
8 Disconnect the starter and remove it (Chapter 10). This must be done as the rear bearing of the armature is in the bellhousing and if the starter is left in position damage may occur to the armature when you lift the gearbox out.
9 Support the gearbox with a jack and undo the five bolts holding the gearbox to the engine.
10 Undo the two bolts holding the gearbox support to the body and then remove the support from the gearbox after undoing the centre-bolt of the support (see photo 3.3a) or the side mounting (3.3b and 3.3c).
11 Carefully prise the gearbox away from the engine until the gearbox mainshaft is withdrawn from the bearing in the flywheel and then from the splines of the clutch driving plate. Support the gearbox all the while, and make sure no stress comes on the mainshaft. When the mainshaft is clear the box may be lifted away and removed from below.

It is not all that heavy but it is awkward so two people will be required for this operation.
12 Replacement is a reversal of the removal procedure

4 Gearbox - removal and replacement (engine away from vehicle)

1 If the engine is already out and the radiator removed, then the removal of the gearbox is much simpler. It will already be supported from underneath.
2 Remove the driveshaft flanges.
3 Disconnect the connecting link from the gearchange rod.
4 Disconnect the speedo-drive and clutch withdrawal cable and tie them out of the way.
5 Remove the rear support bracket (two nuts) from the body, and disconnect the cable from the reverse light switch.
6 Lower the box at the back and then lift it out through the bonnet opening. Two people are required.
7 Replacement is a reversal of the removal procedure.

5 Gearbox - dismantling into the three major sections

1 Clean the box carefully and dry it. Remove the drain plug and allow the 2 litres of oil to run out. Replace the plug.
2 Cover the top of the bench with clean paper and wipe all the tools. From now on work with clean hands.
3 A number of clean receptacles will be needed to contain the parts as they are dismantled.
4 Arrange the layout drawings so that they can be consulted easily and have a note book and pencil available.
5 Read through each section before starting work and plan the job you are going to do.
6 Remove the nuts from the studs holding the gearshift housing to the gear carrier. There are ten of them. Store them and the washers that go with them.
7 It may be necessary to rotate the gearshift shaft to disengage the gearshift lever from the selector rods. This will be apparant as the shift housing is drawn off the studs away from the gear carrier. **Do not** use force - a gentle tap is all that is necessary to break the joint.
8 Collect the shim and the gasket. A new gasket will probably be required. If any of the following parts are to be replaced then a different thickness of shim may be required.

a) Bearing for driveshaft in the gearcarrier housing.
b) Bearing for pinion.
c) Gearshift housing (casing).
d) Gear carrier (casing).

Remember this when you come to inspect the various parts.
9 The gearshift housing may now be drawn off, and laid to one side.
10 Next remove the eleven nuts holding the gear carrier to the final drive casing. Remove the gear carrier from the final drive housing. This may be a little more difficult as there is a dowel to contend with as well as the normal joining compound.

Again you may be in trouble for if either the . . . . .

a) transmission or final drive, housings
b) pinion ball bearing
c) 1st gear needle bearing

. . . . .have to be replaced, the position of the pinion in relation to the housing must be determined **before** dismantling and on assembly the pinion must be set to this position.
11 Lay the two housings down and study the mechanisms that are now exposed to view. See Fig. 6.1.
12 You will have had a very good reason for going so far. If it was transmission whine in all gears then there is a possibility of pinion and crownwheel trouble. Examine these for signs of wear, scuffing or undue heating.

If one gear in particular was noisy then locate that one and see what is awry.

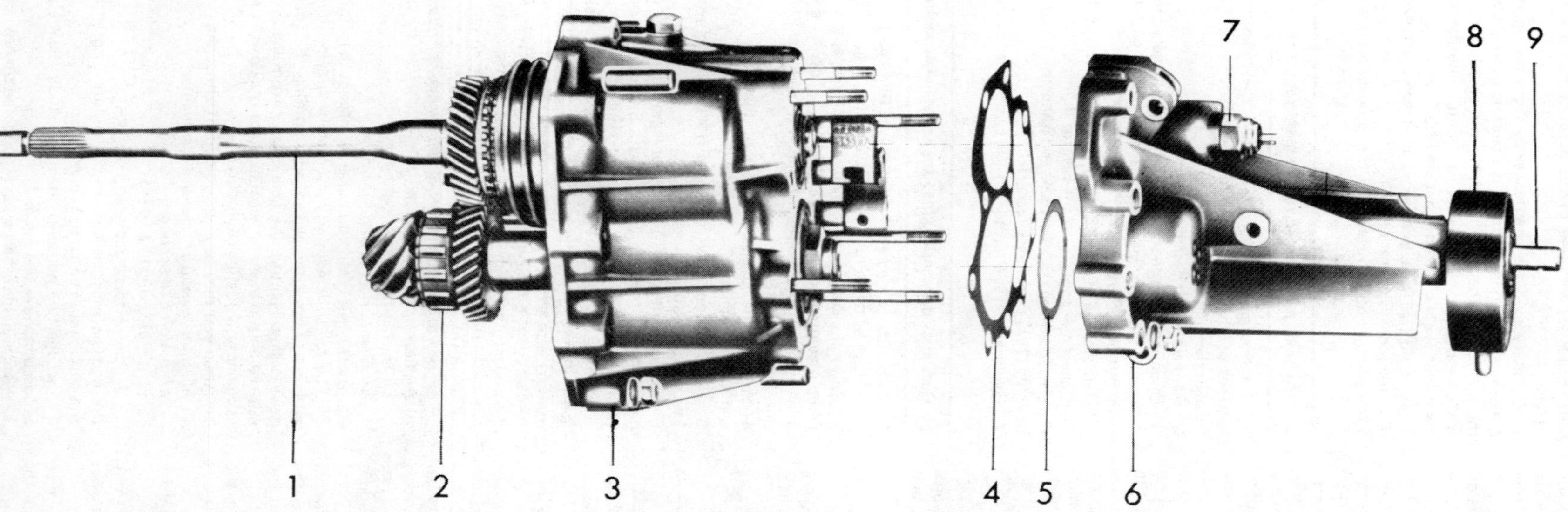

Fig. 6.1 Gear carrier of gearshift housing - exploded view

1 Mainshaft
2 Pinion shaft
3 Gear carrier
4 Gasket
5 Shim
6 Gearshift housing
7 Switch for reversing light
8 Rubber mounting
9 Gearshift lever

Note: the thickness of the gasket and shim must not be altered otherwise the pinion and differential will have to be reset

If it was difficult to engage gears then examine the shift mechanism and the synchro hubs. The damage may be apparant.

Do not take anything further to pieces until you have had a very careful look at it all.

13 This is the point of no return. If you cannot identify what is wrong, or if what is wrong means replacing one of the parts listed in paragraphs 8 and 10, then our sincere advice is to put the three parts together again and take them to the agent for servicing. The measuring of the tolerances and selection of the shims required calls for special jigs which you do not have. The better the mechanic you are the more you will appreciate this, and if you do take the assemblies apart only to find that the tolerances have been affected do not be surprised if the official agent charges you for a new gearbox when you take all the bits in for him to reassemble.

14 On the other hand if you can locate the trouble and it does not affect the tolerences listed then you can carry on dismantling, that is after you have checked that the spares required are available.

15 In either case, a complete set of gaskets will be required. These are sold as a pack.

6 Gearshift housing - overhaul

1 Refer to Fig. 6.2. The shift lever is held in two bushes which may be renewed if necessary. It is unlikely that this will happen but the oil seal at the outer end may need replacement. The shift housing may be removed without disturbing the remainder of the transmission. The rear mounting (photo 3.3) may be removed and a new one fitted without disturbing the shift housing but it may be necessary to move the exhaust pipe to one side.

2 To replace the rubber mounting first support the gearbox and undo the shift mechanism. The old mounting will probably be perished. Remove the rear support crossmember. Cut the rubber mounting off with a knife, clean up the shaft, press on a new mounting. The mounting fits on the gearshift housing and although the position of the stud which fits into the crossmember is not critical it is as well to mark the position of the old mounting on the casing before removal and fit the new one in the same place.

3 If oil is leaking out of the seal at the end there is no need to panic, there is some inside. However, this job should be tackled as soon as possible, and the level of the oil in the gearbox checked frequently if the job has to wait for some time.

4 It will make the job easier if the exhaust pipe is moved to one side. Undo the gearshift mechanism from the inner shift lever. Support the gearbox and remove the rear support. Undo the ten nuts from the studs joining the gearshift housing to the gear carrier. The gearshitt housing may now be drawn away. It may be necessary to rotate the inner shaft lever to disengage it from the operating dog fixed to the gear housing, and the wire to the reversing light switch must be disconnected as the shift housing is removed.

5 The thickness of the gasket between the two housings is critical and if a new one is required then it must be the same thickness. This also applies to the shim which fits over the pinion shaft bearing. These are part of the arrangement for determining the engagement of the pinion and crownwheel, and must be refitted carefully.

6 Once the housing is clear it is a simple matter to extract the shaft, hook out the old seal and fit a new one. At the same time the fit of the shaft in the bushes may be checked and new bushes fitted if necessary. The housing may then be replaced. Be careful that the operating lever on the end of the inner shift lever engages correctly with the operating dog on the gear carrier. On later models an extra spring is fitted to overcome this problem (Fig. 6.3 refers).

7 Gear carrier - dismantling and reassembly

1 This Section deals with the removal and reassembly of the mainshaft and pinion shaft of the box from the gear carrier. The overhaul of these shafts is dealt with separately.

2 Refer to Fig. 6.4. Remove the spring pin from the 3/4 selector fork so that the fork may move freely on the shaft. Engage 3rd gear. To

3.3a Rear mounting of gearbox 'A' square-headed bolt holding gearchange stirrup 'B' bolt holding support to body, (another behind exhaust pipe) 'C' bolt holding rubber mounting to support bracket.

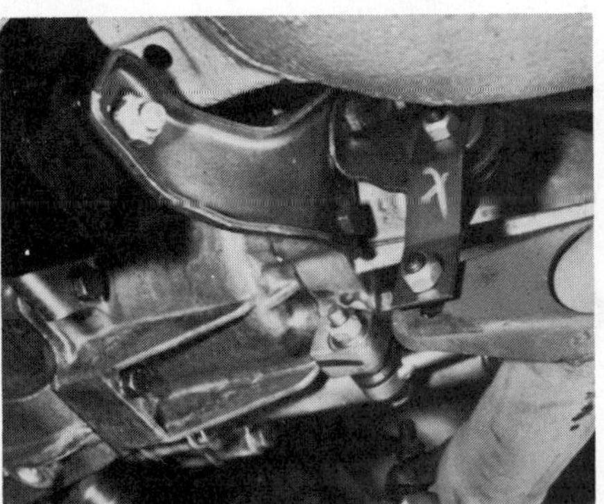

3.3b The later pattern of rear mounting

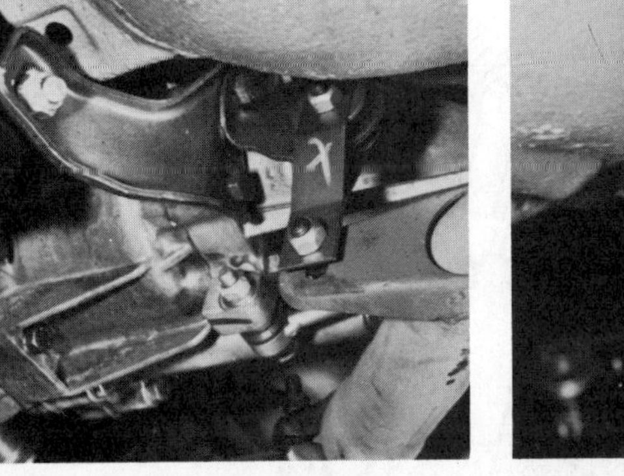

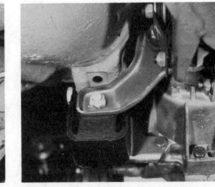

3.3c Another view of the later mounting

3.5 Removing the speedometer drive from the L.H. final drive casing

3.6 Undoing the socket head bolts of the drive shafts

7.10 The reverse gear in the casing before assembly of the shafts

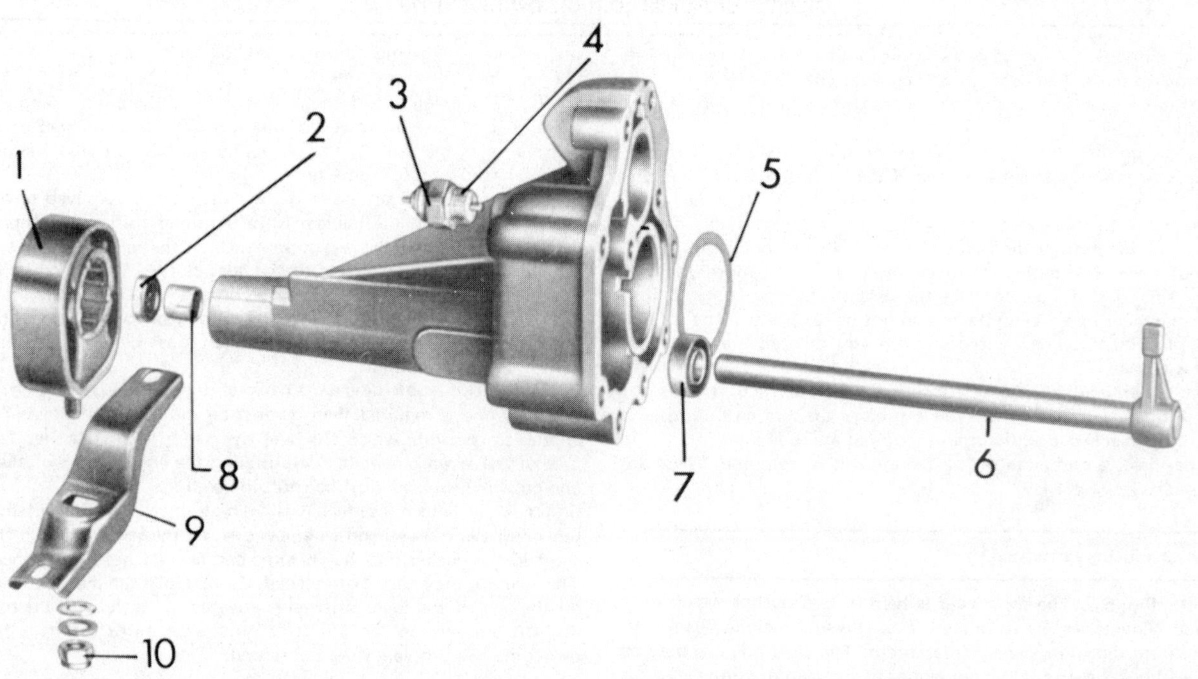

Fig. 6.2 Gearshift housing - exploded view

1 Rubber housing
2 Oil seal
3 Rubber boot
4 Reversing light switch
5 Shim
6 Gearshift lever
7 Bush (inner)
8 Bush (outer)
9 Support bracket
10 Clamp nut

7.11a The two shafts and the selector shaft ready to go into ther gear carrier housing

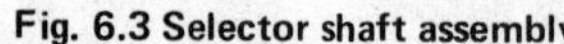

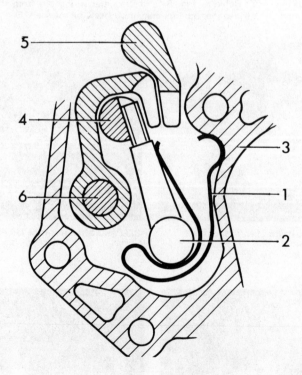

Fig. 6.3 Selector shaft assembly

The spring has been added to facilitate correct assembly

1 Spring
2 Inner shift lever
3 Housing
4 Selector shaft 3/4 gear
5 Selector shaft reverse gear
6 Selector shaft 1/2 gear

7.11b The shafts entering the casing

do this move the fork along the selector rod leaving the rod in the neutral position.

3 Now engage reverse gear and then put the gear train back in the final drive housing. The gear trains will be locked and the nut on the end of the pinion shaft may be undone and removed. Take the gear train out of the final drive housing and remove the 3/4 gear fork. Remove the spring pin from the operating dog of 1/2 gear and remove the dog. On the end of the mainshaft is a circlip. Remove this and the thrust washer under it.

4 The next operation requires a bearing puller. VW suggest a 'RILLEX 6304' tool. Unless a puller is available the job is very difficult. We did manage to drive the shaft out with a brass drift and a lot of patience. We do not recommend this procedure, but it is possible.

5 Remove the bearing holding the mainshaft in the transmission housing and the mainshaft may be taken away complete with gears.

6 Reverse gear and its shaft may now be pressed out, and then the pinion shaft may be pressed out. The outer race will stay behind, the inner race will go with the shaft.

7 The selector rod is best left in position. We do not recommend that you proceed further. If the pinion shaft bearing is to be replaced then there is the problem of the position of the pinion and the shim (S_2) which must be measured. We do not recommend that the DIY owner should remove the plungers and springs of the interlock mechanism either. Both of these jobs are best left to the agent, with his gauges and jigs.

8 The two shafts and the reverse gear may now be serviced.

9 When you are satisfied that the components are in good order the problem of assembly must be tackled.

10 Place the carrier with the bearings in position on the bench. Fit the reverse gear selector to its bolt and fit the reverse gear and shaft so that you are clear how it should be done. Now remove the shaft and the selector but leave the gear in its approximate position. (photo)

11 Fit the two shafts together and put the selector 1/2 gear with its shaft in position (photo). The selector ring groove should be to the front.

12 Enter the shafts into the bearings and 1/2 selector shaft into the casing (photo). The selector shaft will stop when the end of it meets the detent ball. From the front with a screwdriver in the bore ease this ball up against the spring so that the shaft will go into position.

13 Use a hide hammer and tap the shafts gently into the bearings. It is a bit of a fiddling job: go slowly or you will chip the gears. When the pinion shaft has gone in far enough fit the bearing ring on the outside and the retaining nut. Tighten this hand-tight.

14 The mainshaft is a tight fit in the inner race so some patience is required. If you are not careful you will drive the whole race out of the casing. If it does start to come out reverse the box, support the end of the mainshaft and drive the race back into its housing. As the gearshafts go forward be careful that 3rd speed gear on the mainshaft does not foul the housing for the reverse shaft bearing.

15 Pause now and pick up the reverse gear. Fit the shaft in from the rear and coax the gear onto the shaft. Again patience is required but it will go. The shaft then enters the front bearing of the reverse gear and the pin at the rear of the shaft fits in the slot in the casing. Fit the reverse gear rocker lever onto the bolt in the casing and screw the bolt home to 25 lb ft (3.5 kg m) torque. Check that the rocker lever moves easily in all positions and that the selector does not bear hard on the reverse gear. It should have between 0.020 and 0.060 in (0.50 and 1.52 mm) clearance.

16 Now move 1/2 gear selector and the reverse selector until they are in the neutral position and then fit the 3/4 selector rod and fork faces 4th gear (photo). Again, it will be necessary to use a screwdriver to lift the detent ball bearing to allow the selector rod to enter fully. Do not pin the 3/4 selector fork yet.

17 All the bits are in position now but there is more to do. The mainshaft is not yet fully in position, nor is the pinion shaft nut tightened. Engage reverse gear and then move 3rd gear into mesh so that the pinion shaft is locked in position. Tighten the pinion shaft nut to 72 lb ft (10 kg m). Now tap the mainshaft forward until the shim and circlip may be installed, and then tap the shaft back again until the circlip just touches the shim.

18 Now install the operating dogs on the selector rods (photo).

19 Finally install a new gasket of the correct thickness (the same as the old one), fit the shim over the pinion shaft and the gear carrier is ready to be assembled to the gearchange housing. It is wise to use a good cold jointing compound such as 'Hermatite Golden' on the joint and the nuts should be tightened to 15 lb ft (kg m).

8 Mainshaft - dismantling and reassembly

1 Refer to Fig. 6.5. It will be seen that the shaft itself is machined with 15 different diameters, two helical gears and one plain gear. On this are mounted the third speed gear needle bearing and third gear, the synchroniser hub for 3/4 speed gear, fourth speed gear and its needle bearing.

2 The circlip and shim have already been removed. Pull off 4th speed gear and its needle bearing. Now remove the circlip. The complete synchroniser hub must be pressed off the shaft, if it is tight. The one we dismantled came off quite easily. Tape the unit together, we will be discussing synchro units later in this Chapter.

3 Third speed gear and its needle bearing came off quite easily. The needle bearing is a split bearing. Watch which way it is located.

4 The shaft is now stripped except for the spring pin. Be careful not to lose this item.

5 Examine the various gears and needle bearings. Check the synchro unit and replace any part which is worn or defective. If a new gear is installed then the shim, which goes on last may have to be adjusted (see paragraph 11).

6 Clean the shaft carefully and examine the gears for chips, spalling or cracks. If undue wear is present then look for the reason. If you cannot find it consult the agent. Do not replace the shaft until you are satisified that the reason for wear has been located and the fault cured (photo).

7 Install the split needle bearing for 3rd gear. Be careful to get it the right way round (photo).

8 Now fit the 3rd gear and press on the synchro hub. The chamfer on the hub inner splines faces 3rd gear (photo). Refit the circlip (photo).

9 Install the needle bearing and then the 3/4 gear synchroniser ring with 4th gear (photo). You will see that the spring peg (photo) fits in the shim which is installed next (photo).

7.16 Fitting the 3/4 selector rod and fork

7.18 The operating dogs installed on the selector levers

7.19 The transmission casing ready for assembly with the gearchange housing

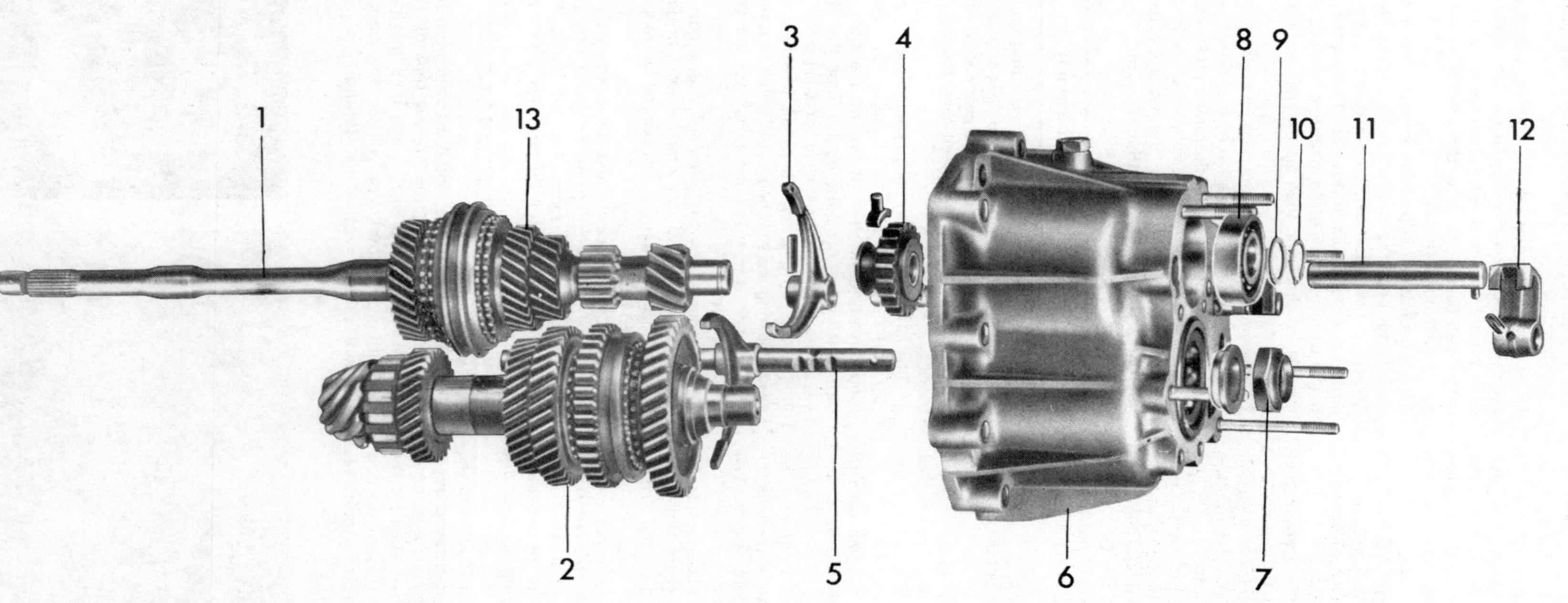

Fig. 6.4 Gear carrier and gearshafts - exploded view

1 Mainshaft
2 Pinion shaft
3 Shift fork 3/4 gear with pin
4 Reverse gear
5 Selector rod and fork 1/2 gear
6 Gear carrier
7 Nut for pinion shaft
8 Mainshaft bearing
9 Shim
10 Circlip
11 Reverse gearshaft
12 Operating dog 1/2 gear
13 3rd gear

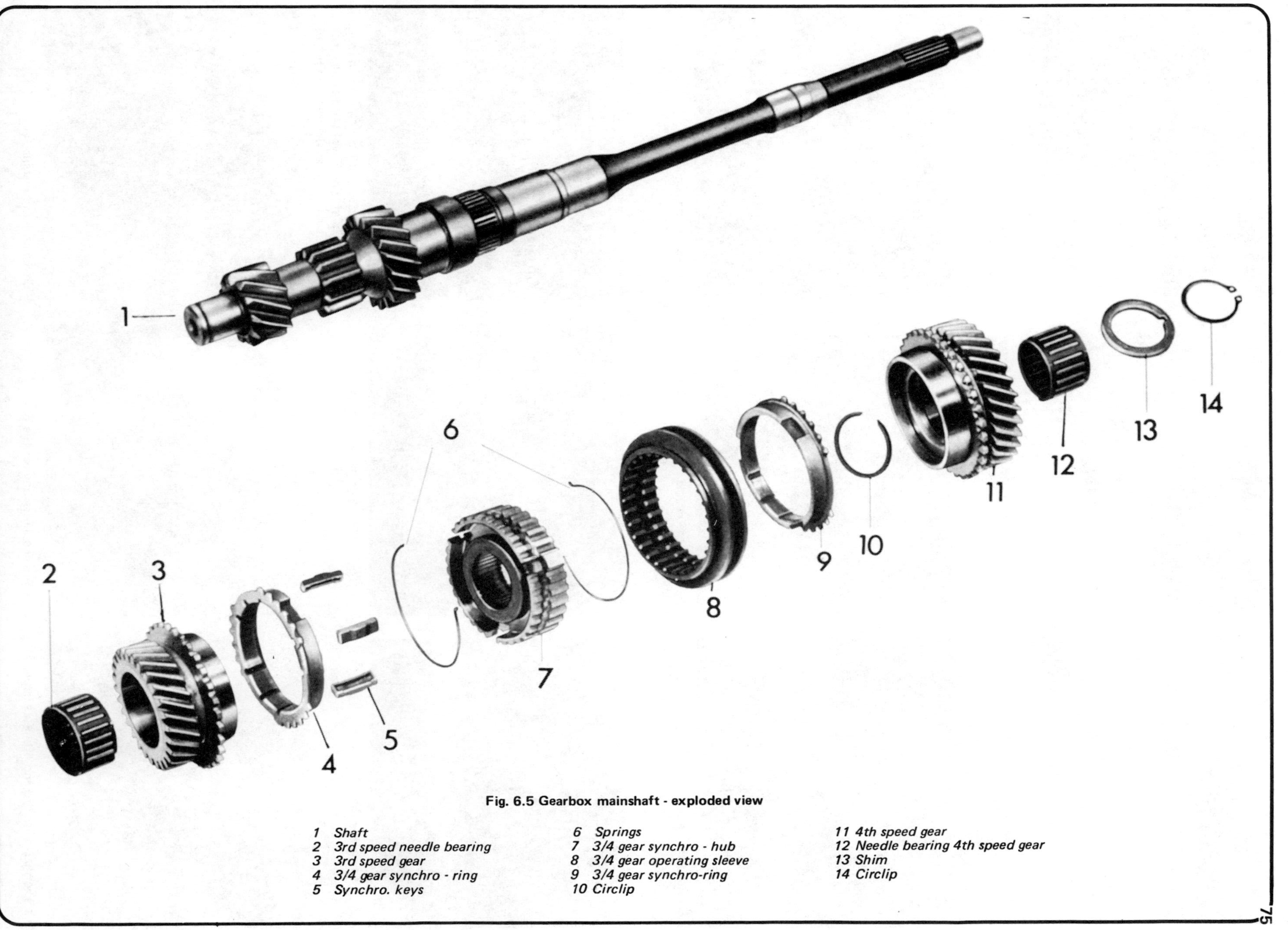

Fig. 6.5 Gearbox mainshaft - exploded view

1 Shaft
2 3rd speed needle bearing
3 3rd speed gear
4 3/4 gear synchro - ring
5 Synchro. keys
6 Springs
7 3/4 gear synchro - hub
8 3/4 gear operating sleeve
9 3/4 gear synchro-ring
10 Circlip
11 4th speed gear
12 Needle bearing 4th speed gear
13 Shim
14 Circlip

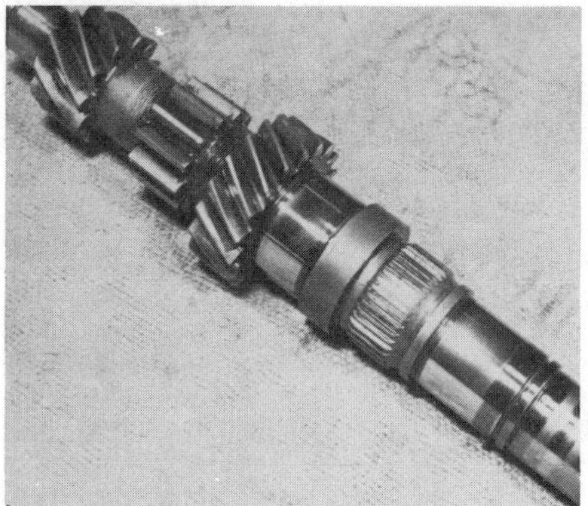
8.6 The shaft ready for reassembly

8.7 Fitting the split needle bearing for 3rd gear. Note which way round it goes

8.8a 3rd gear and the synchro hub

8.8b Refit the circlip

8.9a Install the needle bearing and then 3/4 synchronising with 4th gear

8.9b The spring peg ...

8.9c ... fits in the shim

8.10 The circlip holds the shim in place

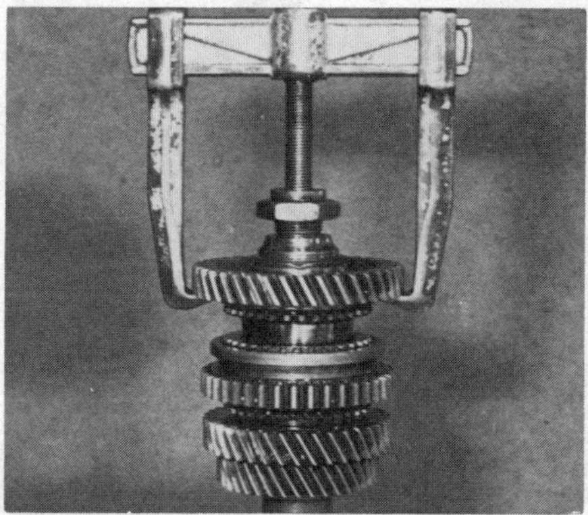
9.1 Removing 1st gear from the pinion shaft. The nut was left on to avoid damage to the thread. It is taken off as the gear is removed

9.4 The shaft with 3rd and 4th gears in place

9.6a The needle bearing for the hub

9.6b Second gear installed and ...

10 Finally refit the circlip and the shaft is ready to go back in the gearbox.
11 If a new gear has been installed the thickness of the shim may need to be altered. The axial play of 4th gear should be between 0.003 and 0.012 inches. Try to keep to the lower limit. Three thicknesses of shim are available 3.5 mm, 3.6 mm and 3.7 mm. The axial play can be measured with a feeler gauge.

9 Pinion shaft - dismantling and reassembly

1 Refer to Fig. 6.6. Using a suitable puller remove the 1st gear, shim and the bearing inner race together (photo).
2 Remove the circlip and with the puller claws behind second gear remove second gear with the complete synchro hub.
3 We do not recommend removal of the 3rd and 4th gears by any but VW trained mechanics. Apart from the fact that they must be pressed off removal of these gears alters the location of the pinion. We suggest this job should be taken to the official agent.
4 Examine the shaft and needle bearings for wear or damage (photo).
5 The inspection of synchro hubs is discussed in Section 10.
6 Install the needle bearing (photo), then second gear (photo).
7 Press on the complete synchro unit. The shift fork groove in the operating sleeve and the groove on the hub should be nearest of 1st speed gear.
8 Next install the needle race for 1st gear (photo) and then 1st gear (photo).
9 Finally press on the inner race (photo).
10 We have talked about pressing things on, how you do this depends on the tools available. A proper press with suitable mandrels is the ideal but a piece of pipe fitted over the shaft and tapped gently seems to do the job well enough. The shaft should not be held in a vice or it will be damaged. Stand the pinion on a piece of soft wood to avoid damge to the teeth.

9.7 ... the synchro hub

10 Synchroniser hubs - inspection and assembly

1 Unless the transmission is the victim of neglect or missuse, or has covered very high mileages, the synchro hub assemblies do not normally need replacement. If they do they must be renewed as a complete assembly. It is not practical to fit an inner hub or outer sleeve alone - even if you could buy one.
2 When synchro baulk rings are being renewed it is advisable to fit new blocker bars (sliding keys) and retaining springs in the hubs as this will ensure that full advantage is taken of the new, unworn cut-outs in the rings.
3 Whether or not a synchro hub is dismantled intentionally or accidentally there is one basic essential to remember: The splines of the inner hub and outer sleeve are matched - either by selection on assembly or by wear patterns during use. Those matched on assembly have etched lines on the inner hub and outer sleeve so that they can be easily realigned. For those with no marks, a paint dab should be made to ensure correct reassembly. If the hub falls apart unintentionally and there are no marks made then you will have to accept the fact that it may wear more quickly (relatively speaking) in the future. But do not have a heart attack if this happens - it will still work for a long time to come.
4 When examining for wear there are two important features to look at:

a) The fit of the splines. With the keys removed, the inner and outer sections of the hub should slide easily with minimum back-lash or axial rock. The degree of permissible wear is difficult to describe in absolute terms. No movement at all is exceptional yet excessive 'slop' would affect operation and cause jumping out of gear. Ask someone with experience for advice.

b) Selector fork grooves and selector forks should not exceed the maximum permissible clearance of 0.3 mm (0.012 inch). The wear can be on either the fork or groove so it is best to try a new fork in the existing hub first to see if the gap is reduced adequately. If not, then a new hub assembly is needed. Too much slack between fork and groove induced jumping out of gear. Where a hub also carries gear teeth on the outer sleeve these should, of course, be in good condition - that is unbroken and not pitted or scored.

5 The fit of the synchro hub ring on the gear is important. Press the synchro ring onto the gear and check the gap 'a' with feelers. For 1st/2nd gears and 3rd/4th gear it should not be more than 0.024 in (0.6 mm). This is illustrated in Fig. 6.7.
6 Note the way chamfers and springs should be fitted in Figs. 6.8 and 6.9.

11 Final drive - dismantling, inspection and reassembly

1 We have already stated that we consider the dismantling and re-asembly of the differential a task not to be undertaken by the DIY motorist. It is not difficutl but the problem of setting it up and mating the pinion with the crownwheel needs gauges and jigs. If you get it

9.8a The needle race for 1st gear ...

9.8b ... followed by 1st gear

9.9 The inner race of the bearing

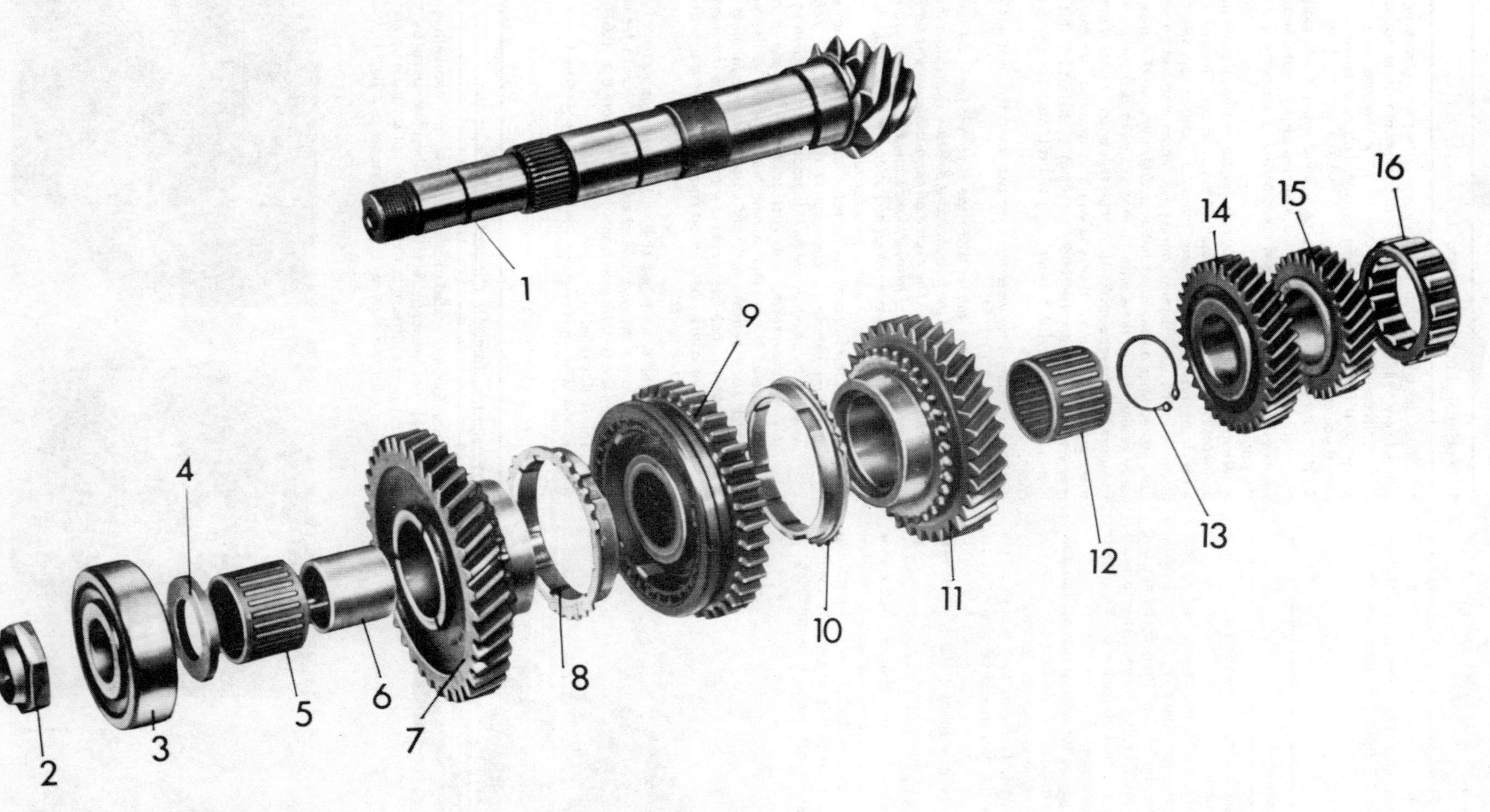

Fig. 6.6 Gearbox pinion shaft - exploded view

1 Shaft
2 Nut
3 Bearing (in casing)
4 Shim
5 1st gear needle bearing
6 Inner race of needle bearing
7 1st speed gear
8 1/2 gear synchro-ring
9 1/2 synchro-hub (complete)
10 Synchro-ring
11 2nd speed gear
12 2nd speed gear needle bearing
13 Circlip
14 3rd speed gear } *Do not remove*
15 4th speed gear }
16 Roller bearing (fits in final drive housing)

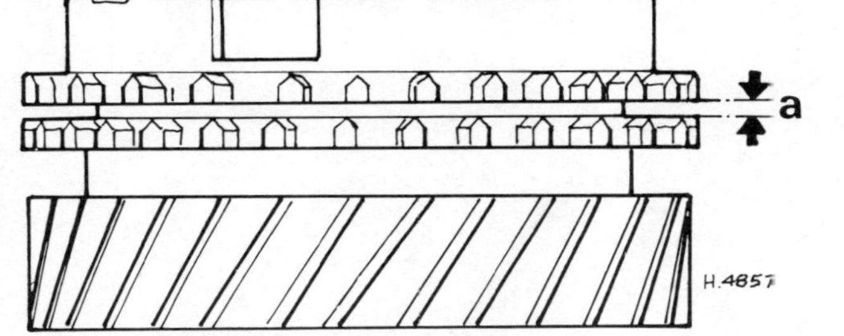

Fig. 6.7 Checking synchro-rings
'a' must not be more than 0.024 ins (0.6 mm)

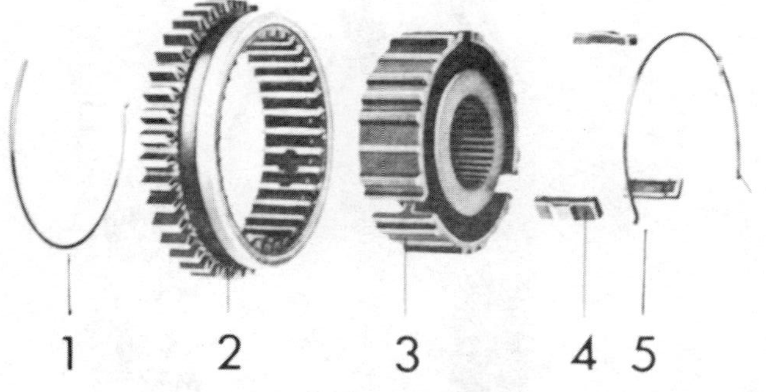

Fig. 6.8 Synchro-hub (1/2 gear) - exploded view

1 Spring
2 1/2 gear operating sleeve - groove for shift fork faces 1st gear
3 1/2 synchroniser-hub - groove on the splines faces 1st gear
4 Synchroniser key
5 Spring. Fit 120 degrees offset from '1'. Angled end fits in hollow key

Fig. 6.9 Synchro-hub (3/4 gear) - exploded view

1 Spring
2 3/4 gear operating sleeve
3 3/4 gear synchroniser-hub - chamfer on internal splines faces 3rd gear
4 Key
5 Spring. Fit 120 degrees offset from '1'. Angled end fits in hollow key

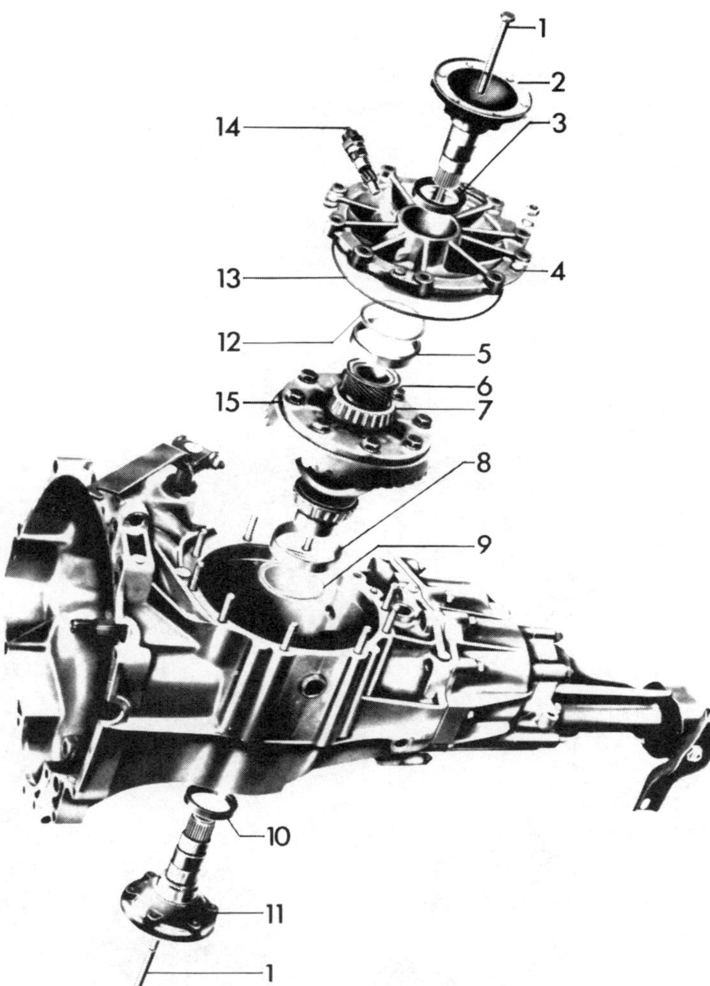

Fig. 6.10 Final drive and differential - exploded view

1 Drive flange bolt
2 Drive flange (left)
3 Oil seal
4 Cover plate
5 Outer race of taper bearing
6 Crownwheel bolt
7 Speedo drive gear
8 Outer race of taper bearing
9 Shim
10 Oil seal
11 Drive flange (right)
12 Shim
13 'O' ring (cover oil seal)
14 Speedo drive
15 Differential

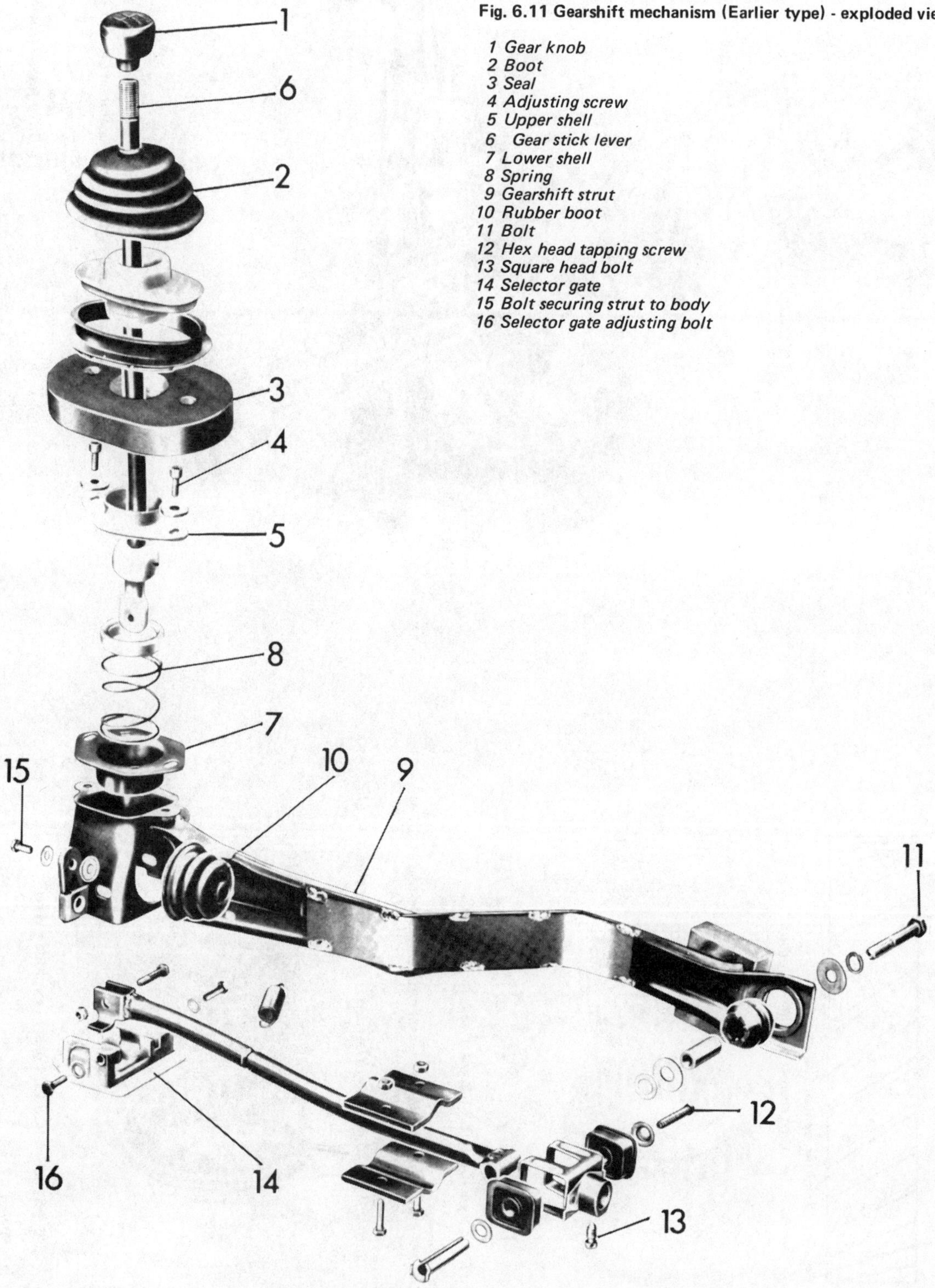

Fig. 6.11 Gearshift mechanism (Earlier type) - exploded view

1 Gear knob
2 Boot
3 Seal
4 Adjusting screw
5 Upper shell
6 Gear stick lever
7 Lower shell
8 Spring
9 Gearshift strut
10 Rubber boot
11 Bolt
12 Hex head tapping screw
13 Square head bolt
14 Selector gate
15 Bolt securing strut to body
16 Selector gate adjusting bolt

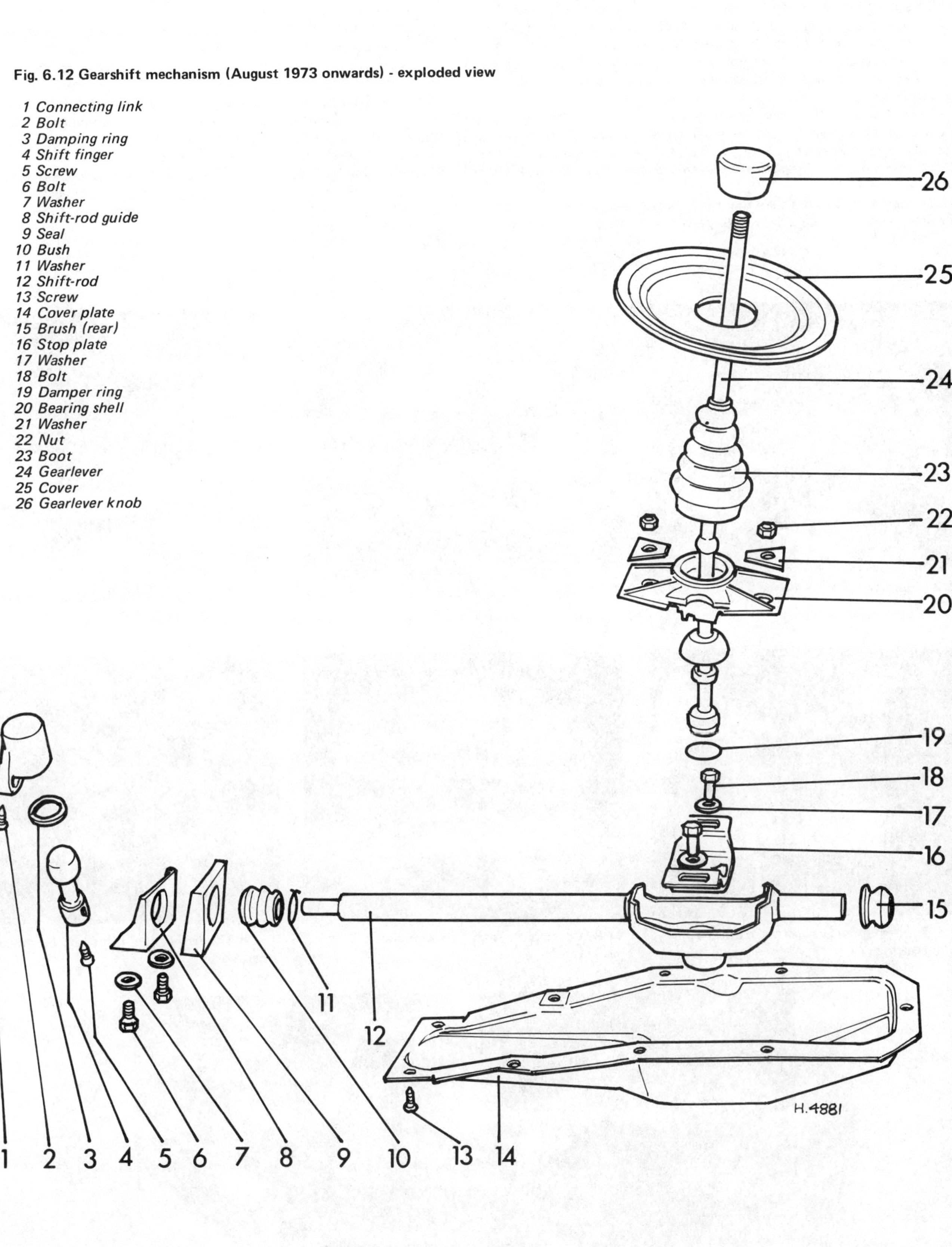

Fig. 6.12 Gearshift mechanism (August 1973 onwards) - exploded view

1 Connecting link
2 Bolt
3 Damping ring
4 Shift finger
5 Screw
6 Bolt
7 Washer
8 Shift-rod guide
9 Seal
10 Bush
11 Washer
12 Shift-rod
13 Screw
14 Cover plate
15 Brush (rear)
16 Stop plate
17 Washer
18 Bolt
19 Damper ring
20 Bearing shell
21 Washer
22 Nut
23 Boot
24 Gearlever
25 Cover
26 Gearlever knob

wrong the result will be a noisy transmission ending in an expensive repair.

2 This does not mean to say that the components of the final drive may not be taken apart and examined. Oil leaks may be cured and troubles traced to their origin, but before dismantling the differential consult the agent. He will tell you what is excessive wear and what can be safely reassembled. You will need a complete set of seals and gaskets.

3 The oil seals in the drive flanges may be replaced without removing the transmission from the car. Remove the wheel driveshaft, drain off the oil, undo the centre-bolt of the drive flange and withdraw the drive flange (photo). The oil seal may be levered out with a screwdriver and a new one pressed in.

4 The left and right seals are slightly different. The one which fits into the flange on the same side as the speedometer drive has a broken line round its outer surface (photo). Do not fit the wrong one, the other has an unbroken groove. If this is all that is necessary then refit the drive flange, tighten to 14 lb ft (2 kg m) and refit the driveshaft. Remember to replace the oil. For any further work the transmission is best dismantled from the car, if only for reasons of cleanliness.

5 The nuts on the studs holding the gear carrier to the final drive housing should be removed and the casing lifted away (photo). The joint may be stuck so proceed with caution. **Do not** try to push a wedge in between the surfaces. Watch out for oil. There will still be some in the casing and it comes out when the bellhousing is inverted, and there is bound to be some trapped in the differential.

6 Refer to Fig. 6.10. Lay the housing on the bench and start with the left-hand side, the one where the speedometer drive is held.

7 Undo the centre-bolt of the drive flange and remove the drive flange

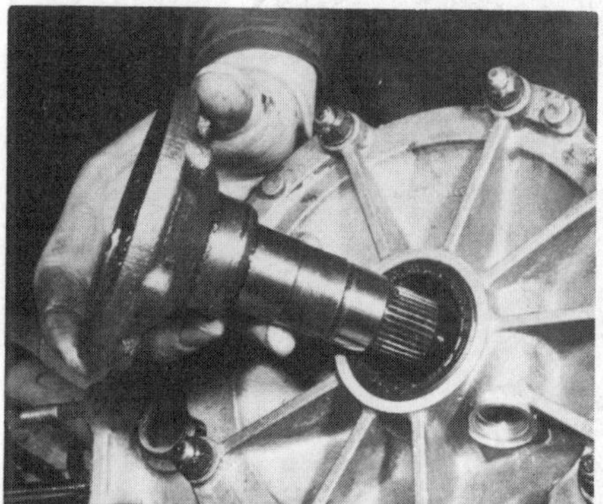
11.3a Remove the drive flange

11.3b Lever out the oil seal

11.3c The oil seal with the broken groove on the speedometer groove side

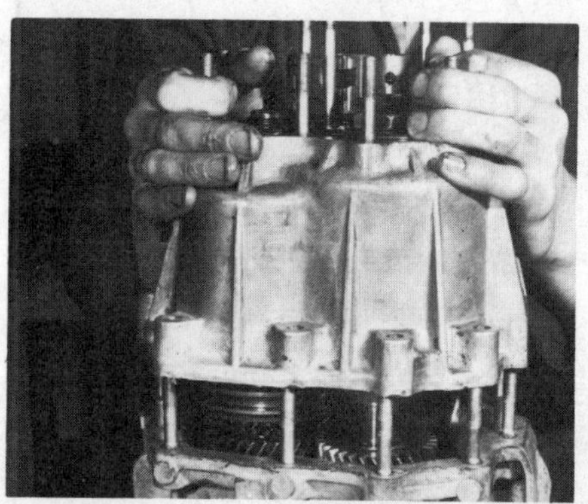
11.5 Removing the gear carrier from the final drive housing

11.8a Cover plate ready for removal

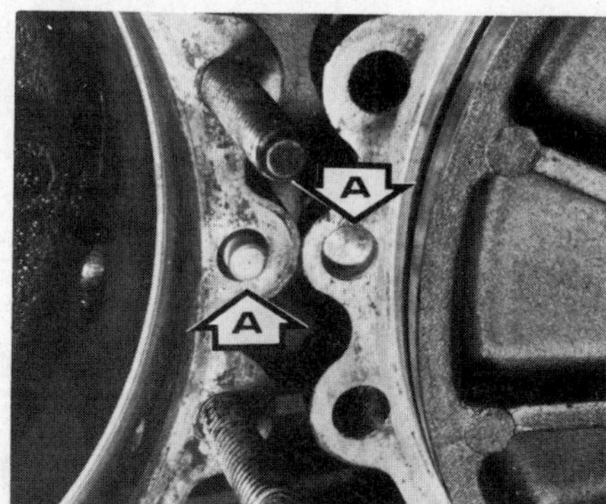

11.8b The cover plate is located by dowels (marked 'A')

11.9 Removing the differential

11.14 A new oil ring should be fitted to the cover plate

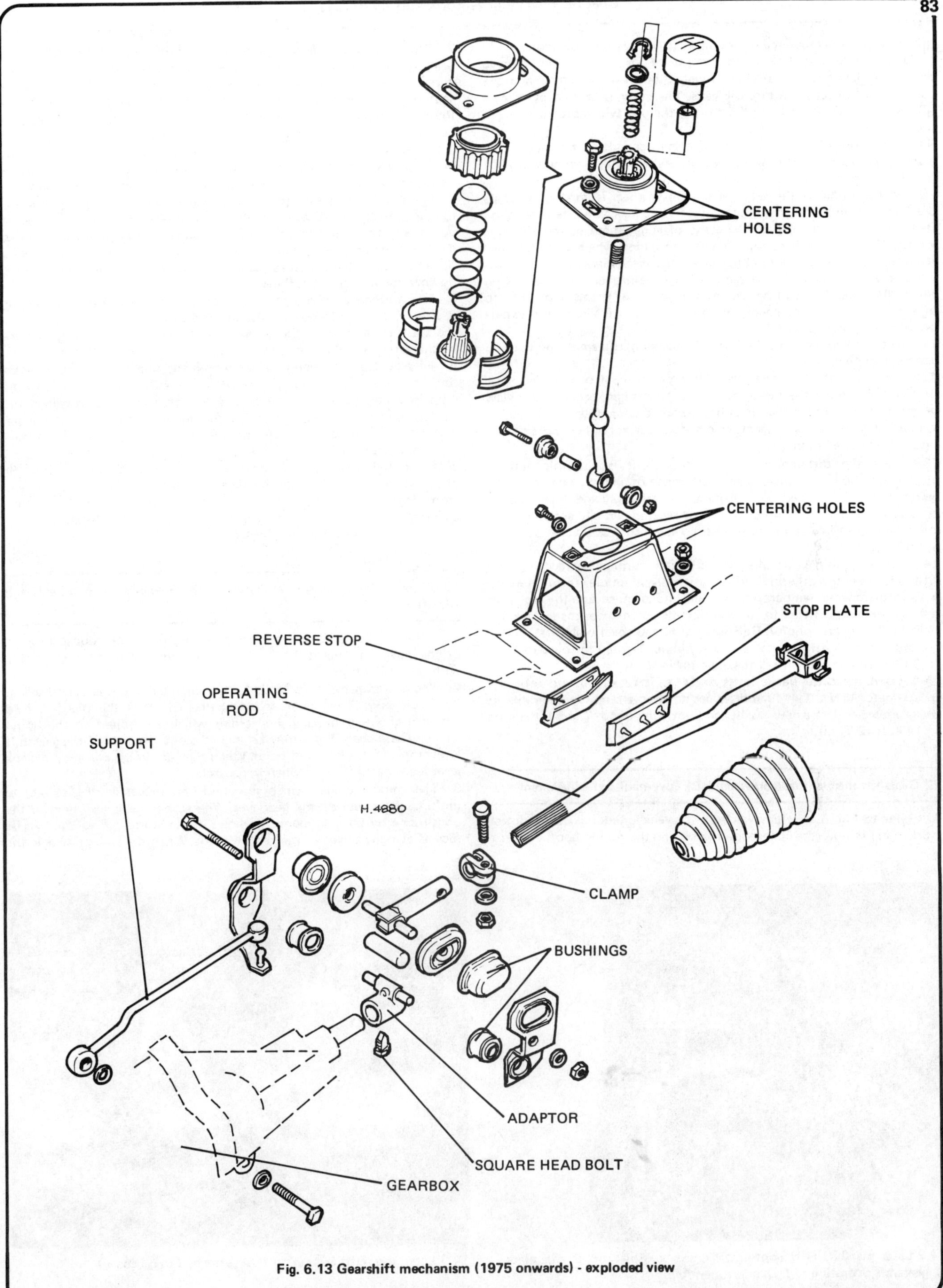

Fig. 6.13 Gearshift mechanism (1975 onwards) - exploded view

(photo 11.3a). Remove the speedometer drive if not already done.

8 Undo the 10 nuts holding the final drive cover (photo) and remove the cover. **Do not** try to drive a wedge between the cover and the casing, this will cause future oil leaks. The cover is located by dowels (photo) and should be levered off using the part which protrudes from the casing.

9 In the bore of the cover will be a shim and the outer race of the differential taper roller bearing. The differential may now be lifted out for examination (photo).

10 The condition of the teeth of the crownwheel is important. Chips cracks or rough scoring mean that either some foreign matter has found its way into the gearing, or the depth of engagement of the pinion is wrong. The marks will be repeated on the pinion which will also need renewal. Apart from the marking stated the wear marks on the crownwheel teeth should be in the centre of the teeth about half way down the tooth face. This will be seen as a bright area. If this is on the top of the tooth or at one edge then the adjustment is wrong and expert opinion should be sought.

11 The taper bearings must be in good condition, run smoothly with no appreciable play.

12 If the speedometer drive-gear is damaged it must be replaced. This involves pulling off the taper race as the gear is hard against it. In view of the fact that a new gear must be purchased we suggest you leave the whole job to the official agent, who has the correct puller and a proper press for re-installation.

13 Finally the differential itself. Although it is a simple enough mechanism the crownwheel is an interference fit and must be heated to be refitted. It is matched with the pinion on assembly and must go back in exactly the same position. We do not recommend any action on this unless you are a skilled motor mechanic, in which case you do not need our advice.

14 Clean everything carefully and lubricate running surfaces lightly. With all parts correctly serviced the assembly is simple. Install new oil seals in the covers, see paragraphs 3 and 4 and make sure the seal with the broken line is fitted to the speedometer drive side. Install new oil rings in the covers (photo). Refit the right-hand cover plate first, install the differential, refit the left-hand cover plate. Tighten the nuts to 18 lb ft (2.5 kg m) and then install the drive flanges.

15 Tighten the drive flange bolts to 14 lb ft (2 kg m) and refit the speedometer drive. The final drive casing is now ready to assemble to the gear carrier. Use a new gasket and joint compound. Tighten the nuts to 14 lb ft (2 kg m).

12 Gearshift mechanism (earlier models) - overhaul and adjustment

1 Refer to Fig. 6.11. Removal from the vehicle requires quite a lot of work. First remove the change lever knob and the rubber boot.

2 From under the car loosen the exhaust from its bracket behind the primary silencer and from the engine and lower it. Remove the locking wire from the square-headed bolt which fastens the gearshift rod to the gearbox shift rod. Remove the gearshift strut to mounting nut and both the nuts holding the gearbox mounting to the frame (see paragraph 3). Support the transmission as necessary. Remove the screws holding the gearshift strut at the rear of the frame, prise the gearshift strut off the pin and take the gearshift out downwards. Once the mechanism is removed it may be checked for wear and parts replaced as necessary.

3 It may be possible to remove the bolt holding the shift rod housing to the gearshift strut without removing the transmission rear support but it is difficult and the little extra trouble may be well worth while.

4 The selector gate is held in the gearshift strut by two screws which fit into slots. Remove these and the selector gate may be removed downwards without disturbing anything else.

5 The mechanism operates by turning the gearshift rod and by sliding it parallel to the gearbox mainshaft. The pivot for both movements is the spherical section of the gearshift lever which is held firmly in place by the spring and the two bearing shells.

6 To adjust the turning motion slacken the two screws fastening the shells together. This is done from inside the body. Press the lever to the right (towards the 3 and 4 gear selector positions) as far as it will go and then tighten the screws, meanwhile holding the lever in position. Now, with the lever in neutral move it to the left. If it fouls the selector gate the gate must be moved.

7 From under the car slacken the two screws holding the gate into the housing and move the gate axially until the gear lever may be moved from right to left without fouling the gate. Tighten the screws and then check that all four gears and reverse can be selected. If not adjust again, or dismantle to seek further damage.

13 Gearshift mechanism (August 1973 onwards) - overhaul and adjustment

1 Refer to Fig. 6.12. This simpler mechanism was introduced to some of the range in August 1973. The mechanisms are not interchangable with the earlier type.

2 The gearlever has three collars, two spherical and one cylindrical at its lower end. The upper spherical one which is the pivot is held between the two bearing shell plates which are bolted to the body-frame. These shell plates may be moved along the axis of the gearshift lever, moving in elongated holes. When they are in the correct plate the lever leans backwards 5° when in neutral.

3 The middle collar, which is cylindrical, moves in the stop-plate limiting the travel of the gearlever. The stop-plate is also held to the bodyframe by bolts in elongated holes in the stop-plate so this can be moved at right-angles to the gearshift axis. When the stop-plate is in the

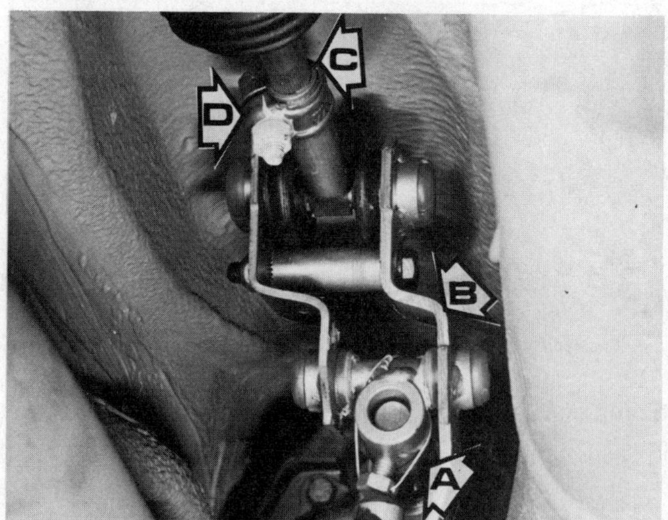

14.2 Later gearshift (1975 onwards) A. gearbox shift rod. B. side plate. C. gearshift operating rod. D. adjustment clip

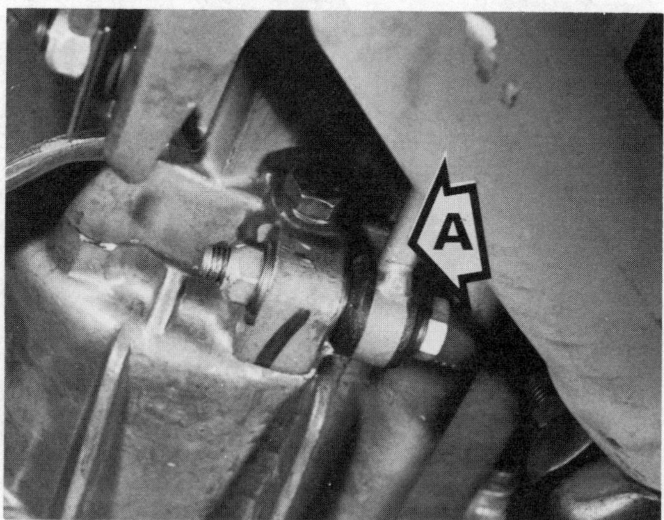

14.3 Later gearshift. Support rod 'A' attached to gearbox

correct place the gearlever in second gear position should be able to move sideways between 3/8 and 5/8 in (10 to 15 mm). Moving the plate to the right increases play, to the left decreases play.

4 The lowest collar engages in a well in the shift rod. The shift rod is held in bushes by the cover plate which is bolted to the base of the body underneath. The shift rod can thus rotate, or slide, axially, as the gearlever knob is moved to select gears. Attached on end of the shift rod is the shift finger, a small lever with a spherical end. This is held in place by a square-headed bolt, and the spherical end fits into the connecting link which is fixed to the gearshift shaft of the gearbox. Thus moving the shift rod will rotate or move axially the shift finger and the movement will be transferred to the gearshift shaft of the gearbox by the connecting link.

5 The cover plate may be removed after the eight screws have been undone. When refitting seal it to the body with 'D.10 compound', or a similar jointing material. If the connecting link and finger are removed then the shift rod and cover will come away and new bushes may be installed. When refitting install the rod in the cover bushes but do not tighten the two bolts holding the shift rod guide. Fit the cover to the body, make sure the bottom of the gearlever is securely in the well of the shift rod, install the connecting link and slide the rod forward. Move the shift rod guide so that the rod is laterally in the centre of the hole in the connecting link. Now tighten the bolts holding the shift rod guide. Push the rod back and install the shift finger. In the vertical plane a tolerance between the rod and the centre of the hole in the connecting link is allowed. Finally test and adjust the linkage if required. Pay special attention to ensure reverse gear engages correctly.

14 Gearshift mechanism (January 1975 onwards) - overhaul and adjustment

1 In early 1975 yet another type of gearshift was introduced (refer to Fig. 6.13).

2 The adapter is fixed to the gearbox selector shaft by a square-headed screw and the screw is wired (photo). The side plates carry the movement to the shift mechanism operating rod.

3 The mechanism is steadied by a support rod fixed to the gearbox (photo).

4 The movement is conventional otherwise. The gearlever moves about a ball held in plastic bearings and controlled by stop-plates.

5 Unfortunately, it is necessary to possess VW tool 3009 (a jig) in order to adjust the mechanism correctly, so this will have to be left to the agent. It is necessary to install the jig and eliminate all play in the balljoint. The shift finger is then moved so that all gears engage without jamming. If necessary move the shift lever bearing to one side as required.

15 Fault diagnosis - manual gearbox

It is sometimes difficult to decide whether all the effort and expense of dismantling the transmission is worthwhile to cure a minor irritant such as a whine or where the synchromesh can be beaten by a rapid gearchange. If the noise gets no worse consideration should be given to the time and money available, for the elimination of noise completely is almost impossible, unless a complete new set of gears and bearings is fitted. New gears and bearings will still make a noise if fitted in mesh with old ones.

Symptom	Reasons	Remedy
Synchromesh not giving smooth change	Worn baulk rings or synchro hubs	Fit new ones.
Jumps out of gear on drive or over-run	Weak detent springs Worn selector forks Worn synchro hubs	Fit new ones. Fit new ones. Fit new ones.
Noisy rough whining and vibration	Worn bearings, chipped or worn gears	Dismantle and fit new.
Gear difficult to engage	Clutch fault Gearshift mechanism out of adjustment	Check free-play. Check and adjust.

Chapter 7 Automatic transmission and final drive

For modifications, and information applicable to later models, see Supplement at end of manual

Contents

Specifications

Gear ratios

1st gear	2.65
2nd gear	1.59
'D'	1.00
Reverse	1.80
Final drive	4.09

Shift points (typical)

	Shift	Full throttle mph	Full throttle kph	Kick-down mph	Kick-down kph
75 BHP engine*	1 - 2	19 - 22	31 - 35	31 - 40	46 - 57
	2 - 3	53 - 61	85 - 98	60 - 68	96 - 109
	3 - 2	42 - 34	67 - 54	64 - 58	102 - 93
	2 - 1	16 - 13	25 - 21	37 - 29	59 - 46
85 BHP engine	1 - 2	20.5 - 22	33 - 35	32.5 - 40	52 - 64
	2 - 3	55 - 60.5	88 - 97	63 - 69	101 - 110
	3 - 2	42.5 - 37	68 - 59	65 - 60.5	104 - 97
	2 - 1	16.3 - 15	26 - 24	38 - 32	61 - 50

** These vary according to engine code - consult official agent.*

Torque convertor

Stall speed (rpm) ... 1900 to 2100 (Note this will fall about 125 rpm per 3000 ft of altitude

Oil capacity

	Litres	Pints US	Pints Imp.
Torque convertor and gearbox (ATF):			
Initial	6	12.5	10
Refill	2.8	6	5
Final drive (Hypoid oil SAE 90)	0.9	2.1	1.75

Torque wrench settings

	lb ft	kg m
Engine to transmission	40	5.5
Convertor cover plate	10	1.5
Oil sump to gearbox	7.2	1
Torque convertor to driveplate	22	3
Transmission carrier to floor	22	3
Transmission carrier to mounting	29	4
Drive flanges	47	6.5
Differential flange to final drive housing	20	2.7
Governor housing to shaft	2.5	0.3
Wishbone to steering knuckle	18	2.5

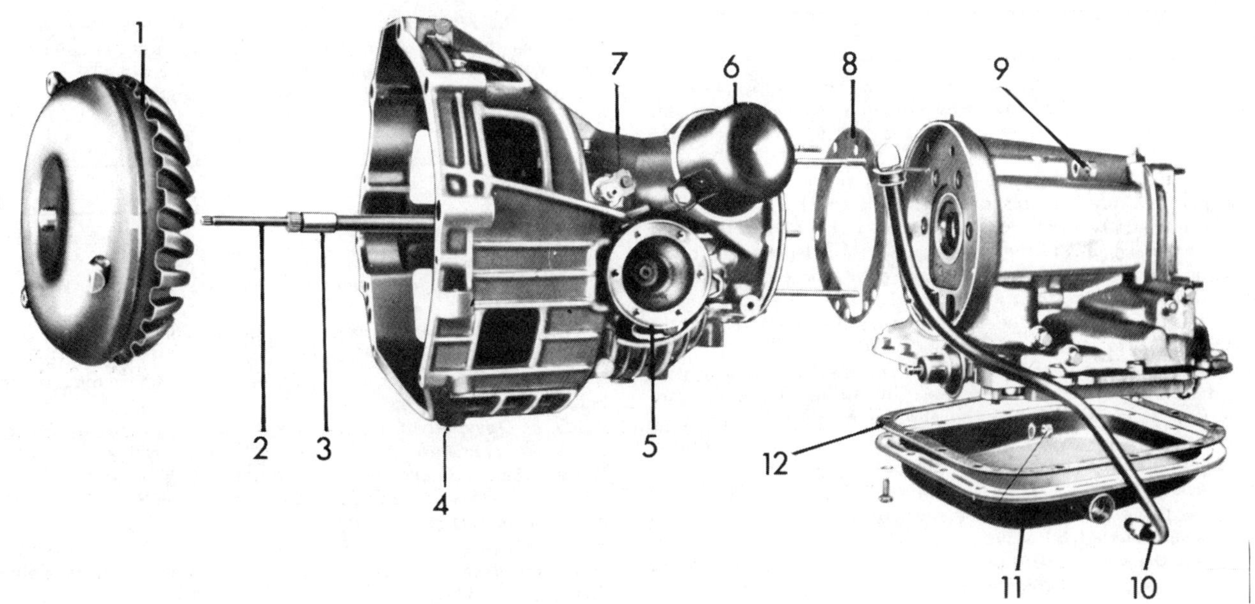

Fig. 7.1 Automatic transmission - exploded view

1 Torque converter
2 Impeller shaft (to oil pump)
3 Turbine shaft (to gearbox)
4 Final drive housing
6 Governor
7 Speedometer drive
8 Gasket
9 Automatic gearbox
10 ATF filler and dipstick tube
11 ATF sump
12 Gasket

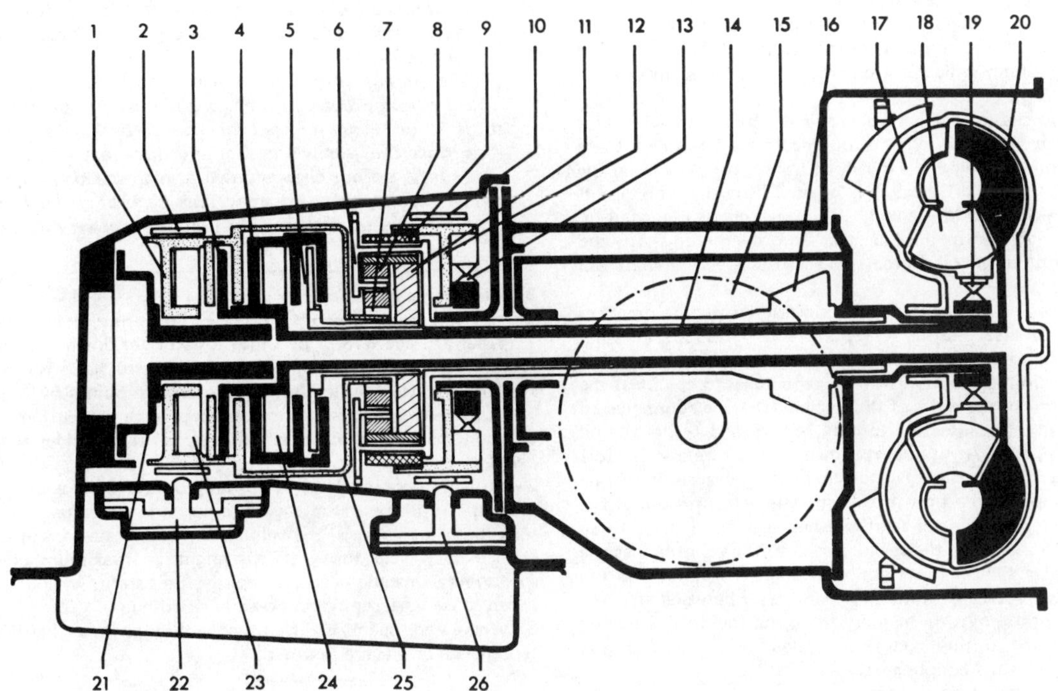

Fig. 7.2 Schematic layout of main components of an automatic transmission

1 Direction and reverse clutch drum
2 2nd gear brake band
3 Direct and reverse clutch
4 Forward clutch drum
5 Forward clutch
6 Planet carrier
7 Small sun gear
8 Large planet pinion
9 Large planet pinion
10 1st gear and reverse brake band
11 Large sun gear
12 Annulus gear
13 1st gear one-way clutch
14 Turbine shaft
15 Final drive gear
16 Drive pinion
17 Impeller
18 Stator
19 One way clutch for stator
20 Turbine
21 Oil pump housing
22 Piston for 2nd gear brake band
23 Piston for direct and reverse gear clutch
24 Piston for forward clutch
25 Driving shell
26 Piston for 1st and reverse gear brake band

1 General description

1 Refer to Fig. 7.1. The unit consists of three parts and is contained in castings which are bolted together and then attached to the engine casing at the rear. They, together with the engine, form an integral power unit.
2 The torque converter casing is bolted to the engine flywheel. Inside the casing are two turbine discs, one (the middle one) is mounted on a one way clutch (freewheel) so that it may turn only in the same direction as the engine, and the other may rotate independently but is mounted on a shaft which is splined to the drive-gear in the automatic gearbox. On the inside face of the casing next to the flywheel are turbine vanes (the impeller). The middle one is called the stator and the third one the turbine.
3 The drive goes from the turbine to the planetary gear system contained in the transmission box. Here by means of a number of epicyclic gear trains with brakes and clutches operated by hydraulic pressure through a complicated valve chest the necessary reduction in rpm is determined for the load and speed of the vehicle. Three main control devices provide the correct combination, the manual valve operated by the gearshift cable and lever by the driver, the second primary valve operated by vacuum from the engine intake manifold which makes the gearbox sensitive to engine load and speed, and the third control is the governor which controls ATF pressure and is sensitive to the road speed.

Thus it will be appreciated that the setting of the various springs and plungers in the valve chest is critical, as is the adjustment of clutches and brake bands, and for that reason we do not recommend that the unit be dismantled.
4 The drive is carried from the epicyclic system through the pinion shaft which is splined into the output gear of the train. The pinion shaft is supported at the rear end by a taper roller bearing in the second casting which also houses the differential and carries the driveshaft flanges. The bellhousing at the end houses the torque converter round which it goes and is bolted to the engine casing.
5 The pinion shaft is hollow and through it goes yet another hollow shaft which is driven by the torque converter primary rotor and takes power to the ATF pump which is situated at the extreme end of the epicyclic box.
6 The transmission case of the epicyclic box is fitted with ATF, as is the torque converter and the ATF is pumped round both of them providing lubrication, cooling and a means of transmitting power in the torque converter. The final drive casing is isolated from the ATF circuit and contains Hypoid oil. Oddly enough, the governor is mounted on the final drive casing, driven by a helical gear from the pinion shaft, and is in the ATF circuit. It will be appreciated that the governor shaft seal is an important item.
7 When the engine is started the torque converter casing commences to rotate with the flywheel and the ATF pump is driven supplying ATF under pressure to the torque converter and the valve chest.

As speed builds up the ATF is driven by centrifugal force out of the ends of the impeller into the vanes of the turbine (the one connected to the epicyclic system). It causes the turbine to turn and throw the oil back towards the impeller. At this point it meets the centre disc (stator) which is turning with the primary rotor (impeller) because of its one way clutch. This impedes the flow of oil increasing the pressure of the flow through the secondary rotor (turbine) and speeds up the turbine by multiplying the torque. As the speed of the turbine approaches the speed of the impeller the oil flows easily through the stator and the multiplication factor decreases until the speed ratio between the two wheels is 0.84:1. At this point the engine torque and the turbine torque are the same and the torque converter ceases to act as a torque convertor and acts as a fluid coupling only.
8 What happens to the torque depends upon the position of the manual selector valve. If the gearlever is in 'N' or 'P' then the epicyclic rotates freely and no power is transmitted to the wheels. When the lever is moved to 'D', '1', '2' or 'R' the various valves in the chest operate and move the controls of the clutches and brake bands so that the epicyclic train produces the correct ratio to the final drive. The secondary primary valve operates as the vehicle goes along according to engine load, causing the gear to change to suit the load, and the governor presides over the whole operation regulating the pressure of the ATF delivered by the pump according to the road speed of the vehicle.
9 It will be seen now why we suggest you leave well alone. It will also be appreciated that if the engine is not running the pump will not circulate the ATF so the vehicle cannot be push started because the turbine will not work. Furthermore, if the ATF is not circulating the oil will get hot and since the lubrication is done by the ATF if the vehicle is towed for any length of time the oil will boil and the bearings suffer accordingly.

2 Operation

1 These instructions are defined in the excellent vehicle handbook issued with the car, but to recap briefly.
2 *'P' or Parking lock,* only used when stopped. Locks the front wheels.
3 *'N' or Neutral,* as for manual transmission, engine running, oil pump working but no gears engaged.
4 *'R' or Reverse,* as for manual transmission. Vehicle must be stopped before this gear is engaged.
5 *'D' or Drive.* When this position is selected, the handbrake on, and the engine running at tick-over speed, the car will remain stationary. Release the handbrake and press the accelerator pedal and the car will move off, change into 2nd and 3rd gear according to load and speed.
6 *'2' or Second gear.* As for 'D' but the box will not select 3rd gear. Maximum speed in '2' is 68 mph (110 km/hr) so do not select '2' at speeds above this, because the move from 'D' to '2' will take place and may cause skidding or mechanical damage. Useful for hilly country but expensive fuel-wise.
7 *'1' or First gear.* As for '2' but will not select 2nd or 3rd gear. Maximum speed for selection on full throttle 40 mph (65 kph). With engine idling the change will happen at 22 mph (35 kph).
8 For the full driving technique read the Instruction Book.
9 There are five more operational points to remember.

a) *It is not possible to push or tow start the car as the transmission oil pump works only when the engine is running.*
b) *If the car is towed the selector should be in 'N', and a limit of 30 miles of towing should not be exceeded as lubrication of the transmission is inadequate when the engine is not running and overheating and seizure may occur. Do not tow at more than 30 mph (40 kph).*
c) *If there is a fault in the transmission the car must be towed with the driving wheels clear of the road; ie: a suspended tow.*
d) *If '2' or '1' are selected for overrun braking when on a slippery surface the gear will change and there may be a skid you did not expect. Do not change down at high speeds in these conditions.*
e) *The cooling fins and areas must be kept clean. The transmission fluid heats up and on long climbs can get very hot indeed.*

3 Kick-down position

1 When the accelerator pedal is pressed right down past the 'hard spot' to the kick-down position yet another control valve is brought into the system. Its effect is to move the gearshift points of first and second gears to correspond with maximum engine revolutions. The valve is operated by a solenoid controlled by a switch under the acceleration pedal.
2 So if you are in a hurry and stamp on the pedal when you are in top gear, the gearbox will change into second, the engine will move up to maximum revolutions, the vehicle will accelerate very quickly and then change back into top with the engine at maximum power with the speedometer needle climbing rapidly. Be careful where this is done for it can cause wheel spin and possibly skidding.
3 When the pedal is lifted back through the 'hard spot' normal gearchange points are resumed.

4 Maintenance and lubrication

1 Change the oil in the final drive housing every 20,000 miles.
2 Run the vehicle for about ten miles and then park on level ground. Remove the drain and filler plugs (Fig. 7.3) and allow the oil to run out. Replace the drain plug and fill to the level of the filler plug. About 1 litre (2 US pints, 1¾ Imperial pints) are required.
3 The automatic transmission fluid level should be checked every 6,000 miles (10,000 km). Locate the dipstick in the engine compartment, it is at the side of the engine oil filter and goes down a long tube to the automatic gearbox. Set the vehicle on a level surface

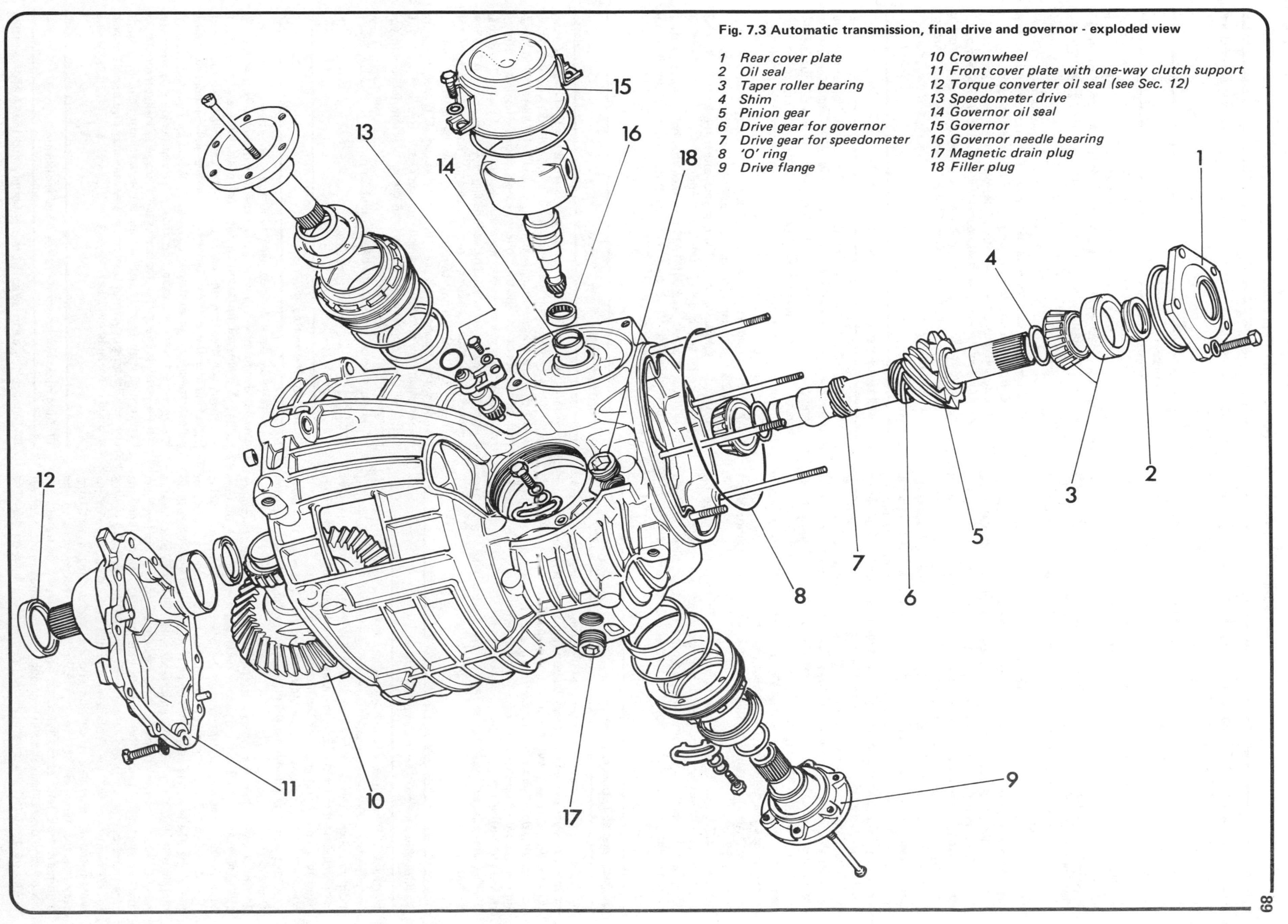

Fig. 7.3 Automatic transmission, final drive and governor - exploded view

1 *Rear cover plate*
2 *Oil seal*
3 *Taper roller bearing*
4 *Shim*
5 *Pinion gear*
6 *Drive gear for governor*
7 *Drive gear for speedometer*
8 *'O' ring*
9 *Drive flange*
10 *Crownwheel*
11 *Front cover plate with one-way clutch support*
12 *Torque converter oil seal (see Sec. 12)*
13 *Speedometer drive*
14 *Governor oil seal*
15 *Governor*
16 *Governor needle bearing*
17 *Magnetic drain plug*
18 *Filler plug*

and with the selector at 'N' run the engine at idling speed until the ATF is warm, and check the level of the oil on the dipstick while the engine is still running. The oil level should be between the two marks on the dipstick. Check twice to see that the dipstick was properly seated.

4 The difference between the two marks is about 0.4 litres (1 US pint, 0.7 Imperial pint). Top-up as necessary but do not overfill or the ATF will need to be drained down to the top mark. Use a funnel and a piece of plastic tube if ATF is to be poured in, it is an unpleasant fluid so do not spill it on the engine.

5 While checking the ATF level take a sample from the end of the dipstick and check its appearance for carbon and smell of burnt linings. If these are present the fluid should be changed and the reason for the burning located and corrected.

6 It is recommended that the ATF be changed every 30,000 miles (45,000 km) but this will be at shorter intervals if the car is used in hilly country or for towing. The interval should then be 20,000 miles.

7 The changing of ATF is a messy job and is best left to the service station. Do not attempt it unless you have a clean dust-free garage. If you must do it then take out the drain plug and let the fluid run out. Replace the plug and remove the automatic gearbox sump. Wash the sump clean and dry it thoroughly. Fit a new gasket and refit the sump to the box. Tighten the bolts to 7 lb ft (1 kg m), leave for 15 minutes and tighten again to the same torque. Fill via the dipstick tube with 4 Imperial pints (5 US pints, 2.4 litres) of Dexron R ATF. Any Dexron R with a five figure number preceeded by the letter B may be used.

8 Start the engine and engage all the gears in turn. Do not drive more than a few yards. Check the level of the ATF and add ATF until the oil level just shows on the dipstick. Now go for a short drive and then check the level again. Fill with ATF until the level is between the marks. Check the sump bolts for tightness again.

9 **Do not tow the vehicle or start the engine while the gearbox is not full of ATF.**

10 If the ATF level is above the top mark ATF must be drained off until the level is correct or damage to the mechanism will result.

11 Apart from checking oil levels, keeping the box clean to assist cooling, and checking connections, no further maintenance is necessary.

5 Tests and adjustments (general)

1 Before any accurate adjustments to the automatic transmission may be carried out the engine must be running correctly. Ignition and carburettor settings must be within the specified limits (eg: idling adjustments, valve tappets, ignition timing, etc). If these are all in order then inspect the transmission for leaks or external damage and correct these before proceeding.

2 The fluid levels must be correct before testing takes place (see Section 4).

6 Kick-down switch - testing and adjustment

1 Check the kick-down switch operation. With the ignition switched on, press the accelerator pedal down as far as it will go. There should be a distinct click from the kick-down solenoid in the gearbox, as the valve is operated. If there is not then the system is not working. The switch is fixed to a small bracket under the accelerator pedal (see Fig. 7.4). It is possible to move it slightly by loosening the screws. There are two wires to it, one from the supply and the other going to the automatic gearbox solenoid.

2 Check that when the ignition is on there is current in the supply cable. Now check that the accelerator pedal is not prevented, by mal-adjustment at the carburettor end of the operating cable, from going right down to its stop. The throttle operating lever should be resting on the spring. If the accelerator is not going right down, adjust the cable so that it will. Fully depress the accelerator and hold it in place with a weight. Adjust the throttle cable at the carburettor so that the lever just touches the stop. Lock the cable in this position. Now allow the accelerator pedal to lift until there is between 0.020 and 0.040 in. (0.5 to 1.0 mm) between the cable lever and the stop. At this point the switch should operate. It can be checked by putting a test lamp between the terminal of the kick-down switch which goes to the automatic box and earth. With the accelerator fully depressed the switch should be closed and the lamp alight. If the adjustment is correct at the point stated the switch should open and the lamp go out. The switch may be moved on the bracket to adjust it or removed and replaced, if necessary.

7 Selector cable - checking operation

1 Correct adjustment for the 'P', 'R', 'N', 'D' and '1' ranges are necessary. The system will not work if they are out of adjustment in the selector mechanism. Adjustment is discussed in Section 15, paragraph 4. To test, switch the engine on and run up to 1100 rpm with the lever at 'N' and the handbrake hard on.

a) Move the lever to 'R'. The engine speed should drop noticeably.
b) Move to 'P' and drop the safety stop. The speed should increase. Pull the lever against the stop - the speed must not alter.
c) Engage 'R' again - speed should drop.
d) Move to 'N' - no gears engaged so the speed should rise again.
e) Move to 'D' and again the engine speed should drop noticeably.
f) The lever should move from 'D' to '1' and back again, through '2', without any resistance.

8 Stall speed test

1 The engine must be warm and the ATF lukewarm. **Do not carry out this test for more than 20 seconds** or the transmission will overheat.

2 The object is to check whether the torque converter is functioning correctly, and the running symptoms are poor acceleration and low maximum speed. A tachometer to measure engine speed is necessary.

3 Put all the brakes hard on and with the lever at 'D' run the engine for a brief period at full throttle. The engine speed should drop to between 2200 rpm and 1900 rpm immediately and remain constant.

4 If the stall speed is above 2200 rpm then either the forward clutch is slipping, or 1st gear one way clutch is slipping.

5 If the stall speed is about 1700 rpm then the engine needs overhaul but if it drops to 1500 rpm then the stator one way clutch in the torque converter is defective.

9 Road test

1 Apart from checking that shift speeds are as per Specification there is no special virtue in a road test. As it is your vehicle you will know whether there are any rough changes, slipping clutches or odd noises and at what point in the journey they occur. However, after a reasonably long run examine the transmission for oil leaks. These may come from several sources. The bellhousing may be dripping ATF. This means the torque converter seal is leaking. You can overhaul this yourself. Oil leaks from the final drive may be rectified without removing the transmission, and there may be an ATF leak from the transmission box sump plate, which you can rectify (see Section 4.7). If the final drive contains ATF then the pinion seal has failed and you cannot do that one yourself.

There may be the obvious bearing noises from the final drive. This is discussed later.

10 Action after testing

1 When you have decided what you think is wrong it would be a sensible idea to make a plan of action and then discuss this with the VW agent. If there are problems in the final drive, torque converter, or automatic gearbox that you cannot solve you can still save a lot of cash by taking the transmission out of the vehicle and sending the faulty unit to the agent for exchange or repair. It would be a good idea to get his agreement to that action first though. If you decide it is a job you can do yourself check that the spares are available. Finally, although we have found with few exceptions the agents are most helpful, they do not run Schools of Instruction and a busy man may give a short answer to an ill considered question.

11 Automatic transmission - removal and replacement

1 Remove the earth strap from the battery and then disconnect the

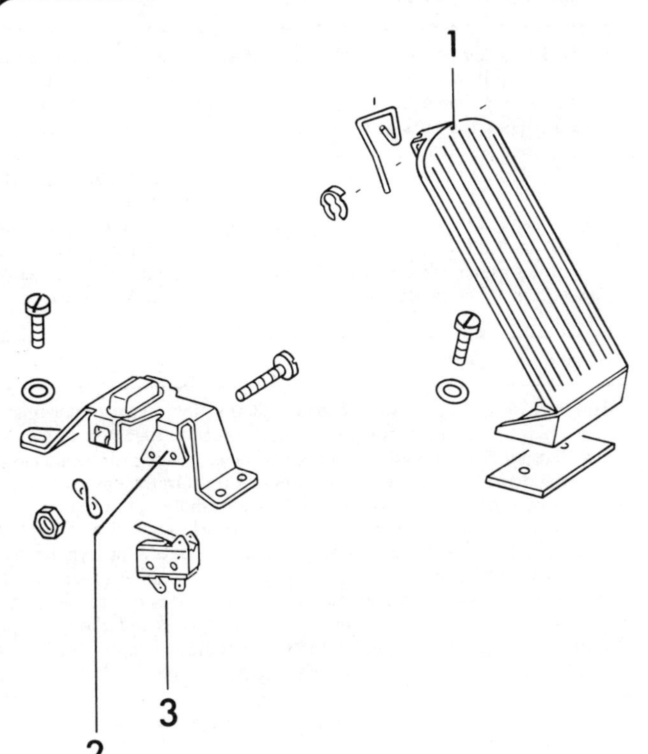

Fig. 7.4 Kick-down switch

1 *Accelerator pedal*
2 *Bracket*
3 *Kick-down switch*

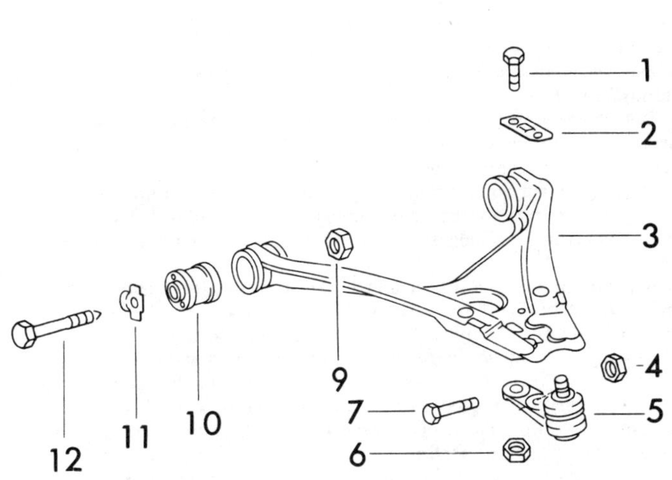

Fig. 7.5 Exploded view of front suspension wishbone and balljoint

1 *Screw*
2 *Plate*
3 *Wishbone*
4 *Nut*
5 *Balljoint*
6 *Nut*
7 *Bolt*
9 *Nut*
10 *Bush*
11 *Lockplate*
12 *Pivot bolt*

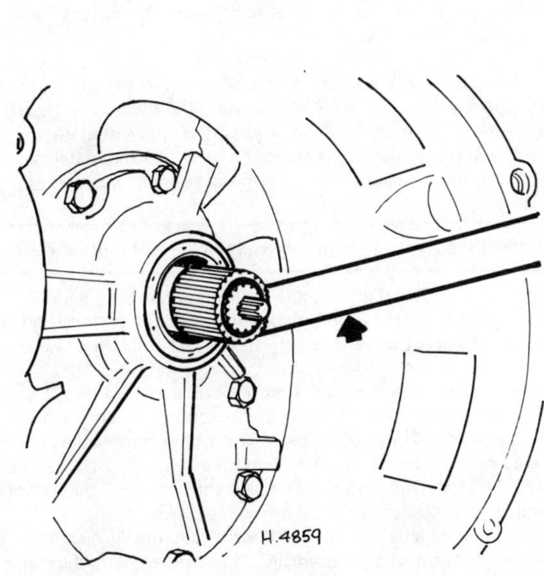

Fig. 7.6 Extracting the torque converter seal

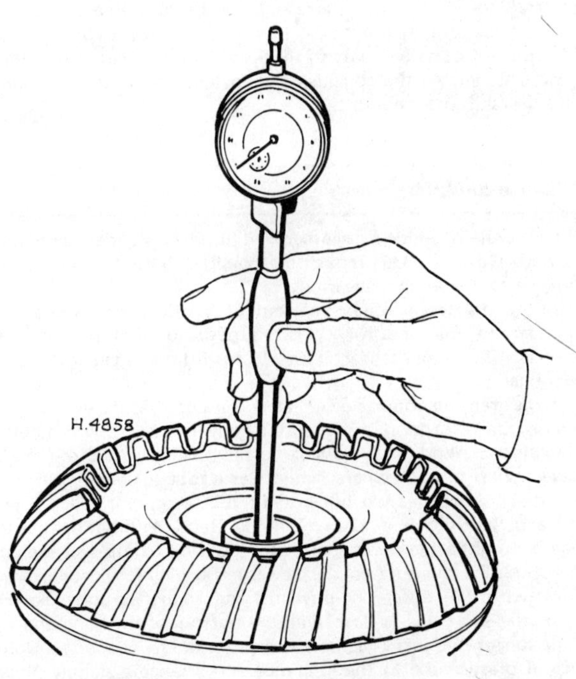

Fig. 7.7 Measuring the internal diameter of the torque converter bush

speedometer drive from the final drive casing and tie the cable out of the way.
2 Undo the exhaust pipe from the engine and the silencer and tie it to one side.
3 Disconnect and remove the starter (Chapter 10).
4 Remove the small cover plate from the bottom of the bellhousing.
5 Working through the hole where the starter was fitted turn the transmission until the bolts holding the driveplate and converter to the flywheel are visible. Remove the first one, turn the converter again and remove the second one, then the third one. The converter is now free from the flywheel.
6 Detach the vacuum hoses and wires from the transmission. Tag them for easy replacement. Undo and remove the selector cable from the transmission (see Section 15).
7 Mark the position of the balljoint on the left-hand wishbone with a scriber and remove the balljoint nut and pull the joint outwards. Be careful about this marking or you will have to reset the camber (see Fig. 7.5).
8 Remove both driveshafts from the transmission. Use the correct key and a lot of care. Tie the driveshafts out of the way.
9 Remove two of the upper transmission/engine bolts.
10 Now undo the gearbox carrier from the mounting and the underside of the body. This is the bracket that the support plate, bolted onto the end of the gearbox, rests on with its rubber mounting. The back end of the box will drop slightly. Undo the three nuts holding the support plate to the back of the gearbox and remove it.
11 The engine and gearbox are now joined by one upper and two lower engine/transmission bolts. Take out the remaining upper bolt. Undo the union on the ATF dipstick/filler pipe and take the pipe off. Catch any ATF that comes out.
12 Support the gearbox with a jack and remove the two lower transmission bolts. The complete transmission may now be removed from underneath the car, by lowering the jack. The torque converter is loose and must be fixed with a strap or strut or it will fall out.
13 The jack problem is a real one. The easiest way is to make a wooden platform to fit under the transmission and use a garage floor jack. The car will have to be raised to get the transmission out from underneath. It all depends on what resources you have.
14 Replacement is the reverse of removal. Install the converter and lift the unit into position. Insert the two lower transmission bolts and reconnect the filler/dipstick pipe. Fit the support plate to the back of the gearbox and install the gearbox carrier. The box is now fully supported so all the other pieces may be fitted. Be careful to put the balljoint back on the wishbone in exactly the same place.
15 Torque all bolts and nuts to the Specification given at the beginning of the Chapter. At the conclusion of installation, check the operation of the gearshift mechanism.

12 Torque converter - repairs

1 The unit is welded together and if seriously damaged must be renewed. However, two repairs are possible, both to cure an oil leak from the converter/shaft bearing.
2 Before discussing repairs a word of warning. When refitting the converter to the one way clutch support do not rock or tilt the converter. Turn the converter slowly to-and-fro when installing it on the splines.
3 If the transmission has overheated so much that the ATF is polluted with carbon or other debris then the converter must be drained of the contaminated fluid. It is possible to siphon this out. From the home-brewers shop or somewhere similar get a rubber bung 1 3/8 in. (34.8 mm) diameter. Bore two holes to fit the bung, one about 6 in. (150 mm) and the other 8 in. (205 mm) long. Bend the tubes so that the top piece is a right-angle bend about 2 in. (50 mm) radius, and the outlet is horizontal. Fit the bung in the converter bushing (the converter should be flat with the starter ring upwards) and adjust the tubes so that the end of the short one is flush with the bottom of the bung and the end of the longer one just touches the bottom of the converter. Connect a piece of plastic tube to the long tube and arrange a siphon. Now blow down the shorter tube to start the siphon going and leave the converter to drain for at least eight hours. Blow, don't suck, the fluid not only does not taste nice, **it is poisonous.**
4 The seal is held in spigot of the front cover plate (see Fig. 7.3). It may be levered out and the seat cleaned with a sharp tool. The new seal is a very soft silicone compound which must not be exposed to petrol or paraffin. Dip it in ATF and push it in gently as far as it will go.
5 If the seal was damaged then there may be damage on the hub of the converter. Check the outside of the hub for scoring and uneven wear.
6 It is as well to check the bush inside the converter at this point. It must not be more than 1.436 in. (34.25 mm) in diameter and not more than 0.001 in. (0.03 mm) out of round. If it is then it must be replaced. The new bush is finished to size and must not be reamed out. The limits are 1.347 to 1.375 in. (34.025 to 34.095 mm). Unless you have an internal micrometer and a suitable press we suggest you leave this job to the agent, but it can be done with patience and the correct tools.

13 Final drive - repairs

1 Refer to Fig. 7.3. It will be seen that the final drive arrangements are very similar to those for the manual gearbox. Please read Section 11, of Chapter 6 for details of photos and instructions for replacing oil seals in the drive flanges, while the transmission is in the car.
2 The unit may be separated from the automatic gearbox once the transmission has been removed from the car. Refer to Fig. 7.1. Undo the nuts of the four through bolts at the end of the automatic box. There is a fifth nut to undo. To get at this the sump of the automatic gearbox must be removed and the nut will be seen opposite the centre-line rib of the final drive housing. When this is removed the two units may be separated. A new gasket for the automatic gearbox sump (see Section 4, paragraph 7) and the joint between the two units will be needed.
3 Examination of the differential and bearings is also discussed in Section 11 of Chapter 6.

14 Governor - dismantling and reassembly

1 The governor is driven by the helical gear on the pinion shaft.
2 If the transmission has failed due to burning of the brake bands or clutches then as well as draining the converter it will be necessary to clean the governor (refer to Fig. 7.8).
3 Remove it from the casing by undoing the clip and taking off the cover. The governor may now be extracted. Look at the thrust-plate and the shaft for wear. The shaft may be replaced by a new one if it is damaged but the new shaft must be fitted to the old governor. If a new governor is to be fitted the whole transmission must go to the agent for the governor to be reset on the test rig.
4 The seals should be replaced with new ones (lip toward the governor body).
5 To clean the governor it is necessary to dismantle it. Remove the two screws from the thrust-plate and take off the thrust-plate and housing. The weight and the transfer plate will fall out. Remove the circlips from the pin and the remainder of the parts may be dismantled.
6 Wash it all carefully and dry it thoroughly. Reassembly is the reverse process. Dip the parts in ATF as you assemble them. The transfer plate drillings should have the narrow end of the taper next to the weight, and the thrust-plate apex must be at the centre of the housing.
7 Refit the shaft, install the governor and refit the cap and clip.

15 Gearshift mechanism - adjustment, removal and replacement

1 Refer to Fig. 7.9. The console is illuminated by a small bulb. The lever moves only in one plane pivotting about its bottom end. A small way below the pivot a cable is attached which transfers the motion to the valve chest of the automatic box.
2 To remove the selector lever first remove the gear knob. Remove the brushes and the console. It may be necessary to remove the exhaust pipe on some cars. Undo the screws which hold the bracket to the floor plate. Detach the cable from lever and take it away to the rear, undoing the sleeve nut in the casing. The gearshift should then come away downwards. Installation is the reverse of removal.
3 To renew the cable remove the console and undo the cable from the lever at the bottom of the assembly. Now underneath the car, remove the circlip holding the cable end to the transmission selector lever. Draw the cable out of the gearshift mechanism.
4 To adjust the cable, set the lever in position 'P'. Take the cover plate off the lever assembly and loosen the clamp on the cable. Now under the car again push the levers on the gearbox right back against the stop.

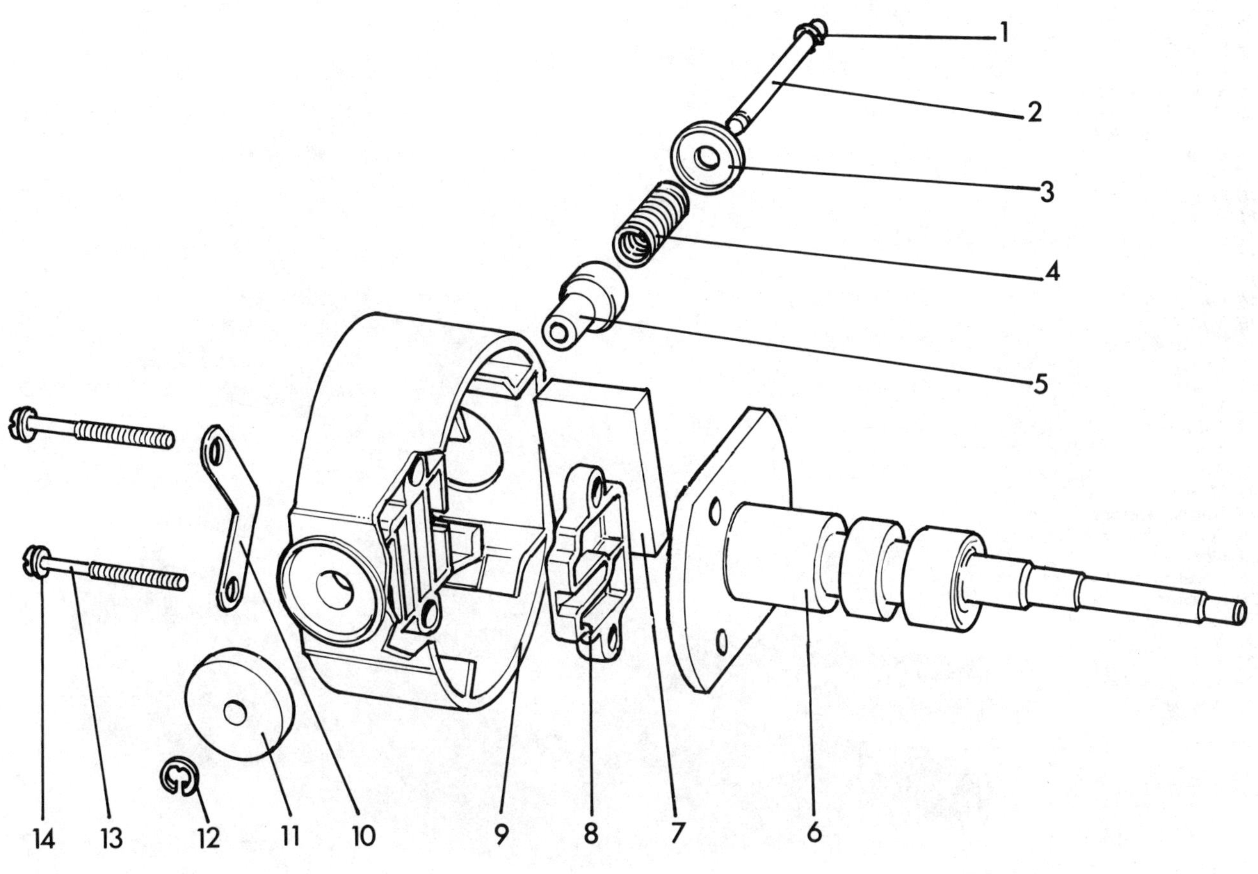

Fig. 7.8 The governor

1 Circlip
2 Pin
3 Spring cup
4 Spring
5 Valve
6 Governor
7 Balance weight
9 Housing
10 Thrust plate
11 Centrifugal weight
12 Circlip
13 Bolt (M5)
14 Washer

Push against the spring pressure with a pair of pliers. Hold the lever in this position and tighten the clamp on the cable in the gearshift.

5 Check the operation as in Section 7, of this Chapter.

6 It will be seen that a small roller runs in the groove of the segment. This roller should touch each end of the groove as the lever is operated. When it is at one end of the groove the selector lever must be at 'P'. Bend the detent lever so that this happens if necessary. The Neutral/ Park switch consisting of the contact bridge and the contact plate must be adjusted so that the starter motor operates only in the 'N' and 'P' positions.

16 Automatic gearbox - repairs

1 We do not recommend any D-I-Y repairs to the automatic gearbox other than replacement of the ATF and the cleaning of the sump. Dismantling is simple, overhaul is limited to replacing worn parts, **but** the box has to be assembled again. There are 12 different springs, each operating a valve, of different wire diameters, free-lengths etc, in the valve chest alone, an oil pump and a complicated epicyclic gear train. If tests show that gears are slipping, or the ATF smells of carbon or burning leave the repair of the automatic gearbox to the official agent whose mechanics have done a course of instruction and have all the jigs, gauges and adjustment schedules. It will be much more economical in the long run.

17 Modifications

1 On some models a different final drive casting is fitted. It, in effect, is two castings joined on the centre-line of the final drive (see Fig. 7.10). For the tasks outlined in Section 13 the modified casting makes no difference. The governor is mounted differently.

2 On 1975 models, there is a new selector lever and cable. A portion of the cable is inside the car under the carpet. The clamp can be adjusted only from inside the car so a second person is needed to do the test in Section 15.4.

3 A new driveplate was introduced in November 1974. It may be necessary to fit shims if this is installed. Check with the official agent.

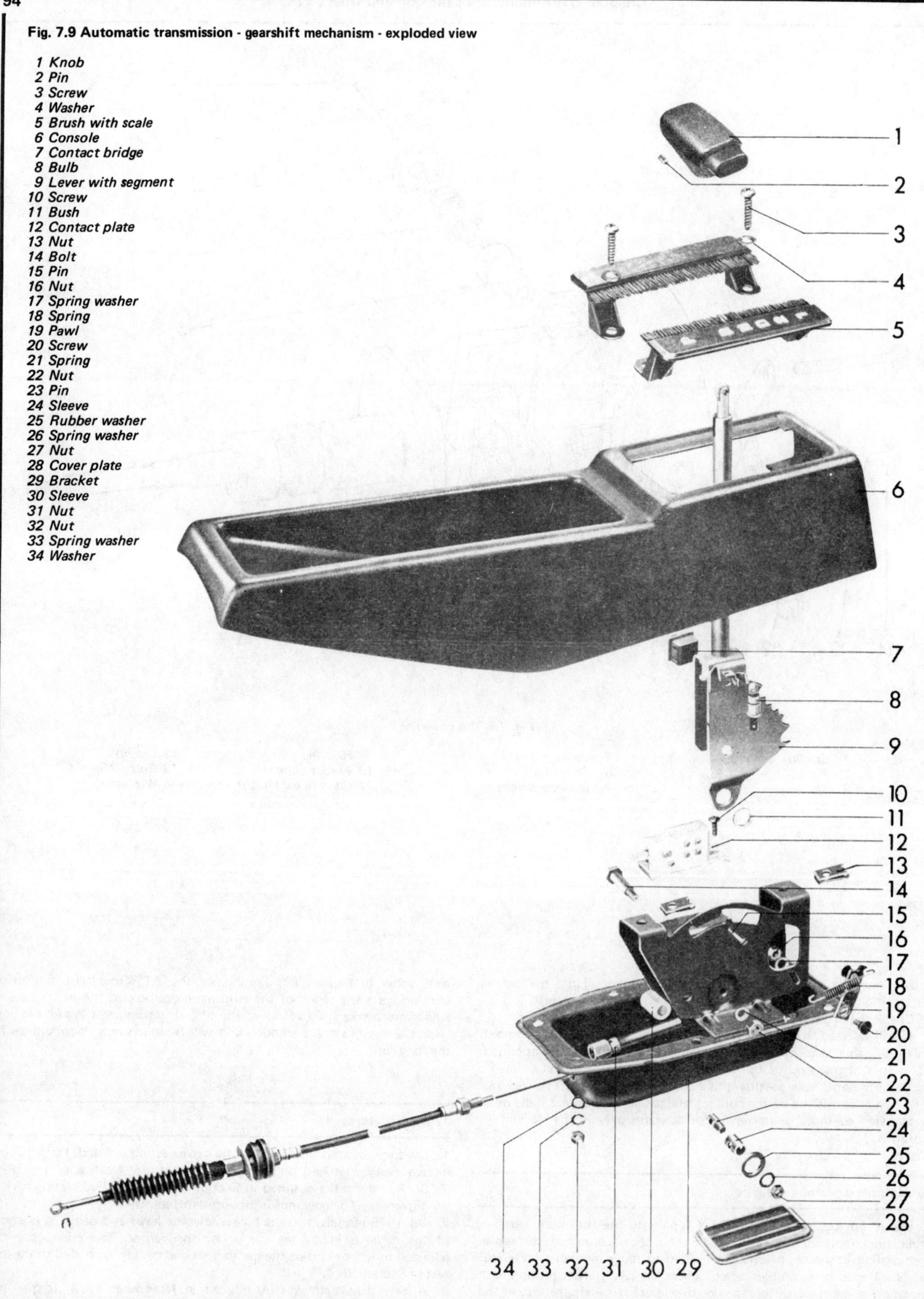

Fig. 7.9 Automatic transmission - gearshift mechanism - exploded view

1 Knob
2 Pin
3 Screw
4 Washer
5 Brush with scale
6 Console
7 Contact bridge
8 Bulb
9 Lever with segment
10 Screw
11 Bush
12 Contact plate
13 Nut
14 Bolt
15 Pin
16 Nut
17 Spring washer
18 Spring
19 Pawl
20 Screw
21 Spring
22 Nut
23 Pin
24 Sleeve
25 Rubber washer
26 Spring washer
27 Nut
28 Cover plate
29 Bracket
30 Sleeve
31 Nut
32 Nut
33 Spring washer
34 Washer

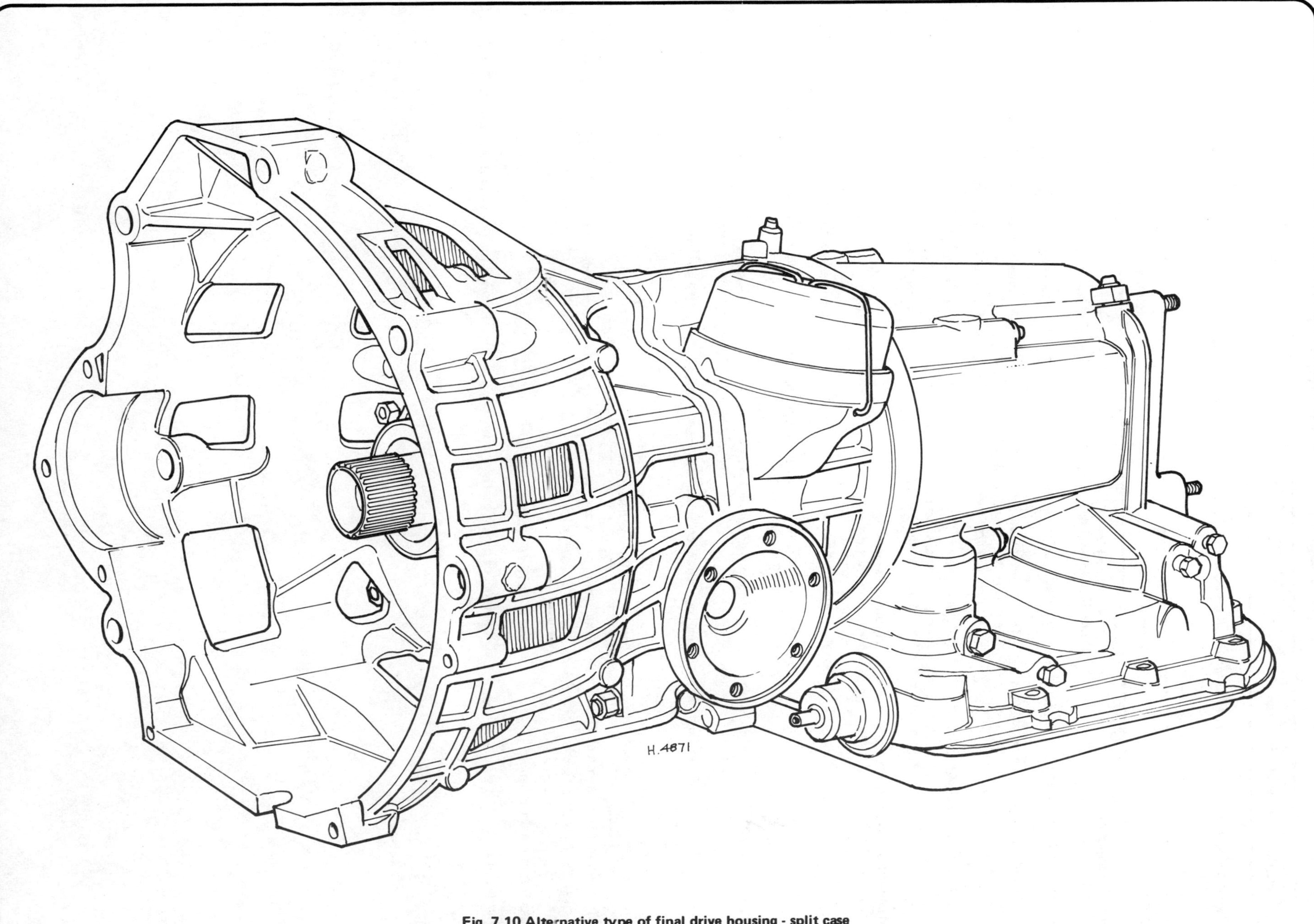

Fig. 7.10 Alternative type of final drive housing - split case

18 Fault diagnosis - automatic transmission

This list is by no means complete but it contains all that the owner can rectify. The official agent is the best person to consult about a faulty automatic transmission

Symptom	Reason/s	Remedy
No drive in any gear	ATF fluid level low Transmission box defective	Fill. Official agent.
Drive in some gears but not all	Transmission box defective	Official agent.
Power output unsteady engine surges on upshift	ATF fluid level incorrect Selector mechanism out of adjustment Oil strainer requires cleaning	Measure and correct. Adjust. Remove pan and clean.
Speed shifts at too low speed	Governor dirty Primary throttle valve needs setting Valve body assembly dirty	Remove and clean. Official agent. Official agent.
Speed shifts at too high speed	Vacuum hose leaking Kickdown lever distorted Kickdown solenoid defective ATF pressure too low	Replace. Repair. Repair. Official agent.
Kickdown will not operate	Lever distorted, solenoid defective, wiring open circuit switch broken	Trace and correct. Replace switch/solenoid.
Heavy leakage of ATF on floor and vehicle	Torque convertor seal casing defective or cracked	Replace seal. Fit new convertor.
Heavy loss of ATF. NONE on floor or vehicle. Smoky exhaust	Leaking vacuum chamber or primary throttle	Official agent.
Parking lock will not hold vehicle	Selector lever out of adjustment Parking lock linkage defective	Adjust. Repair.
ATF dirty and smells of carbon and burning	Brake bands or clutches wearing in auto transmission box	Dismantle and take box to Official agent k (check with him first). Replace oil in convertor.
Oil leaks from final drive flanges	Seals in flanges worn out	Replace.
Differential noisy	Differential or pinion bearings worn	Remove final drive unit and take to Official agent.

Chapter 8 Rear suspension

For modifications and information applicable to later models, see Supplement at end of manual

Contents

Specifications

Type	Trailing arms with beam axle and diagonal (Panhard) arm. Compound axle beam with torsion tube.
Shock absorbers	Hydraulic, telescopic, double action. Borge or Fichtel and Sachs.
Springs	Coil. Three types are available according to model of car. Consult official agents spares dept.
Rear wheel camber	$-30' \pm 30'$
Maximum permissible deviation between sides	30'
Total toe-in of rear wheels	$\pm 50'$
Hub bearings	Taper roller

Torque wrench settings	**lb ft**	**kg m**
Trailing arm to vehicle body pivot bolt	43	6
Shock absorber bolts (top and bottom)	43	6
Diagonal arm pivot bolts (both ends)	61	8.5

1 General description

1 The drive function has been transferred to the front wheels and all that is left for the rear wheels is to follow along supporting the body and providing extra braking power.

2 The main part of the rear suspension structure is the axle beam. On each end of it is a stub axle. It is attached to the body by two trailing arms, the front of which are pivotted in bonded rubber bushes on the bodyframe and at the rear fixed rigidly to the axle beam.

3 Vertical movement of the axle is controlled by a coil spring mounted between the body and the axle on each side and this movement is damped by a shock absorber on each side between the body and the trailing arm, located between the spring and the pivot on a bracket attached to the axle beam (photo), **not** inside the spring.

4 Further control is exerted by the diagonal arm which is fixed between the left-hand end of the axle beam and the forward end of the right-hand trailing arm. It is pivotted at both ends (photos).

5 The axle beam consists of the inverted 'U' section covering a torsion tube. Both are fastened to the stub axle mounting face so that the axle consists of the torsion tube, 'U' section, two trailing arms, two brackets for the shock absorbers, and two platforms for the coil springs, all as an integral piece. Also welded to the axle is the rear pivot of the panhard rod.

6 The camber of the rear wheels is set and is not adjustable. The same applies to the toe-in.

7 The rear wheels run on taper roller bearings.

2 Rear axle - checking for distortion

1 If the tyre treads on the rear wheels begin to wear unevenly although tyre pressures have been maintained correctly, then the rear axle assembly is distorted.

2 To check this the camber angles must be measured. A special protractor or clinometer is required to do this accurately. The vehicle should be raised on a lift or over a pit.

3 Support the axle beam on jacks as near horizontal as possible and remove the wheels. Measure the angle of the axle beam to the horizontal and note which end is higher.

4 Using the brake drum surface as a reference datum, measure the camber angle of the drums on each side of the vehicle. Add the angle of the axle beam to the horizontal to the camber angle of the drum at the higher end of the axle and subtract it from the camber angle of the drum at the lower end. The result in each case should be minus $30' \pm 30'$. If either side is outside this tolerance, then the beam is distorted. Unfortunately there is no adjustment.

5 It would be as well to have this measurement checked by the official agent before going further.

6 Once these readings are confirmed what happens next depends on the owner. Unless something is done the car will go on wearing out tyres at an expensive rate.

7 If both sides are out of tolerance the axle is probably bent due to harsh driving and/or overloading. If one side only is out of tolerance it may possibly be due to a distorted stub axle, or even faulty hub

1.3 View of the right-hand rear suspension
A is the trailing arm, B the shock absorber, C the bump stop, D axle beam

1.4a View of the forward end of the right-hand trailing arm. A is the pivot of the trailing arm, B the pivot of the diagonal arm, C the trailing arm

1.4b The left-hand end of the diagonal arm and the shock absorber bolt and bracket on the axle beam

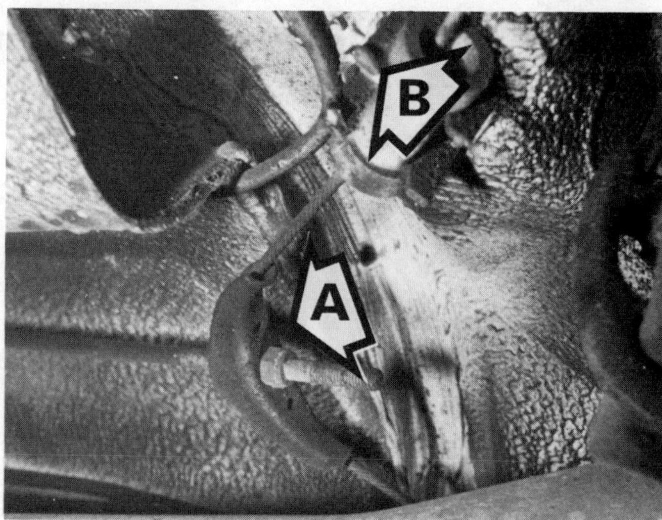

3.2 The handbrake equalizer bar (A) and the plastic bush (B) for the handbrake cable

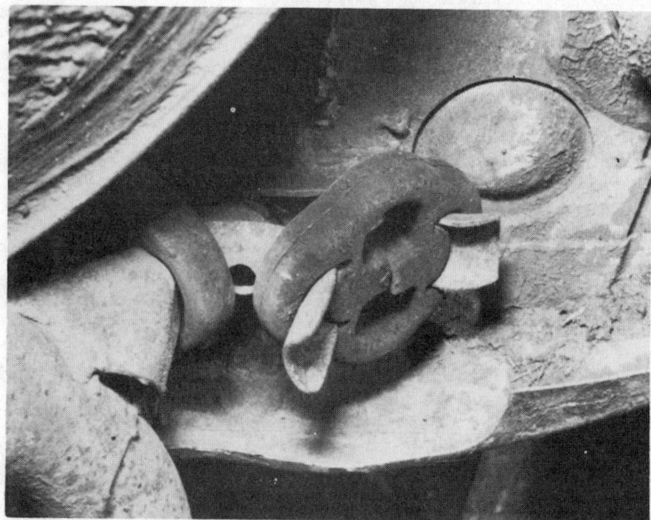
3.3 Silencer mounting hook

bearings. Check the drum for truth when rotated. It is possible to remove the stub axles from both sides and measure the inclination of the bearing face, in the same way that the camber angle of the brake drum was measured. If, after allowing for the slope of the axle beam, the angle on the faulty side is the same as that on the side which was in tolerance, within ± 30', then the axle beam is not distorted and the fault is in the hub or stub axle. The stub axle may be removed and checked (see Section 5, paragraph 4).

8 What ever is distorted must be renewed. **On no account try to straighten the faulty part.** That process will lead to stresses being set up and consequent fractures when travelling. It will not remain straight anyway, unless heat treated and that process is beyond the scope of even the Official agent.

9 The axle beam should be removed for careful inspection and servicing.

3 Rear axle - removal, repair and replacement

1 Jack up the vehicle and support the body. Remove the roadwheels.

2 Undo and remove the nuts for the handbrake equalizer bar (photo). and press out the plastic bush for the handbrake cable (photo).

3 Unhook the silencer (photo) and detach the brake cables from the body.

4 Undo and plug the hydraulic brake pipe unions. Make sure no dirt gets into these pipes. Fasten them in plastic bags.

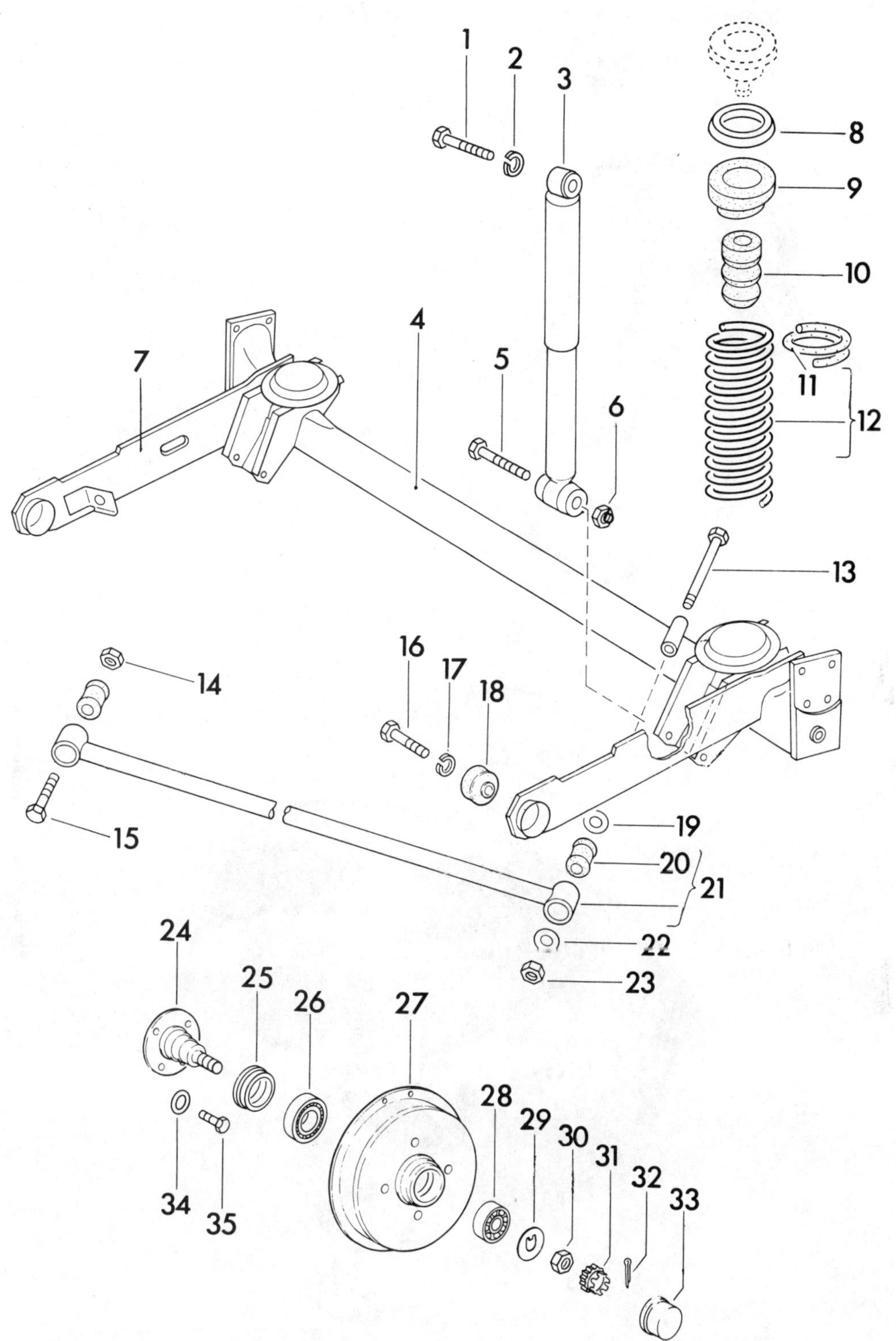

Fig. 8.1 Rear suspension - exploded view

1 Shock absorber pin
2 Spring washer
3 Shock absorber
4 Axle beam
5 Shock absorber lower pin
6 Nut
7 Trailing arm
8 Upper damper cap
9 Upper damper ring
10 Bump stop
11 Coil hose
12 Coil spring
13 Diagonal arm pivot pin
14 Nut
15 Diagonal arm pivot nut
16 Trailing arm pivot pin
17 Washer
18 Bushing
19 Washer
20 Bushing
21 Diagonal arm
22 Washer
23 Nut
24 Stub axle
25 Oil seal
26 Inner race
27 Brake drum
28 Outer race
29 Thrust washer
30 Nut
31 Lock ring
32 Split pin
33 Hub cap
34 Lockwasher
35 Bolt holding stub axle to axle beam (4)

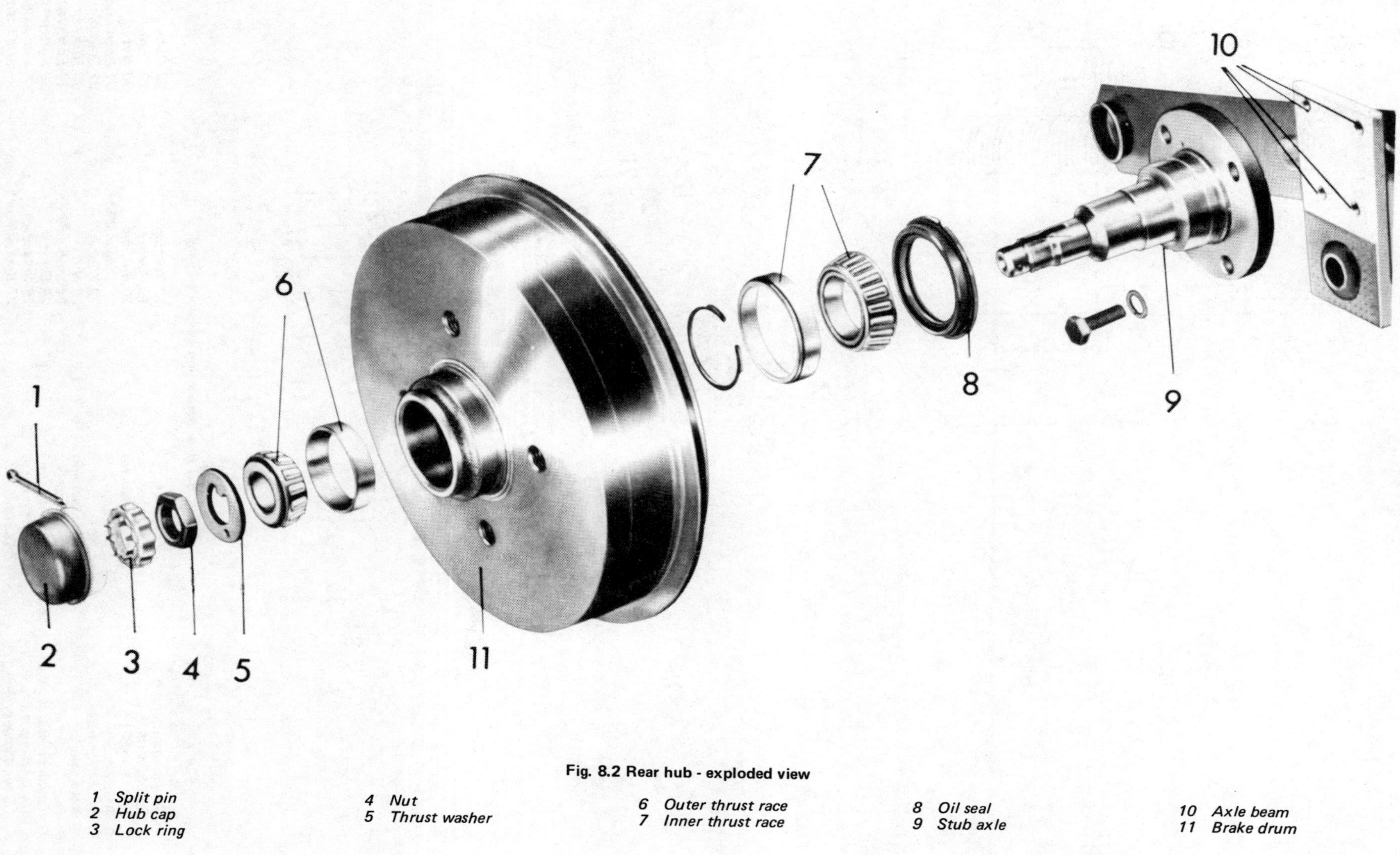

Fig. 8.2 Rear hub - exploded view

1 Split pin
2 Hub cap
3 Lock ring
4 Nut
5 Thrust washer
6 Outer thrust race
7 Inner thrust race
8 Oil seal
9 Stub axle
10 Axle beam
11 Brake drum

5 Undo and remove the shock-absorber lower bolts. Leave the shock-absorbers in place.
6 Undo the pivot bolt of the diagonal arm and the pivot bolts of the trailing arms and remove the pivot bolts from the bushing. It will be necessary to raise the axle beam a little to do this. Once the bolts are out the axle beam, complete with hubs and brake drums may be removed.
7 Replacement is the reverse of removal. Torque all bolts to Specification. Bleed the hydraulic system and adjust the parking brake (see Chapter 9).
8 When installing the rear axle it is important to make sure that the rubber bushings in the pivot of the trailing arm are not under tension. The pivot pins should not be tightened unless the trailing arm is in the mid-position of its normal vertical travel as the car moves along. To achieve this, the axle should be raised until the stub axle centre-line is 2 ¾ in. (70 mm) higher than the pivot pin centre-line. The stub axle centre-line will then be 10 5/8 in. (270 mm) from the lower edge of the wheel housing. With the axle in this position, torque the pivot pin to 43 lb ft/5.94 kg m. (This has been increased from 32 lb ft/4.42 kg m). Always use new pivot pins.
9 A modification introduced in October 1974 has a different type of rubber bush in the pivot of the trailing arm. The new one has slots on each side and the sleeve is also altered. These are **not** interchangeable with the older type.
10 If banging or knocking noises are heard from the axle beam suspect the torsion tube which may be knocking against the 'U' section. This may be eliminated by inserting a suitable rubber stop between the two parts at the point of contact.

The noise may also be generated by coils of the coil spring knocking together. It will most probably be the 1st coil at the top or at the bottom. The spring must be removed and a piece of damping hose fitted over the first coil at each end. It is not necessary to remove the axle to remove the spring. Undo the lower pin of the shock-absorber from the trailing arm and either raise the body or remove the wheel and lower the axle until the spring comes off its seating. Be careful it seats correctly on reassembly. Note that the upper damper ring is different left and right. The spare part number of the hose is '321 511 123A'. The manufacturers suggest the inside of the hose be coated with vaseline, the hose started onto the spring and then expanded with compressed air, after which it will slide on. It must not project more than 3/16 in. (5 mm) past the end of the spring coil.
11 Replacement of the bushings in the trailing arms and the diagonal arm is a straight-forward job if you have a press or a suitable extractor. Smear the outside of the bushing with brake cylinder paste, or a little soft soap. Do not try to hammer them in, they must be pressed in using a suitable mandrel, and be careful to start them square or damage to the bushing will occur.

4 Shock-absorbers - removal, replacement and testing

1 The shock absorber may be removed without disturbing the remainder of the suspension.
2 If it seems to be weak, or is 'bottoming' a simple test will help you to decide. Push down on the rear corner of the car as far as you can and let go. The vehicle should rise sharply and then settle immediately. If it oscillates then the shock absorber is not working properly.
3 Jack-up the car and remove the rear wheel. Set the car on an axle stand and put a jack under the axle. Lift the axle until the shock absorber is slightly compressed. Remove top and botom bolts and remove the shock absorber. It is our experience that these bolts are usually difficult to extract so make sure the car is properly supported whilst you are underneath.
4 Hold the bottom bushing in a vice and work the shock absorber up and down over the whole of its stroke. Repeat this several times. The pressure should be even and uniform throughout the whole stroke. If possible, get the official agent to compare it with a new one. The units are slightly overfilled on assembly, so a small leak is no worry but a considerable leak means that the seals have perished, and the unit must be renewed.
5 The shock absorber is not repairable nor, as far as we can ascertain, are new bushes available. It is worth asking though. If these can be obtained then it is a simple matter to press out the old bushes and fit new ones. The metal sleeve and rubber bush come out together. Clean up the bore in the eye of the shock absorber, coat the new bush with some talcum powder or a silicone spray and press it in until the shoulder on the bush meets the shock absorber eye. Now press in the sleeve from the same side.
6 It is not necessary to replace shock absorbers in pairs, nor even to have two of the same make, so long as they move with the same characteristic. If one has failed and you have the time, it is as well to check the other while you have the tools and jacks available.
7 Replacement is the reverse of removal.

5.2 Remove the split pin and then the locking ring. Always fit a new split pin on assembly

5 Hub bearings and stub axle - removal, replacement and adjustment

1 Refer to Fig. 8.2. The hub is carried on a stub axle bolted to the axle beam. The brake shoes and backplate are also fastened to the stub axle. Details of removal are given in Chapter 9. The roadwheel is bolted to the brake drum and the drum is held on the shaft in two taper roller bearings. An oil seal is provided to keep the grease in the bearing and the brake lining free from contamination.
2 Put chocks under the front wheels and jack-up the car and remove the rear wheel. Tap off the hub cap and remove the split pin (photo) and undo the hub nut; remove the thrust washer and pull off the brake drum. The bearings will come with the drum, except for the outer track of the inner race. This may be held by a circlip or may be located by a shoulder on the drum. Remove the bearings and drive the outer race of the inner bearing from the drum using a drift. You will see three spaces are provided for the drift to rest on the race. Prise out the oil seal. Clean out all the old grease.
3 Test the bearings by washing them clean and swilling them out with clean white spirit. Examine the tracks and rollers for wear. Lightly oil them, assemble the races and rollers together and spin them. No roughness or noise should be apparent. If there is then replace them. If they are in good order grease them with M.P. grease and set on one side.
4 If there is any doubt about the stub axle it may be removed and checked at this point. Remove the four bolts holding the brake backplate and stub axle to the axle beam, and wriggle the stub axle out to the back. To check it, have it set in a lathe and measured for run-out. This must not exceed 0.009 inches (0.25 mm) at the outer wheel bearing seat.
5 If all is correct refit the bearings to the drum and shaft, work about 25 grams of grease into the hub. Refit the new oil seal to the drum, put a little grease on the lip of the bearing to ease it into position, fit the drum to the stub axle and the thrust washer and nut.
6 Tighten the nut to 10 lb ft (1.38 kg m), while rotating the wheel to seat all the bearings properly, then slacken off the nut and tighten it again finger tight. Fit the locking ring and a new split pin.
7 Replace the wheel and lower the vehicle to the ground.

Chapter 9 Braking system, wheels and tyres

For modifications, and information applicable to later models, see Supplement at end of manual

Contents

Specifications

Type ... Hydraulic tandem master cylinder, may be servo assisted, operating front disc brakes and rear drum brakes. Dual circuit diagonally connected

Handbrake ... Mechanically operated, equalizer bar operating cable on rear brakes only

Front brakes	**European manual**		**Automatic and USA**	
	mm	in.	mm	in.
Disc measurements thickness:				
New	10	0.4	12	0.47
After machining (minimum)	8.5	0.33	10.5	0.41
Disc maximum run-out allowed	0.1	0.004	0.1	0.004
Disc diameter	239	9.4	239	9.4
Cylinder diameter	44	1.73	44	1.73
Friction pads (thickness new)	10		14	

Rear brakes				
Drum diameter:				
Nominal	180	7.08	200	7.87
After machining (maximum)	181	7.13	201	7.92
Hydraulic cylinder diameter	14.3	0.563	17.46	0.69
Lining width	30	1.2	30	1.2
Lining minimum thickness:				
Riveted linings	5	0.2	5	0.2
Bonded linings	3.5	0.14	3.5	0.14

Master cylinder	**Non-servo**		**Servo**	
	mm	in.	mm	in.
Internal diameter:				
European models	17.46	0.688	19.05	0.768
USA models	—	—	20.64	0.8126
Piston (free-play rod to piston)	1	0.004	1	0.004

Brake fluid specification	SAE J 1703R	
Brake pressure regulators (Sections 26 and 27)		
Pressure sensitive regulators - test pressures:	**Front/left**	**Rear/right**
Psi	498	384
Kg/cm2	35	27
Load sensitive regulators - test pressures:		
1st reading:		
Psi	710	455 - 484
Kg/cm2	50	32 - 34
2nd reading:		
Psi	1422	768 - 796
Kg/cm2	100	54 - 56

Brake bleeding sequence

1	Right Rear
2	Left Rear
3	Right Front
4	Left Front

Wheel size:

European and most USA models	4 ½J x 13H - 2B *
Some USA models	5J x 13 *

** Check with operators handbook issued with the vehicle.*

Tyres **	**Standard**	**Optional**
1300 cc models	Crossply 6.15/155/134PR	Radial 155 S.R.13
1500 cc (75HP) models	Radial 155 S.R.13	Radial 175/70 S.R.13 on wheel 5J x 13
1500 cc (85 HP) models	Radial 165/70/S.R.13	Radial 175/70 S.R.13 on wheel 5J x 13

*** Note: these are correct at the time of publication, but consult the official agent for up-to-date information.*

Tyre pressures	**psi**	**kg/cm2**
Saloon/Sedan:		
Front and rear (light load)	25	1.8
Front and rear (full load)	25	1.8
Estate/Wagon (Variant):		
Front and rear (light load)	25	1.8
Front (heavy load)	25	1.8
Rear (heavy load)	28	2.1

Torque wrench settings	**lb ft**	**kg m**
Caliper to steering knuckle	45	7
Disc to hub	5	0.7
Splash plate to hub	6	0.8
Backplate to stub axle	22	3
Wheel to drums	65	9
Servo to adapter	14	1
Master cylinder to servo	11.5	1.5
Brake hoses to caliper/wheel cylinders	8	1
Brake hoses to master cylinder	8	1

1 General description

1 Disc brakes with floating calipers on the front wheels and drum brakes on the rear wheels. Two sizes of disc and two sizes of drum according to the size of engine and weight of car are fitted.

2 A tandem brake master cylinder, power assisted by a servo mechanism, with diagonally connected hydraulic circuits, provides insurance against brake failure.

3 The handbrake is cable operated with an equalizer bar, operating on the rear wheels only. On some models a self-adjusting rear brake is fitted.

4 Disc brake calipers are supplied by Teves and Girling. They are of different design and although interchangable must be installed in pairs with the correct hoses.

5 Two types of servo are fitted, the technical specification for each is the same and they are interchangable. One is by Teves and the other by Bendix. A service kit is available to fit a servo mechanism on vehicles issued without servo units.

6 Two types of brake pressure regulator to limit the hydraulic pressure to the rear brakes and prevent the wheels locking have been fitted. The first, pressure sensitive consisted of two units, one for each rear wheel mounted on brackets on the servo unit. A later one introduced in June 1974 is a load-sensitive spring operated spring cylinder mounted on the inside of the right rear wheel arch.

7 The diagonal connection means that the right front and left rear wheels are braked by one circuit and the left front and right rear by a second independant circuit. Thus if one system fails there is still braking on both axles.

8 The sequence for bleeding is right rear, left rear, right front and left front. This is elaborated in Section 29.

2 Braking system - inspection and adjustment

1 The braking system is such a tribute to design that most drivers are taken by surprise when it goes wrong. The way to avoid this unpleasant happening is by regular inspection and by understanding the symptoms of ailing brakes.

2 Many vehicles are fitted with self-adjusting rear brakes - which

means that no active maintenance is required. For the few not so fitted a regular inspection of the shoes and adjustment as necessary is imperative. The handbrake will tell you when excessive wear is taking place. This is discussed in the Section on rear brakes.

3 The front discs are self-adjusting but again rear inspection does not entail much hard labour and may save not only a lot of money but also heartache. This operation is explained in the Section on front brakes.

4 The maintenance of pipes and hoses is also gone into at some length.

5 At the conclusion of this Chapter a fault diagnosis chart is included, but this only diagonses trouble when it has happened, the smart operator gets busy before then.

6 The brakes should operate smoothly and consistently. Any variation in performance must be investigated and cured right away.

7 Pulling to one side, or the other, however slight, means that all four brakes must be checked for adjustment forthwith. It only means jacking-up the vehicle and spinning each wheel in turn. Get someone to apply the footbrake gently and it is easy to find which wheel is at fault.

8 Loss of fluid from the header tank is serious. It is going somewhere it shouldn't and it is no use just topping-up and carrying on. Leaks at the front calipers or the various pipes can be spotted by just looking underneath the car. Leaks in the rear wheel cylinders may require removal of the drums before they can be located.

9 If the pedal goes much further down than usual when there are no leaks in the system and the brakes are properly adjusted then the trouble is at the master cylinder. **Do not** wait until it goes right down to the floor, there will not be any braking force at all then.

10 If the brakes drag, get hot, or even lock on then the trouble is probably either maladjustment of the connecting rod, or foreign matter clogging the compensating ports in the master cylinder. It may be as simple as something stopping the foot brake pedal from returning to its stop. It may be a problem in the servo which will not allow the master cylinder pushrod to return fully and so it is closing the compensating ports when they ought to be open.

If only one brake gets hot then that one should be dismantled checked and readjusted. If both rear brakes get hot then the handbrake may be malfunctioning (or you may have left it on of course, this happens to everyone at sometime or other).

Generally speaking slight overheating will not do too much damage, but it will eventually melt grease and cause oil seals to fail. It can crack discs or even drums if left too long.

11 Although the servo gives very little trouble, when it does it can be difficult to track down the problem. If the pedal does not go right down but very high pressure is needed to operate the brake then the servo vacuum has failed. This is discussed in Section 25 and should be tackled right away.

12 Adjustment of rear brakes is discussed in Section 13 and 17, adjustment of the handbrake (parking brake) is Section 34. There is no adjustment for the front brakes.

13 Finally the question of "sponginess" in the pedal. This is nearly always air in the sytem. It can easily be cured by bleeding the brakes as discussed later on, but the worry is how did it get here. If having checked all the unions for leaks (and fluid at 800 lbs per square inch will come out of any leak), and having bled the brake satisfactorily once, the sponginess returns then the next port of call is the official agent. It will be less expensive than the hospital!

3 Front disc brakes - general description

1 Earlier models are fitted with Teves floating caliper. The standard model has disc thickness 0.4 in (10 mm) but automatic transmission and all models for USA have a slightly thicker disc 0.47 in (12 mm). The Teves caliper has a fixed mounting frame bolted to the stub axle and a floating frame held in position on the mounting frame and able to slide on the mounting frame in a direction 90° to the face of the disc. Fixed to the floating frame is a hydraulic cylinder with piston and seals. The friction pads are held in the mounting frame by pins and a spreader spring.

When the brake pedal is pressed the piston is forced against the inner (direct) brake pad pushing it against the disc. The reaction causes the floating frame to move away until the floating frame presses against the outer (indirect) pad, pushing that one against the disc. Further pressure holds the disc between the two pads.

2 Later models may be fitted with Teves or Girling caliper. The Teves are as described above but the Girling work on a slightly different principle. It is commonly known as Girling 'A' type single cylinder caliper. The cylinder is fixed to the stub axle and contains two pistons. The caliper body which carries the pads is free to slide along grooves in the cylinder body. One piston pushes the direct pad against the disc and the other piston pushes the floating caliper so that the indirect pad is forced against the disc.

3 Despite the obvious structural differences the two calipers are interchangable but must be changed as pairs (ie; two Teves or two Girlings but not one of each). The hoses are different. The Girling has a shorter hose with a left-hand thread. It has a groove machined round the hexagon for easy identification. The brake pads are the same for both calipers. When installing new pads a complete kit should be used. The 10 mm disc has 10 mm thick linings, the 12 mm disc has linings 14 mm thick.

4 On some vehicles a warning light is fitted on the fascia (dash) board to indicate when the pads are worn to the limit. This is operated by a break-off element attached to the pad. This is discussed fully in Section 8.

4 Disc pads (Teves caliper) - inspection and renewal

1 Brake pads wear much more quickly than drum brake linings. They should be checked at least every 10,000 miles. The minimum lining thickness is 1/8 in (3 mm). If the pads wear below this thickness then damage to the disc may result. A badly worn pad is shown in the photo and compared with a new one in the next photo. The dealer has a gauge, tool VW/Audi 60-200, with which he can tell whether replacement is required without taking the pads out. If this gauge is not available then they must be removed for measurement.

2 The pads are different. The inner one is flat on both sides, the outer one has a slot cut in its outer face (photo) which engages with a boss on the caliper.

3 To remove the pads, jack-up the front of the car and remove the wheels. Using a suitable drift tap out the pins (photo) securing the disc pads. On some cars there may be a wire securing clip fitted round these pins. This should be pulled off. If there is no clips the pins will have sleeves.

4 Remove the spreader and pull out the inner, direct pad. If you are going to put the pads back then they must be marked so that they go back in the same place. Use a piece of wire with a hook on the end to pull the pad out. Now lever the caliper over so that there is space between the disc and the outer pad, ease the pad away from the caliper onto the disc and lift it out.

5 Clean out the pad holder and check that the rubber dust cover is not damaged. Insert the outer pad and fit it over the projection on the caliper (photo). It will be necessary to push the piston in to insert the inner pad. This will cause the header tank to overflow unless action is taken to prevent it. Either draw some fluid out of the tank with a pipette or slacken the bleeder screw (see photo 4.7a). We prefer the first method but do not suck the fluid out with a syphon. It is posionous. Use a pipette that has been used for brake fluid only, **not** the battery hydrometer.

6 Push the piston in and check that the angle of the edges of the raised face of the piston are at 20° to the face of the caliper (photo). Make a gauge out of cardboard as shown in the photo. If the angle is more or less turn the piston until the angle is correct.

7 Insert the inner pad (photo), fit the spreader and install the pins (photo). Fit a new locking wire if the type of pin requires it.

8 Do not forget to shut the bleed screw if it was opened as soon as the piston has been forced back. We do not like this method because there is a chance of air entering the cylinder and we do not like spare brake fluid about on the caliper while working on the friction pads.

10 Work the footbrake a few times to settle the pistons. Now repeat the job for the other wheel.

11 Replace the roadwheels, lower to the ground and take the car for a test run.

5 Disc pads (Girling) - inspection and replacement

1 In general, the method is the same as for the Teves caliper with the following differences.

2 Lever off the pad spreader spring with a screwdriver, and **pull** out the pins with pliers after removing the screw which locks them in position.

3 Remove and replace the pads as with the Teves caliper. Install the

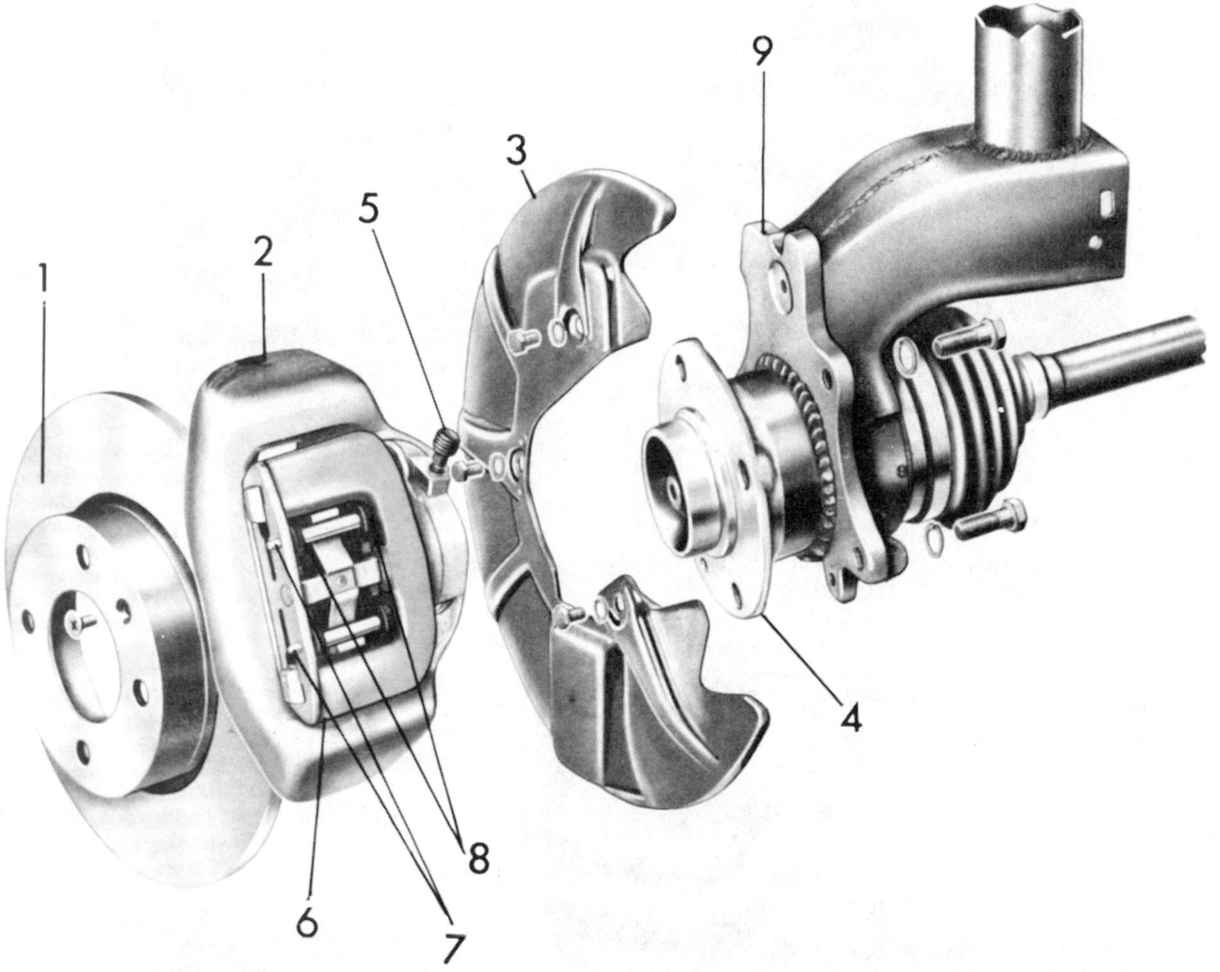

Fig. 9.1 Front brake (Teves) - exploded view

1 *Disc*
2 *Floating caliper*
3 *Splash plate*
4 *Drive flange*
5 *Bleed screw*
6 *Fixed mounting*
7 *Pins*
8 *Brake pads under spreader*
9 *Stub axle*

4.1a This brake pad was worn well below the limit

4.1b Badly worn pad compared with a new one

4.2 The back of the outer pad showing the slot

Fig. 9.2 Floating caliper - Girling

Note the arrow on the spreader. This must point in the direction of the rotation of the disc when the car moves forward.

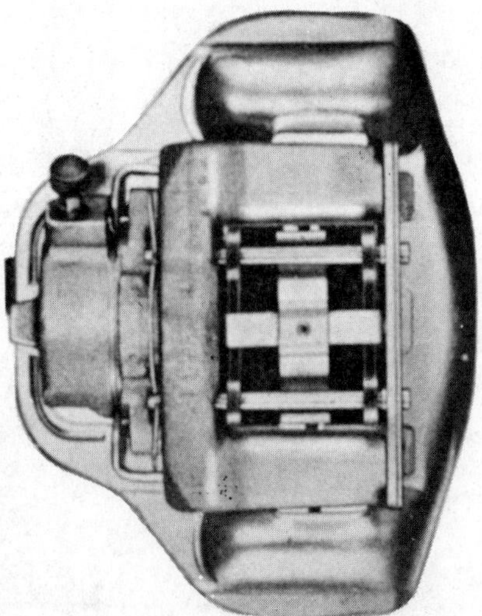

Fig. 9.3 Floating caliper - Teves

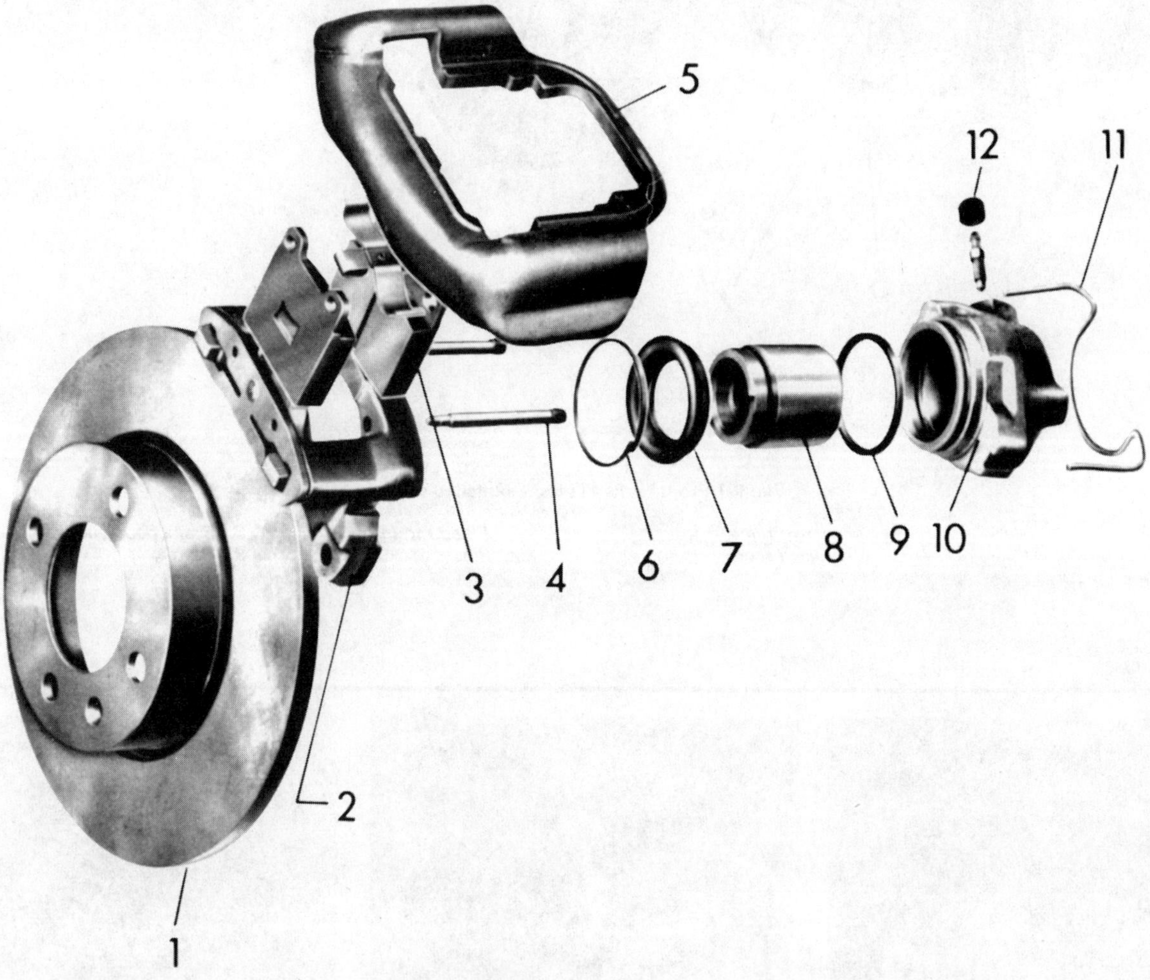

Fig. 9.4 Front disc brake - exploded view showing contents of cylinder

1 Disc
2 Mounting frame
3 Brake pads
4 Pins
5 Floating caliper
6 Retainer ring
7 Dust cap
8 Piston
9 Seal
10 Cylinder
11 Guide spring
12 Bleed nipple

4.3 Tap out the pins and remove the spreader

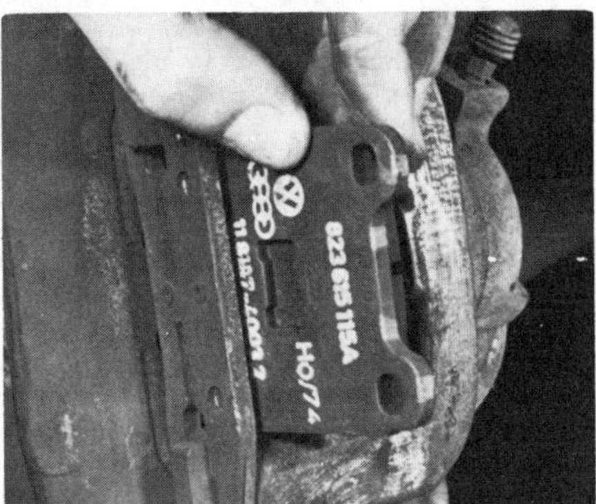
4.5 Install the outer pad

4.6 Check the angle of the piston projections

4.7a Insert the inner pad 'A' is the bleeder screw

4.7b Refit the spreader and pins

6.1 Left-hand front disc showing caliper in place

6.4 Right-hand front disc. Removing the caliper bolts

6.5 Withdrawing the right-hand caliper. This photo and 6.4 were taken whilst removing the subframe. The hydraulics and brake pads are still in place

pins and the locking screw. A repair kit for brake pads will include new pins and retainer so use them.

4 The pad spreader spring is pressed on. The arrow must point in the direction of rotation of the disc when the car is travelling forward.

6 Calipers, pistons and seals (Teves) - removal, inspection and renewal

1 Support the front of the car on stands and remove the wheels (photo).

2 If it is intended to dismantle the caliper then the brake hoses must be removed, plugged and tied out of the way.

3 Mark the position of the brake pads and remove them (Section 4), if the caliper is to be dismantled.

4 Remove the two bolts holding the caliper to the stub axle (photo). This should not be done while the caliper is hot.

5 Withdraw the caliper from the car and take it to a bench.

6 Refer to Fig. 9.4. A repair kit should be purchased for the overhaul of the caliper.

7 Ease the floating frame away from the mounting frame. Now press the brake cylinder and guide spring off the floating frame. The cylinder may now be dismantled.

8 Remove the retaining ring and the rubber boot. The next problem is to remove the piston which is probably stuck in the piston seal. The obvious way is to blow it out using air pressure in the hole which normally accomodates the hydraulic pressure hose. However, be careful. The piston may be stuck in the seal but when it does come out it will come quickly. Fit the cylinder in a vice with a piece of wood arranged to act as a stop for the piston. If you do not, as most people do not, have a ready supply of compressed air use a foot pump. If it will not come out that way then a trip to the local garage is indicated.

9 When the piston is out of the cylinder clean carefully the bore of the cylinder and the piston with brake fluid on methylated spirits.

10 It is difficult to define wear on the piston. When it has been cleaned it should have a mirror finish. Scratches or dull sections indicate wear.

The inside of the bore must be clean with no scratches or distortion. If there is any doubt replace the whole unit. In any case replace the seal and dust excluder. Dip the cylinder in clean brake fluid. Coat the piston and seal with brake cylinder paste (ATE) and press the piston and seal into the cylinder. Use a vice with soft jaws. Install a new dust excluder and its retaining ring. Fit a new locating spring and knock the cylinder onto the floating frame with a brass drift.
11 Refit the floating frame to the mounting frame and set the piston recess at an inclination of 20° to the lower guide surface of the caliper (where the pad rests).
12 Bolt the mounting frame onto the stub axle and install the pads. Refit the wheel and lower to the ground.

7 Caliper, pistons and seals (Girling) - removal, inspection and renewal

1 Refer to Fig. 9.5. The general rules for overhaul are the same as for the Teves but the complication of the extra piston is more work.
2 Remove the cylinder and floating mounting from the stub axle and press them apart. Again use compressed air to dislodge the pistons and be careful that they do not come out suddenly. Clean the pistons and bore carefully. Use a Girling kit of seals and parts. Wash the cylinder and pistons with clean brake fluid and reassemble.

8 Break-off element - description and renewal

1 A simple device consisting of a pair of contacts held on the spreader in such a way that when the pads have worn to a safe limit the break-off elements are broken by the brake pad plates and the light shines on the fascia board.
2 The wires are carefully taped to the brake hose line and connected in to the main cable harness behind the battery.
3 When replacing the worn pads, fit a new break-off element. Trace the wiring and remove the old wiring plugging in at the connector behind the battery.

9 Pad wear indicators - general

As from September 1974 a different type of wear indciator is fitted. The chamfer on the disc has a lug about 1 in (25 mm) long flush with the face of the disc. The brake pads have an extension piece on the bottom. When the pads are worn to the limit the extension on the pad makes contact with the lug on the disc. This causes the pad to vibrate and the piston to oscillate a small amount, thus producing a pulse effect on the brake pedal. Pad replacement is then a matter of urgency. This type of pad **must not** be fitted to earlier models.

10 Front disc brakes - squeaking pads

If the pads squeal or squeak excessively relief from this problem may be obtained by removing and cleaning the pads and holders and then applying a substance known as 'Plastilube'. This substance **must not** be applied to friction surfaces but to the ends, sides and back of the pad. It should also be applied to the pins and spreader and the sliding surfaces of the floating caliper.

11 Discs - checking, removal and replacement

1 Two thicknesses of disc are fitted 10 mm (0.4 in) to vehicles with manual gearboxes and 12 mm (0.47 in) to automatic gearbox models and vehicles bound for the USA.
2 The discs may be removed and machined if scored until the thickness reaches a minimum of 8.5 mm (0.33 in) or 10.5 mm (0.41 in). The maximum run-out allowable is 1 mm (0.004 in). Variation of thickness is 0.02 mm (0.001 in) maximum.
3 Removal is quite simple. Remove the pads and calipers but do not disconnect the hydraulic hose. Hang the calipers out of the way.
4 The disc is held to the hub by one small screw. Remove this and the disc may be drawn off for the hub for servicing.
5 If the vehicle has been left for a while and the discs have rusted seriously they can be salvaged by the agent without removing them from the vehicle. Special polishing blocks can be inserted in place of the pads and the wheels driven to polish the discs.
6 The machining of the disc should be left to a specialist, and if one side is done it is sure that the other side will need doing soon, so why not make a good job of it and have then both done? The new pads will last longer this way.

12 Rear brakes - general description

1 A number of variations are found. Automatic gearbox vehicles and all models bound for the USA have drums of diameter 200 mm (7.87 in). The others have drums of 180 mm (7.08 in).
2 Three types of layout may be found for the vehicles not having self-adjusting brakes, and two for those having self-adjusting rear brakes. All five types are described as although the different makes and types of vehicle within the VW/Audi organization tend to use one type of brake it may be possible to find one of the others fitted. Adjustment is described for each type.
3 All are hydraulically operated, two shoe (leading-trailing) drum brakes with a single hydraulic cylinder containing two pistons. The variations are in the details and methods of adjustment.
4 In each case the handbrake is cable operated with an equalizer bar, the cable pulling a lever which operates the brake mechanism for parking or emergency stops.
5 It is easy to determine which types of adjuster you have if you cannot find the information in the handbook. Look at the back of the brake. If there is a rubber plug just below the bleed nipple where the pipe enters the brake then this is the pushrod adjuster type. By measuring the diameter of the outside of the drum you will determine whether the brake is the 180 mm (7.08 in) type or the 200 mm (7.87 in) type.
6 If there is not a rubber plug then look for two hexagon headed bolts equally spaced just above the horizontal diameter of the drum. If you

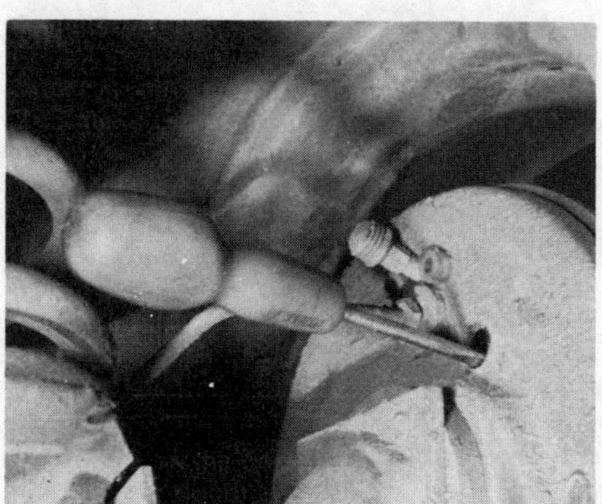

13.2 Using a screwdriver to adjust the rear brake

13.4a Removing the brake drum

13.4b Removing the 'U' spring

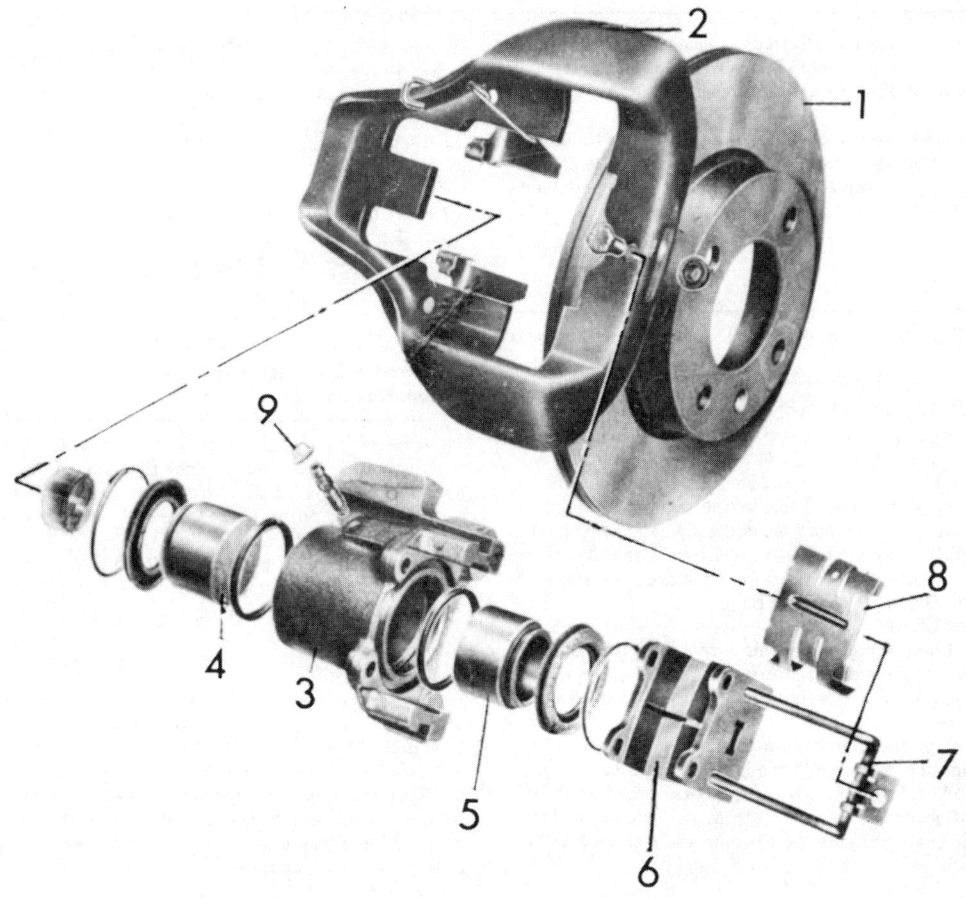

Fig. 9.5 Front disc brake - Girling pattern

1. *Disc*
2. *Floating caliper*
3. *Cylinder (bolted to stub axle)*
4. *Piston pushing caliper*
5. *Piston pushing brake pad*
6. *Brake pads*
7. *Pin*
8. *Spreader*
9. *Bleed screw*

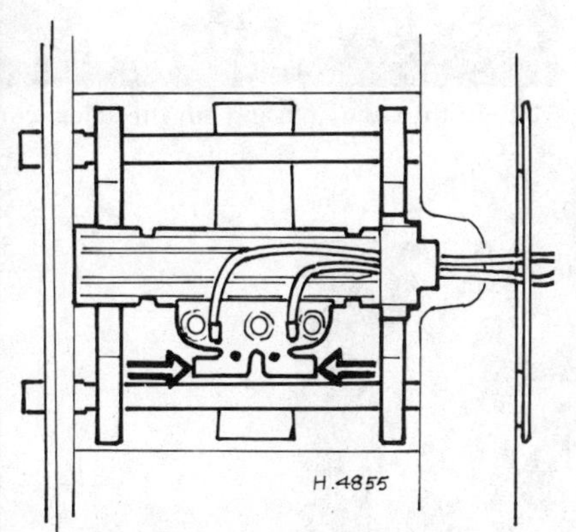

Fig. 9.6 Break-off element (arrows show contacts)

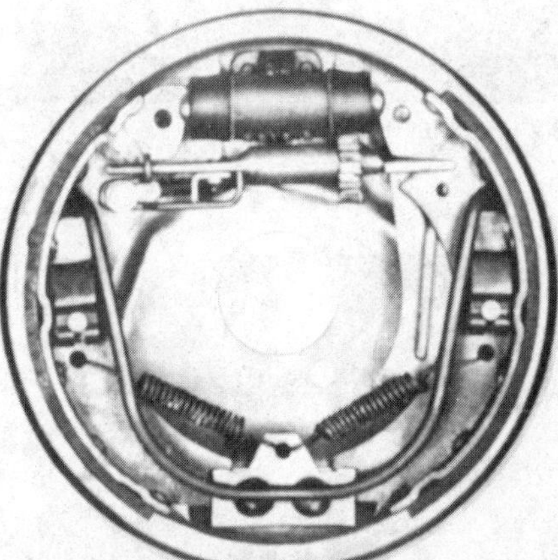

Fig. 9.7 Rear brake (180 mm) - manual pushrod adjustment

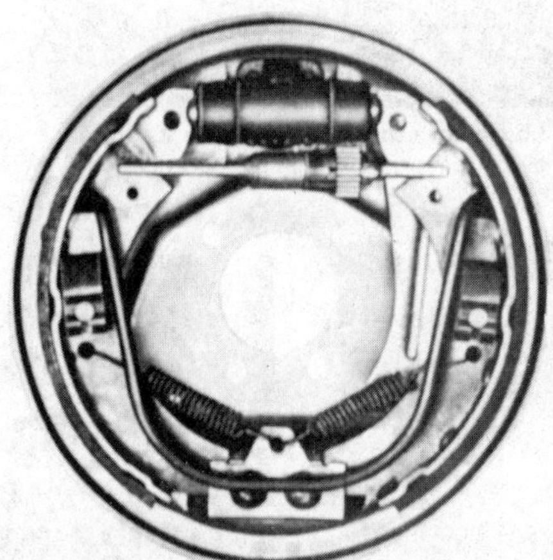

Fig. 9.8 Rear brake (200 mm) - manual pushrod adjustment

can locate these then the system is adjusted by eccentric cams, one for each shoe. On this type of brake there is usually an inspection hole in the backing plate, filled by a rubber plug. Remove this and you can see the linings.

7 The system described in paragraph 6 does not have a self-adjusting version, but the pushrod adjuster type does. Look through the adjuster hole in the backplate. The manual type has uniform shaped teeth. Those for the self-adjuster type are saw-shaped teeth.

13 Drum brake (180 mm/7.08 in diameter) - pushrod adjustment (manual)

1 Refer to Fig. 9.7. This brake is adjusted through a hole in the backplate. Remove the rubber plug and a toothed wheel will be seen inside the plate.

2 Jack-up the rear wheels, chock the front wheels and ensure the handbrake is off. Through the small hole in the left-hand rear brake backplate, using a screwdriver (photo) lever the adjuster wheel teeth downwards (handle of the screwdriver up) until the shoes bind on the drum. Now back-off (work the other way) until the drum rotates without touching the shoes. Replace the rubber plug.

3 Repeat on the other wheel.

4 To dismantle the brake remove the wheel and the hub dust cap. Remove the split pin, lock plate and thrust washer and draw off the drum (photo). Remove the large 'U' type spring (photo). This keeps the shoes against the pistons.

5 Remove the return springs from the bottom of the shoes undo and remove the steady pins. To do this hold the head of the pin at the back and pull off the clip 'A' (photo). The front shoe may now be removed from the pivot and lifted away. The adjuster may be removed and then remove the handbrake cable from the lever behind the rear shoe and lift the shoe away.

6 Inspection of drums and shoes is discussed in Section 18.

7 Assembly is the reverse of removal. Install the handbrake cable on the lever behind the rear shoe, fit it to the pivot and piston and install the spring (photo).

8 Fit the steady pin and put the adjuster in place (photo).

9 Now install the front shoe with spring. Fit the adjuster in place (photo). Install the steady pin.

10 Refit the 'U' spring, slacken off the adjuster until you can install the drum. Refit the drum and adjust the bearing correct (see Chapter 8). Adjust the shoes as in paragraph 2.

14 Drum brake (180 mm/7.08 in diameter) - pushrod adjustment (automatic)

1 Refer to Fig. 9.8. There is an extra lever in the system hinged on the front shoe and held in place by a spring. Each time the brakes are operated the lever presses down on the adjuster turning the threaded portion of the pushrod a very small amount but moving the shoes a fraction towards the drum.

2 When setting the brakes initially this lever must be pressed down so that the adjuster may be moved.

3 In all other respects the brake is as the one described in Section 13.

15 Drum brake (200 mm/7.87 in diameter) - pushrod adjustment (manual)

1 Refer to Fig. 9.9. The principal of operation is the same as the 180 mm diameter brake but the 'U' spring is replaced by two coil springs. The handbrake lever is of different configuration and is on the outside of the brake shoe.

13.5 Remove the clip 'A' and the steady pin may be removed through the backplate

13.7 Installing the rear shoe

13.8 Fit the steady pin and put the adjuster in place

13.9 Refit the front shoe

13.10 Install the 'U' spring

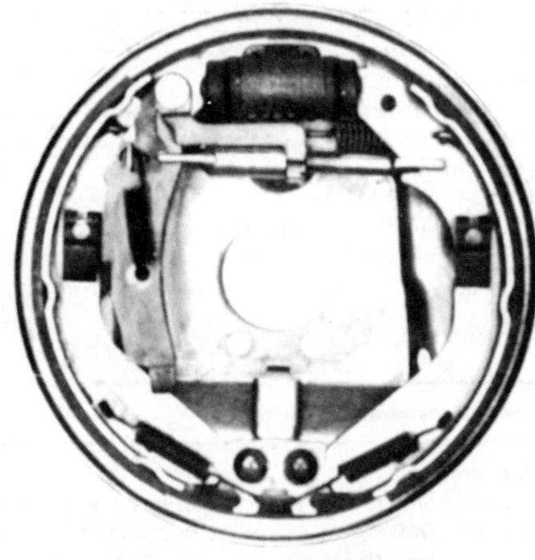

Fig. 9.9 Rear Brake (200 mm) - manual pushrod adjustment

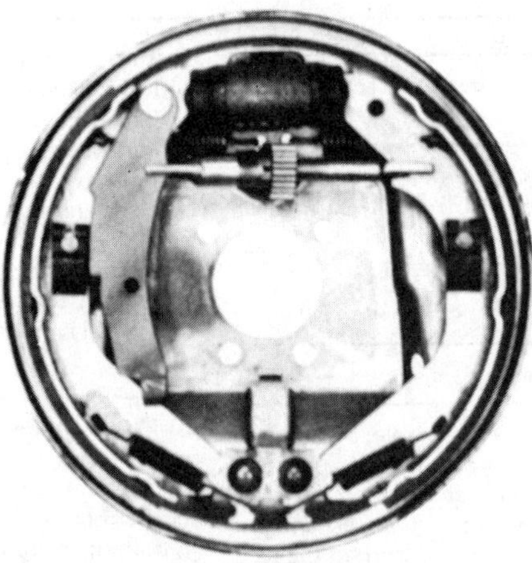

Fig. 9.10 Rear brake (200 mm) - automatic adjustment

Fig. 9.11 Rear brake - eccentric adjustment

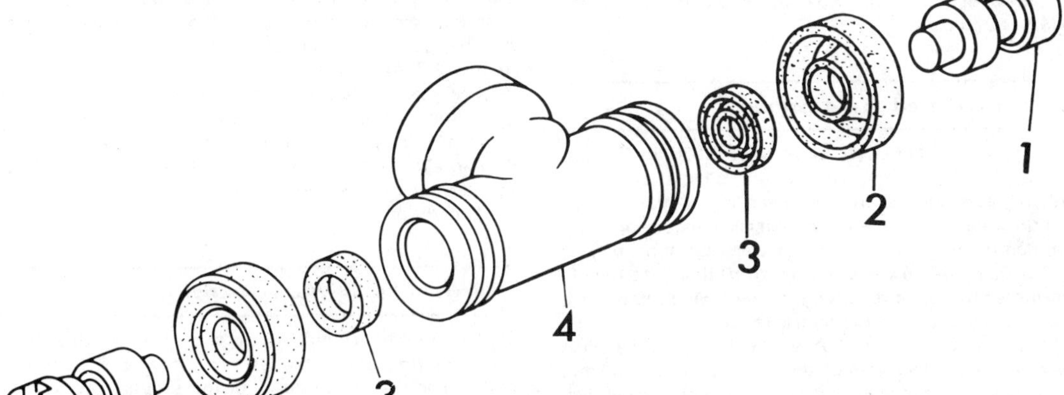

Fig. 9.12 Hydraulic wheel cylinder - exploded view (alternative type)

1 Piston
2 Dust cap
3 Seal
4 Cylinder

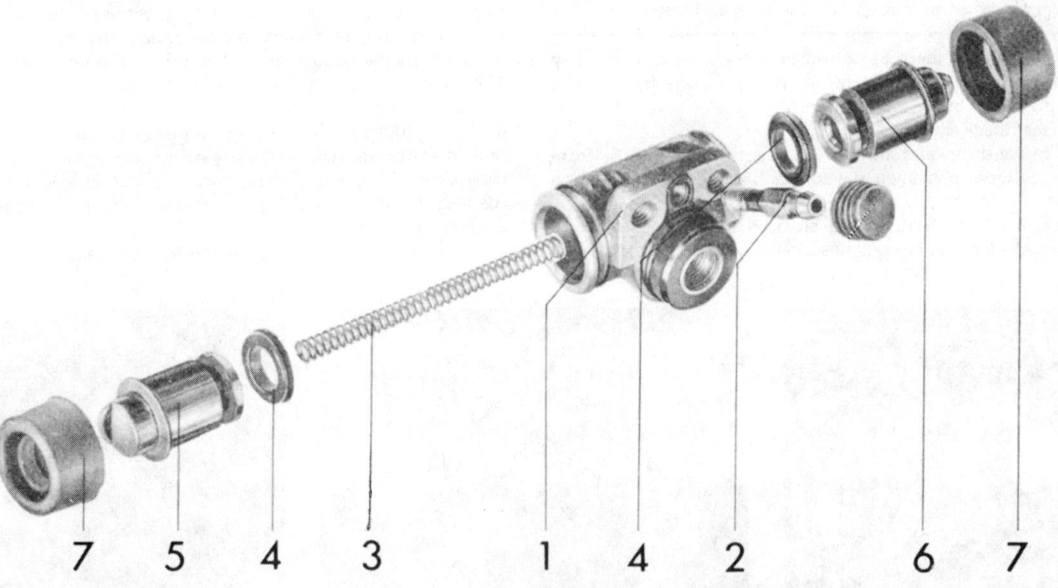

Fig. 9.13 Hydraulic wheel cylinder - exploded view

1 Cylinder
2 Bleed screw
3 Spring
4 Seal
5 Piston
6 Piston
7 Dust cap

16 Drum brake (200 mm/7.87 in diameter) - pushrod adjustment (automatic)

1 Refer to Fig. 9.10. The brake reassembles the one described in paragraph 15, except for the automatic adjuster. This is shown in the illustration.
2 Adjustment initially is as in Section 14, paragraphs 1 and 2.

17 Drum brake (both sizes) - eccentric adjustment

1 Refer to Fig. 9.11. This is basically a very simple, efficient mechanism. The shoes are pivotted at the bottom and forced apart at the top by a hydraulic system. They are held in place by coil springs and located by steady pins. Adjustment is by turning an eccentric located halfway along the shoe. The eccentrics must be turned clockwise to push the shoe to the drum. The shoes must be adjusted independantly.
2 The 180 mm (7.08 in) variety is fitted to 1300 cc and 1500 cc manual gearbox types, the 200 mm (7.87 in) to automatic gearbox vehicles and all USA bound cars.

18 Brake shoes and drums - inspection and overhaul

1 The surface of the brake shoe must be at least 0.020 in (5 mm) above the rivet heads. The linings must be free from oil contamination, have level smooth surfaces, and be free from scoring. If the existing shoes do not fulfil these conditions then new linings are required.
2 The four linings on the rear axle must be renewed simultaneously. It is not recommended that D-I-Y owners attempt to fit linings to the old shoes. It is much better to obtain replacement shoes which have been rivetted on in a jig and planished to a concentric radius.
3 Drums must be smooth and unscored. Any grooving or scoring must be machined away. There are two sizes of drum, the nominal 180 mm (7.08 in) drum must not be machined out to a diameter greater than 181 mm (7.13 in). The 200 mm (7.87 in) drum limit is 201 mm (7.92 in).
4 Inspect the drum for cracks, and ovality. Machining is a job for the specialist.

19 Wheel cylinders (rear drum brakes) - dismantling and overhaul

1 If the wheel (slave) cylinders are seized or show signs of leaks they must be overhauled or replaced. There are two sizes one for the 180 mm (7.08 in) diameter brake, the other for the 200 mm (7.87 in) diameter brake (see Specification).
2 Remove the brake drum and shoes. Disconnect the brake hose from the back of the cylinder and undo the screws holding the cylinder to the backplate.
3 Refer to Figs. 9.12 and 9.13. There are two types of cylinder in use. They are almost identical but one has a central spring and the other does not so be careful when ordering spares. Check your chassis number with the official agent's storeman.
4 To dismantle remove the dust caps and blow the pistons out with compressed air. Examine the bore and pistons for wear or scratches and if anything but a mirror finish is visible then discard the complete cylinder and fit a new unit.
5 If the pistons and bore are in good order wash with brake fluid or methylated spirits, dry and coat with brake paste before re-installing. Always fit seals and dust caps. Be careful when fitting the seals to get them the right way round.

20 Master cylinder and servo - general description

1 The master cylinder and header tank together with the servo mechanism if fitted, stoplight and fail safe light switches are mounted in the engine compartment just in front of the brake pedal (photo). Two types of servo are fitted either Bendix or Teves. They are interchangable.
2 This is a welcome change from other VW/Audi arrangements as the mud and water do not reach this all important item. Furthermore the pushrod operating the master cylinder is short and accessible (photo).
3 The master cylinder for vehicles without servo mechanism is 17.46 mm (0.687 in) diameter. It is illustrated at Fig. 9.14.
4 The master cylinder for vehicles with servo mechanism is either 19.05 mm or 20.64 mm (0.768 or 0.813 in) diameter. It is illustrated in Fig. 9.15. The larger diameter is in use in USA.
5 A brake servo kit, part No. 321 698 486 is available to be installed in place by the non-servo type of master cylinder. This is discussed in Section 25, of this Chapter.

21 Brake hydraulic system - description of operation

1 The master cylinder has two pistons, the front or secondary supplying pressure to the left-hand front wheel and the right-hand rear wheel. The rear, or primary, piston supplies pressure to the right-hand front wheel and the left-hand rear wheel. Inspection of the unit will show four pipes leading from the main casting to the hydraulic wheel cylinders.
2 Brake fluid is supplied from the header tank, the white plastic container which feeds both circuits through the master cylinder.
3 When the brake pedal is pressed the pushrod moves the primary piston forward so that it covers the port to the header tank. Further movement causes pressure to build up between the two pistons exerting pressure on the secondary piston which also moves forward covering the port to the header tank. The pressure now builds up in the pipes. The pipes are joined to the cylinder via unions containing residual pressure valves.
4 If the pipes of the secondary piston circuit fracture or the system fails in some way the secondary piston will move forward to the end of the piston compressing the conical spring and sealing the outlet port to the left front and right rear brakes. The primary piston circuit will continue to operate.
5 Failure of the primary piston circuit causes the piston to move

20.1 The header tank, master cylinder and servo unit

20.2 The brake pedal. 'A' is the adjusting nut for the master cylinder

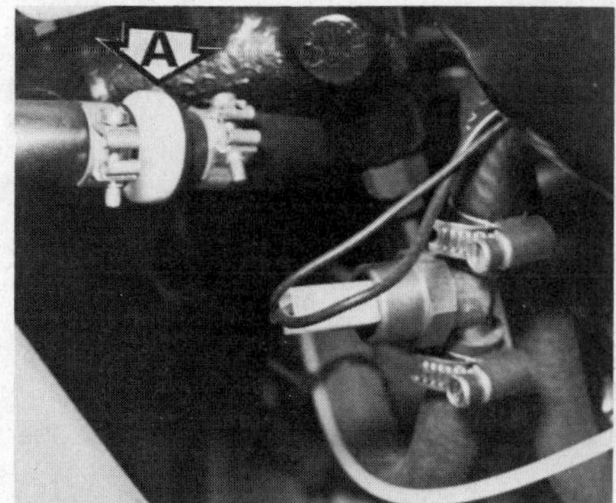

25.3 The non-return valve in the servo line 'A'

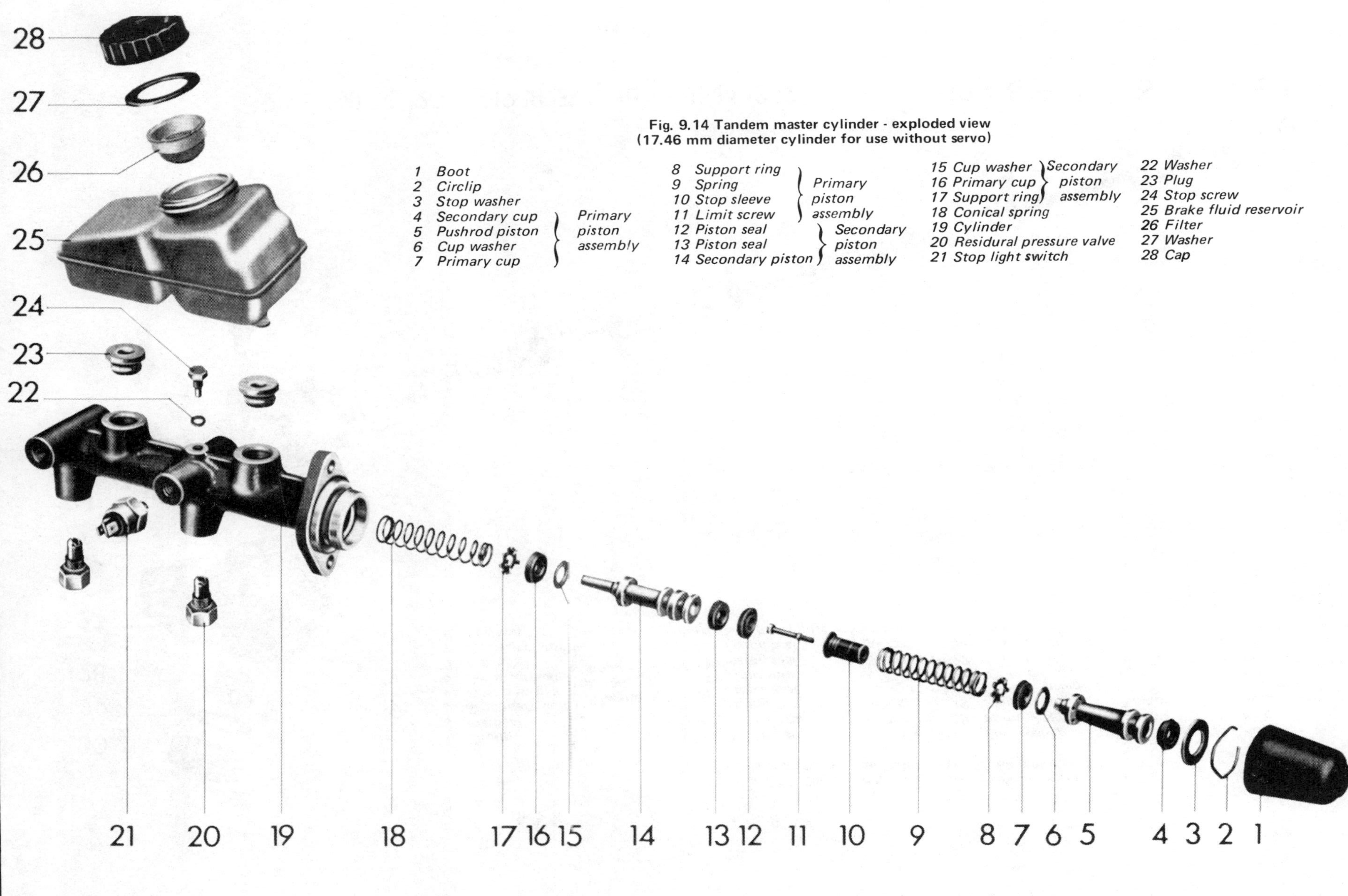

Fig. 9.14 Tandem master cylinder - exploded view (17.46 mm diameter cylinder for use without servo)

1 Boot
2 Circlip
3 Stop washer
4 Secondary cup } *Primary piston assembly*
5 Pushrod piston } *Primary piston assembly*
6 Cup washer } *Primary piston assembly*
7 Primary cup } *Primary piston assembly*
8 Support ring } *Primary piston assembly*
9 Spring } *Primary piston assembly*
10 Stop sleeve } *Primary piston assembly*
11 Limit screw } *Primary piston assembly*
12 Piston seal } *Secondary piston assembly*
13 Piston seal } *Secondary piston assembly*
14 Secondary piston } *Secondary piston assembly*
15 Cup washer } *Secondary piston assembly*
16 Primary cup } *Secondary piston assembly*
17 Support ring } *Secondary piston assembly*
18 Conical spring
19 Cylinder
20 Residural pressure valve
21 Stop light switch
22 Washer
23 Plug
24 Stop screw
25 Brake fluid reservoir
26 Filter
27 Washer
28 Cap

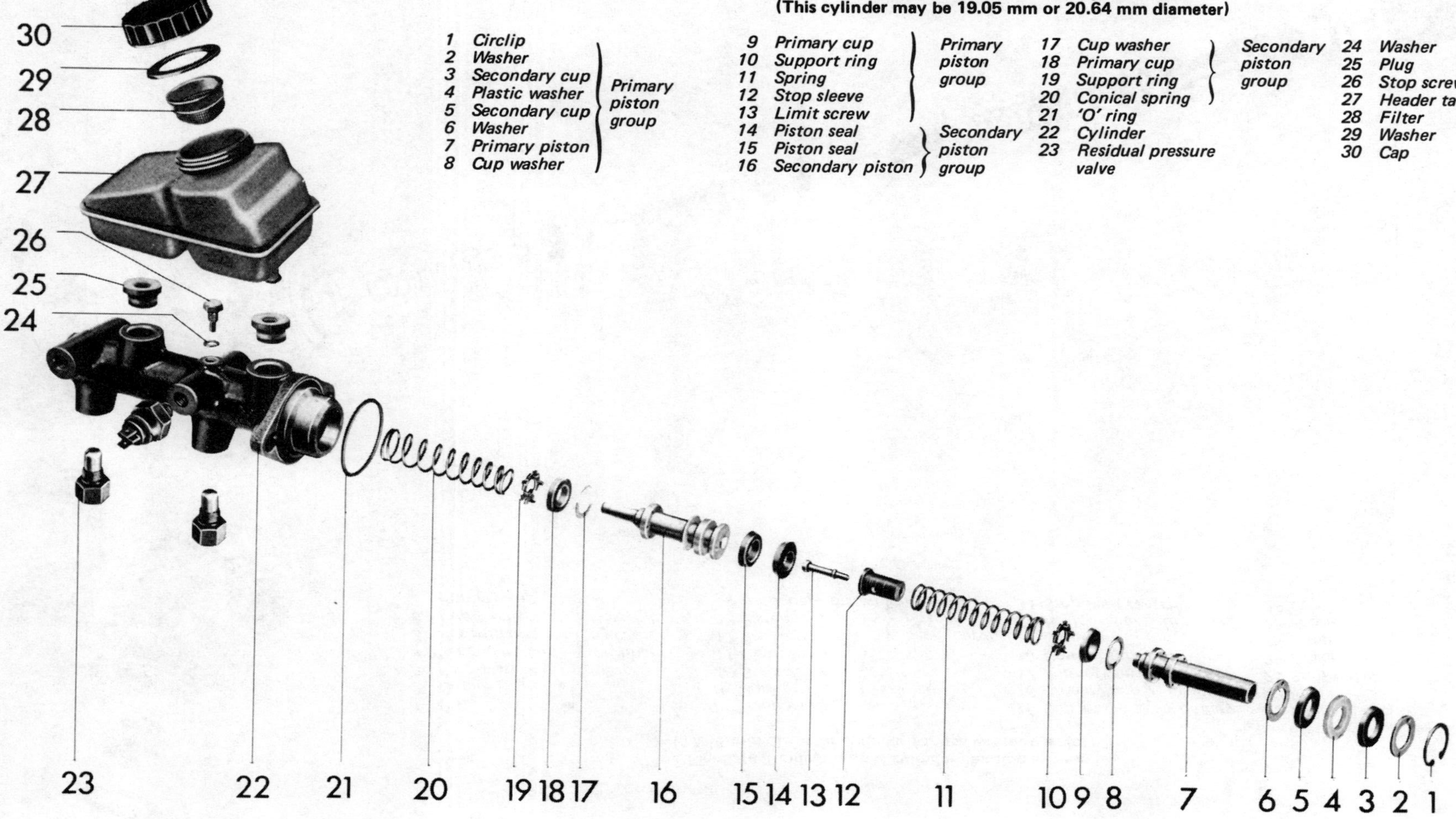

Fig. 9.15 Tandem master cylinder - exploded view
(This cylinder may be 19.05 mm or 20.64 mm diameter)

1 Circlip
2 Washer
3 Secondary cup
4 Plastic washer
5 Secondary cup
6 Washer
7 Primary piston
8 Cup washer
(1–8: Primary piston group)
9 Primary cup
10 Support ring
11 Spring
12 Stop sleeve
13 Limit screw
(9–13: Primary piston group)
14 Piston seal
15 Piston seal
16 Secondary piston
(14–16: Secondary piston group)
17 Cup washer
18 Primary cup
19 Support ring
20 Conical spring
(17–20: Secondary piston group)
21 'O' ring
22 Cylinder
23 Residual pressure valve
24 Washer
25 Plug
26 Stop screw
27 Header tank
28 Filter
29 Washer
30 Cap

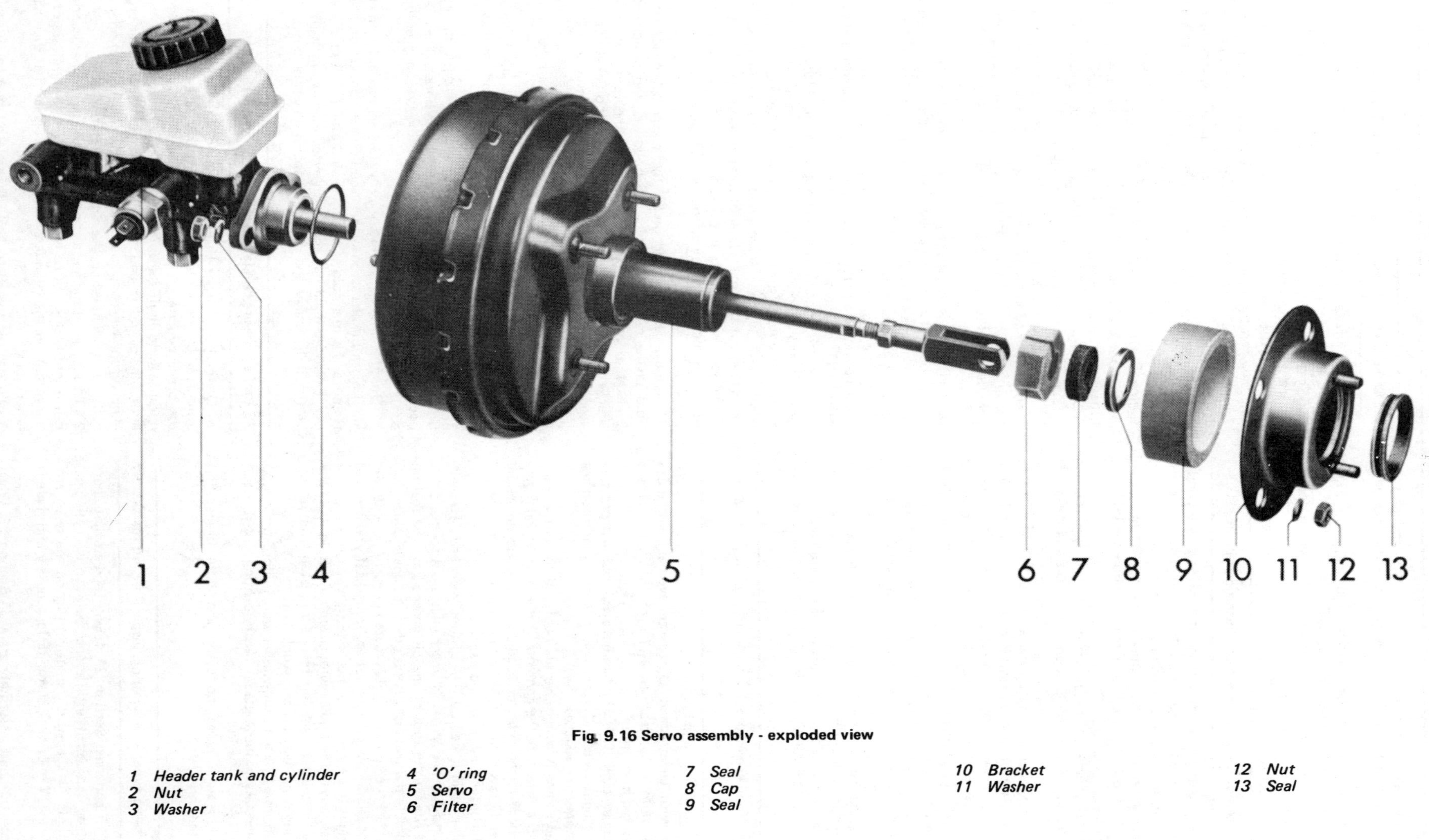

Fig. 9.16 Servo assembly - exploded view

1 Header tank and cylinder
2 Nut
3 Washer
4 'O' ring
5 Servo
6 Filter
7 Seal
8 Cap
9 Seal
10 Bracket
11 Washer
12 Nut
13 Seal

forward until the stop sleeve contacts the secondary piston and the primary piston simultaneously when pressure will again be applied to the secondary piston circuit.
6 The various springs and seals are designed to keep the pistons in the right place when the sytem is not under pressure.
7 Pressure switches, are screwed into the cylinder body which operate the brake stoplights and warning lamps.

22 Master cylinder - removal, replacement and pushrod adjustment

1 Depending upon whether a servo unit is fitted or not the cylinder may be removed, after disconnecting the pipes and switches - marking them for easy replacement, either by undoing the nuts from the bolts connecting it to the servo unit, or by removing the cover from under the fascia board and unbolting the cylinder from the bulkhead bracket from inside the car.
2 When replacing the cylinder, if to the servo unit, fit a new 'O' ring and bolt the cylinder to the servo unit. Connect up pipes and wires and bleed the system.
3 If no servo is fitted, then it may be necessary to adjust the free travel of the pushrod after bolting the unit in place and connecting up. The brake pedal is attached to the pushrod by a yoke which has a locking nut. Slacken off the locking nut and rotate the pushrod until a clearance (free travel) of approximately ¼ in (4 to 7 mm) can be measured at the foot pedal pad.
4 If, for some reason, both servo and master cylinder have been removed the adjustment of the pushrod is a little different. Install the servo unit and the master cylinder. Remove the pin that secures the yoke to the brake pedal, slacken the locknut and with the pedal in the normal off position turn the pushrod until the yoke pin can be fitted between the yoke and pedal without moving the pedal. Replace the pin and tighten the locknut. The allowance is automatic in the servo unit.

23 Master cylinder (non-servo type) - dismantling, inspection and reassembly

1 Clean the outside of the cylinder carefully and set it on a clean bench. Work only with clean hands. Obtain an overhaul kit and a quantity of brake fluid in a clear jar. Refer to Fig. 9.14 for the cylinder without a servo mechanism.
2 Remove the header tank. Undo and remove the residual pressure valves and the brake light switch. On cars with a warning lamp on the fascia there are two pressure switches.
3 Remove the stop screw. Now remove the boot and the circlip may be levered out. With a little luck the contents of the cylinder will come sliding out of the bore if the cylinder is tilted. If they do not apply gentle air pressure and blow them out. Take them out one at a time and lay then down in the order they should go back.
4 The front spring is slightly conical. The pistons may need new seals. These are not easy to fit. The VW/Audi mechanics use a special taper mandrel which just fits on the ends of the piston and ease the seal on over the taper. Assemble the two pistons with their groups of parts.
5 Examine the bare of the cylinder. If it is scored or rusty the cylinder must be renewed. It is possible to hone out slight marks if you can find someone with the right tools, but our advice is to fit a new one.
6 Wash out all passageways and holes with clean brake fluid, hold the cylinder vertical and install the complete secondary piston from underneath. If you do it any other way the bits will fall off.
7 Now install the primary piston, stop washer and circlip. Fit the stop screw. It may be necessary to move the secondary piston to fit the stop screw fully.
8 Fit the residual pressure valves, boot and install the brake fluid reservoirs. Refit to the car.

24 Master cylinder (servo type) - dismantling, inspection and reassembly

1 Refer to Fig. 9.15 and read Section 23. It will be seen that apart from the bore diameter there is little difference between the cylinders. The end of the cylinder is shaped differently to fit on the servo and there is an extra 'O' ring. The primary piston differs slightly and there is no rubber boot.
2 Dismantling, inspection and reassembly are as in Section 23. When the unit is complete it is installed onto the servo unit.

25 Servo unit - testing, repair, removal and replacement

1 If the brakes seem to need more or less pressure than normal a check of the servo is indicated.
2 First of all trace the hoses and check their condition. There must be no leaks or obstructions.
3 Check the vacuum check valve. This is to be found in the vacuum line between the induction manifold and the servo (photo). Remove it from the hose line and clean it carefully. There is an arrow on the valve. Blow into the valve in the direction of the arrow, the valve should open. Blow in the opposite direction and the valve must seat. The valve is there to stop pressure from the manifold eg; a backfire, arriving in the vacuum side of the servo, ie; it is a non-return valve, so that the induction suction can only suck, and not blow.
4 If all of the above are correct and the servo is still not assisting the brakes the trouble is either a leaky servo diaphragm or something wrong with the master cylinder. Check that the sealing ring between the master cylinder and the servo is not leaking.
5 If the pedal pressure increases only at a certain position each time then there may be wear in the master cylinder pushrod allowing air to get into the vacuum side of the servo. This will only be on elderly brake cylinders, and it is time the master cylinder was overhauled.
6 The repairs possible to the servo are very limited. Refer to Fig. 9.16. The 'O' ring between the servo and the master cylinder should always be replaced with a new one when the units are separated. At the rear end of the servo the seals for the brackets should be renewed when the units are dismantled.

The cap damping washer may be removed from the sleeve and renewed, note that the slots in the damping washer and filter should be offset 180° on reassembly.

Apart from this the unit cannot be serviced further as it is sealed. Be careful when assembling the servo to the bracket not to tighten the nuts to torque greater than 11 lb ft (1.5 kg m) or damage to the case may occur. Two types of servo are fitted Teves or Bendix, they are interchangable but the spares are not interchangable (see illustration).
7 To remove the servo unit first disconnect the hoses, then remove the master cylinder - do not disconnect the pipes but move the cylinder to one side.
8 Remove the covering under the fascia board to get at the nuts holding the servo bracket to the bulkhead and remove the servo and bracket. It may be possible to remove the four nuts from the servo/bracket studs and remove the servo from the bracket but there is always a possibility of pushrod adjustment on reassembly so why do a difficult job without reason.
9 If the vehicle does not have a servo unit it is possible to purchase a kit (part No. 321 698 486) to install a servo.
10 This includes a new master cylinder and all the parts required.
11 Remove the old cylinder and straighten the ends of the existing brake lines carefully, avoiding kinks or wrinkles.
12 Install the servo and new cylinder and attach the extensions of brake pipe to the brake pipe and master cylinder. These are necessary because the postion of the cylinder has moved some six inches forward to fit in the servo and bracket.
13 On the intake manifold provision is made for a tapping. An aluminium pin is cast into the vacuum hose connection blanking it off. Remove the manifold (Chapter 2) and either drill or hammer out this pin. Refit the manifold and fit the vacuum hose with the check valve.
14 Bleed the brakes and check the operation of the servo.

26 Brake pressure regulators (pressure sensitive) - general

1 On earlier vehicles fitted with servo units these pressure sensitive units may be found mounted on the lower face of the servo unit below the brake cylinder. There is one in each rear wheel brake line and its purpose is to limit the pressure that may be applied to the rear brake hydraulic cylinders and so achieve maximum braking effort without allowing the wheel to lock and cause a skid. The cylinder on the right controls the right rear brake. Fig. 9.18 refers.
2 To rest get someone to press the brake pedal hard and then release it. A slight knock will be felt in both cylinders on release of the pedal as the pistons in the cylinders reseat. If this is not felt then a pressure test is necessary.
3 To do this two 0 to 1400 lbs per square inch (0 to 100 kg/cm^2) gauges are required to be connected to the bleed nipples of the right

Fig. 9.17 Servo assembly - alternative types

A Bendix *B Teves*
These are interchangable

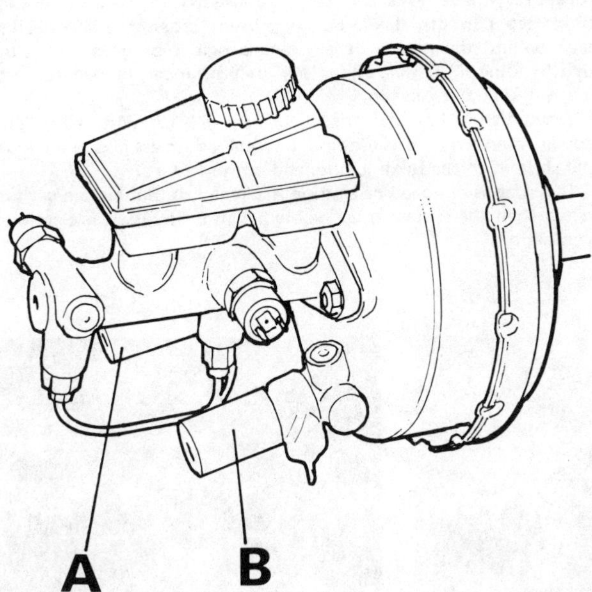

Fig. 9.18 Brake pressure regulator - pressure sensitive

A Regulator for right rear wheel
B Regulator for left rear wheel

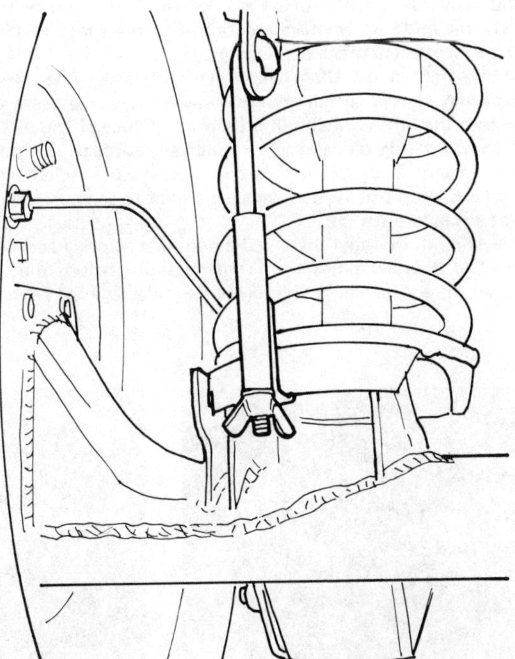

Fig. 9.19 Tool VW/Audi 552 used to set the axle in the correct relation to the body, before testing the pressure sensitive regulator

rear brake and the left front caliper. The necessary tube and adapters will be required. Both gauges should be bled through after connection.
4 The system should be pumped up until the gauge attached to the caliper reads 498 lb/sq in (35 kg/cm^2). At this point the gauge attached to the rear brake should read 384 lb/sq in (27 kg/cm^2).
5 Repair is by replacement only. We strongly urge that if you do this job yourself it be tested by the agent on completion.

27 Brake pressure regulators (load sensitive) - general

1 On some of the later USA models instead of the two pressure sensitive regulators one load sensitive regulator is fitted (photo).
2 Testing is by measuring pressures as in Section 26 but this time the front and rear pressures must be measured twice. Furthermore, the suspension spring must be compressed with a special tool (VW 552) to determine the relative positions of the regulator on the body and the spring anchor on the axle (see Fig. 9.19).
3 The pressures to be measured are:

Left front caliper — 710 psi (50 kg/cm^2) and
1422 psi (100 kg/cm^2)
Right rear brake — 455 - 484 psi (32 - 34 kg/cm^2) and
768 - 796 psi (54 - 56 kg/cm^2)

Adjustment is by altering the spring tension, reading too high - reduce spring tension and vice-versa.
4 Again we recommend that this adjustment be checked by the official agent.

28 Hyraulic pipes and hoses - inspection and renewal

1 The magnitude of the pressure in the hydraulic lines is not generally realized. The test pressures are 1420 lbs per square inch (100 kg sq cm) for the front brakes.

These pressures are with the braking system cold. The temperature rise in the drums and discs for an emergency stop from 60 mph is as much as 80°C (176°F), and during a long descent may reach 400°C (752°F). The pressure must be even further raised as the temperature of the brake fluid in the cylinder rises.

The normal pressure in the hydraulic sytem when the brakes are not in use is negligible. The pressure builds up quickly when the brakes are applied and remains until the pedal is released. Each drive will know how quickly the build up is when equating it to the speed of his own reaction in an emergency brake application.
2 Recent research in the USA has shown that brake line corrosion may be expected to lead to failure after only 90 days exposure to salt spray such as is thrown up when salt is used to melt ice or snow. This in effect makes a four year old vehicle automatically suspect. It is possible to use pipe made of a copper alloy used in marine work called 'Kunifer 10' as a replacement. This is much more resistant to salt corrosion, but as yet is not a standard fitting.
3 All this should by now have indicated that pipes need regular inspection. The obvious times are in the autumn before the winter conditions set in, and in the spring to see what damage has been done.
4 Trace the routes of all the rigid pipes and wash or brush away accumulated dirt. If the pipes are obviously covered with some sort of underseal compound do not disturb it. Examine for signs of kinks or dents which could have been caused by flying stones. Any instances of this means that the pipe section should be renewed. **but before actually taking it out read the rest of this Section.** Any unprotected sections of pipe which show signs of corrosion or pitting on the outer surface must also be considered for renewal.
5 Flexible hoses, running to each of the front wheels and from the underbody to each rear wheel should show no external signs of chafing or cracking. Move them about to see whether surface cracks appear. If they feel stiff and inflexible or are twisted they are nearing the end of their useful life. If in any doubt renew the hoses. Make sure also that they are not rubbing against the bodywork.
6 Before attempting to remove a pipe for renewal it is important to be sure that you have a replacement source of supply within reach if you do not wish to be kept off the road for too long. Pipes are often damaged on removal. If an official agency is near you may be reasonably sure that the correct pipes and unions are available. If not, check first that your local garage has the necessary equipment for making up the pipes and has the correct metric thread pipe unions available. The same goes for flexible hoses.
7 Where the couplings from rigid to flexible pipes are made there are support brackets and the flexible pipe is held in place by a 'U' clip which engages in a groove in the union. The male union screws into it. Before getting the spanners on, soak the unions in penetrating fluid as there is always some rust or corrosion binding the threads. Whilst this is soaking in, place a piece of plastic film under the fluid reservoir cap to minimise loss of fluid from the disconnected pipes. Hold the hexagon on the flexible pipe coupling whilst the union on the rigid pipe is undone. Then pull out the clip to release both pipes from the bracket. For flexible hose removal this procedure will be needed at both ends. For a rigid pipe the other end will only involve unscrewing the union from a cylinder or connector. When you are renewing a flexible hose, take care not to damage the unions of the pipes that connect into it. If a union is particularly stubborn be prepared to renew the rigid pipe as well. This is quite often the case if you are forced to use open ended spanners. It may be worth spending a little money on a special pipe union spanner which is like a ring spanner with a piece cut out to enable it to go round the tube.
8 If you are having the new pipe made up, take the old one along to check that the unions and pipe flaring at the ends are identical.
9 Replacement of the hoses or pipes is a reversal of the removal procedure. Precautions and care are needed to make sure that the unions are correctly lined up to prevent cross threading. This may mean behind the pipe a little where a rigid pipe goes into a fixture. Such bending must not, under any circumstances, be too acute or the pipe will kink and weaken.
10 When fitting flexible hoses take care not to twist them. This can happen when the unions are finally tightened unless a spanner is used to hold the end of the flexible hose and prevent twisting.
11 If a pipe is removed or a union slackened so that air can get into the system then the system must be bled. This is discussed in Section 29 of this Chapter.

27.1 The load sensitive regulator. Adjustment is by moving the spring anchor 'A'

29.1a The bleed nipple on the rear drum 'A'

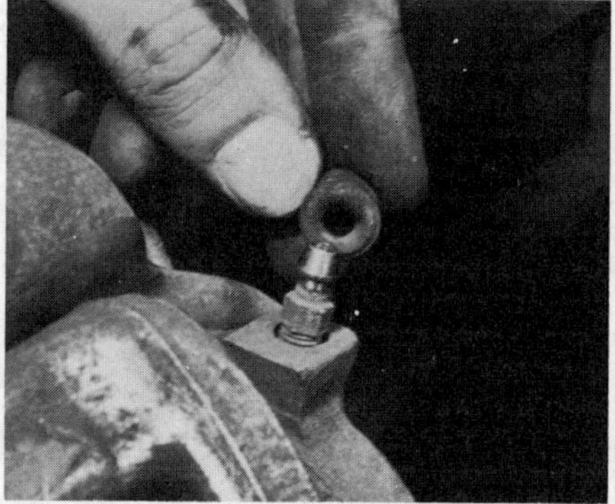

29.1b The bleed nipple, cap removed, on the caliper

29 Brake hydraulic system - bleeding

1 First locate the bleed nipples on all four brakes. The rear wheel bleed nipples are at the back of the drum at the centre of the hydraulic cylinder (photo). A small dust cap covers the nipple. This will probably be covered with mud. Clean the mud from the back of the drum, wipe the dust cap and the area around it with a clean rag and the operation may start.

The front disc brake bleed nipples are on the inside surface of the caliper (photo).

When all four wheels have been cleaned sufficiently sweep up the mud and then wash your hands, this is a job where cleanliness pays.

2 As fluid is to be pumped out of the system make sure you have plenty of new clean fluid. It must conform to SAE recommendation J1703, J1703R but better still, get the official VW fluid. If the wrong fluid is used the whole system may become useless through failure of piston seals. Top-up the header tank generously, and keep topping it up at intervals throughout the whole job.

3 Start with the rear right-hand wheel. A piece of rubber or plastic hose 5/32 in. (4 mm) inside diameter and about two feet (600 mm) long is required. Fit this over the bleed nipple and immerse the other end in a jar or bottle with about 4 inches of clean brake fluid in it. Fix the hose so that the end of it cannot come out of the brake fluid, and stand the bottle on the ground in a secure place.

4 You will need a helper whose job is to depress the brake pedal when requested. It is as well to rehearse the operation before opening the bleed nipple valve. Open the valve about one turn and depress the pedal slowly to the floor of the vehicle. As soon as it is on the floor close the bleed valve **before** the pedal is released. Now release the pedal slowly. Brake fluid and air bubbles should have passed down the tube into the bottle. Repeat the operation until no further air bubbles are observed. Make the final tightening at the end of the last down-stroke. Check the header tank level after every two strokes and top-up if necessary.

5 When you are satisified that the rear right-hand brake line is clear of air bubbles then wipe down the brake caliper and proceed to the next task; in order left rear, right front caliper, left front caliper.

6 After each session clean down the brakes with care and wash your hands. Brake fluid is poisonous and it is a splendid paint remover. Use a soapy solution and wash any paintwork that has been splashed.

7 Finally, the brake fluid in the jar or bottle should be discarded. This is not too easy. I bury mine three spits deep - bubbles and all.

30 Brake fluid - changing

1 The brake fluid is hygroscopic, which means that allowed to come into contact with the open air it will absorb moisture. If it does then when the brakes get hot the water will boil and the brakes will not work properly - at the moment they are needed most.

2 VW/Audi recommend that the fluid should be changed every two years - they give a variety of reasons - but the fact that they do recommend it should be reason enough.

3 The change over is simple to do. First of all clean the rear drums, particularly by the bleed nipples, and give the front calipers the same treatment.

4 Connect all four bleed nipples to plastic pipe and suitable containers, then open all four bleed nipples and get a helper to pump the brake pedal until no further fluid comes out.

5 Close the nipples, fill the system with clean brake fluid and then bleed the system as in Section 29.

31 Tyres - selection, inspection and maintenance

1 These can be an expensive problem if neglected. The most important matter is to keep them inflated at the correct pressure. A table of pressures is given at the start of the Chapter.

If the vehicle is driven over rough ground, or over glass in the road the tread should be inspected to see whether stones or glass fragments are lodged in the tread. These should be removed forthwith.

2 A careful study of the tread once a week will pay dividends. Tyre should wear evenly right across the tread but they rarely do, they are usually replaced because of misuse. A table is given showing some of the main troubles. Study it and watch your tyre treads.

Wear description	Probable cause
Rapid wear of the centre of the tread all round the circumference	*Tyre overinflated.*
Rapid wear at both edges of the tread, wear even all round the circumference	*Tyre underinflated.*
Wear on one edge of the tyre	
(a) Front wheels only	*Steering geometry needs checking.*
(b) Rear wheels only	*Check rear suspension for damage.*
Scalloped edges, wear at the edge at regular spacing around the tyre	*Maybe wheel out of balance, or more likely wear on the steering knuckle.*
Flat or rough patches on the tread	*Caused by harsh braking. Check the brake adjustment.*
Cuts and abrasions on the wall of the tyre	*Usually done by running into the kerb.*

3 If the tyre wall is damaged the tyre should be removed from the wheel to see whether the inside of the cover is also damaged. If not the dealer may be able to repair the damage.

4 Tyres are best renewed in pairs, putting the new ones on the front and the older ones on the rear. Do not carry a badly worn spare tyre, and remember to keep the spare properly inflated.

5 The much debated question of radials against crossply seems to have been solved for these vehicles. The 1300 cc engined vehicles are fitted with crossply tyres as standard, with radials as an optional extra; the 1500 cc engined vehicles are fitted with radials as standard. Much thought goes into these recommendations and we suggest that for 1500 cc vehicles the radial be kept.

6 **There are two golden rules to observe about tyres:**

a) Never have a crossply and a radial tyres on the same axle.

b) If there are two radials and two crossplys, the radials must be on the rear axle.

7 Crossplys are slightly cheaper and give a smoother ride at lower speeds but radials seem to last longer, stand up to hard driving and provide superior roadholding.

32 Wheels - description and balancing

1 Tyres and wheels should be balanced dynamically when even a new tyre is fitted. Mark the position of the balance weights and note the size of them. They have been known to fly off. This will affect the steering in the case of the front wheel.

2 If you suspect a wheel is out of balance, jack-up that wheel and spin it gently. Mark the bottom position when it comes to rest. Spin it several times more and note the bottom position each time. If the wheel comes to rest in the same position each time then the wheel and tyre are definitely out of balance and should be taken for balancing. It is best to do this test with the wheel on the rear axle where it may spin more freely.

3 Even though the wheel may be balanced statically (as in paragraph 2) it may still be out of balance dynamically. The only way to check for certain is to have it tested by a specialist.

33 Wheels - inspection

1 The standard wheel fitted is 4½J x 13-2B with an offset of 1.77 in (45 mm). A few models have 5J x 13 wheels.

2 There are two simple checks to do on the wheel.

(a) Jack the wheel off the ground and spin the wheel. Place a heavy weight so that it almost touches the rim and watch the clearance between the weight and rim as the wheel spins to see that the rim is not distorted.

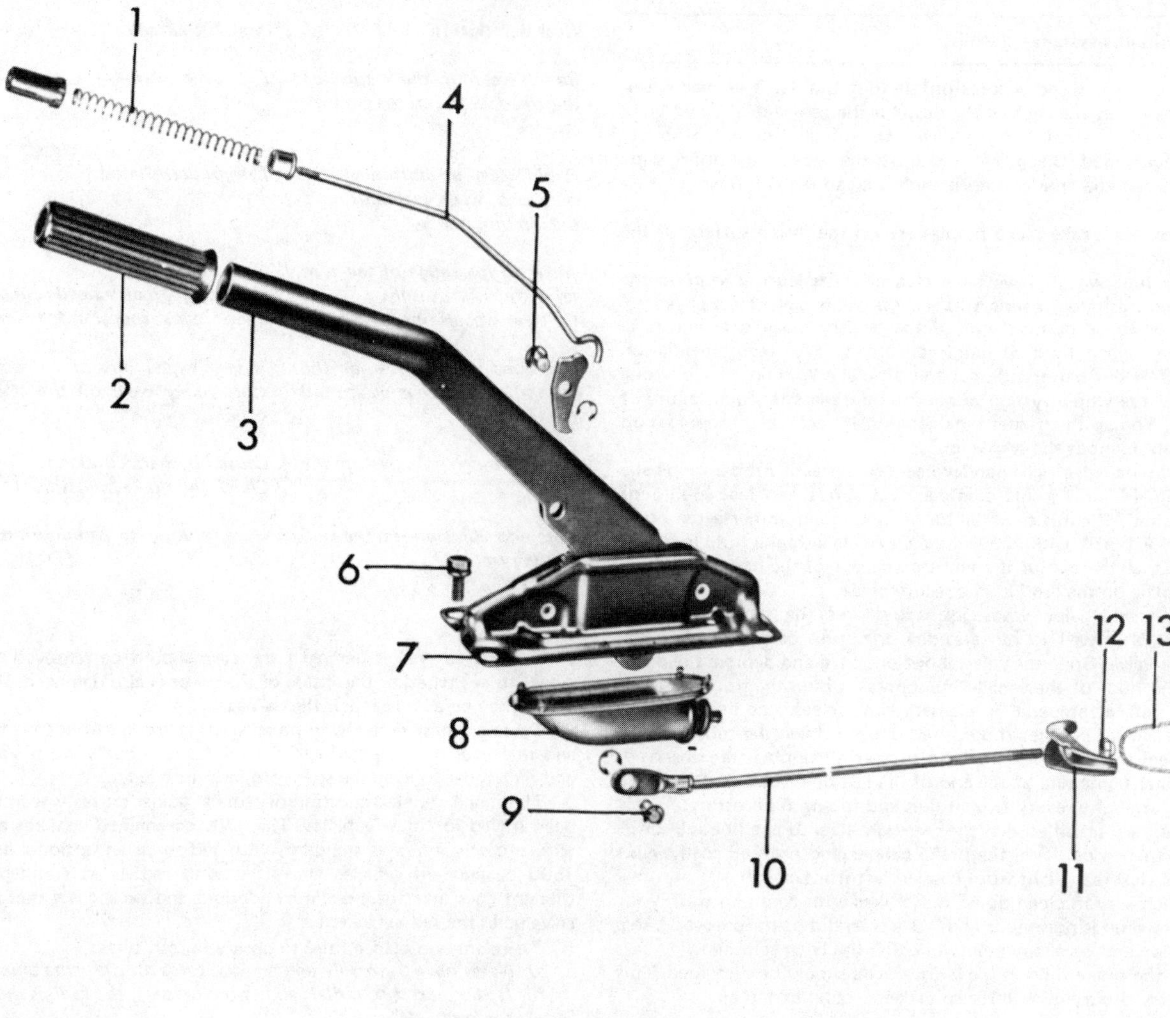

Fig. 9.20 Handbrake - exploded view

1 Spring	*5 Pin*	*8 Boot*	*11 Equalizer bar*
2 Lever grip	*6 Bolt*	*9 Pin*	*12 Nut*
3 Lever	*7 Bracket*	*10 Pull-rod*	*13 Cable*
4 Locking pawl rod			

33.3a The holes for the hub cap removal tool

33.3b The special tool and lever fitted for removing the hub cap

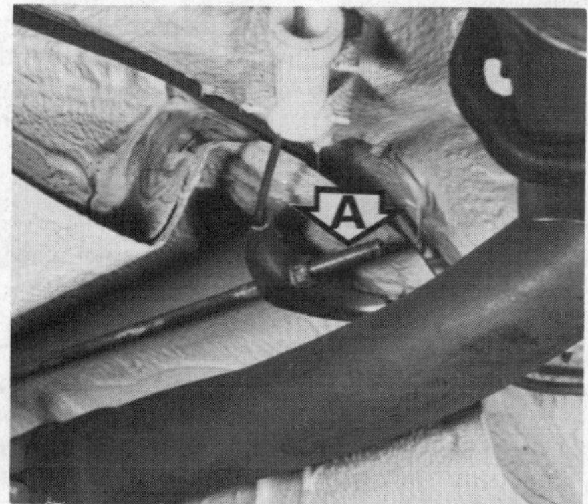

34.2 The equaliser bar 'A' for the handbrake cable

(b) Examine the holes through which the fixing bolts are fitted. If the bolts are allowed to get loose while the car is in service these holes may be elongated. Check the rim for cracks between bolt holes.

3 Earlier models have plastic covered wheel bolts which have no covering. Some of the later models have chromium hub caps. These are removed by inserting a special tool in the holes in the rim of the hub cap and levering the cap off (photos). The tools are supplied with the car.

34 Handbrake - adjustment, removal and replacement

1 The hand (or parking) brake acts through a mechanical linkage to the rear drum brakes. The action at the rear brake is covered in Section 13.6.

2 Refer to Fig. 9.20. The handbrake lever is shown with the ratchet. This is inside the car, and is bolted to the bottom plate. Attached to the bottom of the lever, under the car is the pull rod. The joint is inside a rubber boot. The pull rod is attached to an equalizer bar. By adjusting the nut behind the equalizer bar the cable which goes from the equalizer bar to the two rear brake parking brake levers may be tightened or slackened as required.

3 To adjust the handbrake, first jack-up the rear wheels of the car. Set the handbrake ratchet on the second tooth, or on vehicles with an automatic adjuster pull onto the 4th tooth, and tighten the nut behind the equalizer bar until it is not possible to rotate either wheel by hand. Release the handbrake lever and check that both wheels spin freely.

4 To replace the cable it is unfortunately necessary to dismantle both rear brake mechanisms to unhook the outer ends.

5 To remove the handbrake lever slacken the nut at the equalizer bar, remove the boot and undo the connecting pin. Undo the four screws holding the lever to the bottom plate and remove it upwards.

6 Installation is the reverse of removal. Lightly grease the equalizer bar and the pins. It may be necessary to replace the nylon cable guides when replacing the cable. These may be pressed out and new ones pressed in.

35 Fault diagnosis - braking system

Before diagnosing faults in the brake system check that irregularities are not caused by any of the following faults:

1. *Incorrect mix of Radial and Crossply tyres*
2. *Incorrect tyre pressures*
3. *Wear in the steering mechanism, suspension or shock absorbers*
4. *Misalignment of the bodyframe*

Symptom	Reason/s	Remedy
Pedal travels a long way before the brakes operate	Seized adjuster on rear shoes or shoes require adjustment	Check, repair, and adjust.
	Disc pads worn past limit	Inspect and renew as necessary.
Stopping ability poor, pedal pressure firm	Linings, pads, discs or drums worn, contaminated, or wrong type	Renew pads, linings, discs and drums as necessary.
	One or more caliper piston or rear wheel hydraulic cylinder seized	Inspect and repair as necessary.
	Loss of vacuum in servo	Test servo.
Car veers to one side when brakes are applied	Brake pads on one side contaminated with oil	Remove and renew. Repair source of oil leakage.
	Hydraulic pistons in calipers seized or sticking	Overhaul caliper.
	Wrong pads fitted	Install correct pads.
Pedal feels spongy when brakes are applied	Air in the hydraulic system	Bleed brakes and check for signs of leakage. Top-up header tank.
	Spring weak in master cylinder	Repair master cylinder.
Pedal travels right down with no resistance and brakes do not operate	Fluid reservoir empty	Check refill and bleed all brakes.
	Hydraulic lines fractured	Trace through and replace as necessary.
	Seals in master cylinder have failed	Dismantle cylinder and rebuild with new seals.
Brakes overheat or bind when car is in motion	Compensating port in master cylinder blocked	Rebuild cylinder.
	Reservoir air vent blocked	Clean vent.
	Pushrod requires adjustment	Adjust.
	Brake shoes return springs broken or strained	Replace.
	Caliper piston seals swollen	Replace.
	Unsuitable brake fluid	Drain and rebuild system.
Brakes judder or chatter and tend to grab	Linings worn	Replace.
	Drums out of round	Replace.
	Dirt in drums or calipers	Clean.
	Discs run-out of true excessive	Replace.
Brake shoes squeak (rear brakes)	Dirt in linings	Clean.
	Backplates distorted	Fit new backplates.
	Brake shoe return springs broken or distorted	Fit new springs.
	Brake linings badly worn	Fit new linings.

Symptom	Reason/s	Remedy
Disc pads squeak	Wrong type of pad fitted Pad guide surfaces dirty Spreader spring deficient or broken Pads glazed Lining on pad not secure	Fit new pads. Clean. Fit new spring. Fit new pads. Fit new pads.
Foot pedal must be pressed harder in one position only	Groove in master cylinder pushrod due to wear at sealing cups. Air entering vacuum side of servo	Rebuild master cylinder, new pushrod required.
Very high pedal pressure required to operate brakes, linings found to be in good condition and correctly adjusted	Servo has failed	Check hoses are tight and vacuum check valve is working. If so, then remove and service servo. If necessary fit a new one.

Chapter 10 Electrical system
Part I: generating and starting systems

For modifications, and information applicable to later models, see Supplement at end of manual

Contents

Specifications

Battery type	Lead acid, six cells with central connection for computer. Negative earth. 12 volt	
Battery capacity		
1300 and 1500 cc models with 35 amp alternator	36 amp hour	
1500 cc automatic models with 55 amp alternator	45 amp hour	
All models with air-conditioning	55 amp hour	
Alternator		
Type	K.I. Bosch, rotating field with static windings for output current. Built in rectification by diodes mounted in the end plate 490 watt output or 770 watt	
Mean regulating volts	14	
Nominal output speed	4000 rpm	
	in.	mm
Brush length (new)	3/8	10
Brush length (wear limit)	7/32	5
Maximum ovality of slip-rings	0.0001	0.03
Voltage control	Transistor type with replaceable bushes EE 14 Bosch, built into alternator	
Starter motor		
Type	Solenoid operated pinion drive with overrun clutch	
Make	Bosch EF 12	
Volts	12	
Output (HP)	0.7	
Armature:	ins.	mm
Axial play (max.)	0.012	0.3
Radial run-out (max.)	0.0001	0.003
Commutator minimum diameter	1.357	34.5
Brushes minimum length	0.5	13

1 General description

1 The car may be fitted with a 36 amp/hour or 45 amp/hour battery. The latter is fitted to vehicles equipped with the 55 amp alternator for starting the larger engines and automatic gearboxes. If the car is air-conditioned a 54 amp/hour battery is fitted. These batteries are fitted with a centre tapping to the computor plug.

2 The alternator may be of 35 amp or 55 amp output. The difference in appearance is that the 55 amp stator is 6.5 mm longer than the 35 amp, giving longer windings. The rotor winding is also different. The difference in power output 490 watts or 770 watts.

The alternator is mounted on a hinge bolt with an adjusting strap to the left-hand front of the engine and is driven by a 'V' belt which also drives the water pump. The voltage regulator is part of the alternator, is transistorized, and carries the brushes to the slip-rings.

3 The alternator has a diode carrier holding field current diodes and the main current diodes. The carrier acts as a heat sink to cool the diodes. The diode will pass current only one way, thus acting not only

as a rectifier from AC to DC, but also doing away with the need for a cut-out.

4 The starter motor is carried in bearings in the bell housing. It has a solenoid operated pinion drive. When the starter switch is closed the solenoid is energised and moves the pinion into mesh with the ring on the flywheel, switching on the main current after meshing has taken place. The pinion is thrown out of mesh by a one way clutch arrangement when the engine begins to drive the starter.

2 Battery - removal and replacement

1 The battery is mounted on the bulkhead inside the bonnet. The exact position depends on the type of vehicle.

2 It is held in position by a metal clamp on the base secured by a bolt (photos).

3 First remove the earth connection (ground strap) and then the positive connection. Finally the centre terminal, then undo the clamp and lift the battery off the car.

4 Before re-installation check that no corrosion has been caused by battery leaks. Remove any such corrosion with an alkali solution, ammonia or bicarbonate of soda (baking powder) will do. Where corrosion has extended to metal, remove the rust until the metal is bright and repaint right away.

5 Installation is the reverse of removal. Grease the terminals with a little petroleum jelly (vaseline). **Do not** use grease.

3 Battery - maintenance and inspection

1 Normal weekly battery maintenance consists of checking the electrolyte level of each cell to ensure that the separators are covered by ¼ inch of electrolyte. If the level has fallen, top up the battery using distilled water only. Do not overfill. If a battery is overfilled or any electrolyte spilled, immediately wipe away the excess as electrolyte attacks and corrodes any metal it comes into contact with very rapidly.

2 As well as keeping the terminals clean and covered with petroleum jelly, the top of the battery, and especially the top of the cells, should be kept clean and dry. This helps prevent corrosion and ensures that the battery does not become partially discharged by leakage through dampness and dirt. If topping up the battery becomes excessive and the case has been inspected for cracks that could cause leakage, but none are found, the battery is being over-charged and the regulator should be checked.

3 When removing the battery be careful not to strain the terminal posts. If these are twisted too much they may cause the plates inside to move with consequent battery failure.

4 With the battery on the bench at the three monthly interval check, measure its specific gravity with a hydrometer to determine the state of charge and condition of electrolyte. There should be very little variation between the different cells and if a variation in excess of 0.025 is present it will be due to either:

a) Loss of electrolyte from the battery at some time caused by spillage or a leak, resulting in a drop in the specific gravity of electrolyte when the deficiency was replaced with distilled water instead of fresh electrolyte.

b) An internal short circuit caused by buckling of the plates or a similar malady pointing to the likelihood of total battery failure in the near future.

5 The correct readings for the electrolyte specific gravity at various states of charge and conditions are:

	Temperate	*Tropical*
Fully charged	*1.285*	*1.23*
Half charged	*1.20*	*1.14*
Discharged	*1.12*	*1.08*

6 The hydrometer is a glass tube tapered at one and and fitted with a rubber bulb at the other end. Inside there is a float.

The tapered end of the tube is inserted into the filler hole of the cell to be tested and the bulb squeezed. When it is released acid is drawn into the tube. Enough must be drawn to allow the float to float freely.

The float has a scale on it and where the surface of the acid meets the float is the point to be read on the scale.

7 It is rare indeed for a battery to freeze but it can happen. If the battery is discharged and the specific gravity is low it may happen more easily. It will not happen while the engine is running so the first intimation will be a refusal to start, for a frozen battery will not supply current. Remembering that there is a solid lump of acid take care how it is handled. It must be thawed slowly. If it can be removed from the car so much the better but if it is frozen in any attempt to remove it by force will break the case. Indeed, the case may have split due to the expansion of the electrolyte so watch carefully as it does thaw or there may be an acid leak of considerable proportions which will do a lot of damage. If this happens take the battery out of the car as quickly as possible, but wear rubber gloves, to avoid being burned.

If the battery thaws out and no leaks appear then it will be of use again. However check the specific gravity and charge if necessary.

For interest value, acid at specific gravity 1.120 (ie; the battery is flat) will freeze at 12°F (−11°C), at 1.200 S.G. at −17°F (−27°C) and a fully charged battery at 1.285 is safe until −68°C (−90°F), so keep the battery well charged in cold weather, and if you do have to leave the car in a snowdrift get the battery out before it freezes.

8 If the battery loses its charge repeatedly then it is probably sulphated or damaged internally. First check the specific gravity of each cell. If some are high (1.285) and the odd one is lower then that is where the trouble lies. The S.G. throughout the six cells should not vary by more than 0.025.

The remaining test is a brutal one, which will probably kill an ageing battery anyway. It consists of short circuiting the battery through a "pair of tongs" equipped with a shunt and a voltmeter in such a way that a current of about 110 amps is passed for 5 to 10 seconds. The voltage between the terminals should not drop below 9.6 volts.

4 Battery - charging

1 In winter time when heavy demand is placed upon the battery such as when starting from cold and much electrical equipment is continually in use, it is a good idea occasionally to have the battery

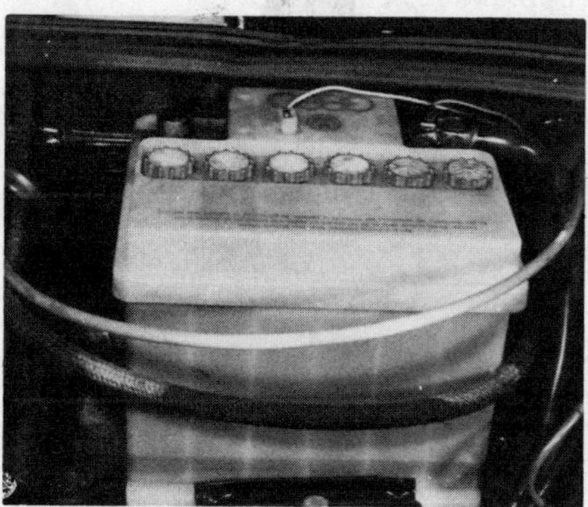
2.2a The battery - note centre tapping

2.2b Battery alternative position

7.3 The alternator mounted on the side of the engine. Note the adjusting strap

fully charged from an external source at the rate of 3.5 to 4 amps. Always disconnect it from the car electrical circuit when charging.
2 Continue to charge the battery at this rate until no further rise in specific gravity is noted over a four hour period.
3 Alternatively, a trickle charger, charging at the rate of 1.5 amps, can be safely used overnight. Disconnect the battery from the car electrical circuit before charging or you will damage the alternator.
4 Specially rapid 'boost' charges which are claimed to restore the power of the battery in 1 to 2 hours can cause damage to the battery plates through over-heating.
5 While charging the battery note that the temperature of the electrolyte should never exceed 100°F (37.8°C).
6 Make sure that your charging set and battery are set to the same voltage.

5 Battery - electrolyte replenishment

1 If the battery has been fully charged but one cell has a specific gravity of 0.025, or more, less than the others it is most likely that electrolyte has been lost from the cell at some time and the acid over diluted with distilled water when topping-up.
2 In this case remove some of the electrolyte with a pipette and top up with fresh electrolyte. It is best to get this done at the Service Station, for making your own electrolyte is messy, dangerous, and expensive for the small amount you need. If you must do it yourself add 1 part of sulphuric acid (concentrated) to 2.5 parts of water. **Add the acid to the water**, not the other way round or the mixture will spit back as water is added to acid and you will be badly burnt. Add the acid a drop at a time to the water.

Having added fresh electrolyte recharge and recheck the readings. In all probability this will cure the problem. If it does not then there is a short circuit somewhere.
3 Electrolyte must always be stored away from other fluids and should be locked up, not left about. If you have children this is even more important.

6 Alternator - safety precautions

1 The alternator has a negative earth circuit. Be careful not to connect the battery the wrong way or the alternator will be damaged.
2 **Do not** run the alternator with the output wire disconnected.
3 When welding is being done on the car the battery and the alternator output cable should be disconnected.
4 If the battery is to be charged in-situ both the leads of the battery should be disconnected, before the charging leads are connected to the battery.
5 Do not use temporary test connections which may short circuit accidentally. The fuses will not blow, the diodes will burn out.
6 When replacing a burnt out alternator clear the fault which caused the burn out first or a new alternator will be needed a second time.

7 Alternator - drivebelt adjustment

1 The alternator is driven by a belt from the crankshaft pulley. The belt also drives the water pump.
2 The alternator has two lugs on its casing. A bolt threaded through these is mounted in a bracket bolted to the cylinder block. This bolt forms the hinge on which the alternator is mounted. The head of the bolt is a hollow (socket) hexagon which is accessible through a hole in the timing belt cover. This bolt must be slackened before the alternator belt tension may be adjusted.
3 On the top of the alternator is yet another lug (photo), through which a bolt is fitted to a slotted strap. The strap is hinged on the cylinder block.
4 Thus the alternator may be rotated about the hinge bolt to tighten the drivebelt. The tension in the drivebelt is correct when the belt may be depressed with a thumb a distance of 3/8 in. (9.5 mm) halfway between the crankshaft and alternator pulleys. The bolts should be tightened to hold the alternator in this position.
5 It may be difficult to slacken the socket head bolt. In this case do not go on until the bolt hexagon is destroyed, do as we did, remove the strap, and then remove the bracket with alternator complete. Undo the wiring plug, remove the belt and then take the alternator away. The socket head bolt may then be held in a vice and undone that way.

8 Alternator - testing

1 There is a way of testing the alternator in the car, but it requires a lot of expensive equipment and does not provide much conclusive evidence. Refer to Fig. 10.1. The following are required. A battery cut-out switch, a variable resistance capable of consuming up to 500 watts, an ammeter reading 0-30 amps, a voltmeter reading 0-20v, and a tachometer.
2 The battery cut-out switch is illustrated in Fig. 10.2.
3 Connect up as shown in the diagram in the following manner. Disconnect the battery earth strap and the positive cable. Connect the cut-out switch to the battery positive terminal and then connect the car positive lead to the cut-out switch.
4 So far no interference with the normal circuit. Now arrange an alternative one to take the place of the battery. From the battery cut-out switch connect the variable resistance and ammeter in series to the chassis (earth) of the car. Arrange a voltmeter so that the volts drop between the battery cut-out switch and earth. Reconnect the battery earth strap. The following test figures are for both 35 amp and 55 amp alternators.
5 Start the engine and run it up to 2,800 rpm. Set the variable resistance so that the ammeter reading is between 20 and 30 amps. Now

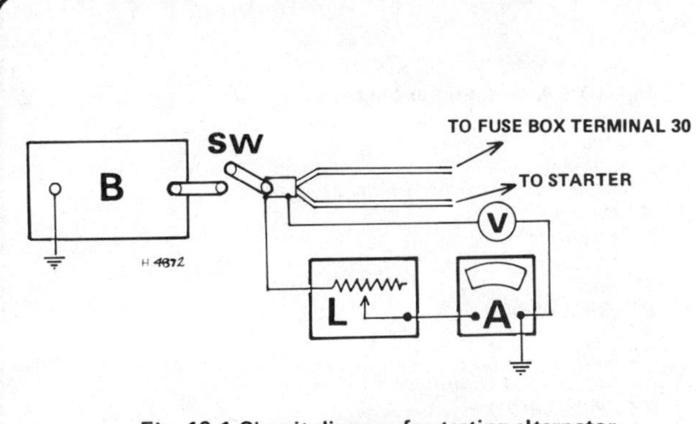

Fig. 10.1 Circuit diagram for testing alternator

B Battery
SW Battery cut-out switch
L Variable resistance (load)
A Ammeter 0 - 30 amps
V Voltmeter 0 - 20 volts

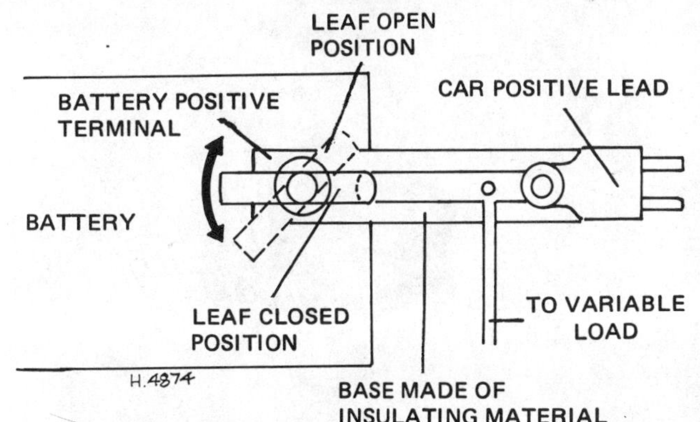

Fig. 10.2 Diagramatic arrangement battery cut-out switch. VW/Audi recommend 'Sun Electric' No. 7052 - 003

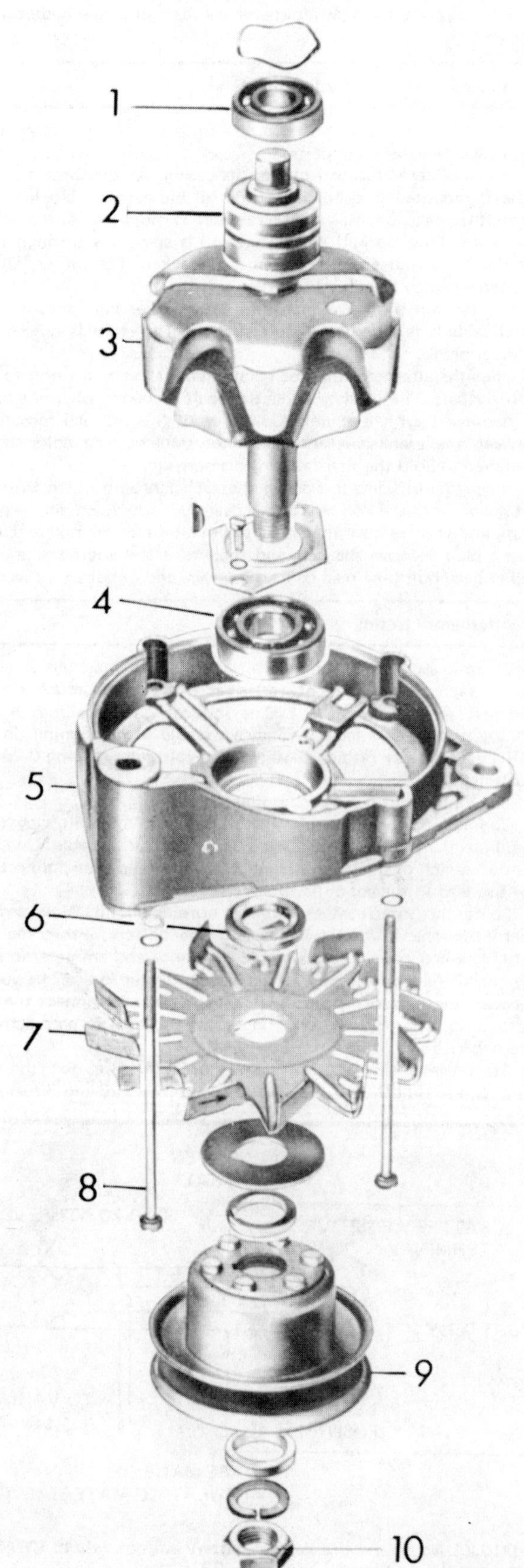

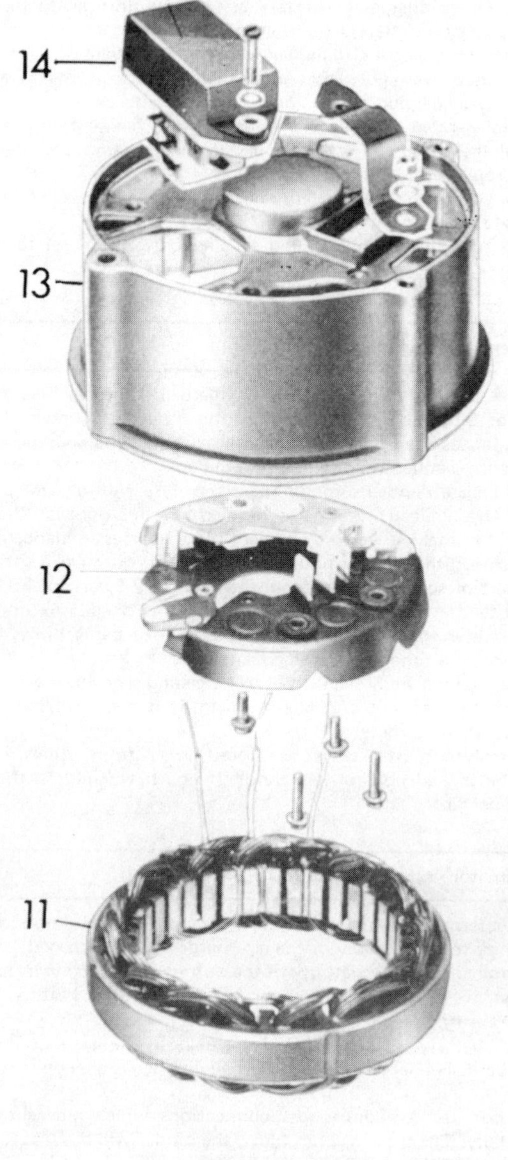

Fig. 10.3 Alternator - exploded view

1 Bearing
2 Slip-rings
3 Claw pole rotor with field windings
4 Bearing
5 Endplate
6 Spacer ring
7 Fan
8 Through-bolt
9 Pulley
10 Nut
11 Stator with windings
12 Diode carrier
13 Alternator housing
14 Regulator with carbon brushes

Note: Part 11, stator. This is the 35 amp stator. The 55 amp stator is 6.5 mm (¼ inch) longer than this one

open the battery cut-out switch, that is, cut the battery out of the circuit so that the current flows only through the resistance. Alter the resistance to bring the current back to 25 amps. Now read the voltmeter. It should read between 12.5 and 14.5 volts.

6 If the voltmeter reading is outside these limits close the cut-off switch, stop the engine and replace the alternator regulator with a new one (or a borrowed one). Repeat the test. If the desired 12.5 to 14.5 volts is obtained then the old regulator was faulty. If not then the alternator is faulty and must be changed. It seems a lot to do for little reward but the only other way is to take the alternator to an official agent for testing.

9 Alternator - overhaul

1 The regulator is fitted into the alternator housing. Remove a small screw and it may be removed. Refer to Fig. 10.3.

2 Inside it will be seen the two slip ring brushes. These must be free in the guides and at least 5 mm (0.2 in.) long. The new length is 10 mm (0.4 in.). The brushes may be renewed by unsoldering the leads from the regulator, fitting new brushes and resoldering the leads. (Fig. 10.4).

3 Undo the pulley nut and remove the pulley, the spacer ring, the large washer and the fan. Note which way the fan fits to make assembly easier. There is an arrow showing the direction of rotation.

4 Remove the bracket from the housing which held the wiring plug and if not already removed, take away the regulator.

5 Undo the housing bolts and separate the components. The armature will stay in the endplate and the housing bearing will stay on the shaft. Have a good look at the various components. Clean off all the dust using a soft brush and then wipe clean with trichlorethylene. Any smell of burnt carbon or signs of over-heating must be investigated. Check the slip-rings for burning, scoring and ovality. You will have had reason to check the bearings before dismantling, but have a further look now. At this point you must make up your mind whether to do the repair yourself, or whether to take the alternator to a specialist. If you have the tools and the skill it is possible to replace the bearings, replace the diode carrier complete, clean up the slip-rings and to fit a new rotor or stator. It is **not** possible to repair the windings, replace individual diodes, replace the slip-rings or repair the fan.

6 Dealing with the rotor first. The rotor may be removed from the endplate by using a mandrel press. Then take the screws out of the cover over the endplate bearing and press the bearing out of the frame. The slip-ring end bearing may be pulled off using an extractor on the **inner** race. If you pull on the outer race the bearing will be scrapped. Replace the bearings with new if necessary.

7 The slip-rings may be cleaned up by setting the rotor in a lathe and either cleaning them with emery or by taking a very fine skim.

8 Test the rotor electrically. Check the insulation resistance between the slip-rings and the shaft. This must be infinity. If it is not there is a short circuit and the armature must be replaced. Get an auto-electrical specialist to confirm your findings first. Check the resistance of the winding. Measure this between slip-rings. It should be about 4 ohms. If there is an open circuit or high resistance, then again the rotor must be renewed.

9 The stator and the diode carrier are connected by wires. Make a simple circuit diagram so that you know which wire goes to which diode and then unsolder the connections. This is a delicate business as excess heat will destroy the diode and possibly the winding. Grip the wire as close as possible to the soldered joint with a pair of long nosed pliers and use as small a soldering iron as possible.

10 The stator winding may now be checked. First check that the insulation is sound. The resistance between the leads and the frame must be infinity. Next measure the resistance of the winding. It should be of the order of 1.3 ohms between leads. A zero reading means a short circuit, and of course a high or infinity reading, an open circuit.

11 The diode carrier may now be checked. Each diode should be checked in turn. Use a test lamp or an ohmmeter. Current must flow only one way; ie, the resistance measured one way must be high and the other way (reverse the leads), low. Keep the current down to 0.8 milliamps and do not allow the diode to heat up. If the resistance both ways is a high one, then the diode is open circuited, a low one, short circuited. If only one diode is defective the whole assembly (diode plate) must be replaced.

12 Reconnect the stator winding to the diode circuit, again be careful not to overheat the diode, and reassemble the stator and diode carrier to the housing.

13 A new diode carrier, or a new stator may be fitted, but be careful to get the correct parts.

14 Assembly is the reverse of dismantling. Be careful to assemble the various washers correctly.

15 It has been found that voltage surge in the electrical system damages the alternator diode. If this happens when requesting repair of the diode plate ask for and install a condenser (part no. 059 035 271) to preventing this occurring again (see Fig. 10.5).

10 Starter motor - testing in car

1 The starter motor is bolted to the bellhousing behind the right front wheel. There are three connections to the solenoid (see photos). Terminal 'A' (terminal 50) goes to the ignition starter switch, 'B' (terminal 16), goes to terminal 15 on the ignition coil direct and 'C' (terminal 30), the big one, goes to the battery positive terminal direct.

2 If when the ignition is switched on the starter will not turn the engine over it does not necessarily mean the starter is at fault. So before taking the starter out a routine check should be done.

3 Check the state of charge of the battery. Remove the leads from the battery terminals, clean the leads and terminals and reassemble correctly. The quickest way to check the battery is to switch on the headlights. If the lights come on brightly and stay bright then the

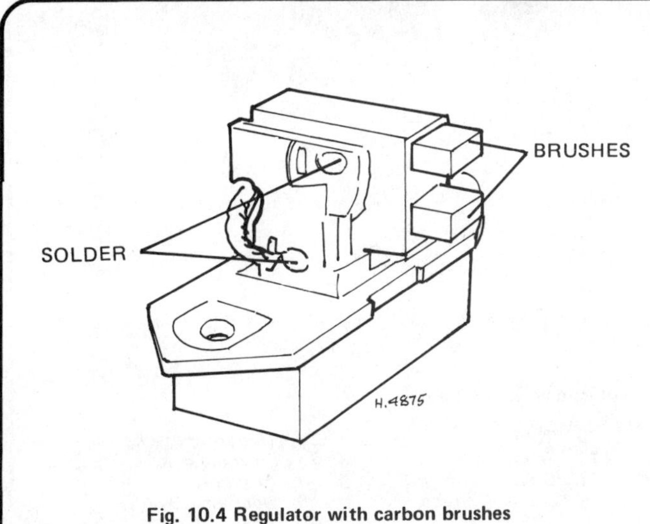

Fig. 10.4 Regulator with carbon brushes

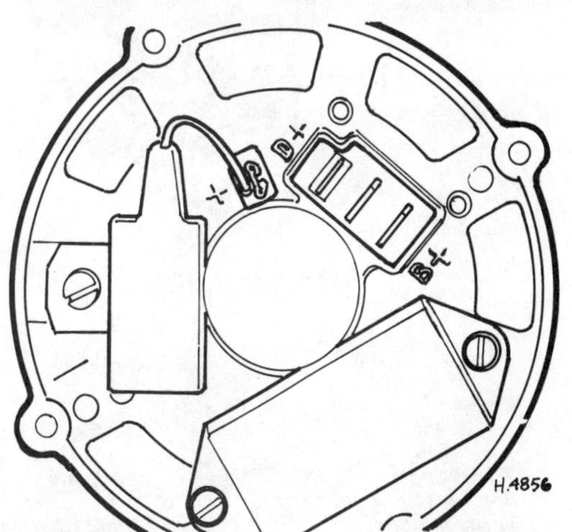

Fig. 10.5 Alternator - modification to prevent damage from surging. Install condenser as shown

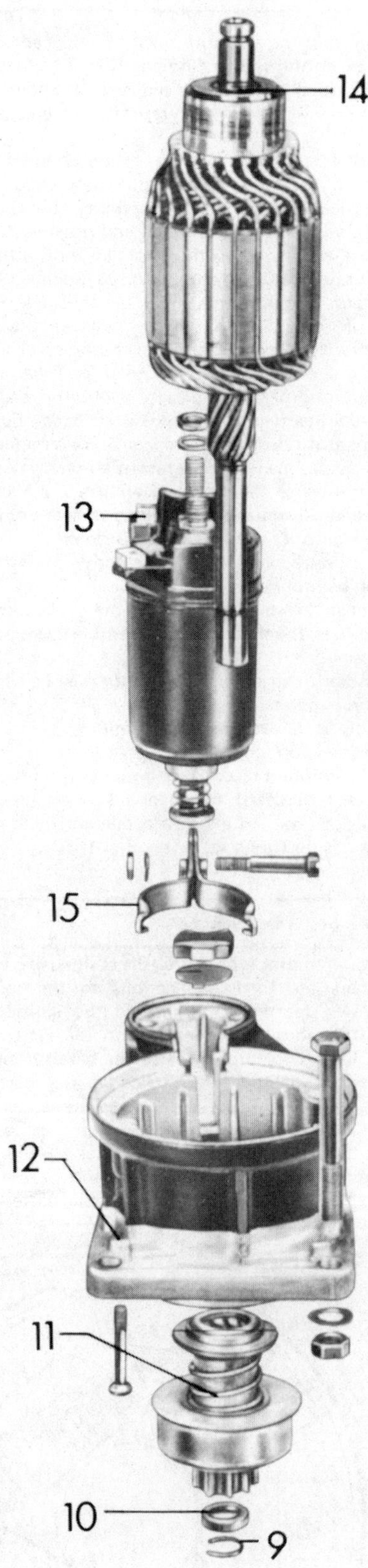

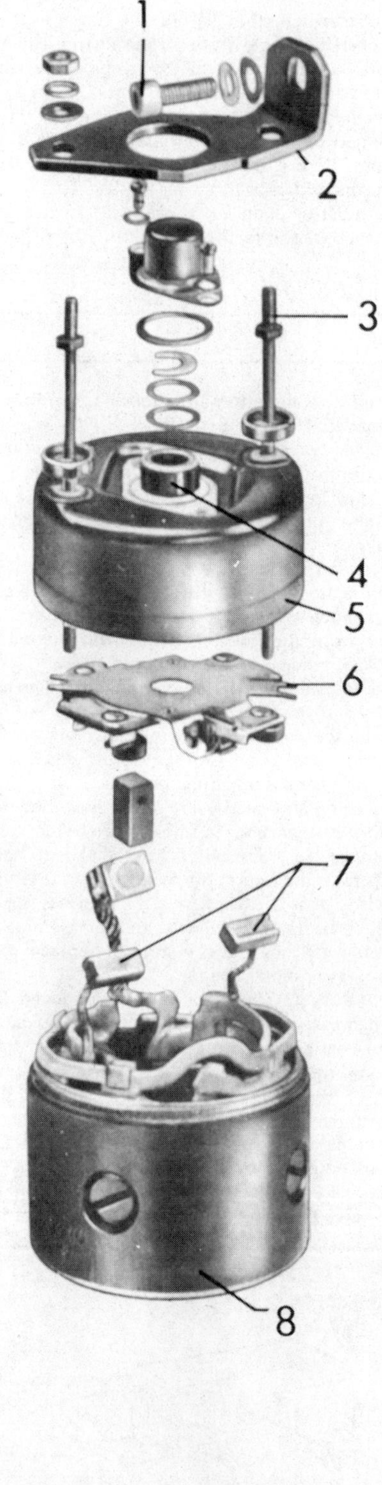

Fig. 10.6 Starter motor - exploded view

1 Bracket bolt	*5 Endplate*	*9 Circlip*	*12 Mounting bracket*
2 Bracket (starter to block)	*6 Brush plate*	*10 Stop-ring*	*13 Solenoid case*
3 Through-bolts	*7 Field winding brushes*	*11 Drive pinion with one-way clutch*	*14 Armature*
4 Bush in endplate	*8 Stator body (housing)*		*15 Operating lever*

10.1a The starter and solenoid on the engine. Terminals are: A to the starter switch, B to terminal '15', C to battery, D solenoid to starter, E socket head bolt on support bracket

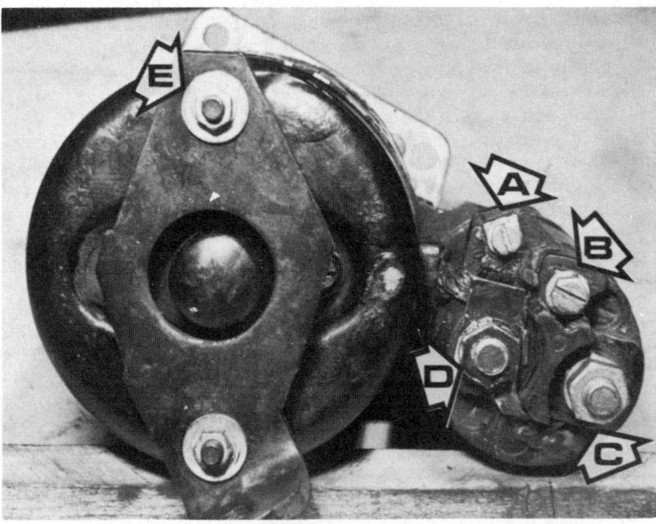

10.1b A view of the starter on the bench. Terminal markings as for 11.1 A terminal '50', B terminal '15', C terminal '30', D solenoid to starter terminal

11.1 Removing the starter

12.3a Remove the end cap ...

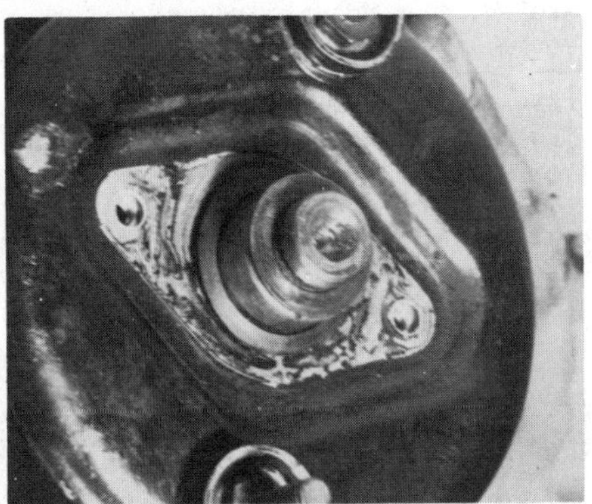
12.3b ... to reveal the circlip thrust washers and shims

battery is in good order. If the lights are dim, or come on bright and dim quickly then the battery is discharged. Remedy this state of affairs before dismantling the starter.
4 If the battery is in good order and the ground strap (earth lead) is firmly fixed to the chassis then turn to the starter connections. Are they tight, free from corrosion and water. On automatic transmission vehicles check that the starter cut-out switch is in good order (Chapter 7).
5 Get down by the starter and have someone operate the ignition switch. Does the solenoid work (make a clunking noise), if so disconnect the cable from terminal 30 and fit it to the connector strip terminal (D). If the starter now revolves when the ignition is switched on then the solenoid contacts are worn or faulty and the starter must be removed for overhaul.
6 If the starter still does not work bridge terminals '30' and '50'. If the starter works then the fault is in the ignition switch wiring, not the starter.
7 If all the above tests have been done and there is still no life then the starter must be removed for test and overhaul.
8 If the starter turns the engine slowly, and the battery and connections are in good order then the starter should be removed for testing and overhaul. It is probably brush or commutator trouble, or it may be problems with the field windings.
9 If the starter works erratically or will not disengage then the fault is a mechanical one, and the starter must be removed for overhaul.
10 Only after checking all these points should the starter be dismantled.

11 Starter motor - removal and replacement

1 Remove the earth strap from the battery. Disconnect the starter leads and remove the starter after removing three nuts from the mounting bracket, and one socket head bolt from the support plate (photo). The socket head bolt is item 'E' on photo 11.1a.
2 Replacement is the reverse of removal. Be careful to enter the shaft into the bearing in the bellhousing before lining up the bolts.

12 Starter motor - overhaul

1 Clean the exterior carefully and clean and oil the pinion and shaft (refer to Fig. 10.6).
2 Refer to photo 11.1b and remove the support plate nuts (E). Remove the connector strip terminal nut (D) and from the other end remove the two bolts holding the solenoid to the mounting bracket. Now lift the solenoid pull rod so that it is clear of the operating lever and remove the solenoid.
3 At the front end of the starter is a cap held by two screws. Remove this (photo) and under it there is a shaft with a circlip and bush (photo). Remove the circlip (photo).
4 Now remove the through bolts (photo) and remove the cover.
5 The brush gear is now visible (photo). Lift the brushes out of the holder and remove the brush holder. The starter body holding the field coils may now be separated from the endplate. This will leave the armature still in the mounting bracket.
6 To remove the mounting bracket from the drive end of the shaft,

first push back the stop ring with a suitable tube so that the circlip underneath may be released from its groove. It is now possible to remove the mounting bracket and pinion from the shaft.

7 Finally remove the operating lever pin from the mounting bracket and remove the pinion assembly.

8 Clean and examine the pinion, shaft and lever and inspect for wear. If possible run the armature between centres in a lathe and check that the shaft is not bent. Check the fit of the drive pinion on the shaft. Check that the pinion will revolve in one direction only (one way clutch) and that the teeth are not chipped.

9 Examine the commutator. Clean off the carbon with a rag soaked in petrol or trichlorethylene. Minor scoring may be removed with fine emery paper. Deep scoring must be removed by machining in a lathe. Commutator copper is harder than the commercial grade, and requires the lathe tool to be ground differently. Unless you have had instruction on machining commutators we suggest that the skimming and under-cutting be left to the expert. The minimum diameter for the commutator is 1.358 in. (34.5 mm).

10 Test the armature electrically. Check the insulation between the armature winding and the shaft. To do this connect the negative terminal of the ohmmeter to the shaft and place the positive probe on each commutator segment in turn.

11 Burning on the commutator is usually a sign of an open circuited winding. If you have access to a 'growler' have the armature checked for short circuits.

12 Inspect the field windings for signs of abrasion or stiff and damaged insulation, particularly where the leads leave the coil. Check the field coil for short circuit to the pole piece and for open circuits. Replace if necessary.

13 The brushes must be at least ½ in. (13 mm) long and must slide easily in the holder. There are two schools of thought about brush replacement. One says that the entire field coil must be replaced or the brush plate with the armature current brushes. The VW/Audi method is somewhat different.

14 Isolate the brushes, pull them out of the holders and hold them away from the winding and crush the old brush with a powerful pair of pliers until the lead is free from the brush. Clean the end of the lead and prepare it for soldering. The new brush, obtainable from official agents, is drilled and has a tinned insert. Push the end of the lead into the drilling and splay it out, then using silver solder, solder the brush to the lead.

15 If it is your first attempt at soldering it could be better to get expert help. Use a large soldering iron (250 watt plus) do not let any of the solder creep along the wire and file off any surplus. Do not let the lead get too hot or damage will occur to the field coils. Use a flat pair of pliers to hold the lead as close to the brush as possible while soldering. These will act as a heat sink and will also stop the solder getting in the core of the lead.

16 One final word about brushes. Check that you can get new ones before crushing the old ones.

17 Assembly is the reverse of dismantling. Fit the drive pinion and operating lever to the mounting bracket. Fit the drive pinion to the armature shaft. Refit a new lock ring (circlip) and install the stop ring (groove towards the outside) over the lock ring. Check that the stop ring will revolve freely on the shaft.

18 Fit the starter body over the armature to the mounting bracket. See that the tongue on the body fits in the cut-out of the mounting bracket and that the body seats properly on the rubber seating. Smear a little joint compound round the joint before assembly.

19 Fit the two washers onto the armature shaft and install the brush holder over the commutator. This we found easier to do with a pen than in actual fact. In order to get the holder in place with the brushes correctly assembled we found that we didn't have enough fingers so we cut two lengths of wire and bent them as shown (photos) to hold up the brush springs while the brushes were fitted over the commutator. Once the four brushes are in place the wires may be withdrawn.

20 Wipe the end of the shaft and oil it, then fit the endcover onto the housing and install the through-bolts. Again seal the joint, and seal the ends of the through-bolts. Now refit the shims and the circlip. If a new armature has been fitted the endplay must be checked. It should not exceed a maximum of 0.072 in., minimum of 0.004 in. (0.1 to 0.3 mm) and is adjusted by fitting appropriate shims.

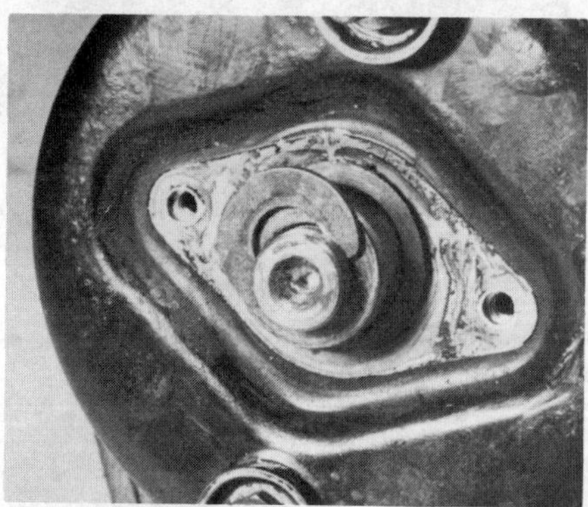

12.3c Remove the circlip

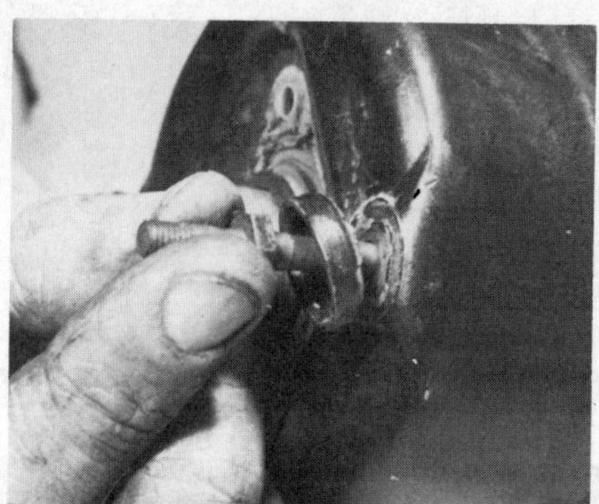

12.4 Remove the through bolts. These must be sealed on assembly

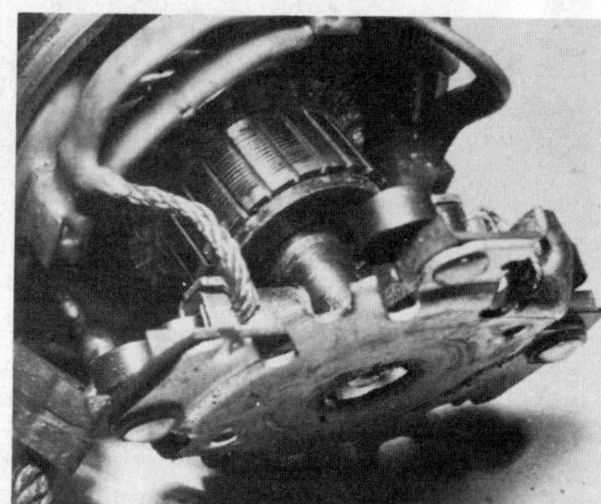

12.5 Lift off the brush plate. This commutator needs attention

12.18a Using two clips to hold the brush springs on assembly. This way the plate may be fitted without trouble

12.8b The wire clip 'A' fits under the brush spring so that the brush may be easily lifted to enter the plate over the commutator

21 Check that the solenoid lead grommet is in place and refit the solenoid. Use a seal compound on the joint faces, move the pinion to bring the operating lever to the opening and reconnect pullrod. Seat the solenoid firmly on the mounting bracket in the sealing compound and install the bolts. Reconnect the wire to the starter body (D).
22 The starter may now be refitted to the car.
23 The pinion end of the shaft fits into a bearing in the clutch housing and this can be checked only when the transmission is dismantled. The commutator end of the shaft fits into a bearing bush in the endplate. The old bush may be pressed out if necessary and a new one pressed in. The endplate should be dipped into hot oil for five minutes before the bush is pressed in to give a shrink fit. Grease the bush with multi-purpose grease before installing the shaft.

13 Starter motor - bench test

1 Because the pinion end bearing is in the clutch housing, it is not possible to rotate the starter under load or at speed when not fitted to the engine. The customary bench tests are therefore not applicable to this starter.

14 Fault diagnosis - charging circuit

Symptom	Reason/s	Remedy
Alternator warning light does not come on when the ignition switch is closed	1 Bulb burned out 2 Battery flat 3 Connector between alternator and relay not correctly fitted 4 Carbon brushes not seating on slip ring 5 Open circuit between battery, ignition switch and warning light 6 Rotor windings damaged	1 Replace. 2 Charge. 3 Refit. 4 Check for length and free movement. Replace if necessary. 5 Check continuity. 6 Check and fit new rotor if necessary.
Alternator warning light does not go out as engine speed increases	1 Regulator damaged 2 Field winding diodes open circuit	1 Check and replace if necessary. 2 Dismantle alternator, check diodes. Replace diode carrier if required.
Alternator warning light remains on when the ignition is switched off	1 Positive diode (main load diode) short circuited	1 Dismantle alternator check diodes, replace diode plate if necessary.

15 Fault diagnosis - starting circuit

Symptom	Test and possible reason	Remedy
1 Starter does not operate when key is turned to 'start' position	Turn on the lights for this test: 1 Lights go out - loose connections, corroded terminals, flat battery 2 Lights go dim - battery run down 3 Connect a cable between terminals '30' and '50'. If starter now turns either cables or ignition switch is faulty 4 Lights stay bright. Connect cable from terminal '30' to connector strip terminal - starter now turns	 Check circuit and replace battery. Recharge or replace battery. Replace cables, starter to ignition switch and/or ignition switch. Solenoid needs service or replacement.
2 Drive pinion sticks in mesh with starter ring	1 Coarse thread damaged 2 Solenoid not working	Overhaul starter. Replace solenoid.
3 Starter turns slowly and will not start engine	1 Battery run down 2 Loose connections 3 Brushes not making proper contact 4 Commutator dirty, burnt or damaged 5 Windings damaged	Charge or replace. Check circuit. Overhaul or replace starter. Overhaul or replace starter. Overhaul or replace starter.
4 Erratic starting ie; sometimes it will and sometimes it will not, particularly from cold	1 Battery has internal fault Load test battery with tongs	Replace battery if necessary.

Chapter 11 Electrical system Part II: lights, instrument panel and electrical accessories

For modifications, and information applicable to later models, see Supplement at end of manual

Contents

Specification

Bulb chart *	**DIN Designation**	**Part no.**	**Type**
Headlamp:			
Round (filament)	A12V 45/40W	N17 705 3	Twin filament
Round (halogen)	YD 12V 60/55W	N17 763 2	Halogen H.4
Square	As above	As above	As above
Double headlamp (halogen)	YA 12V 55W	N17 761 2	Halogen H.1
Parking light	HL 12V 4W	N17 717 2	Tubular
Front turn signal	RL 12V 21W	N17 732 2	Ball
Rear turn signal	RL 12V 21W	N17 732 2	Ball
Brake/tail light	SL 12V 21/5W	N17 738 2	Twin filament
Reversing light	RL 12V 21W	N17 732 2	Ball
License plate lights (2)	HL 12V 4W	N17 717 2	Tubular
Interior light	K12V 10W	N17 723 2	Festoon
Glovebox	J12V 2W	N17 722 2	Tubular
Warning lamps for switches and heater levers	W 12V 1.2W or JG 12V 1.2W	N17 751 2	Glass base
Instrument lights	VA 12V 3W	N17 752 2	Glass base
Fog lights (halogen)	YC 12V 55W	N17 762 2	Halogen H.1
Rear fog light	RL 12V 21W	N17 732 2	Ball

* *Note - Check this chart against your own vehicle bulb chart which is found in the operators handbook.*

Sealed beam lamp (USA) ... G.E.C. sealed beam SBM IAE 122.7 in. diameter, 45 watt

Wiper motor ... 12V, 2 speed, worm-drive permanent magnet field

Rear window demister ... 110 - 120 watt

Fan blower ... 65 watt, 2 speed

Air-conditioner blower ... 180 watt, 3 speed

Fuses

This is a typical layout. Check your own against the handbook or see Section 20. This layout was taken from a 1300 cc model.

Fuse No.	Fuse serves	Amperage
1	Headlamp low beam (left)	8
2	Headlamp low beam (right)	8
3	Headlamp high beam (left)	8
4	Headlamp high beam (right)	8
5	Radiator fan, fresh air fan, turn signals, heated rear window (sw only), warning lights, stabilizer	8
6	Horn	8
7	Turn signals, emergency light	8
8	Heated rear window (main circuit)	16
9	Windscreen wipers, cigar lighter	16
10	Brake lights, interior lights	8
11	Windscreen wipers	16
12	Washer pump	16
13	Taillight (right) and parking light (right)	8
14	Taillight (left) and parking light (left)	8
15	License plate, switch and heater lights	8
16	Air-conditioner	25
17	Fog lights	16

Relay location

See fuse cover and vehicle operators handbook.

A	Radiator fan
B	Headlights
C	Combi relay (dimmer, headlight flasher)
D	Turn signal and emergency flasher
E	Heated rear window
F	Wipers
G	Wash wipe - intermittent wipers
H	Fog lights

1 General description

1 The various models have a common system of electric wiring and accessories although the number and exact type of accessories depends on the option package and year of the vehicle. In most cases wiring and fixing provision is already built in to models not fitted with extras such as fog lamps, and fitting of these extras is a simple task. All such extras must be earthed to the chassis with a separate connector.

2 A very marked step in technique is evident. The fuse and relay console in the engine compartment has now 17 fuses and possibly ten relays. The purpose of these relays is two-fold. Firstly, the heavy current required for headlamps, fog lamps, fan motor, air-conditioner, horn, rear window heater, and flashers, may be routed only from the generating circuit, via the relay, to the accessory. The operation of the relay switching on the current is by a much smaller current from the switch on the dashboard (fascia) which enables the second step. By using relays the current to and from instruments may be carried by a printed circuit and the size of switches and wiring behind the fascia board reduced to a minimum. Indeed it would not be very difficult to install all the accessories if the main current had to be led to switches on the fascia.

3 Measuring instruments on the fascia have a controlling voltage stabilizer plugged in to the circuit.

4 The car is wired to a computor plug so that the official agents computor may check the car against standard values in a very short time. In our opinion this service is invaluable and should be used as intended. It does however, preclude the addition of extra electrical accessories, unless these are VW/Audi standard ones, or can be easily disconnected before the check is done. The operator must be informed of any such additions before he starts his inspection.

5 The more expensive types of vehicle have built in tachometer (rev counters), oil pressure gauge and voltmeter fitted as standard. These may be added to the standard vehicle and will assist considerably in maintenance.

6 Four types of headlight are fitted. These are detailed elsewhere in this Chapter, otherwise the lamp layout is standard. Filament or Halogen type are fitted to single headlamps. Double headlamps have halogen bulbs.

7 The speedometer is included in this Chapter because it is very much part of the fascia board although completely mechanical.

8 Guide lines only are given for fitting radio and fog lamps. If items other than VW/Audi accessories are fitted the owner may be confronted with problems which we cannot forsee: so comment is confined only to what not to do, rather than how to overcome such problems.

9 The wiring diagram presents us with a problem. There are so many versions. The ones we have provided are basic. Your vehicle may vary a little. The VW organization now provide only current flow diagrams, which, unless you are trained in the use of them can be misleading. If there are serious wiring problems we suggest you consult the official agent. He has the up-to-date information on your vehicle whereas advice given by us can only be up-to-date at the time of publication.

10 The wiring harness is divided into four portions and may be obtained from the official agencies for replacement if so required. These are:

- *a) The battery harness*
- *b) The front harness supplying current from the relay board to the front lamps, horn and radiator fan.*
- *c) The main harness*
- *d) The rear harness which deals with the rear lights and window heater*

A diagram is given which shows the general layout, divided accordingly (Fig. 11.1).

2 Headlamps - general

1 Four separate types of headlamp installation are fitted to this range of vehicles. They are:

- *a) Bulb and reflector fitted to 1300 cc models, round reflector.*
- *b) Bulb and reflector square, wide beam, fitted to 1500 cc models.*
- *c) Twin headlamp, halogen bulbs fitted to the higher powered models.*
- *d) Sealed beam units fitted to USA models.*

2 The fixing and beam adjustment is generally the same, as is the switching mechanism. The main differences are in the type of bulb and the method of renewing it.

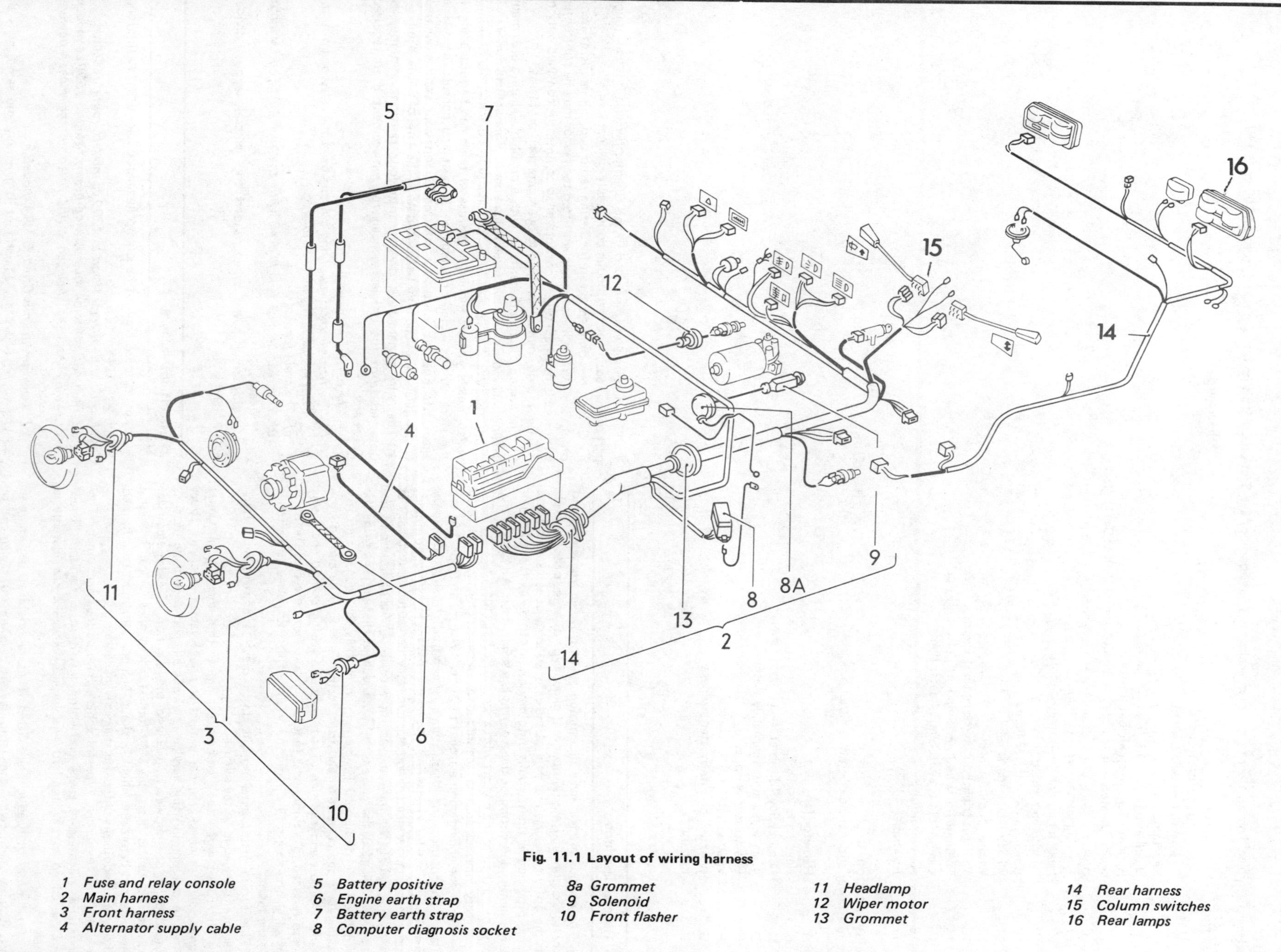

Fig. 11.1 Layout of wiring harness

1 Fuse and relay console
2 Main harness
3 Front harness
4 Alternator supply cable
5 Battery positive
6 Engine earth strap
7 Battery earth strap
8 Computer diagnosis socket
8a Grommet
9 Solenoid
10 Front flasher
11 Headlamp
12 Wiper motor
13 Grommet
14 Rear harness
15 Column switches
16 Rear lamps

3 Single headlamp (round reflector) - removal, replacement and bulb renewal

1 To remove the bulb first extract the rubber grommet at the back of the headlamp cover (photo). Then pull off the cover. Some covers do not have this plug but the wire is fed in the side of the lamp (photo).
2 Under this will be found another cover and a plug (photo). Remove the plug and pressing in the cover remove it from the retaining ring (photo).
3 This now exposes the lamp holder (photo) which may be turned in its bayonet fitting and pulled out carrying the bulb. Using a duster remove the bulb and replace it with a serviceable one. **Do not** touch the bulb with bare fingers, it won't hurt you but the moisture from your skin will etch lines on the bulb when it lights up.
4 Assembly is the reverse of removal. Make sure the covers seat properly or the lamp will leak water and require a new reflector. A typical layout is shown at Fig. 11.2.
5 To remove the reflector it is necessary first to remove the grille. This is held by five screws. The screws holding the headlamp (not the focus screws) may then be undone and the lamp drawn out from the front. The frame and reflector are held together by clamps (photo) which must be turned to separate the parts. It would be better to replace them as an assembly.
6 Focusing is done by moving two screws one for vertical and the other for horizontal adjustment (photo). Although for clarity's sake the photo shows the lamp out of the car, the adjustment may be done without disturbing the headlight as the screws are accessible from inside the engine compartment without undoing any part of the lamp (see photo 3.1).

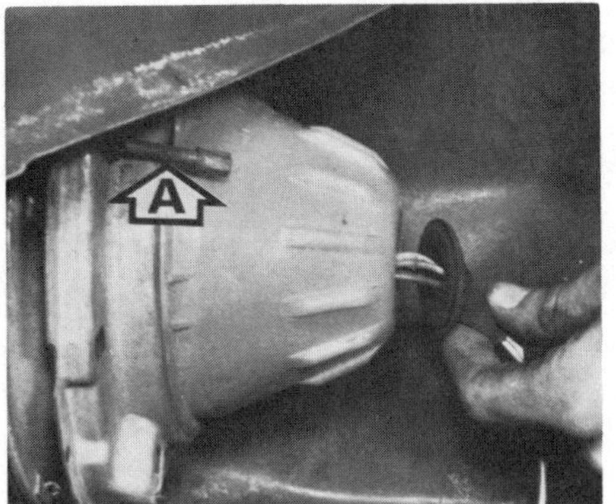

3.1a Remove the plug from the back of the cover. 'A' is one of the focussing screws

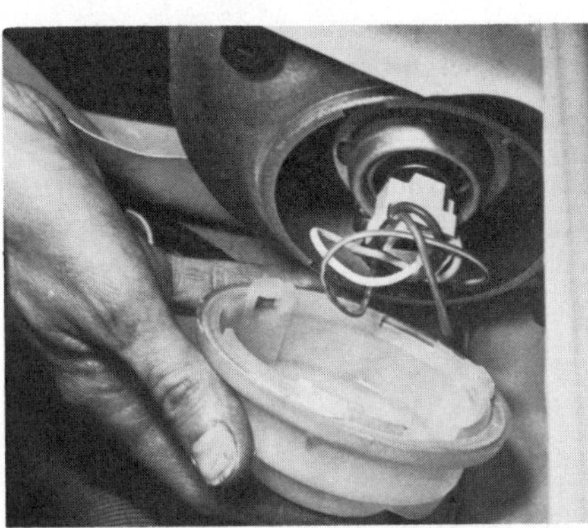
3.1b Another type of cover does not have a plug but the lead goes in the side

3.2a Remove the plug and ...

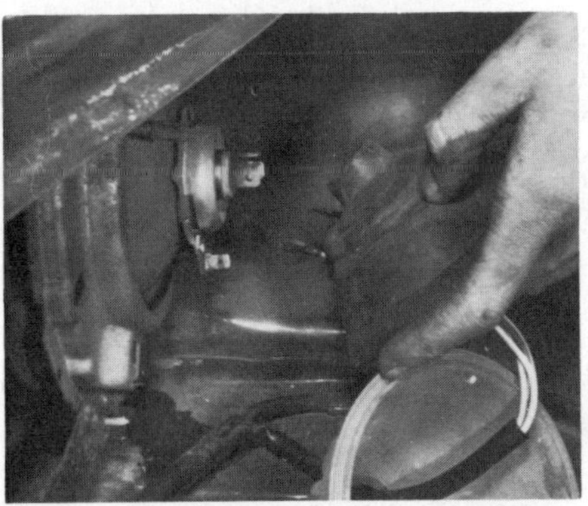
3.2b ... then the rubber cover

3.3a The bulb holder in place ...

3.3b ... may be removed by turning the bayonet fitting

3.5a With the grille removed the lamp may be detached

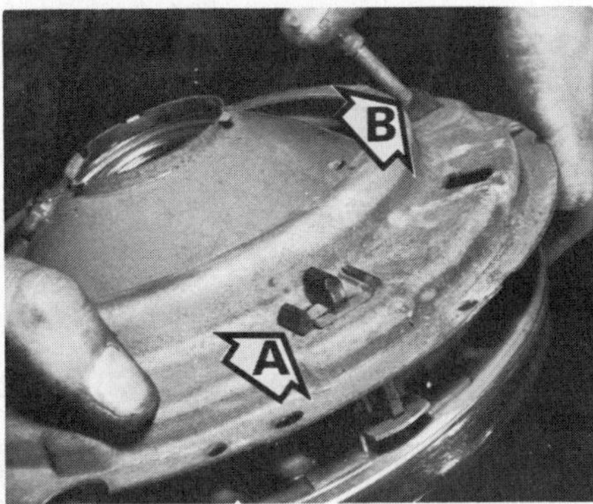

3.5b The fastener clips are at 'A' and the focussing screw 'B'

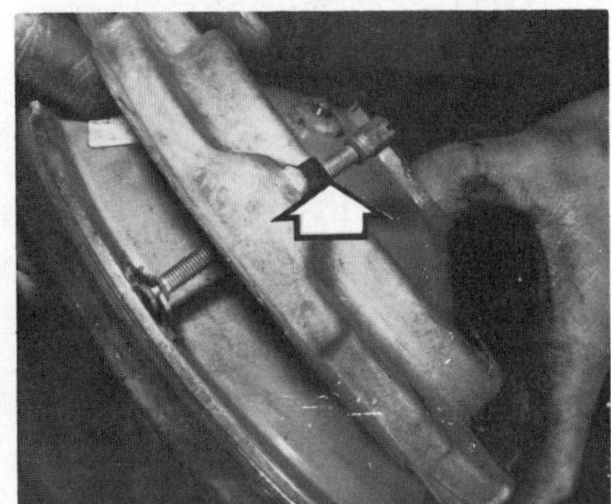
3.6 The focussing screw. Do not move this unless you intend to refocus the lamps

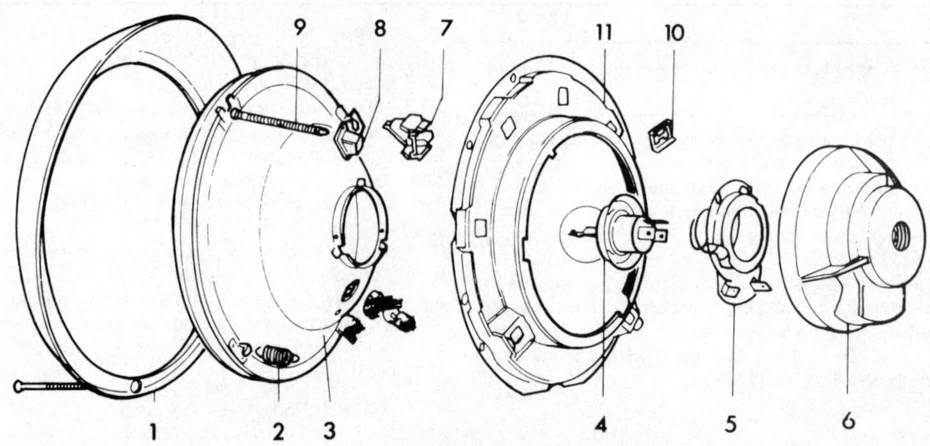

Fig. 11.2 Single headlamp (round pattern) - exploded view

1 Rim
2 Spring
3 Headlight unit
4 Bulb for headlight
5 Bulb holder
6 Cover for bulb holder
7 Retainer
8 Adjuster screw nut
9 Adjuster screw
10 Clip
11 Retaining ring

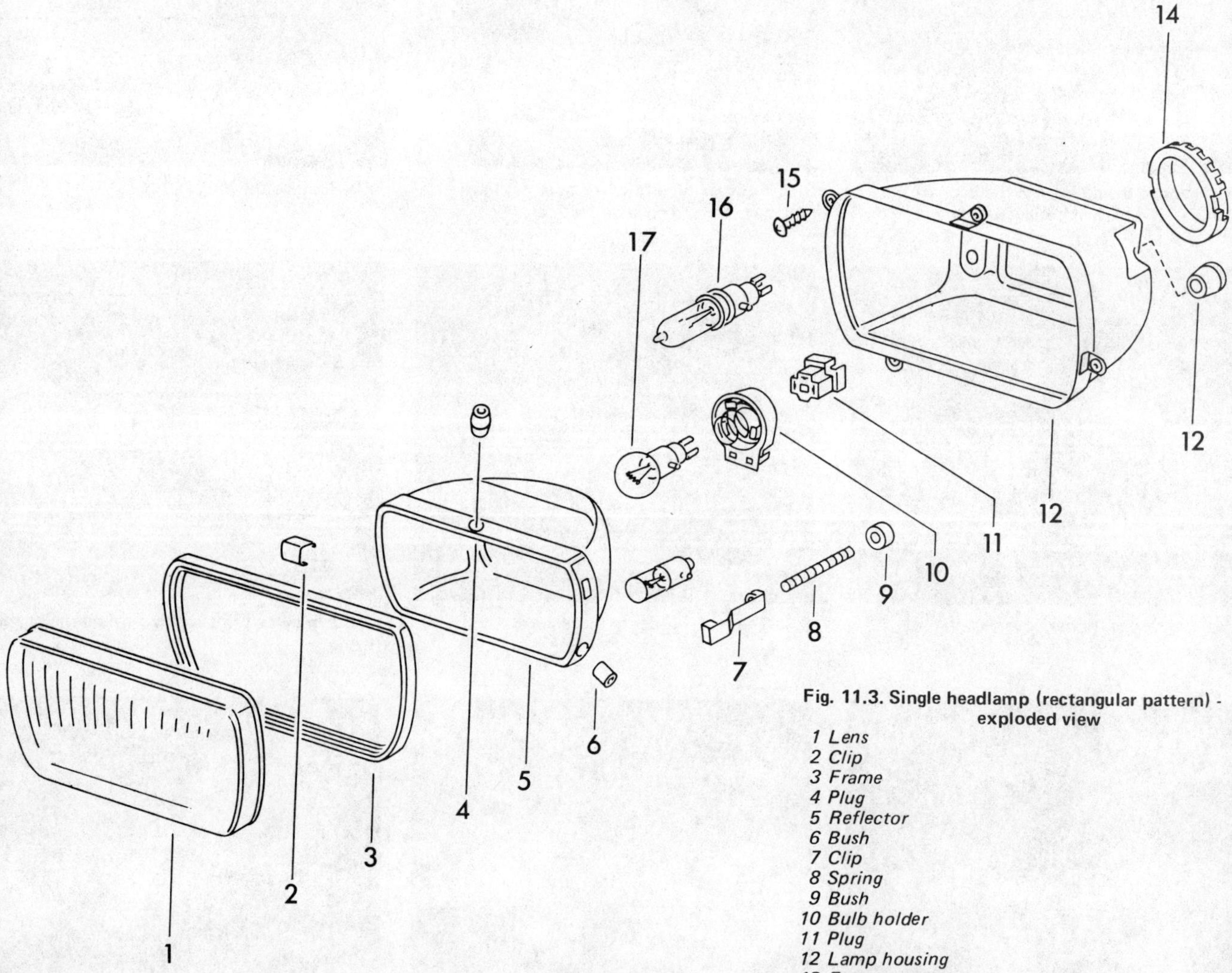

Fig. 11.3. Single headlamp (rectangular pattern) - exploded view

1 Lens
2 Clip
3 Frame
4 Plug
5 Reflector
6 Bush
7 Clip
8 Spring
9 Bush
10 Bulb holder
11 Plug
12 Lamp housing
13 Focus screw nut
14 Cover
15 Screw
16 Halogen bulb
17 Ball type bulb

4 Single headlamps (square reflector) - removal, replacement and bulb renewal

1 Removal and replacement of bulbs is exactly as in Section 3. A diagram is given of the layout.
2 The principle of headlamp removal, replacement and focusing is as in Section 3.

5 Single headlamps (sealed beam units) - removal and replacement

1 These are to be found mostly in the USA. The advantages of better focusing, more light, and easier maintenance are offset by greater expense when failure occurs. If the light filament fails the whole unit must be renewed (see Fig. 11.4).
2 Remove the radiator grille, remove the chromium ring mounting screws and pull the sealed beam unit out. On some vehicles it may be necessary to turn the ring and unit in a counter-clockwise direction before removing it. Pull the plug off the back and fit a new sealed beam unit. Be careful that the lettering on the headlight housing and the chrome ring are at the top and the lettering on the glass of the sealed beam unit is at the bottom.
3 Adjustment of the beam is again by control screws from inside the engine compartment.

6 Double headlamps - removal, replacement and bulb renewal

1 The twin lamps are mounted into a frame onto which they are held by chrome rings and mounting screws. Disconnect the grille and loosen the mounting screws drawing the headlamp forward. It will then be possible to disconnect the wires at the back of the reflector and remove the cap at the back of the light. The bayonet socket may then be removed.
2 If it is only bulb renewal that is required, there is no need to dismantle the lamp assembly. From inside the bonnet locate the twin lamps. The outer one is dipped beam and the inner main or high beam. Pull the connector off the bulb, unhook the spring clip and swing it away. Remove the bulb and replace with a new one. After changing bulbs the headlamp alignment should be checked.

7 Headlamps - beam adjustment

1 Because of the many different local regulations and the increasing argument about what is, and what is not, a correctly aimed headlamp beam we are not offering any advice as to where the beam should point, only how to make it point in that direction. The actual focus point should be obtained from your local dealer or police authority.
2 Movement of the lamp is controlled by the two screws, already discussed in Sections 3, 4, 5 and 6.
3 Having ascertained how the beam is to be aimed on dip, whether it must swing to the right or left when dipped, and the measurements of the displacement, set the car on level ground about 20 feet (6.09 metres) from a vertical wall or door. The vehicle tyre pressures should be correct and there should be the equivalent of the drivers weight in the driving seat.
4 Mark with relation to the centre-line of the car and the height of the lamps from the ground, the equivalent positions of the lamps on the wall. Using this as a datum, mark the area to which the lights should be directed on dipped beam. Cover one light and switch on. Using the adjusting screws direct the beam to the area required. Cover that light and repeat with the other one.

When the beams are correctly focussed on dip the main beams will automatically be correct.

8 Front turn signal light - bulb renewal

1 This lamp is carried in the bumper bar. The lead is joined to the harness by a plug just inside the engine compartment.
2 Remove the lens by undoing two screws and lifting it away (photo). Remove the bulb from the bayonet socket. Do not handle it with bare fingers. Replace the bulb (photo) and refit the lens.
3 If by mischance the porcelain is broken this may be removed by undoing two screws under the bumper bar and removing the porcelain downwards. It is a tight fit so be careful (photo).

9 License plate light - bulb renewal

1 There are two of these bulbs concealed in the lower edge of the rear boot lid just above the license (number) plate.
2 Open the boot and remove the screws holding the lens (photo). Ease

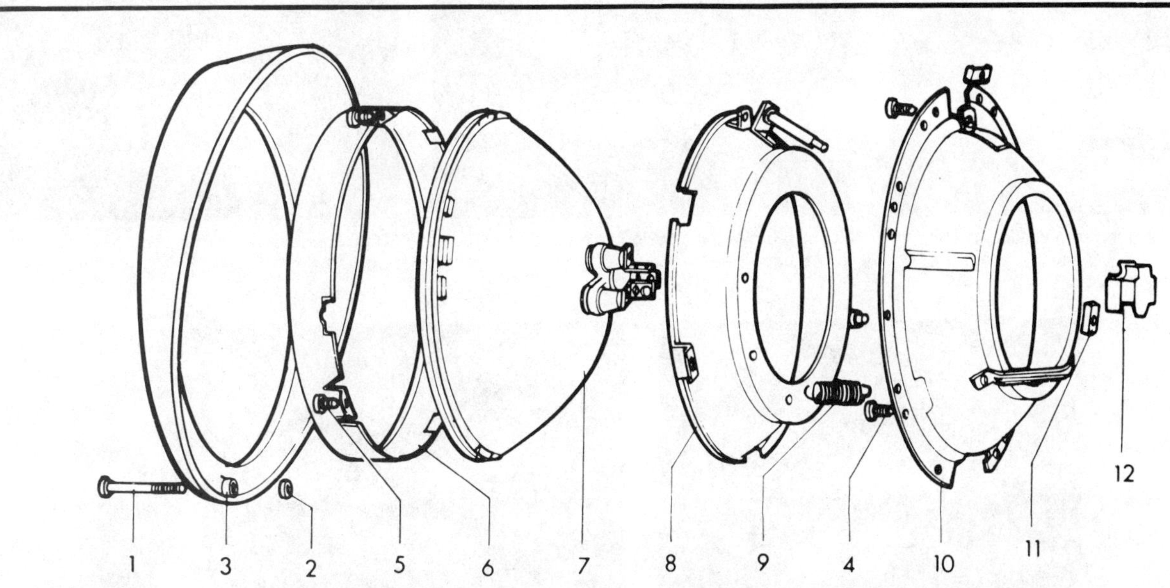

Fig. 11.4 Single headlamp (sealed beam) - exploded view

1 Rim securing screw
2 Rubber washer
3 Rim
4 Securing ring screw
5 Retaining ring screw
6 Retaining ring
7 Sealed beam unit
8 Aiming ring with 2 aiming screws
9 Retaining ring spring
10 Securing ring
11 Tapped plates
12 Terminal

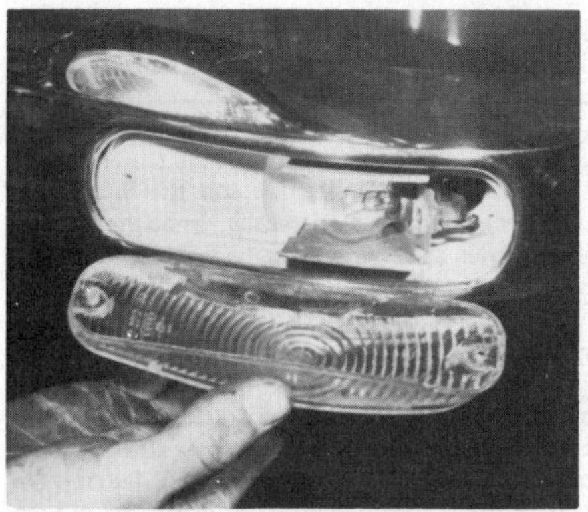
8.2a Remove two screws and lift the front turn signal lens away from the bumper

8.2b Remove the bulb from the bayonet socket

8.3 Removing the porcelain through the hole in the bumper

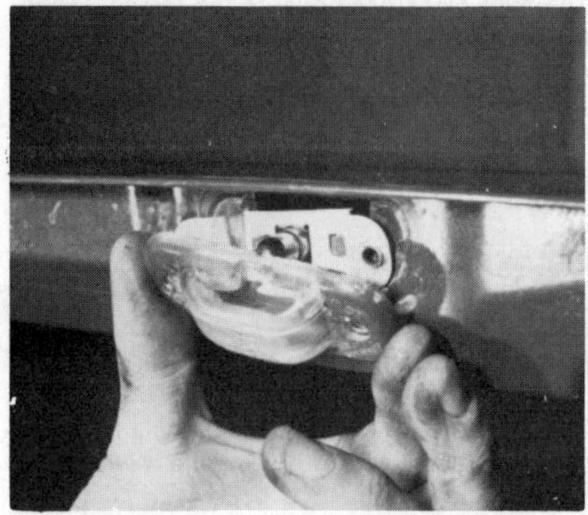
9.2a Remove the lens from the bottom of the rear boot lid ...

9.2b ... and remove the bulb

9.3 On later Saloons/Sedans the light is mounted on the bumper

10.1 The Estate/Wagon has a vertical taillamp cluster

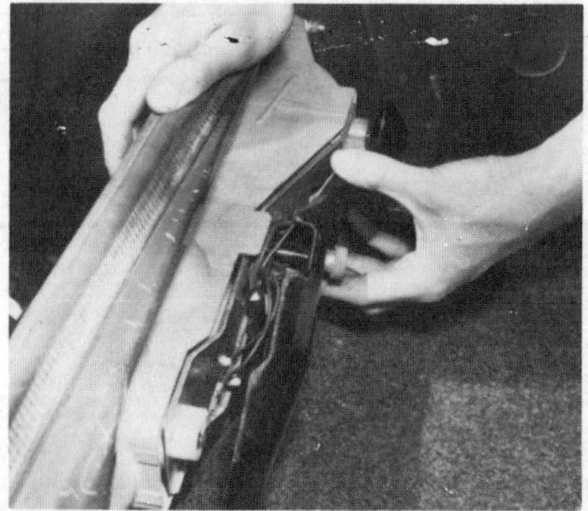
10.2a Remove the knurled knob and ease the plate away

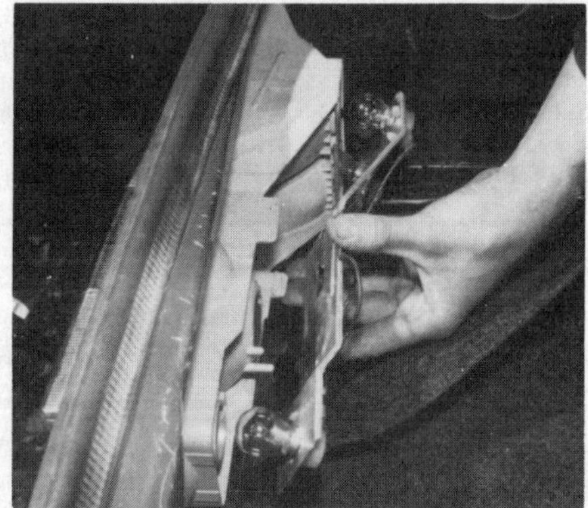
10.2b Remove the metal plate to get at the bulbs

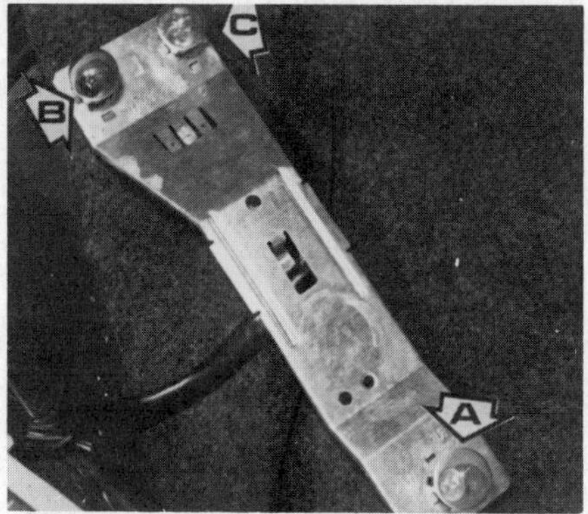

10.2c Plate showing (A) back-up light (B) double fillament brake/tail light and (C) turn signal

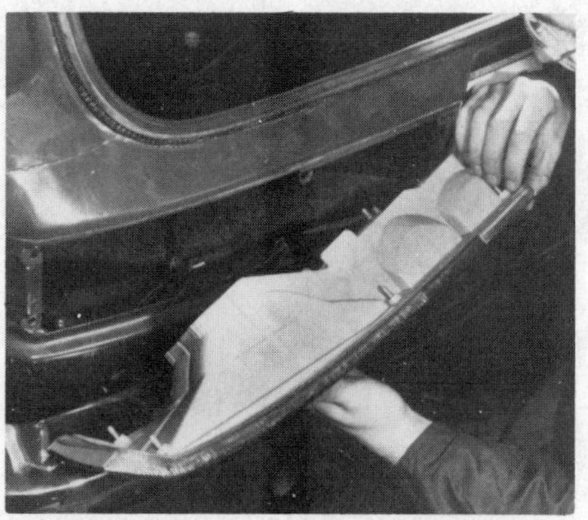
10.3 The plastic lens removed in one piece

the bulb holder out until it is possible to turn the bulb and withdraw it (photo). Install a new bulb and refit the lens.
3 On some of the later saloons/sedans these lights are mounted on the bumper (photo). Servicing is by the same method.

10 Rear light cluster - bulb renewal

1 There are at least two variations of this fitting. One is a horizontal cluster for the saloon/sedan, the other a vertical cluster for the estate/wagon/variant (photo). There may be slight variations on both of these but the method of servicing and repair is the same. The one illustrated is a 1300 cc saloon/sedan.
2 Access to the bulb is from inside the car boot. Remove the knurled knob from the black plastic cover and lift it away (photo). Inside the cover is a metal plate carrying the bulbs. This may now be removed and the bulbs extracted (photo). The single bulb at the one end (photo) marked 'A' is the back-up light, 'C' is the turn signal bulb and the brake and tail lights are in one twin filament bulb. This bulb can only be inserted if the thicker pin was pointing outside when the bulb was inserted. On American versions the plate is larger and four bulbs are installed, the double filament being replaced by two single filaments.
3 The lens is a large multi-coloured plastic item which comes off in one piece when the nuts and bolts are undone (photo). It should be sealed to the body on replacement.

11 Interior lights - bulb renewal

These are held into the linings by a lug at one end and a spring clip at the other. Lever them out with a small screwdriver. Replace the festoon bulb making sure the contacts are tight. Install the housing at the switch end first and then press in the other end until the spring clip is in place.

12 Side marker lights - bulb renewal

On American versions of the vehicle there are four small red lights one on each side at the front and one on each side at the back. To replace the bulb remove the lens by undoing the two screws, and lift the lens away. Replace the bulb and then the lens. Be careful that this joint is watertight for this lamp gets a lot of water thrown at it.

13 Fog lamps - fitting guidelines

1 The vehicle is wired for fitting fog lamps whether they are fitted or not. Similarly provision is made for standard switches so there is really little point in fitting any other type than the VW/Audi type. A switch will cost very little, the relay and lamps are more expensive but compare well with other proprietory fog lamps.
2 The location of the switch is to the left of the steering wheel. Cut the necessary slot and fit the fog switches. Pick up the wiring which is tied back under the fascia. There are two multipin sockets not in use, (see photo 2.1 of Chapter 5), which will reach the fascia at the right place. The one with four spare pins is the rear fog lamp, the other the front fog lamp and they fit onto the switches. The leads which go to the flasher units in the engine compartment (Section 8) have one spare terminal in the multi-pin plugs which may be used for the supply to the fog lamp and the earth wire from the lamp may be bolted to the frame.
3 A relay (part no. 823 951 253) must now be fitted to the console in the position shown on the cover. The lamp is positioned under the front bumper to shine on the roadside about ten yards in front of the car.
4 The rear fog lamp is a warning lamp only of much greater power than the existing red rear lamps. The supply for the rear fog lamp may be found in the boot of the saloon/sedan or rear compartment of the estate/wagon/variant. A two pin socket is taped to one side.
5 Part numbers for switches are: Front – 823 941 535A; Rear – 823 941 563B.
6 If you wish to fit fog lamps other than this way, remember the following do nots:

a) Do not plug them into the headlight supply. The relay will not like it.

b) Do not run them straight back to the battery unless an adequate fuse is included, and remember that such an installation will not only require a heavy duty switch but also a heavy duty connector.

c) Do not run them in parallel with the main beam. That defeats the object. The law about where lamps are on the front of a vehicle is strict, so be sure you fit them in the correct place.

14 Direction indicators and emergency flashers - general

1 The direction indicators are controlled by the left-hand column switch. The removal of this is discussed in Section 18 of this Chapter.
2 A switch on the fascia board operates all four flashers simultaneously, and although the direction indicators will not work when the ignition is switched off the emergency switch over-rides this and the flasher signals continue to operate.
3 All the circuits are routed through the relay on the console and its fuse.
4 If the indicators do not function correctly a series of tests may be done to find which part of the circuit is at fault.
5 The most common fault is in the flasher lamps, defective bulbs, and dirty or corroded contacts. Check these first, then test the emergency switch. Remove it from the circuit and check its operation. If the switch is in good order replace it and again turn on the emergency lights. If nothing happens then the relay is not functioning properly and it should be renewed. If the lights function on emergency but not on operation of the column switch then the wiring and column switch are suspect (see Section 18).

15 Instrument panel and warning lights - removal and replacement

1 Refer to Fig. 11.5. The instruments and warning lights are held in one panel in the fascia board. To get at them the cover must be removed from under the dashboard and the instrument panel insert pulled forward.
2 Undo and remove the battery earth lead. Reach behind the fascia and undo the speedometer union nut.
3 On each side of the panel there is a spring. This must be disconnected and then the panel may be drawn forward.
4 Pull out the multi-pin plug and the panel may be removed.
5 The warning lights are held in sockets plugged into the printed circuit. Turn the holders in an anticlockwise direction and they may be removed.
6 When replacing the sockets, push the contact lugs of the holder into the plate carrying the printed circuit and turn the socket in a clockwise direction.

16 Speedometer and speedometer drive - removal and replacement

1 Remove the battery earth lead and the cover from under the fascia board. It is not necessary to remove the speedometer if only the drive cable is to be renewed, but installation will be simplified if the springs holding the panel insert are removed, so that the insert may be drawn forward (refer to Fig. 11.6).
2 Undo the speedometer drive from the transmission and remove the cable from the clips. The cable is held in a grommet in the engine compartment bulkhead. Ease the cable forward through this grommet so that the panel insert may be moved forward. Pull back the rubber boot and undo the knurled nut. Remove the drive through the engine compartment taking the bulkhead grommet with it. The nut can be undone without removing the panel insert if you have a small hand, it is worth a try anyway.
3 When installing a new cable make sure you have the right length of cable, the one for the automatic transmission (55 in./1.39 m), is almost 6 in. (152 mm) longer than the one for manual transmission (49.5 in./1.25 m). **Do not** grease the cable at the speedometer end and check that there are no kinks or twists in the outer cable.
4 Install the cable to the speedometer first and then to the transmission.
5 The speedometer may be removed from the panel insert by undoing the two retaining screws.

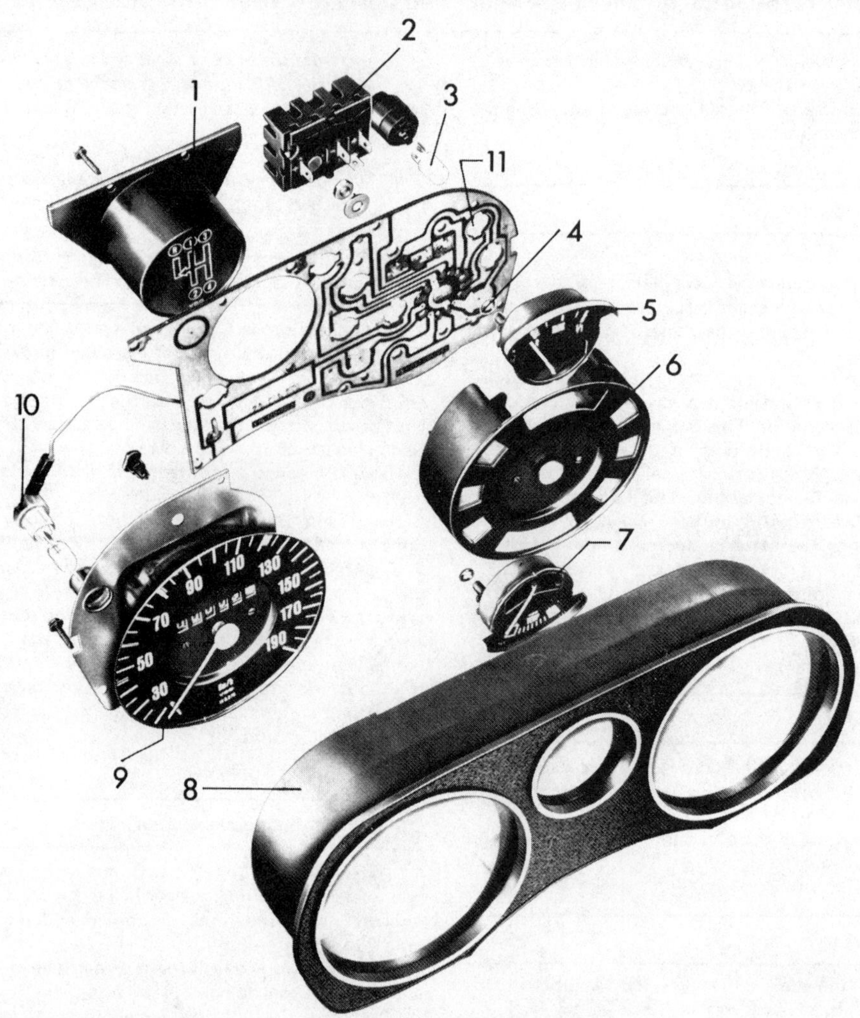

Fig. 11.5 Instrument cluster - exploded view

1 Blanking cover, location for clock or tachometer
2 Voltage regulator
3 Lamp
4 Printed circuit
5 Fuel gauge
6 Cover
7 Temperature gauge
8 Cover
9 Speedometer
10 Light for speedometer
11 Socket hole for lamp

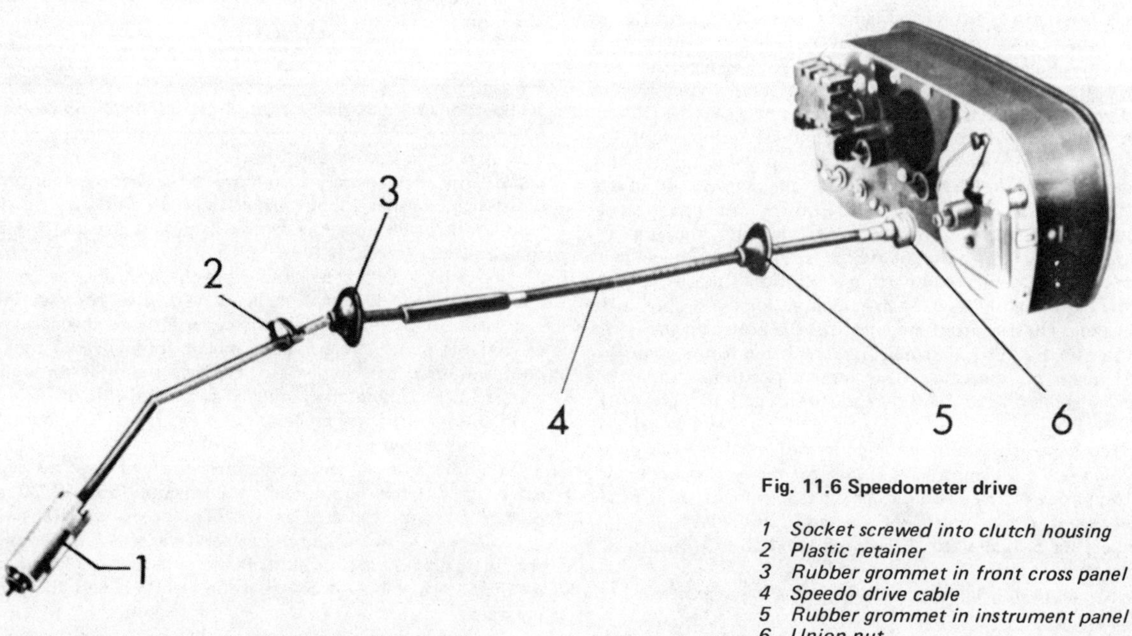

Fig. 11.6 Speedometer drive

1 Socket screwed into clutch housing
2 Plastic retainer
3 Rubber grommet in front cross panel
4 Speedo drive cable
5 Rubber grommet in instrument panel
6 Union nut

17.1 Squeeze the sides of the cap and remove it

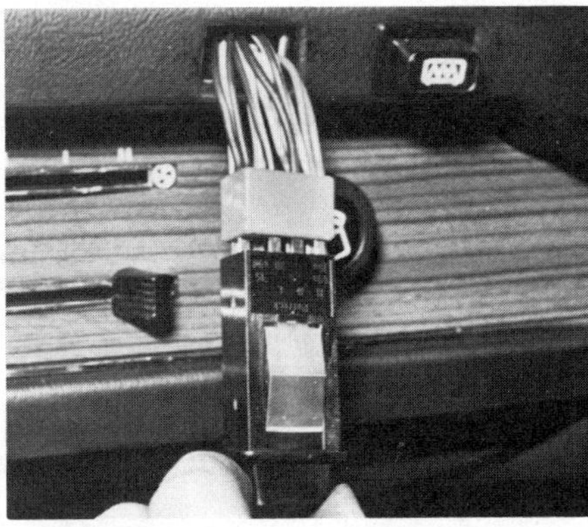

17.2 Pull the switch out of the fascia and separate the plug

18.2 Pull off the horn pad ...

18.3 ... and disconnect the horn wire (A)

18.4 Remove the steering column nut

18.5a Remove the 4 screws holding the switch mounting to the steering column and ...

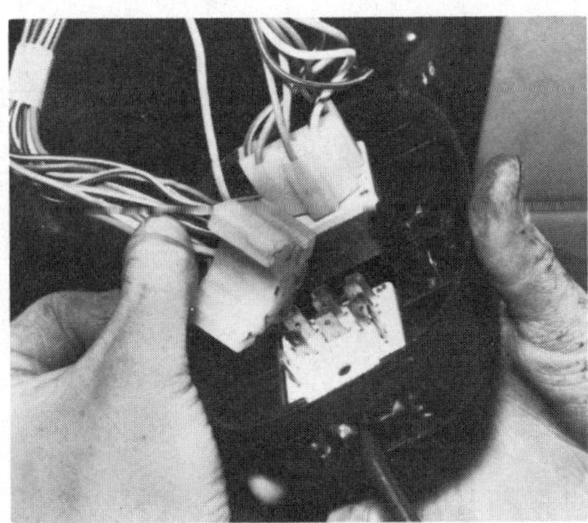

18.5b ... remove the mounting. Remove the multi-pin plugs

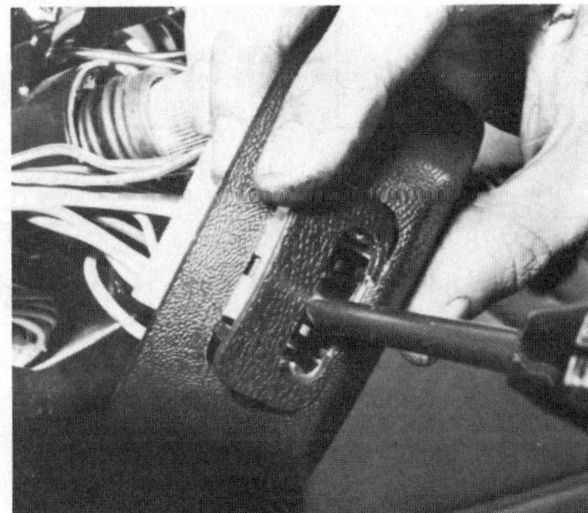

18.6a Remove the plastic cover from the switch stem ...

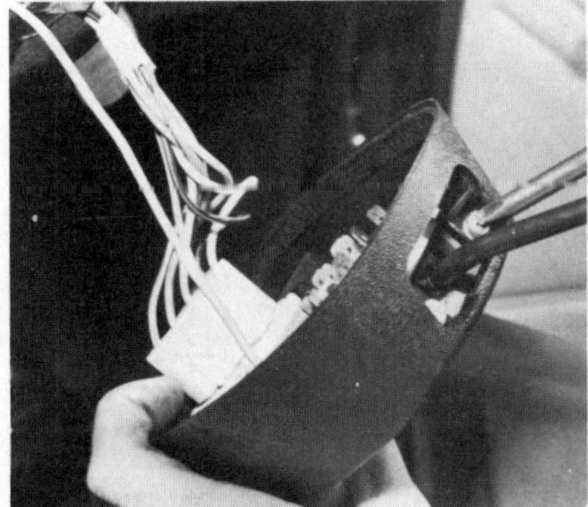

18.6b ... remove the screws ...

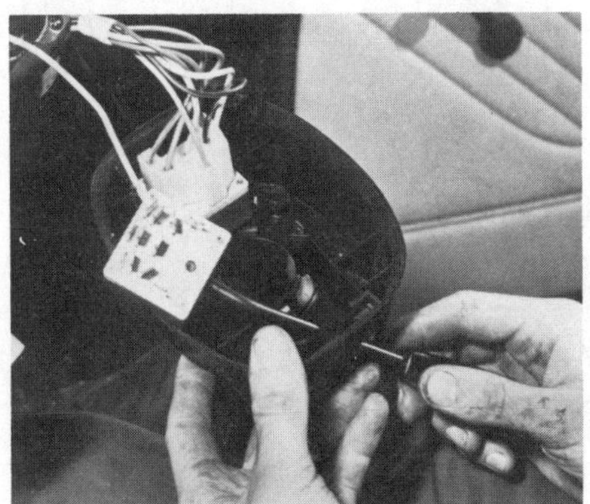

18.6c ... and remove the switch

18.7 The slip-rings must be clean. The inner one is connected to terminal '15a', the outer one to the horn via the relay box

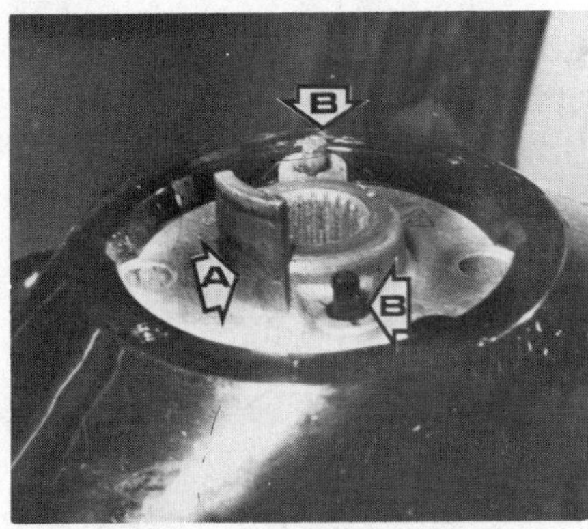

18.11 The underside of the steering wheel 'A' is the cancelling lug 'B' are the brushes

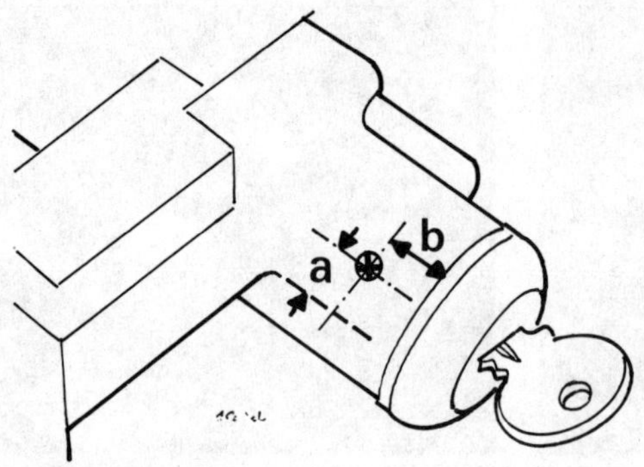

Fig. 11.7 Starter/ignition switch - position of hole to be drilled 3 mm (1/8 in.) to remove lock

a = 8 mm (0.315 in)
b = 11.5 mm (0.45 in)

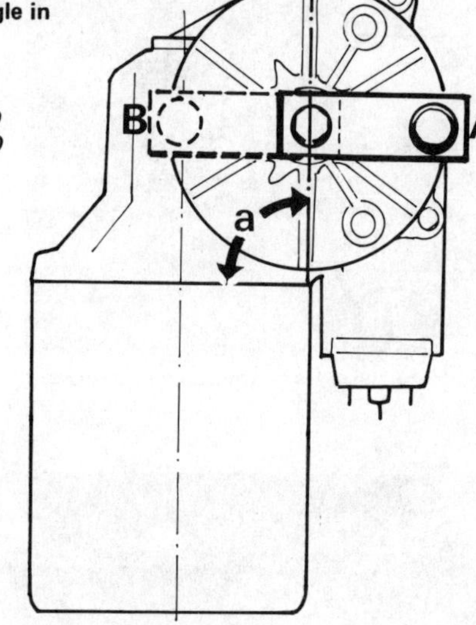

Fig. 11.8 Diagramatic arrangement of wiper motor crank angle in the 'PARK' position

a = 90°
A = crank position LHD
B = crank position RHD

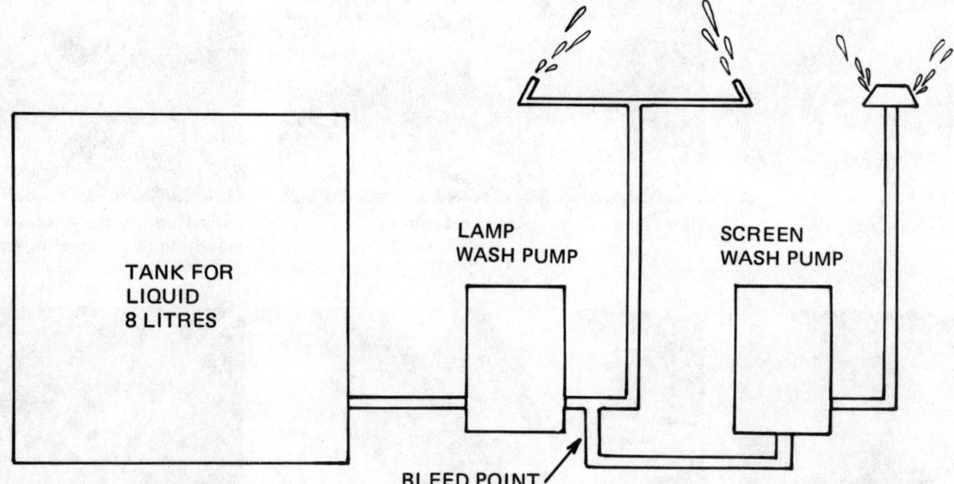

Fig. 11.9 Diagramatic layout of hose connections screen and headlamp washing circuits

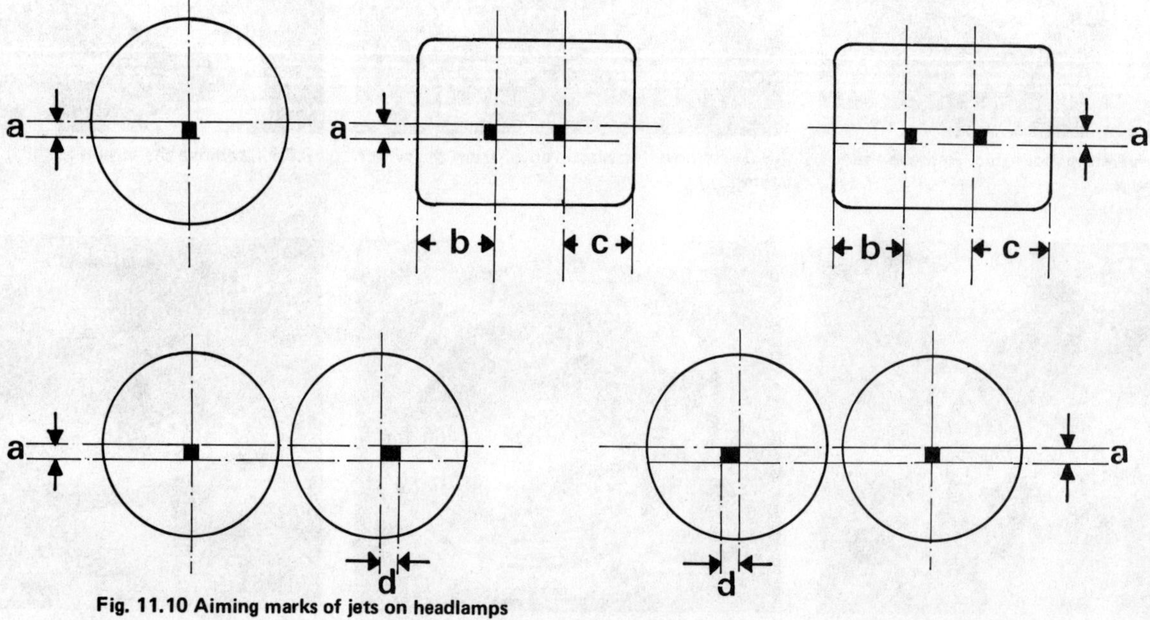

Fig. 11.10 Aiming marks of jets on headlamps

a = 10 mm, b = 70 mm, c = 60 mm, d = 15 mm. Width of area except double headlamps = 1 mm

17 Switches - removal from fascia

1 The switch may be removed very easily. Squeeze the cap in from the side and remove it (photo). Extract the bulb using a piece of plastic tube which just fits over it, do not handle with bare fingers.
2 The switch may then be pulled out of the fascia and will bring the multipoint connector with it. This may then be pulled off the switch (photo).

18 Steering column switches and horn switch - removal and replacement

1 The removal and replacement of the various switches on the steering column is dealt with without reference to the items which they control. Reference will be made to those in separate Sections, but as the dismantling of one switch involves the removal of the others, it is as well to study the entire assembly in one Section. Before starting work, disconnect the earth lead from the battery.
2 The hardest job is removing the horn pad. It is pulled off its dowels but it really does need a very hard pull. We thought we were going to break the plastic when suddenly the pad came away (photo).
3 Disconnect the wire from the pad to the column (photo).
4 Undo the steering wheel retaining nut (photo) and remove the steering wheel. **Do not use undue force. If the steering wheel refuses to budge, a suitable puller must be used, otherwise the integral safety section of the steering column may be damaged.**
5 Undo the four crosshead screws (photo) and lift the entire switch ring off the column. The multi-pin plugs may be disconnected. They are different shapes, so there is no worry about which goes where on reassembly.
6 Remove the small piece of plastic cover round each switch stem (photo) and unscrew the self-tapping screws holding the switch in place (photo). The switch may now be removed from the housing for test and possible replacement.
7 The slip rings should be cleaned and polished and the condition of the brushes in the steering wheel checked. These must be free to move in the guides (see photo 18.11).
8 The remaining switch is the ignition switch/steering lock which presents quite a problem. The removal of the entire assembly is dealt with in Chapter 12 under the heading of removing the steering column. The wiring to the switch is carried on a multi-pin plug which may be removed by pulling off. The switch is retained in the housing (see Fig. 12.5), and may be removed after undoing the small grub screw. The switch is operated by an extension of the steering lock. Before removing set the key in the off position. When installing see that the thread in the housing lines up with the hole in the starter/ignition switch. Then install the locking screw and secure with paint.

9 Removal of the lock is yet another problem. Refer to Fig. 11.7 There may or may not be a centre-punch mark in the position shown. If not then make one. Drill through the housing *only* with a 3 mm drill (1/8 in.). Now push a piece of wire through the hole and push down the spring. Turn the key slightly clockwise and pull the cylinder out. When installing the lock cylinder the key should not be in the lock. Push the cylinder in until the locking spring latches into position.

10 Reassembly of the steering column switches is the reverse of removal. Replace the stalk switches in the housing and fit the screws and plastic covers. Plug in the multi-pin plugs to the switches and install the assembly onto the column with the four screws.
11 When installing the steering wheel the roadwheels should be in the straight-ahead position and the cancelling lug on the steering wheel (photo) must be to the right. The turn signal switch should be in the neutral position. Be careful about this or the lug may damage the cancelling cams when the steering wheel is installed. Torque the steering wheel nut to 36 lb ft (5 kg m).

19 Horn circuit - testing

1 The horn is mounted on the right front body frame member (photo). When correctly installed the horn casing must not touch the vehicle body. Check that the connections are tight.
2 If the horn is still in the guarantee period when it goes wrong, do not try to adjust it — or the guarantee will become void.
3 If it is not then there are alternatives. If it makes a noise, but not the right one, remove the seal on the back and turn the adjusting screw.
4 If the horn makes no noise at all, check the wiring and fuse. When the ignition is on and the horn pad is pressed there should be at least 9 volts at the horn terminal. If there is not then the circuit must be traced and tested.
5 The circuit as far as the slip-rings, is described in Section 18. If the carbon brush on the underside of the steering wheel is broken, a new brush may be obtained from a VW/Audi dealer. The slip-rings must be replaced as an assembly.
6 The inner slip ring is connected to the fusebox (no. 6). The cable from the outer-ring goes to the relay box also. The one cable from the horn goes to the same terminal in the relay box as the cable from the outer slip ring and the other (earthing) cable to the combined relay/fusebox. The actual terminals may vary according to model, so consult the wiring diagram for your model.
7 Follow the wiring through, testing at each terminal, check the fuse, and if all still seems in order but no noise comes from the horn, then try connecting it direct to the battery, momentarily. If it makes the right kind of noise then suspect the relay (if fitted). The only way to test this is by replacing it with a new one.

20 Fuse panel and relays - removal and replacement

1 The fusebox and relay panel which form the heart of the electrical circuits are housed under the bonnet in the engine compartment (photos). There are seventeen fuses which vary from one of 25 amps for the air-conditioner, five 16-amp fuses for the larger accessories, and eleven 8-amp fuses for the lights and smaller accessories. A typical fuse table is given in the Specification but this will vary from model to model. Check the layout in the operators handbook issued with the vehicle.
2 On some quite peaceful morning, with the table of fuses in front of you, check each circuit by switching the circuit on, checking that it works, switching off, removing the fuse, checking that it does not work, replacing the fuse and checking that the system works again. Make your

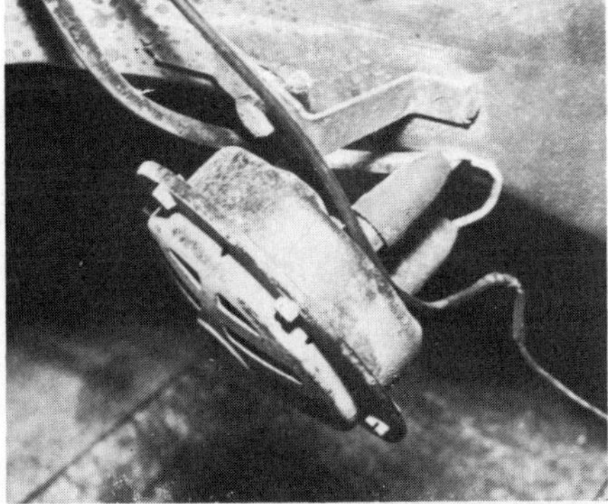

19.1 The horn is on the right-hand front body member

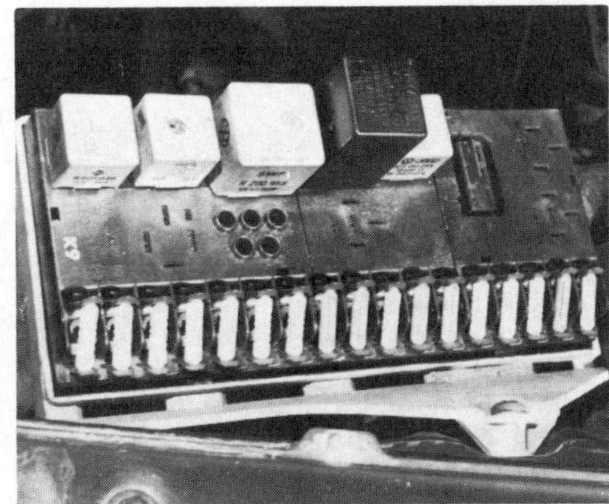

20.1a The fuse and relay console

20.1b Another location and layout of the fuse /relay console own table of fuses and keep it with spare fuses in an envelope in the glovebox. The quickest way to stop the horn blowing is to remove the fuse.

3 When a fuse 'blows' there is no point in just replacing it. The fault must be traced and rectified before installing a new fuse.

4 **Never** replace a fuse with one of a higher current rating. That is the quickest way to start a fire, or at the least an expensive 'burn-out'.

5 The number and type of relays fitted depends on the electrical equipment fitted to the car, but as extra equipment is added the space and wiring for the extra relay (fog lamp for instance) is already there.

6 If for some unfortunate reason the panel is cracked or broken it may be removed and replaced by a patient operation. The panel is held in the housing by lugs which protrude into the housing on the engine side of the housing. Disconnect the battery earth strap. Ease the casing away from the panel and the panel may be drawn upwards. There are three lugs.

7 Remove the wiring from the broken panel, noting from which point each connection is taken. Install them all on the new panel and refit the panel to the housing. Transfer the relays from the old panel to the new one. Reconnect the battery.

21 Heated rear window - general

1 If this accessory is not fitted and it is wished to fit one, then the task is made easier by the fact that the necessary wiring is already installed.

2 In the boot a white coloured wire is a spare lead which goes back to terminal 8 of the fuse/relay console. Connect this wire to one side of the window element and earth the other end.

3 Next to the emergency flasher switch on the fascia is a space for an extra switch. Fit a standard VW/Audi switch. Remove the cover from under the fascia and among the wiring is a spare multi-pin plug with terminals '31', '86h', 87hc', '15a' and '15r'. Plug this in to the switch.

4 The space for the relay is marked on the cover of the console. Fit a standard VW/Audi relay and the job is complete.

22 Radio - fitting guidelines

1 Provision is made for the fitting of a radio in the fascia board of the vehicle. Five standard sets are available according to taste and availability of cash, including one radio/cassette tape player.

2 In the UK these sets are usually supplied by Motorola, although others are available. It is best to consult with one of the official agencies as to the set most suited to your needs and fit it according to the instructions supplied. Different sets have characteristics suitable to certain localities and most of them have blind spots (eg; VHF will give patchy reception in built-up or hilly areas), so again accept the advice of the local expert.

3 The aerial/antenna is usually installed on the left-hand front wing and the lead brought through the engine compartment. This may require holes to be drilled. These should always be sealed with grommets.

4 Supression is generally built in to the various electrical components when the car is made. However, electrical 'noise' may appear and can only be traced by isolating components to see whether the noise disappears (eg: switch off the engine and if the noise disappears then the trouble is ignition or alternator). Take off the alternator belt and run the engine to see whether the alternator is causing the trouble.

5 It is imperative that a small fuse be fitted to the supply cable. A 2 amp VW/Audi standard (part no. 111 035 307) is recommended.

23 Windscreen wiper and washer - general description

1 The early basic vehicle was fitted with a two speed wiper and a mechanical foot pump for the washer system.

2 Subsequent models have an electric washer pump and an intermittent wiper control as well as two speed continuous wiping.

3 In August 1973 a headlight washer system was introduced as an optional extra.

4 A rear window wiper is also available for estate/wagon type vehicles.

5 The wiper/washer is controlled from the right-hand steering column switch. The speed control is fixed by the horizontal movement of the lever and the washer works when the lever is lifted towards the steering wheel.

6 Two lengths of wiper blade are fitted, 15 in. (380 mm) and 15 ¾ in. (400 mm). Make sure that you use the correct replacement.

24 Windscreen wiper mechanism - removal, inspection and replacement

1 The cover for the wiper spindle nut which hides the joint of the blade and spindle is hinged (photo). Turn this back and remove the nut. Note how the blade is fitted, remove the nut and pull off the blade (photo). Repeat for the other wiper blade. Undo the battery earth strap.

2 Remove the gland nut from each side (photo).

3 Pull off the multi-pin plug (photos) and then remove the bracket nut (photo).

4 Lower the frame away from the body and remove it (photos).

5 Repair is by replacement. Whatever is wrong with the electrical circuit may only be cured by fitting a new one. The replacement of the column switch is discussed in Section 18. The brush gear is not a service part so the motor must be replaced if faulty.

6 Inspect the linkage for wear or corrosion. The parts of the linkage are replaceable, if required. However, the links are different on left-hand and right-hand drive vehicles.

7 If electrical 'noise' has caused problems with the radio the motor may be replaced by a fully suppressed one. This carries a yellow paint stripe.

8 Before assembling set the motor to the 'park' position. Refit the battery earth strap, plug the motor into the circuit (but do not fit it to the body) and run the motor for a few minutes. Switch off and the motor will stop in the 'Park' position. Install the crank at 90° to the wiper motor body, away from the body for LHD vehicles and towards the body for RHD vehicles (see Fig. 11.8).

9 Install the motor to the wiper frame and refit to the vehicle body.

10 Install the arms in the 'Park' position. The blade should be 1 3/8 in. (35 mm) from the edge of the screen. Tighten the nut to 7 lb ft (1 kg m).

25 Windscreen wipers - fault diagnosis

Symptom	Probable reason	Remedy
Motor does not work, runs slowly or runs and then stops	1 Loose connections 2 Brushes worn 3 Linkage stiff or seized 4 Armature burnt out 5 Column switch defective	1 Check wiring. 2 New motor. 3 Dismantle, clean and lubricate. 4 Replace motor. 5 Replace switch.
Wiper arms do not park correctly	1 Cable to terminal '53' of the motor loose or broken 2 Drive crank not in correct position 3 Open circuit between terminals '53' and '31b'	1 Check and repair. 2 See Fig 11.8. 3 Replace switch.
Motor continues to run when switched off	1 Switch burnt or defective	1 Replace switch.

Motor runs slowly, high pitched noise from wiper motor and gearbox	1 The gear housing is not seated properly, is not lubricated or is worn and out of alignment	1 Examine gears, lubricate and adjust. If worn replace motor complete.

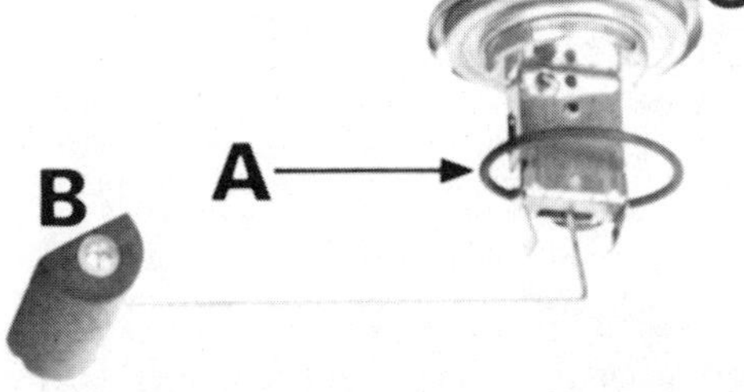

Fig. 11.11 Fuel gauge transmitter unit

A 'O' ring
B Float
C Tank fitting

24.1 Turn back the hinged cover and undo the nut. The wiper arm can then be lifted off the splines

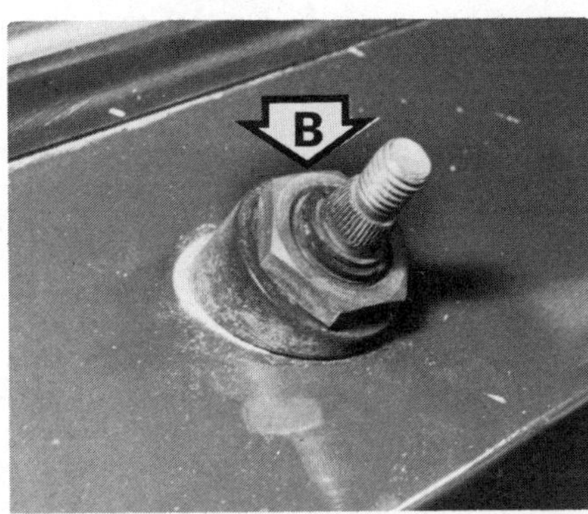

24.2 Remove the gland nut (B)

24.3a The plug, bracket and motor are all close together

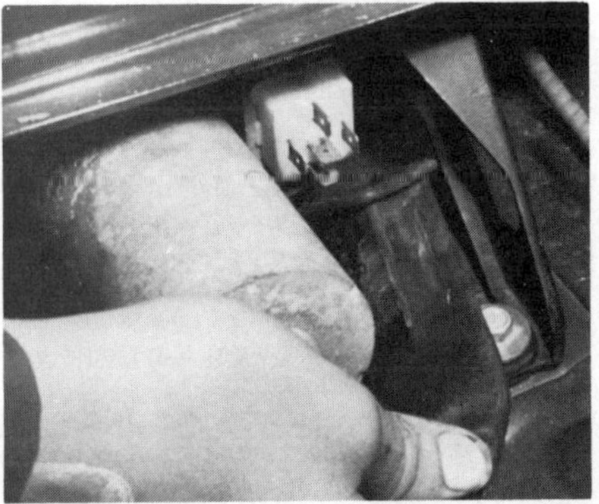

24.3b Remove the lead from the plug ...

24.3c ... and undo the bracket nut

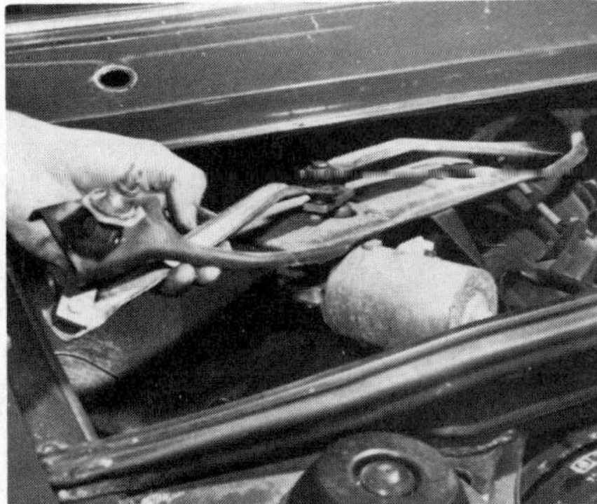

24.4a Remove the wiper mechanism

24.4b The motor and connections viewed from underneath

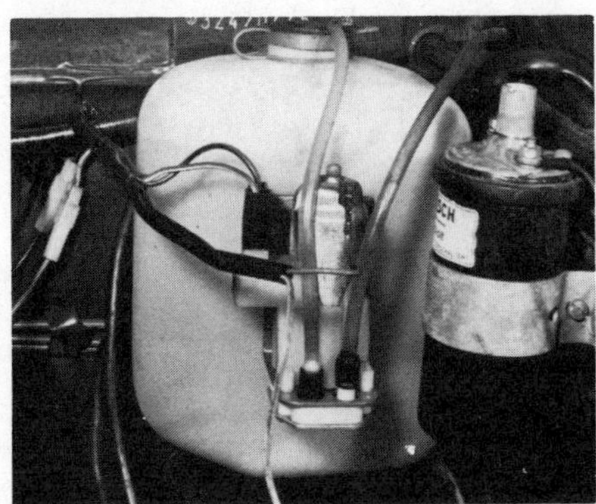

26.2 The container and pump

30.2 The computer plug in the engine compartment

26 Windscreen washer - repair and adjustment

1 The electric pump is controlled by the same stalk switch on the steering column as the wiper, see Section 18 for removal and replacement.
2 The washer liquid is held in a tank on the engine bulkhead (photo). The pump is located on the front of the tank.
3 To remove the pump first detach the battery earth strap. Pull off the plug from the pump noting which way round it goes. Pull off the plastic pipes and ease the pump body away from the plastic lugs on the tank.
4 Neither the pump nor the column switch can be repaired, and must be replaced. The jet may be cleared and correctly directed using a needle.
5 The washer pump on the early models is connected to the same (16 amp) fuse as the wiper (12) and uses the same relay (G), but check the layout on later models.

27 Headlamp washer system - general

1 Installed in 1973 with an extra water container, the twin container was discontinued in 1974 in favour of one larger container for the washer fluid. A diagram of connections is shown at Fig 11.9.
2 The system washes only, and does not wipe. An extra pump is installed which is operated by a relay allowing a jet for 0.3 seconds. The emission is further controlled by a pressure valve set at 35 psi (2.6 bar).
3 When the system is filled the lines must be bled (as with brakes). This is done by pulling off the hose at the junction leading to the headlamp jets until liquid emerges. Then reconnect the hose, switch on the ignition and the headlights and operate the column switch until water emerges from the jets. Be careful that all connections are correctly installed and use only the VW/Audi special water hose.
4 Training the jet is a difficult job unless the correct tool (VW 819) is available. This is a cylindrical mandrel which fits in the jet hole and reaches up to the lens. The top of the tool is moved about until it contacts the lens with certain limits (see Fig. 11.10).

28 Headlight washer system - fault diagnosis

Symptom	Possible cause	Remedy
One jet only squirts	Pressure valve stuck	Close off jet which does work and switch on to clear the blockage.
No jets, but pump can be heard to work	1 No fluid in tank 2 Pressure valve defective	1 Fill. 2 Replace.
No jets, pump not working	1 Column switch faulty 2 Relay defective 3 Pump defective	1 Check continuity - replace switch if necessary. 2 Check continuity - replace relay if necessary. Connect pump direct to 12V supply. If it does not work, remove and fit a new pump.
1 Jets squirt for longer than 1 second	Relay defective	Replace relay.
2 Jets squirt when lights are not switched on	Relay defective	Replace relay.

29 Fuel gauge and transmitter unit - general

1 To remove the gauge, first take off the cover under the fascia centre panel, undo the speedometer union nut, detach the springs (2) which hold the instrument console in position and pull the instrument console forward. The voltage stabilizer and fuel gauge may now be removed (see Fig. 11.5).
2 Removal of the sender unit from the petrol tank is described in Chapter 3, Section 3.3. Disconnect the leads and hoses, remove the screws holding the gauge unit in position and withdraw the gauge and pipe together (see Fig. 11.11).
3 Testing is simple. First check the fuse (no. 5). There is no relay in the system but other units are connected to the same fuse. See that they all function correctly. If the fuse is blown then there is a wiring short circuit. Check the wiring. There may be an open circuit - fuse not blown but no signal from the transmitting unit.
4 If the gauge registers full all the while there is a short circuit. Disconnect the wire from the sender unit, and if the gauge still reads full then the short circuit is in the wiring. If the gauge now reads empty then the transmitter unit is faulty. Remove the transmitter from the tank and connect it across a battery. Connect a voltmeter across the instrument terminals and work the arm of the float unit up and down. The reading on the meter should fluctuate smoothly. If it does not then the unit must be replaced.

30 Computer diagnosis - general

1 In 1970 VW introduced the computer diagnosis system. It is a truely immense step forward in preventative maintenance. The system is devised to assess the state of maintenance of all the major and many minor components of the vehicle. Over 80 points are checked, many of them automatically.
2 A multi-pin plug is installed in the engine compartment (photo). The operator at official agency will check the correct pressures of your tyres and then plug in a large cable to the diagnosis plug. He selects the correct master card for your vehicle, installs it, and from there on a computer takes over. The operator has a hand set connected to the computer which has a small window showing the number of the test to be carried out. As each check is done the print out is marked '+' if the measurement agrees with the vehicle specification or '–' where it is beyond tolerance.
3 The items which are not measured automatically are checked by the operator, where all is well he presses a button marked '+' on the hand set, where all is not well the '– ve' button is pressed.
4 The items which are measured by the equipment automatically are the steering geometry, ignition and charging systems and cylinder compression. Lights and battery condition are checked automatically.

The steering geometry is checked by photo electric beams and mirrors as the steering wheel is turned through 180°, 90° each side of the straight ahead position. This is done within a 20 second period and measures toe and camber and prints out the answer in degrees and minutes. The ignition and charging systems are measured by the resistance of the various circuits. It is important that all connections are clean and that cable sizes are standard.

The cylinder compression is measured by calculating the load on the starter motor when the engine is turned over. The state of the battery and the temperature of the engine oil is measured and taken into account for this check.

There is no doubt that the system is quick, accurate and calculated to tell the unhappy customer all the awful things wrong with his vehicle in the shortest possible time.

5 If the vehicle is used a lot then this system is without doubt the finest way to take care of its working parts. The system does not repair, it diagnoses only, but a record such as the computer gives is worth many hours of hard work inspecting all these things manually, and of course it measures accurately items which the owner of the car cannot measure without expertise and a lot of expensive equipment.
6 Finally, it does away with opinion. It measures and compares with the vehicle Specification. After that it is up to the owner what repairs he does, and which he leaves to the official agent to do.

Key to wiring diagrams in pages 148 to 152. For later models see Chapter 14

1R	Headlight, right
1L	Headlight, left
2R	Turn signal, right
2L	Turn signal, left
3	Oil pressure switch
5	Governor
6	Alternator
7	Starter
8	Ignition coil
9	Distributor with contact breaker
10	Resistor, ignition coil
11	Spark plugs
12	Battery
13	Back-up light switch
14	Brake light switch
15	Relay
15a	Relay, fan motor (coolant)
15b	Relay, rear window defogger *
15c	Relay, fog lights *
15d	Relay, automatic intermittent washer/wipers **
15e	Relay, wiper motor, turn signal and hazard lights
15f	Flasher relay
15g	Main light relay
15h	Relay, headlamp flasher, high and low beams
15i	Relay, halogen high and low beams *
15j	Relay, air conditioning *
17	Blower motor, heater and ventilation
18	Resistor, blower motor
19	Combination instrument
19a	Electronic voltage stabilizer
19b	Instrument light
19c	Temperature gauge
19d	Fuel gauge
19e	Oil pressure indicator
19f	Turn signal indicator
19g	Alternator charge indicator
19i	High beam indicator
19j	Clock **
20	Wiper motor
21	Washer motor **
22	Wiper/washer switch
23	Turn signal/low beam switch
25	Socket (cigar lighter) **
26	Horn button
27	Hazard warning light switch
28	Light switch
29	Steering wheel/ignition lock
30	Temperature transmitter
31	Idle cut-off valve
32	Door contact switch, right
33	Door contact switch, left
34	Courtesy light with switch
35	Fuel level transmitter
36R	Tail light, right
36L	Tail light, left
36h	Turn signal
36i	Tail light
36k	Brake light
36l	Back-up light
37	Licence plate light
38	Switch, tail fog light *
39	Glove compartment light **
44	Horn
46	Rear window defogger *
46a	Switch, rear window defogger
47	Twin circuit brake indicator *
48	Switch, indicator bulb for position 47 *
51	Acoustic turn signal indicator *
52	Parking light switch
53	Fan motor, coolant
54	Thermo-switch, fan motor
55	Switch, fog lights *
56	Fog lights *
57	Tail fog lights *
58	Fuse, radio *
59	Radio *
65	Diagnosis plug
66	Battery ground strap from engine block
66a	Ground, engine block
66b	Ground point
67	Safety belt warning system relay
68	Electronic switch for brake lining wear control
69	Brake lining wear control, right
70	Brake lining wear control, left
71	Safety belt warning system light
72	Safety belt lock, left
73	Safety belt lock, right
74	Contact strip in passenger seat
75	Contact strip in driver's seat
76	Instrument panel lighting control
77	Parking brake control light switch
78	Side marker light, rear
79	Side marker light, front
80	Transmission switch
81	Buzzer contact in ignition switch
82	Automatic choke
83	Cold starting thermo-switch
84	Starter cut-out switch and back-up light switch
85	Back-up light, left
36	Back-up light, right
87	Selector lever console illumination
88	Kick-down switch
89	Kick-down solenoid

* *Optional extra some models*
** *Not applicable to all models*

Colour code

BK	Black
BR	Brown
RD	Red
OR	Orange
YW	Yellow
GN	Green
BL	Blue
GY	Grey
WH	White
MV	Mauve

Wiring diagram - VW Passat

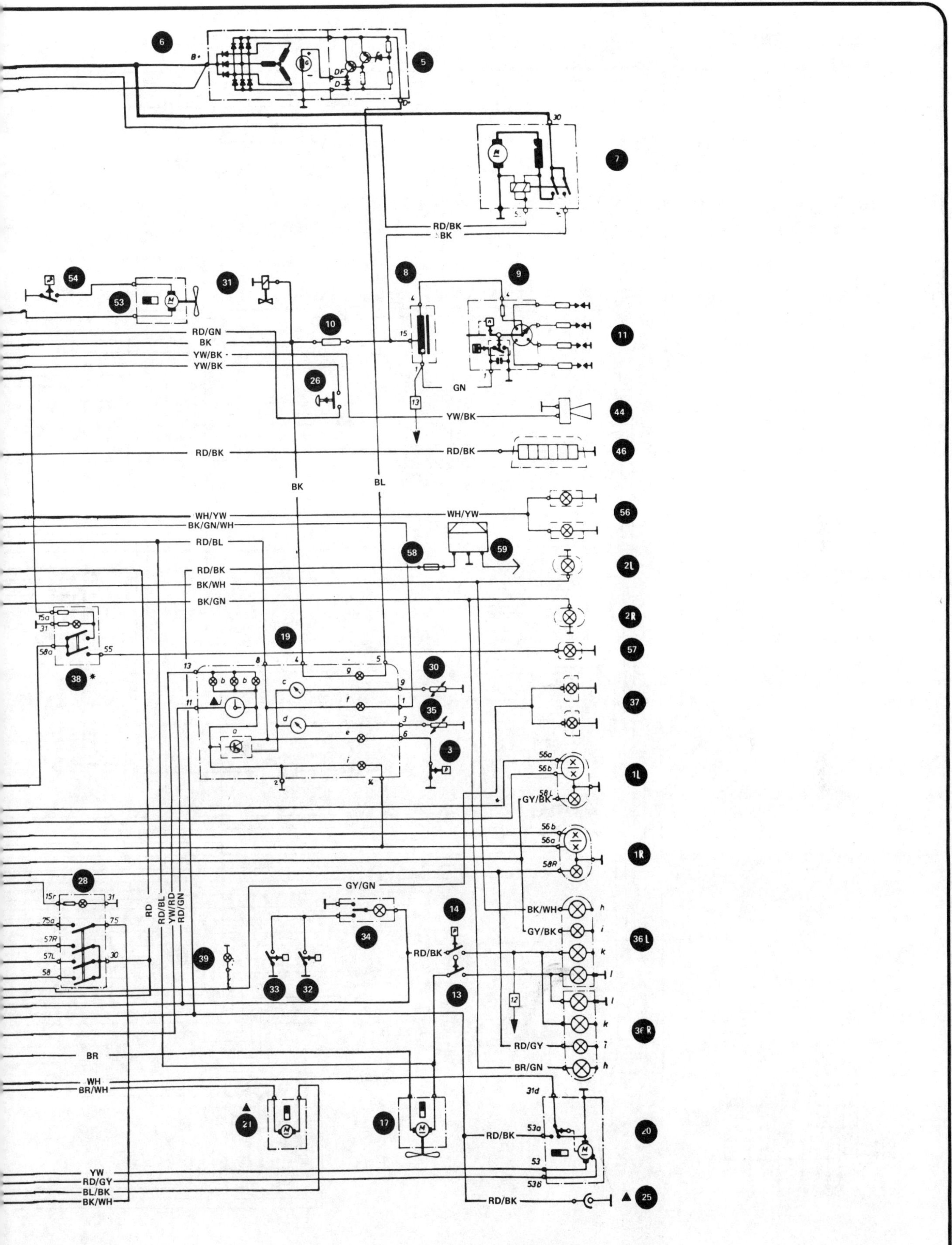

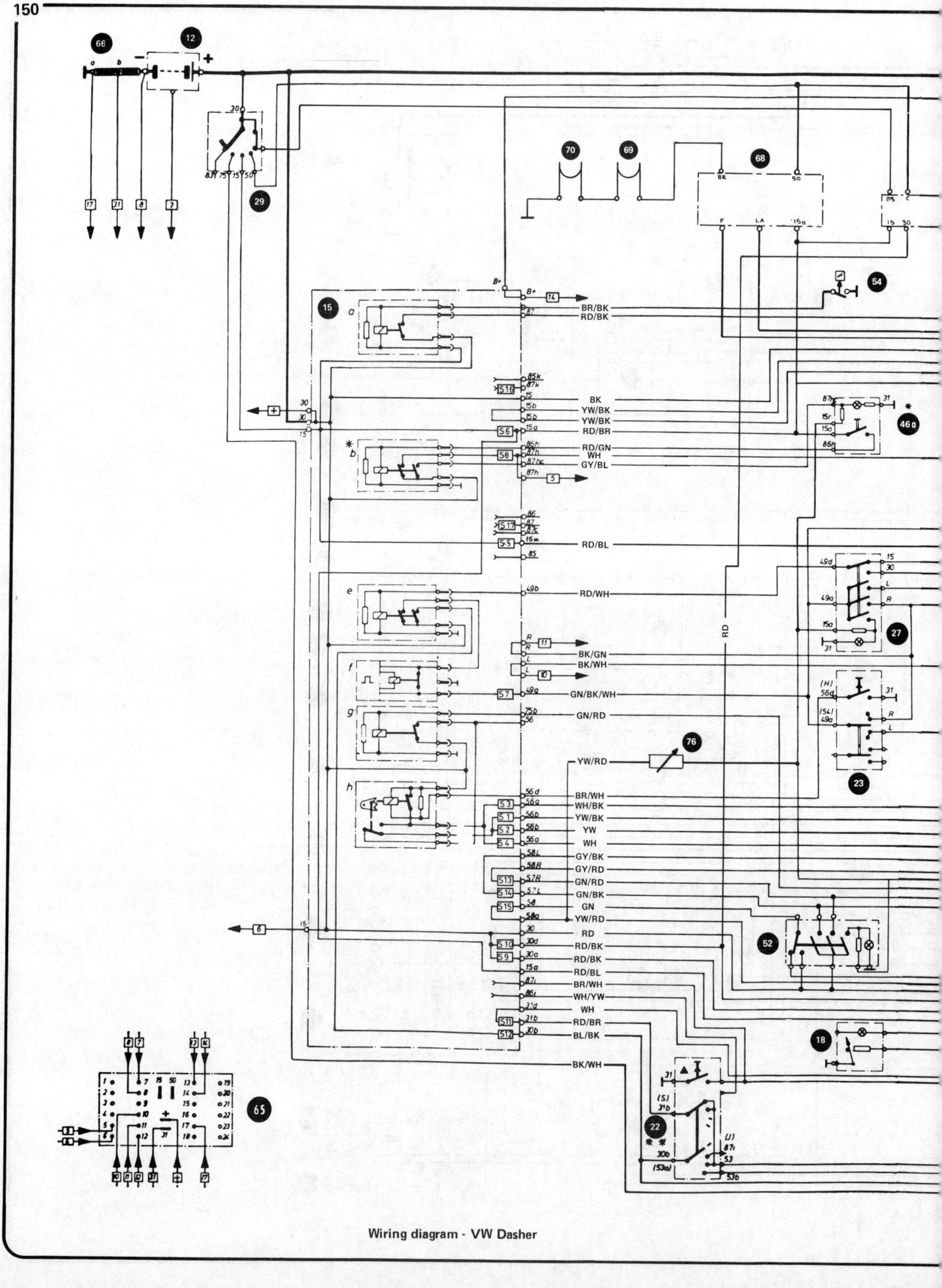

Wiring diagram - VW Dasher

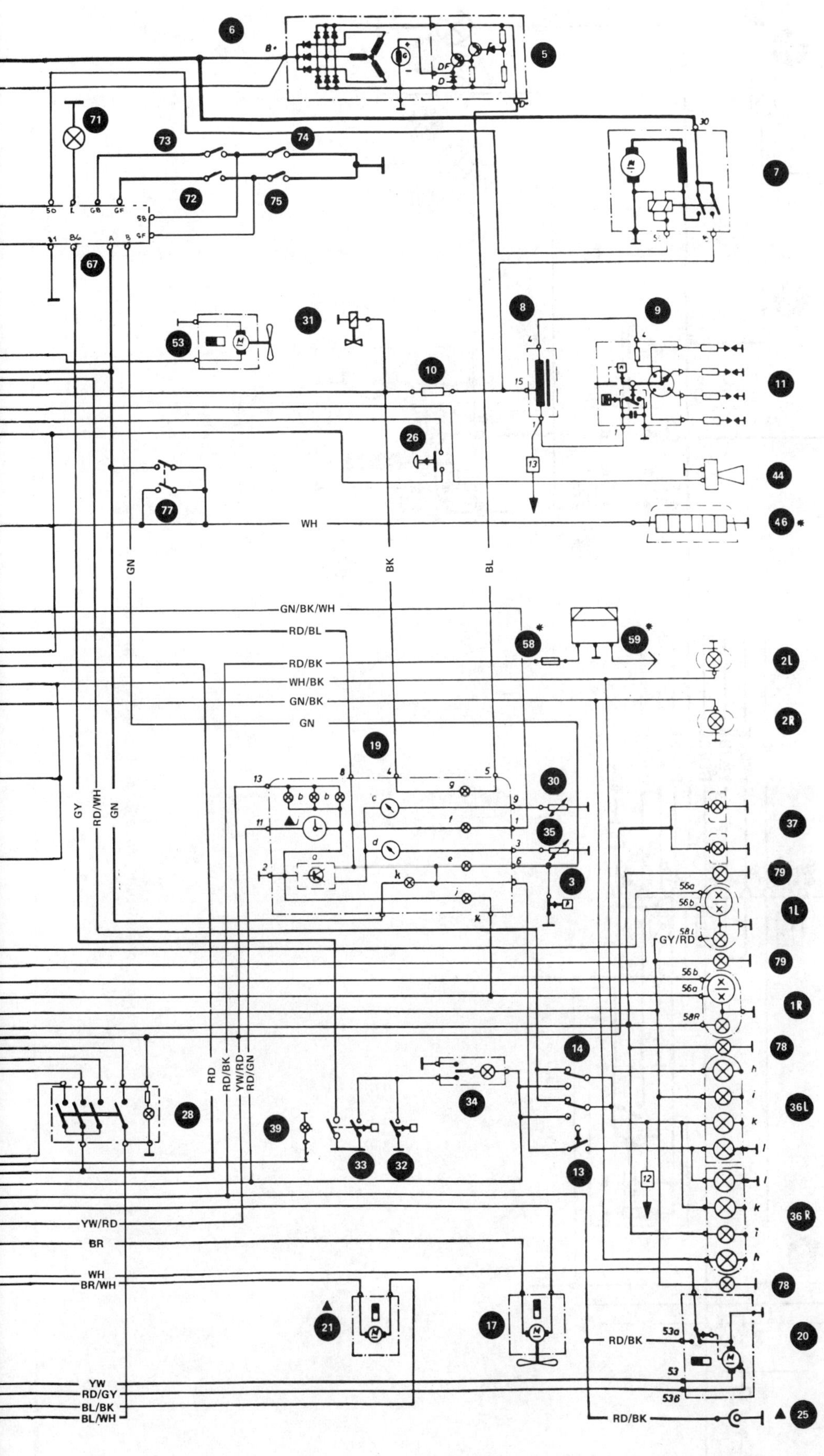

WH
GN
BK
BL
GN/BK/WH
RD/BL
RD/BK
WH/BK
GN/BK
GN
GY
RD/WH
GN
GY/RD
RD
RD/BK
YW/RD
RD/GN
YW/RD
BR
WH
BR/WH
RD/BK
RD/BK
YW
RD/GY
BL/BK
BL/WH

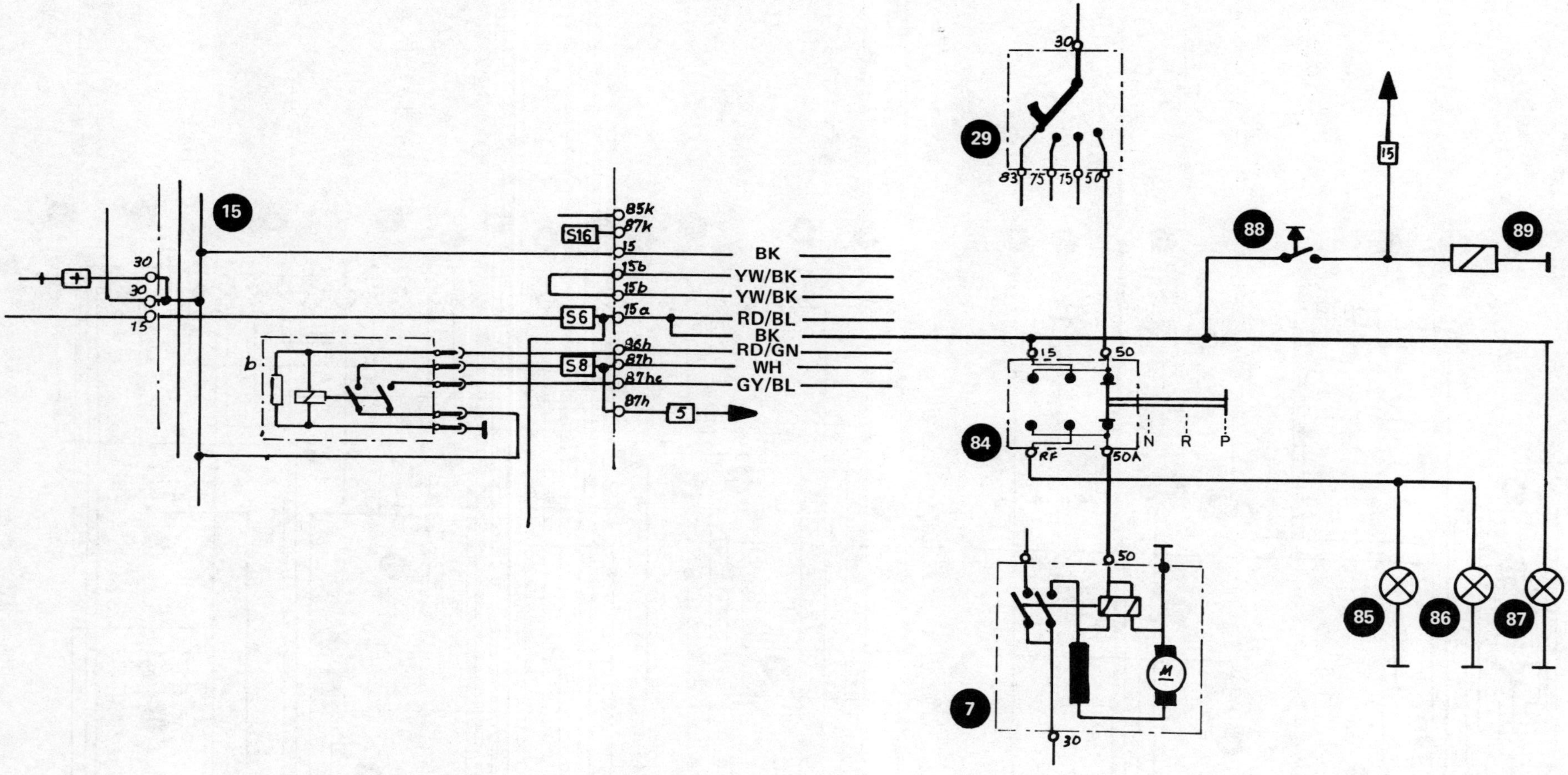

Additional circuitry for all models fitted with automatic transmission

Chapter 12 Steering, front suspension and driveshafts

For modifications, and information applicable to later models, see Supplement at end of manual

Contents

Specifications

Front track ... 52.7 in. (1340 mm)

Turning circle (approx) ... 34 ft (10.3 metres)

Front suspension ... MacPherson strut with the shock absorber in the centre of the coil spring. Stub axle mounted on the steering knuckle. Stabilizer bar between steering knuckles and subframe

Coil springs ... There are eight sizes of coil spring according to the type of body and size of engine. Consult the official agents spares department for the correct type for your vehicle

Shock absorbers ... Either Borge or Fichtel and Sachs. Telescopic, double-acting hydraulic (standard). Gas filled shock absorbers are an option on GT models

Steering balljoints

Maximum play (vertical) ... 0.10 inch (2.5 mm)

Driveshafts

Type ... Double homokinetic or zeppa joints

Length:

Manual transmission ... Both shafts 19.92 ins. (506 mm)

Automatic transmission ... Right 17.2 ins. (437 mm); Left 20.9 ins. (531 mm)

Steering gear ... Rack and pinion, collapsable column

Steering geometry ... Varies by type and model (see Section 19). All models negative roll radius

Steering ratio

Early models ... 19.2

Later models ... 20.2

Steering wheel turns (lock-to-lock) ... 3.94

Torque wrench settings	**Size (mm)**	**lbs ft**	**kg m**
Driveshaft to wheel:			
18 mm nut	18	145	20
20 mm nut	20	175	24
Wheel to hub	12	58	8
Coil spring to body	8	18	2.5

Wishbone to subframe ...	—	50	7.0
Stabilizer to subframe ...	6	7	1
Wishbone to steering knuckle ...	8	18	2.5
Brake caliper to steering knuckle	10	43	6.0
Brake disc to wheel hub ...	6	5	1
Splash guard to steering knuckle	6	7	1
Wishbone joint to wishbone	10	47	6.5
Stabilizer to wishbone ...	6	7	1
Driveshaft to transmission ...	8	25	3.5
Rack and pinion unit to body ...	8	14	2
Tie-rod to rack ...	10	40	5½
Bar to slider ...	8	14	2
Camber adjustment nuts ...	8	11	1½
Camber adjustment nuts ...	14	28	4
Tie-rod to tie-rod lever ...	10	28	4
Steering column to pinion ...	8	22	3
Steering wheel to column ...	18	36	5
Outer tube bearing to pedal base	6	7	1
Subframe to body ...	—	50	7.0
Strut to turret ...	—	18	2.5
Strut gland nut ...	—	108	15.0
Strut piston rod nut ...	—	43	6.0

1 General description

1 The front end of the car is mounted onto a subframe which holds the front suspension. It may be removed as one assembly quite easily if the engine is supported from above (photo).

2 On each side of the subframe is a wishbone frame hinged to the frame and fastened to the balljoint of the suspension strut at the apex of the frame (photo). Two types of frame have been fitted. These are discussed later.

3 The relative movement of the wishbone frames and the subframe is controlled to a certain extent by a stabilizer bar bolted across them (photo).

4 The balljoint is fastened to the apex of the wishbone and supports the steering knuckle. The shock-absorber fits into the steering knuckle at its lower end and is fastened to the car body at the top by a nut on the piston rod (photo). A platform on the steering knuckle supports the coil spring (photo), which is compressed between this platform and the upper spring cup which is held against the car frame by the piston rod.

5 Thus the weight of the car is supported by the coil spring, the vertical movement is controlled by the shock absorber, and the suspension strut is able to rotate in a horizontal plane being mounted on a balljoint.

6 The wheel bearing and hub are inserted into a housing at the lower end of the suspension strut, thus the vertical movement of the wheel is transferred to the strut when the vehicle is being driven.

7 Drive is supplied to the front wheel by a splined shaft which fits into the hub and is splined at the other end into the transmission final drive unit. This shaft has two double homokinetic Rzeppa joints (or in plain language constant velocity joints) which convey the drive at a

1.1 The subframe and suspension struts lowered from the vehicle

1.2 The wishbone, ball joint and wheel hub

1.3 The subframe inverted showing the stabilizer bar (A)

1.4a The mounting of the MacPherson Strut into the body

1.4b The suspension strut

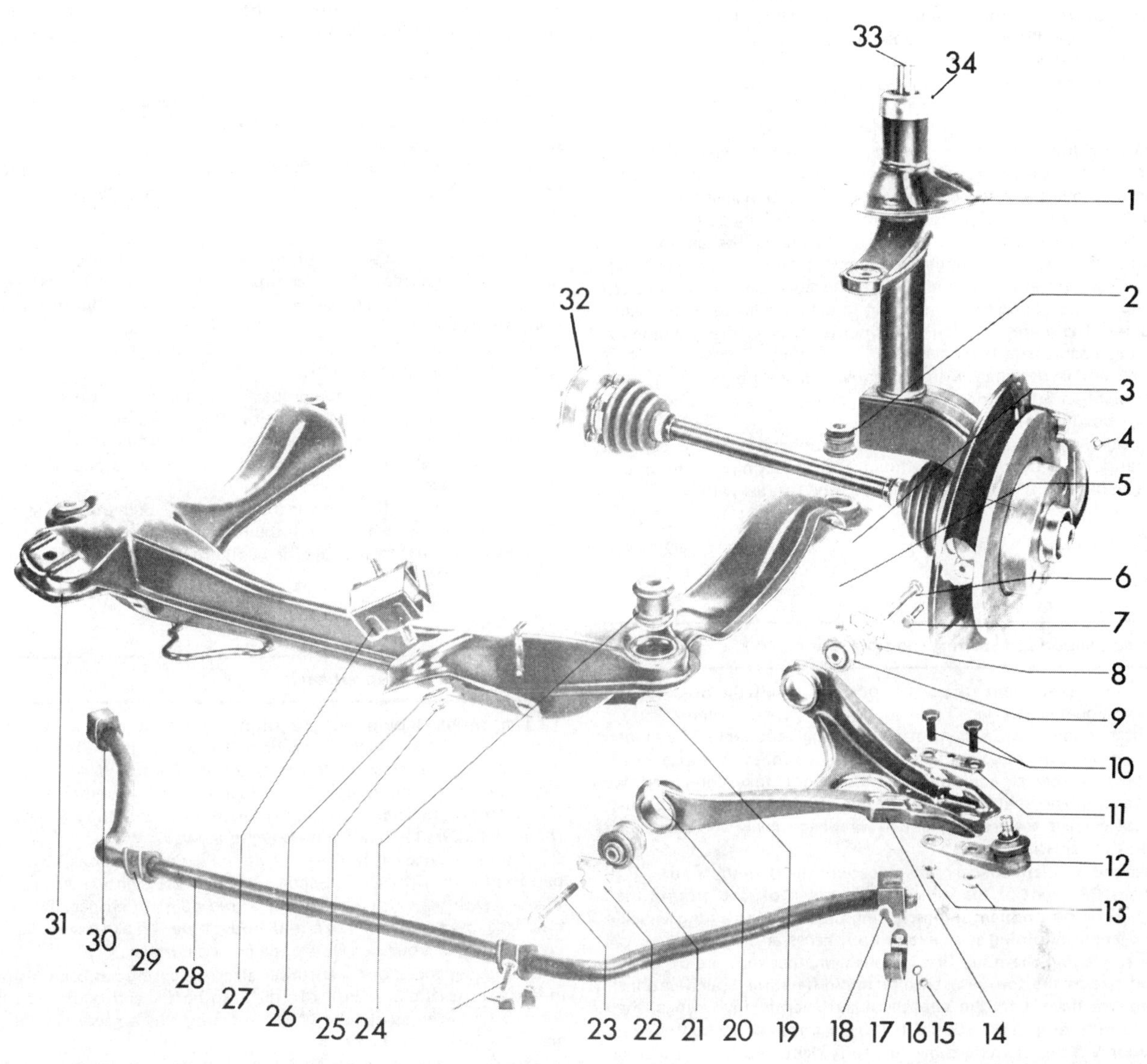

Fig. 12.1 Front suspension - exploded view

1 Steering knuckle spring platform
2 Bush
3 Splash plate
4 Nut
5 Bolt
6 Bolt
7 Bolt
8 Lockplate
9 Bush
10 Bolt
11 Lockplate
12 Steering knuckle balljoint
13 Nut
14 Wishbone
15 Washers
16 Washer
17 Clip
18 Bolt
19 Washer
20 Bolt
21 Bush
22 Lockplate
23 Bolt
24 Bush
25 Nut
26 Washer
27 Engine mounting
28 Stabilizer bar
29 Clip block
30 Rubber block
31 Subframe
32 Driveshaft
33 Shock absorber
34 Cap

constant rate while the wheel is moving in a vertical plane and being rotated in a horizontal plane for steering.

8 The steering is effected by a rack and pinion mechanism mounted across the rear of the engine compartment, just above the transmission unit. The pinion is turned by the steering column shaft. This shaft and its casing are arranged to be collapsible if the vehicle is involved in an accident. The steering gear slide moves to the left or right as the pinion rotates carrying with it the inner ends of the tie rods. These are attached to horns projecting from the upper rear of the steering knuckle by balljoints, so that movement of the steering gear rotates the suspension struts in a horizontal plane achieving the steering function.

9 On some models a steering damper is mounted between the steering gear and the body frame to promote a smoother steering action.

10 The left-hand tie rod is in three parts which enable the length of the rod to be adjusted so setting the corect 'toe-in' to the steering geometry. The right-hand tie rod is not adjustable. Camber is adjusted by moving the balljoints on the steering knuckles relative to the wishbone frames. There are no other adjustments to the steering geometry, king pin angle and castor being fixed.

11 The system is designed with a negative roll radius which ensures steady straight-ahead steering even when one front tyre is punctured. This is explained in detail in Section 19.

12 The brake caliper and splash plate are attached to the steering knuckle and may be removed without disconnecting the hydraulic system. The brake disc is bolted to the hub, and rotates with it.

2 Front suspension and steering - possible repairs

1 Repair by replacement of parts is possible to all the areas of the front suspension and steering. There are however, two problems.

2 The first is the measurement of the steering geometry. The adjustment is simple but measurement to the tolerences required needs experience and special equipment. It does not take long and we strongly recommend that it be done by the official agent. If the adjustment is not correct the front tyres will wear excessively and cost much more than the adjustment.

3 The second problem concerns the release of the driveshaft nuts.

Provided the front of the vehicle is not raised off the ground then there should be no problem in unscrewing the nut using a long knuckle bar with a length of piping as an extension if necessary.

When tightening the nuts, first establish whether they are of 18 mm or 20 mm size as the torque wrench setting differs (see Specifications). If you do not have a torque wrench of sufficiently high range, then tighten the nuts to at least 100 lbf ft (13.6 kgf m) and make your first stop at your VW dealer to have the nuts fully tightened to the specified torque.

Always use a new nut if the original is removed for any reason.

4 On the assumption that you are prepared to do this the following repairs are described:

a) *Replacement of hubs and wheel bearings.*
b) *Replacement of suspension struts complete or in parts.*
c) *Replacement of shock absorbers.*
d) *Replacement of driveshaft and constant velocity joints.*

5 The repair of the steering gear is less complicated but requires a puller to dismantle the steering balljoints. If the steering column is to be removed, then the bolts holding the column to the frame must be drilled out which presents a possible difficulty.

6 The rack and pinion unit may be adjusted, by an adjusting screw on models from 1974 onwards. Wear on earlier types is adjustable, by altering the setting of the pinion in the rack. This may be achieved by varying the shims in the box. Wear of this type may be also corrected by using spare kit No. 321 498 061A which virtually converts it to the later type.

7 The complete steering gear may be removed through the opening in the right-hand wheel housing after unbolting it from the frame. Repairs to the rack and pinion are not possible, the assembly must be replaced completely. The collapsible boots may be renewed once the gear is out of the car.

8 The steering column may be dismantled and fitted with new brushes and bearings. Balljoints and tie-rod bushes may be replaced, as may the bushes of the steering damper.

3 Suspension strut - removal and replacement

1 With the vehicle still on its wheels remove the dust cap from the front hub and then undo the hub nut (refer to Section 2, paragraph 2). Refer to Fig. 12.2.

2 Jack-up the vehicle, remove the front wheel and set the vehicle firmly on axle stands. Undo the two bolts holding the brake caliper to the steering knuckle and pull the caliper away. Tie the caliper firmly to the vehicle frame.

3 Undo the screw holding the brake disc to the hub and remove the brake disc. Next remove the three bolts holding the splash plate and remove the splash plate.

4 Undo the two nuts holding the steering knuckle to the wishbone (mark the relative position of the wishbone and balljoint if the same joint is to be reassembled or camber must be readjusted) and lower the wishbone. If there is any difficulty it may be advisable to remove the stabilizer bar.

5 Using a wheel puller remove the tie-rod balljoint from the suspension strut (photo 15.2).

6 From inside the engine compartment, remove the two nuts, spring washers and plates securing the strut to the mounting (photo 1.4a). **Note** *Do not, under any circumstances, undo the central nut.*

7 Now, turning the strut pull it off the driveshaft and lower it away from the vehicle.

8 Replacement is the reverse of removal. Guide the upper part into the vehicle mounting and install the hub at the same time.

9 Torque all nuts to the specified amount and have camber checked as soon as possible.

4 Suspension strut - overhaul

1 The spring should not be dismantled from the strut except to replace either the shock absorber or the spring itself. It is held under considerable compression and releasing it, unless VW/Audi tool 340 is available, is a dangerous job. We therefore counsel that the strut be taken to the official agent for dismantling and fitting a new coil or shock absorber. These must be bought anyway.

2 If you do succeed in dismantling the spring the shock absorber may be tested as in Chapter 8, Section 4. There are eight varieties of spring, marked with yellow, green, white or red paint in striper. The spring is classified by the engine size and body type - make sure you get the correct one for your car. Quote the chassis number.

3 Removing the shock absorber after the spring has been dismantled presents no difficulty. Pull off the stop buffer and boot and unscrew the cap from the strut tube. When refitting this a new cap is necessary and a new seal underneath it.

Now, holding the steering knuckle in the vice by the lug for the tie-rod balljoint, hold an open-ended spanner under the piston rod nut and tap the whole assembly out by hitting the spanner. The new shock absorber should not be driven in, the bore of the knuckle must be cleaned and worked until the shock absorber may be pushed in by hand.

5 Wheel bearings - removal and replacement

1 Faulty wheel bearings will cause excessive wheel rim rock, steering wobble, juddering action of the disc brakes and excessive tyre wear. They will also emit noise. If left for any length of time they will cause excessive wear of other components of the hub and thus add more expense.

2 Unfortunately they cannot be adjusted, only replaced and if the bearing is pressed out of the hub, VW/Audi state categorically that a new bearing must be fitted (refer to Fig. 12.2).

3 Remove the suspension strut as in Section 4. Remove the brake disc and splash plate. It is not necessary to remove the coil spring and shock absorber from the strut but obviously if both bearing and spring require renewal the spring should be removed first. Using feeler gauges measure the clearance between the hub flange and the steering knuckle. Whichever way, support the strut in a horizontal plane and press out the hub from the steering knuckle. The wheel bearing outer race and ball case

will remain in the steering knuckle, the inner race will come away with the hub. Clamp the hub in a vice and pull the inner race off the hub with a wheel puller using a VW/Audi tool 295a or a substitute to press on in the centre of the hub.

4 The outer race is positioned in the steering knuckle by two large circlips (68 mm dia x 2.5 mm thick). These must now be removed, one from each side. The remainder of the wheel bearing may now be pressed out of the steering knuckle.

5 Clean all parts carefully and examine for wear. **Do not** wash the new bearing with solvent. It is prepacked and requires no more grease.

6 Refit the *outer* circlip in the groove of the steering knuckle bore and press the new bearing up to it using VE tool 40-20. This is a piece of tube which bears on the *outer* race only. Do not press the bearing in by pushing on the inner race. Now refit the *inner* circlip. Make sure both circlips are firmly in the grooves.

7 The next bit is really tricky. The hub has to be pressed into the bearing with **both** races are supported. This can best be done by placing the hub on the support plate of the press and pushing the inner race of the bearing over the hub, supporting the strut conveniently as the hub enters the bearing and making sure the alignment is correct. If you have access to the special tools use VW/Audi 402 as a support for the hub, and a combination of 412, 432 and 519 to press in the bearing. If not use a piece of tube which presses **only** on the inner bearing of the race. Press the hub into the bearing until the clearance between the hub flange and the knuckle is the same as that which was measured in paragraph 2.

8 Refer back to Section 4, reassemble the splash plate, disc, and then the strut to the vehicle. Refit the drive shaft and calipers; refit the wheel and take the vehicle to the official agent for the camber to be reset and the driveshaft nut to be correctly assembled.

6 Steering knuckle balljoint - removal and replacement

1 The amount of play in a vertical plane of the balljoint must not

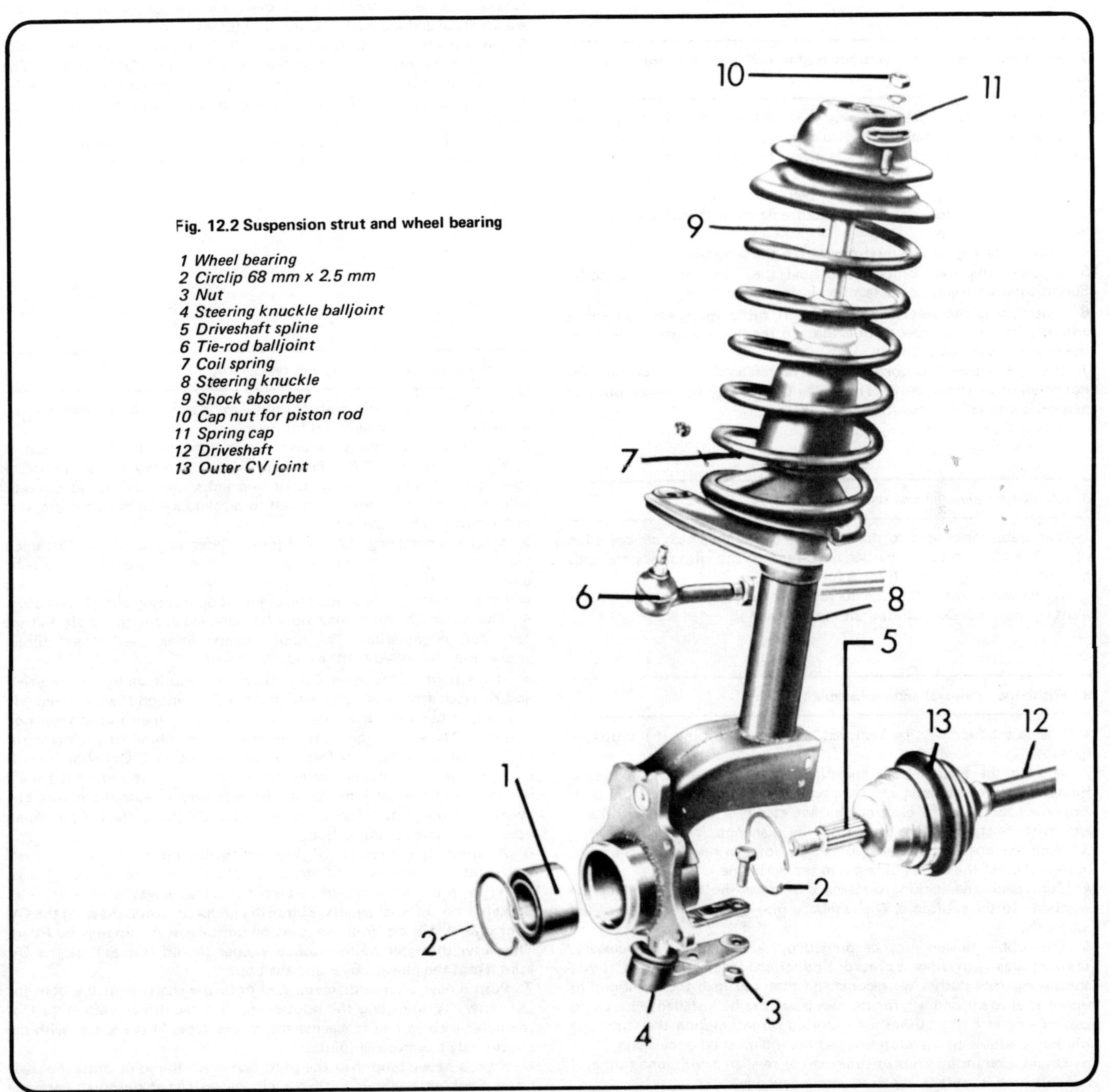

Fig. 12.2 Suspension strut and wheel bearing

1 Wheel bearing
2 Circlip 68 mm x 2.5 mm
3 Nut
4 Steering knuckle balljoint
5 Driveshaft spline
6 Tie-rod balljoint
7 Coil spring
8 Steering knuckle
9 Shock absorber
10 Cap nut for piston rod
11 Spring cap
12 Driveshaft
13 Outer CV joint

exceed 0.10 in (2.5 mm). This should be measured with a vernier gauge: one anvil on the steering knuckle and the other under the wishbone. The front wheel must be jacked clear of the ground. The measurement in this position will be the larger one. Now using VW/Audi tool 281a or a suitable lever pull the wishbone up and press the steering knuckle down until no more movement may be obtained. Measure again in the same place and subtract the second measurement from the first. This will give the vertical play.

2 The balljoint is fastened to the wishbone by two bolts (photo). Mark the position of the balljoint bracket relative to the wishbone if it is intended to replace the same joint so as to preserve the camber angle. Remove the bolts, undo the clamp bolt holding the top of the balljoint to the steering knuckle and draw the balljoint out downwards.

3 Some earlier types had a different fastening of the balljoint to the wishbone. This pattern of wishbone is referred to as a 'Vee type'. In this case a special tool (40-200) is required to turn the adjusting nut after the securing nuts have been undone. The tool is inserted from the front on the right-hand wishbone and the rear on the left-hand one.

7 Subframe (complete - without engine and transmission) - removal and replacement

1 It is necessary to take the weight of the engine and transmission from above before commencing to remove the subframe. A diagram showing the tool for doing this is given, but there are other ways. A hoist could be used or a floor crane.

2 Remove the stabilizer bar as described in Section 8.

3 Detach the wishbones from the subframe by withdrawing the pivot bolts.

4 Unbolt the engine side mountings from the subframe.

5 Unscrew the four bolts which hold the subframe to the body. Support the subframe as the last bolt is unscrewed.

6 Assembly is the reverse of removal. If difficulty is experienced in entering the engine bearer studs. Slacken the bonded mountings from the engine mounting brackets.

7 If the subframe is distorted it must be replaced with a new one. Do not attempt to straighten it. The rubber bushes may be pressed out and new ones pressed into the frame.

8 Stabilizer - removal and replacement

The stabilizer is held to the frame by two clips which are bolted in place. The outer ends of the bar are bolted to the wishbones and thus provide a damping, anti-roll force (photo 1.3).

If the bar is distorted due to accident damage or other reasons it must be renewed. **Do not** attempt to straighten it.

9 Wishbone - removal and replacement

1 The wishbone may be removed without disturbing the subframe (photo).

2 Jack-up the front wheels and support the vehicle on axle stands. Remove the front wheels and then remove the stabilizer bar from both wishbones. Slacken the clips holding the stabilizer bar to the subframe and twist the stabilizer bar away from the wishbone.

3 Mark the position of the stub axle balljoint in relation to the wishbone and undo the bolts holding it to the wishbone.

4 Turn back the locking plates and remove the bolts holding the wishbone to the subframe. The wishbone may now be drawn out of the subframe.

5 The rubber bushes may be pressed out and replaced if necessary. This requires know how, a press or a puller and special mandrels. If you are buying new bushes we recommend that you take the wishbone to the official agent and ask for the new bushes to be installed. This could save money as if the bushes are distorted on installation the wishbone will not assemble to the subframe and the job must be done again.

6 **On no account** attempt to straighten or re-align a wishbone frame. If it is distorted it must be replaced with a new one.

10 Driveshafts - removal and replacement

1 Once again the problem of the front hub nut rears its ugly head. Read Section 2, paragraph 2 of this Chapter, and make your own arrangements. Having overcome this problem, with the nut slackened jack-up the front wheels and set the car on axle stands. There is no need to remove the wheels.

2 Using a suitable splined key undo and remove the bolts holding the *inner* joint flange to the transmission. These are socket-head bolts tightened to 25 lb ft (3 kg m) (photo). Make sure the key fits properly for if the socket bolt head is damaged you will be in serious trouble. Note how each pair of bolts has a locking plate.

3 Once the joint is unbolted pull it away from the transmission and enclose it in a polythene bag. This stops dirt and grit entering the joint and keeps the grease of the joint from going where it is unwanted.

4 Turn the wheels to full lock, remove the wheel nut and the left-hand driveshaft may be withdrawn. Before removing the right-hand shaft the exhaust pipe must be removed from the manifold and the gearbox bracket. The above applies to the shafts for manual transmission. These are identical and are both 506 mm (19.92 in) long.

5 For vehicles with automatic transmission the right-hand shaft is 437 mm (17.2 in) long and the left-hand one 531 mm (20.9 in) long. The left-hand shaft may be removed only after the steering knuckle balljoint has been disconnected (Section 6) and the pivot mounting pushed outwards.

6 Installation is the reverse of removal. Remember that all nuts and bolts must be tightened to the correct torque and if the balljoint has been removed then the camber angle must be checked.

11 Driveshafts - dismantling and reassembly

1 Having removed the shaft from the car it may be dismantled for the individual parts to be checked for wear.

2 The rubber boots, clips and thrust washers may be replaced if necessary but the CV joints may only be replaced as complete assemblies. It is not possible to fit new hubs, outer cases, ball cages or balls separately for they are mated to a tolerance on manufacture; it is not possible to buy them either.

3 Start by removing the outer joint (Refer to Fig. 12.4). Cut open the 34 mm clip and undo the 88 mm hose clamp. The boot may now be pulled away from the joint. Open the circlip with a pair of circlip pliers and top the side of the joint. The circlip should spring out of its groove.

4 The outer CV joint may now be removed from the shaft and set aside for examination. The boot, clamp, dished washer and thrust washer may be pulled off the end of the shaft.

5 If the boot of the inner CV joint is damaged it should be removed and replaced from the outer end and the CV joint on the inner end left in place. If however, the inner joint is suspected then this too must be removed. The end of the shaft will look like the photo so a fair amount of cleaning is necessary before the job may proceed. Once the joint is clean, using circlip pliers remove the circlip from the end of the shaft and press off the CV joint. It will be necessary to ease the plastic cap away from the joint before pressing off the CV joint. The CV joint may now be set aside for inspection.

6 Assembly is the reverse of dismantling. Fit the inner CV joint first. It should be filled with 90 grams of Molybdenum-disulphide grease, filling in equal amounts from each side. The grease is obtainable in packets from official agents. Pump the grease in while pressing the CV joint onto the shaft. Pull the joint on until a new circlip may be fitted. The outer diameter of the dished washer should rest against the CV joint. Refit the plastic cover and the boot.

7 Push a new 34 mm diameter clip onto the shaft, then the boot for the outer CV joint and the boot clamp. Fit the dished washer so that the outer diameter rests against the spacer. Now fit the spacer with the convex side towards the joint.

8 Press a new circlip into the joint and drive the joint onto the shaft using a rubber hammer until the circlip seats in the groove. Pack the

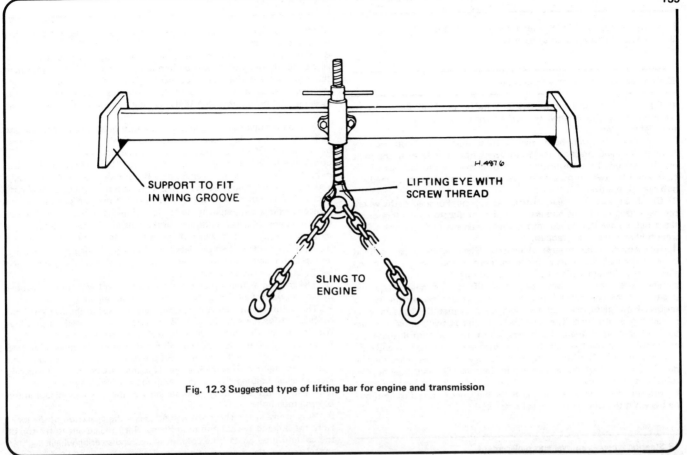

SUPPORT TO FIT IN WING GROOVE

LIFTING EYE WITH SCREW THREAD

H.4976

SLING TO ENGINE

Fig. 12.3 Suggested type of lifting bar for engine and transmission

6.2 The ball joint 'A' is fastened to the wishbone by two bolts

9.1 The wishbone frame. A hinge joints to subframe, B steering knuckle ball joint bracket, C stabilizer bar

10.2a Driveshaft inner C.V. joint. Remove the bolts 'A'

10.2b Driveshaft inner C.V. joint seen from underneath

11.5 This is what the end of the shaft looks like when it is disconnected so wrap it in a polythene bag

14.3 The clamp (A) holding the cclumn to the pinion

joint with 90 grams of MOS_2 grease and then refit the boot.
9 Re-install the shaft as in Section 10.

12 Constant velocity joints - inspection

1 Both joints should be washed in paraffin until all the grease is removed. They should then be washed with more clean paraffin and then lightly oiled.
2 The inner joint may be dismantled by turning the ball hub and cage through 90° and pressing them out away from the face of the joint which rests on the transmission. The balls may be pressed out of the cage and if the two grooves on the ball hub and ball cage are aligned the hub may be removed.
3 Check all parts for wear, pitting and scoring. Polished paths where the balls have run in the hub are no reason for discarding the hub but if these paths have developed into grooves then the hub will not swivel smoothly and must be scrapped.
4 Reassembly is the reverse of removal. The chamfer on the splined bone of the ball hub must point to the contact shoulder on the driveshaft and to the larger diameter of the outer ring.
5 The outer race is dismantled in a different manner. Mark the position of the ball hub in relation to the cage and the housing with a scriber. Now pivot the ball hub and cage so that the balls may be removed one at a time. The cage has six openings, two opposite to one another are larger than the others. Turn the cage until these are coincident with the flats on the outer joint and slide the hub and cage out of the joint. Turn the joint hub until one of the segments may be pushed into the rectangular opening in the cage. The hub may now be rolled out of the cage.
6 Inspection of the outer race is as for the inner race and again if any part is worn the whole joint must be replaced.

13 Steering wheel - removal and replacement

1 This is discussed in detail in Chapter 11 under the heading of column switch. Pull off the horn pad, remove the steering wheel nut and pull off the steering wheel.
2 When replacing be careful to fit the cancelling lug in the correct position (see Chapter 11).

14 Steering column - removal, overhaul and replacement

1 Refer to Fig. 12.5. Disconnect the battery earth strap. Remove the steering wheel and column switch (see Chapter 11). The top of the outer column tube and the steering column are now exposed. Remove the stop-ring, snap-ring, washer and support ring and the column will be left protruding from the ball race in the top of the column tube.
2 The hardboard covers under the fascia must be removed (see Chapter 11), and the bracket holding the column tube to the vehicle frame is accessible.
3 The screws holding the column tube flange to the frame are accessible. These should now be removed. In the engine compartment the bolt holding the clamp connecting the steering column to the steering gear is accessible (photo). Undo this clamp and push the steering column up into the body so that the column is clear of the steering gear.
4 The only thing holding the column and tube in place is the steering lock bracket and this is secured with screws, the heads of which have been sheared off to discourage theft. It is therefore necessary to centre-punch the bolts and then to drill them out. Use a 5/16 in drill (8.5 mm). Drill down until the bracket may be removed, remove the bracket and then the remainder of the bolts. This operation is not all that easy and if you are not confident that you can do it then we suggest you get someone who is competent to do the job. If in the course of drilling out the screws you damage the threads in the hole in the frame then you are in serious trouble, as it will not be possible to install a new column.
5 With the bolts drilled out leave the bracket hanging by the wiring. The column and tube may now be withdrawn from the vehicle and separated into its component parts.
6 The bearing at the top of the tube may be replaced, and the rubber bushes between the flange tube and the column renewed.
7 The deformation element attaching the bracket to the frame should be checked for tears or signs of deformation and replaced if necessary. We recommend that this be done by skilled personnel.
8 When reinstalling the steering column first assemble the column into the tube and refit the flange tube. Fit the column to the steering pinion but do not tighten the clamp as yet. Fit the new bolts to the steering lock bracket holding the column tube in position. Do not tighten the bolts yet. Refit the steering lock making sure the lock lugs engage in the column tube holes.
9 Now screw in the shear screws and check the operation of the lock. Refit the bolts to the column tube flange. Refit the details to the top of the column tube, install the column switch and steering wheel. Tighten the clamp to the steering pinion and check that the steering works correctly. Now tighten the shear screws until the heads shear off.
10 Replace the covers under the fascia and reconnect the battery earth strap.

15 Tie-rods - removal, replacement and adjustment

1 Refer to Fig. 12.6. The right-hand tie-rod is in one piece with a balljoint on the outer end. The left-hand tie-rod is made in three pieces so that the length may be adjusted to determine the amount of toe-in of the front wheels.
2 It is necessary to use an extractor (wheel puller) to remove the balljoints from the suspension struts (photo). Slacken the balljoint nut and using the extractor as shown in the photo break the joint. Remove the extractor and the nut and pull the joint apart.
3 The rods are held at the centre by two bolts and a clamp plate.

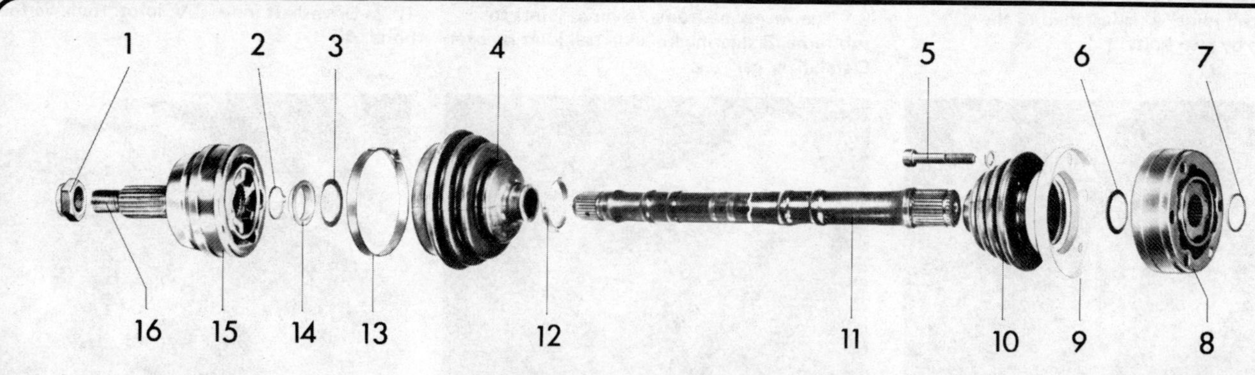

Fig. 12.4 Driveshaft and CV joints - exploded view

1 Axle nut
2 Circlip
3 Dished washer
4 Boot
5 Socket head bolt
6 Dished washer
7 Circlip
8 CV joint inner
9 Cap
10 Boot
11 Shaft
12 Clip (34 mm)
13 Clamp (88 mm)
14 Thrust washer
15 CV joint outer
16 Axleshaft

Remove the bolts and pull the rods away from the steering gear (photo). The rods may then be removed from the clamp (photo).

It is possible to remove the through-bolt of the clamp, slacken the tie-rod securing screws and then remove one screw and pull out that tie-rod. Replace the screw and repeat for the other rod. Reverse the procedure on installation and you will avoid a difficult five minutes trying to pick up the threads through the rubber. We learnt the hard way.

4 The inner ends of the tie-rods are eyes holding rubber bushes. Should these become worn or distorted they may be pressed out and new bushes inserted. Use a suitable mandrel and smear the new bush lightly with brake cylinder paste when installing.

5 The left-hand tie-rod is adjusted for length by slackening the clamp holding the centre tube to the inner portion, undoing the locknut clamping the centre tube and the outer portion and rotating the centre tube to lengthen or shorten as required. The locknut should be tightened to 30 lb ft (4 kg m).

16 Rack and pinion unit - removal and replacement

1 Refer to Fig. 12.6. Undo the clip securing the flange tube to the pinion (photo 14.3), and drive the flange tube off using a soft drift. It may be necessary to remove the panel under the fascia board to do this.

2 Disconnect the tie-rods from the steering gear (photo 15.3a).

3 Remove the two nuts from the studs on the left-hand end of the steering gear (photo) and the nut and bolt holding the right-hand end (photo). The steering gear may now be removed through the opening in the right-hand wheel housing. The wheels must be turned to full right lock when extracting the gear.

4 When installing the steering fit the tie-rod bolts before fitting the steering gear to the car. When the gear is in place remove one tie-rod

15.2 Using a wheel puller to break the tie-rod ball joints

15.3a The tie-rods removed from the steering gear ...

15.3b ... and pulled out of the clamps

16.3a The studs connecting the steering gear to the frame on the left side of the body and ...

16.3b ... the bolt holding the other end

17.1a Earlier models, removing the top from the pinion box ...

17.1b ... shows the spring and the shims ...

17.1c ... remove these and the friction plunger is visible ...

17.1d ... which is in two parts

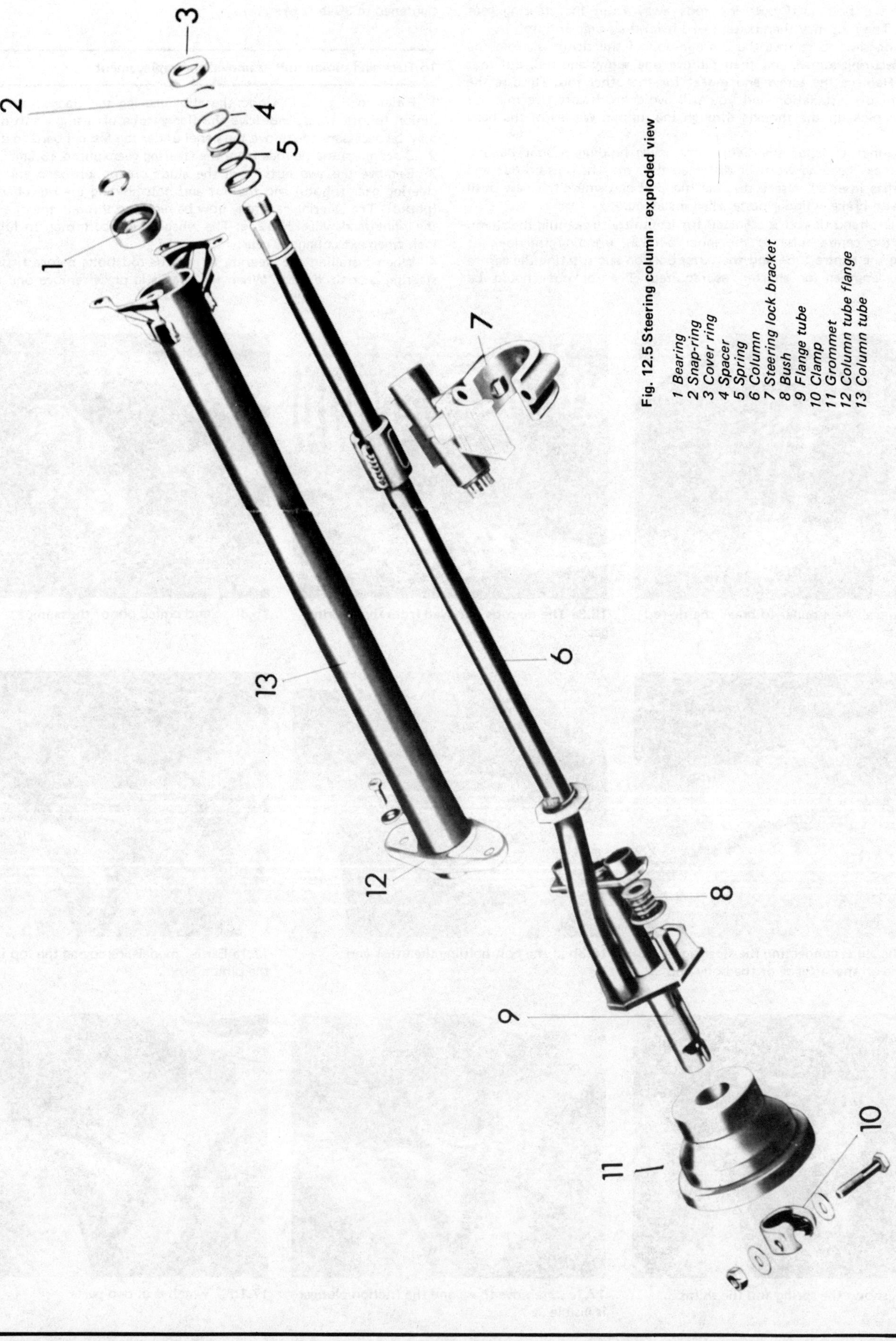

Fig. 12.5 Steering column - exploded view

1 Bearing
2 Snap-ring
3 Cover ring
4 Spacer
5 Spring
6 Column
7 Steering lock bracket
8 Bush
9 Flange tube
10 Clamp
11 Grommet
12 Column tube flange
13 Column tube

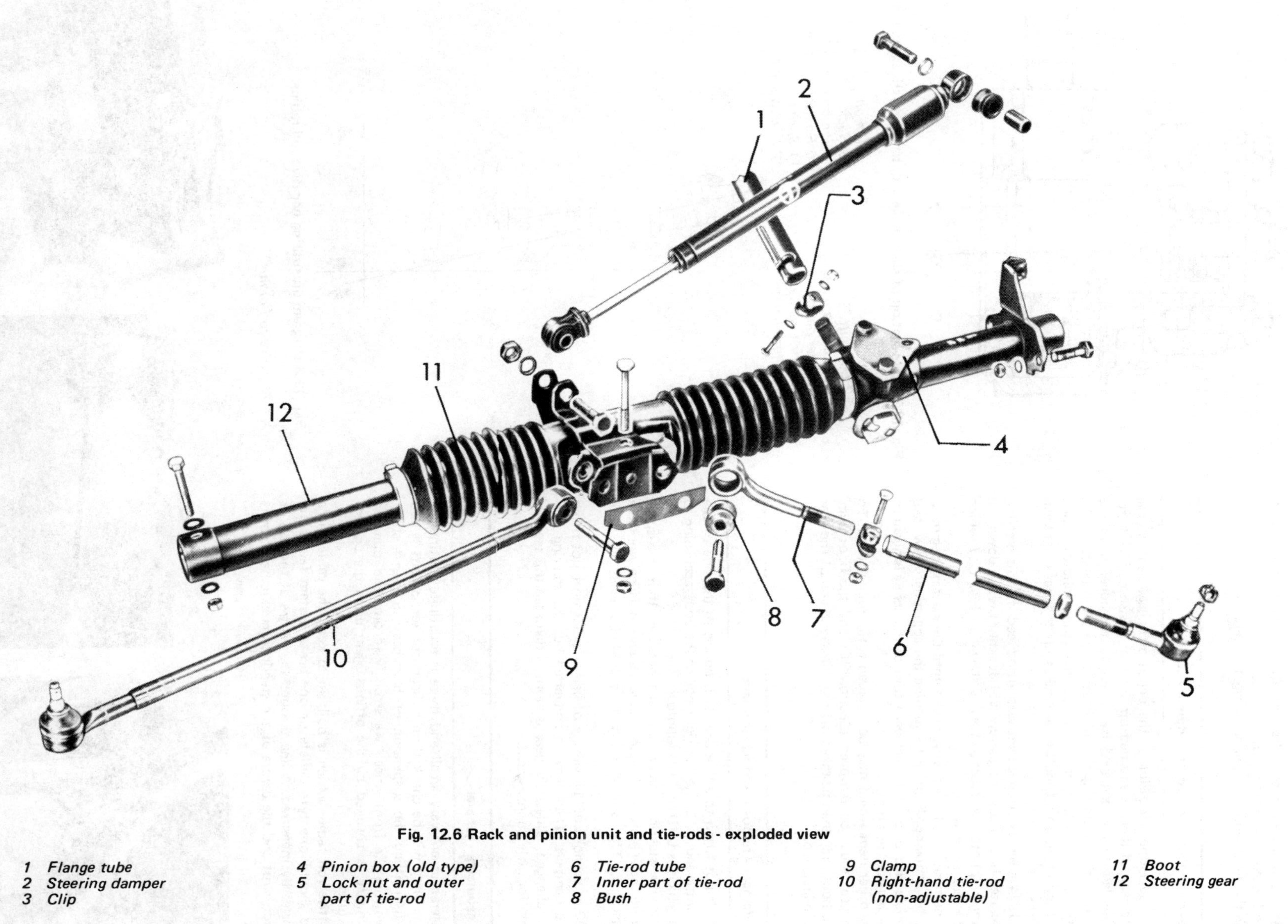

Fig. 12.6 Rack and pinion unit and tie-rods - exploded view

1 Flange tube
2 Steering damper
3 Clip
4 Pinion box (old type)
5 Lock nut and outer part of tie-rod
6 Tie-rod tube
7 Inner part of tie-rod
8 Bush
9 Clamp
10 Right-hand tie-rod (non-adjustable)
11 Boot
12 Steering gear

bolt and fit that tie-rod. Tighten the bolt and then fit the other tie-rod in the same manner. Finally install the clamp. As can be seen from photo 15.3a, we removed both bolts with the gear in the car and we had a little difficulty in refitting them.
5 Refit the flange tube to the pinion and tighten the clip.

17 Rack and pinion unit - repair and adjustment

1 The only adjustment possible is the depth of engagement of the pinion in the rack. If there is a rattle from the gear this should be done. On earlier models this is achieved by removing the cover from the pinion box (photo) and altering the thickness of the shims between the cover and the box. This further compresses the spring (photo) which presses the friction plunger (photos) and takes up the slack between pinion and rack.
2 In May 1974 a better arrangement was introduced. In this method no shims are used but an adjusting screw with locknut presses down the friction plunger (photo). A cross-section is shown in Fig. 12.7 which illustrates the rack and pinion.
3 In both methods the plunger is depressed until the steering begins to bind, either by removing shims or by turning the adjusting screw, and then a shim is added or a small backward turn of the screw is given so that the steering does not bind.
4 The only other item which may be repaired is the rubber boot. To do this the gear must be removed (Section 16) and the boot clips undone. The boot may then be taken off the right-hand end of the gear and a new one installed.

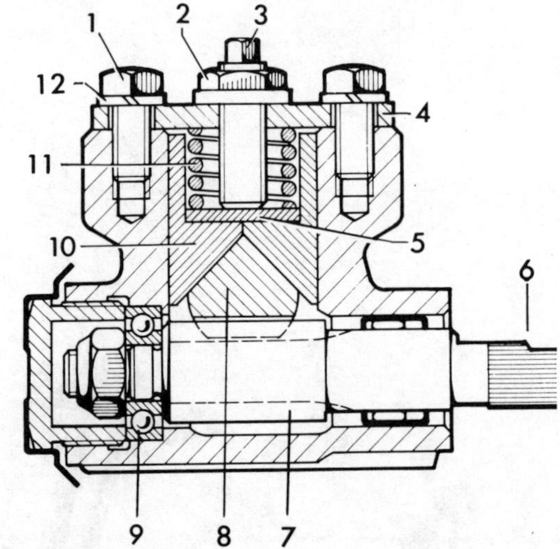

Fig. 12.7 Cross-section of steering gear (later models) - exploded view

1 Nut
2 Locknut
3 Adjusting screw
4 Cover plate
5 Thrust washer
6 Pinion shaft
7 Pinion
8 Rack
9 Pinion bearing
10 Friction plunger
11 Spring
12 Lockwasher

18 Steering damper - removal and replacement

1 This item is not fitted to all models. It is bolted to the side of the gear in the centre and to the left or right side of the body according to whether the vehicle is LHD or RHD (photos).
2 Repairs to the steering damper are not possible. If it is suspect remove it from the vehicle and holding the larger end in a vice work the piston to-and-fro. The stroke pressure should be even in both directions.
3 The 1300 cc versions of the vehicle of earlier types were not fitted with steering dampers. They may be converted but the steering gear must also be changed. Unless the gear is worn or damaged this seems a lot of expense for little improvement.

19 Steering geometry - general

1 These tolerances are very small and there is a definite routine for setting them. They will be checked on a diagnostic service but if you have been dismantling the suspension or have been in even a slight accident involving the front wheels we strongly recommend that the steering geometry is checked by the official agent using the correct tools and fixtures.
2 The negative roll radius which is built in to keep the vehicle in a straight line should one tyre deflate or one brake system fail is not adjustable or easily measured. A line through the centre of the top of the suspension strut and the centre of the steering knuckle balljoint is

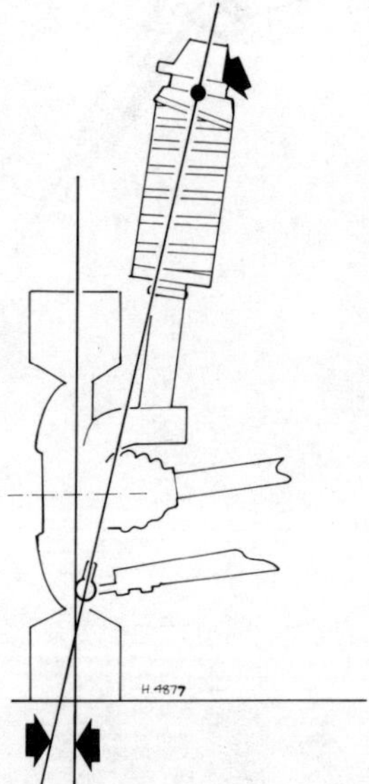

Fig. 12.8 Diagram illustrating negative roll radius

X = Negative roll radius

17.2 Later models have an adjusting screw (A)

18.1a The piston rod of the steering damper bolted to the slide of the steering gear

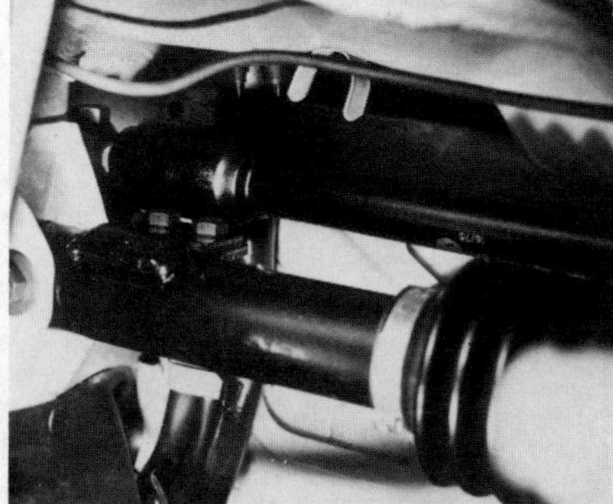

18.1b The outer end of the steering damper

extended to cut the level plane on which the wheels stand. As the wheel suspension strut expands and contracts this line will pivot about the upper joint, which is fixed, as the steering knuckle balljoint pivots about the wishbone hinge. It is known as the roll radius. If the vertical centre-line of the tyre is drawn to intersect the plane on which the tyre stands this will give the centre of the area of tyre contact with the ground. Should the roll radius line intersect the ground plane inside the centre of contact the suspension is said to have positive roll radius. However, the suspension we are considering has an intersection outside the centre of contact, which gives it a negative roll radius. The actual mathematics of the force distribution should the tyre deflate, or other exceptional occasion arise are beyond the scope of this manual but they do prove that this property of negative roll radius stabilizes the steering which would otherwise become unmaneagable in certain conditions.

3 Detailed information on checking and adjusting the front wheel alignment will be found in Chapter 14.

20 Fault diagnosis - front suspension and steering

Before diagnosing faults in the steering mechanism check that irregularities are not caused by:

1 *Binding brakes*
2 *Incorrect mixtures of radial and crossply tyres*
3 *Incorrect tyre pressures*
4 *Accident damage to the frame or suspension*

Symptom	Reason/s	Remedy
Steering wheel may be rotated considerably before the roadwheels turn	1 Play between the pinion and rack 2 Tie-rod joints worn 3 Column coupling slack or bushes worn	1 Adjust. 2 Renew. 3 Tighten or replace.
Vehicle difficult to steer in a constant straight-line - wandering	1 As above 2 Wheel alignment incorrect indicated by worn tyres 3 Worn wheel bearings 4 Worn suspension balljoints	1 As above. 2 Correct alignment. 3 Renew. 4 Renew.
Steering stiff and heavy	1 Incorrect wheel alignment 2 Rack and pinion binding 3 Tie-rod balljoints or suspension balljoints require lubrication	1 Adjust. 2 Adjust. 3 Lubricate or renew if very worn.
Wheel wobble and vibration	1 Roadwheels out of balance or buckled 2 Wheel alignment incorrect 3 Wear in linkage or suspension 4 Steering damper ineffective	1 Balance or renew. 2 Check and reset. 3 Adjust or replace. 4 Renew.
Excessive pitching and rolling on corners during braking	1 Defective shock absorbers or broken springs	Check and renew as necessary.

This sequence of photographs deals with the repair of the dent and paintwork damage shown in this photo. The procedure will be similar for the repair of a hole. It should be noted that the procedures given here are simplified – more explicit instructions will be found in the text

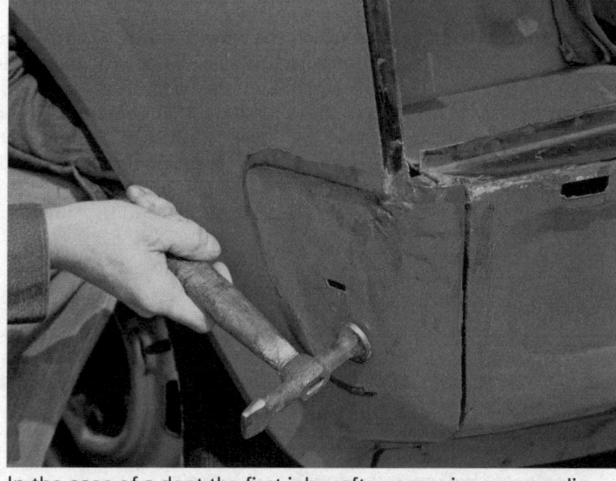

In the case of a dent the first job – after removing surrounding trim – is to hammer out the dent where access is possible. This will minimise filling. Here, the large dent having been hammered out, the damaged area is being made slightly concave

Now all paint must be removed from the damaged area, by rubbing with coarse abrasive paper. Alternatively, a wire brush or abrasive pad can be used in a power drill. Where the repair area meets good paintwork, the edge of the paintwork should be 'feathered', using a finer grade of abrasive paper

In the case of a hole caused by rusting, all damaged sheet-metal should be cut away before proceeding to this stage. Here, the damaged area is being treated with rust remover and inhibitor before being filled

Mix the body filler according to its manufacturer's instructions. In the case of corrosion damage, it will be necessary to block off any large holes before filling – this can be done with aluminium or plastic mesh, or aluminium tape. Make sure the area is absolutely clean before ...

... applying the filler. Filler should be applied with a flexible applicator, as shown, for best results; the wooden spatula being used for confined areas. Apply thin layers of filler at 20-minute intervals, until the surface of the filler is slightly proud of the surrounding bodywork

Initial shaping can be done with a Surform plane or Dreadnought file. Then, using progressively finer grades of wet-and-dry paper, wrapped around a sanding block, and copious amounts of clean water, rub down the filler until really smooth and flat. Again, feather the edges of adjoining paintwork

The whole repair area can now be sprayed or brush-painted with primer. If spraying, ensure adjoining areas are protected from over-spray. Note that at least one inch of the surrounding sound paintwork should be coated with primer. Primer has a 'thick' consistency, so will find small imperfections

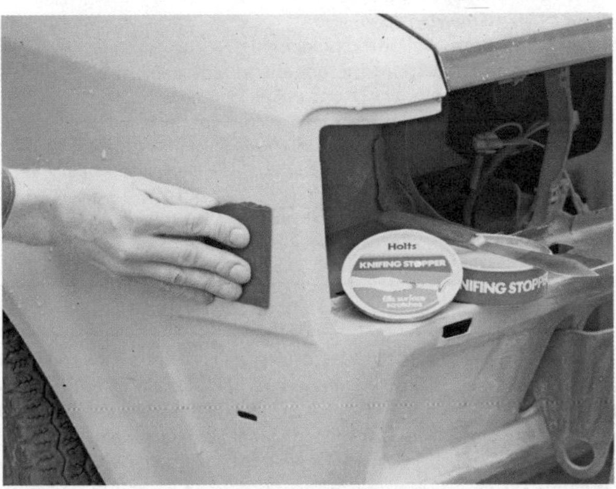

Again, using plenty of water, rub down the primer with a fine grade wet-and-dry paper (400 grade is probably best) until it is really smooth and well blended into the surrounding paintwork. Any remaining imperfections can now be filled by carefully applied knifing stopper paste

When the stopper has hardened, rub down the repair area again before applying the final coat of primer. Before rubbing down this last coat of primer, ensure the repair area is blemish-free – use more stopper if necessary. To ensure that the surface of the primer is really smooth use some finishing compound

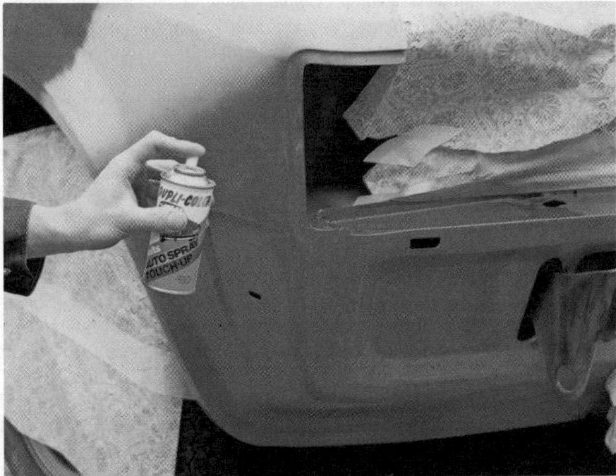

The top coat can now be applied. When working out of doors, pick a dry, warm and wind-free day. Ensure surrounding areas are protected from over-spray. Agitate the aerosol thoroughly, then spray the centre of the repair area, working outwards with a circular motion. Apply the paint as several thin coats

After a period of about two weeks, which the paint needs to harden fully, the surface of the repaired area can be 'cut' with a mild cutting compound prior to wax polishing. When carrying out bodywork repairs, remember that the quality of the finished job is proportional to the time and effort expended

Chapter 13 Bodywork and fittings

For modifications, and information applicable to later models, see Supplement at end of manual

Contents

1 General description

1 The bodywork is of unit construction. The diagram shows the type of layout for a two door Sedan/Saloon, the other bodies are similar but vary in detail. The bonnet is removable and so is the boot cover, or in the case of the Estate/Wagon version the rear door. The doors are easily removable, and with care the front wing (fender) may be unbolted from the shell and replaced if necessary.
2 The underbody is sealed with a PVC compound which should be renewed if damaged as it will hold water in as well as keep it out.
3 The bodyshell is made from deep drawn sheet steel with a high fatigue strength.

2 Maintenance - bodywork and underframe

1 The general condition of vehicle's bodywork is the one thing that significantly affects its value. Maintenance is easy but needs to be regular and particular. Neglect, particularly after minor damage, can lead quickly to further deterioration and costly repair bills. It is important also to keep watch on those parts of the car not immediately visible, for instance, the underside and inside all the wheel arches.
2 The basic maintenance routine for the bodywork is washing - preferably with a lot of water, from a hose. This will remove all the solids which may have stuck to the car. It is important to flush these off in such a way as to prevent grit from scratching the finish. The wheel arches and underbody need washing in the same way to remove any accumulated mud which will retain moisture and tend to encourage rust. Paradoxically enough, the best time to clean the underbody and wheel arches is in wet weather when the mud is thoroughly wet and soft. In very wet weather, the underbody is usually cleaned of large accumulations automatically and this is a good time for inspection.
3 Periodically it is a good idea to have the whole of the underside of the vehicle steam cleaned, so that a thorough inspection can be carried out to see what minor repairs and renovations are necessary. Steam cleaning is available at commercial vehicle garages but if not there are one or two excellent grease solvents available which can be brush applied. The dirt can then be hosed off.
4 After washing paintwork, wipe it with a chamois leather to give an unspotted clear finish. A coat of clear protective wax polish will give added protection against chemical pollutants in the air. If the paintwork sheen has dulled or oxidised, use a cleaner/polisher combination to restore the brilliance of the shine. This requires a little more effort, but is usually caused because regular washing has been neglected. Always check that drain holes are completely clear so that water can drain out. Brightwork should be treated the same way as paintwork. Windscreens and windows can be kept clear of the smeary film which often appears if a little ammonia is added to the water. If they are scratched, a good rub with a proprietary metal polish will often clear them. Do not use any form of wax or chromium polish on glass.

3 Maintenance - upholstery and floor coverings

1 Mats and carpets should be brushed or vacuum cleaned regularly to keep them free of grit. If they are badly stained remove them for scrubbing or sponging and make quite sure they are dry before replacement. Seats and interior trim panels can be kept clean by a wipe over with a damp cloth. If they do become stained (which can be more apparent on light coloured upholstery) use a little liquid detergent and a soft nailbrush to scour the grime out of the grain of the material. Do not forget to keep the head lining clean in the same way as the upholstery. When using liquid cleaners inside the car do not over-wet the surfaces being cleaned. Excessive damp could get into the seams and padded interior causing stains, offensive odours or even rot. If the inside of the car gets wet accidentally, it is worthwhile taking some trouble to dry it out properly, particularly where carpets are involved. **Do not** leave heaters inside for this purpose

4 Minor body damage - repair

See also the photo sequence on pages 166 and 167

Repair of minor scratches in the bodywork

If the scratch is very superficial, and does not penetrate to the metal of the bodywork, repair is very simple. Lightly rub the area of the scratch with a paintwork renovator (eg; T-Cut), or a very fine cutting paste, to remove loose paint from the scratch and to clear the surrounding bodywork of wax polish. Rinse the area with clean water.

Apply touch-up paint to the scratch using a thin paint brush, continue to apply thin layers of paint until the surface of the paint in the scratch is level with the surrounding paintwork. Allow the new paint at least two weeks to harden; then blend it into the surrounding paintwork by rubbing the paintwork in the scratch area with a paintwork renovation (eg; T-Cut), or a very fine cutting paste. Finally apply wax polish.

If the car is painted with a two coat metallic finish an entirely different technique is required. The materials may be obtained from the official agent. Two types of repair are possible, the $80^{o}C$ drying method and the Air-Drying method. A 'wet-on-wet' procedure for the topcoat and clear varnish is used. The repair can be done satisfactorily

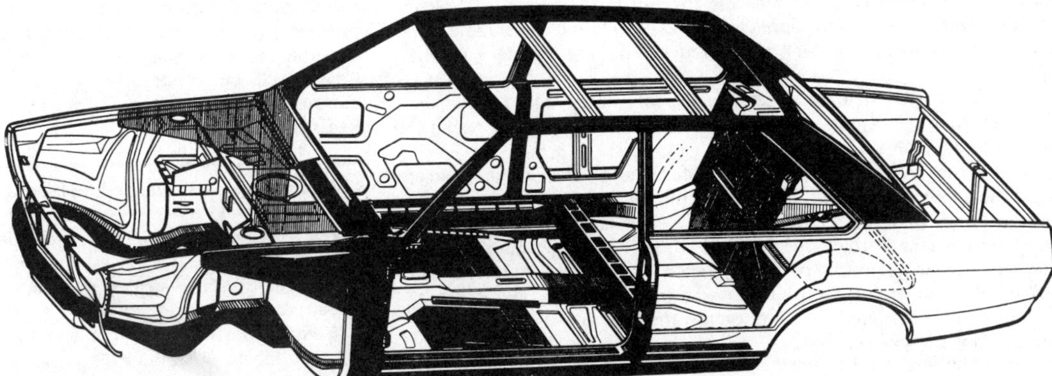

Fig. 13.1 Typical layout of a unit-construction bodyshell

only if the specified top coat and varnish are used with the specially developed synthetic thinner. After filling with Filler L145 if required sand down with the 400-500 wet and dry paper. Apply the first topcoat using synthetic resin metallic paint LKL or spraying viscosity 15-17 seconds (DIN cup 4 mm). Let the paint flash off for 25 minutes, then apply the second layer of Air-Drying L100 clear varnish with hardener L101 mixed in proportion 8:1. This becomes unusable after six hours. The repair is dust dry after 30 minutes but requires up to eight days for complete drying. As can be seen it is a complicated process and you are advised to go to the official agent for advice if you have not done the job before. If you have other than a metallic finish then proceed as follows.

An alternative to painting over the scratch is to use Holts "Scratch-Patch". Use the same preparation for the affected area; then simply pick a patch of a suitable size to cover the scratch completely. Hold the patch against the scratch and burnish its backing paper; the patch will adhere to the paintwork, freeing itself from the backing paper at the same time. Polish the affected area to blend the patch into the surrounding paintwork. Where a scratch has penetrated right through to the metal of the bodywork causing the metal to rust, a different repair technique is required. Remove any loose rust from the bottom of the scratch with a penknife; then apply rust inhibiting paint (eg; Kurust) to prevent the formation of rust in the future. Using a rubber or nylon applicator fill the scratch with bodystopper paste. If required, this paste can be mixed with cellulose thinners to provide a very thin paste which is ideal for filling narrow scratches. Before the stopper-paste in the scratch hardens wrap a piece of smooth cotton rag around the tip of a finger. Dip the finger in cellulose thinners and then quickly sweep it across the surface of the stopper-paste in the scratch; this will ensure that the surface of the stopper-paste is slightly hollowed. The scratch can now be painted over as described earlier in this Section.

Repair of dents in the bodywork

When deep denting of the car's bodywork has taken place, the first task is to pull the dent out, until the affected bodywork almost attains its original shape. There is little point in trying to restore the original shape completely, as the metal in the damaged area will have stretched on impact and cannot be reshaped fully to its original contour. It is better to bring the level of the dent up to a point which is about 1/8 inch (3 mm) below the level of the surrounding bodywork. In cases where the dent is very shallow anyway, it is not worth trying to pull it out at all.

If the underside of the dent is inaccessible, it can be hammered out gently from behind, using a mallet with a wooden or plastic head. Whilst doing this, hold a suitable block of wood firmly against the impact from the hammer blows and thus prevent a large area of bodywork from being 'belled-out'.

Should the dent be in a section of the bodywork which has a double skin or some other factor making it inaccessible from behind, a different technique is called for. Drill several small holes through the metal inside the dent area - particularly in the deeper sections. Then screw long self-tapping screws into the holes just sufficiently for them to gain a good purchase in the metal. Now the dent can be pulled out by pulling on the protruding heads of the screws with a pair of pliers.

The next stage of the repair is the removal of the paint from the damaged area, and from an inch or so of the surrounding 'sound' bodywork. This is accomplished most easily by using a wire brush or abrasive pad on a power drill, although it can be done just as effectively by hand using sheets of abrasive paper. To complete the preparations for filling, score the surface of the bare metal with a screwdriver or the tang of a file, or alternatively drill small holes in the affected areas. This will provide a really good 'key' for the filler paste.

To complete the repair see the Section on filling and respraying.

Repair of rust holes or gashes in the bodywork

Remove all paint from the affected area and from an inch or so of the surrounding 'sound' bodywork, using an abrasive pad or wire brush on a power drill. If these are not available a few sheets of abrasive paper will do the job just as effectively. With the paint removed you will be able to gauge the severity of the corrosion and therefore decide whether to replace the whole panel (if this is possible) or to repair the affected area. Replacement body panels are not as expensive as most people think and it is often quicker and more satisfactory to fit a new panel than to attempt to repair large areas of corrosion.

Remove all fittings from the affected areas except those which will act as a guide to the original shape of the damaged bodywork (eg; headlamp shells etc.,). Then using tin snips or a hacksaw blade, remove all loose metal and any other metal badly affected by corrosion. Hammer the edges of the hole inwards in order to create a slight depression for the filler paste.

Wire brush the affected area to remove the powdery rust from the surface of the remaining metal. Paint the affected area with rust inhibiting paint (eg; Kurust); if the back of the rusted area is accessible treat this also.

Before filling can take place it will be necessary to block the hole in some way. This can be achieved by the use of one of the following materials: Zinc gauze, Aluminium tape or Polyurethane foam.

Zinc gauze is probably the best material to use for a large hole. Cut a piece to the approximate size and shape of the hole to be filled, then position it in the hole so that its edges are below the level of the surrounding bodywork. It can be retained in position by several blobs of filler paste around its periphery.

Aluminium tape should be used for small or very narrow holes. Pull a piece off the roll and trim it to the appropriate size and shape required, then pull off the backing paper (if used) and stick the tape over the hole; it can be overlapped if the thickness of one piece is insufficient. Burnish down the edges of the tape with the handle of a screwdriver or similar to ensure that the tape is securely attached to the metal underneath.

Polyurethane foam is best used where the hole is situated in a section of bodywork of complex shape, backed by a small box section (eg; where the sill panel meets the rear wheel arch - most cars). The unusual mixing procedure for this foam is as follows. Put equal amounts of fluid from each of the two cans provided into one container. Stir until the mixture begins to thicken, then quickly pour this mixture into the hole, and hold a piece of cardboard over the larger apertures. Almost immediately the polyurethane will begin to expand, gushing frantically out of any small holes left unblocked. When the foam hardens it can be cut back to just below the level of the surrounding bodywork with a hacksaw blade.

Bodywork repairs - filling and re-spraying

Before using this Section, see the Sections on dent, deep scratch, rust hole and gash repairs.

Many types of bodyfiller are available, but generally speaking those proprietary kits which contain a tin of filler paste and a tube of resin hardener (eg; Holts Cataloy) are best for this type of repair. A wide, flexible plastic or nylon applicator will be found invaluable for imparting a smooth and well contoured finish to the surface of the filler.

Mix up a little filler on a clean piece of card or board - use the hardener sparingly (follow the maker's instructions on the packet), otherwise the filler will set very rapidly.

Using the applicator, apply the filler paste to the prepared area; draw the applicator across the surface of the filler to achieve the correct contour and to level the filler surface. As soon as a contour that approximates the correct one is achieved, stop working the paste - if you carry on too long the paste will become sticky and begin to 'pick-up' on the applicator. Continue to add thin layers of filler paste at twenty-minute intervals until the level of the filler is just 'proud' of the surrounding bodywork.

Once the filler has hardened, excess can be removed using a Surform plane or Dreadnought file. From then on, progressively finer grades of abrasive paper should be used, starting with a 40 grade production paper and finishing with 400 grade 'wet-and-dry' paper. Always wrap the abrasive paper around a flat rubber, cork or wooden block - otherwise the surface of the filler will not be completely flat. During the smoothing of the filler surface the 'wet-and-dry' paper should be periodically rinsed in water. This will ensure that a very smooth finish is imparted to the filler at the final stage.

At this stage the 'dent' should be surrounded by a ring of bare metal, which in turn should be encircled by the finely 'feathered' edge of the good paintwork. Rinse the repair area with clean water, until all of the dust produced by the rubbing-down operation is gone.

Spray the whole repair area with a light coat of grey primer - this will show up any imperfections in the surface of the filler. Repair these imperfections with fresh filler paste or bodystopper, and once more smooth the surface with abrasive paper. If bodystopper is used, it can be mixed with cellulose thinners to form a really thin paste which is ideal for filling small holes. Repeat this spray and repair procedure until you are satisfied that the surface of the filler, and the feathered edge of the paintwork are perfect. Clean the repair area with clean water and allow to dry fully.

The repair area is now ready for spraying. Paint spraying must be carried out in a warm, dry, windless and dust free atmosphere. This condition can be created artificially if you have access to a large indoor working area, but if you are forced to work in the open, you will have to pick your day very carefully. If you are working indoors, dousing the floor in the work area with water will 'lay' the dust which would otherwise be in the atmosphere. If the repair area is confined to one body panel, mask off the surrounding panels; this will help to minimise the effects of a slight mis-match in colours. Bodywork fittings (eg; chrome strips, door handles etc) will also need to be masked off. Use genuine masking tape and several thicknesses of newspaper for the masking operation.

Before commencing to spray, agitate the aerosol can thoroughly, then spray a test area (an old tin, or similar) until the technique is mastered. Cover the repair area with a thick coat of primer; the thickness should be built up using several thin layers of paint rather than one thick one. Using 400 grade 'wet-and-dry' paper, rub down the surface of the primer until it is really smooth. While doing this, the work area should be thoroughly doused with water, and the 'wet-and-dry' paper periodically rinsed in water. Allow to dry before spraying on more paint.

Spray on the top coat, again building up the thickness by using several thin layers of paint. Start spraying in the centre of the repair area and then, using a circular motion, work outwards until the whole repair area and about 2 inches of the surrounding original paintwork is covered. Remove all masking material 10 to 15 minutes after spraying on the final coat of paint.

Allow the new paint at least 2 weeks to harden fully; then using a paintwork renovator (eg; T-Cut) or a very fine cutting paste, blend the edges of the new paint into the existing paintwork. Finally, apply wax polish.

5 Major body damage - repair

1 Where serious damage has occurred or large areas need renewal due to neglect it means certainly that completely new sections or panels will need welding in and this is best left to professionals. If the damage is due to impact it will also be necessary to check the alignment of the body structure. In such instances the services of a agent with specialist checking jigs are essential. If a body is left misaligned it is first of all dangerous as the car will not handle properly - and secondly, uneven stresses will be imposed on the steering, engine and transmission, causing abnormal wear or complete failure. Tyre wear will also be excessive.

6 Front wings - removal and replacement

1 If a front wing (fender) is badly damaged it may be removed and replaced by a new one. It is secured to the bodyshell by self-tapping screws (each with a washer) and one crosshead screw. The latter is at the rear of the wing.

2 Remove the front bumper and the lower trim moulding, if fitted, and then locate the screws. The front wheel should be removed and the car fixed firmly on axle stands. The screws are to be found all round the joint of the wing to the bodyshell, along the top (6) between the lower front and the front panel (2) and under the wheel arch (5). We apologise if the count is wrong for your car but that is where we found them. They are not easy to undo so if easing oil will not do the trick it may be necessary to chip or grind off the head and then drill out the shank after the wing has been removed.

3 When the wing is removed clean off all rust patches from the body-shell and paint with zinc primer. When this is dry apply a suitable top coat.

4 When refitting the wing apply a coat of mastic between fitting surfaces and tighten the bolts progressively. Once the wing is in position the entire inside should be carefully coated with permanant underseal.

7 Bonnet - removal and replacement

1 The bonnet, or engine compartment cover, is hinged at the rear and held shut with by a lock operated from inside the vehicle. It is held to the hinge by two bolts on each side. Remove these, and it may be lifted off and taken away. Two people are needed to lift it, not because it is heavy but to avoid scratching the paint.

8 Bonnet cable and lock - removal, refitting and adjustment

1 Inside the car remove the centre cover under the fascia, then the cover on the side of the bonnet lock handle and the glovebox. The cable now accessible at the inside end. Before it can be removed it must be released from the lock which is mounted in the centre of the cross-member just above the radiator grille.

2 Open the bonnet and it will be seen that the left-hand side of the lock is secured by two hexagon head screws. Remove these and the cable may be detached from the lock.

3 Now back inside the car undo the crosshead screws which hold the bonnet catch release handle bracket to the side of the car and lift the bracket away from the trim. In the centre of the upper end of the operating handle is a small clamping plate. Bend this outwards and the handle may be released from the bracket. The cable may now be pulled out of the handle and out of the car. If you are wise you will tie a piece of thin wire or cord to the inside end and pull that into the place the cable occupied to make fitting a new cable more simple.

4 Replacement is the reverse of removal. Do not forget the water trap grommet. If a new cable is obtained from the official agent it will be the correct length, if you use other material the length must be determined by trial and error. Fasten the cable in the handle and assemble the handle to the car. Lead the cable through the correct run and measure the right amount to operate the lock correctly.

5 Remove the radiator grille. This is secured by screws at the ends and in the centre. Some models differ and the screws may be inside the 'centre-lines' of the lamps. Again on some models the grille is held at the top by clips, as well as the screws. Whichever way it is, remove the grille.

6 It will now be seen that the lock carrier plate is held by two clips. Squeeze these together and press out the lock carrier plate. Remove the bonnet lock and detach the connecting rod. Undo the cable on the left lock.

9 Bumpers - removal and replacement

1 On European type vehicles the bumpers are bolted to the frame

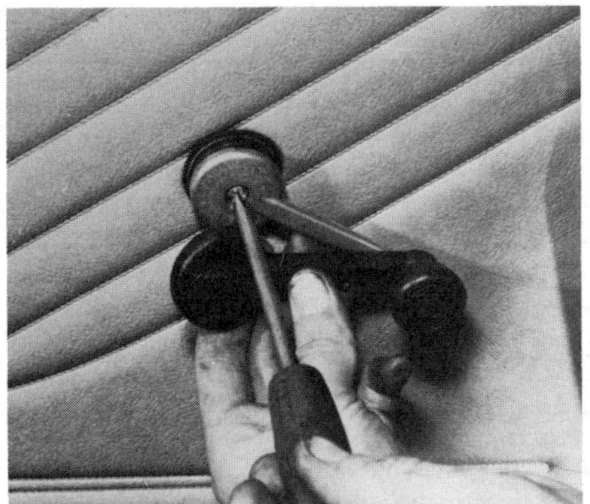
11.1 Removing the window winder

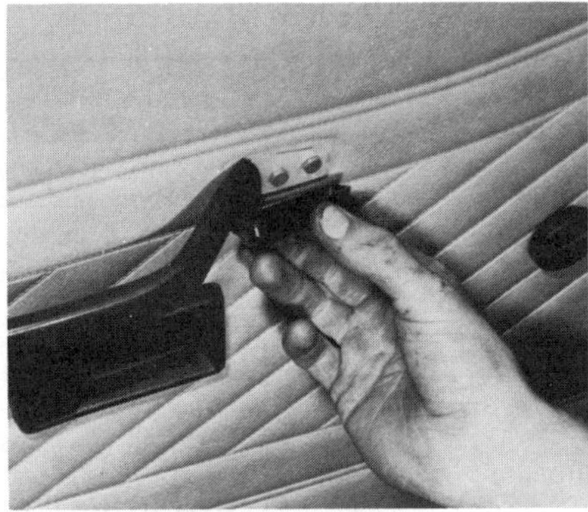
11.2 Removing the door strap

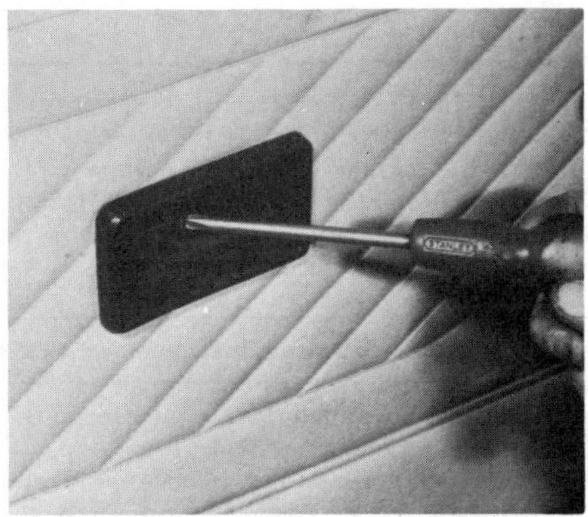
11.3 Removing the cover from the door lock handle

12.1 The door check strap (A)

13.3a Removing the crosshead screw from the door handle

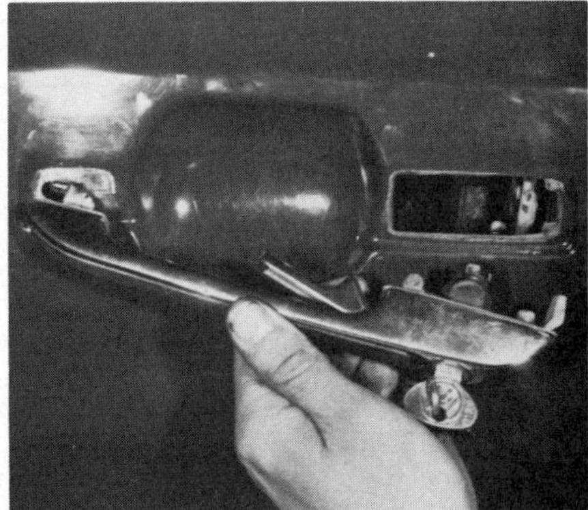
13.3b Lift the handle forward and draw it out of the door

13.4 Remove the small screw, eccentric, spring, and lockwasher ...

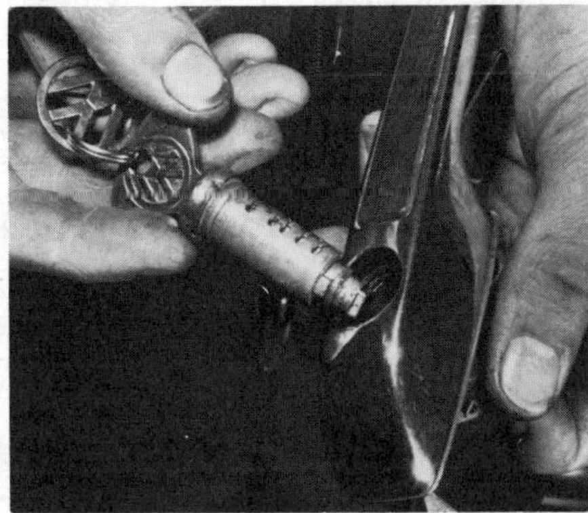
13.5 ... withdraw the lock to the back

14.1 The door lock inside the door. Disconnect linkage 'A'

14.2 Undo the two screws marked 'A' to remove the lock

15.2 The slide channel of the window winder

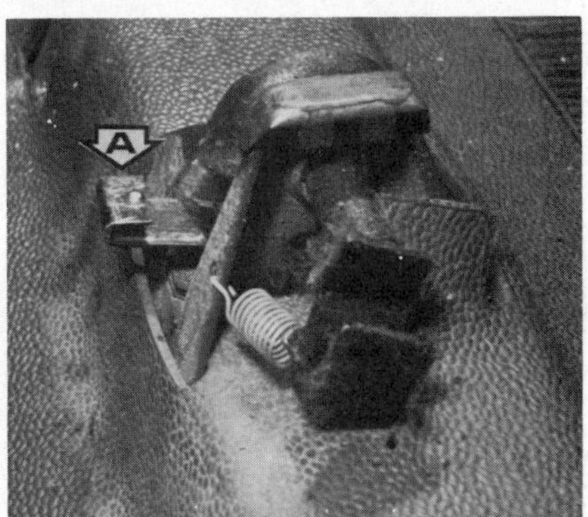

16.3 The rear mounting of the front seat. 'A' is the spring which must be pushed down

direct. Undo and remove the parking lights and then the bumpers may be unbolted and removed. If the bumpers have been bent or twisted it is necessary to replace them with new ones.
2 On USA models the bumpers are carried on buffers. These are bolted to the frame. In the event of damage the whole assembly should be removed and replaced.

10 Luggage compartment cover - removal and replacement

1 Open the cover and undo the hinge bolts. A second person will be required to hold the cover while this is done.
2 To replace the lock first remove the screws securing the upper part of the lock to the cover. Now unscrew the nut securing the lock cylinder to the cover and remove the lock cylinder. Finally remove the two bolts securing the lower part of the lock.
3 Installation is the reverse of removal.

11 Door interior trim - removal and replacement

1 Open the front door and unscrew the lock plunger from the top of the door. Prise off the cover from the window winder and unscrew the centre screw (photo). Remove the handle.
2 Slide the plastic clips off the door pull and remove the four screws exposed underneath (photo).
3 Undo the crosshead screw in the centre of the door latch and remove the cover (photo).
4 The trim may now be levered away from the door. There are 11 plugs holding it in position all down the two sides and along the base. Use a thin wooden or plastic lever to ease the clips out. They come away with a distinct pop.
5 Replacement is the reverse of removal. Fit the top of the trim first and then ease the other parts into position.
6 The trim is removed from the rear door in the same way. Remove the arm rest, window winder and inside door handle and pry the trim away from the door.

12 Doors - removal and replacement

1 Remove trim (Section 11) and remove the polythene sheet. Press out the sleeve from the door check strap (photo).
2 If you are replacing the same door mark the position of the hinges. Unscrew the door from the hinges. The hexagon headed bolts are easily accessible from inside the door. You will need a helper to hold the door while the hinges are detached.
3 There are three bolts and a spring washer to each hinge.
4 When replacing the door install the bolts and tighten them hand-tight. Set the door to the marks on the hinges and check the alignment of the door. Close it gently and see that it fits properly. Open it carefully and tighten one bolt in each hinge. Check the alignment again and if all is correct tighten all the bolts. Replace the check strap sleeve and refit the trim.
5 It is a good idea to look round the door interior while the trim is off. The one we dismantled was rusty both on the door and the window winder. Remove the rust and paint the affected portions.

13 Door handles - removal and replacement

1 It is not necessary to remove the trim to remove the door handles.
2 Insert the key in the lock and keep it there while removing the front door handle (Refer to Fig. 13.2).
3 Remove the crosshead screw from the end of the door (photo). There are three, make sure you undo the correct one, it is in a small indentation. The handle may now be moved forward slightly and drawn away from the door (photo).
4 To remove the lock from the handle undo the small screw and remove the lockwasher, eccentric and spring (photo).
5 The lock may now be removed from the handle (photo). There is a rubber seal round the lock cylinder which will probably require renewal.
6 Replacement is the reverse of removal. Lubricate the lock before installation with VW/Audi lock lubricant G4 or a suitable light oil. The ends of the spring must bear against the housing stop under tension.
7 To remove the rear door handle locate the rubber plug inside the door at the back of the handle and prise it out of the trim. Underneath is the head of the securing screw. Remove this and the handle may be removed in a similar fashion to the front handle.

14 Door locks (front) - removal and replacement

1 Remove door trim (Section 11). Press the clip off the linkage (photo) and disconnect the linkage (Refer to Fig. 13.3).
2 Remove the two screws, holding the remote control lever in the centre of the door, disengage the long link and then disconnect it from the lock.
3 Undo the two screws holding the lock to the door (photo) and remove the lock through the door opening.
4 When assembling make sure the door handle operating lever engages with lock operating lever.

15 Window glass and winders (front doors) - general

1 If the glass is broken or the mechanism is jambed we recommend that this job be left to the official agent. The job involves the removal of trim strips and you will probably break the trim strips and clips when removing them.
2 To inspect the winder remove the door trim panel (Section 11) and replace the winder handle. Revolve the handle and the operating lever should move in the slot of the fixture on the bottom of the window (photo). This may be rusted or clogged. Clean it out and lubricate with general purpose grease. Lubricate the gears and check that the lifter

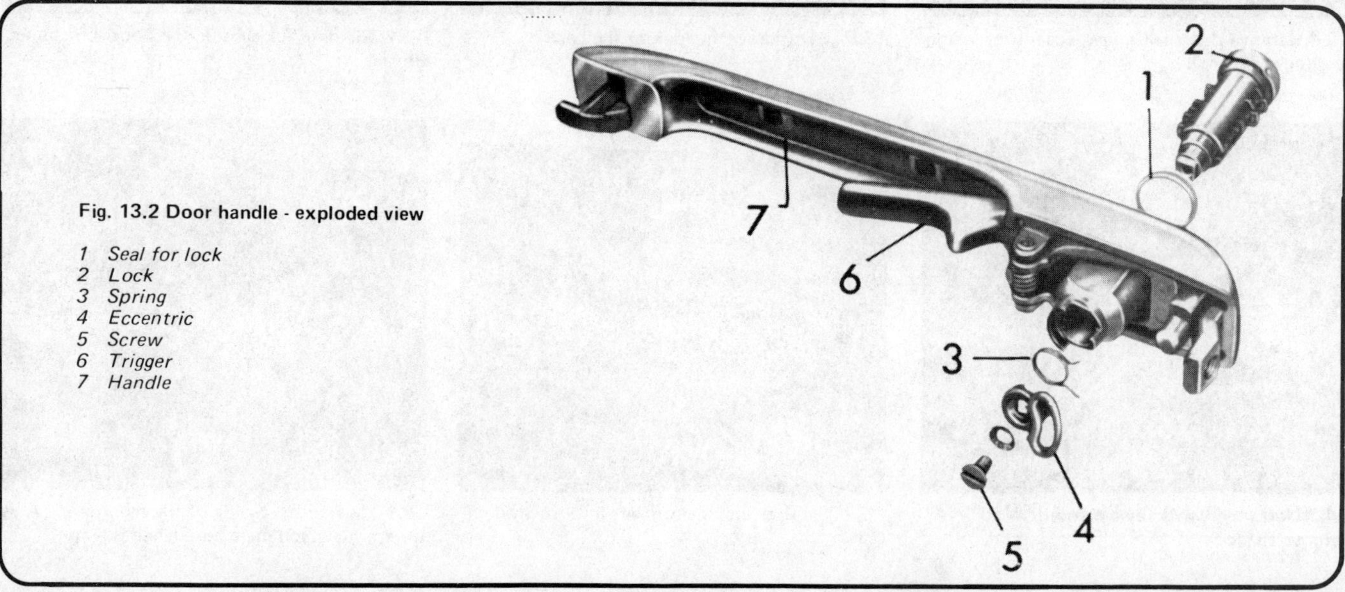

Fig. 13.2 Door handle - exploded view

1 Seal for lock
2 Lock
3 Spring
4 Eccentric
5 Screw
6 Trigger
7 Handle

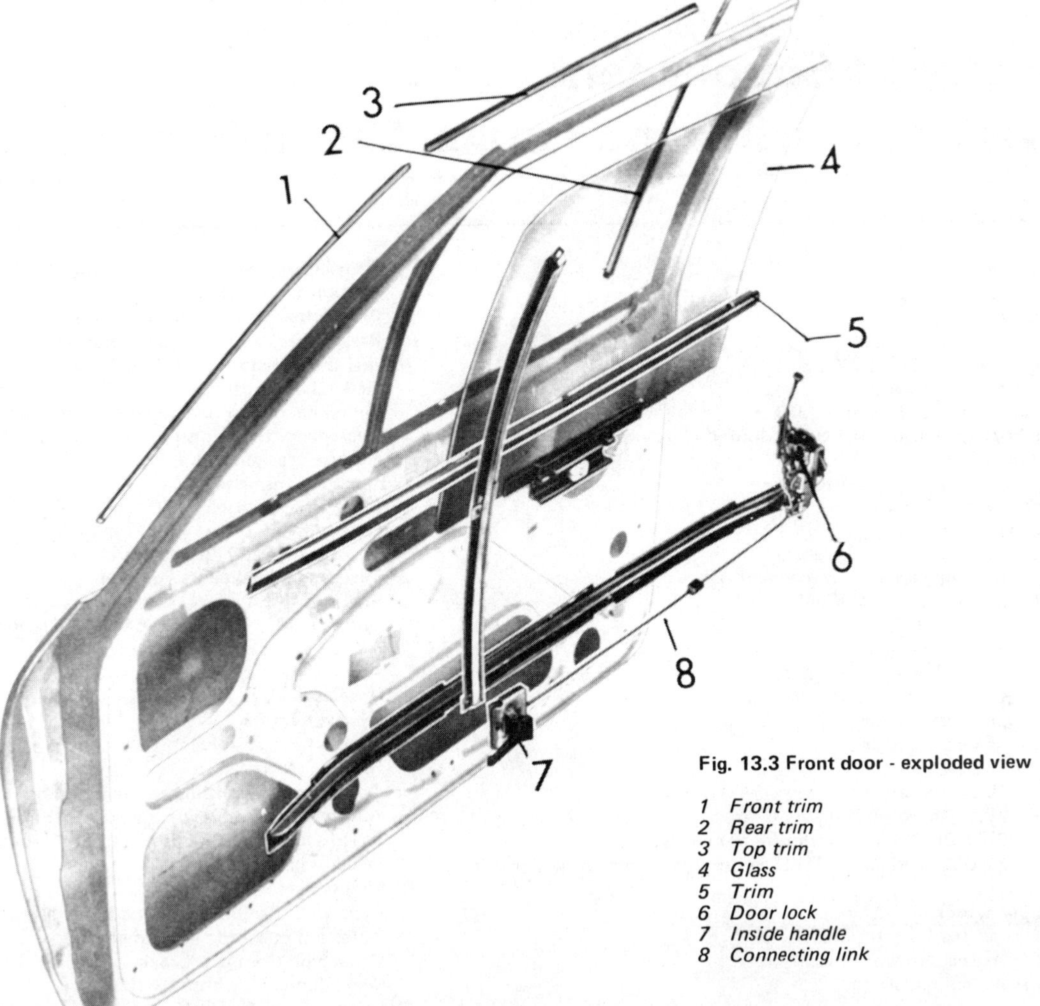

Fig. 13.3 Front door - exploded view

1 Front trim
2 Rear trim
3 Top trim
4 Glass
5 Trim
6 Door lock
7 Inside handle
8 Connecting link

cable is running properly over the rollers.
3 The removal of the glass and winder involves dismantling the centre guide channel and as we stated in paragraph 1 we consider this is best left to the expert, if the window is to work correctly and be weather proof.

16 Seats (front) - removal and replacement

1 This simple operation proves suprisingly difficult until one gets the knack of it. At the back of the slides are small covers. Remove these by pushing them off.
2 Depress the longtitudinal adjustment lever and set the seat backward into the last position but one, and with the screwdriver on the stop spring depress the stop spring and push the seat out to the rear.
3 The photo shows the stop spring with the seat removed. The piece on the spring fits into the upper slide of the seat.
4 Replacement is a reversal of removal.

17 Seats (rear - Sedan/Saloon) - removal and replacement

1 Push the seat back slightly to release the retainers and then pull it up a little. The seat may now be lifted out.
2 At the lower edge of the backrest are a number of plates held in brackets. Bend the tabs open, push the backrest down and unhook it. It may now be lifted out of the vehicle.
3 Replacement is a reversal of removal.

18 Exterior mirrors - general

1 Remove the door interior trim (Section 11). The fixing bolts for the mirror may now be seen, remove with a socket wrench.
2 Provision is made for the fitting of a second mirror (photo). Remove the trim from the inside of the door and push out the chromium plated insert. The second mirror may now be assembled.
3 There are two types of mirror available. The one described fits from the inside. There is another type which screws in from the outside.

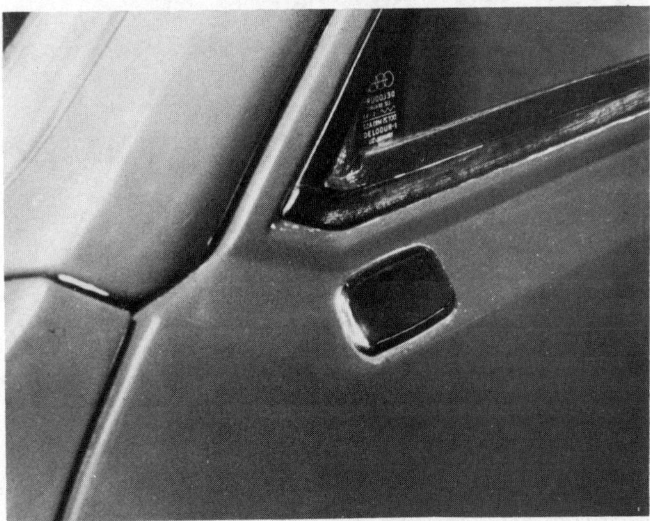

18.2 The position of the second exterior mirror

Chapter 14 Supplement
Revisions and information on later models

Contents

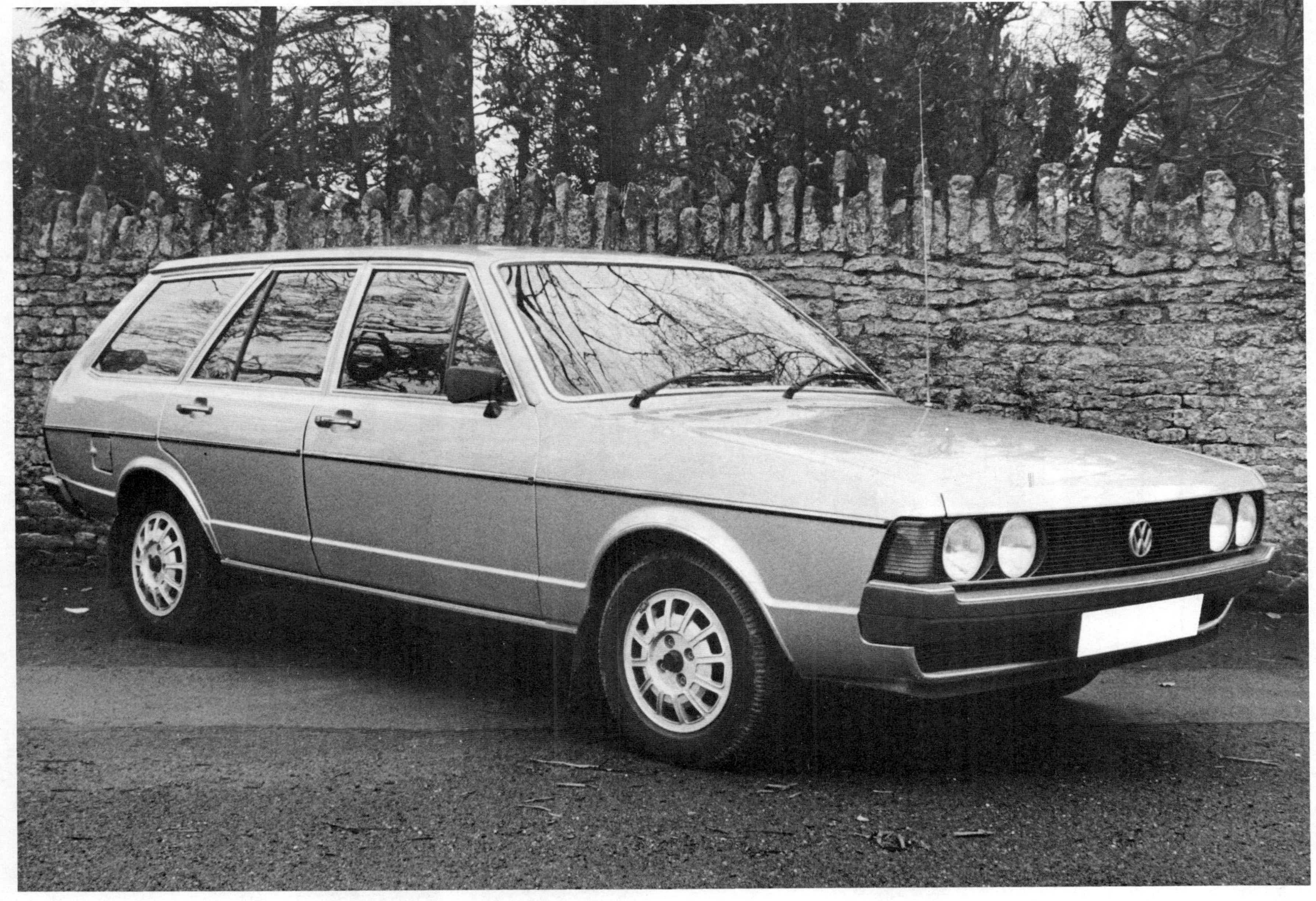

1981 model Passat Estate

1 Introduction

1 The various Sections of this Supplement should be read in conjunction with the text contained in the original Chapters of the manual. There have been many detailed changes to the models in the range during the years of production, but the major modifications are few (photos) and include the following:

1588 cc engine (commonly referred to as '1600 cc')
Fuel injection system
Electronic (breakerless) ignition

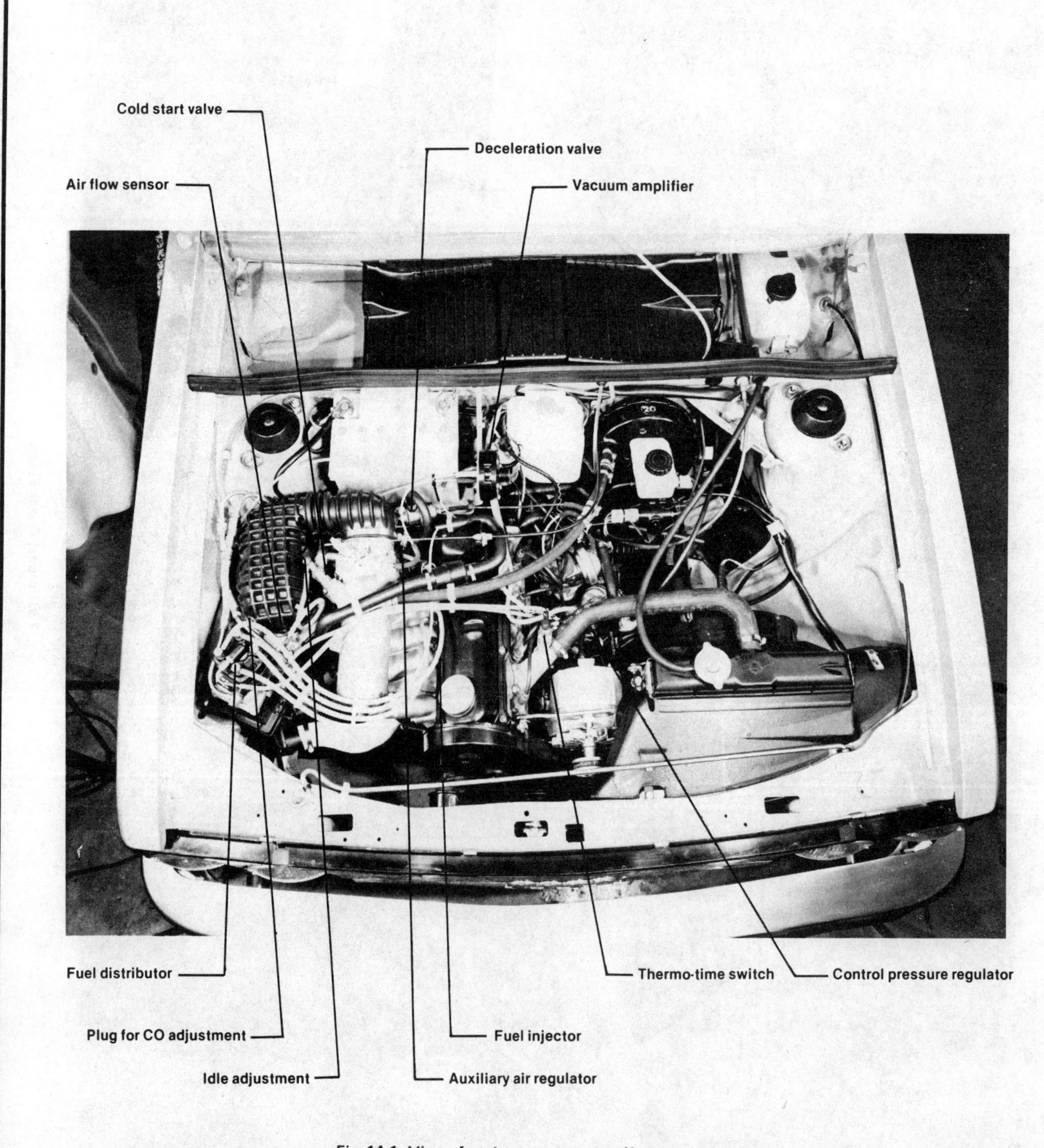

Fig. 14.1 View of engine compartment (fuel injection)

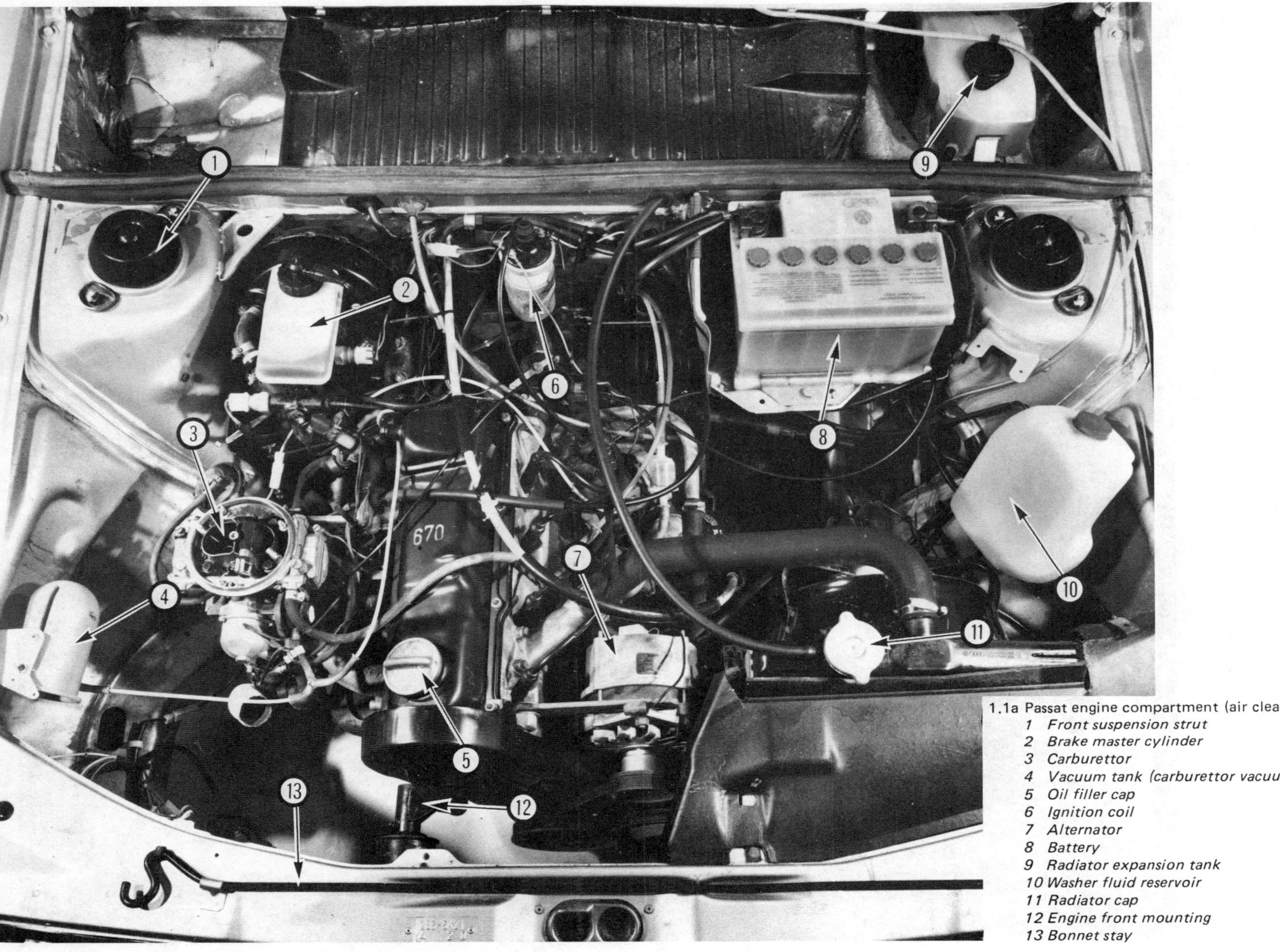

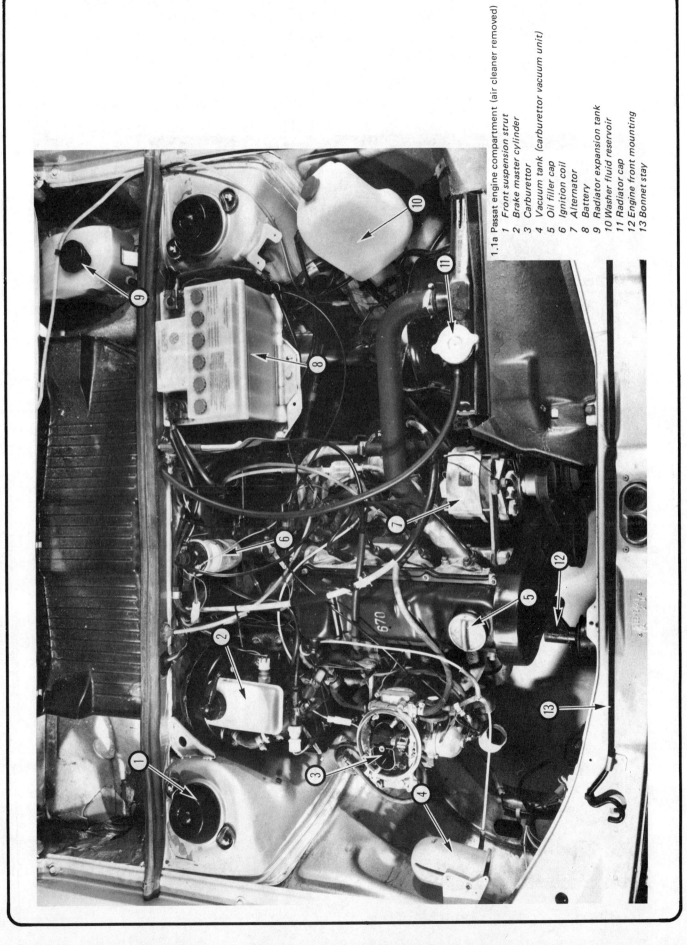

1.1a Passat engine compartment (air cleaner removed)
1 *Front suspension strut*
2 *Brake master cylinder*
3 *Carburettor*
4 *Vacuum tank (carburettor vacuum unit)*
5 *Oil filler cap*
6 *Ignition coil*
7 *Alternator*
8 *Battery*
9 *Radiator expansion tank*
10 *Washer fluid reservoir*
11 *Radiator cap*
12 *Engine front mounting*
13 *Bonnet stay*

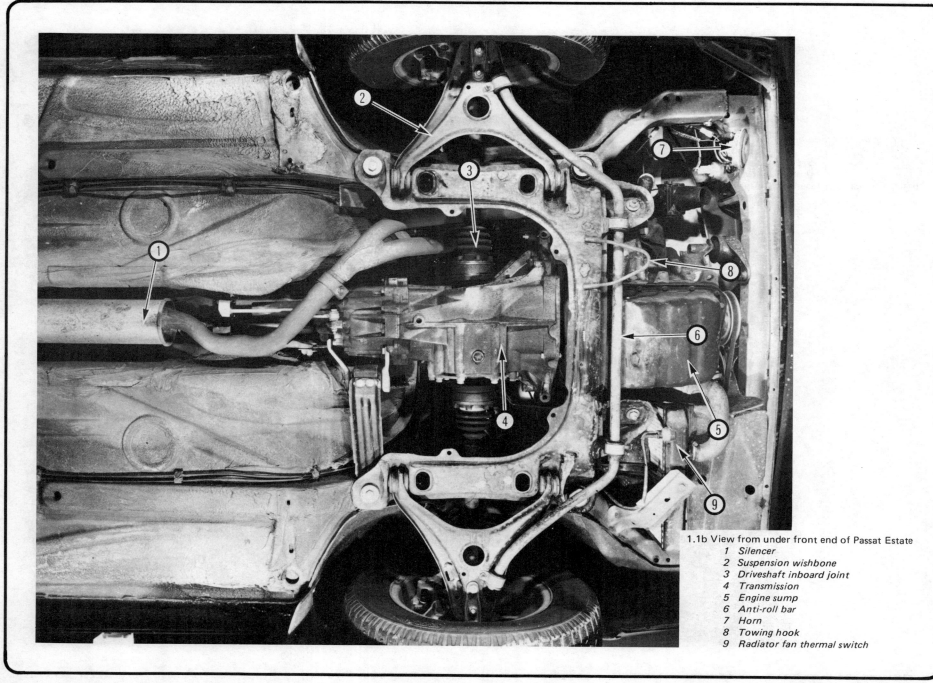

1.1b View from under front end of Passat Estate
1 *Silencer*
2 *Suspension wishbone*
3 *Driveshaft inboard joint*
4 *Transmission*
5 *Engine sump*
6 *Anti-roll bar*
7 *Horn*
8 *Towing hook*
9 *Radiator fan thermal switch*

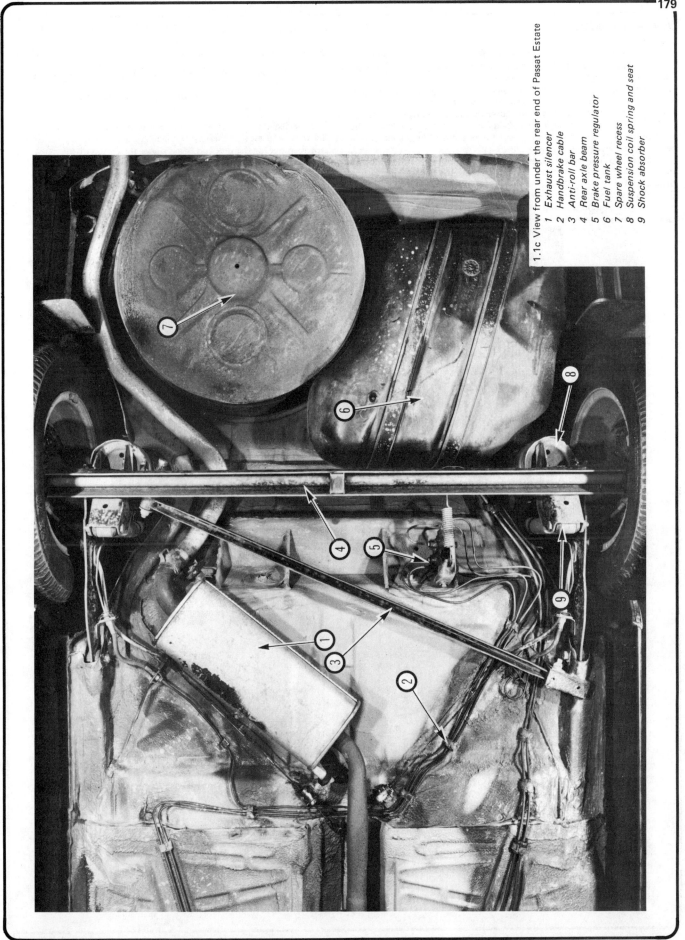

1.1c View from under the rear end of Passat Estate

1. *Exhaust silencer*
2. *Handbrake cable*
3. *Anti-roll bar*
4. *Rear axle beam*
5. *Brake pressure regulator*
6. *Fuel tank*
7. *Spare wheel recess*
8. *Suspension coil spring and seat*
9. *Shock absorber*

Jacking and towing

Jacking

2 For roadside wheel changing, a jack is supplied in the vehicle tool kit. Use this only at the jacking points (two on each side). These are indicated by triangles recessed into the sill (photos).

3 If a roadwheel is to be removed, prise off the hub cap (where applicable) and just release the wheel retaining bolts before raising the vehicle. Chock the wheel diagonally opposite the one being removed.

4 If the road wheels have been balanced on the vehicle, mark the relative position of the roadwheel and the hub mounting flange before removing the wheel.

5 Tighten the roadwheel bolts to their final torque when the weight of the vehicle is once again on its wheels. Smear the bolt threads with a little grease.

6 If the vehicle is to be raised for repair or overhaul purposes, ideally a trolley jack should be used. Alternatively, use a bottle or screw jack supplemented by axle stands.

7 A jack must only be used at one of the following positions when lifting the vehicle for working under it.

(a) To raise the front, jack under the transverse or longitudinal floorpan reinforcement

(b) To raise the rear, jack under the welded flange at the joint of the floorpan and side-member

8 Provided the lifting pad of the jack is at least 4 in (100 mm) wide, the front end may be raised if the jack is placed under the centre of the crossmember, or the rear end lifted under the centre of the axle beam.

Towing

9 The towing hooks, although primarily intended for lashing-down purposes, may be used for short emergency towing. For extended towing work always have the front wheels raised off the ground on a proper towing rig (photos).

1.2a Spare wheel location on Estate

1.2b Tool stowage on Estate

Fig. 14.2 Tool kit jack in use

Fig. 14.3 Raising the front of the vehicle

Fig. 14.4 Raising the rear of the vehicle

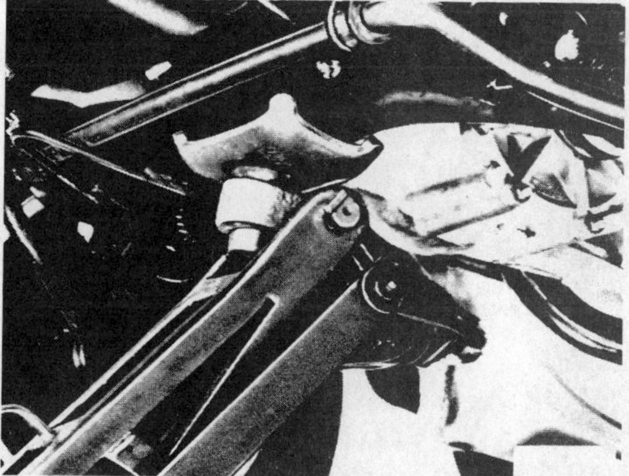

Fig. 14.5 Jack under the front crossmember

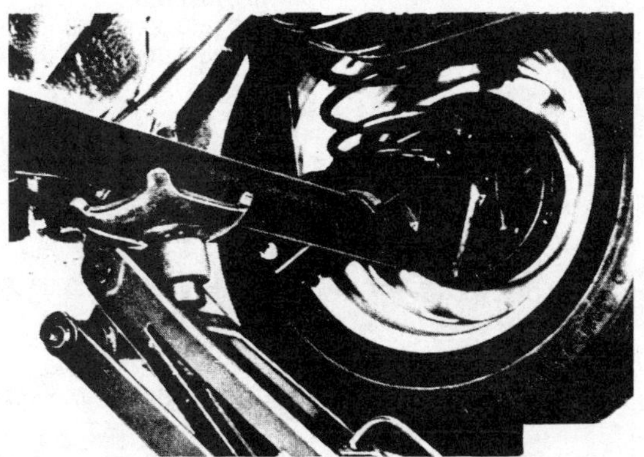

Fig. 14.6 Jack under the rear axle beam

1.9a Rear towing hook

1.9b Front towing hook

2 Specifications

These Specifications are revisions of, or supplementary to, the Specifications at the beginning of the previous Chapters. 1600 cc engine Specifications are as given for 1500 cc engines in Chapter 1, except for the differences listed below.

Engine (1600 cc)

General

Bore	79.5 mm (3.130 in)	
Stroke	80.0 mm (3.150 in)	
Displacement	1588 cc (96.9 cu in)	
Performance (DIN):	**kW (hp) @ rpm**	**kgf m (lbf ft) @ rpm**
Engine code:		
XX	74 (100) @ 6000	13.4 (96) @ 4000
YN	55 (75) @ 5600	12.1 (87) @ 3200
YP	63 (85) @ 5600	12.7 (92) @ 3200
YS	81 (110) @ 6100	14.0 (101) @ 5000
YG, YK, YH	61 (83) @ 5800	13.0 (94) @ 3300
YT	51 (70) @ 5600	12.3 (89) @ 3200
Compression ratio (by engine code):		
XX	9.8 : 1	
YS	9.5 : 1	
YN, YP, YG, YT	8.2 : 1	
YK, YH	8.0 : 1	

Valve timing

	Engine code YT	**All other codes**
At 1 mm valve lift and zero valve clearance:		
Inlet opens	6° ATDC	4° ATDC
Inlet closes	32° ABDC	46° ABDC
Exhaust opens	42° BBDC	44° BBDC
Exhaust closes	0° (TDC)	6° ATDC

Valve clearances	**Hot, mm (in)**	**Cold, mm (in)**
Inlet	0.20 to 0.30 (0.008 to 0.012)	0.15 to 0.25 (0.006 to 0.010)
Exhaust	0.40 to 0.50 (0.016 to 0.020)	0.35 to 0.45 (0.014 to 0.018)

Valve guides

Maximum rock:

Inlet	1.0 mm (0.039 in)
Exhaust	1.3 mm (0.051 in)

Camshaft

Bearing running clearance	0.02 to 0.05 mm (0.0008 to 0.0020 in)

Piston rings

Clearance in groove:

New	0.02 to 0.05 mm (0.0008 to 0.0020 in)
Wear limit	0.15 mm (0.0059 in)

Pistons and cylinders

Piston crown markings:

Arrow direction	Towards front of engine
Weight group marking	Two letters below arrow
Grade marking (see below)	Opposite weight group marking

Repair stage	Piston diameter		Cylinder bore		Honing
	mm	in	mm	in	group
Standard:					
Grade 1	79.48	3.1290	79.51	3.1302	951
Grade 2	79.49	3.1295	79.52	3.1307	952
Grade 3	79.50	3.1299	79.53	3.1310	953
1st rebore:					
Grade 1	79.73	3.1390	79.76	3.1402	976
Grade 2	79.74	3.1394	79.77	3.1406	977
Grade 3	79.75	3.1398	79.78	3.1409	978
2nd rebore:					
Grade 1	79.98	3.1490	80.01	3.1500	001
Grade 2	79.99	3.1493	80.02	3.1505	002
Grade 3	80.00	3.1497	80.03	3.1508	003
3rd rebore:					
Grade 1	80.48	3.1685	80.51	3.1698	051
Grade 2	80.49	3.1690	80.52	3.1700	052
Grade 3	80.50	3.1693	80.53	3.1705	053

Maximum bore size before 1st rebore:

Grade 1	79.55 mm (3.1319 in)
Grade 2	79.56 mm (3.1323 in)
Grade 3	79.57 mm (3.1327 in)
Bore taper or out-of-round limit	0.05 mm (0.002 in)
Piston-to-bore clearance:	
New	0.03 mm (0.0012 in)
Wear limit	0.07 mm (0.0028 in)

Lubrication system

Oil pressure warning light operating pressure	0.3 to 0.6 kg/cm^2 (4 to 8 lbf/in^2)
Oil pressure at 2000 rpm, 80°C (176°F)	2 kgf/cm^2 (29 lbf/in^2) minimum
Oil capacity (with filter change)	3 litres (5.3 Imp pints, 3.2 US quarts)

Fuel system

Carburettor data (UK models)

Solex 35/40 DIDTA

Application	1600 cc engine code XX, 1973 to 1975	
Calibration:	**1st stage**	**2nd stage**
Venturi dia (mm)	24	28
Main jet	X 117.5	X 150
Air correction jet	140	120
Pilot jet	47.5	–
Pilot air jet	175	–
Auxiliary fuel jet	60	–
Auxiliary air jet	130	–
Enrichment with ball	57.5	100
Injection rate/stroke, slow (cc)	0.75	1.05
Float needle valve dia (mm)	1.75	
Float needle valve washer thickness (mm)	0.5	
Throttle valve gap (mm)	0.80 ± 0.05	
Drill size	68 or 1/32 in	

Choke valve gap (mm)	4.0 $\pm$ 0.15
Drill size	25
Fuel octane requirement	98 RON (UK 4-star)
Idle speed	900 to 1000 rpm
CO content at idle	1.3 to 1.7%

Solex 35 PDSIT

Application	1600 cc engine code YN, 1976
Calibration (values in brackets are for automatic transmission, where different):	
Venturi diameter (mm)	27
Main jet	X140
Air correction jet	110
Pilot jet	55
Pilot air jet	150
Injection rate/stroke, slow (cc)	1 to 1.4 (0.35 to 0.65)
Float needle diameter (mm)	1.5
Needle washer thickness (mm)	1.0
Throttle valve gap (mm)	0.75 to 0.85 (0.85 to 0.95)
Equivalent drill size	No. 68 or 1/32 in (No. 65)
Choke valve gap (mm)	4.25 to 4.55 (3.85 to 4.15)
Equivalent drill size	No. 17 or 11/64 in (No. 22)
Fuel octane requirement	91 RON (UK 2-star)
Idle speed	900 to 1000 rpm
CO content at idle	1.3 to 1.7%

Zenith 2B2 (1975 models)

Application	1600 cc engine code YP, 1975	
Calibration:	**Stage 1**	**Stage 2**
Venturi diameter (mm)	24	28
Main jet	X117.5	X125
Air correction jet	135	92.5
Pilot fuel jet	52.5	40
Pilot air jet	135	125
Auxiliary fuel jet	42.5	–
Auxiliary air jet	130	–
Progression fuel jet	100	–
Progression air jet	200	–
Pump injection tube	45	45
Enrichment valve	65	–
Needle valve diameter (mm)	2	2
Float level setting (mm)	28	30
Injection rate/stroke, slow (cc)	0.75 to 1.05	
Throttle valve gap (mm)	0.6 to 0.7 (manual), 0.9 (automatic)	
Equivalent drill size	72 or 65	
Choke valve gap (mm)	4.35 to 4.65	
Equivalent drill size	10	
Fuel octane requirement	91 RON (UK 2-star)	
Idle speed	900 to 1000 rpm	
CO content at idle	0.7 to 1.3%	

Zenith 2B2 (1976 on models)

Application	1600 cc engine code YP, 1976 on
Calibration and other values as given above for 1975 models, except for the following:	
Progression fuel jet	130 (manual)
Progression air jet	180 (manual)
Pump injection tube	40 (manual)
Injection rate/stroke, slow (cc)	1.15 to 1.45 (manual)
Throttle valve gap (mm)	0.7 to 0.8 (automatic)
Equivalent drill size	69
Choke valve gap (mm)	3.0 to 3.3 (manual)
Equivalent drill size	31
CO content at idle	0.5 to 1.5%

Zenith 181

Application	1300 cc engine codes FY, FZ, 1979/80
Calibration:	
Venturi diameter (mm)	25
Main jet	117.5
Air correction jet	95
Idle fuel jet	52.5
Idle air jet	130
Auxiliary fuel jet	42.5
Auxiliary air jet	120
Enrichment (height above atomizer, mm)	24
Needle valve diameter (mm)	1.5
Pump injection tube	0.3/0.4
Injection rate/stroke, slow (cc)	0.75 to 1.05
Choke valve gap (mm)	3.35 to 3.65
Fuel octane requirement	91 RON (UK 2-star)

Idle speed	900 to 1000 rpm
Fast idle speed	4300 to 4700 rpm
CO content at idle	0.5 to 1.5%

Zenith 1B3

Application	1600 cc engine code YN, 1979/80
Calibration:	
Venturi diameter (mm)	26
Main jet	125 (manual), 122.5 (automatic)
Air correction jet	100
Idle fuel jet	50
Idle air jet	130
Auxiliary fuel jet	37.5
Auxiliary air jet	130
Needle valve diameter (mm)	2.0
Pump injection tube	0.55
Injection rate/stroke, slow (cc)	0.75
Choke valve gap (mm)	4.15 to 4.45
Fuel octane requirement	91 RON (UK 2-star)
Idle speed	900 to 1000 rpm
Fast idle speed:	
Manual	3700 to 4100 rpm
Automatic	3500 to 3900 rpm
CO content at idle	0.5 to 1.5%

Zenith 2B5

Application	1600 cc engine code YP, 1979/80	
Calibration:	**Stage 1**	**Stage 2**
Venturi diameter (mm)	24	28
Main jet	117.5	125
Air correction jet	135	92.5
Idle fuel jet	52.5	40
Idle air jet	135	125
Auxiliary fuel jet	42.5	–
Auxiliary air jet	130	–
Progression fuel jet	–	130 manual, 100 automatic
Progression air jet	–	180
Needle valve diameter (mm)	2	2
Enrichment valve	65	–
Float level (mm)	27 to 29	29 to 31
Pump injection tube	37.5/40	37.5/40
Injection rate/stroke, slow (cc)	0.8 manual, 0.75 automatic	
Choke valve gap (mm)	3.75 manual, 3.55 automatic	
Fuel octane requirement	91 RON (UK 2-star)	
Idle speed	900 to 1000 rpm	
Fast idle speed:		
Manual	3550 to 3650 rpm	
Automatic	3350 to 3450 rpm	
CO content at idle	0.5 to 1.5%	

Carburettor data (US models)

Solex 32/35 DIDTA

Application	1500 cc engine codes XW and XZ (manual), XV and XY (auto), 1974	
Calibration:	**Stage 1**	**Stage 2**
Venturi diameter (mm)	24	27
Main jet	120 (XY), 122.5 (XZ), 130 (XV), 135 (XW)	140 (XV, XW), 142.5 (XZ), 145 (XY)
Air correction jet	130 (XZ), 140 (XV, XY), 150 (XW)	140
Idle fuel jet	g45 (XY, XZ), g52.5 (XV, XW)	–
Idle air jet	180	–
Auxiliary fuel jet	42.5 (XV, XW), 60 (XY, XZ)	–
Auxiliary air jet	110 (XV, XW), 130 (XY, XZ)	–
Injection tube	45	–
Injection rate/stroke, slow (cc)	0.75 to 1.05	–
Needle valve diameter (mm)	1.75	–
Float level (mm)	16 to 17	–
Choke valve gap (mm):		
XV, XW	3.55 to 3.85	–
XY, XZ	3.35 to 3.65	–
Fast idle gap (mm), choke on highest step:		
XV, XW, XY	0.75 to 0.85	–
XZ	0.6 to 0.7	–
Fuel octane requirement	91 RON (regular)	
Idle speed	850 to 1000 rpm	
CO content at idle:		
XV, XW	0.4 to 1.6%	
XY, XZ	1.0 to 2.0% (air injection disconnected)	

Zenith 2B3

Application	1500 cc engine codes XS (manual), XR (automatic)	
Calibration:	**Stage 1**	**Stage 2**
Venturi diameter (mm)	24	27
Main jet	117.5	137.5
Air correction jet	140	92.5
Idle fuel jet	52.5	52.5
Idle air jet	130	110
Auxiliary fuel jet	42.5	–
Auxiliary air jet	127.5	–
Needle valve diameter (mm)	2	2
Float level (mm)	27.5 to 28.5	29.5 to 30.5
Injection tube	50	–
Injection rate/stroke, slow (cc)	0.75 to 1.05	–
Choke valve gap (mm)	3.8 to 4.2	–
Fast idle gap (mm), choke on highest step	0.45 to 0.50	–
Fuel octane requirement	91 RON (unleaded with catalytic converter)	
Idle speed	850 to 1000 rpm	
CO content at idle	1.5 to 2.5% (measured ahead of catalytic converter, air injection disconnected)	

Fuel injection system

Application	1600 cc engine codes YG, YK, YH, 1975 and later
Fuel pump delivery rate:	
To 1976	750 ml/30 sec
1977 on	900 ml/30 sec
Control pressure:	
Engine cold	1.35 to 1.65 bar (19 to 23 lbf/in^2)
Engine warm	3.4 to 3.8 bar (48 to 54 lbf/in^2)
System pressure	4.50 to 5.20 bar (64 to 74 lbf/in^2)
Fuel injectors:	
Opening pressure	2.5 to 3.5 bar (35 to 50 lbf/in^2)
Pressure difference permissible between injectors (maximum)	0.6 bar (8.5 lbf/in^2)
Idle speed*	850 to 1000 rpm
CO level:*	
49 States	1.5% manual, 1.0% automatic
California	0.5% manual and automatic

** Refer also to vehicle tune-up decal*

Ignition system

Ignition timing (1976 on)	Timing	Engine rpm	Vacuum hoses
UK models:			
Engine codes ZA, ZF	9° BTDC	900 to 1000	Disconnected
Engine codes YP, YS, and YN up to Chassis No. 329XXX	TDC	900 to 1000	Connected
Engine code YN from Chassis No. 32AXXX	9° BTDC	900 to 1000	Disconnected
US models*	3° ATDC	850 to 1000	Connected

** Digital idle stabilizer disconnected (models with breakerless ignition)*

Dwell angle

US models (conventional ignition)	44° to 50°

Spark plugs

UK models:	
Engine codes XX and YS	Champion N6YC or equivalent
All other engines	Champion N7YC or equivalent
US models (breakerless ignition)	Bosch WR7DS, Beru RS35 or Champion N8GY
Electrode gap (breakerless ignition)	0.6 to 0.7 mm (0.024 to 0.028 in)

Manual gearbox

Gear ratios (later models)	1975	1976 on
1st	3.4 : 1	3.4 : 1
2nd	1.95 : 1	2.06 : 1
3rd	1.37 : 1	1.29 : 1
4th	0.94 : 1	0.88 : 1
Reverse	3.17 : 1	3.17 : 1
Final drive	4.11 : 1	4.11 :1

Automatic transmission

General

Maker's type No.	089

Gear ratios:

1st	2.55 : 1
2nd	1.45 : 1
3rd	1 : 1
Reverse	2.46 : 1
Final drive	3 : 9

Shift speeds (typical)

	Full throttle		Kickdown	
	kph	mph	kph	mph
1 - 2	31 to 38	19 to 24	57 to 62	35 to 39
2 - 3	79 to 85	50 to 53	104 to 106	65 to 67
3 - 2	49 to 57	31 to 35	99 to 101	62 to 64
2 - 1	24 to 27	15 to 17	51 to 55	32 to 34

Lubricant capacity

Initial fill	10.3 Imp pints (6.0 litres, 6.3 US quarts)
Refill	5.2 Imp pints (3.0 litres, 3.2 US quarts)
Final drive	1.3 Imp pints (0.75 litre, 0.8 US quart)

Lubricant type

Automatic transmission	ATF Dexron or Dexron II
Final drive	Castrol Hypoy B EP90 or equivalent

Torque wrench settings	lb ft	kgf m
Converter housing-to-engine bolts	40	5.5
Mounting bolts to body	29	4.0
Driveshaft bolts	32	4.5
Torque converter/driveplate bolts	22	3.0
Suspension balljoint to wishbone	47	6.5

Braking system

Girling disc brakes (1979 on)

Piston diameter	48.0 mm (1.89 in)
Disc diameter	239.0 mm (9.41 in)
Disc thickness:	
81 kW engine	20.0 mm (0.79 in) (ventilated)
55, 63 kW engine	12.0 mm (0.47 in)
Minimum disc thickness after regrind:	
81 kW engine	18.0 mm (0.71 in)
55, 63 kW engine	10.0 mm (0.39 in)
Pad thickness - new:	
81 kW engine	14.0 mm (0.55 in)
55, 63 kW engine	10.0 mm (0.39 in)
Pad thickness - wear limit:	
81 kW engine	10.0 mm (0.39 in) including backplate
55, 63 kW engine	7.0 mm (0.28 in) including backplate

Torque wrench settings - Girling disc brakes	lbf ft	kgf m
Caliper guide bolts (ventilated disc)	29	4.0
Caliper guide self-locking bolts	26	3.6

Electrical system

Motorola alternator

Maximum output	35 or 55 amps
Rotor winding resistance	3.9 to 4.3 ohms
Stator winding resistance:	
35 amp	0.23 to 0.25 ohms
55 amp	0.15 to 0.17 ohms

Fuse application (typical) - later models

Fuse number and rating* (amps):	
1 (8)	Low beam, left
2 (8)	Low beam, right
3 (8)	High beam, left, high beam warning light
4 (8)	High beam, right
5 (16)	Rear window heater, main current
6 (8)	Brake light, emergency flasher
7 (8)	Cigar lighter, radio, clock, interior light
8 (8)	Fuel gauge, temperature gauge, oil pressure light, turn signal warning light, turn signal, wash/wipe circuit
9 (8)	Reversing light, gearshift illumination (automatic), choke and fuel cut-off valve

Fuse number and rating* (amps):	
10 (8)	Horn
11 (8)	Fresh air fan, heated rear window (control), wipers, washer, headlight washer, voltmeter, oil temperature, oil pressure gauge (as applicable)
12 (8)	Number plate light, foglights (control), rear foglight
13 (8)	Tail and sidelights, right
14 (8)	Tail and sidelights, left
15 (16)	Radiator fan

**8 amp fuses are white, 16 amp are red*

Steering and suspension

Steering and suspension angles (unladen)

Front suspension:	
Castor	0° to 1° positive
Camber	0° to 1° positive
Toe	2.5 mm (0.098 in) toe-in to 0.5 mm (0.020 in) toe-out
Rear suspension - 1976 and 1977 models:	
Camber	0° 30′ negative to 0° 30′ positive with a maximum side-to-side difference of 0° 30′
Toe	0° 25′ toe-in to 0° 25′ toe-out with a maximum side-to-side difference of 0° 15′
Rear suspension - 1978 and later models:	
Camber	0° 40′ negative to 0° 40′ positive with a maximum side-to-side difference of 0° 30′
Toe	0° 50′ toe-in to 0° 50′ toe-out with a maximum side-to-side difference of 0° 20′

Driveshaft lengths (later models)

1.5/1.6 litre, manual transmission	508.4 mm (20.02 in) left and right
1.6 litre, automatic transmission:	
Left	566.4 mm (22.30 in), tubular
Right	467.5 mm (18.41 in), solid

Torque wrench settings

	lbf ft	kgf m
Tie-rod clamp pinch-bolt	22	3.0
Tie-rod end locknut	29	4.0

Bodywork

Dimensions and weights

Overall length (except US)	4.190 m (164.96 in)	
Overall length (US)	4.255 m (167.52 in)	
Overall width	1.600 m (62.99 in)	
Overall height (unladen)	1.360 m (53.54 in)	
Ground clearance	107 mm (4.21 in)	
Kerb weight:*		
Saloon (two-door)	860 kg	1896 lb
Hatchback (two-door)	880 kg	1938 lb
Saloon (four-door)	885 kg	1951 lb
Hatchback (four-door)	905 kg	1996 lb
Estate car (Wagon)	920 kg	2029 lb
For automatic transmission add	25 kg	55 lb

** With fuel, oil, water, no occupants or luggage*

Maximum roof rack load	75 kg	165 lb
Maximum trailer weight:*		
1300 cc:		
With brakes	850 kg	1872 lb
Without brakes	450 kg	992 lb
1500 cc, 1600 cc:		
With brakes	1000 kg	2202 lb
Without brakes	450 kg	991 lb

** Subject to local regulations*

3 Engine

General description - 1600 cc

1 The 1600 cc engine is identical with the 1500 cc engine except that the bore has been increased to 79.5 mm. The stroke remains the same and the crankshaft, intermediate shaft and bearings are identical. The cylinder head is slightly modified and a new camshaft is fitted giving changed valve timing. The valves and their seatings are identical with the 1500 cc engine.

2 Two different types of piston are fitted, the governing dimension being the depth of the dish in the crown. This is shown in Fig. 14.7. The American engines may only be supplied with pistons of the same type as installed.

3 The valve clearance adjustment is identical with the 1500 cc model, using the same part numbers for replacement discs.

4 The procedure for removal and refitting of the engine is as described in Chapter 1, but on models equipped with a fuel injection engine, the following additional operations will be required before the engine can be removed:

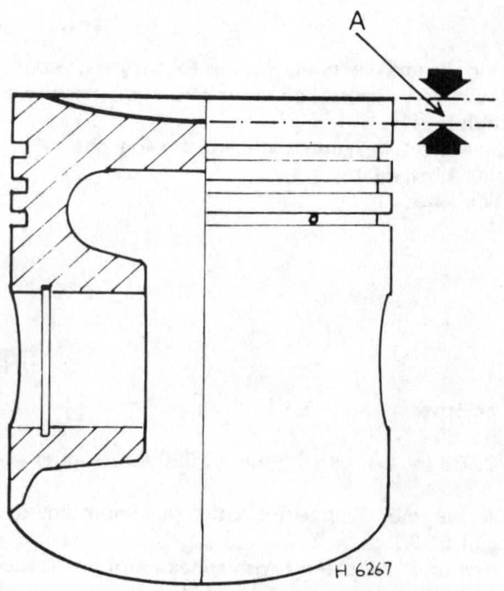

Fig. 14.7 Dished crown type piston
A (YN and YP engine codes) = 6.3 mm/0.248 in)
A (YS engine code) = 7.5 mm (0.295 in)

(a) Disconnect the vacuum hoses from the intake manifold, distributor and emission devices
(b) Disconnect the air intake duct
(c) Remove the cold start valve
(d) Remove the fuel injectors
(e) Remove the accelerator cable
(f) Remove the airflow sensor with fuel distributor and place to one side
(g) Remove the air filter housing with preheater
(h) On vehicles so equipped, detach the inlet pipe from the EGR valve
(j) Disconnect the lead from the cold start valve, the auxiliary air regulator and the thermotime switch

5 The combustion chamber of the cylinder head is modified. The 1600 cc head is identified by the cast-in part number '049 103 373'. The new camshaft may be identified by shoulders near the first and third cams, these shoulders are not present on the 1500 cc camshaft. The part number of the new shaft is '049 109 101'.

Engine number - 1300 cc

6 On later models with 1300 cc engines, the engine number is located on a machined surface adjacent to the alternator bracket.

Crankshaft thrust washers - 1300 cc

7 On later 1300 cc engines, separate semi-circular thrust washers are used at No 3 main bearing to control crankshaft endfloat instead of the composite flanged type shells used on earlier models.

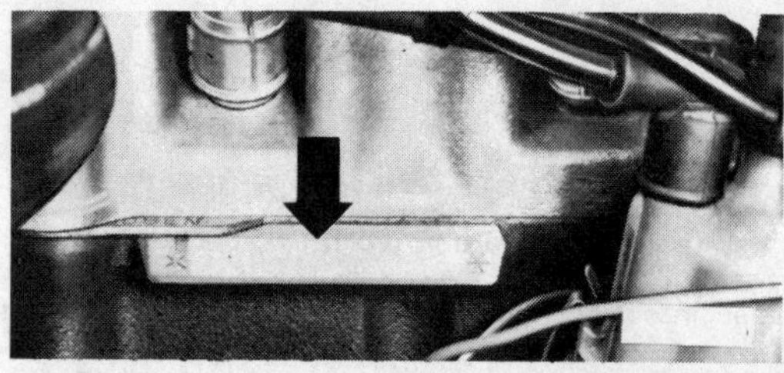

Fig. 14.8 Location of engine number on later 1300 cc models

4 Cooling, heating, exhaust and air conditioning systems

Thermostat

1 The thermostat operating range differs on later models to give an opening at higher coolant temperatures.
2 Due to the interrelationship of the coolant thermostat, radiator thermo-switch, temperature sender unit and gauge, it is imperative that the correct thermostat is fitted to the appropriate vehicle. Do not fit a thermostat of higher opening temperature in place of the original unit.

Radiator or expansion bottle cap

3 The pressure rating of later model caps differs from earlier models. Again make sure that a replacement is exactly as specified for your vehicle.

Heating and fresh air system

4 The heater/fresh air system remains as shown in Chapter 2 until August 1976. After this date a three-speed radial blower is installed.
5 The two halves of the blower housing are fastened together with clips which may be levered off with a screwdriver. The heat-exchanger cover may be removed by pressing in the retaining tabs and then it may be pulled off. If the heat exchanger is removed the seal should be stuck in position on reassembly, or the heat exchanger will rattle. When refitting the operating rod press the female end into the lever and the male end into the cut-off flap lever, otherwise the rod will touch the clip securing the heater to the body. The blower is held in position by one screw.
6 To adjust the control levers when reassembling the heat-exchanger, set the control levers in the 'off' position, close the flaps and the control valve, secure the cables and assemble the operating rod.

Exhaust system

7 The Passat exhaust system is not modified but the Dasher system has a catalytic converter added on some models. This is discussed with the other emission controls in Section 4. It entails some dismantling of the exhaust system every 30 000 miles (48 000 km). When reassembling the exhaust system on all models the distance between the body crossmember and the rear surface of the mounting hook must be 7/8 in (21 mm). When lining up the silencer the distance from the rear surface of the shift gate and the front surface of the silencer must be 1¾ in (44 mm) and there must be a vertical clearance of ¾ in (19 mm) between the exhaust pipe and the shift gate. These dimensions apply also to the Passat. The side of the rear clamp with the bolt should be face outwards (towards the rear wheel).
8 The exhaust pipe must be correctly assembled and aligned when the engine is reinstalled. The clamps should be slackened and the pipe and silencer should be moved so that the support loops at the front and rear of the silencer are uniformly loaded. Bend the supporting hooks if necessary. Slacken the clamp behind the silencer and align the tailpipe so that it is free from strain.

Air conditioning system - general

9 Refer to Section 5, Chapter 1.
10 It is recommended that disconnection of the refrigerant circuit be left to your dealer or a refrigeration engineer. This is not because of any potential danger but because evacuation and recharging of the system requires special equipment, and because the entry of moisture (carried in the air) can cause damage to the system.
11 Regular maintenance should be carried out to include the following.

Compressor drivebelt adjustment

12 On models up to 1978, slacken the compressor mounting bolts and then turn the nut (Fig. 14.10) until the belt tension is correct. This is when the belt can be deflected by moderate finger pressure, at the midpoint of its longest run, through 15 mm (0.6 in). Retighten the mounting bolts.
13 A new belt can be fitted after the adjustment link has been completely slackened off.
14 On post-1978 models a different make of compressor is used which incorporates a different type of drivebelt adjuster.
15 To tension the drivebelt, release the compressor and alternator mounting bolts and pass a rod through the holes in the lugs at the base of the compressor. Prise the rod downward to give the specified belt tension, which corresponds to a deflection of between 5 and 10 mm (0.2 and 0.4 in). Tighten the mounting bolts.

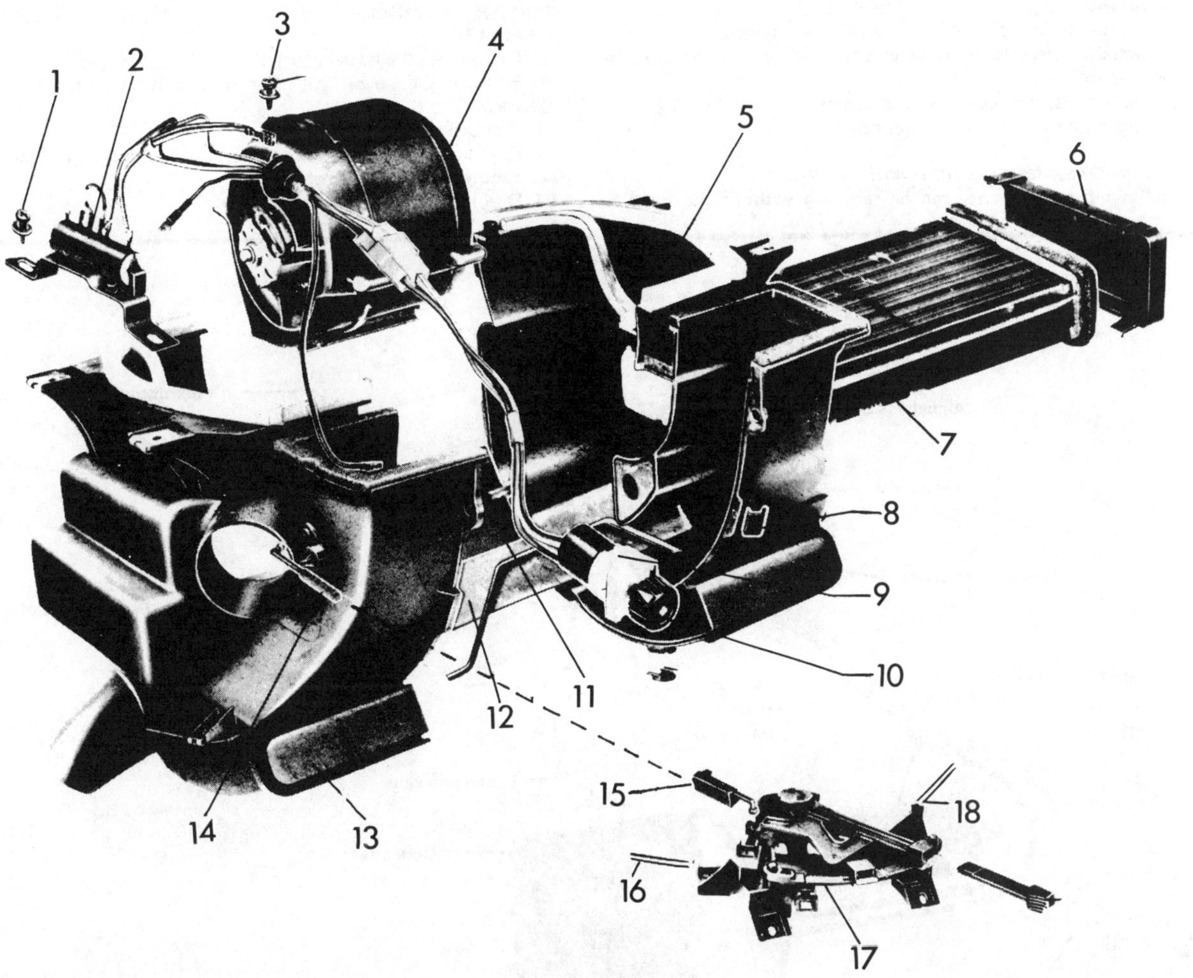

Fig. 14.9 Heater assembly (1976 on)

1 Series resistance securing screw
2 Series resistance
3 Screw securing blowers to fresh air housing
4 Blower motor
5 Fresh air housing
6 Cover for heat exchanger
7 Heat exchanger
8 Clip
9 Switch
10 Switch knob
11 Flap for cut-off
12 Control flap
13 Cap
14 Operating rod (flap end)
15 Operating rod (control end)
16 Heater valve cable
17 Control levers
18 Control flap cable

Fig. 14.10 Air conditioner compressor drivebelt adjuster (arrowed)

Fig. 14.11 Compressor drivebelt deflection

a = 15 mm (0.6 in)

Other maintenance

16 During winter it is advisable to operate the system for a short period at weekly intervals to provide adequate lubrication for the seals in the system.

17 Check the condenser regularly and remove dirt or flies from its fins using compressed air or a cold water hose.

Air conditioning system - component removal

18 The following components can be removed without the need to discharge the system.

Fresh air fan

19 Disconnect the battery negative lead.

20 Remove the cover from the air conditioner unit by swivelling it sideways.

21 Remove the resistors.

22 Extract the three fan fixing screws and withdraw the fan.

Air conditioner/heater controls

23 Drain the cooling system.

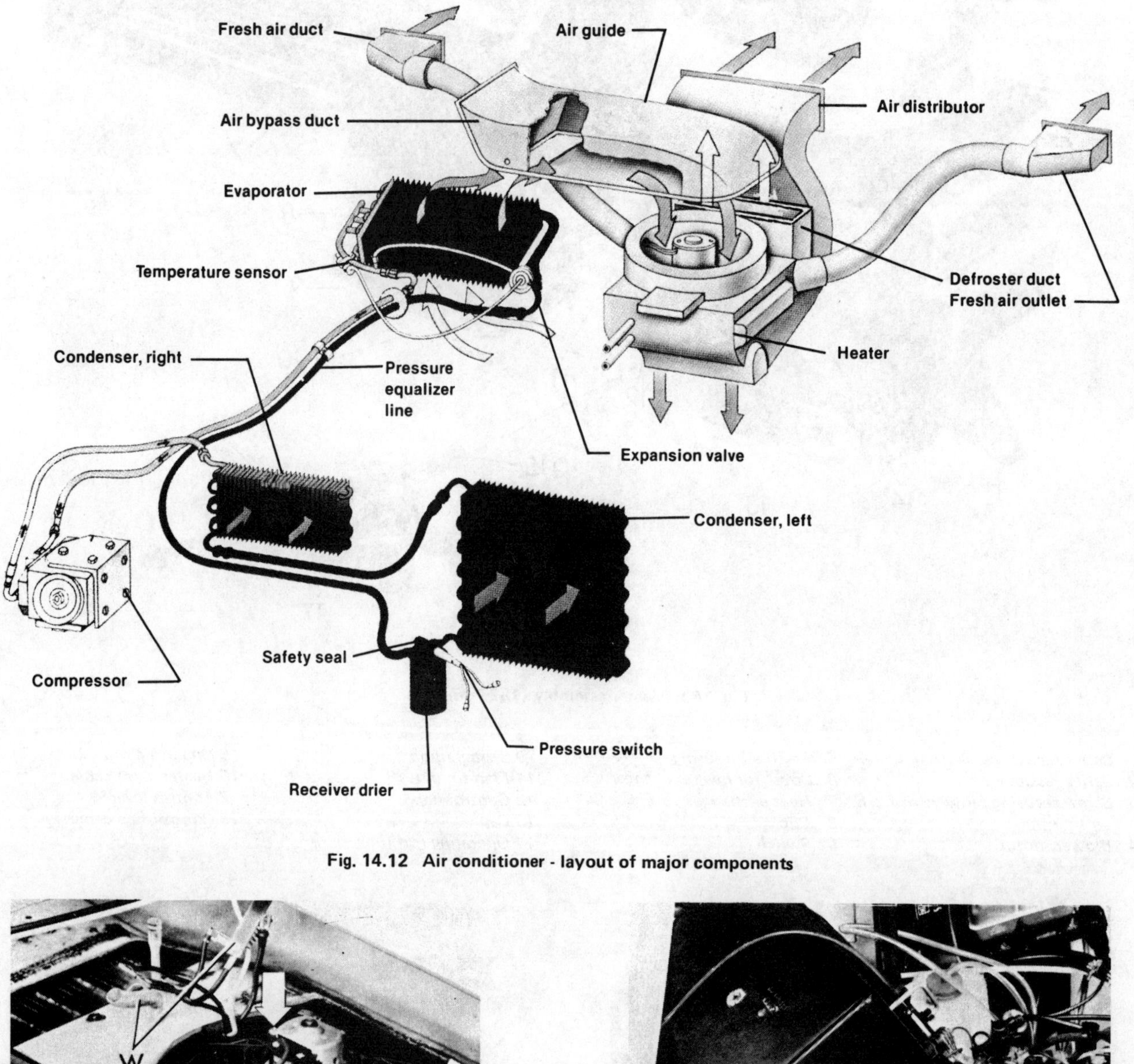

Fresh air duct
Air guide
Air distributor
Air bypass duct
Evaporator
Temperature sensor
Defroster duct
Fresh air outlet
Heater
Condenser, right
Pressure equalizer line
Expansion valve
Condenser, left
Safety seal
Compressor
Pressure switch
Receiver drier

Fig. 14.12 Air conditioner - layout of major components

Fig. 14.13 Fresh air booster fan (models with air conditioning). Mounting screws arrowed

W Resistors

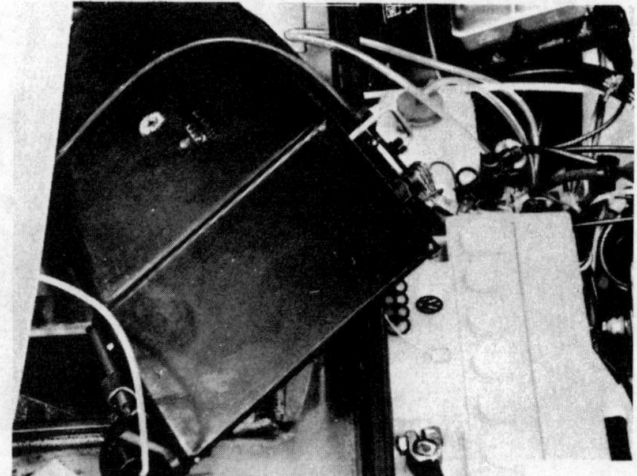

Fig. 14.14 Removing air conditioner cover

24 Move the windscreen washer fluid reservoir aside.
25 Unbolt the ignition coil and move it aside.
26 Slacken the heater hose clamps and disconnect the hoses.
27 Pull the knobs from the heater control levers.
28 Extract the two screws and remove the controls and brackets.
29 Pull the lead from the terminal on the fresh air blower. Disconnect the vacuum hose.
30 Disconnect the rotary knob lever cable and prise off the cable clamp.
31 Pull the fresh air housing downwards complete with control assembly.

Fresh air vents

32 These can be removed if their hoses are first disconnected and the securing tags squeeezed inwards.
33 *If the air conditioning system is first discharged,* the following components can be removed.

Compressor

34 Disconnect the hoses from the compressor and cap or plug them.
35 Slacken the four mounting bolts (Fig. 14.17).
36 Disconnect the earth strap at the base of the compressor.
37 Disconnect the compressor clutch cable.
38 Remove the drivebelt and then lower the unit and remove it from the vehicle.

Evaporator

39 Remove the battery from the engine compartment.
40 Remove the glove compartment.
41 Release the evaporator housing cover.
42 Prise off the cable clamp and disconnect the cable.
43 Disconnect the vacuum pipe from the vacuum unit.
44 Release the low pressure hose clamp by unscrewing the screw which is located in the battery tray. Disconnect the hose from the compressor and plug or cap the openings.

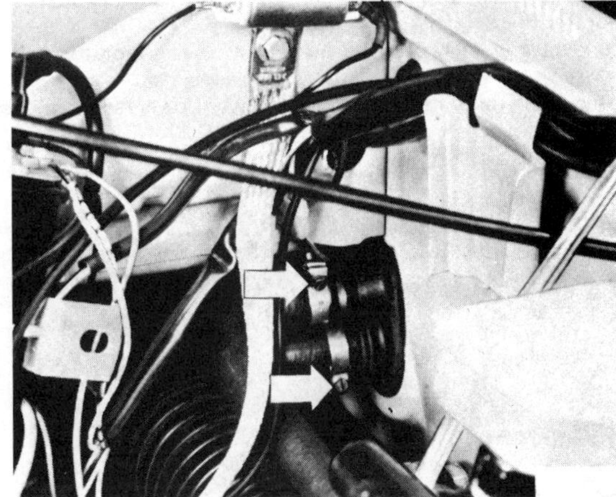

Fig. 14.15 Heater hose clamps (arrowed) at bulkhead

Fig. 14.17 Compressor mounting/adjuster bolts

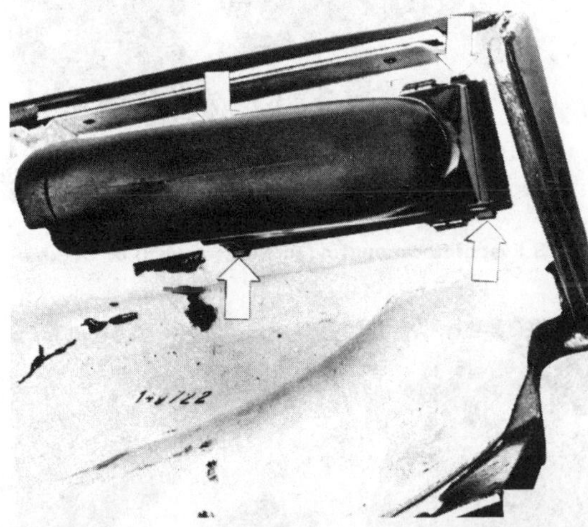

Fig. 14.16 Fresh air vent securing tags (arrowed)

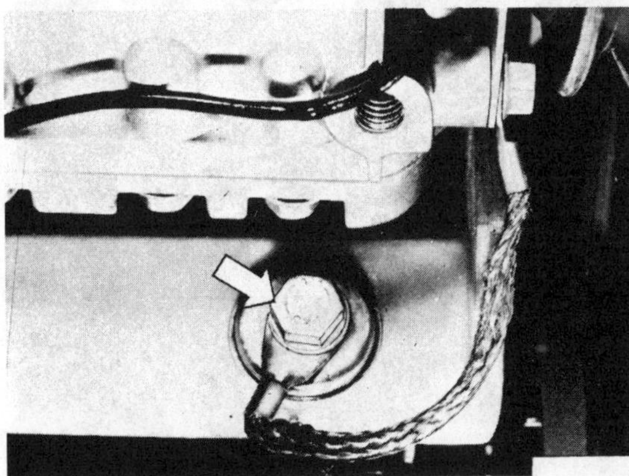

Fig. 14.18 Compressor earth lead

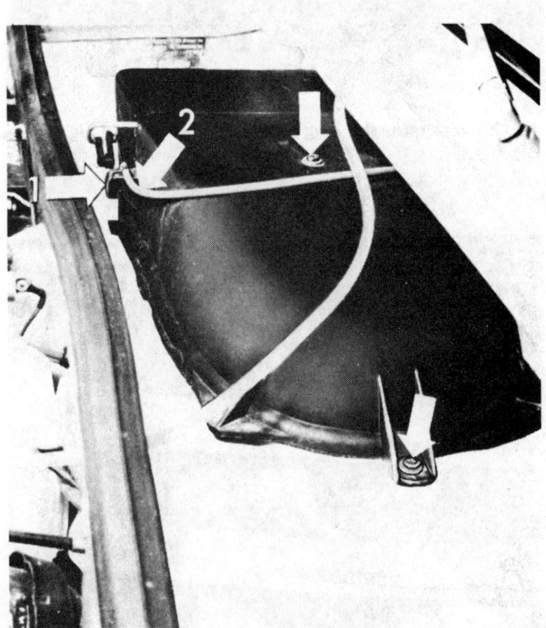

Fig. 14.19 Air conditioner evaporator. Cover securing screws arrowed

1 Clamp *2 Cable*

45 Unscrew the drip tray and carefully pull the capillary tube out of the evaporator.
46 Disconnect the high pressure hose from the evaporator and plug the openings.
47 Extract the evaporator mounting screws. Lower and remove the unit from the vehicle.

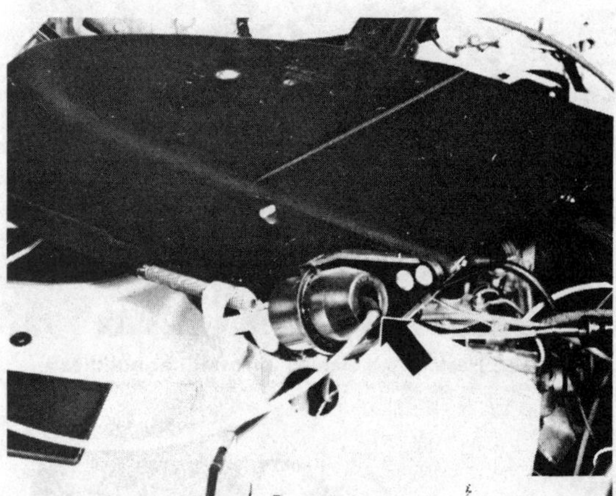

Fig. 14.20 Evaporator vacuum line (arrowed)

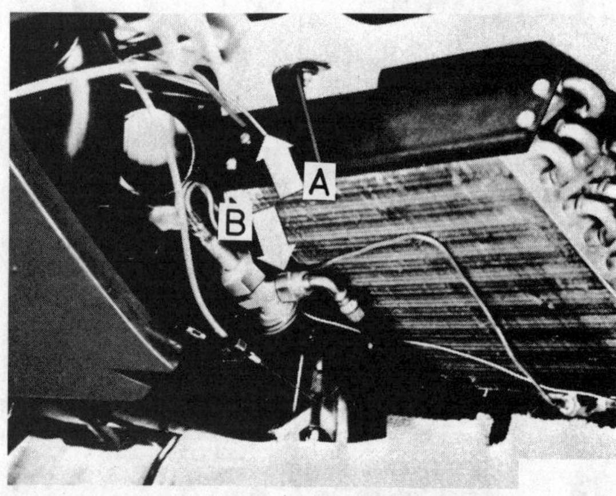

Fig. 14.22 Evaporator showing capillary tube (A) and high pressure hose (B)

Fig. 14.24 Condenser (left-hand) disconnection points. Hose connections arrowed

A Pressure switch connecting plug

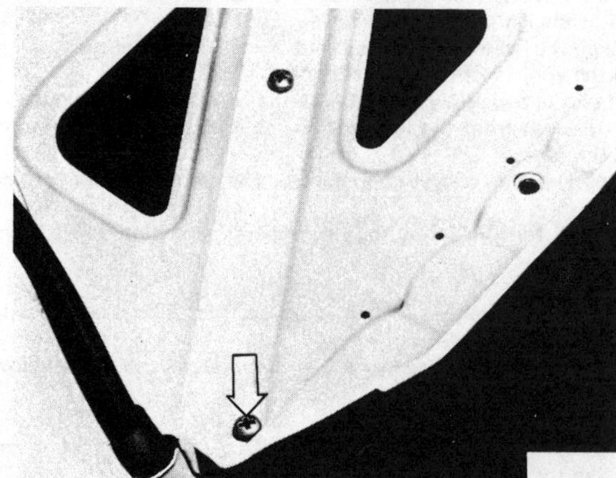

Fig. 14.21 Evaporator mounting screw (arrowed) in battery tray

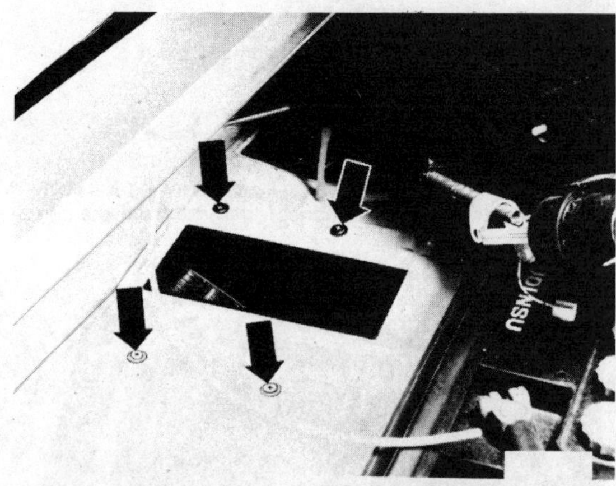

Fig. 14.23 Evaporator mounting screws (arrowed) on bulkhead

Fig. 14. 25 Condenser (right-hand) disconnection points (arrowed)

Fig. 14.26 Right-hand condenser mounting screws (arrowed)

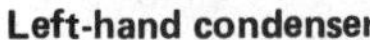

Fig. 14.27 Air conditioning receiver/drier

A Pipeline
B Mounting screws

Left-hand condenser

48 Drain the cooling system.
49 Remove the radiator grille.
50 Disconnect the condenser and receiver drier hoses. Plug or cap the openings.
51 Pull the lead from the pressure switch connector on the receiver dryer.
52 Remove the radiator complete with condenser and air deflector.

Right-hand condenser

53 Remove the radiator grille.
54 Disconnect both condenser hoses and plug the openings.
55 Extract the condenser mounting screws, pull the unit forward and remove it.

Receiver/dryer

56 Disconnect the pipeline from the condenser, plug the openings.
57 Extract the mounting screws and remove the receiver/drier.

Fault diagnosis - air conditioning

Symptom	Reason(s)
Blower motor does not operate	Blown fuse Defective relay Defective resistor Defective microswitch
No airflow	Faulty vacuum unit or hose
Heater matrix unwantedly warm or hot	Defective control valve or incorrectly set cable
Evaporator unwantedly cold	Defective temperature switch
No warm air	Faulty vacuum unit or hose
No fresh air	Hose disconnected
No cooling	Faulty compressor drivebelt Fault in receiver/drier Obstructed condenser
Intermittent cooling	Moisture in system Slipping compressor belt Faulty thermostatic switch

5 Fuel system - general

1 Adjustment procedures for some earlier carburettors have been modified and additional types of carburettor have been fitted to later vehicles. Full details are given both in the Specifications and in the text of this Chapter (Section 5A).

2 Detail changes have also been carried out to the fuel supply system. These are described in Section 5B.

3 Certain 1600 cc models are equipped with a fuel injection system. This arrangement ensures lower emission levels to comply with North American legislation. It is described in Section 5C.

4 Developments in the emission control system are described in Section 5D.

5A Fuel system - carburettors

Solex 35/40 DIDTA carburettor

Description and adjustment

1 The construction of the carburettor is given in Chapter 3 Sections 9 and 10. The jet sizes and some adjustments are given in the Specifications at the start of this Chapter.

2 Tests and adjustments are carried out as for the 32 TDID and amplified below.

3 To adjust the throttle valve gap basic setting first open the choke to its full extent and close the throttle. Refer to Fig. 14.28. Turn the screw 'a' until there is a gap between the stop and the screw, turn the screw the other way until it just touches the stop, ie would just grip a piece of cigarette paper, and then turn it in a further ¼ of a turn. The idle speed and CO content must be checked after this.

4 To set the 1st stage throttle gap remove the carburettor from the car, close the choke and check the gap between the throttle butterfly valve and the bore with a No 68 drill. A 1/32 in drill may be used if a No 68 is not available. Adjust by turning the nuts on the connecting rod shown in Fig. 14.29. Then adjust the idle speed and CO content.

5 To set the 2nd stage throttle gap, take the carburettor off the car and turn it upside down. Refer to Fig. 14.30. Slacken the adjusting screw 'a' until the throttle is just closed, screw it back in half a turn and lock it in place. Put a dab of paint on to secure it further. Work the flap gently to check that it does not bind at all.

6 The setting of the choke valve is as described in Chapter 3. Use a No 25 drill and adjust by bending the lever as shown in Fig. 14.31.

7 The carburettor may be fitted with a thermo-switch in the choke heater circuit as shown in Fig. 14.32 and described in paragraphs 10 to 12.

Solex 35 PDSIT carburettor - general

Construction and adjustment

8 The construction of the 35 PDSIT is as shown in Chapter 3 and the methods of testing and adjusting the unit are as given in that Chapter.

Immersion tube and gasket

9 In July 1975 the immersion tube in the upper half of the carburettor has been omitted after the introduction of the idle air control system and a new carburettor gasket has been installed (part number 056 129 281 A). When renewing the gasket be careful to obtain the correct one or the idle speed of the engine will be affected.

Choke heating system

10 In August 1975 on the YN engine (Passat) a two-stage electric heating system is installed for the automatic choke. This is from chassis number 62 000 051 onwards. Refer to Figs. 14.32 and 14.33.

11 The thermo-switches are located in the engine coolant bypass circuit. When starting from cold both switches are closed and 12 volts is supplied to the choke heater unit. At 52°F (11°C) switch 'a' opens and the current flows only through switch 'b' and the 3 ohm resistance. The voltage drops to 9 volts. At temperature 77 to 82°F (25 to 28°C) switch 'b' opens and the heater is no longer operative.

Fig. 14.28 Basic throttle setting (Solex 35/40 DIDTA carburettor)

a Adjustment screw

Fig. 14.29 1st stage throttle gap setting (Solex 35/40 DIDTA)

a Adjustment nuts
b Twist drill as gauge

Fig. 14.30 Second stage throttle gap setting (Solex 35/40 DIDTA)

a Adjustment screw

Fig. 14.31 Choke valve gap adjustment (Solex 35/40 DIDTA)

12 The switches may be removed and checked for operation in a pan of warm water as for a thermostat.

Zenith 2B2 carburettor

General description

13 The carburettor has two venturi tubes, two float chambers and two throttle valves. However, it is not, as would seem, two separate carburettors. The throttle valve of stage II remains shut until released by the movement to full throttle of the butterfly valve of stage I.

14 Once the system of locking levers releases stage II throttle, it is then controlled by a vacuum capsule and opens according to the depression in the venturis of both stages. Fig. 14.34 shows the layout of the interlock and the diagrammatic layout of the vacuum capsule.

15 At idling speed most of the fuel is supplied by stage I. The fuel flows through the main jet to the idling fuel jet and mixes with the idle air supply to form the idle mixture. It is then delivered via drillings in the carburettor body into the choke tube just below the throttle valve. The composition of this mixture is governed by the mixture regulating screw, which governs the CO value.

16 During the idling period, stage II also supplies fuel to its own venturi via a similar system of drilling and jets.

17 Further supply of fuel during the idle period is provided through the auxiliary fuel jet and auxiliary air jet of stage I. These intermingle in the emulsion tube and enter the inlet via the same passage below the throttle flap of stage I. The flow of this fuel is controlled by the bypass air control screw. The entire supply can be shut off by the magnetic (solenoid) cut-off valve which operates when the ignition is switched off.

18 Stage II does not have an auxiliary supply system, bypass control screw, mixture regulating screw or cut-off valve. All idle adjustments and mixture control adjustments are done on stage I.

19 As the throttle valve is opened the accelerator pump comes into action and the bypass of stage I is further activated. Then the main jet system comes into action and delivers fuel to the atomiser in the venturi. The butterfly valve of stage II is still closed, and the only contribution from stage II is via the basic idle system.

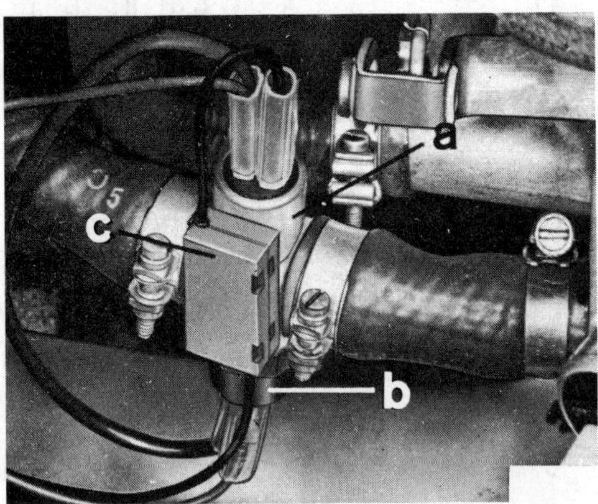

Fig. 14.32 Electric choke pre-heater (Solex 35 PDSIT)

a Thermoswitch opening at 82°F (28°C)
b Thermoswitch opening at 52°F (11°C)
c Resistor

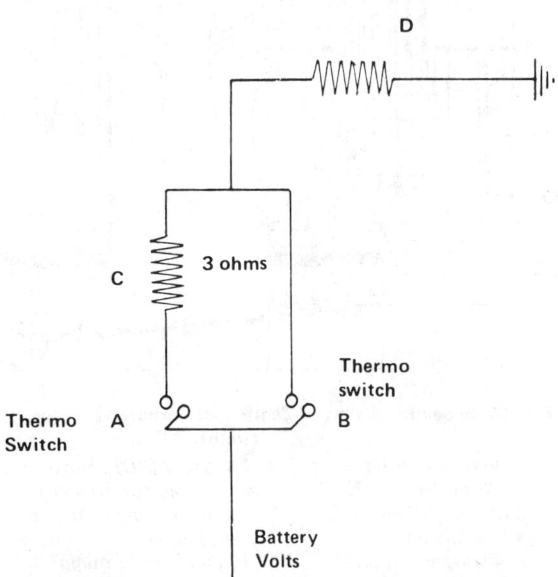

Fig. 14.33 Automatic choke heater circuit diagram

A Thermoswitch opening at 77 to 82°F (25° to 28°C)
B Thermoswitch opening at 52°F (11°C)
C 3 ohm series resistance
D Choke heater

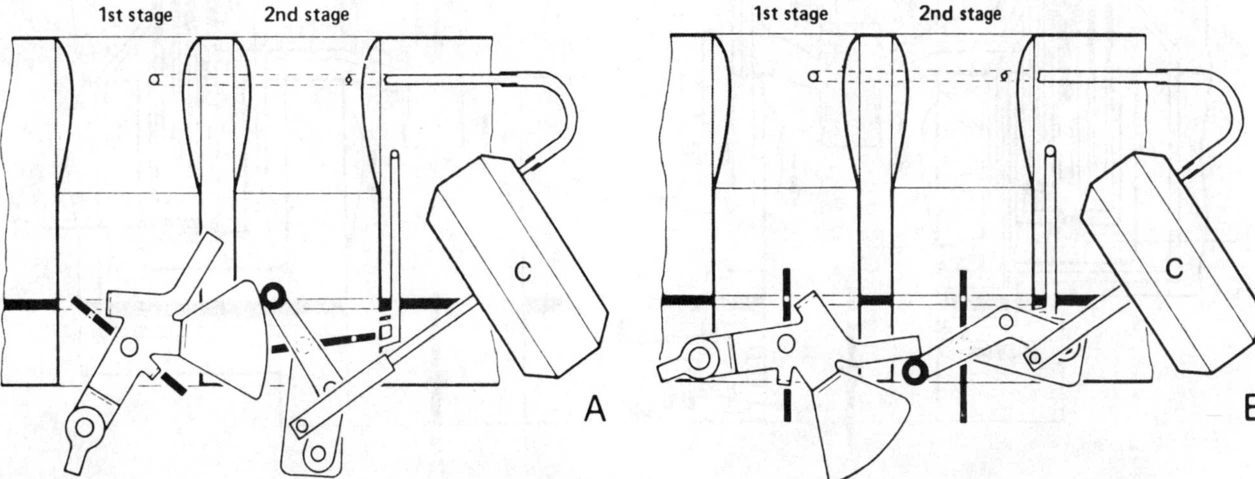

Fig. 14.34 Throttle interlock mechanism (Zenith 2B2 carburettor)

A The first stage throttle is opening during the transitional stage from idling to full throttle. The second stage throttle is locked shut by the lever mechanism

B The interlock mechanism is non-operative at full throttle conditions and the 2nd stage throttle is now open and controlled by the vacuum capsule 'c'

20 As full load conditions are approached, the supply of fuel from stage I increases through the main jet system. The interlock mechanism of the throttle valve of stage II is released, allowing the butterfly valve to open, and fuel is supplied via the main jet of stage II to the atomiser in stage II venturi. The enrichment tube of stage II also supplies fuel to the stage II venturi.

21 The position of the butterfly valve of stage II is governed by a vacuum capsule which is operated by the increasing depression in the venturi of both stages I and II.

22 Fig. 14.35 shows a layout of a cross-section of stage I and Fig. 14.36 of stage II, both under idle conditions. Fig. 14.37 shows a cross-sectional view of the carburettor at full load.

23 The specification is changed after January 1976 (see Specifications).

24 Fig. 14.38 shows an exploded view of the components of the carburettor.

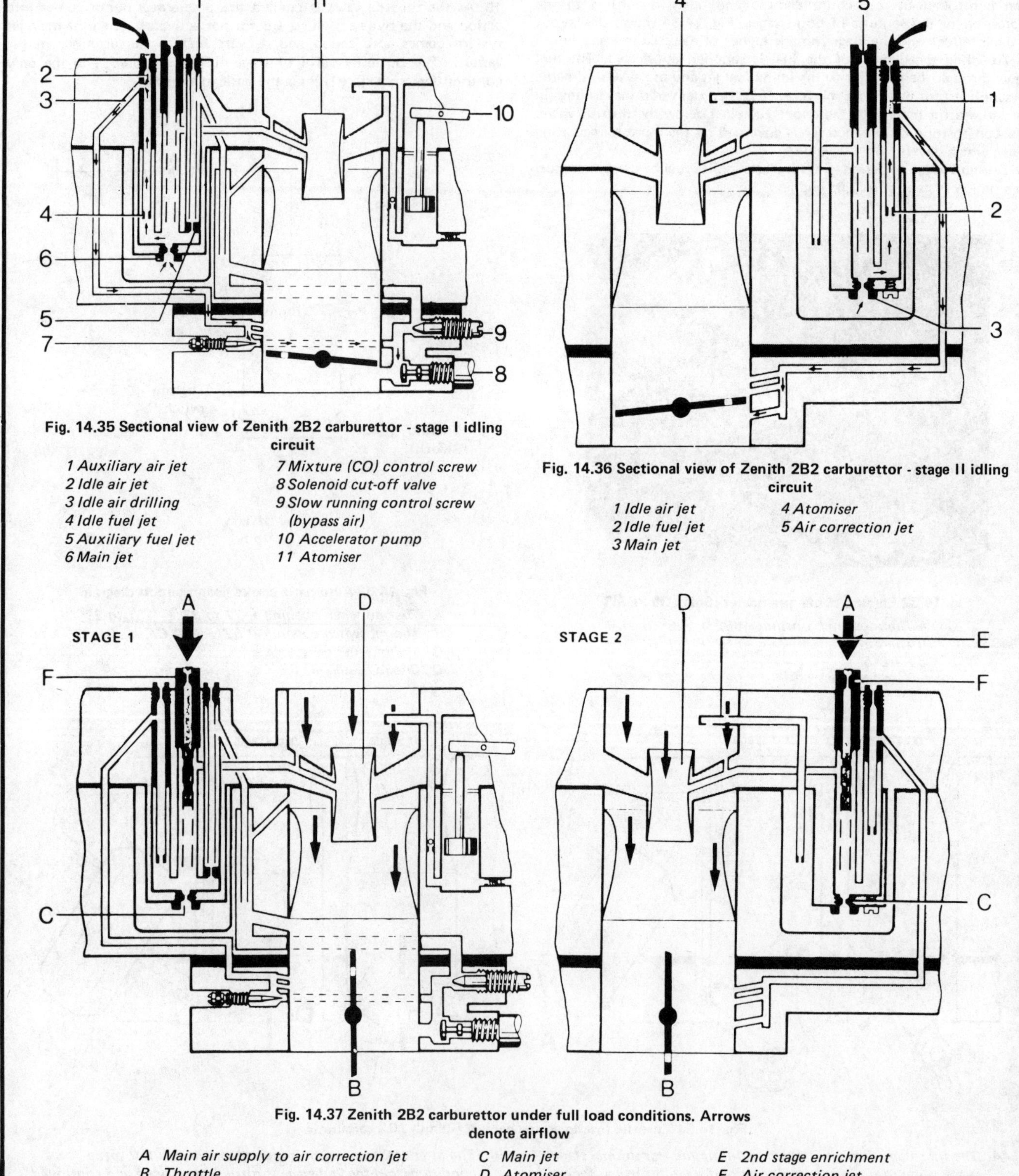

Fig. 14.35 Sectional view of Zenith 2B2 carburettor - stage I idling circuit

1 Auxiliary air jet
2 Idle air jet
3 Idle air drilling
4 Idle fuel jet
5 Auxiliary fuel jet
6 Main jet
7 Mixture (CO) control screw
8 Solenoid cut-off valve
9 Slow running control screw (bypass air)
10 Accelerator pump
11 Atomiser

Fig. 14.36 Sectional view of Zenith 2B2 carburettor - stage II idling circuit

1 Idle air jet
2 Idle fuel jet
3 Main jet
4 Atomiser
5 Air correction jet

Fig. 14.37 Zenith 2B2 carburettor under full load conditions. Arrows denote airflow

A Main air supply to air correction jet
B Throttle
C Main jet
D Atomiser
E 2nd stage enrichment
F Air correction jet

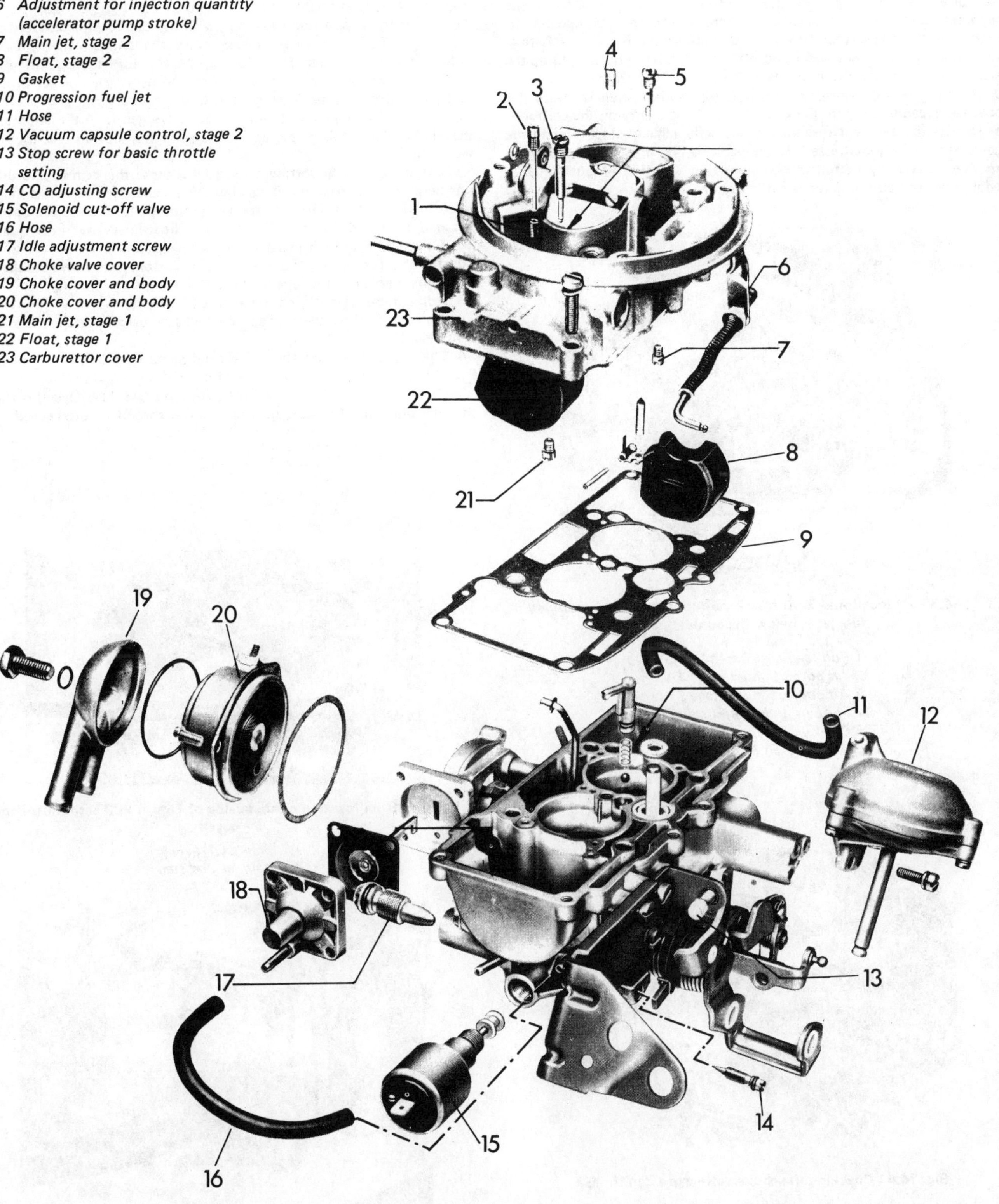

Fig. 14.38 Exploded view of Zenith 2B2 carburettor

1 *Bypass air fuel jet*
2 *Air correction jet, stage 1*
3 *Pilot fuel and air jet, stage 1*
4 *Progression air jet*
5 *Pilot fuel and air jet, stage 2*
6 *Adjustment for injection quantity (accelerator pump stroke)*
7 *Main jet, stage 2*
8 *Float, stage 2*
9 *Gasket*
10 *Progression fuel jet*
11 *Hose*
12 *Vacuum capsule control, stage 2*
13 *Stop screw for basic throttle setting*
14 *CO adjusting screw*
15 *Solenoid cut-off valve*
16 *Hose*
17 *Idle adjustment screw*
18 *Choke valve cover*
19 *Choke cover and body*
20 *Choke cover and body*
21 *Main jet, stage 1*
22 *Float, stage 1*
23 *Carburettor cover*

Removal, overhaul, static adjustment and refitting

25 Apart from cleaning the jets, setting the choke and throttle flaps and checking the accelerator pump injection capacity, the only other repair possible is the adjustment of the float level. These tests are included here because they must be done with the carburettor removed from the car.

26 To remove the carburettor, first take off the air cleaner. Disconnect the accelerator cable and take off and plug or clip the fuel hose. Remove the battery earth strap and then disconnect the wiring from the magnetic cut-off valve, the automatic choke and the microswitch (if fitted) on the accelerator linkage. Tag these wires for easy refitting. Label the vacuum hoses and remove them. Undo the bolts holding the carburettor to the manifold and take the carburettor away.

27 Refitting is the reverse of removal. Be careful when refitting the accelerator cable to secure the outer cable in the clamp on the carburettor so that there is no stress on the butterfly valve of stage 1 when the accelerator is fully depressed. If the pedal is not fully depressed when the valve is exactly at full throttle position you will be pushing the pedal down and straining the throttle linkage.

Fig. 14.39 Jet locations - Zenith 2B2 carburettor. Stage 1 auxiliary fuel jet is below the auxiliary air jet

1 Full load enrichment stage 2
2 Air correction jet stage 1
3 Air correction jet stage 2
4 Pilot air and fuel jet stage 1
5 Pilot air and fuel jet stage 2
6 Auxiliary air jet stage 1

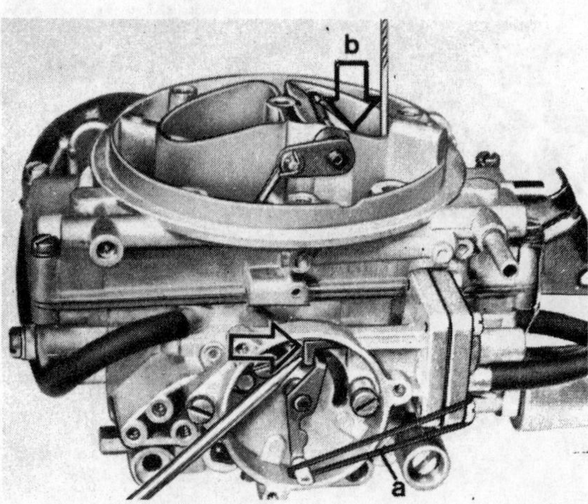

Fig. 14.41 Checking the choke valve gap - Zenith 2B2

a Hold the operating lever with a rubber band. Then push the lever in the direction of the arrow to take up the play
b Check the choke valve gap with a drill (see specifications)

28 Refer to Fig. 14.39. The various jets may be removed or blown clear with compressed air. **Do not** use wire or a pin to clear them. If they cannot be cleared with compressed air, new jets must be fitted.

29 Remove the screws clamping the two halves of the carburettor together, take off the top half and turn it upside down. The main jets are now exposed and may be serviced. Fig. 14.40 refers.

30 The automatic choke is described in Chapter 3, Section 15. When assembling the choke the mark on the cover must line up with the mark on the upper part of the carburettor.

31 To set the choke flap valve gap, with the carburettor removed from the car, remove the choke cover, close the choke valve, press the pullrod on to the stop. Refer to Fig. 14.41. Hold the operating lever with a rubber band or a similar device and using the correct drill size (see Specifications) as a gauge check the choke valve gap. Refer to Fig. 14.42. The adjusting screw for the valve gap is in the endplate of the choke. Turn this screw until the gap is correct and seal the screw with paint.

32 The basic throttle setting for stage 1 is set at the factory and should not be altered. If however it has been it should be adjusted as follows. Refer to Fig. 14.43. Turn the screw 'A' out until there is a gap between the end of it and the stop. Operate the throttle several times quickly. Turn the screw until it just touches the stop, and then turn it in one-quarter of a turn more. If this adjustment is done, the slow-running and CO adjustments must be checked when the engine is running.

33 Adjustment of the first stage throttle gap is shown in Fig. 14.44. Turn screw 'A' until the appropriate drill size gauge (see Specifications) is just held.

34 The adjusting screw for the second stage throttle gap is shown in Fig. 14.45. Unscrew the limit screw until there is a gap between the end of it and the stop. Set the choke open and the 1st stage throttle at the idle position. The vacuum unit pullrod should be disengaged from

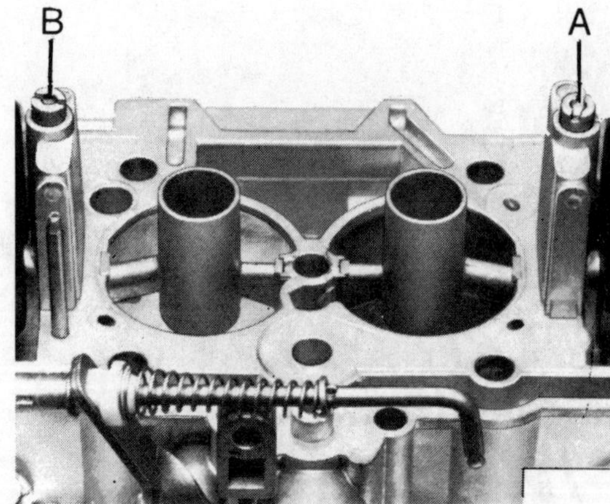

Fig. 14.40 Jet location on underside of Zenith 2B2 carburettor top cover

A Main jet 1st stage
B Main jet 2nd stage

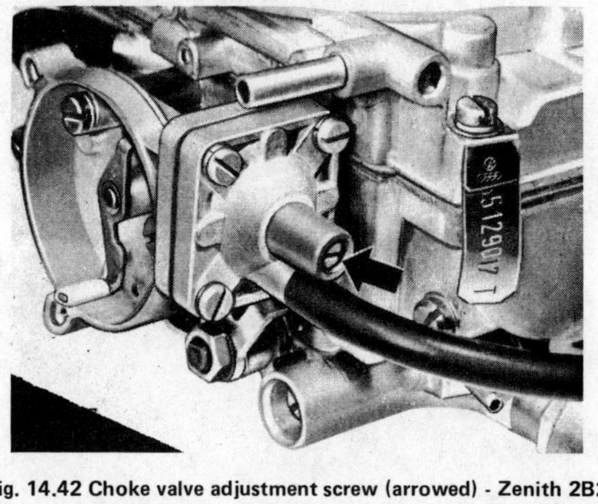

Fig. 14.42 Choke valve adjustment screw (arrowed) - Zenith 2B2

the operating lever. Turn the screw in, until it will just grip a thin piece of paper between it and the stop, remove the paper and turn the screw in a further one-quarter turn.

35 The measurement and adjustment of the accelerator pump output must be done with the carburettor assembled but not bolted to the manifold. Make sure the float chambers are full and that a supply of fuel to the carburettor is available. A piece of hose and a funnel connected to the carburettor inlet will do. Hold the carburettor over a large funnel and operate the throttle lever until fuel begins to run from the carburettor into the funnel. Now hold a measuring glass under the funnel and operate the throttle fully ten times. Allow the fuel to run into the glass and divide the quantity by ten. The correct amount varies according to the engine to which the carburettor is fitted (see Specifications). To adjust the amount refer to Fig. 14.46 and turn screw 'A' as shown. If the necessary amount is not injected with full adjustment check the injection pump piston and make sure the injection tube is not blocked.

36 While the carburettor is off the vehicle check the float settings. Refer to Fig. 14.47. Measure the dimensions as shown. If necessary, bend the tongue of the float hinge which contacts the needle valve. Take the float out to do this and treat the tongue very gently or you will need a new float. The tolerance allowable is 0.020 in (0.5 mm).

37 If it is necessary to renew the vacuum capsule which controls stage 11, disconnect the throttle operating rod and remove the screw holding the capsule to the body. When fitting the capsule adjust the length of the vacuum capsule rod which operates the throttle valve arm. To do this, before connecting it to the operating arm slacken the locknut, hold the choke valve fully open and both throttle flaps closed, and turn the

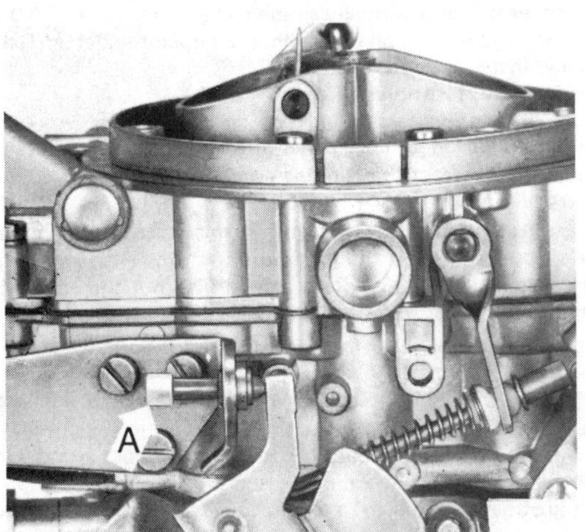

Fig. 14.43 Throttle valve basic setting screw (A)

Fig. 14.44 Throttle valve stage 1 setting screw (A) - Zenith 2B2 carburettor

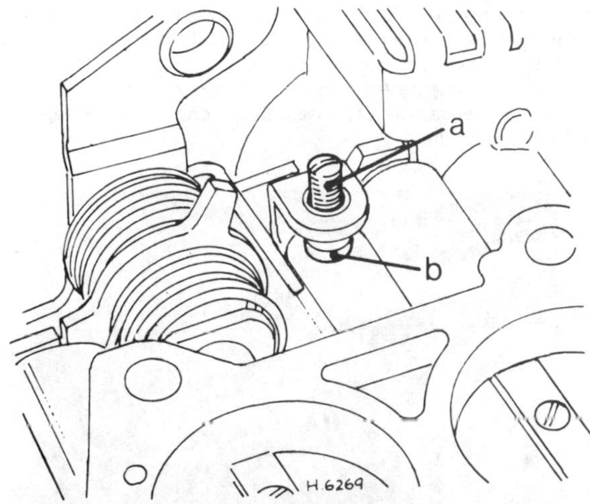

Fig. 14.45 Throttle valve stage 2 setting screw (a) and stop (b) - Zenith 2B2 carburettor

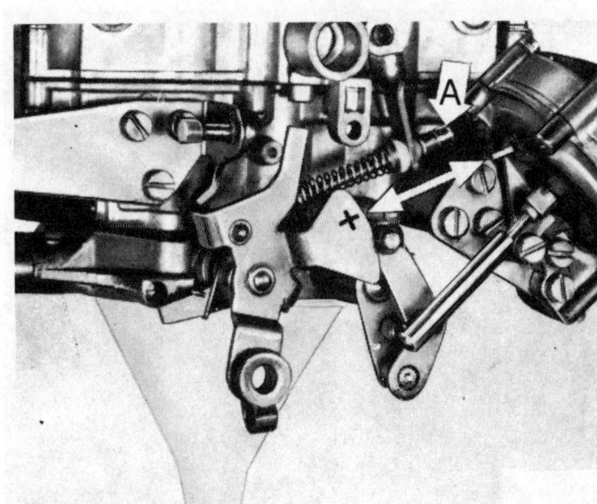

Fig. 14.46 Accelerator pump rod (A) - Zenith 2B2 carburettor

Turn screw in direction + or – to increase or decrease injection quantity

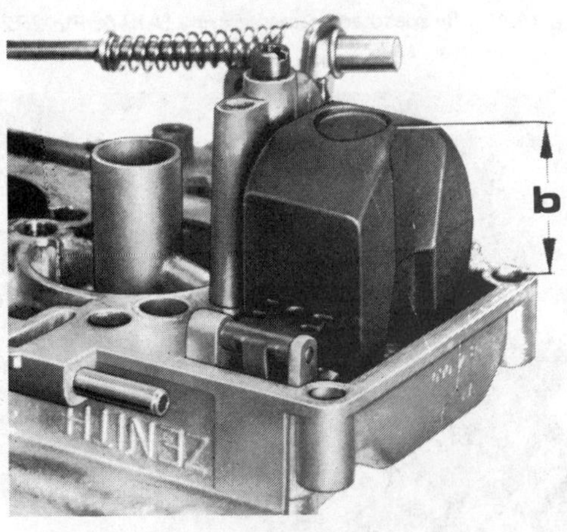

Fig. 14.47 Float level checking diagram - Zenith 2B2 carburettor

Invert cover to measure dimension b
b (1st stage) = 28.0 mm (1.10 in)
b (2nd stage) = 30.0 mm (1.18 in)

capsule rod until the ball socket in the rod extends 0.04 to 0.08 in (1.0 to 2.0 mm) beyond the ball on the throttle operating lever. Tighten the locknut and install the rod to the lever.

Idle speed and mixture adjustment

38 Before attempting to do the running adjustments make sure that valve timing, ignition timing, dwell angle and clearances are correct. Unless these are correct the running adjustments will not come within the required limits.

39 It is essential to have a tachometer (rev counter) and an exhaust gas analyser - you cannot do the job without them. With the carburettor correctly installed start the engine and run it until the engine is warm (oil temperature 140°F/60°C) and the choke is fully open.

40 To adjust the idle speed refer to Fig. 14.48. Turn screw 'A' to vary the idle speed.

41 Having set the idle speed it is now necessary to adjust the CO content. This is done by turning screw 'A' shown in Fig. 14.49. A good quality infra-red analyser should be used. On cars not fitted with EGR the probe is inserted in the tailpipe and the reading repeated several times. Adjustment of the CO content may affect the idle speed. If so readjust the idle speed and recheck the CO content again. Continue until both readings are within specification.

42 On cars fitted with EGR and catalytic converters the procedure is more complicated. Disconnect the hose from the activated charcoal filter (for the fuel tank) from the air cleaner. Disconnect the hose from the air injection pump to the diverter valve and plug the hole in the diverter valve. Plug the analyser into the electricity supply and push the probe into the port provided on the side of the EGR filter. The cooling fan **should not** be running during this test. Turn the adjusting screw until the required CO content is achieved.

43 Once the level is achieved check the idle speed again and if necessary adjust it. Then repeat the CO check. Carry on until both adjustments are in the required limits.

Zenith 1B1 carburettor

General description

44 This carburettor is of single barrel design, with a manually-operated choke (cold start device), and is used only on the 1300 cc engine.

Idle speed and mixture adjustment

45 The adjustment screws are fitted with tamperproof seals which will have to be removed should the need for adjustment arise. Satisfy yourself that you are not contravening local or national anti-pollution regulations before removing the seals.

46 Have the engine at normal operating temperature with all electrical accessories switched off.

47 Disconnect the crankcase vent hose from the air cleaner.

48 Check that the choke valve plate is fully open, and that the ignition timing and dwell angle are correctly set.

49 Connect a tachometer to the engine in accordance with the manufacturer's instructions. Start the engine and then adjust the idle speed to the specified value. Should the radiator fan come on during the adjustment, switch off the engine and allow it to cool for a few minutes before continuing.

50 Using an exhaust gas analyser with its probe inserted into the exhaust tailpipe, check that the CO level is as specified. If it is not, turn the mixture screw in or out as necessary. A slight correction of the idle speed may be necessary after this.

51 Reconnect the vent hose. This may cause the CO level to rise, but this is caused by the accumulation of oil fumes in the crankcase during idle and will soon clear after the engine has been run at higher speeds.

52 Fit new tamperproof seals on completion.

Fig. 14.48 Idle speed adjustment screw (A) (Zenith 2B2)

Fig. 14.49 Mixture screw (A) (Zenith 2B2)

Fig. 14.50 Idle speed adjustment screw (arrowed) (Zenith 1B1 carburettor)

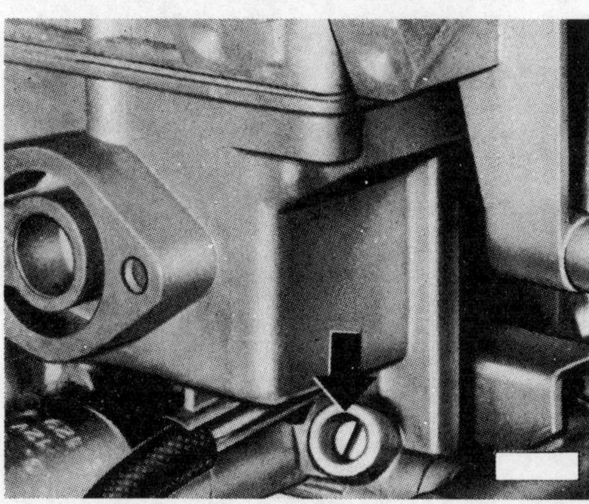

Fig. 14.51 Mixture screw (arrowed) (Zenith 1B1 carburettor)

Fast idle speed - adjustment

53 Have the engine at normal operating temperature and the idle speed correctly set, but the engine not running.

54 Pull the choke cable fully out. Check that the alignment arrow on the choke assembly disc is opposite the centre of the fixing screw. If not, adjust after releasing the screw (Fig. 14.52).

55 Start the engine without touching the accelerator pedal.

56 Check the engine speed, which should be within the specified fast idle range. If it is not, turn the adjusting screw.

Choke pull-down - checking

57 Remove the air cleaner. Have the engine running at the specified idle speed.

58 Pull the choke cable fully out.

59 Close the choke valve plate gently with the fingers. If the plate moves through its travel until the last 4.0 mm (0.18 in), when resistance is felt, the pull-down arrangement is operating correctly. No resistance indicates a split diaphragm in the vacuum capsule or a leak in the vacuum system.

Choke valve gap - adjustment

60 Remove the air cleaner and then pull the choke operating cable fully out.

61 Slacken the choke cover securing screws and turn the cover in an anti-clockwise direction until the valve plate is completely closed. Retighten the cover screws.

62 Using a screwdriver, push the choke operating rod to its stop in the direction of the pull-down unit. The valve plate should now be open slightly and the gap should be measured using a twist drill or similar. If the gap is not within the specified tolerance, turn the screw on the vacuum unit.

Overhaul

63 With the carburettor removed from the engine, clean off all external dirt and grease.

64 Extract the top cover securing screws and lift the cover from the main body.

65 Clean out the float chamber.

66 The jets can be removed from the cover. The main jet can be removed after inverting the cover.

67 Clean the jets by blowing air from a tyre pump through them. Never attempt to clear them by probing with wire.

68 The external items such as the choke, cut-off valve and partial load enrichment valve may be removed if necessary after extracting the securing screws.

69 Renew any worn or damaged items and check that the jet calibration markings agree with those shown in the Specifications. Any wear in the throttle valve plate spindle will indicate the need for a new carburettor. This will normally only occur after a high mileage.

70 Obtain a repair kit for your particular carburettor. This will contain all the necessary gaskets, seals and other renewable items.

71 Reassembly is a reversal of dismantling, but observe the following points as the work progresses.

72 If the choke cover has been removed, make sure when refitting it that as the bi-metal spring is attached to the operating lever, so the opening lever is located to the left-hand side of the operating lever.

73 Twist the choke cover within the limits of its elongated screw holes to align the positioning marks. When tightening the fixing screws, press the bottom part of the cover against the guide lugs.

74 The float level is non-adjustable.

75 Carry out the running adjustments as described earlier once the carburettor is refitted to the engine.

Accelerator pump stroke - adjustment

76 This operation is rarely required unless hesitation or lack of power during acceleration is noticed.

77 Remove the carburettor and hold a funnel under its base so that fuel can be directed into a measuring glass. The float chamber must be full of fuel - see paragraph 35.

78 With the finger, hold the choke valve plate operating lever in the fully open position.

79 Slowly operate the throttle valve plate operating lever ten times through its full stroke. Check the volume of fuel collected, divide it by 10 and compare the result with the discharge volume given in the Specifications.

80 Where necessary, vary the discharge volume by releasing the clamp screw and turning the cam (Fig. 14.60).

Throttle cable - adjustment

81 Depress the accelerator pedal to its full extent. In this position there should be a clearance of 1 mm (0.04 in) between the throttle

Fig. 14.52 Fast idle adjustment (Zenith 1B1 carburettor). Alignment mark is arrowed

1 Choke valve operating lever
2 Fast idle adjustment screw
3 Alignment setting screw

Fig. 14.53 Choke valve gap adjustment (Zenith 1B1 carburettor)

1 Screwdriver depressing choke rod
2 Twist drill used as gauge

Fig. 14.54 Choke valve gap adjustment screw (arrowed) - Zenith 1B1 carburettor

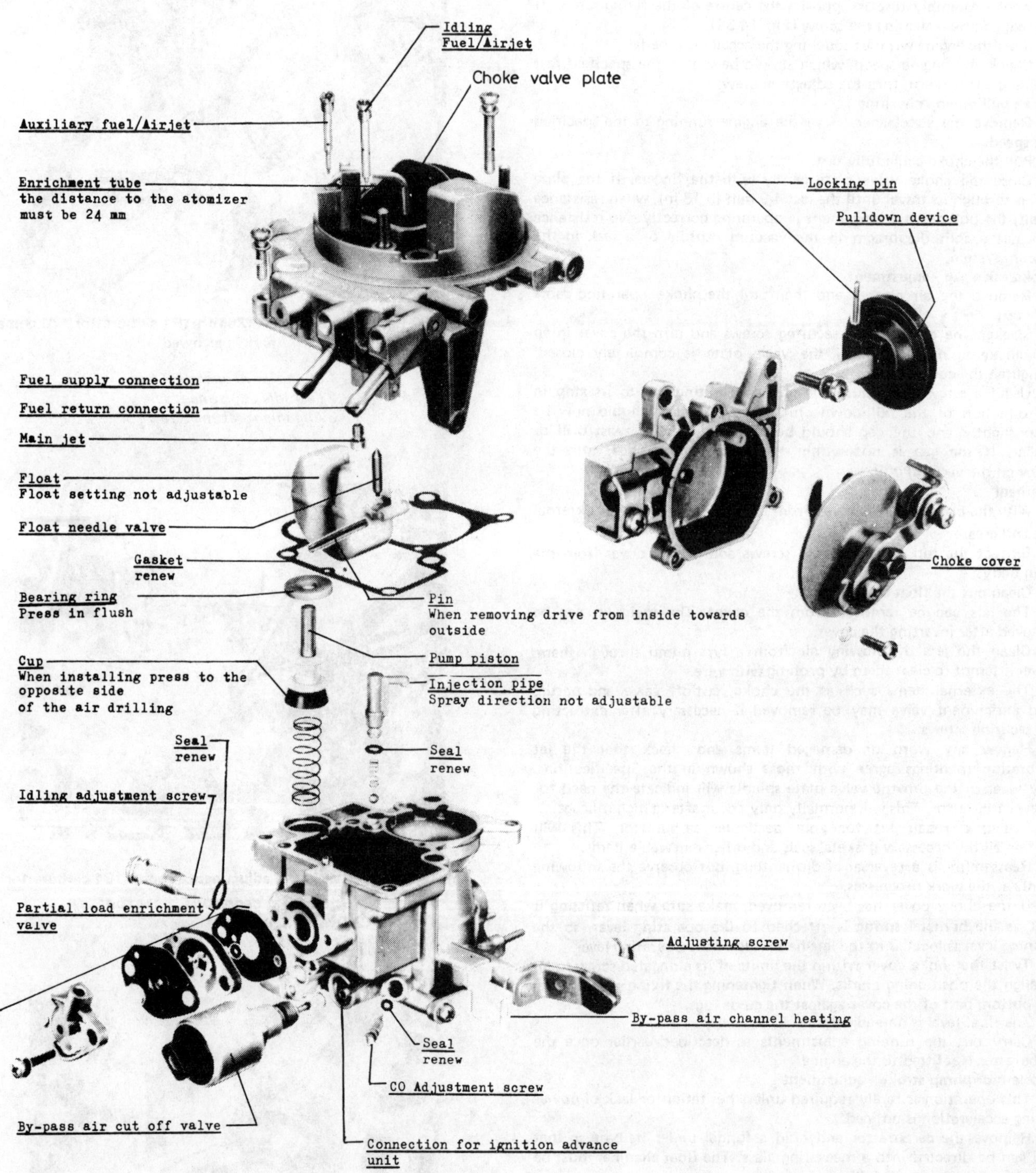
Idling
Fuel/Airjet
Choke valve plate
Auxiliary fuel/Airjet
Enrichment tube
the distance to the atomizer
must be 24 mm
Locking pin
Pulldown device
Fuel supply connection
Fuel return connection
Main jet
Float
Float setting not adjustable
Float needle valve
Gasket
renew
Bearing ring
Press in flush
Pin
When removing drive from inside towards
outside
Choke cover
Pump piston
Cup
When installing press to the
opposite side
of the air drilling
Injection pipe
Spray direction not adjustable
Seal
renew
Seal
renew
Idling adjustment screw
Partial load enrichment
valve
Adjusting screw
By-pass air channel heating
Seal
renew
CO Adjustment screw
By-pass air cut off valve
Connection for ignition advance
unit

Fig. 14.55 Exploded view of Zenith 1B1 carburettor

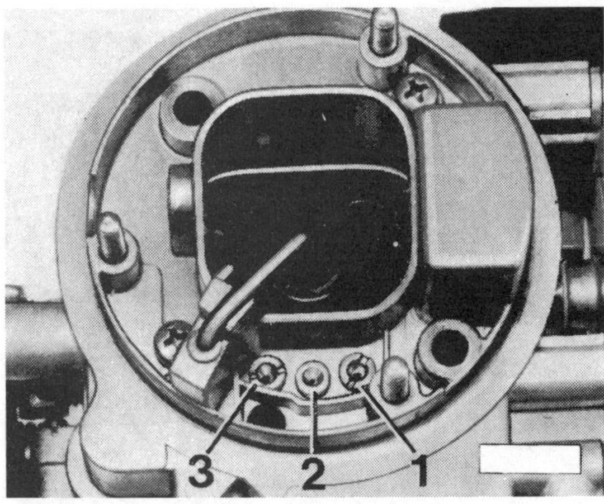

Fig. 14.56 Location of jets in Zenith 1B1 carburettor

1 Idle fuel/air *3 Auxiliary fuel/air*
2 Air correction jet/emulsion tube

Fig. 14.57 Main jet (arrowed) - (top cover inverted) on Zenith 1B1 carburettor

Fig. 14.58 Fitting the choke cover (Zenith 1B1 carburettor)

1 Bi-metal spring *3 Opening lever*
2 Choke valve operating lever

Fig. 14.59 Choke cover alignment marks (arrowed) on Zenith 1B1 carburettor

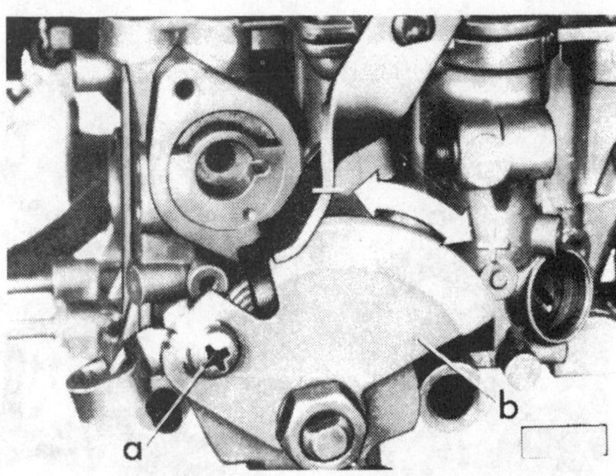

Fig. 14.60 Accelerator pump operating cam - Zenith 1B1 carburettor. Turn cam plate in + or — direction to adjust

a Clamp screw *b Cam plate*

Fig. 14.61 Throttle cable adjustment clip (arrowed) - Zenith 1B1 carburettor

valve lever and its stop. Move the clip to another groove if necessary to achieve this.

82 Where gross maladjustment is encountered, release the accelerator pedal pinch-bolt and move the pedal until the distance from the stop to the pedal contact point is as shown in Fig. 14.63. Push the pedal upper lever as far as the stop towards the engine compartment and tighten the pinch-bolt. Adjust the throttle cable as previously described.

Choke operating cable - connection

83 Clamp the choke outer cable at the carburettor so that it projects beyond the clamp by 5 mm (0.2 in).

84 Engage the inner cable in the trunnion.

85 Pull the choke knob on the facia so that there is a clearance between the base of the knob and its facia contact of 4 mm (0.16 in).

86 Check that the choke valve plate is fully open, with the lever on the carburettor fully against its stop, and clamp the cable in the trunnion.

87 Some later models have a bi-metal spring unit fitted to the choke valve plate spindle of the carburettor. It controls the point of closure of the choke valve according to ambient temperature.

88 Models fitted with this type of carburettor have an exhaust gas heated manifold and an in-line fuel filter.

Zenith 1B3 carburettor

General description

89 This carburettor is of similar general design to the 1B1 described previously, but it incorporates an automatic choke which is heated both by engine coolant and electrically.

90 Where this type of carburettor is used, an electrically assisted preheater is located in the intake manifold. The preheater is a combination unit and houses two thermostatic switches, one for the automatic choke and one for the intake manifold warm-up facility. On later models the intake manifold heating is carried out by electrical means only.

91 Also on later models equipped with the 1B3 carburettor, a fuel reservoir is located in the fuel line between the pump and the carburettor. This device stabilises the fuel supply to the carburettor by routing excess fuel back to the tank through a return line.

Idle speed and mixture adjustment

92 The operations are similar to those described in paragraphs 45 to 52, but note the following

(a) Air conditioning (when fitted) must be switched off

(b) Before starting the engine for carburettor adjustment, depress the accelerator pedal fully and release it. The fast idle adjusting screw should not then be in contact with the fast idle cam. If it is, turn the cam as necessary to clear it

Fast idle speed - adjustment

93 Have the engine at normal operating temperature with the idle speed correctly set. Remove the air cleaner.

94 Open the throttle lever on the carburettor and set the fast idle screw on the highest step of the cam.

95 Start the engine without touching the accelerator pedal.

96 Check the fast idle speed against that specified. Adjust if necessary by breaking off the cap and turning the adjusting screw.

Choke pull-down - checking

97 Refer to paragraphs 57 to 59. Note the vacuum tank used in the choke pull-down circuit (photo).

Choke valve gap - adjustment

98 Remove the air cleaner.

99 Actuate the throttle so that the fast idle screw is located on the highest step of the cam.

100 Apply a screwdriver to the adjusting screw and press the choke operating rod towards the vacuum pull-down unit as far as it will go (Fig. 14.69).

101 Now check the choke valve plate gap using a twist drill or similar as a gauge. If the gap is not as specified, turn the fast idle screw.

Overhaul

102 This is essentially as described for the 1B1 carburettor, but observe the following additional points of differences.

103 Before removing the carburettor, remember to disconnect the coolant hoses. Provided the ends of the hoses are supported in their highest positions, there should be little loss of coolant and no need to drain the cooling system. Make sure that the engine is cold, however, otherwise the cooling system will be pressurised.

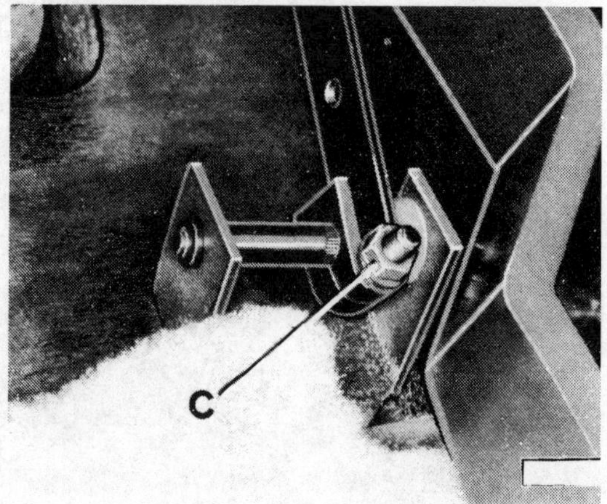

Fig. 14.62 Accelerator pedal pinch-bolt (c)

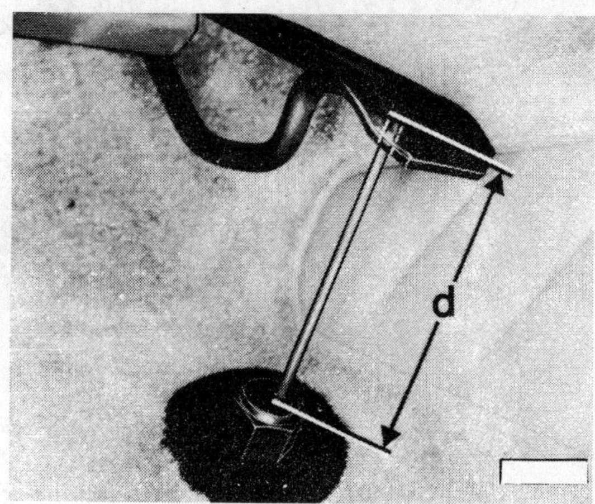

Fig. 14.63 Accelerator pedal arm setting

d = 90 mm (3.6 in)

Fig. 14.64 Choke cable clamp (A) and pinch-bolt (B) on Zenith 1B1 carburettor

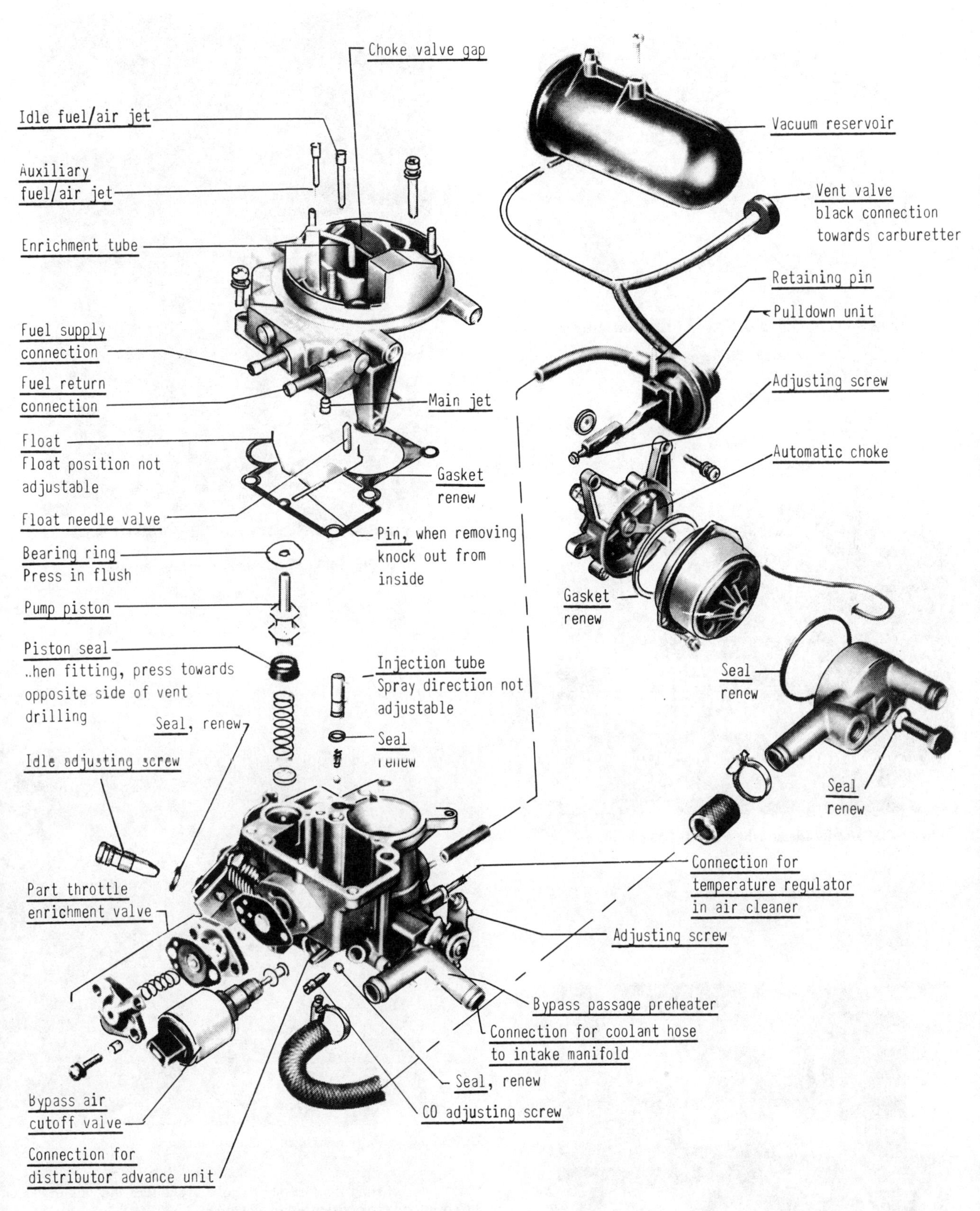
Choke valve gap
Idle fuel/air jet
Auxiliary fuel/air jet
Enrichment tube
Fuel supply connection
Fuel return connection
Main jet
Float
Float position not adjustable
Gasket renew
Float needle valve
Pin, when removing knock out from inside
Bearing ring
Press in flush
Pump piston
Piston seal
..hen fitting, press towards opposite side of vent drilling
Injection tube
Spray direction not adjustable
Seal, renew
Seal
renew
Idle adjusting screw
Part throttle enrichment valve
Bypass air cutoff valve
Connection for distributor advance unit
CO adjusting screw
Seal, renew
Connection for coolant hose to intake manifold
Bypass passage preheater
Adjusting screw
Connection for temperature regulator in air cleaner
Seal
renew
Seal
renew
Gasket
renew
Automatic choke
Adjusting screw
Pulldown unit
Retaining pin
Vent valve
black connection towards carburetter
Vacuum reservoir

Fig. 14.65 Exploded view of Zenith 1B3 carburettor

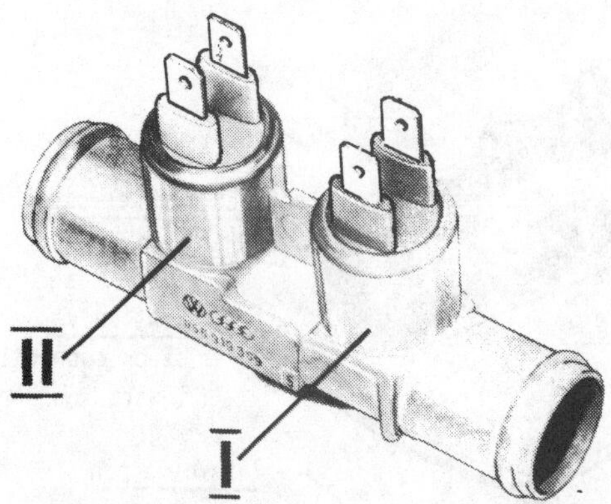

Fig. 14.66 Preheater (used with Zenith 1B3 carburettor)

I Automatic choke thermoswitch
II Intake manifold thermoswitch

Fig. 14.68 Fast idle adjustment - Zenith 1B3 carburettor

A Fast idle cam
B Fast idle adjustment-screw

Fig. 14.69 Choke valve gap adjustment-screw (I) on Zenith 1B3 carburettor. Arrow points to pull-down unit

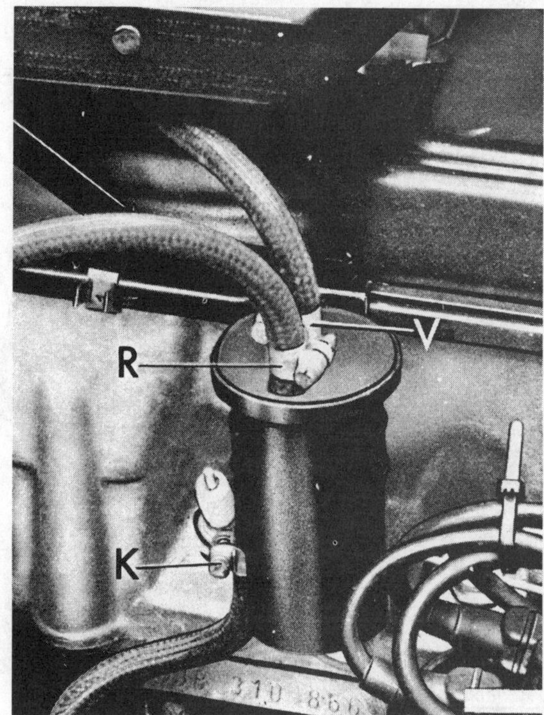

Fig. 14.67 Fuel reservoir on later engines

K From fuel pump
R Fuel return line
V To carburettor

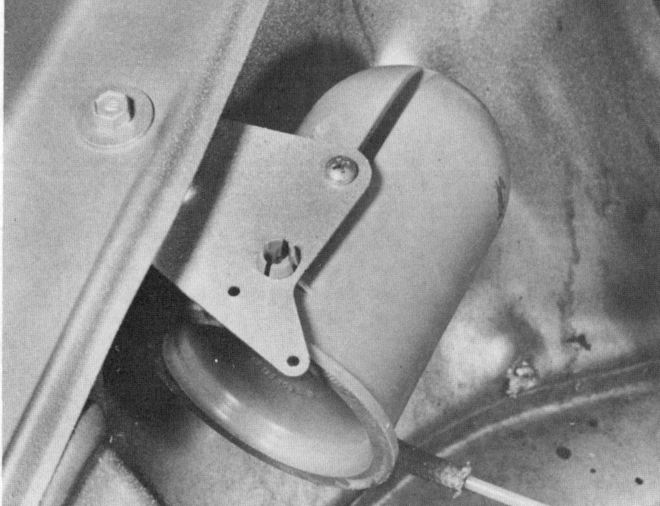

5A.97 Vacuum tank used with 1B3 carburettor

104 When refitting the automatic choke, make sure that the marks on the cover and the housing are in alignment.

105 Check that the end of the enrichment tube is level with the upper surface of the choke valve plate as shown (Fig. 14.72). Failure to set this correctly will cause uneven pulling when cold, or cold start problems.

Accelerator pump stroke - adjustment

106 Refer to paragraph 76, then proceed as described in paragraph 77.

107 Open the throttle slightly and turn the fast idle cam so that the

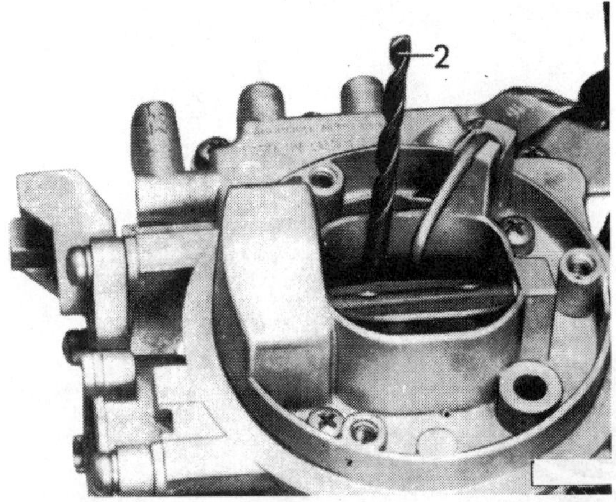

Fig. 14. 70 Choke valve gap check using twist-drill (2) - Zenith 1B3 carburettor

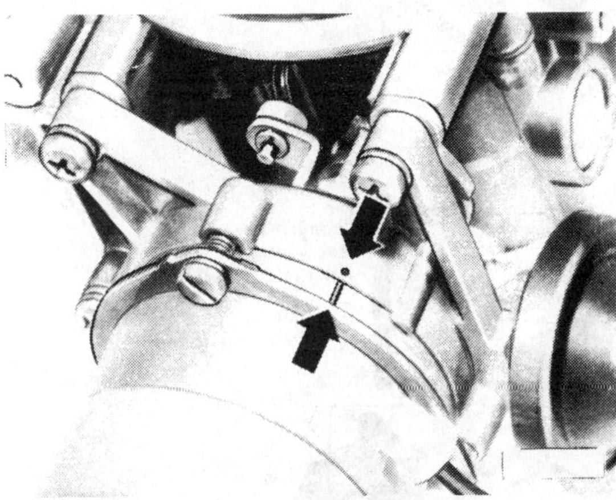
Fig. 14.71 Automatic choke housing alignment marks (arrowed) on Zenith 1B3 carburettor

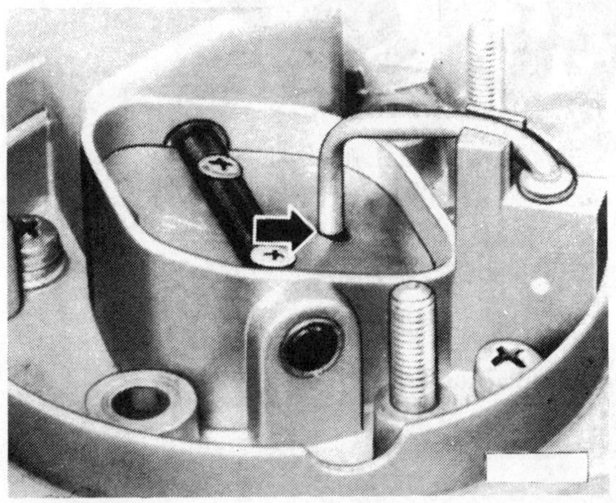
Fig. 14.72 Enrichment tube (arrowed) - Zenith 1B3 carburettor

fast idle screw is not in contact with the cam.

108 Carry out the operations described in paragraphs 79 and 80.

Zenith 2B5 carburettor

General description

109 This is a dual barrel carburettor, with an automatic choke which is heated both electrically and by coolant.

110 A preheater is used to heat the intake manifold and the automatic choke as described for the 1B3 carburettor.

Idle speed and mixture adjustment

111 The operations are similar to those described in paragraphs 45 to 52 for the 1B1 carburettor but note the location of the adjusting screws (Figs. 14.75 and 14.76).

112 Switch off the air conditioner (if applicable) and make sure that the fast idle screw of the automatic choke is not in contact with the step of the cam.

Throttle valve (1st stage) - basic setting

113 The adjusting screw is preset during production and fitted with a tamperproof cap. Break off the cap for access to the screw.

114 Have the engine at normal operating temperature with the air cleaner removed. Unscrew the adjusting screw until it clears its stop (Fig. 14.78).

115 Open and close the throttle quickly and then turn the adjusting screw until it just contacts its stop, then give the screw a further quarter of a turn.

116 Check the idle speed and mixture setting as previously described. Finally, fit a new tamperproof cap.

Fast idle speed - adjustment

117 Have the engine at normal operating temperature. Remove the air cleaner and the tamperproof cap from the fast idle screw.

118 Open the throttle slightly so that the choke valve plate can be fully closed with the fast idle screw resting on the highest step of the cam.

119 Connect a tachometer to the engine in accordance with the manufacturer's instructions and then start the engine without touching the accelerator pedal.

120 If the fast idle speed is not as specified, turn the screw in or out to correct it.

121 Fit a new tamperproof cap on completion.

Throttle valve (2nd stage) - basic setting

122 The adjustment screw is set in production and should not normally be touched. However, if necessary after overhaul or renewal of components, carry out the following operations with the carburettor removed from the engine.

123 Open the choke valve plate fully with the fingers and check that the 1st stage throttle valve plate is in the idle position.

124 Break off the tamperproof cap from the screw (Fig. 14.79).

125 Turn the screw until there is a gap between its end and the stop.

126 Unhook the vacuum unit pullrod and then eliminate bearing and lever play by applying slight pressure to the throttle valve lever.

127 Turn the adjustment screw in until it just contacts the stop and then give it a further quarter turn.

128 Reconnect the vacuum unit pullrod and fit a new tamperproof cap to the screw.

129 Check the idle speed and mixture adjustment when the carburettor is returned to the engine.

Accelerator pump stroke - adjustment

130 Follow the instructions described in paragraphs 76 to 79.

131 If adjustment is required, turn the nut on the pump rod. Lock the nut on completion with a sealant such as a dab of paint.

Choke valve gap - adjustment

132 This operation is only possible if a vacuum gauge and switching valve are available. If not, leave the work to your dealer.

133 Remove the air cleaner.

134 Extract the screws which secure the automatic choke.

135 Detach the Y connector from the upper hose of the pull-down unit. Plug the open end of the hose.

136 Disconnect the vacuum hose from the carburettor. Connect a vacuum gauge between the hose and the carburettor. Start the engine and run it until the vacuum gauge indicates 400 m bar. Operate the switching valve so that vacuum is applied and maintained to the choke pull-down unit. Switch off the ignition.

137 Actuate the throttle valve so that the fast idle screw is on the highest step of the cam. Check that the return spring is correctly connected.

138 Now measure the choke valve plate gap using a twist drill or

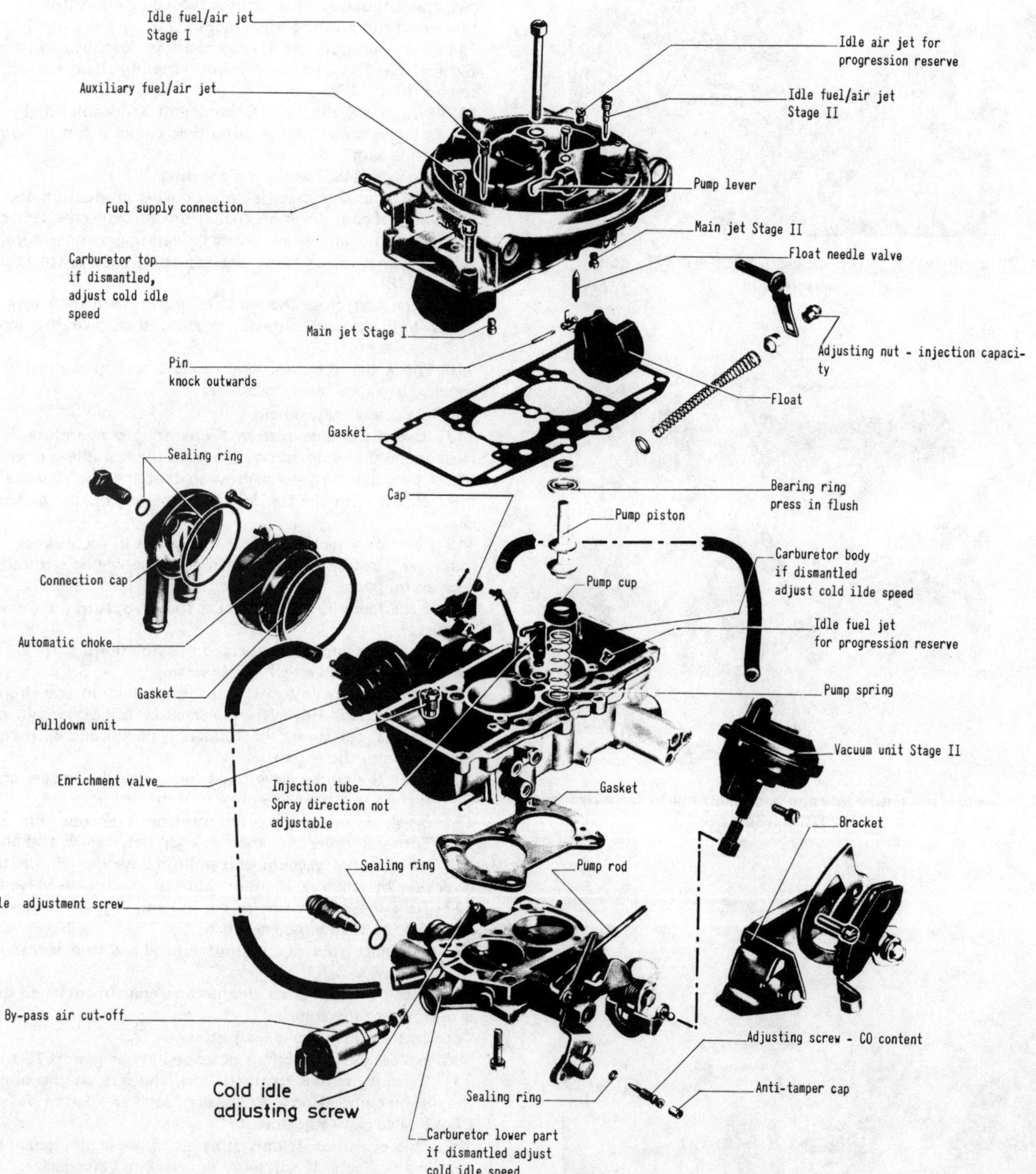
Idle fuel/air jet
Stage I
Idle air jet for
progression reserve
Idle fuel/air jet
Stage II
Auxiliary fuel/air jet
Pump lever
Fuel supply connection
Main jet Stage II
Carburetor top
if dismantled,
adjust cold idle
speed
Float needle valve
Main jet Stage I
Adjusting nut - injection capacity
Pin
knock outwards
Float
Gasket
Sealing ring
Bearing ring
press in flush
Cap
Pump piston
Connection cap
Carburetor body
if dismantled
adjust cold ilde speed
Pump cup
Idle fuel jet
for progression reserve
Automatic choke
Gasket
Pump spring
Pulldown unit
Vacuum unit Stage II
Enrichment valve
Injection tube
Spray direction not
adjustable
Gasket
Bracket
Sealing ring
Pump rod
Idle adjustment screw
By-pass air cut-off
Adjusting screw - CO content
Anti-tamper cap
Sealing ring
Cold idle
adjusting screw
Carburetor lower part
if dismantled adjust
cold idle speed

Fig. 14.73 Exploded view of Zenith 2B5 carburettor

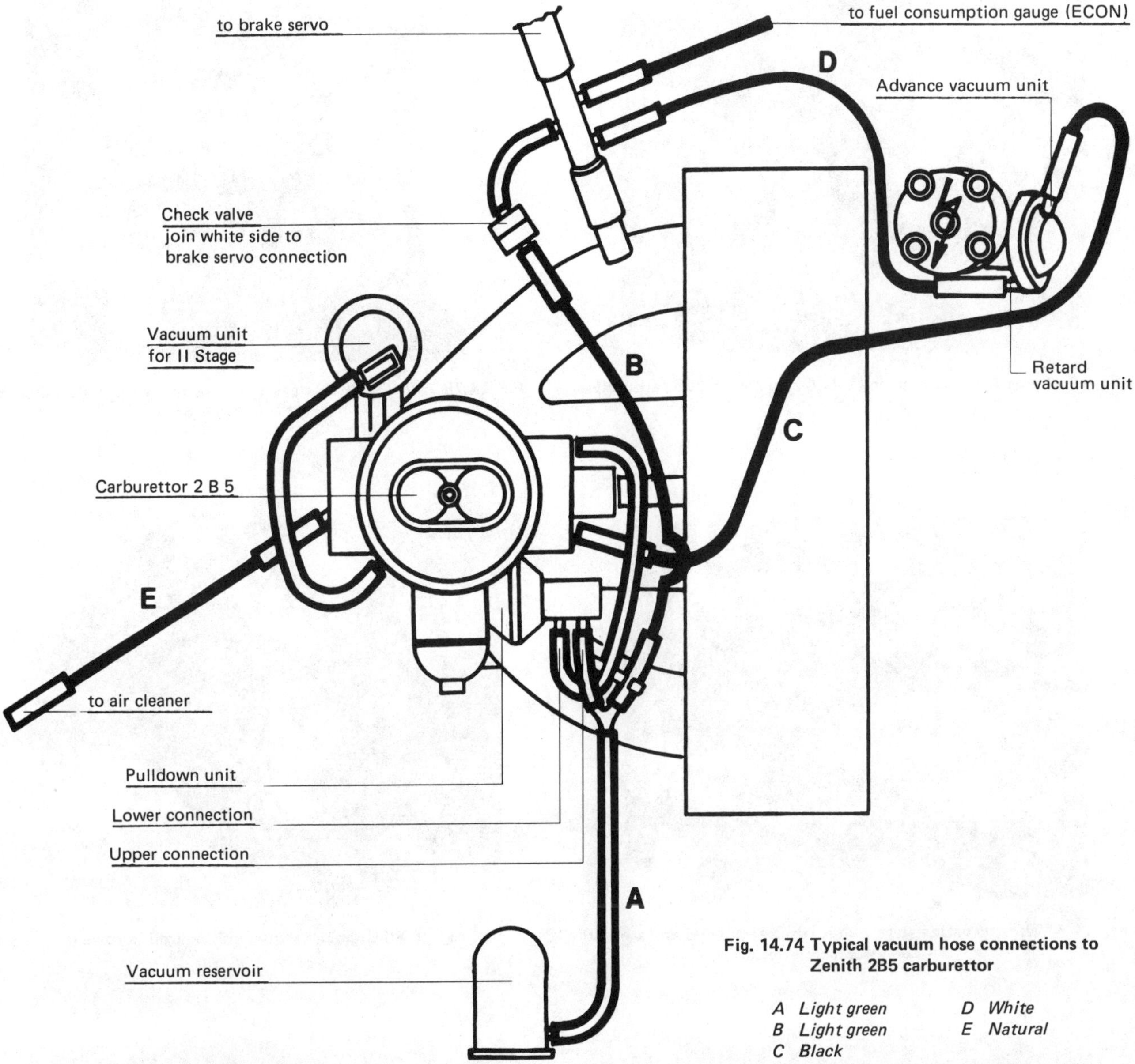

to brake servo

to fuel consumption gauge (ECON)

D

Advance vacuum unit

Check valve
join white side to
brake servo connection

Vacuum unit
for II Stage

B

Retard
vacuum unit

C

Carburettor 2 B 5

E

to air cleaner

Pulldown unit

Lower connection

Upper connection

A

Vacuum reservoir

Fig. 14.74 Typical vacuum hose connections to Zenith 2B5 carburettor

A Light green
B Light green
C Black
D White
E Natural

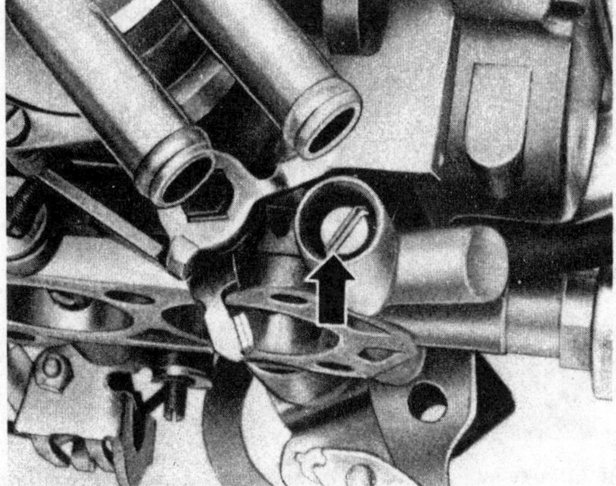

Fig. 14.75 Idle speed screw (arrowed) - Zenith 2B5 carburettor

Fig. 14.76 Mixture adjustment screw (arrowed) - Zenith 2B5 carburettor

Fig. 14.77 Fast idle screw (b) and cam (a) on Zenith 2B5 carburettor

Fig. 14.78 Throttle valve - stage 1 basic setting screw (a) on Zenith 2B5 carburettor

Fig. 14.79 Throttle valve - stage 2 basic setting screw (a) and stop (b) on Zenith 2B5 carburettor

Fig. 14.80 Unhook vacuum unit pullrod (arrowed)

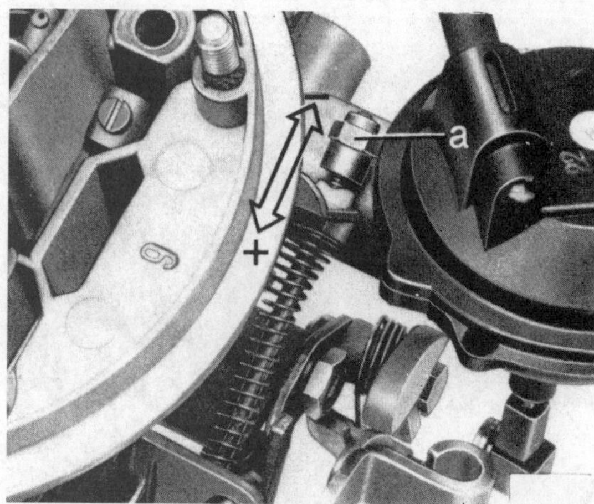

Fig. 14.81 Accelerator pump pushrod - Zenith 2B5 carburettor

a Adjustment nut

Fig. 14.82 Choke pull-down unit Y connector - Zenith 2B5 carburettor. Plug arrowed hose

Fig. 14.83 Automatic choke screw (b) on highest step of cam (a) - Zenith 2B5 carburettor

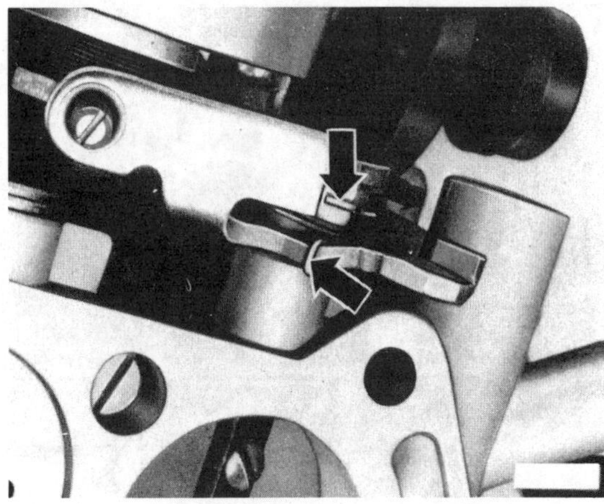
Fig. 14.84 Ends of return spring (arrowed) correctly connected on Zenith 2B5 carburettor

Fig. 14.85 Measuring choke valve plate gap on Zenith 2B5 carburettor. For drill size see Specifications

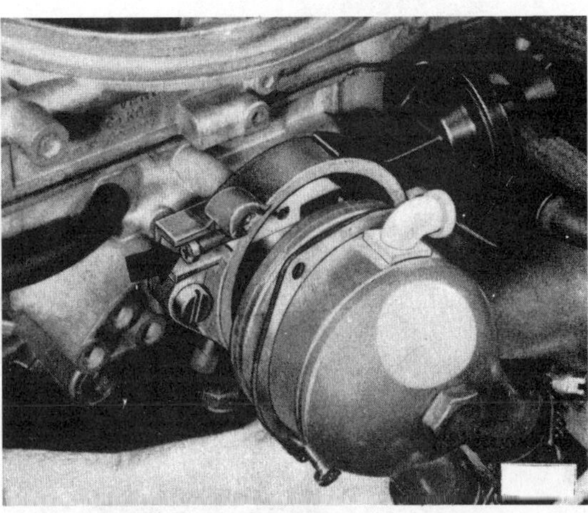
Fig. 14.86 Choke valve gap adjustment screw (arrowed) - Zenith 2B5 carburettor

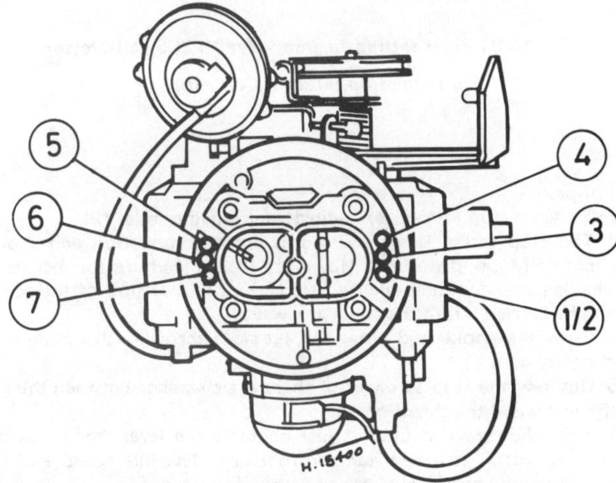

Fig. 14.87 Jet location – Zenith 2B5 carburettor

1/2 *Auxiliary fuel/air jet*
3 *Air correction jet with emulsion tube - stage 1*
4 *Idle jet - stage 1*
5 *Idle jet - stage 2*
6 *Air correction jet with emulsion tube - stage 2*
7 *Idle air jet - progression reserve*

gauge rod. If the gap is not as specified, turn the small screw (arrowed in Fig. 14.86).

Overhaul

139 Extract the top cover fixing screws and remove the cover.

140 Note the location of the jets if they are to be removed for cleaning.

141 Refer to paragraphs 63 to 71 for general details of carburettor overhaul.

142 Set the automatic choke housing so that the marks are in alignment and then tighten the fixing screws.

143 The float level may be adjusted if the top cover is held in the attitude shown (Fig. 14.91).

Zenith 2B3 carburettor

General description

144 This carburettor is of dual barrel type. It is similar in many respects to the 2B5 carburettor, but the method of actuation of the automatic choke is electrical only.

145 The unit is normally fitted to US vehicles equipped with a full emission control system.

Idle speed and mixture adjustment

146 With the engine at normal operating temperature, adjust the idling speed to the specified level by turning the idle speed screw (Fig. 14.93). On vehicles not so equipped, connect a tachometer to the engine for precise setting of the idle speed.

Fig. 14.88 Jet location - Zenith 2B5 carburettor

10 Idle fuel jet - progressive reserve
11 Enrichment valve

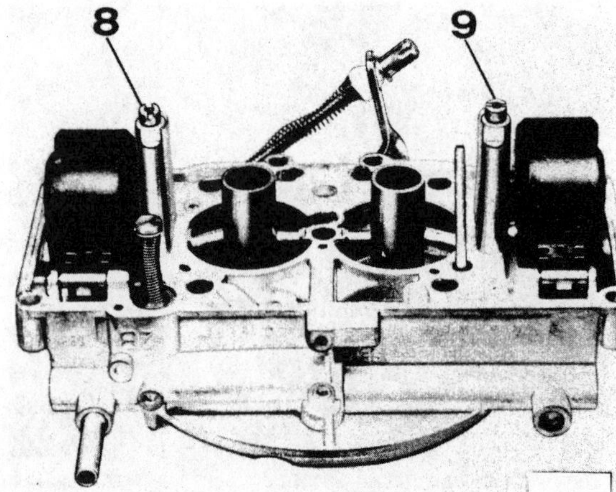

Fig. 14.89 Main jet locations - Zenith 2B5 carburettor

8 Main jet - stage 1
9 Main jet - stage 2

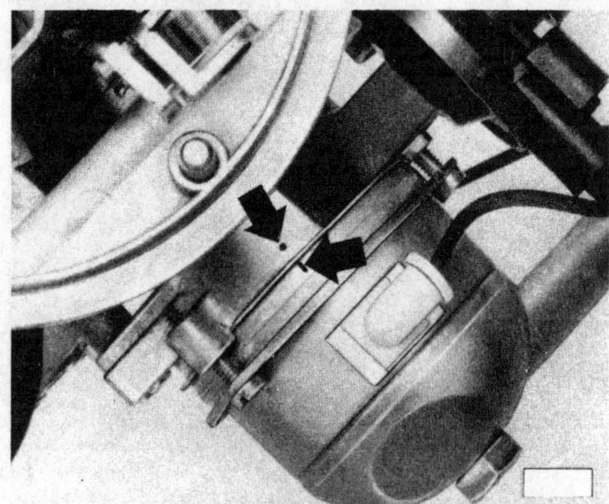

Fig. 14.90 Automatic choke alignment marks (arrowed) - Zenith 2B5 carburettor

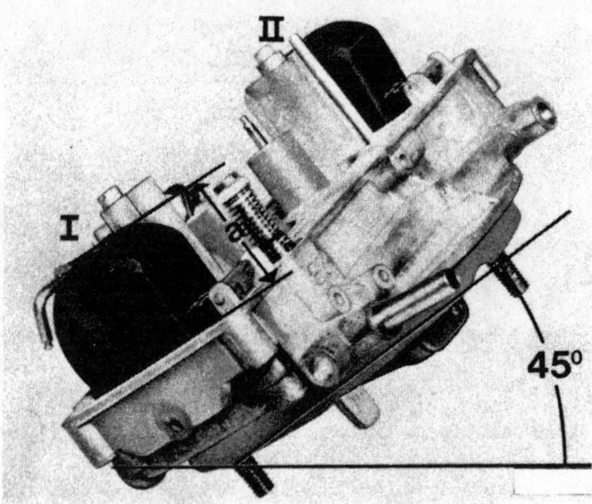

Fig. 14.91 Float setting diagram - Zenith 2B5 carburettor

For dimension (a) see Specifications

147 If the mixture must be adjusted, remove the tamperproof seal from the mixture adjusting screw (where this is permitted by law). Connect an exhaust gas analyser by inserting its probe into the exhaust pipe ahead (upstream) of the catalytic converter at the connecting aperture provided.

148 Disconnect the hose which runs between the air pump and the diverter valve. Plug the opening on the diverter valve.

149 With the engine at normal idling speed and at operating temperature, check the CO level in the exhaust gas. Adjust if necessary to the specified value by turning the adjusting screw.

150 Once the adjustment is completed, reconnect the air pump hose and check the CO level at the exhaust tailpipe. The level must be less than 0.4% if the original adjustment has been correctly carried out.

Choke valve gap - checking and adjustment

151 Extract the screws and remove the cover from the automatic choke.

152 Open and close the choke valve plate completely, then push the choke rod in the direction of the arrow (b) to its stop (Fig. 14.95).

153 Hold the choke in the closed position using a rubber band. Equalize the bush and lever clearances by pushing gently in the direction of arrow (a) (Fig. 14.95). Check the choke valve plate gap using a twist drill or similar. The gap should be as specified, if it is not, turn the screw on the vacuum unit. Lock the screw on completion with a dab of paint.

Throttle valve stop (1st stage) - adjustment (engine code YP)

154 The stop screw is set and sealed during production and should not normally be disturbed. However, if the carburettor has been overhauled or new components fitted, the basic setting of the screw should be carried out in the following way.

155 Open the choke and close the 1st stage throttle valve plate with the fingers.

156 Unscrew the stop screw until there is a clearance between the end of the screw and the throttle lever.

157 Turn the screw in until it just contacts the lever, then give it a further ¼ turn. Fit a new tamperproof cap. The idle speed and CO level should now be adjusted as previously described.

Throttle valve stop (1st stage) - adjustment (all other engines)

158 With the engine at normal operating temperature and idling, pull the distributor vacuum hose from the carburettor and connect a vacuum gauge. Screw in the idle adjusting screw until the gauge shows a vacuum reading, then unscrew it until the vacuum drops to zero. Unscrew the screw a further ¼ turn. Check and adjust the idle speed and CO level with the distributor vacuum hose reconnected.

Throttle valve gap (1st stage) - adjustment

159 With the carburettor removed from the engine, close the choke valve fully and then check that the throttle valve plate (fast idle) gap

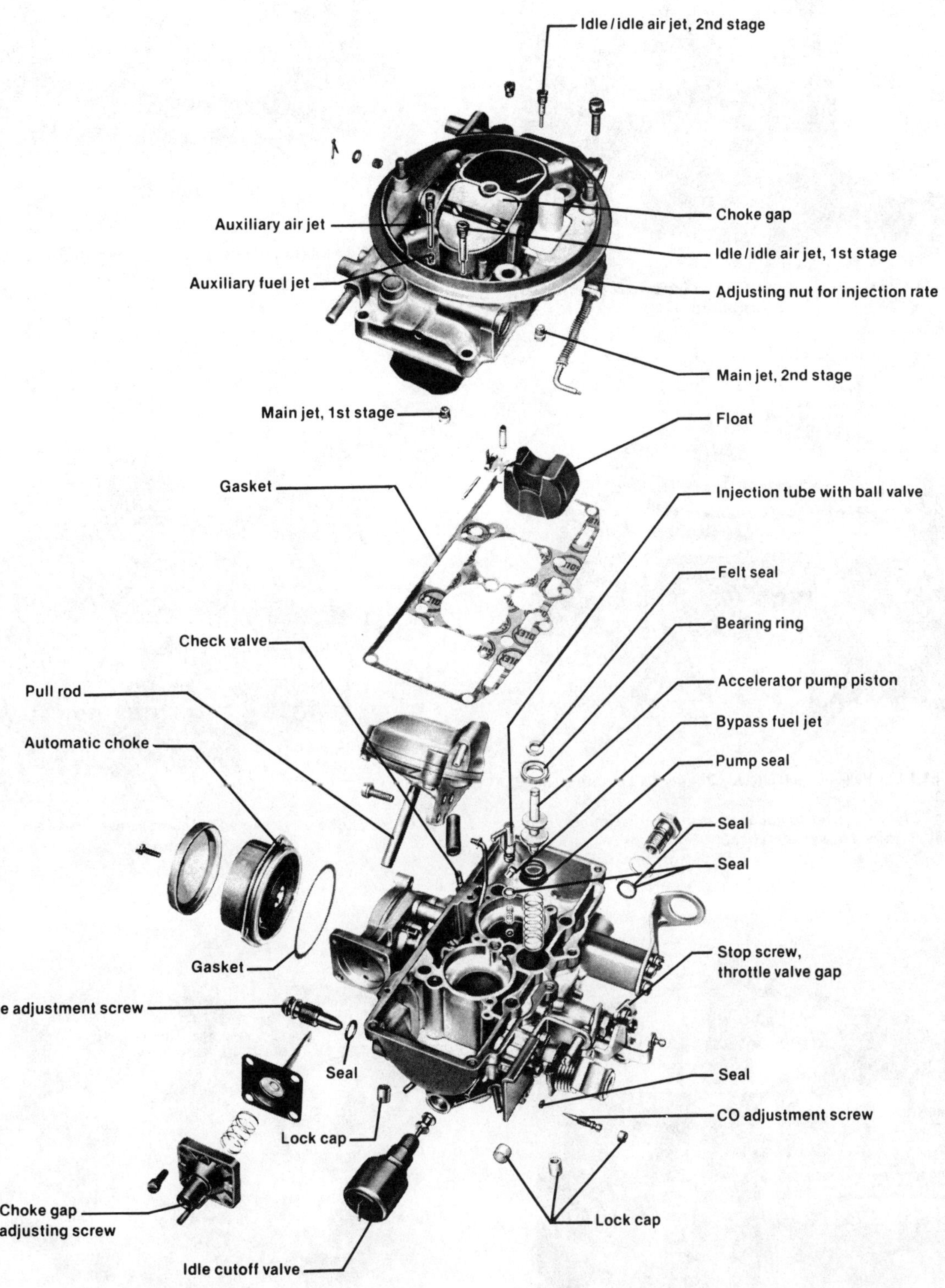
Idle / idle air jet, 2nd stage
Auxiliary air jet
Choke gap
Idle / idle air jet, 1st stage
Auxiliary fuel jet
Adjusting nut for injection rate
Main jet, 2nd stage
Main jet, 1st stage
Float
Gasket
Injection tube with ball valve
Felt seal
Bearing ring
Check valve
Accelerator pump piston
Pull rod
Bypass fuel jet
Automatic choke
Pump seal
Seal
Seal
Gasket
Stop screw,
throttle valve gap
Idle adjustment screw
Seal
Seal
CO adjustment screw
Lock cap
Choke gap
adjusting screw
Lock cap
Idle cutoff valve

Fig. 14. 92 Exploded view of Zenith 2B3 carburettor

Fig. 14.93 Idle speed adjustment screw (arrowed) - Zenith 2B3 carburettor

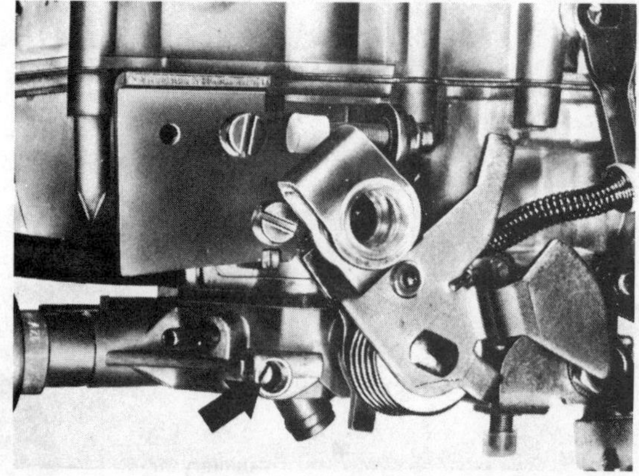

Fig. 14.94 Mixture adjustment screw (arrowed) - Zenith 2B3 carburettor

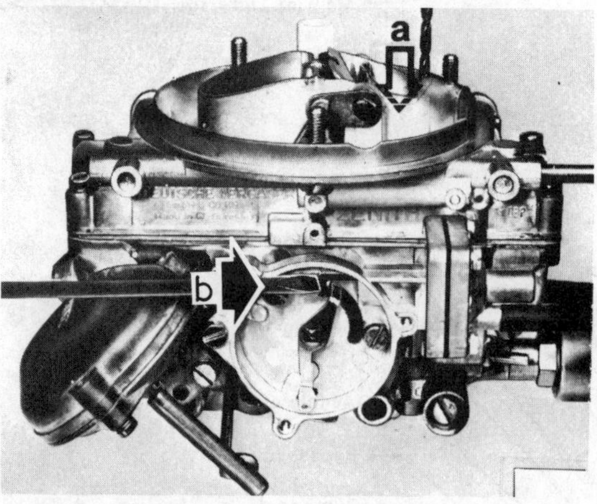

Fig. 14.95 Choke valve gap check - Zenith 2B3 carburettor

(a) Light pressure to equalize bush/lever clearance
(b) Pushing choke rod to stop

Fig. 14.96 Choke valve gap adjustment screw (arrowed) - Zenith 2B3 carburettor

Fig. 14.97 1st stage throttle valve stop screw (arrowed) on Zenith 2B3 carburettor

Fig. 14.98 1st stage throttle valve gap adjustment screw (arrowed) - Zenith 2B3 carburettor

is as specified. If it is not, turn the adjusting screw.

Throttle valve gap (2nd stage) - adjustment

160 With the carburettor removed from the engine, open the choke and close the 1st stage throttle valve plate.

161 Turn the adjusting screw until all clearance has been removed from the lever (Fig. 14.99). Now turn the screw out ¼ turn.

162 The vacuum pullrod should now be checked and adjusted. To do this, disconnect the linkage, loosen the locknut and turn the 2nd stage throttle operating rod until the dimension (a) is as shown in Fig. 14.100. Retighten the locknut and reconnect the ball end of the link rod.

Accelerator pump stroke - adjustment

163 The operations are as described in paragraphs 76 to 79. Note that the volume of fuel must be as specified, and observe location of the pump rod adjusting nut (Fig. 14.101).

Dashpot - adjustment

164 Close the throttle valve plate and have the choke valve plate fully open.

165 Push the dashpot plunger inwards and measure the clearance (a) as shown in Fig. 14.102. If necessary, release the plunger rod locknut and turn the rod to adjust, then retighten the locknut.

Overhaul

166 Refer to paragraphs 63 to 71. Note the location of jets as shown in Figs. 14.103 to 14.105.

167 During reassembly, make sure that the cranked lever of the automatic choke locates between the ends of the bi-metal spring. When fitting the choke housing cover, ensure that the alignment

Fig. 14.100 2nd stage vacuum pullrod adjustment

a = 1.0 to 2.0 mm (0.040 to 0.080 in)

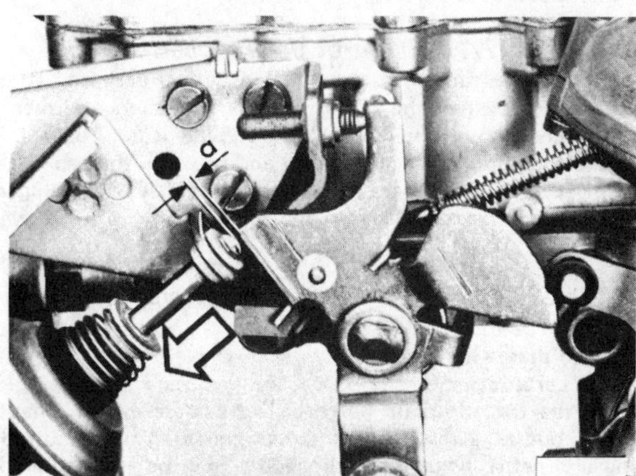

Fig. 14.102 Dashpot plunger clearance - Zenith 2B3 carburettor. Push in direction of arrow

a = 3.0 mm (0.12 in)

Fig. 14.99 2nd stage throttle valve gap adjustment screw (A) and lever (B) on Zenith 2B3 carburettor

Fig. 14.101 Accelerator pump pushrod - Zenith 2B3 carburettor

1 Adjustment nut

Fig. 14.103 Jet location - Zenith 2B3 carburettor

1 Auxiliary air jet
2 Auxiliary fuel jet (below air jet)
3 Air connection jet with mixture tube (1st stage)
4 Idle fuel/air jet (1st stage)
5 Idle fuel/air jet (2nd stage)
6 Air correction jet with mixture tube (2nd stage)
7 Auxiliary fuel/air jet (2nd stage)

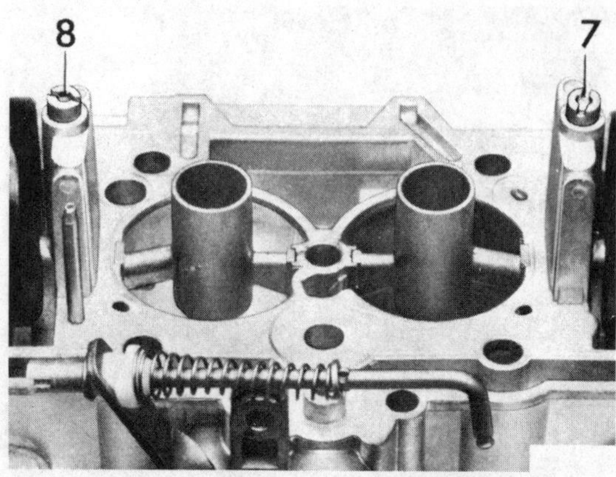

Fig. 14.104 Main jet location - Zenith 2B3 carburettor with top cover inverted

7 1st stage main jet
8 2nd stage main jet

Fig. 14.105 Bypass fuel jet (arrowed) - Zenith 2B3 carburettor

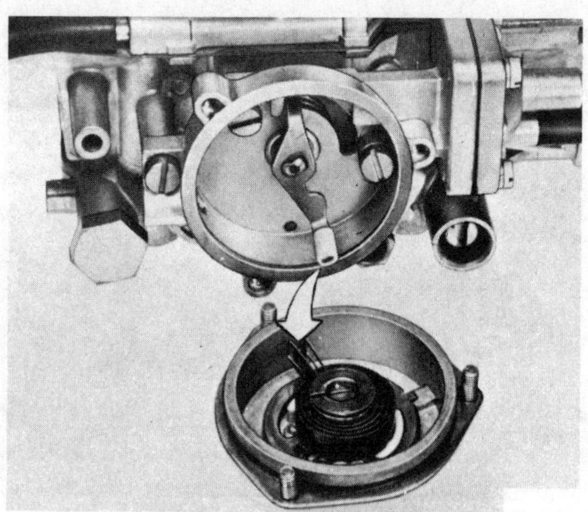

Fig. 14.106 Automatic choke cranked lever engagement with bi-metal spring - Zenith 2B3 carburettor

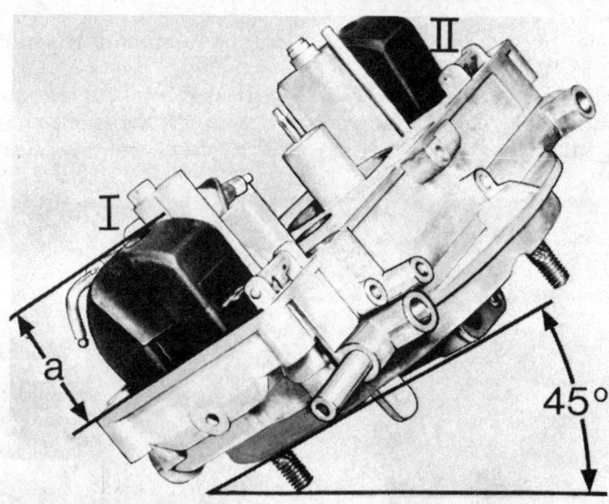

Fig. 14.107 Float setting diagram - Zenith 2B3 carburettor

I 1st stage
II 2nd stage
For (a) see Specifications

Fig. 14.108 Dashpot pushrod setting on Solex 32/35 later model carburettors

a = 1.0 mm (0.039 in)

marks coincide.

168 To measure the float setting, turn the carburettor top cover upside down and hold it at an angle of 45°. The levels of the floats should be as given in the Specifications when measured between the bases of the floats and the surface of the top cover flange. Bend the tang of the float arm to adjust.

Solex 32/35 DIDTA carburettor (later models)

169 Some of these carburettors are fitted with a dashpot. To adjust the dashpot, first extract the spring tensioning washers and then close the throttle valve plate while the choke valve plate is fully open.

170 Push the dashpot plunger fully in and measure the gap as shown in Fig. 14.108. If adjustment is necessary, release the plunger rod locknut and turn the rod. Tighten the locknut and refit the washers on completion.

Solex 35 PDSIT and 32/35 TDID carburettors - revised adjustment procedures

Throttle valve plate - basic setting

Single barrel carburettor

171 Where the throttle plate has been set as described in Chapter 3, Section 17, but as a result hesitation or misfiring has occurred, the following alternative adjustment procedure may be tried to eradicate the problem.

172 To give the throttle valve plate its basic setting, first unscrew the throttle stop screw until it clears its stop.

173 Turn the screw in until its end just touches the stop.

174 Turn the screw in a further quarter of a turn. Basic setting is now complete.

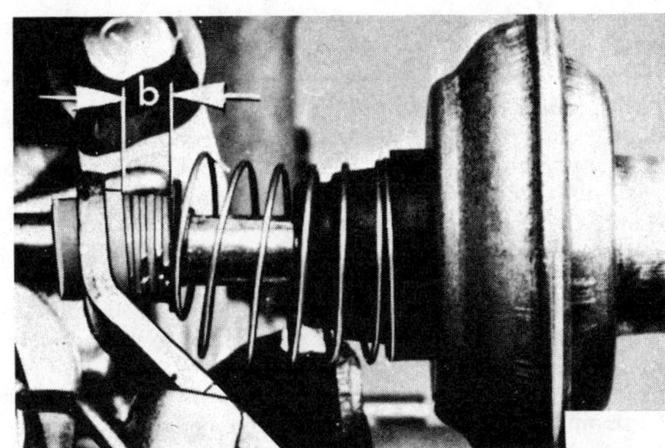

Fig. 14.109 Dashpot spring tensioning washers (b) on Solex 32/35 DIDTA carburettor

Fig. 14.110 Throttle stop screw (arrowed) - Solex PDSIT 35 and 32/35 TDID

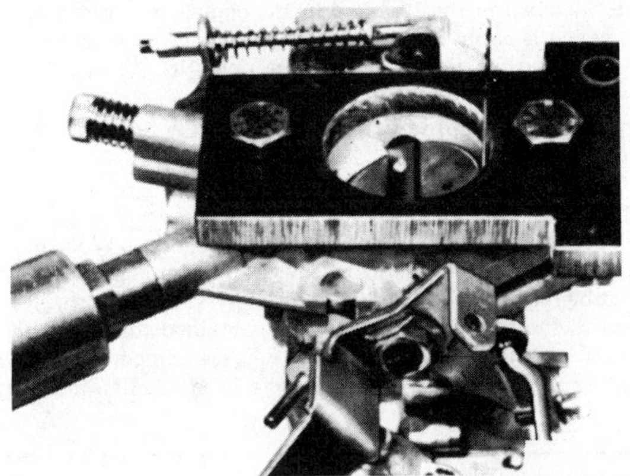

Fig. 14.111 Checking throttle valve plate (fast idle) gap on Solex PDSIT 35

Fig. 14.112 1st stage throttle valve plate basic setting screw (arrowed) on Solex 32/35 TDID

Fig. 14.113 Throttle to choke valve connecting rod on Solex 32/35 TDID. Adjusting nuts are circled, gauge rod is arrowed

175 Fine adjustment to give a satisfactory fast idle at starting can be carried out in the following way.
176 Remove the carburettor.
177 Close the choke valve plate with the finger.
178 Measure the throttle valve gap between the edge of the throttle valve plate and the wall of the carburettor throat. Use a drill or gauge rod of the specified diameter (see Specifications in this Chapter or in Chapter 3). Where adjustment is required, move the position of the nuts on the valve plate connecting rod.

Dual barrel carburettor

179 Give the throttle valve plate its basic setting as described in paragraphs 172 to 174 but note the different location of the screw.
180 Carry out the fine adjustment to the primary (first stage) throttle valve plate, also as previously described for the single barrel carburettor (paragraphs 175 to 178).
181 Should the secondary (second stage) valve plate be out of adjustment then slacken the adjusting screw until the valve plate is just closed. Now turn the screw in one half a turn and secure it with a suitable sealant such as a dab of thick paint.
182 On completion, check for ease of operation and that the valve plates do not stick.
183 Once this adjustment has been completed on either type of carburettor, and the unit refitted to the engine, check the idle speed and mixture setting.

Fig. 14.114 2nd stage throttle valve adjustment screw (arrowed) on Solex 32/35 TDID

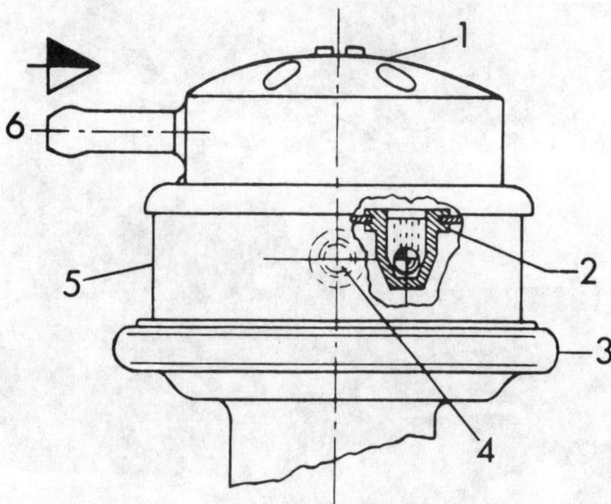

Fig. 14.115 Fuel pump with hot start valve

1 Top half (suction side) of pump
2 Hot start valve
3 Lower half (pressure side) of pump
4 Outlet
5 Pump body
6 Fuel inlet

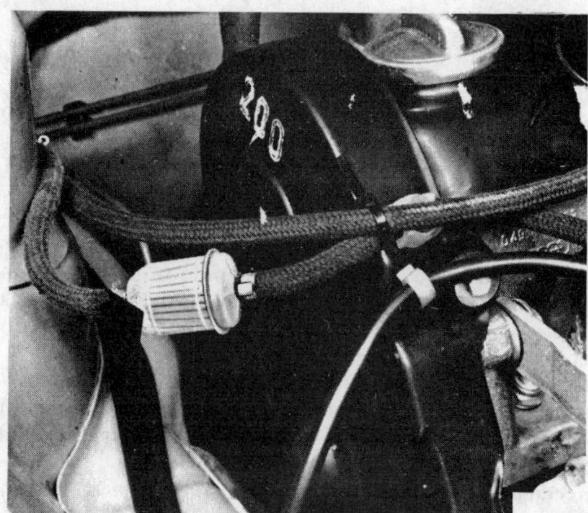

Fig. 14.116 In-line fuel filter

5b Fuel supply system

Fuel pump - carburettor models

1 The fuel pump described in Chapter 3 has been modified twice. A longer operating arm is installed, the old pump operating arm protrudes 1.65 in (42 mm) from the face of the flange, the new one 1.85 in (47 mm). A thick 0.19 in (5 mm) gasket is installed with the new pump and M8 x 30 bolts must be used to secure the pump and gasket. The new pump may be used to replace the old type.

2 To improve hot starting a valve has been fitted in the pump body, to prevent pressure in the pump to carburettor fuel pipe exceeding 3.5 psi (0.26 kg/sq cm).

3 The suction side of the pump is the top half. If the cover gasket leaks the pump will draw in air and the engine may misfire. The air leak will not be evident as there will not be a fuel leak.

Fuel filter - carburettor models

4 Prior to September 1975 a strainer was fitted to the fuel outlet of the fuel tank. In order to clean the strainer it was necessary to remove it from the tank - a lengthy business. In September 1975 a full flow filter was installed in the fuel line in the engine compartment, see Fig. 14.116, which is easily accessible. It should be renewed at the specified intervals. The arrow on the filter must point in the direction of the pump when renewing the filter.

5 From the date of introduction of the full-flow filter the strainer was not fitted in the fuel tank.

Fuel tank - all models

6 Later model fuel tanks are of plastic construction. With this type of tank, no repair is possible and in the event of a leak developing, the tank must be renewed. The tank is secured by straps (photo).

7 Access to the fuel tank sender is still obtained through a small hole (with cover plate) on the floor of the luggage compartment. Note the flow and return hoses connected to the sender unit mounting plate (photo).

5c Fuel injection system

Description

1 The system used is the Continuous Injection System (CIS) of the Bosch K Jetronic type. The system is fitted to certain 1600 cc engines of the Dasher range.

2 Refer to Fig. 14.117 which shows a general layout of the CIS. The flow of air into the inlet manifold is controlled by the two throttle butterfly valves as with a carburettor, but there the resemblance ceases. The purpose of having two butterfly valves and two air passages is not to produce a two stage affair but to divide the airflow. The valves move simultaneously and at equal angles. On its way to the inlet manifold the air passes through a cone shaped orifice, in the centre of which is a circular metal disc known as the sensor plate. The sensor plate is supported by an arm hinged and balanced as shown in Fig. 14.118. The pressure of the airflow causes the sensor plate to move. When there is zero airflow the plate rests in the throat of the cone, as the airflow increases the plate moves upwards, as it decreases the plate moves down again.

3 Also mounted on the sensor plate pivot is a small arm with an adjusting screw on the end which can vary the angle of this arm to the sensor plate lever. Resting on the centre of this arm is a plunger which moves up and down as the sensor plate is moved by the airflow.

4 This plunger, known as the control plunger, operates a small hydraulic valve which controls the flow of fuel to the injectors by covering and uncovering the ports in the valve linking the supply from the fuel pump to the injector supply pipe. The supply of fuel through to inlet port to this plunger would tend to move the plunger away from the sensor arm, or at least prevent it from moving downwards in contact with the arm during the deceleration period. To overcome this a drilling in the fuel distributor allows fuel at system pressure to the plunger bore on top of the plunger, thus keeping the plunger in contact with the sensor arm. The variation of this pressure on top of the plunger is governed by the control pressure regulator about which more is said later in the text.

5 Thus the supply of fuel to the engine matches the air supply giving the correct mixture at all times. The sensor operates on a principal that states that a body which floats suspended in a cone will move in a

5B.6 Fuel tank mounting straps

5B.7 Fuel tank sender unit (Estate)

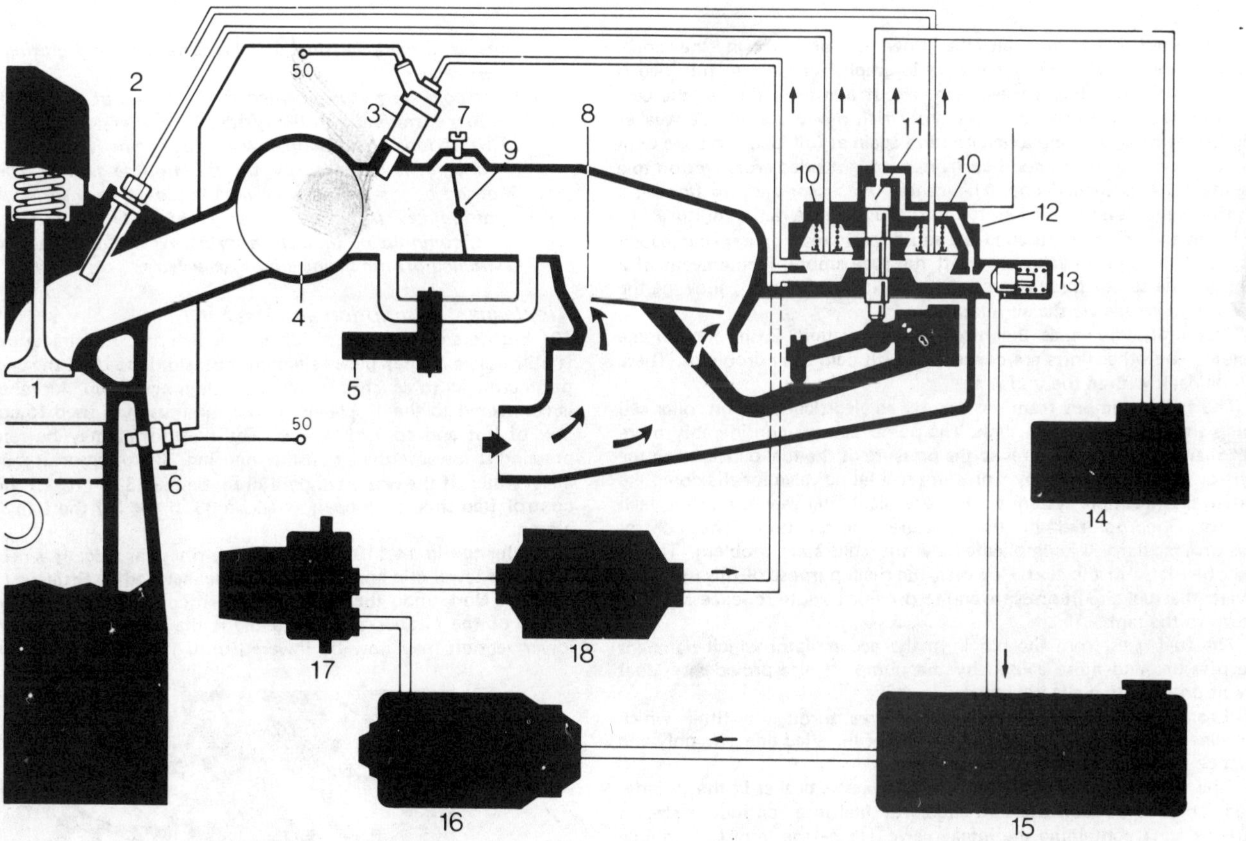

Fig. 14.117 Jetronic fuel injection system - schematic view

1 Inlet valve
2 Injector
3 Cold start valve
4 Air intake distributor
5 Auxiliary air regulator
6 Thermotime switch
7 Idle speed adjusting screw
8 Air sensor plate
9 Throttles (2)
10 Pressure regulating valves (1 per injector)
11 Control plunger
12 Fuel distributor body
13 System pressure regulating valve
14 Control pressure regulator
15 Fuel tank
16 Fuel pump
17 Fuel accumulator
18 Fuel filter

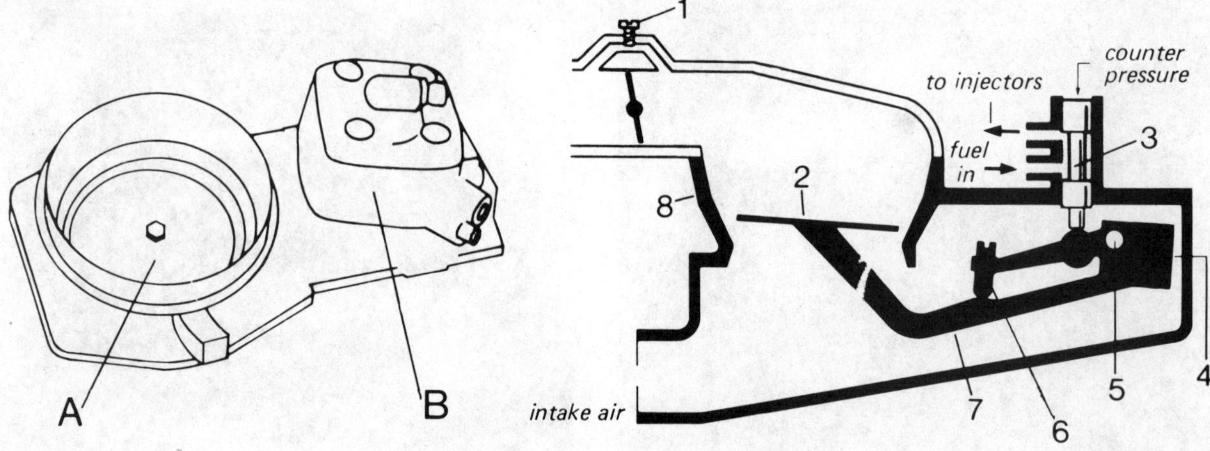

Fig. 14.118 Fuel injection system air sensor unit

A Sensor plate
B Fuel distributor

1 Idle speed screw
2 Sensor plate
3 Control plate
4 Balance weight
5 Pivot
6 Mixture (CO) adjustment screw
7 Sensor beam
8 Air cone

straight line, depending on the flow of air through the cone. Unfortunately the actual air/fuel ratio graph from idle to full load is not a straight line but a wave form about a straight line, as the best performance is obtained with a slightly rich mixture at idle, a weaker mixture at part load and a rich mixture again at full load. To cope with this the cone has been modified from a straight sided cross-section to a slightly egg-cup shaped one. This causes the sensor plate to float at a slightly higher level at idle and full load thus giving a richer mixture.

6 When the engine is stopped the sensor plate rests on a spring-loaded stop and the control valve shuts off the fuel supply. In the event of a backfire the sensor plate depresses the spring-loaded stop, allowing the pressure to escape via the air inlet.

7 This unit, known as the mixture control unit, is the key to the system. The other units are concerned with cold start problems. These will be dealt with in the text.

8 The fuel is pumped from the tank by an electrically driven roller cell pump situated by the fuel tank. The pump delivers considerably more fuel than the engine requires so the pressure of the fuel delivered to the control valve is governed by a pressure regulating valve for the complete system and a simple system of pressure regulating valves, one for each injector, incorporated in the mixture control unit. The control pressure regulator is complicated by the cold start problem. This is described later in the text. However, the main purpose of this unit is to govern the fuel circuit pressure and to provide a route for excess fuel to return to the tank.

9 The fuel goes from the pump to the accumulator which dampens the pressure and noise caused by the pump. It also provides residual circuit pressure to assist hot starting.

10 From the accumulator the fuel passes through a filter which contains a nylon-paper element. This may be installed one way only and must be renewed regularly.

11 The injectors, which are a push fit into plastic bushes in the cylinder head, open at a preset pressure and spray fuel in a continuous stream into the port containing the intake valve. Hence the term Continuous Injection.

12 There are three more items in the system, all concerned with starting problems:

(a) The auxiliary air regulator is a valve, operated by a bi-metallic strip, which allows air to enter the inlet manifold when the throttles are closed during the warm-up period. The valve gate is open when the engine is cold and is closed by the bi-metallic strip as the engine warms up. Without this valve the engine would stall when idling cold.

(b) The thermotime switch which operates the cold start valve is governed by the starter current and the coolant temperature. Depending on the coolant temperature the switch operates between three and ten seconds from the moment the ignition key is turned, cutting off the current to and closing the cold start valve.

(c) The cold start valve, located in the centre of the inlet manifold, squirts extra fuel into the system for a brief period whenstarting. This period, three seconds when the engine is hot, and ten when it is cold, is governed by the thermotime switch. The valve is opened by a solenoid winding and closed by a spring. When the ignition key is turned the solenoid pulls the plunger off the seat, compressing the return spring. When the solenoid current is switched off the spring closes the valve.

Air cleaner - description and servicing

13 A different shape of air cleaner is fitted to fuel injection models. It still uses a pleated paper element, but is mounted on the engine compartment wall to which it is secured by lugs and a clip. A preheater hose is connected to the air cleaner and a thermostat is used to control the mix of hot and cold intake air. The thermostat may be removed by pressing it towards the air cleaner housing. The thermostat may be tested in water. If the water temperature is below 68°F (20°C) then the air control flap should be open, if above 93°F (34°C) the flap should be closed.

14 Refer to Fig. 14.119. To remove the filter cartridge it is necessary to undo the lower clip and move the air cleaner body a little way from the console. Now undo the four clips which connect the upper and lower halves of the cleaner together and lift the upper section slightly. The lower section may now be lowered until it is possible to remove the

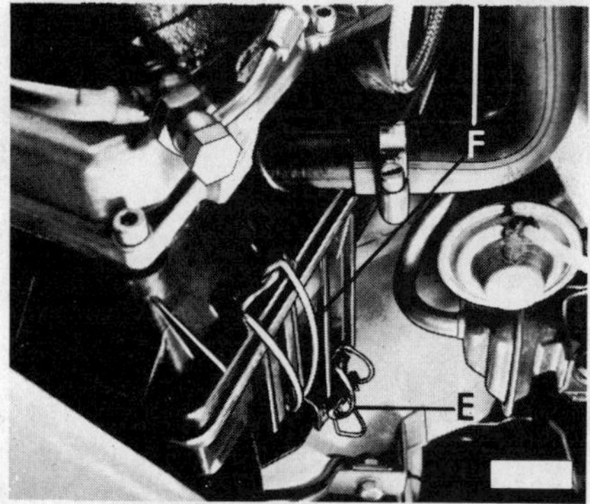

Fig. 14.119 Air cleaner on fuel injection engine

E Lower clip
F Upper clip (1 of 4)

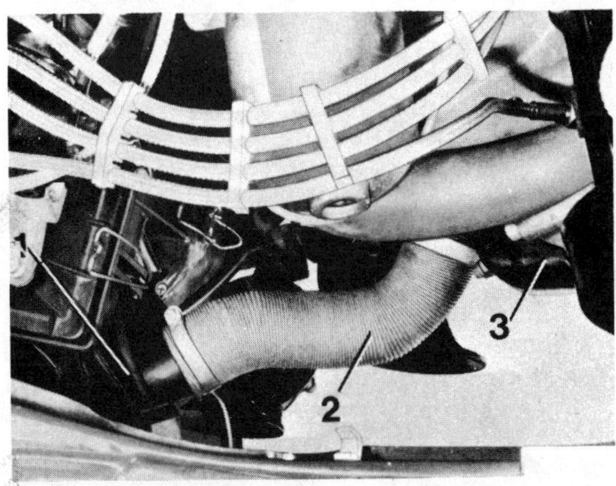

Fig. 14.120 Air cleaner preheater arrangement

1 *Control box with thermostat*
2 *Preheater hose*
3 *Warm air deflector plate*

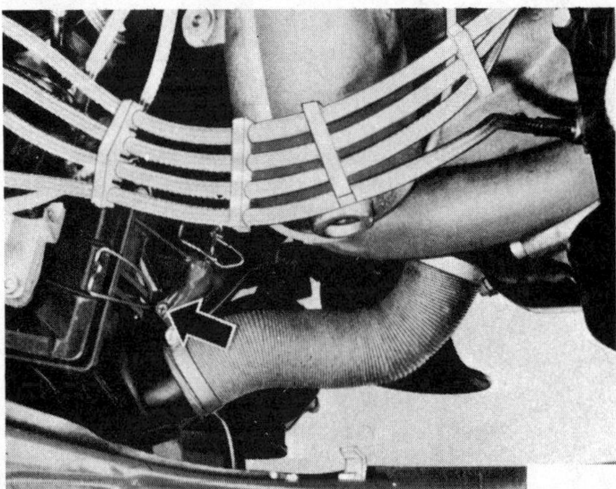

Fig. 14.121 Air preheater control box fixing screw (arrowed)

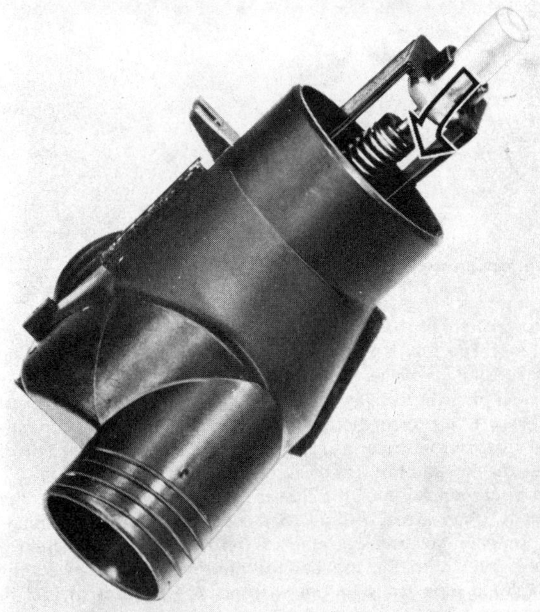

Fig. 14.122 Thermostat located in control box. Direction of motion is arrowed

paper cartridge. Take the cartridge away and set it on a sheet of newspaper. Tap it gently until all dust has been removed. It may be cleaned with an air jet, but not more than 4 to 5 psi (0.28 to 0.35 kg/sq cm) should be used. **On no account use a solvent**, this will clog the cartridge beyond repair. If the cartridge is frayed or torn it should be renewed.

15 Clean the inside of the air cleaner casing carefully with a rag dampened with light oil and wipe the casing dry.

16 To refit the air cleaner first install the cartridge in the lower half of the casing. Fit the two retaining lugs of the lower casing into the rubber bushings on the side of the engine compartment and fasten the lower clip. Now lower the top half of the cleaner onto the lower half, align it carefully and refit the four clips.

17 Servicing intervals are discussed in Chapter 3, Section 5.

Air sensor - description and checking

18 The principle of operation has been stated earlier. As the airflow varies, the plate moves up and down moving the control plunger in the mixture control unit.

19 An aluminium casting is bolted to the top of the air cleaner casing and connected to the black plastic air conducting casing at the top. The joint is held by a circular clip.

20 The mixture control unit is fastened to the top of the air sensor casing by two screws.

21 In order to check the sensor the air intake casing must be pulled away from the sensor unit to expose the moving plate, but first run the engine for a minute or so to build up residual pressure in the fuel lines.

22 First examine the position of the sensor plate in the bore. It must be central with a gap of 0.004 in (0.10 mm) all round between it and the bore. It must also be even with the bottom rim of the air cone when the residual pressure is removed.

23 If the plate is out of centre, the bolt in the centre of the plate should be slackened and removed. Clean the bolt and then install it again, and try to centre the plate. If this is possible remove the bolt again, coat the threads with locking compound, install, centre the disc and tighten the bolt to 2.6 lbf ft (0.35 kgf m).

24 If it is not possible to centre the plate then the whole unit must be removed from the car. It is probably easier to take the mixture control unit off than to undo all the pipes, but if you do this be careful that the plunger does not drop out. Disconnect the unit from the top of the air cleaner. With the unit out turn it upside down and check that the lever is central in its bearings. If the clamp bolt on the sensor arm counterweight is slackened it is possible to move the lever to a central position and with it the plate. If this is possible then the bolt must be refitted with thread locking compound. If this does not centre the plate then a new unit is required.

25 The level of the plate at rest on the stop may be adjusted by bending the clip with small pliers. This can be done in position on the car if the sensor plate is pulled up to its top position, but be careful not to strain it or scratch the polished surfaces. The tolerance is 0.020 in (0.5 mm), but it is not possible to measure it, so judge the level as best you can by eye.

26 Once the plate is central and at the correct level and the system is reconnected to the fuel lines and air cleaner, the mixture control unit in position, and the system charged with residual pressure by turning the ignition on for a few seconds, it is then possible to check the action of the air sensor unit with the ignition turned off. Using a small magnet, lift the plate steadily thus moving the control plunger. The resistance, which is slight, must be even. There may be no hard spots. Push the plate down quickly. There must be no resistance to movement. If there is resistance in both directions, or hard spots in both directions, it is probable that the plate is still not central. If the hard spot is only felt when lifting the plate then the problem is with the plunger. Remove the mixture control unit from the air sensor unit and check the plunger for free movement. If there is a hard spot carefully withdraw the plunger and then wash it with clean fuel to remove any residue. If this method will not cure the hard spot then the mixture control unit must be replaced. **Do not** attempt to remove the hard spot with abrasive, that will only make things worse. A visit to the VW agent is indicated. He may be able to cure the problem, but be prepared to purchase a new mixture control unit.

27 On some vehicles there is an electric switch on the air sensor unit. This is closed when the sensor is in the rest position. When the ignition is turned on this switch supplies current from the ignition switch (terminal 15) to terminal '85' on relay '1'. As the sensor arm rises the switch opens and relay '1' opens. For details see paragraphs 100 to

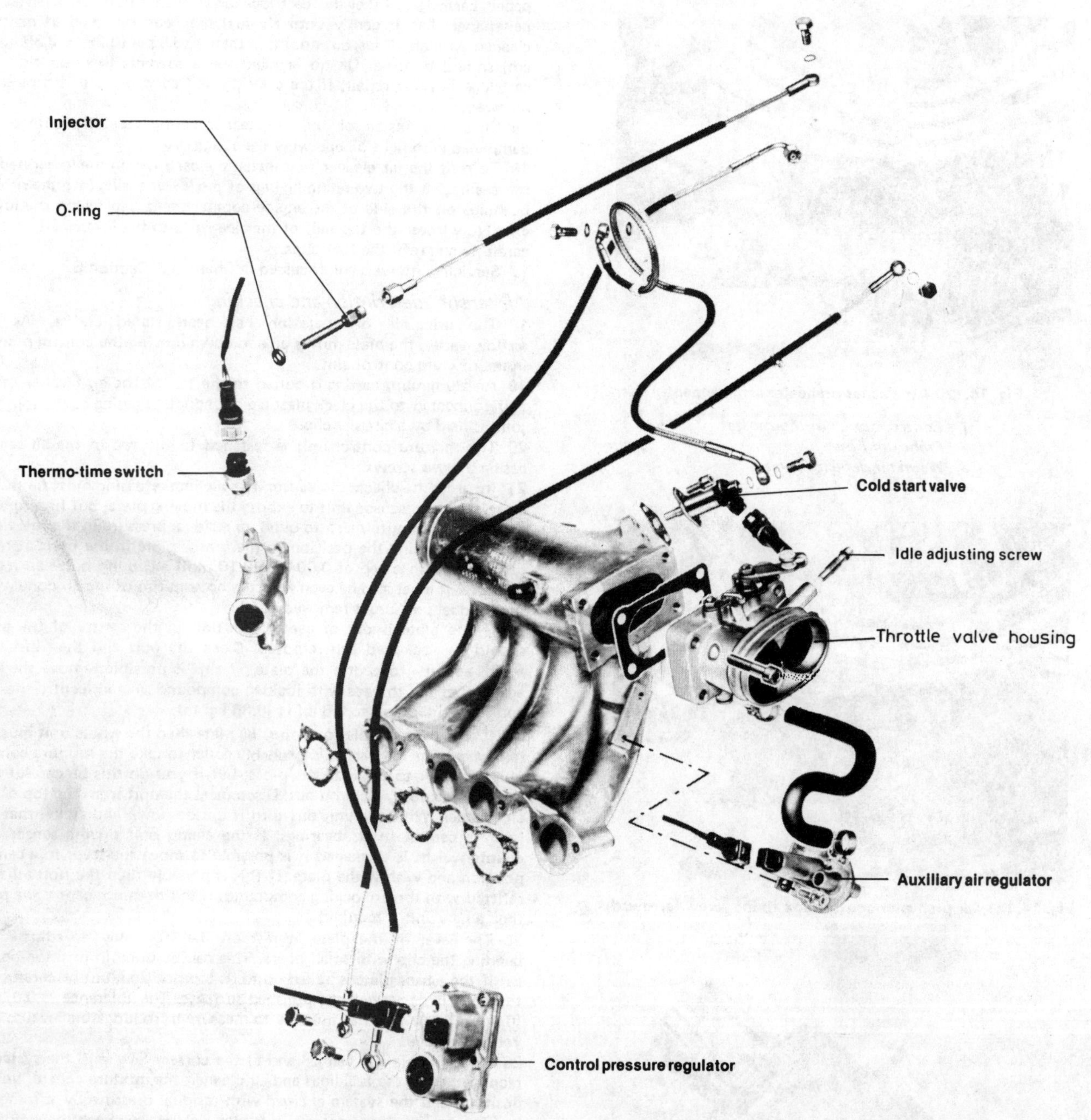

Fig. 14.123 Components of the fuel injection system

108. On vehicles with this switch it should be disconnected when doing tests with the ignition switched on but the engine not started.

Fuel distributor - description and checking

28 This is the unit on top of the airflow sensor unit which has all the pipes connected to it. It is secured to the sensor unit by two cheese-headed screws. If you take it off the sensor unit, be careful that the control plunger does not fall out. Always fit a new gasket if the units are separated. When refitting, tighten the screws to 2.8 lbf ft (0.4 kgf m).

29 The four banjo joints on the top held by hexagon-headed bolts go to the injectors. The one in the centre goes to the control pressure regulator. On the side are the inlet from the pump which has a banjo attachment, the return pipe to the tank which also has a banjo attachment, and a hexagon-headed plug which gives access to the system pressure relief valve.

30 The pressure relief valve controls the overall pressure in the system in the lower half of the fuel distributor, allowing excess fuel to go back to the tank. The fuel is supplied to the lower half via the drilling from the control plunger valve (see Fig. 14.124). Fuel goes to the upper half of the fuel distributor via the metering slot of the control plunger valve. There is a pressure regulating valve for each injector built into the fuel distributor under each injector line outlet. A steel diaphragm separates the top and bottom of each regulating valve.

31 The fuel comes into the lower half, pressing against the four diaphragms, then via a drilling to the control plunger chamber. The control plunger governs the area of the metering port which admits fuel via a drilling to the top half of the regulating valve. In this part of the valve a pipe leads to the injector. The amount of fuel flowing through that pipe is governed by a spring-loaded disc valve. The increase of pressure in the top half of the regulating valve distorts the diaphragm downwards. This allows the spring-loaded valve to open further, and more fuel goes to the injector. The pressure in the top

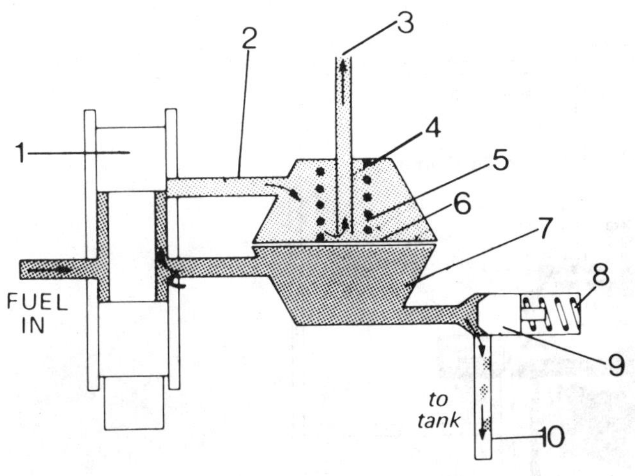

Fig. 14.124 Sectional view of control pressure valves in fuel distributor

1 Metering valve
2 Inlet to upper part of valve and injection line
3 Pipe to injector
4 Valve spring
5 Location of valve (valve not shown) regulating injector pressure
6 Diaphragm
7 System pressure chamber
8 System pressure regulating valve spring
9 System pressure regulating valve piston
10 Return fuel line to fuel tank

half drops, the diaphragm returns towards normal and the valve closes a small amount and the pressure in the top half builds up again. This process is continuous. About 1.5 psi (0.11 kg/sq cm) is used in the upper half of the valve to deflect the diaphragm so the pressure in the upper half is governed to small limits and the control plunger can control the flow of fuel to the injector without being affected by pressure changes. If this unit were not present all sorts of hydraulic flow problems would beset the control plunger when sudden demands for fuel were made by the engine. It does not, however, overcome the problems of the warm-up period which are discussed below in relation to the control pressure regulator.

32 The tests on the mixture control unit are only two in number. The checking of the plunger has been described in the section on the air sensor. The other test concerns the system operating pressure. To do this a pressure gauge is required. This should be connected in the line from the fuel distributor to the control pressure regulator. The operating pressure should be between 65 and 75 psi (4.5 and 5.2 kg/sq cm). Adjustment is by altering the shims under the plug of the relief valve. Refer to Fig. 14.125. If the pressure is outside the limit first check the pump delivery, the fuel filter and fuel lines, as described elsewhere in this Section. If these are in order then remove the plug from the fuel distributor and withdraw the copper ring, shims, spring, piston

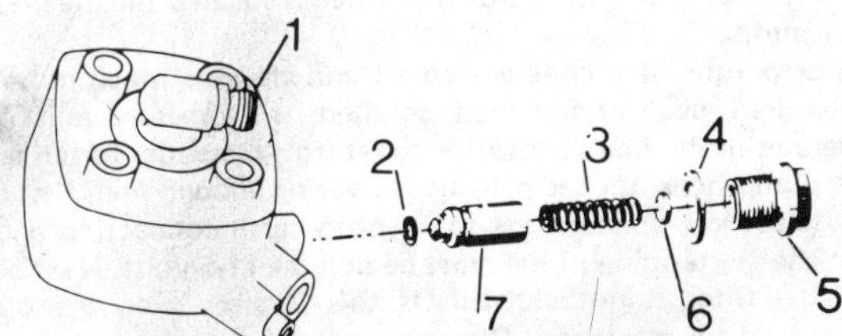

Fig. 14.125 Fuel distributor and pressure relief valve

1 Fuel distributor body
2 Rubber ring
3 Spring
4 Copper ring
5 Plug
6 Shims for pressure adjustment
7 Valve piston

and rubber ring in that order. Wash them all in clean fuel and fit the piston on a wooden dowel and try it in the bore to see whether it moves freely. If it sticks try gently to remove the obstruction, but be careful, the piston is mated to the fuel distributor and damage to either means renewal of both.

33 If the piston moves freely the pressure may be adjusted by altering the shims. Adding or subtracting a 0.004 in (0.1 mm) shim changes the pressure by 0.9 psi (0.06 kg/sq cm), a 0.020 in (0.5 mm) shim changes it by 4.4 psi (0.3 kg/sq cm). Always fit a new copper ring and a new rubber ring.

Control pressure regulator - description and checking

34 As described above, the control pressure regulator's main function is to control the pressure on the top of the control plunger and to help regulate the air/fuel mixture during the warm-up period.

35 The unit is bolted to the cylinder block on the left-hand side of the engine just in front of the distributor. Two pipes and an electrical connector go to it. One pipe goes to the top of the plunger chamber and the other to the fuel return line on the fuel distributor as shown in Fig. 14.126. A cross-section of the unit in diagrammatic form is given at Fig. 14.127. The inlet pipe from the top of the control plunger is open at all times. The outlet pipe is open when the engine is cold because the valve spring is held down by a bi-metallic strip. As fuel flows through the fuel distributor on starting the engine, fuel is bled off from the top of the control plunger, lessening the pressure there and allowing the air sensor to move the control plunger up further for the same volume of inlet air. This opens the metering ports still further and enriches the mixture for cold starting. A heater element is wound round the bi-metallic strip and current is passed through it right from the time the engine is started. This heats the bi-metallic strip which distorts, allowing the spring to push the valve against the control pressure regulator output pipe and close the fuel return to the tank from the control pressure regulator. As the valve closes the pressure on the top of the control plunger increases, forcing the plunger back to its normal working position.

36 The unit is not adjustable. To check whether it is working correctly, fit a pressure gauge in the line between the fuel distributor and the regulator (the input line). Bleed the valve. Remove the electrical leads from the control pressure regulator and start the engine from cold. The pressure will vary according to the outside air temperature, at 50°F (10°C) it should be 14 to 20 psi (0.98 to 1.40 kg/sq cm), at 68°F (20°C), 20 to 25 psi (1.40 to 1.75 kg/sq cm), at 86°F (30°C), 25 to 30 psi (1.75 to 2.10 kg/sq cm) and at 104°F (40°C) 30 to 35 psi (2.10 to 2.46 kg/sq cm).

37 Now refit the electrical leads to the control pressure regulator and run the engine until it reaches normal operating temperature (oil temperature 122°F/50°C). Stop the engine for a few minutes. Remove the electrical connections from the regulator and start the engine and let it idle. The pressure should build up to 48 to 54 psi (3.37 to 3.79 kg/sq cm) right away. If these pressures are not obtainable, check the resistance of the heater coil of the regulator (Fig. 14.128). It should be 20 ohms. If the regulator does not build up to the pressures stated it should be renewed, but it might be as well to have the agent repeat the test before doing anything drastic.

Fuel pump - description and checking

38 A roller cell type of pump is fitted. The roller cell consists of a rotor held on the shaft of the motor armature. There are five cut-outs in the rotor which hold rollers. The rotor is installed in the pressure chamber of the pump. As the rotor spins the rollers are forced out against the pressure chamber wall and collecting fuel at the inlet carry it round to the outlet where the configuration of the pressure chamber wall directs it into the outlet. The pump is driven by a permanent magnet electric motor and is situated under the fuel pressure accumulator under the car and just in front of the right-hand corner of the fuel tank.

39 There is a non-replaceable fuel pressure relief valve which allows fuel to return to the intake side of the pump if the pressure in the system exceeds normal working value. This valve is behind the pump rollers and is not accessible.

40 Integral with the pump delivery outlet is a check valve. This holds the pressure in the delivery pipe to 28 psi (2 kg/sq cm) when the pump is not working and in conjunction with the accumulator and the piston seal in the fuel distributor assists hot starting.

41 The entire pump, brushgear and armature are immersed in the fuel which lubricates and cools the bearings. At first sight this would

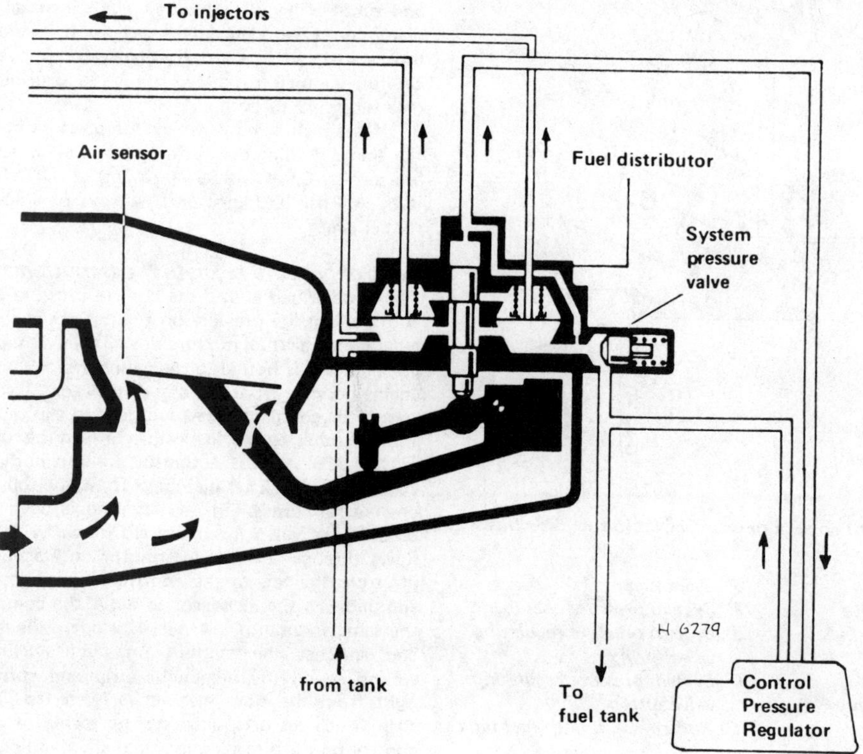

Fig. 14.126 Layout of fuel injection control pressure regulator system

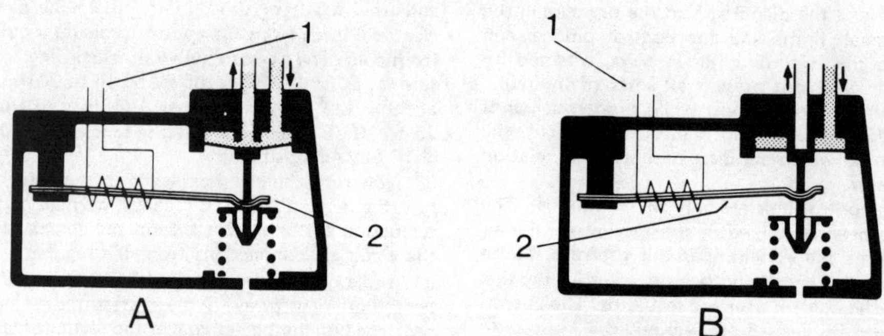

Fig. 14.127 Operating modes of control pressure regulator valve in cold (A) and hot (B) condition

1 Heater 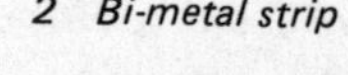 *2 Bi-metal strip*

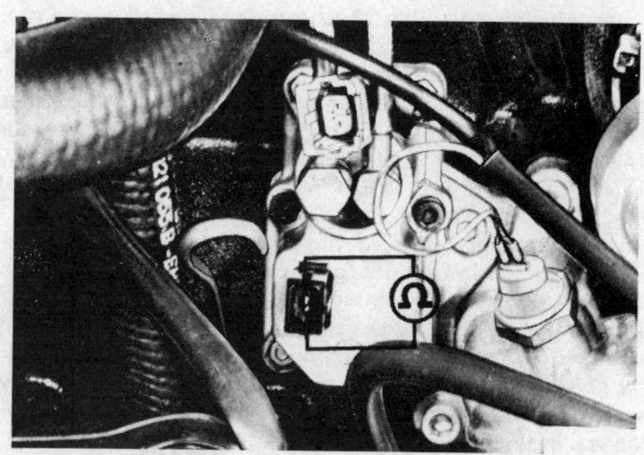

Fig. 14.128 Checking control pressure regulator heater resistance

appear dangerous, but the fuel will not ignite without an air supply so it is safe enough. However the pump must not be allowed to run dry, or it will overheat. For this reason the filter is located on the pressure side of the pump.

42 The pump runs at a constant speed and delivers much more fuel than is required, even at full load, so there is a pressure relief valve which operates in the fuel distributor to return excess fuel to the tank.

43 If the pump does not seem to be delivering enough fuel, first of all check the electrical connections to it, both earth connection and the voltage at the '+' terminal. This must be at least 11.5 volts. Next check that the fuel filter is not clogged. If this is clear then the output quantity should be measured. Disconnect the fuel return pipe at the fuel distributor and place it in a measuring glass of at least 0.9 Imp. qt (1000 cc/1US quart) capacity. Run the pump for exactly 30 seconds and the output should be as stated in the Specifications.

44 The condition of the hydraulic lines may be checked by installing a pressure gauge in the line between the fuel distributor and control pressure regulator. Set the gauge control lever or valve to the closed position, run the pump for 30 seconds to repressurize the system and

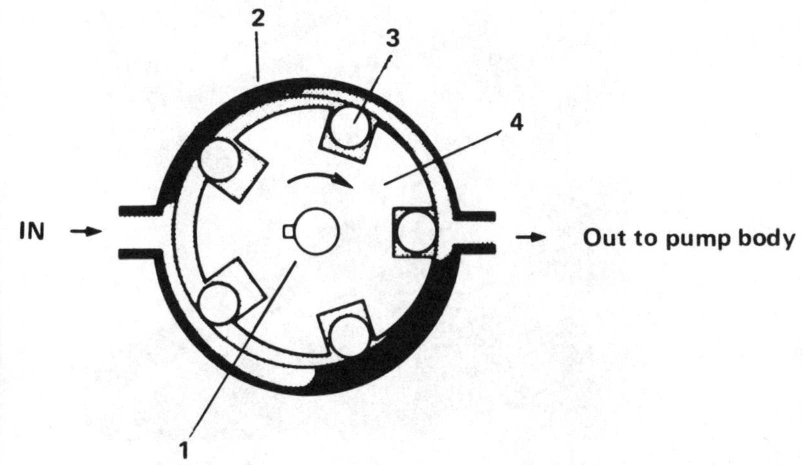

Fig. 14.129 Sectional view of fuel injection system fuel pump

1 Shaft
2 Body
3 Roller
4 Rotor

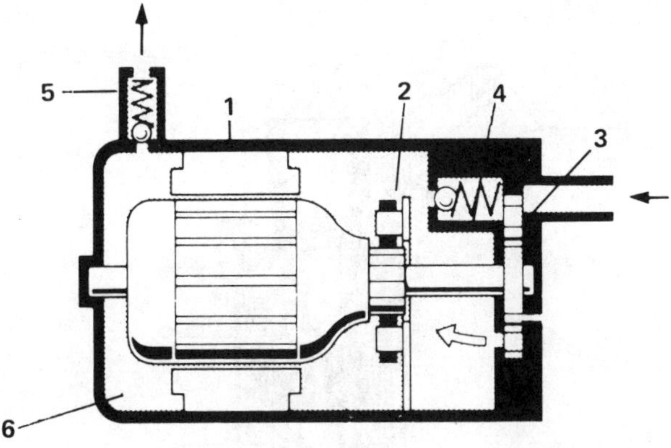

Fig. 14.130 Longitudinal sectional view of fuel pump

1 Permanent magnet
2 Brushgear
3 Roller cell
4 Relief valve
5 Check valve
6 Rotor

Fig. 14.131 Location of fuel injection system pump and accumulator

1 Accumulator
2 Fuel pump

switch off. After 20 minutes check the line pressure; the gauge should read at least 23.5 psi (1.6 kg/sq cm). If it does not then either the check valve on the pump or the rubber seal ring on the fuel distributor pressure relief piston is suspect. However, before renewing these, check the current consumption of the pump motor by putting a 10 ampere ammeter in series with the pump and earth. The ammeter should read between 6.5 and 8.5 amps. If it is higher then the pump is defective. If the current is correct but the output low, then again a new pump is required. If the current flow is correct and the output correct but the pressure drops, renew the check valve.

45 If the motor does not work when the ignition is switched on, check that the voltage of 11.5V is present at the motor terminals. If it is not check the system fuse (see vehicle handbook supplied with the car). If this is in order check the relay. This is in Socket 'L' on the plate under the dash. Remove the relay and with a 1.5 mm^2 cross-section wire and an 8 amp fuse in series connect contacts 'L14' and '15' in the relay plate. If the motor now works then renew the relay.

46 Renewing the check valve may be necessary. To do this lift the right rear wheel, set the car on an axle stand and remove the wheel. Open the tank filler cap to release pressure in the tank. Clean the fuel pump and fuel line carefully and then remove the fuel line on the side by the support bracket. The check valve is inside the screw connector. Remove the screw connector and fit a new one. Fit new seals when refitting the joint.

47 1977 onward models have a modified fuel pump. The electrical connections are fitted on the end of the pump; the output pipe has been moved from the side to the end of the pump and has a larger non-return valve. This has a larger screw connector (12 mm) which must be tightened to 15 lbf ft (2 kgf m) on assembly.

48 The clamp is modified and a larger fuel accumulator is fitted.

49 From chassis No 846 2042 542 the pump relay is altered (see paragraphs 100 to 108).

Fuel accumulator - description and checking

50 The accumulator plays several roles. It damps down the fuel surge as the pump pressure builds up and cuts down the noise generated by the pump. It improves hot starting by helping to retain fuel pressure in the system when the engine is switched off and avoids fuel vapourization and vapour lock. The operation is simple. As the pump forces fuel into the accumulator body past the damper plate, the diaphragm is pushed inwards against the spring until the diaphragm is hard against the stop. Only then does the system pressure begin to build up to its operating value. Without the accumulator in the circuit, operating pressure would be achieved in micro-seconds; with the accumulator in the circuit the time lag is approximately 1 second.

51 When the pump is switched off, the spring forces the diaphragm back slowly to the original position, forcing about 20 cc of fuel through a small hole in the reed valve, maintaining pressure in the system for some 40 minutes.

52 The accumulator is mounted just above the fuel pump. To remove, first clean the pipes and unions, disconnect the pipes and plug them, and then take off the screw that holds the accumulator to the mounting bracket.

53 The only reason for removing the accumulator would be a ruptured diaphragm, which would be evident by a fuel leak from the unit via the air bleed hole and a failure to maintain a residual pressure with possible vapour lock. The initial symptom of failure would be difficult starting when the engine is hot. There is no repair; a faulty unit must be renewed.

54 On 1977 onward models the accumulator has been enlarged to a

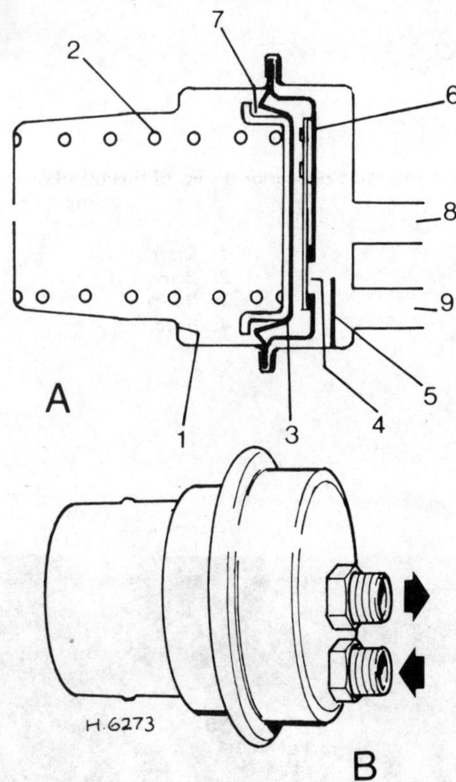

Fig. 14.132 Sectional view (A) and side view (B) of fuel accumulator

1 *Casing*
2 *Pressure spring*
3 *Diaphragm*
4 *Bleed hole*
5 *Damper plate*
6 *Valve*
7 *Spring cap*
8 *Outlet*
9 *Inlet*

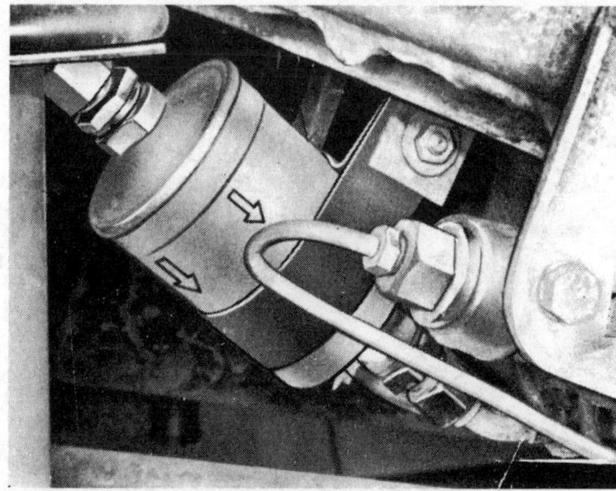

Fig. 14.133 Location of fuel injection system fuel filter in the engine compartment

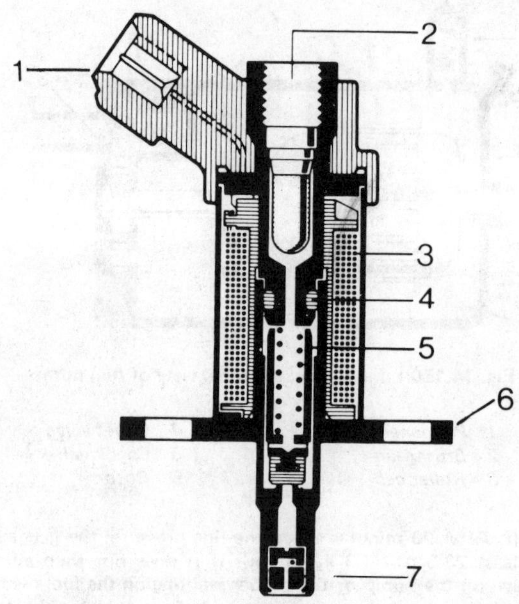

Fig. 14.134 Sectional view of cold start valve

1 *Electrical connections*
2 *Fuel inlet*
3 *Solenoid*
4 *Seal*
5 *Plunger*
6 *Flange*
7 *Nozzle*

Fig. 14.135 Checking fuel injection cold start valve

capacity of 40 cc. Parts are still available for the older models.

Fuel filter - description and checking

55 The filter is situated on the left-hand side of the front floor plate under the bulkhead. If it is damaged or suspect, it must be removed and checked. If fuel does not flow freely through it then a new one should be fitted.
56 To remove it, first clean the pipes and unions. Undo the unions and plug the pipes. Unscrew the clamp bolt and take the filter and clamp away. When installing a new one the arrow on the casing must point towards the engine.
57 It is recommended that the fuel filter be renewed every 10 000 miles (16 000 km).

Cold start valve - description and checking

58 Located in the centre of the intake manifold, the cold start valve is activated by the thermotime switch. The amount of fuel injected varies according to the coolant temperature and the starter current.
59 To test it remove it from the manifold and place it in a glass container; a measuring glass is suitable. Do not remove the fuel pipe or electrical connections. Take the HT lead out of the coil so that the engine may not start and tie it away safely so that it cannot spark. Now operate the starter. This test should be done with a cold engine. The valve will spray fuel into the measuring glass for up to 8 seconds. The spray should be uniform and cone shaped. Switch off, wipe the nozzle dry and check that no drops of fuel form on the nozzle within one minute. If it is faulty it will be necessary to fit a new one.

Thermotime switch - description and checking

60 This unit is screwed into the coolant system. If you have trouble finding it follow the lead from the cold start valve. It has a plug connector covered by a rubber grommet. A cross-section is shown in

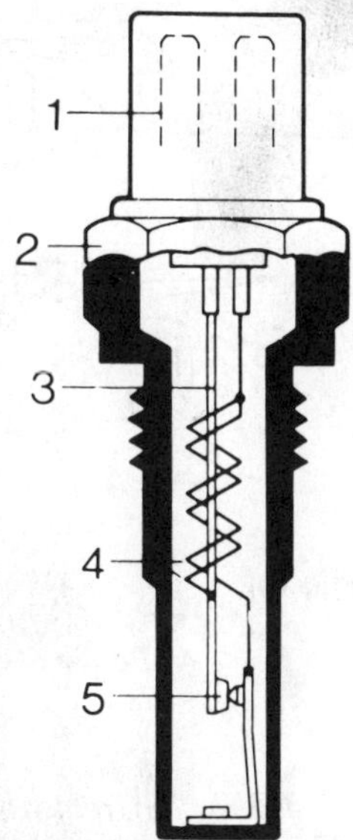

Fig. 14.136 Sectional view of thermotime switch

1 *Electrical connections*
2 *Switch body*
3 *Bi-metallic strip*
4 *Resistance coil*
5 *Contact point*

Fig. 14.137 Location of thermotime switch (arrowed)

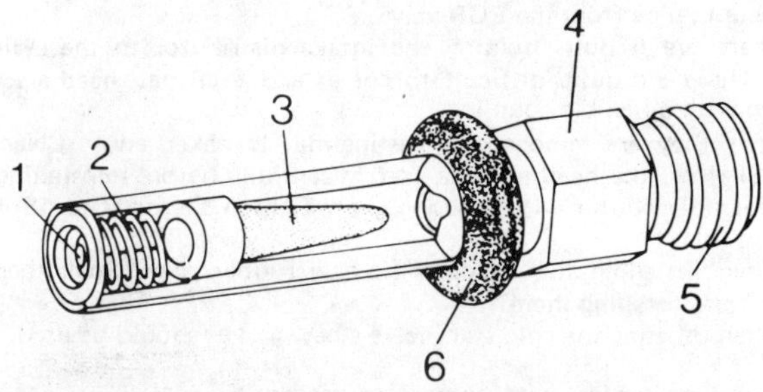

Fig. 14.138 Cutaway view of a fuel injector

1 *Pin*
2 *Spring*
3 *Filter*
4 *Injector body*
5 *Connector*
6 *Sealing ring*

Fig. 14.136. The bi-metallic strip is heated by the temperature of the switch body being raised by warm coolant and by an electric resistance supplied with current during the starting operation. When the engine is cold the electric heater takes as long as 8 seconds to open the switch. When the coolant is hot this may be reduced and above 95°F (35°C) the switch should be open at all times. It follows then that the test must be done with a cold engine. The test is simple enough, remove the centre lead from the HT coil and tie it away safely. The starter may now be operated without the engine firing. Take the plug off the cold start valve and bridge the plug connectors with a voltmeter or a test lamp, ie: the voltmeter or lamp takes the place of the cold start valve. Get someone to operate the starter and check carefully how long the starter operates before the test lamp goes out or the voltmeter shows no reading. At this point the switch opens. If it is longer than 8 seconds the switch should be renewed. Be careful about the temperature at which the test is done. If it is above 95°F (35°C) the switch should not close at all. If it does, then it is defective and you will be flooding a warm engine, with resultant starting troubles. Both the cold start valve and the thermo-switch are supplied with current from terminal '50' of the starter circuit.

Fuel injectors - description and checking

61 A cutaway view of an injector is shown in Fig. 14.138. It will be seen that each injector is fitted with a filter and a vibrator pin to ensure clean atomised fuel only is injected. The pin and spring close the injector when the engine is shot off and ensure residual pressure at the fuel line between the injector and the fuel distributor. This ensures easy starting.

62 The injector is held in the inlet manifold by a rubber bushing. It may be pulled out of the bushing to check its operation. The injector may not be dismantled further and if defective must be renewed.

63 The operating pressure is between 35 and 48 psi (2.5 and 3.5 kg/sq cm). It is not possible to check this unless special equipment can be obtained; if this can be done the opening pressures of the four injectors should not vary by more than 8.5 psi (0.6 kg/sq cm).

64 More important is the quantity injected per minute and the shape of the spray. To check this properly four measuring glasses are required, each of 100 cc capacity. Pull the injectors out of the manifold and arrange for them to be held vertically, each one over a measuring glass. This is a bit tricky as there is not much room, but it can be done. The air cleaner must be removed so that you can get at the sensor plate in the venturi if you are going to run the pump independent of the engine, or alternatively you can remove the spark plugs and distributor centre lead and turn the engine with the starter motor. In the latter case the cold start valve must be rendered inoperative or you will have petrol in the manifold. The injector holes must be plugged too, or the sensor plate may not lift sufficiently to operate the injectors. Whichever way you do it, the idea is to get the pump running and to lift the sensor plate sufficiently to cause the injectors to squirt fuel. Keep them squirting until one of the glasses contains 100 cc of fuel. Close the sensor plate or switch off and check that after 15 seconds there are no drops of fuel on the injectors. While the injectors are spraying fuel check that each one has a symmetrical cone shaped spray and that all four are the same shape.

65 At the end of the test the lowest level must be more than 85 cc, ie: the difference between the full glass and the lowest level is not more than 15 cc. If this fault is present change the injectors on the two lines with the widest variation and repeat the test. If the same injector shows low on the second test then that injector is faulty. If the same fuel line shows low on the second test then the fuel distributor is faulty.

66 The test we have just described is for the person who wants to know that everything is correct. If the engine is running roughly there is an easier test to determine that all the injectors are at least functioning. Pull the injector out of No 1 cylinder and plug the hole. Hold the injector in a measuring glass. Start the engine and let it idle roughly on three injectors. Check that the injector in the measuring glass is giving a symmetrical cone shaped spray. Switch off, and wait 15 seconds. The injector must not drip fuel. Repeat the test with each injector in turn.

67 When refitting the injectors, moisten the rubber seal with a drop of fuel and press the injector firmly. The injector may be removed from the fuel line. When fitting a new one tighten the joint to 18 lbf ft (2.5 kgf m).

68 Inspect the seals carefully before refitting the injectors. If they are hard, cracked, or distorted, renew them. Clean out the hole carefully, and soak the new seal in fuel for ten minutes before installing it.

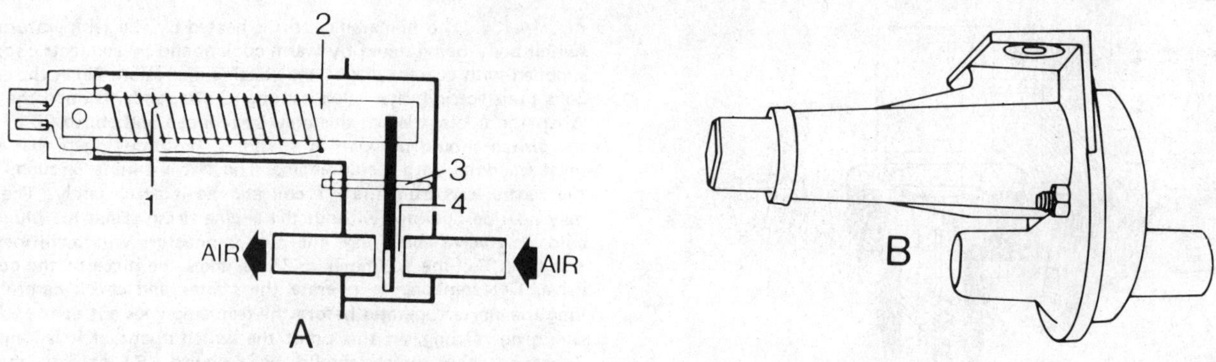

Fig. 14.139 Auxiliary air regulator - cross-section (A) and profile (B)

1 Heating resistance *2 Bi-metallic strip* *3 Pivot* *4 Rotary disc valve*

Flexible fuel lines - removal and refitting

69 More trouble accrues from misguided attempts to fit new plastic fuel lines than is realized. If the fuel line is damaged or old age has brought cracks and leaks it must be renewed.

70 In order to remove the old line from a banjo or similar joint the plastic must be heated at the connection point. Make sure that the fuel line is drained completely. **Do not** use a blowlamp or a naked flame, warm the plastic with a soldering iron until the plastic may be pulled off. **Do not** cut the joint away, you will damage the cone of the joint and thereby create a permanent leak.

71 Now you have to fit the new line. This must be done cold. The tube should be gripped in a suitable circular clamp with the lip of the tube required to cover the metal of the joint protruding. Push the tube on cold until it is fully in position and leave it. **Never** reassemble a joint that has been removed, fit a new line.

72 The VW organisation has a special clamp for holding the tube on installation, VW P385.

Auxiliary air regulator - description and checking

73 When the engine is cold and the throttle is closed the engine will stall unless provision for a richer mixture than normal is made. This is provided by an air bypass round the throttle valve controlled by a rotary gate valve which closes gradually as the engine warms up. Thus there is an increased airflow and the sensor plate moves, operating the valve in the fuel distributor and increasing the supply of fuel to the injectors. Under normal starting conditions the rotary valve is closed completely in about five minutes and the system reverts to normal control. It is so arranged that there is little difference in the idle speed whether the engine is cold or warm.

74 The unit is known as the auxiliary air regulator. Refer to Fig. 14.123 and it will be seen that the unit is bolted to the side of the air intake. Hoses lead from both sides to the air intake system. A cross-sectional view is shown at Fig. 14.139. The heating coil causes the bi-metallic strip to bend, turning the rotary valve on the pivot so that the hole in the disc is moved away from the inlet and outlet tube orifices, preventing the passage of air. When the ignition is switched off the heating coil cools and the valve opens again.

75 Testing of this important unit is simple. While the engine is cold remove both hoses from the unit and using a lamp and a mirror check visually that there is a clean passage through the valve. Refit the hoses and start the engine. Run the engine until it is warm. Pinch one of the hoses while the engine is idling. If the gate has closed the idle speed should not change. If you are not sure stop the engine, pull off the hoses quickly and look through the valve again.

76 If the valve has not closed pull off the electrical plug from the auxiliary air regulator, bridge the plug connectors with a voltmeter, switch the ignition on and check that voltage is present. If there is a no-volt reading the trouble is in the wiring system or the relays. If there is a reading then use an ohmmeter to check the resistance of the heater element. It should be 30 ohms. If the resistance is infinity there is an open-circuit; zero, then there is a short-circuit. In any case a variation from 30 ohms indicates that there is a fault and the unit must be renewed.

Throttle valve housing - description, removal and refitting

77 Refer to Fig. 14.123. The housing is bolted to the air intake distributor. On the other end of it a clamp fastens the black plastic air conducting casing. Inside the housing the throttle valves are mounted on vertical axes. There are two air passages, each with a throttle valve in it. The valve spindles are parallel and protrude through the housing at the top. Each has an operating lever. The throttle cable moves the left-hand valve and the interlock on the top moves the second throttle. The relationship is fixed and there is no adjustment. The accelerator cable linkage is carried on the top of the housing, and just next to the boss for the linkage on the conductor casing side is a boss with a screw in it. This is the idle adjustment crew. Inside the housing wall are drillings leading from one side of the throttle valves to the other to allow air to bypass the throttle for idling. This drilling passage is interrupted by the end of the idle adjustment screw, so that the amount of air passing may be regulated by screwing the screw in or out.

78 To remove the housing, unclip the air cleaner so that the air sensor and conducting casing may be moved. Disconnect the clamp holding the conducting duct to the throttle housing and ease the duct away a little. Undo the throttle cable from the lever and disconnect the auxiliary air valve hoses. Remove the four bolts holding the housing to the air intake distributor and take the housing away.

79 Refitting is the reverse of removal. It would be wise to fit a new gasket. Tighten the bolts to 15 lbf ft (2 kgf m).

Air intake distributor - removal and refitting

80 This should only be necessary if the cylinder head is to be removed with the engine in the car.

81 Remove the throttle valve housing, as described above. It will not be necessary to undo the accelerator cable or the air conducting casing.

82 Remove the four injectors as described previously. Remove the cold start valve and the auxiliary air valve. Label all the hoses as you remove them for ease of refitting. Where applicable remove the EGR pipe and the vacuum pipe from the EGR valve.

83 There are 6 bolts holding the intake distributor to the cylinder head. These are quite difficult to get at and you may need a socket wrench with a flexible coupling.

84 Once they are removed the casting may be taken away. Clean the old gasket off the head and the casting carefully before reinstalling the air intake distributor with a new gasket. Tighten the bolts to 18 lbf ft (2.5 kgf m).

85 When installing the injectors fit new rubber rings. Soak these in fuel before installing them.

86 When refitting the cold start valve a new gasket should be used.

Accelerator cables - fitting and adjustment

87 There are two kinds of cable, one for the manual gearbox model, and a double one for the automatic gearbox. The fitting and adjusting of the cable for the automatic gearbox is described in Section 8.

88 To adjust the throttle cable on the manual transmission model, first push the accelerator pedal onto its stop and hold it there with a heavy weight. Then go to the engine compartment and slacken the

Fig. 14.140 Throttle cable adjustment point (arrowed) on fuel injection system

Fig. 14.141 Idle speed screw (arrowed) on fuel injection system

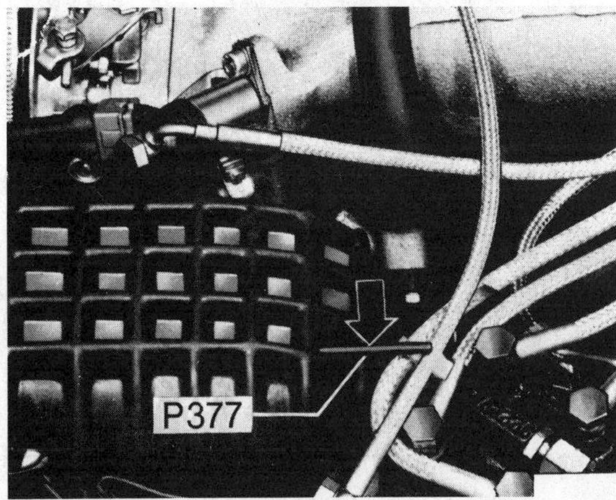

Fig. 14.142 Adjusting mixture (CO) with VW tool P377 (arrowed)

Fig. 14.143 Diverter valve hose connection plugged (arrowed)

bolt which clamps the throttle cable inner wire to the throttle valve actuating arm. Move the clamp on the wire so that both throttle valves are fully open, but only just. Tighten the clamp bolt. Operate the accelerator pedal three times and check that there is just 1 mm of play at the throttle lever when the pedal is hard on the stop. The pedal-to-stop distance should be 95.0 mm.

89 The purpose of this check is to make sure that the throttle opens fully, but that the pedal is on the stop at that point. If the throttles are fully open before the pedal reaches the stop, pressure on the pedal will tend to open the valves further and strain the whole mechanism.

Running adjustments for the fuel injection system

90 There are two adjustments, idle speed and CO content. Before attempting these check the ignition timing, dwell angle, plug gaps, valve clearances, and make sure that all the components of the fuel injection system are operating correctly. It will be necessary to fit a suitable tachometer to the engine and you will need VW Tool P377 or a long 3 mm Allen key to turn the CO content adjuster. A CO content tester (exhaust gas analyser) is also required.

91 Run the engine up to normal operating temperature. The engine oil should be at temperature 120 to 160°F (50 to 70°C). Load the engine with a light load by turning on the headlamps at high beam to load the alternator, and switching on the air conditioner or fan heater. Disconnect the radiator cooling fan.

92 Turn the idle speed screw (Fig. 14.141) until the engine speed is between 850 and 1000 rpm.

93 There is a small rubber plug on the top of the air sensor housing by the side of the fuel distributor. Pull this out and fit the Allen key into the adjusting screw on the air sensor arm (see Fig. 14.142). If the car is fitted with an evaporative emission system disconnect the hose that goes between the activated charcoal canister and the air cleaner. If the emission control system incorporates an air pump, disconnect the air pump-to-diverter valve hose and plug or cap the valve opening (Fig. 14.143).

94 Connect the exhaust gas analyser to the power source and push the probe into the exhaust system tailpipe. This holds good for all models except models sold in California, where the probe should go into the special port in the exhaust pipe just in front of the catalytic converter.

95 A word of warning here. There may be a small notice on the casing by the MacPherson strut which will give acceptable levels for CO, but find out from your local agent what the current level is, or you may adjust the CO content to an illegal value. These limits are changing all the while.

96 To lower the CO content screw the adjuster out. To raise it screw it in. Remove the key, accelerate the engine a little and read the meter. **Do not** accelerate with the key in position or you will bend something.

97 When turning the adjusting screw try not to push down (the sensor arm bearings are delicate): ease the key out gently.

98 When the CO content is correct check the idling speed and readjust if necessary. A small adjustment should not alter the CO content.

99 Refit the rubber plug and the emission hose to the air cleaner and reconnect the cooling fan. Also reconnect the air pump hose (where applicable).

Fuel injection electrical circuits - description and testing

100 Two circuit diagrams are included at Figs. 14.144 and 14.145. These are for cars fitted with an air sensor switch. The first one shows the relays and switches when the ignition is turned on and the starter operated. It will be seen that the switch on the airflow sensor is closed and current is supplied to the control relay (15 amp, green dot) from the ignition switch (terminal 15 to terminal 85). The control relay operates and terminal 87 connects with 30/51.

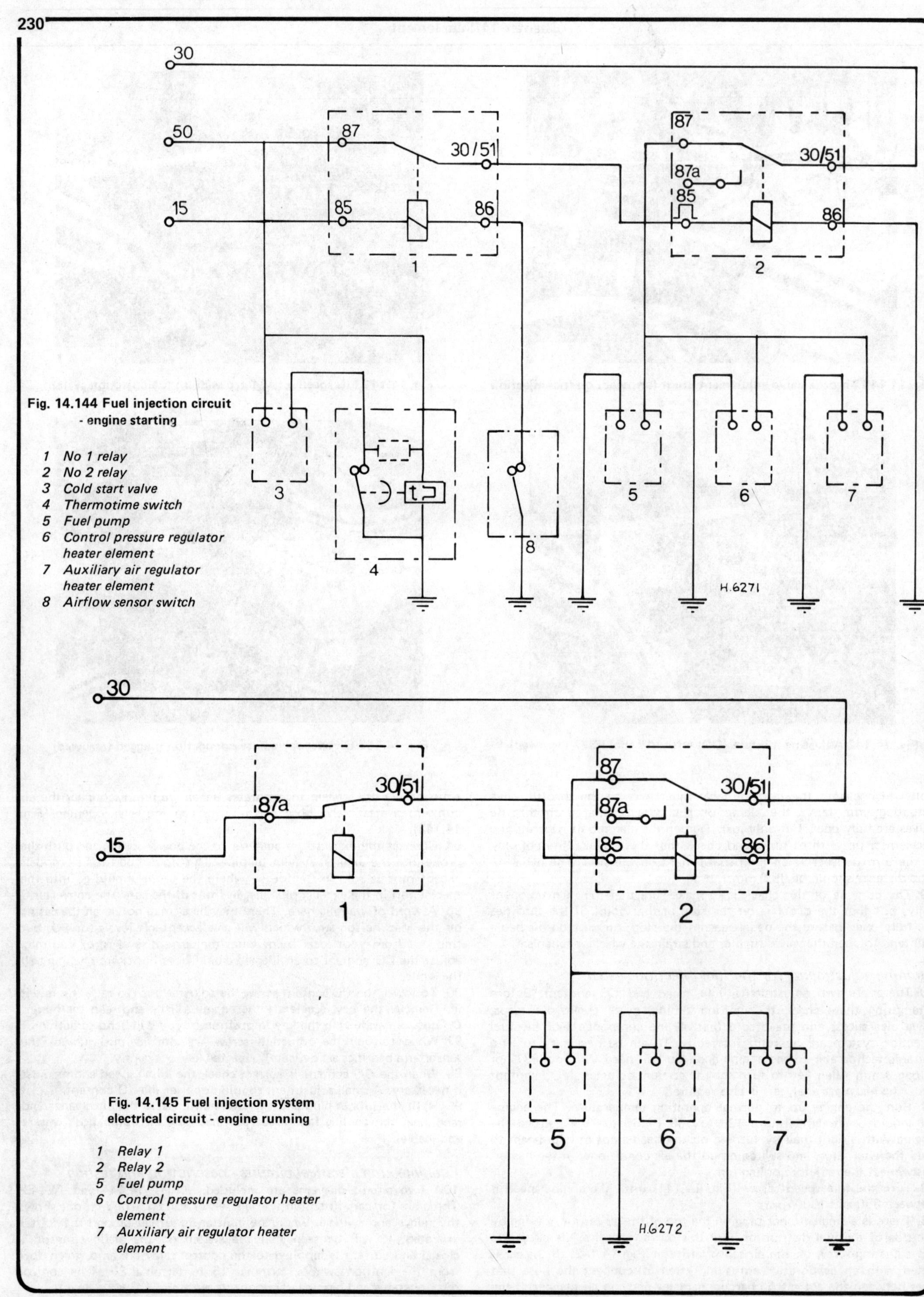

Fig. 14.144 Fuel injection circuit - engine starting

1. No 1 relay
2. No 2 relay
3. Cold start valve
4. Thermotime switch
5. Fuel pump
6. Control pressure regulator heater element
7. Auxiliary air regulator heater element
8. Airflow sensor switch

Fig. 14.145 Fuel injection system electrical circuit - engine running

1. Relay 1
2. Relay 2
5. Fuel pump
6. Control pressure regulator heater element
7. Auxiliary air regulator heater element

101 Current flows from terminal 50 through terminal 85 of 'No 2' relay, (the pump relay, 20 amp, yellow dot). Terminal 86 of relay '2' is earthed so the relay operates. The current from terminal 30 is thus passed to the fuel pump control pressure regulator and auxiliary air regulator.

102 As the starter operates the air sensor moves and opens the air sensor switch. Relay '1' is now switched off and relay '2' receives current through relay '1' from terminal 15 (the ignition switch) via terminal 87a.

103 In 1976 some of the vehicles dispense with the air sensor switch but both relays '321 906 059A' and 'B' (with and without sensor switch) have a 16 amp fuse mounted on the top of the relay which is inserted in the terminal 87 (pump) to terminal 30 (battery) line.

104 On vehicles without the air sensor switch the relay is activated via the ignition coil during starting and running. Diagrams of the relay connections are given in Fig. 14.146.

105 The whole idea of this elaborate procedure is to prevent the pump from running and flooding the engine if the ignition is turned on and the engine not started. For this reason, when performing tests which require the ignition to be turned on but the engine not to be started, on the older vehicles, disconnect the plug at the air sensor switch and the '+ve' wire to the alternator (this is in case the sensor plate has stuck in the open position). On the vehicles without air sensor switches if it is wished to run the pump while the engine is stationary, take the relay off the board and bridge the terminals L13 and L14 on the board with a wire and a 16 amp fuse.

106 On models equipped with an air sensor switch, the pump relay (321 906 059A) has a contact for the airflow sensor and has six connectors. The wires to the airflow sensor and starter terminal 50 to pump relay 50 are discontinued on the modified version (suffix 059B) and the line A3 on the relay plate is connected to the coil terminal 1 instead of the air flow sensor switch (blue 0.5 mm^2 wire).

107 To check the pump relay it is necessary to remove the shelf. Remove the relay and bridge contacts L13 and 14 with a wire and an 8 amp fuse. The pump should then work.

108 To check the fuel pump, first take the HT wire from the centre of the ignition coil and tie it back out of the way (this will prevent the engine from firing) and then disconnect the union in the fuel return line. The short part on the airflow sensor is the one to use. Stick the end of this in a 1000 cc measuring glass and operate the starter for 30 seconds. The pump must deliver fuel at the rate given in the Specifications.

Fault diagnosis - Fuel injection system

109 Before you do anything to the fuel injection system, check that the ignition system is functioning correctly and the valve clearances are correct. Check the ignition timing and the dwell angle; ensure that the spark plugs are clean and correctly gapped, that the battery is fully charged and that there is fuel in the tank.

110 Inspect all the hoses and electrical connections and clean any dirt or grease from the components before you attempt to do anything to them. If you allow any dirt to get into the system the result could be horribly expensive.

111 A tachometer, voltmeter, ohmmeter and a pressure gauge, zero to 100 psi (7 kg/sq cm), are required, plus the use of an exhaust gas analyser, if the system is to be checked completely. However, much can be done with just a test lamp and an ohmmeter.

112 Get a notebook and pencil and write down what you do in the order you do it, and what the result was. If in the end you have to go to the VW agent for help he will then know what has been checked and may save valuable time.

113 Start with the electrical system. Is the pump running, are all the connections to the cold start valve, thermo time-switch, control pressure regulator and so on supplied with the correct voltage? Check the various heater elements to see that the resistance is correct, or at least that they are working. A fault finding chart is given below as a suggestion of the more common problems. In the third column a possible remedy is suggested. Read the sub-Section on that component before doing anything about it. Work methodically.

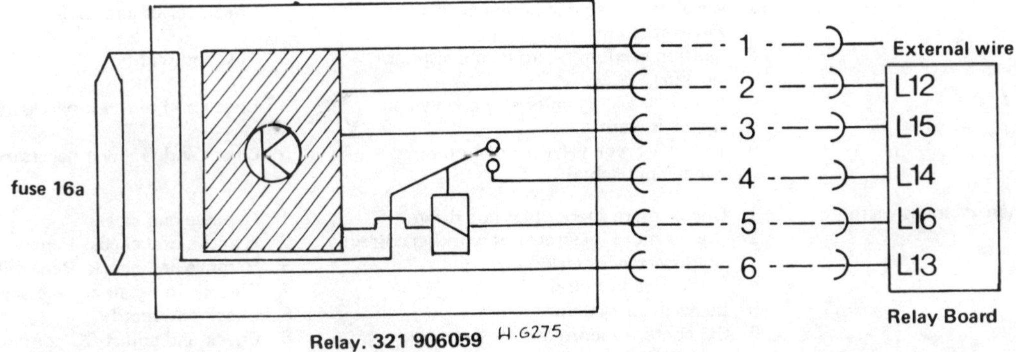

Fig. 14.146 Fuel pump relay connections

Up to chassis 8462042542	Line	After chassis 8462042542
Terminal 50 from starter	*1*	*Discontinued*
Terminal 31B air sensor contact	*2*	*Terminal 1 ignition coil*
Terminal 31 to earth	*3*	*Terminal 31 to earth*
Terminal 87 to fuel pump	*4*	*Terminal 87 to fuel pump*
Terminal 15 from ignition switch	*5*	*Terminal 15 from ignition switch*
Terminal 30 from battery	*6*	*Terminal 30 from battery*

Fault diagnosis - fuel injection system

Symptom	Possible reason	Remedy
Engine will not start from cold (ignition checked for correct operation)	1 Battery flat 2 Thermotime switch not working 3 Cold start valve not operating correctly 4 Auxiliary air valve stuck in the closed position 5 Filter choked and/or damaged	1 Check and charge battery 2 Check and renew if necessary 3 Check and renew if necessary 4 Check visually. Renew if necessary 5 Check that fuel is coming through it

Symptom	Possible reason	Remedy
	6 Fuel pump not working	6 Check electrical connections, short out relay and check, check fuse
	7 Sensor plate stuck in down position or will not lift	7 Check sensor plate and control plunger for operation. Adjust as necessary
	8 Air leaks in air supply	8 Check all clamps and air joints. Tighten if loose
	9 Control pressure regulator not working	9 Check heater unit, renew if necessary
	10 Fuel pressure too low to open injectors	10 Check operation of pressure relief valve in the fuel distributor. Renew if necessary
Engine starts from cold but difficult or impossible to start from hot (ignition checked for correct operation)	1 Cold start valve operating continuously or leaking	1 Check cold start valve and thermotime switch. Renew if necessary
	2 Control pressure regulator valve not closing	2 Check control pressure regulator with engine warm. Renew regulator
	3 No residual pressure, or vapour lock in system	3 Check fuel pump check valve. Check operation of accumulator. Check injectors. Renew if necessary
	4 Sensor plate incorrectly adjusted	4 Check sensor plate and adjust if necessary
	5 Control plunger in fuel distributor sticking	5 Check control plunger. Fit new fuel distributor if necessary
	6 Auxiliary air regulator valve not closing	6 Check auxiliary air regulator. Renew if necessary
	7 CO content too low	7 Check idle and CO content. Renew fuel distributor if necessary
Engine starts but stalls when idling (ignition checked for correct operation)	1 Auxiliary air regulator stuck in the closed position for a cold engine, or open for a hot engine	1 Check and renew if necessary
	2 For warm engine, cold start valve operating or leaking	2 Check valve and thermotime switch, renew if necessary
	3 CO value too low	3 Adjust CO and idle speed
	4 Control pressure regulator faulty	4 Check and renew if necessary
	5 EGR valve does not close at idle (when applicable)	5 Check and renew if necessary
Idle speed too high or engine hunts at idle	1 CO content incorrect	1 Check CO content and adjust
	2 Accelerator cable jamming or throttle valves sticking	2 Check valves and cable
	3 Ignition vacuum retard mechanism not working	3 Test and rectify
	4 Auxiliary air regulator still open when engine is warm	4 Check and renew if necessary
	5 Vacuum check valve is open on servo (when applicable)	5 Check and renew if necessary
Idle speed rough when engine is warm	1 One or more spark plugs not firing	1 Remove and clean
	2 One or more injectors not working correctly	2 Remove and check. Renew if necessary
	3 Cold start valve leaking	3 Remove and check. Renew if necessary
	4 EGR valve not closing	4 Check and repair as necessary
	5 Leaks in air system	5 Check and rectify
	6 CO content incorrect	6 Check and adjust CO content and idle speed
Engine does not accelerate uniformly (flat spots)	1 Check ignition timing and advance and retard mechanism, check dwell angle	1 Adjust as necessary
	2 Sensor plate or control plunger sticking	2 Check and adjust as necessary
	3 Injectors not working correctly	3 Check and renew if necessary
	4 Leaks in air system	4 Check all joints and correct as necessary
	5 Control pressure regulator defective	5 Check and renew if necessary
	6 Cold start valve leaking	6 Check and renew if necessary. Check thermotime switch
	7 Incorrect CO or idle adjustment	7 Check and adjust
Fuel consumption too high (ignition checked for correct adjustment)	1 Brakes binding	1 Check brake system and adjust if necessary
	2 Leaks in fuel system	2 Trace system and repair if necessary
	3 Control pressure regulator defective	3 Test and renew if necessary
	4 Cold start valve leaking	4 Check and renew cold start valve and/or thermotime switch
	5 Sensor plate or control plunger not moving freely	5 Check and adjust or renew
	6 Idle mixture or CO content incorrect	6 Check and adjust
	7 Catalytic converter blocked	7 Go to VW agent for service
Engine runs on when ignition is turned off	1 System pressure too high	1 Adjust system pressure by pressure relief valve
	2 Injectors leaking	2 Test and adjust
	3 Sensor plate sticking	3 Check and adjust

5D Emission control system

General description

1 A full emission control system is fitted to all North American models with either a carburettor or a fuel injection engine.

2 The system may be divided into three parts:

(a) The evaporative emission control system, dealing with the fumes from the crankcase and the fuel tank
(b) The exhaust gas recirculation system. This has been modified extensively from the system used with the 1500 cc engine described in Chapter 3
(c) The catalytic converter. This unit, which is located in the exhaust system promotes the burning of CO and HC emissions. The system is mainly confined to California and may be used only with lead-free fuel

Evaporative emission control system - description and maintenance

3 This system is divided into two sections, PCV (positive crankcase ventilation) and fuel tank venting. There are no moving parts and the only part which may need renewal under normal usage is the charcoal-filled filter of the fuel tank venting. It should be noted that there is not a vent valve in the filler cap.

4 The PCV system consists of a tube going from the engine to the air cleaner via a plastic oil separator. Fumes from the crankcase are sucked into the air cleaner and burned in the engine. Oil vapour and droplets are trapped in the separator and return to the sump when the engine is stationary. The only maintenance is to remove the hose if it seems to be soaked with oil and clean and dry it, or renew it. It is best to examine it externally when you service the air cleaner, and to service it when overhauling the cylinder head.

5 The fuel tank venting system is not easy to check. If the tank is removed be careful to reinstall the pipe from the top of the tank without twists or kinks. Inside the tank is a small expansion chamber which is an integral part of the tank. This takes care of temperature changes and consequent expansion of the fuel volume and surging in the tank. A pipe from this goes to the activated charcoal filter via a fuel vapour restrictor. The filter is located in the engine compartment, usually on the left-hand side. The fume-laden air passes through the filter where the hydrocarbon content is deposited on the charcoal. When the engine is stationary, the clean air seeps out to atmosphere. When the engine is running, a pipe from the air cleaner sucks fresh air through the filter removing the hydrocarbons from the filter and thus burning them in the engine. The filter should be changed every 50 000 miles (80 000 km).

EGR system (Californian models with carburettor) - description and testing

6 As mentioned in Chapter 3, the EGR system on Californian models incorporates an air injection system (AIS) to further reduce emission of hydrocarbons and carbon monoxide.

7 A simplified plan of the EGR system is shown in Fig. 14.147.

8 The following checks and adjustments are additional to those in Chapter 3.

EGR - first stage check

9 With the engine idling, pull the vacuum hose from the EGR valve (Fig. 14.149).

10 Pull the vacuum hose from the anti-backfire valve and attach it to the EGR valve in place of the hose previously disconnected. The idle speed should now drop. If it does not, then the EGR valve filter is blocked, the valve is faulty or the return line blocked. The EGR valve can be cleaned (Fig. 14.151).

EGR - second stage check

11 With the engine idling, operate the microswitch which is located on the throttle valve. The idle speed should drop or the engine stall. If it does not, then the EGR valve or microswitch is faulty, the two-way valve is faulty, or the EGR filter or return line may be blocked.

Anti-backfire valve-check

12 Disconnect the hose from the anti-backfire valve.

13 Start the engine and rev it up momentarily, then let the throttle snap shut. Using the finger, check that a vacuum can be felt at the hose opening on the anti-backfire valve for a period of between 1 and 3 seconds. If not apparent, the valve is faulty or the hoses are blocked or kinked.

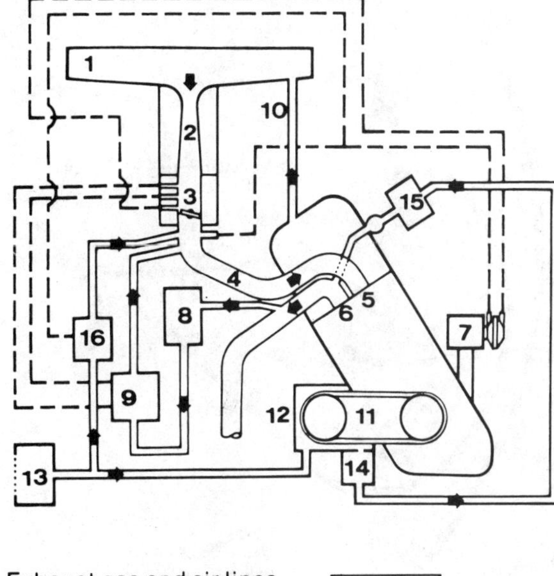

Fig. 14.147 Emission control system with air pump (carburettor models)

1 Air cleaner
2 Carburettor venturi
3 Carburettor throttle valve
4 Intake manifold
5 Cylinder head intake
6 Cylinder head exhaust
7 Dual vacuum unit ignition distributor
8 EGR filter
9 EGR valve
10 Crankcase vent
11 Air pump drivebelt
12 Air pump
13 Air pump filter
14 Pressure relief valve
15 Check valve
16 Anti-backfire valve

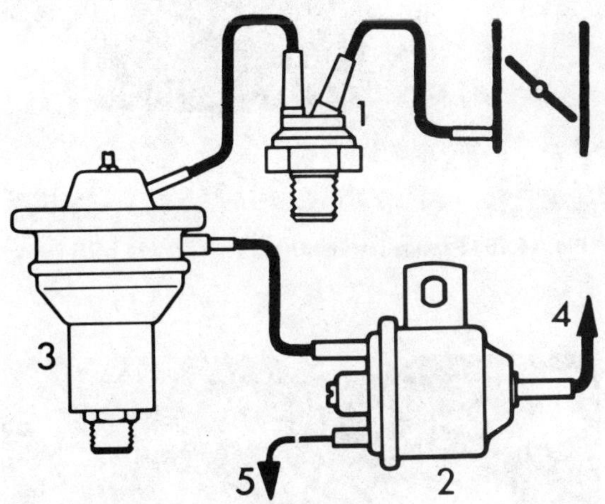

Fig. 14.148 EGR system circuit

1 Temperature valve
2 Two-way valve
3 EGR valve
4 To brake servo
5 Wire to throttle valve in microswitch

Diverter valve - check

14 Pull the vacuum hose from the diverter valve.

15 Connect the vacuum hose of the anti-backfire valve to the diverter valve.

16 Start the engine and allow it to idle.

17 There should be airflow at the diverter valve silencer. If not, the air pump is faulty, the pump filter is clogged, the diverter valve is

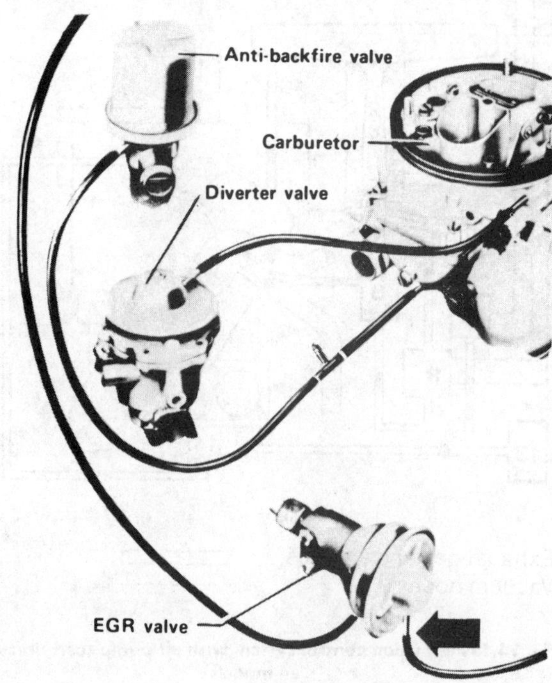

Fig. 14.149 EGR first stage check - disconnect arrowed hose

Fig. 14.151 Passage (arrowed) to be cleaned in EGR valve

Fig. 14.153 Diverter valve check

1 Diverter valve hose *2 Anti-backfire valve hose*

Fig. 14.150 Throttle valve microswitch (arrowed)

Fig. 14.152 Anti-backfire valve hose connector (arrowed)

Fig. 14.154 Protractor on primary (1st stage) throttle valve spindle

faulty or the connecting hoses are clogged.

Throttle valve microswitch - adjusting

18 Detach the automatic choke housing from the carburettor, but leave the coolant hoses attached.

19 Remove the idler arm nut from the throttle valve spindle and attach a protractor.

20 Check that the throttle valve is closed and set the protractor to zero.

21 Open the throttle slowly and check that the microswitch is heard to click at the following valve plate openings as indicated on the protractor:

Manual transmission - 30° and 67°
Automatic transmission - 23° and 63°

Fig. 14.155 Air pump check valve (arrowed)

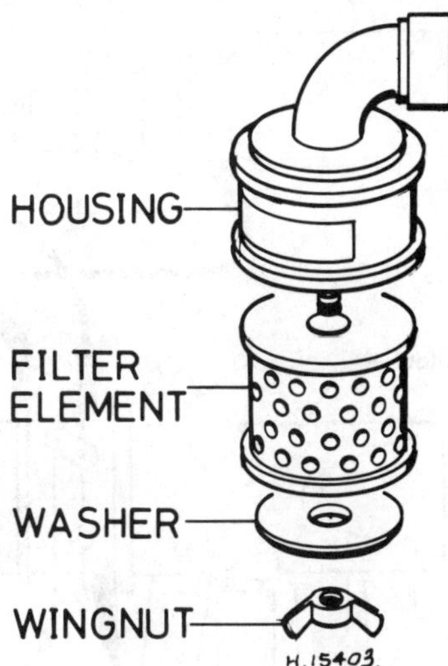

Fig. 14.156 Air pump air filter

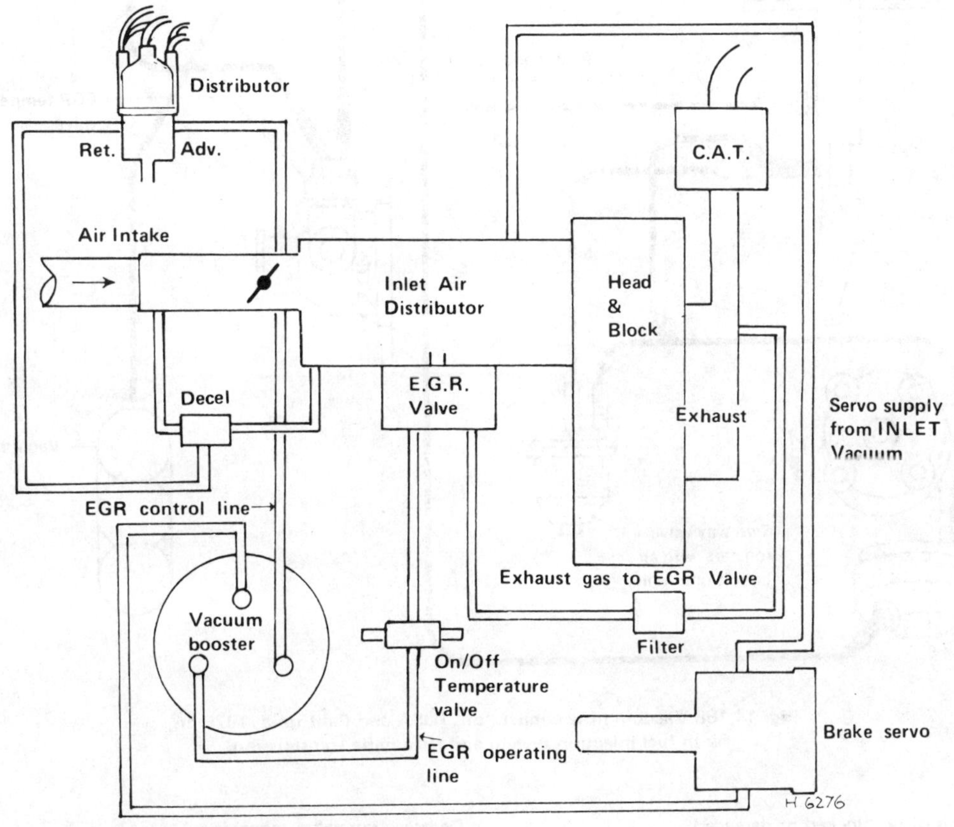

Fig. 14.157 Schematic of typical EGR system used with fuel injection system

22 Where necessary, adjust by moving the position of the microswitch.

Air pump - checking and servicing

23 To test the air pump, disconnect the hose from the check valve and plug or cap the opening in the valve.

24 With the engine idling, check that virtually no air is being emitted from the open end of the hose. If this is not the case, then the air pump is faulty, the drivebelt is slipping or the pump filter is clogged.

25 Check and tension the drivebelt for the air pump at regular intervals and keep the intake air filter clean. Check all hoses for condition and security.

26 Renew the air pump air filter at the specified intervals. Do this by unscrewing the wing nut from the filter casing and extracting the element.

27 Clean out the filter casing before reassembling.

EGR system (fuel injection models) - description and testing

28 The EGR system on these vehicles varies according to operating territory and to whether the vehicle is equipped with an air conditioner. The following checks should be carried out at the recommended service intervals.

EGR valve - checking

29 With the engine at normal operating temperature and idling, pull the vacuum retard hose from the distributor and the vacuum hose from the EGR valve.

30 Connect the distributor vacuum retard hose to the EGR valve. The engine idle speed should drop or the engine should stall. If not, then

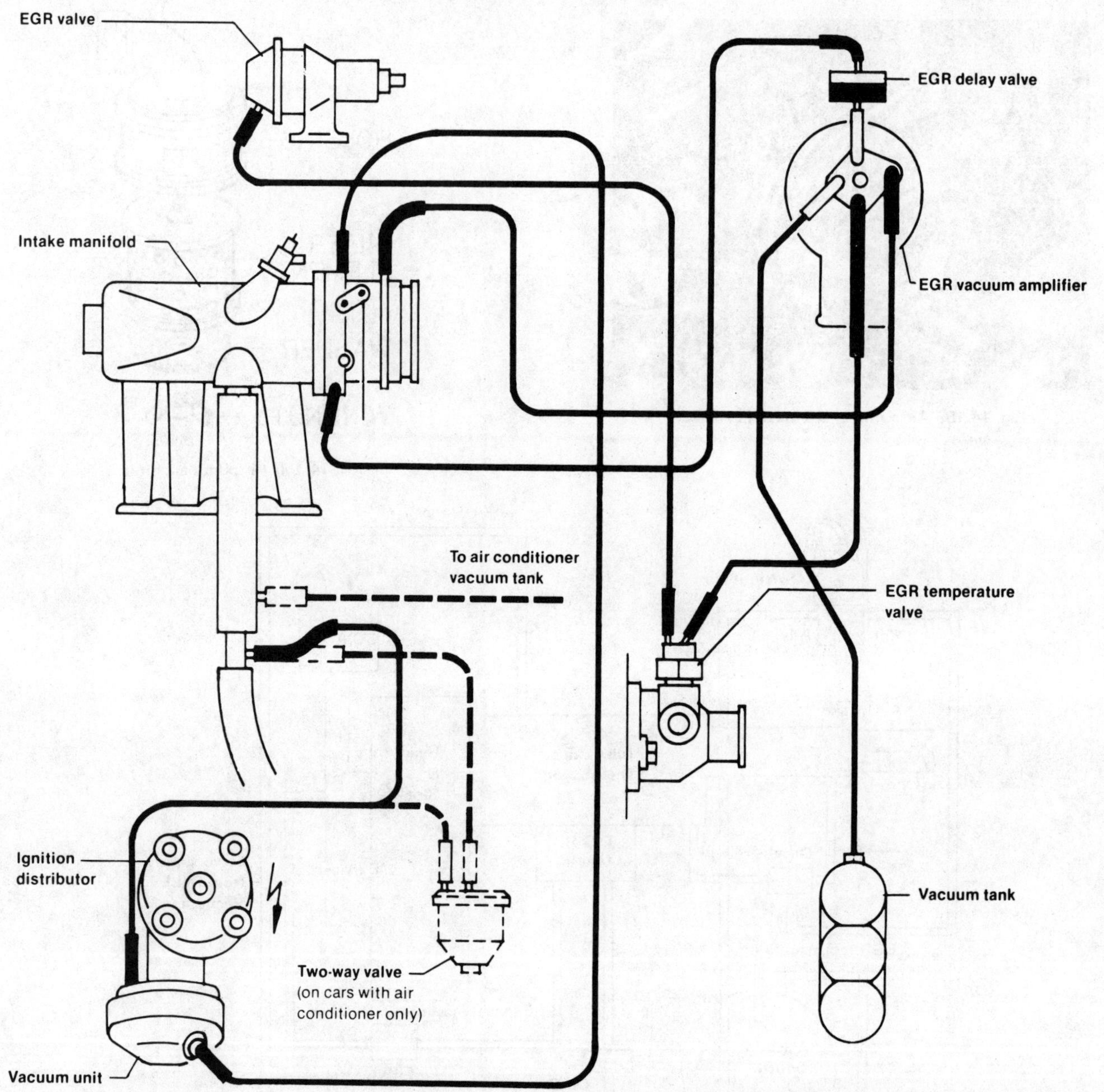

Fig. 14.158 Vacuum hose connections (USA and California, 1976 on, with fuel injection system and automatic transmission)

the EGR valve or hose is dirty, blocked or damaged.

EGR temperature valve - checking

31 With the engine at normal operating temperature and idling, insert a vacuum gauge between the EGR temperature valve and the EGR valve.

32 The vacuum gauge should indicate between 50 and 100 mm (2 and 4 in) Hg. If it does not, the valve is faulty and it should be renewed.

EGR delay valve - removal and refitting

33 If the delay valve is removed and refitted, make sure that the white cover of the valve is located as shown (Fig. 14.162).

Vacuum amplifier - checking

34 With the engine idling, connect a vacuum gauge between the vacuum amplifier and the throttle valve port. The gauge should indicate between 5 and 8 mm (0.2 and 0.3 in) Hg. If it does not, check the throttle valve port for obstruction.

35 Now connect the vacuum gauge between the amplifier and the temperature valve. The gauge should read between 50 and 100 mm (2 and 4 in) Hg. If it does not, renew the vacuum amplifier.

Deceleration valve - checking

36 Pull the hose from the deceleration valve and plug the hose.

37 Start the engine and run it for a few seconds at about 3000 rpm. Let the throttle snap closed and simultaneously use the finger to feel for vacuum at the valve connector. If vacuum is present, then the valve is serviceable.

38 Pull the vacuum hose from the T-piece and plug the T-piece. Start the engine and run it at about 3000 rpm. No vacuum should be felt at the hose connector on the deceleration valve. If it is, renew the valve.

Vent valve - checking

39 Remove the valve and blow into it at 'B'; no air should be emitted from 'C' (Fig. 14.166).

40 Start the engine and allow it to idle. Pull the vacuum hose from the distributor and connect it to 'A' on the vent valve. Now blow into 'B' of the valve, air should be emitted from 'C'.

Vacuum accumulator

41 Due to the vacuum characteristics of the fuel injection engine,

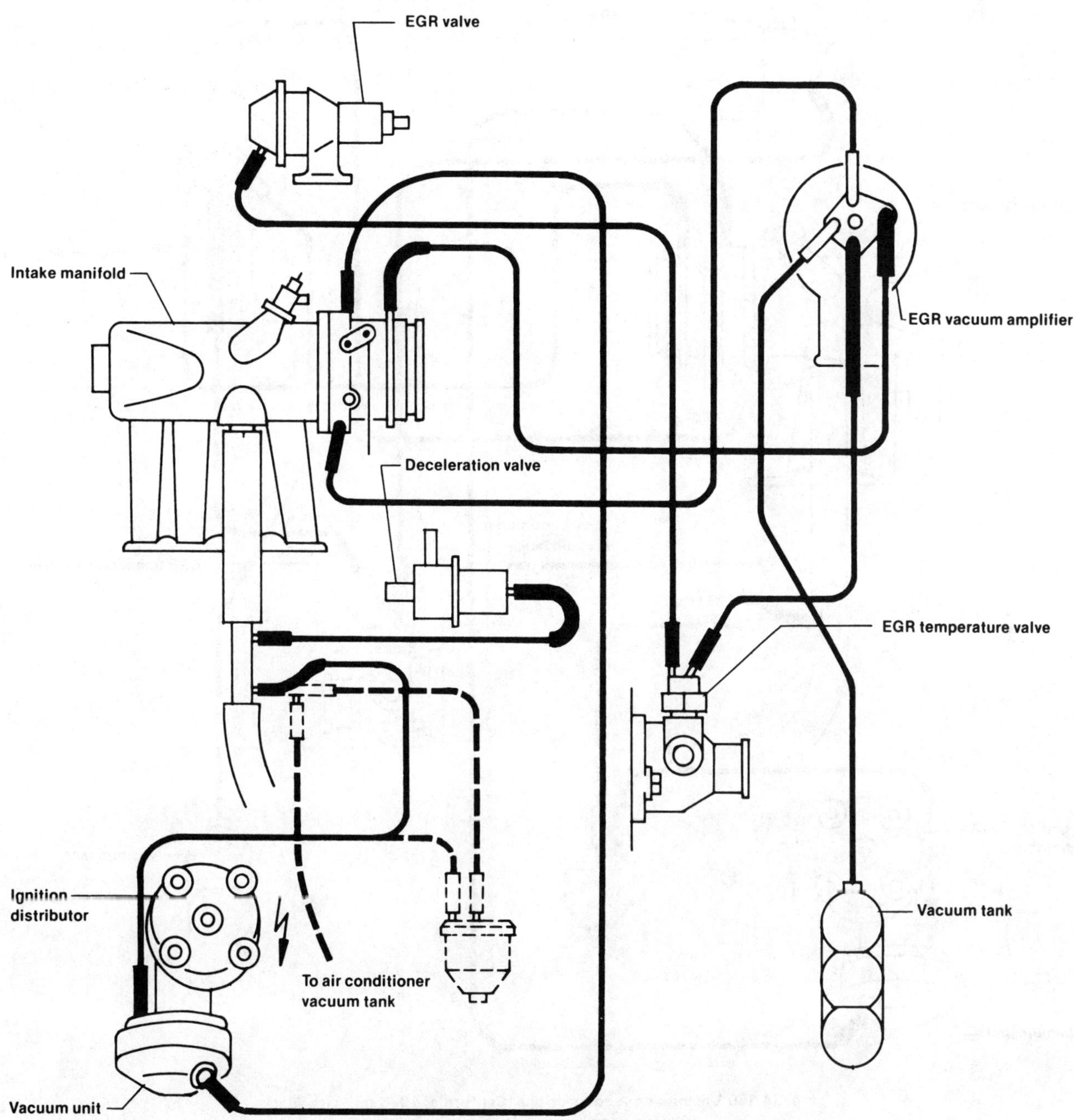

Fig. 14.159 Vacuum hose connections (USA except California, 1976 on, with fuel injection system and manual transmission)

some models use a vacuum accumulator (reservoir) in the emission control system. The accumulator is in the form of a metal tank located under the right-hand front wing.

EGR service indicator (elapsed mileage switch)

42 On some models, an indicator switch and warning lamp are fitted in order to remind the driver that maintenance of the system is due. When the service has been completed, press the white button on the switch to reset it (Fig. 14.168). The indicator lamp in the speedometer should go out.

Catalytic converter (Californian models) - description and maintenance

43 This unit is fitted to cars destined for California. It may be used on vehicles using lead-free fuel only and to this end the filler pipe of the fuel tank is made too small in diameter to admit the nozzles of station pumps other than those supplying lead-free fuel.

44 The converter is similar in appearance to a silencer (muffler). The case, made of stainless steel, is circular with tapered ends terminating in stout flanges, each with three connecting studs. There are no moving parts. Inside the tube is the element. This is constructed from ceramic moulded in the shape of a honeycomb and coated with platinum.

45 On the side of the casing is a temperature sensor. The electrical connection from this goes to a warning light on the vehicle dashboard. If the light flickers then the converter is overheated and steps must be taken to relieve the load on the engine and so reduce the amount of burning in the converter. If the light does not go out then the vehicle must be stopped and the converter allowed to cool before continuing. If this condition continues then the converter should be checked and

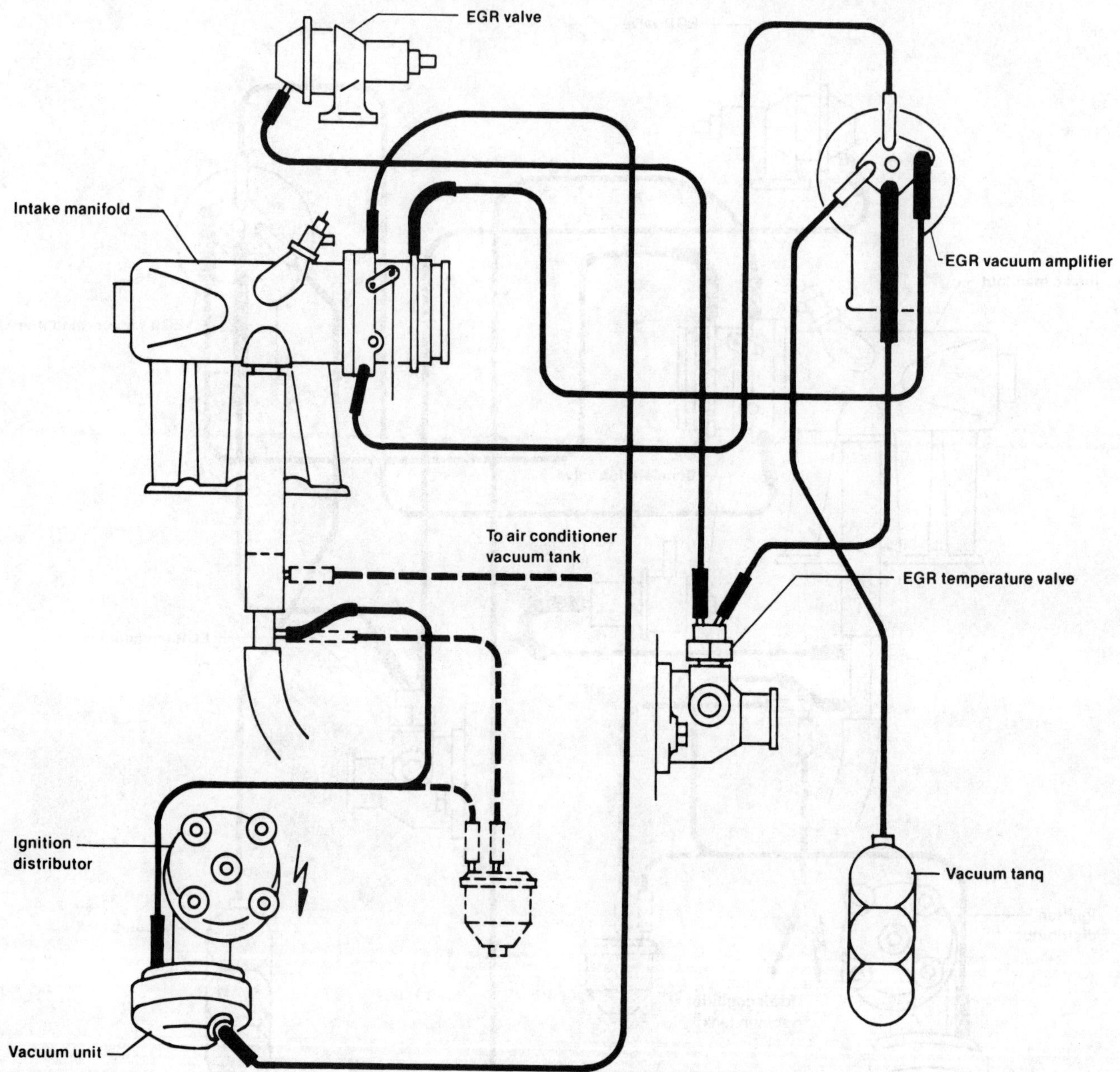

Fig. 14.160 Vacuum hose connections (California, 1976 on, with fuel injection system and manual transmission)

probably renewed.

46 If this unit is installed the engine must not be switched off while the vehicle is moving and in gear. Nor may tow or push starts be done, or any other action which may result in raw fuel being carried over into the exhaust system. Such a condition will court disaster.

47 Painting the car with underseal near the exhaust system, or parking over dry grass or bracken after a long run, should be avoided. The converter does get very hot and can easily start a fire under these conditions.

48 An elapsed mileage switch illuminates the warning light when the catalytic converter is due for routine renewal. The switch is located just below the EGR elapsed mileage switch (Fig. 14.168) and is reset in a similar manner.

49 Apart from the routine renewal due to the fact that the chemical life of the catalyst is complete, the warning light may be operated by an overheated converter due to the fact that the engine is out of tune. Incorrect ignition settings, too rich a fuel mixture, incorrect CO adjustment, and, if fitted, a faulty diverter valve in the air injection system will all cause the converter to overheat and operate the warning light. There is also the possibility of a faulty temperature sensor.

50 Whatever the reason, the converter must be removed from the system and checked. Handle the unit carefully, the ceramic is fragile. It should be possible to see through the unit. It is wise to use goggles to protect your eyes when doing this. There must be a free passage of air through the unit, and no undue deposit in the inlet to the unit. Unless it is completely clear the unit should be renewed.

51 If the CO content check of the fuel system will not adjust with the given limits then the converter should be No 1 suspect. A rattle in the exhaust system may well be due to a fractured ceramic unit.

52 Finally, do not worry if a system fitted with a converter has a soot-covered tailpipe. Under normal conditions a system without a converter will produce soot in the tailpipe only if the mixture is too rich, but such a deposit is normal for systems fitted with a converter.

53 When renewing the converter, make sure that the rest of the exhaust system is in good condition and correctly aligned.

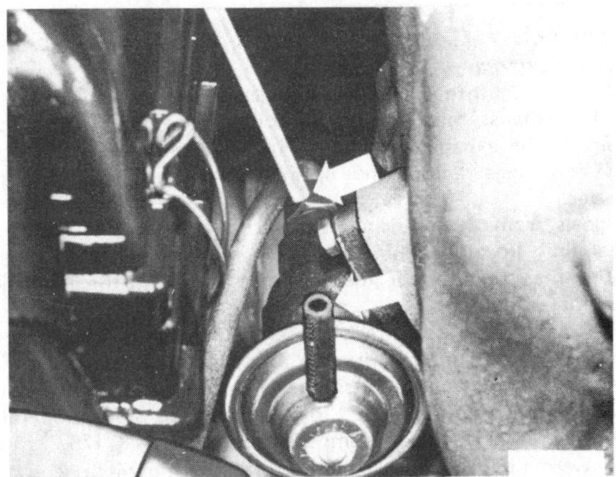

Fig. 14.161 Gauge connecting points (arrowed) for checking EGR temperature valve

Fig. 14.162 EGR delay valve (arrowed). White cover (1) must face vacuum source

Fig. 14.163 Hose connecting points (arrowed) for checking vacuum amplifier (output side)

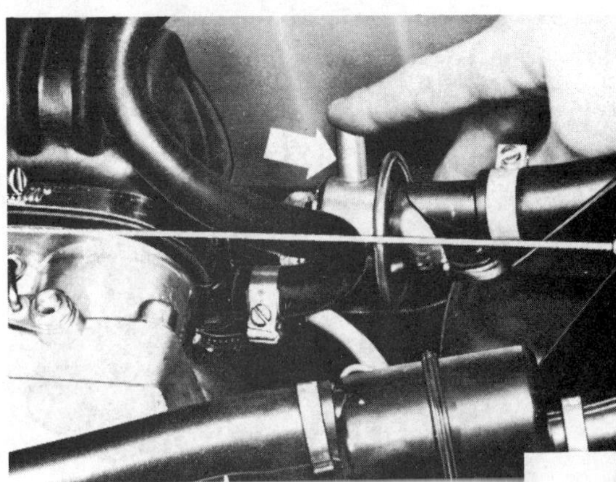

Fig. 14.164 Checking deceleration valve at connector (arrowed)

Fig. 14.165 Deceleration vacuum hose T-piece connector (right-hand arrow) and deceleration valve (left)

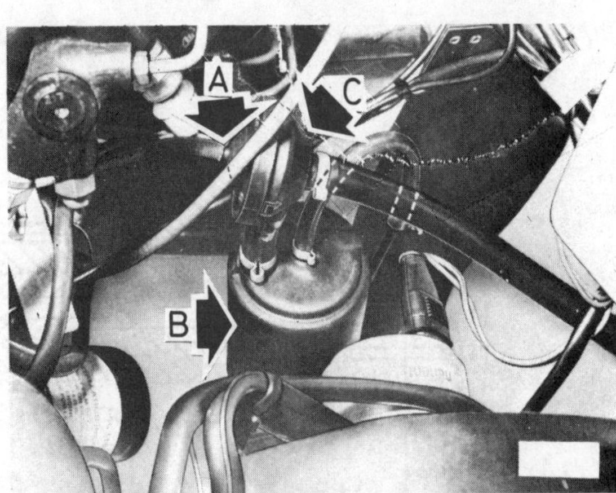

Fig. 14.166 Vent valve checking points. For A, B and C see text

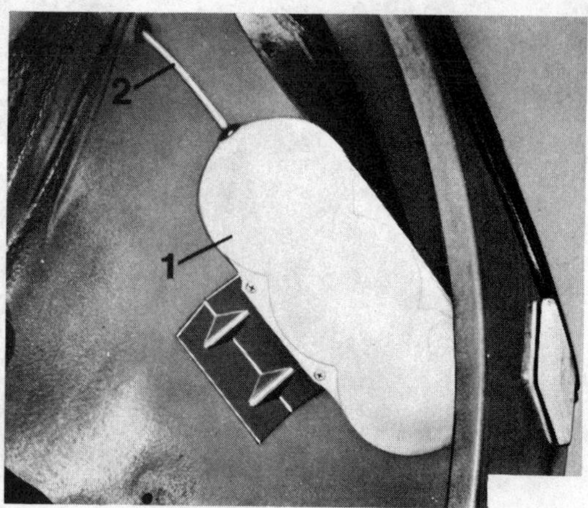

Fig. 14.167 Vacuum tank location

1 Tank 2 Green connecting hose

Fig. 14.168 EGR elapsed mileage switch (arrowed)

Oxygen sensor (Californian models, 1980 on) - description and maintenance

54 On later Californian Dasher models, an oxygen sensor is screwed into the exhaust manifold. Its purpose is to monitor the oxygen content of the exhaust gas so that its level can be maintained within the narrow range required for optimum performance of the catalytic converter.

55 Signals from the oxygen sensor are transmitted to an electronic control unit (located behind the glove compartment) which in turn modifies the operation of the frequency valve in the fuel injection system fuel distributor.

56 The system fuel pressure is therefore constantly varied according to engine requirements to provide an optimum fuel/air mixture and consequently low exhaust emission levels.

57 An additional device is used in this system to prevent operation of the oxygen sensor at coolant temperatures below 24°C (75.2°F) during engine warm-up. The device comprises a thermoswitch screwed into the coolant hose.

58 An indicator lamp located on the instrument panel lights up at 30 000 mile (48 000 km) intervals as a reminder to renew the oxygen sensor. After renewal, depress the switch button to reset it.

Oxygen sensor - renewal

59 With the engine switched off, release the flexible duct from the throttle valve housing, also the small hose from the duct. Remove the duct.

60 Disconnect the lead from the oxygen sensor.

61 Unscrew and remove the oxygen sensor.

62 Installation is a reversal of removal, but coat the threads with anti-seize compound before screwing in the new sensor.

Fig. 14.169 Oxygen sensor (arrowed)

A Permanently attached wire

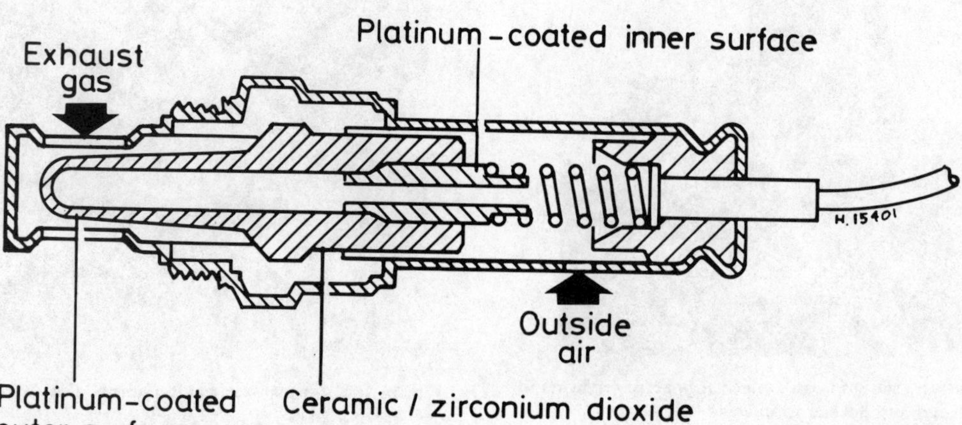

Fig. 14.170 Sectional view of oxygen sensor

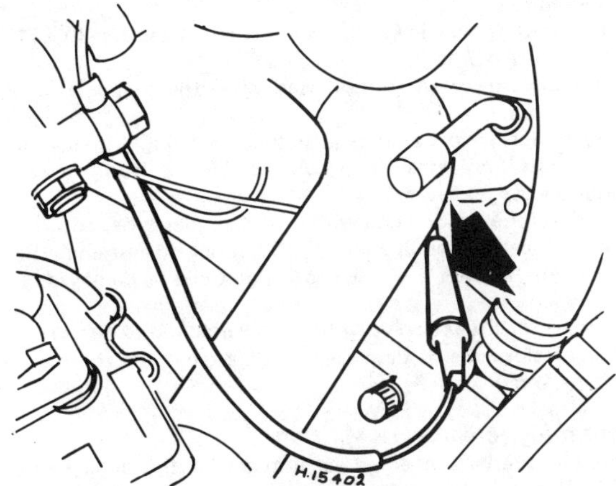

Fig. 14.171 Connecting plug (arrowed) on oxygen sensor lead

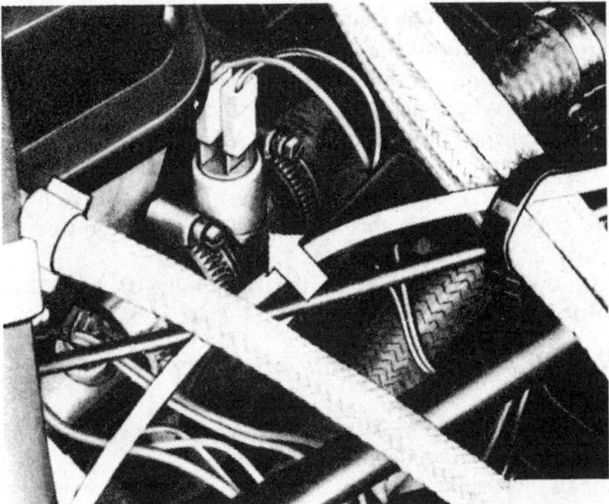

Fig. 14.172 Oxygen sensor thermoswitch (arrowed)

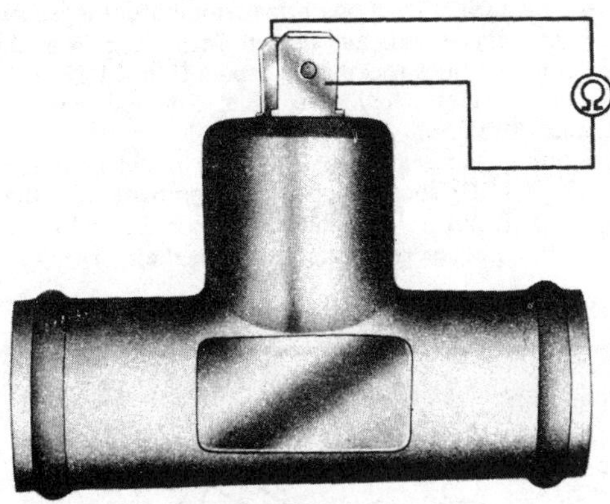

Fig. 14.173 Thermoswitch test circuit

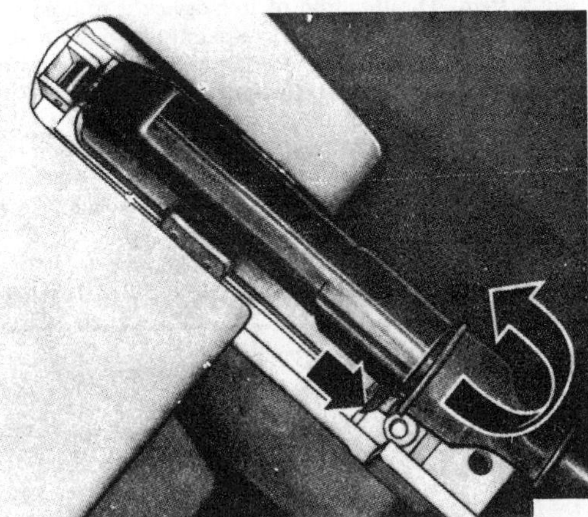

Fig. 14.174 Control unit multiplug

Small arrow indicates retaining catch; large arrow indicates direction of release of connecting plug

Oxygen sensor system - testing

63 Have the engine at normal operating temperature with the ignition switched off.

64 Disconnect the leads from the thermoswitch and using a test lamp or ohmmeter, check the switch for continuity. If there is no continuity, continue with the following test procedure. If the switch is suspect, refer to paragraphs 71 to 75.

65 Disconnect the lead from the oxygen sensor.

66 Using an exhaust gas analyzer as described in paragraphs 93 to 99 of Section 5C, adjust the CO level to between 2.0 and 3.0% with the engine idling. Turn off the ignition and reconnect the oxygen sensor.

67 Start the engine and run it at about 2000 rpm. The exhaust gas analyzer should now register a CO level of 1.5%. If the figure is below this, check for leaks at the sensor and exhaust manifold.

68 If the CO level is above 1.5%, turn off the ignition, disconnect the lead from the oxygen sensor and earth the green wire of the connector plug at the end of the cable.

69 Start the engine. If the CO level is still greater than 1.5%, renew the oxygen sensor.

70 On completion of testing and renewal of components, adjust the idle speed and mixture (CO) to the specified levels for normal operation.

Thermoswitch - testing

71 Drain the cooling system (engine cold) and disconnect the lead from the thermoswitch.

72 Release the hose clips and detach the hoses from the thermoswitch.

73 Place the switch in a pan of water, using a thermometer to check the water temperature levels and a test lamp or ohmmeter to check the thermoswitch for continuity.

74 Gradually heat the water. At a temperature below 20°C (68°F) the test lamp should be illuminated. At a temperature above 25°C (77°F) the lamp should be extinguished.

75 If the thermoswitch does not operate in this way, renew it.

Electronic control unit

76 Renewal of this component should only be considered after all other components of the oxygen sensor system have been checked out.

77 Remove the glove compartment and extract the two screws which hold the control unit in place.

78 Detach the multi-plug from the control unit by pressing down the catch and pulling the cable end of the plug before unhooking the other end of the plug from the pin in the control unit.

79 Refitting is a reversal of removal, but it is most important that you obtain a control unit bearing the same part number as the original, otherwise some rewiring of the plug terminals may be required.

6 Ignition system

Modifications (mechanical breaker system)

1 The system is generally as described in Chapter 4.

2 A modified rotor arm and dust cap have been introduced, and the new type must be installed complete, ie a new rotor arm and a new dust cap.

3 The ballast resistor for the coil has been replaced by a resistance wire, a special piece of cable of fixed resistance from the coil terminal 15 to C15 on the relay plate. This should be tested as for the ballast resistor. Its resistance should be 0.9 ohms; it is a wire with transparent insulation marked with violet stripes.

4 Vehicles with automatic gearboxes are now fitted with a thermo-pneumatic valve in the hose line between the throttle housing and the distributor advance vacuum mechanism. This is in addition to the on/off switch which governs the electrical switching characteristics of the heater element in the choke cover. It is located in the same metal insert in the cooling circuit. The adaptor which is at 90° to the coolant flow

line houses the hose to the distributor, the other one, at an angle, goes to the throttle housing. The switch operates at 137°F (58°C), at which temperature the vacuum line is opened.

5 To assist in ignition timing a dot has been installed on one tooth of the camshaft gearwheel carrying the belt drive from the crankshaft. The dot is on the rear face of the tooth. When this is aligned with the edge of the cylinder head cover adjacent to it, both cams of No 1 cylinder are pointing upwards uniformly and there is no need to remove the cover to check this when resetting the ignition timing or refitting the distributor as in Chapter 4, Section 3.

6 Refer to the Specifications at the beginning of this Chapter for revised ignition settings for later models.

Breakerless (transistorized) ignition system - description and precautions

7 This system incorporates a Hall electromagnetic sender unit instead of the conventional mechanical breaker points.

8 The signals generated by this unit are sensed by a transistorized control unit and amplified.

9 A special ignition coil is used, the 12V current for which is switched on and off electronically by the control unit. A digital idle stabilizer is used in the system. The function of this device is to hold the engine idle speed within the specified range irrespective of any increased load which might be placed upon it by switching on the air conditioning or selecting a drive range for the automatic transmission. The digital idle stabilizer operates from signals from the distributor so that when the idle speed drops below 940 rpm it advances the ignition timing automatically to compensate.

10 No routine maintenance is required with this system, but certain precautions should be observed.

11 Do not hose the car down with the engine running.

12 Always disconnect the battery if electric welding is being carried out on the vehicle.

13 Do not start the engine if the car is still hot (above 80°C/176°F) from a paint drying oven.

14 Do not disconnect an ignition lead while the engine is running as a means of stopping it.

15 If the engine is to be cranked without starting (for compression testing or fuel pump testing etc) pull the HT lead from the centre of the distributor cap and earth it.

16 Only renew the ignition coil with one of similar type.

17 Never connect test equipment of 12V rating to terminal 15(+)° of the ignition coil, or the electronic control unit will be damaged.

Distributor - removal and refitting (breakerless ignition)

18 The operations are as described in Chapter 4 for the mechanical breaker type unit.

Ignition timing (breakerless ignition)

19 Where necessary, connect a tachometer to the engine as shown (Fig. 14.175).

20 Connect a stroboscopic timing lamp in accordance with the manufacturer's instructions.

21 Run the engine until normal operating temperature is reached.

22 Switch off the engine and then detach both plugs from the digital idle stabilizer. Join the plugs together as shown (Fig. 14.176).

23 Start the engine and allow it to idle. The idle speed must be between 880 and 1000 rpm.

24 Point the timing lamp at the sight hole in the bellhousing. The timing mark (3° ATDC) should appear in alignment with the pointer (Fig. 14.177). If it is not, release the distributor clamp bolt and twist the distributor one way or the other to align the marks. Tighten the clamp bolt.

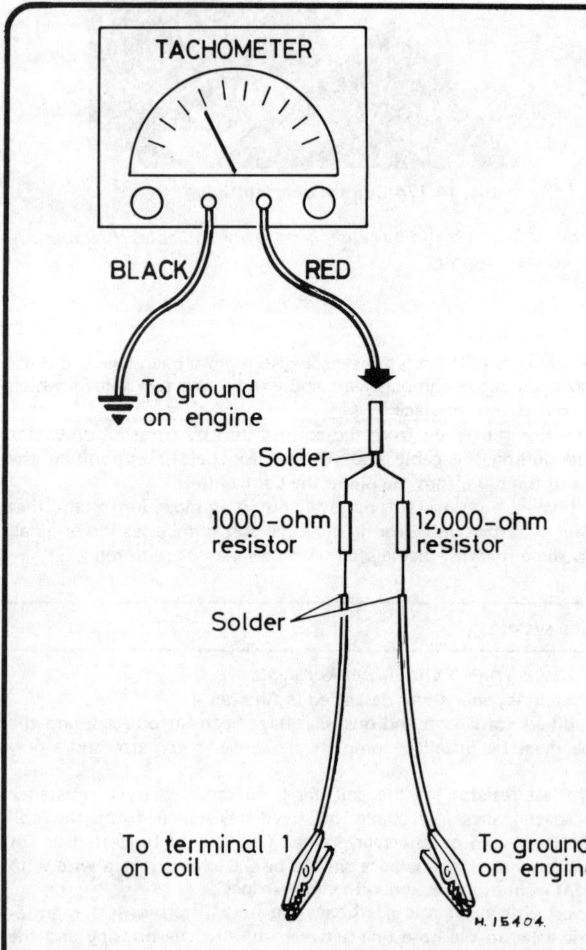

Fig. 14.175 Tachometer correctly connected to breakerless type distributor

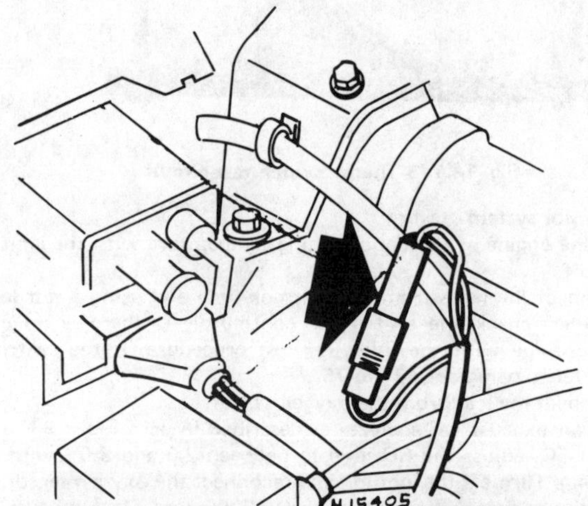

Fig. 14.176 Digital idle stabilizer plugs (arrowed) temporarily connected to each other

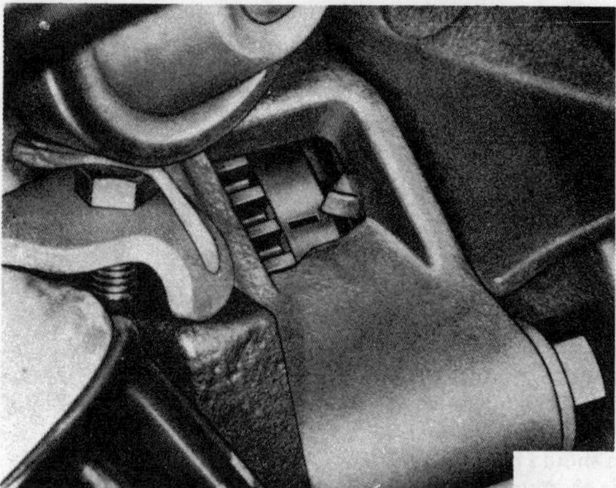

Fig. 14.177 Timing marks in alignment

25 Disconnect the timing lamp and tachometer and remake the idle stabilizer connections.

Breakerless distributor - dismantling and reassembly

26 Remove the distributor cap by prising down the two spring clips.
27 Remove the suppression shield, the rotor and the shield plate.
28 With a pair of snap-ring pliers, extract the snap-ring from the top of the trigger wheel. Remove the trigger wheel.
29 Extract the fixing screws and the snap-ring and washers from the distributor shaft. Withdraw the Hall sender unit from the baseplate.
30 The baseplate may be removed if the vacuum unit is first withdrawn and the side fixing screw extracted from the distributor body.
31 The distributor shaft and centrifugal advance mechanism are not supplied as renewable items, so if they are worn, it will mean a new distributor.
32 Reassembly is a reversal of dismantling. Apply engine oil to the centrifugal advance mechanism and the felt pad in the distributor shaft. Smear the friction surfaces of the baseplate sparingly with grease.

Breakerless ignition system - testing

Control unit

33 With the ignition off, connect a voltmeter between terminal 15(+) of the ignition coil and a good earth. Switch on the ignition: if no voltage is indicated, then there is a fault in the ignition switch or wiring.
34 If voltage is indicated, disconnect the voltmeter and proceed to the next stage of testing.
35 Disconnect the HT cable from the centre of the distributor cap and ground the end of the cable.
36 Disconnect the distributor-to-control unit wiring at the multi-plug connector.
37 Connect the positive (+) red lead of the voltmeter to terminal 1(–) of the ignition coil. Connect the voltmeter negative (–) black lead to a good ground.
38 Switch on the ignition. If the indicated voltage is less than 12 or drops below 12 before one second has passed, switch off the ignition immediately. The control unit is faulty and must be renewed.
39 If the indicated voltage is a constant 12 then proceed to the next testing stage.
40 With the ignition switched off, use a jump lead to connect the green (some models green/white) lead running from the distributor to ground.
41 Switch on the ignition and the voltmeter should indicate 12V. With the ignition still switched on, disconnect the temporary jump lead. The reading should drop to 6V. If it does not then the control unit is faulty.
42 With the ignition switched off, disconnect the voltmeter from the ignition coil. Now reconnect the red (+) lead of the voltmeter to the red lead at the distributor wiring multiple connectors terminal. Connect the black (–) lead of the voltmeter to the brown lead terminal at the multiple connector.
43 Switch on the ignition: the voltmeter should indicate about 10V. If it does not, the control unit is faulty and must be renewed.

Hall sender unit

44 Testing this component will require the use of a test lamp or voltmeter.
45 With the ignition off, connect a voltmeter between terminal 15 (+) of the ignition coil and a ground point on the engine.
46 Switch on the ignition. If there is no voltage indicated on the voltmeter, then the ignition switch is faulty or the feed wire to the ignition coil is broken.
47 Switch off the ignition and disconnect the HT cable from the centre of the distributor cap. Ground the end of the cable to the engine.
48 Connect a 12 volt test lamp between terminal 15 (+) of the coil and an engine ground.
49 Have an assistant crank the engine on the starter for a period of five seconds while the test lamp is observed. If it flickers then the sender unit is satisfactory. If it only emits a steady light then the sender unit must be renewed.

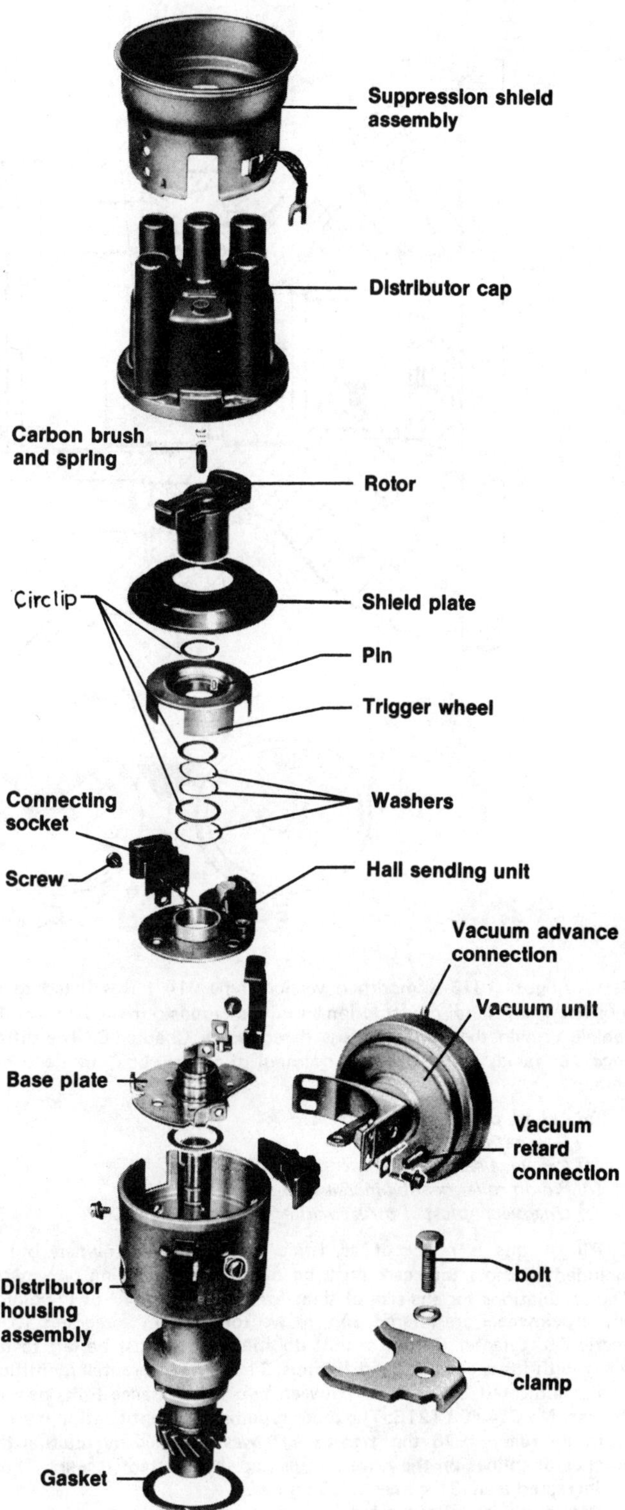

Fig. 14.178 Exploded view of breakerless distributor

7 Manual transmission

General description

1 Until August 1976 the manual gearbox type 014 remained unchanged from the unit described in Chapter 6. The only modification to gearbox 014 that we have noted is the alteration of the number of splines on the drive flange shaft from 31 to 33 in February 1976.

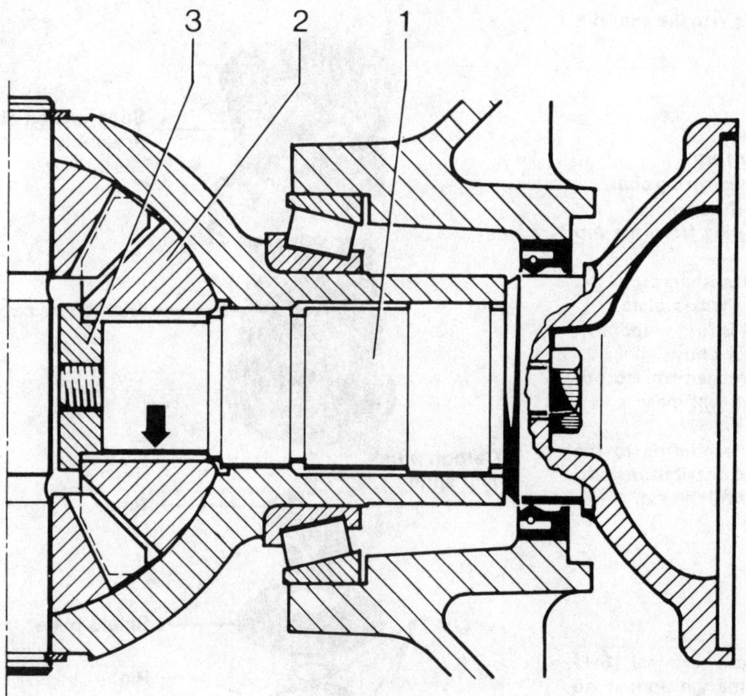

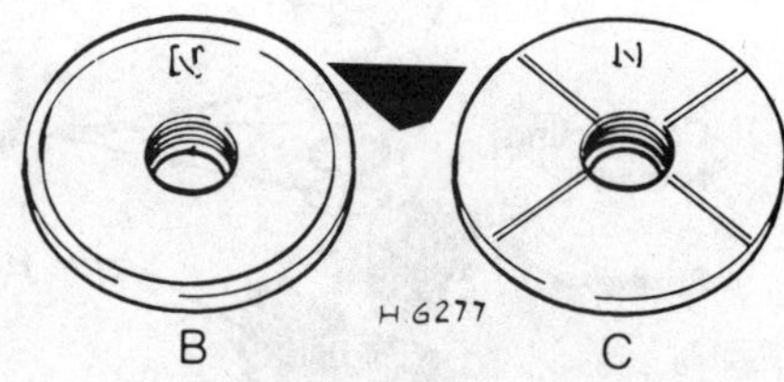

Fig. 14.179 Type 014 manual transmission spline identification on drive flanges and differential gears

1 Drive flange
2 Bevel gear
3 Nut
B 31 splines
C 33 splines

2 In August 1976 a modified version type 014/1 was fitted to all models. The general construction and the methods of removal from the vehicle remain the same as those described in Chapter 6. The differences, as far as they affect the overhaul of the gearbox, are described below:

(a) Length of input shaft increased
(b) Gear ratios changed
(c) Crownwheel diameter increased
(d) Pinion roller bearing increased diameter
(e) One-piece (plastic) thrust washer for bevel gears

3 All of this is really of academic interest to the owner, but is included to show that care must be taken when ordering new parts. The calculations for the size of shim for the engagement of the pinion and crownwheel are altered, but, as we told you in paragraph 13 of Section 5, Chapter 6, you cannot do this job, it must be left to the agent with his special jigs and fixtures. The new differential identification is indicated by an insert between two of the flange bolts bearing the Part No 014 409 121E. The order type has no identification mark.
4 In February 1976 the gearbox 014 was modified by altering the number of splines on the drive flanges and the differential gears. These are increased from 31 splines to 33 splines.
5 One quite important minor change is that the housings are now joined by galvanized bolts instead of studs and nuts. When assembling the housings together it is advisable to use two studs to align the housings properly, then remove the studs and fit the bolts.
6 Minor modifications to the synchromesh gear make it necessary to be able to identify the rings. Prior to May 1975 the springs were as shown in Figs. 6.8 and 6.9. Two additional pockets have been made in each of the 1st and 4th gear synchro-rings. If it is necessary to fit new synchro-rings to gearboxes made before May 1975 the new synchro-ring should be installed with a slightly shorter spring (Part No 014 311 311B) otherwise the shifting plate spring will interfere with the rotary movement of the synchro-ring.

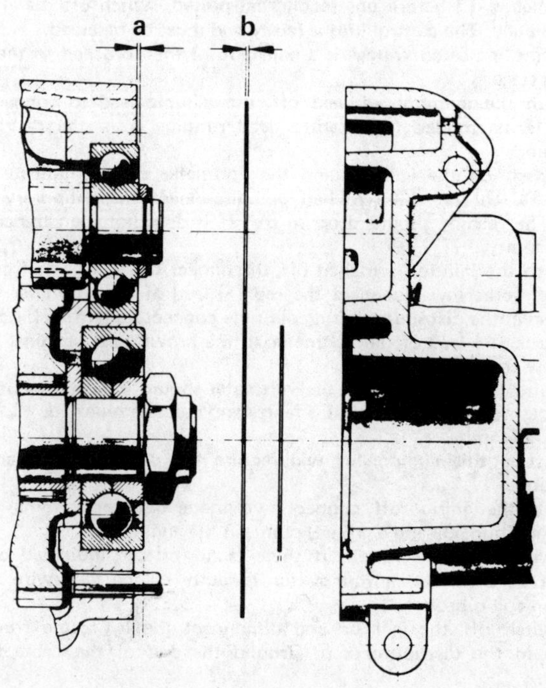

Fig. 14.180 Type 014 manual transmission - sectional view of mainshaft bearings in casing

a Mainshaft bearing protrusion *b Thickness of gasket*

7 From 5th August 1976 the identification groove for 1st gear side has been moved from the top of the external splines to the end face. Thus it may be seen while the gears are mated. The fitting position is as before for the synchroniser unit 1/2 gears - groove towards 1st gear.
8 Refer to Chapter 6, Section 10, paragraph 3. The etched lines were discontinued from 18th October 1976. The items no longer need to be fitted in a certain way, but if one part is renewed then the other should also be renewed.
9 The locking key spring (Figs. 6.8 and 6.9, parts 1 and 5) has been made from thinner wire with effect from 29th September 1976. Old diameter 1.6 mm, new diameter 1.4 mm. New springs may be fitted to the old hubs.
10 The 1st gear synchroniser ring has been altered as from 27th January 1977. The tooth angle has been modified from 120° to 110° to give easier engagement of 1st gear. Three teeth are missing (on purpose). When renewing 1st gear synchro-ring use Part No 014 311 295D which is standard for 2nd - 4th gears.

Pinion bearing in final drive housing - locating pin

11 As already stated the diameter of the outer race of this bearing has been increased with consequent reduction in the length of the locating pin from 63.4 mm to 59.8 mm. On the old cover there was a blind hole which allowed the top of the pin to protrude from the gearbox housing so that it could be gripped and extracted when necessary.
12 The blind hole in the final drive cover is now discontinued and a countersink has been added to the hole in the gearbox housing so that the pin may be gripped. The old and new parts are not interchangeable. Fig. 14.181 refers.

Gearchange mechanism (later type 1975 on) - adjustment

13 Place the gearchange lever in neutral.
14 Release the clamp nut on the remote control rod. Unscrew the gearlever knob and remove the gaiter.
15 The gearbox must be in the neutral position. The lever is set by use of a special jig 3014 which when installed as in Fig. 14.183 sets the lever in the correct plane. Align the centering holes of the housing and lever bearing plate. Install the tool 3014 with the locating pin inserted into the front centering hole and screw in the knurled knob until the screw just contacts the lever base.
16 Now set the shift rod and finger with the gearbox in neutral and tighten the clamp. The jig should now be removed and the box tested for engagement of all four gears and reverse.

Reverse gear relay lever

17 This mechanism has been modified from a relay lever with shift segment to a relay lever with jaw. The difference will be seen from the illustrations.
18 With the modified arrangement, the following adjustment will be required at time of overhaul or if the reverse gear selection becomes unsatisfactory.
19 Push the relay lever downwards (ie away from the bolt) and then screw the relay lever bolt in until it contacts the relay lever. The end of the bolt and the relay lever threaded bush must be flush.
20 Press the relay lever against the end of the bolt and then turn the bolt in an anti-clockwise direction until the threads of the bolt are

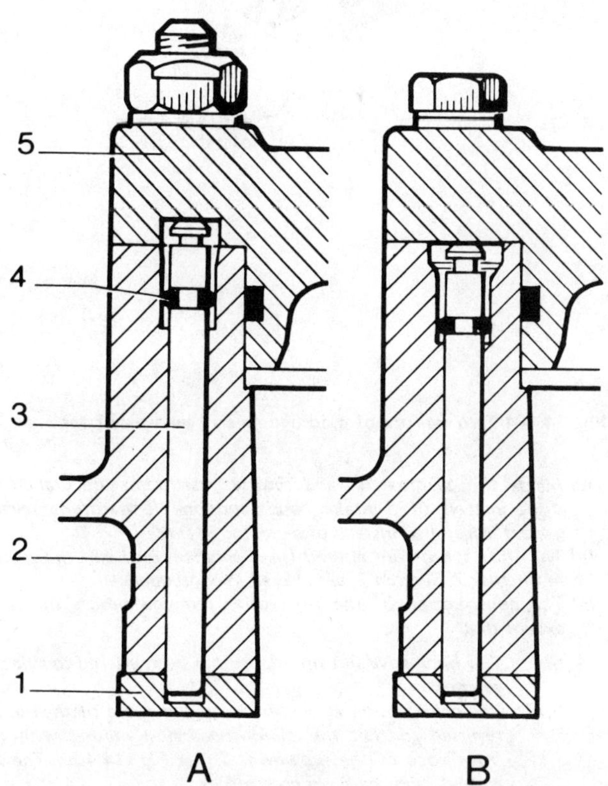

Fig. 14.181 Type 014 manual transmission - sectional view of pinion bearings with modified retaining pin in transmission housing

A Pin as fitted to gearbox 014
B Pin as fitted to gearbox 014/1
1 Pinion bearing outer race
2 Gearbox housing
3 Pin
4 Oil seal
5 Final drive cover

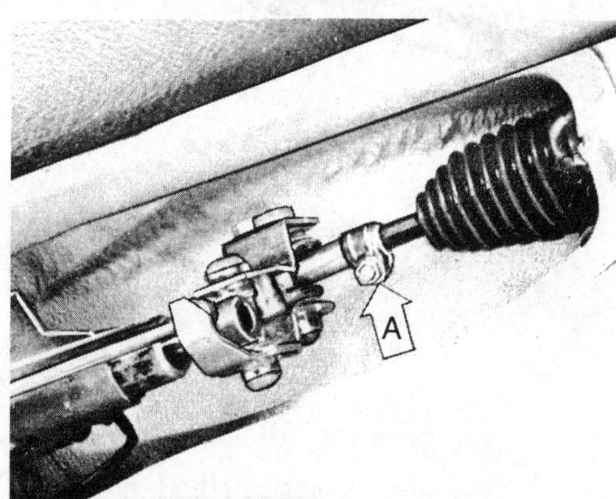

Fig. 14.182 Gearchange rod adjustment clamp (A)

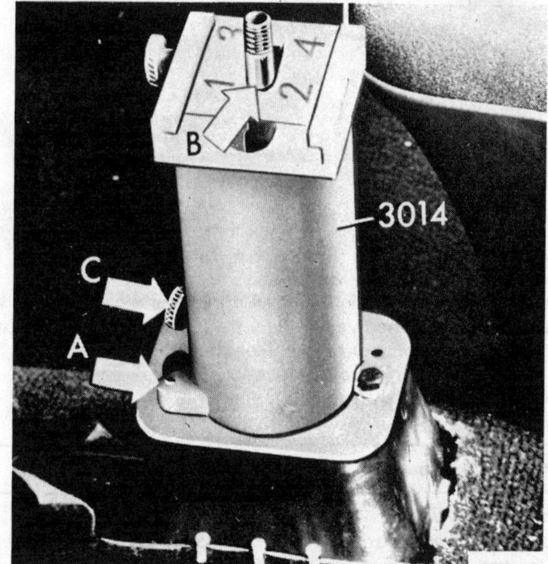

Fig. 14.183 Special gearchange lever setting tool

A Tool locating pin towards front of vehicle
B Gearchange lever
C Knurled screw

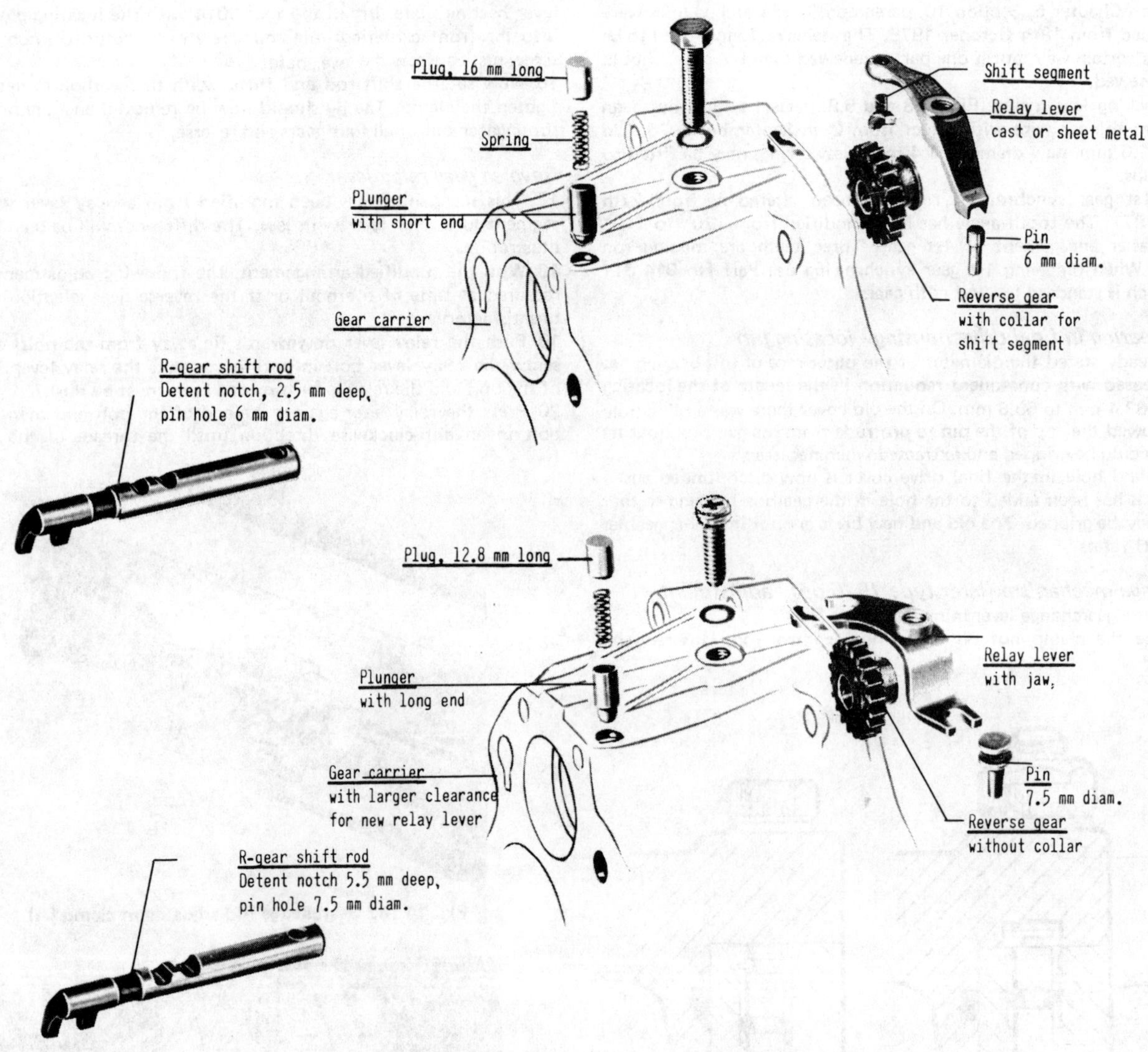

Fig. 14.184 Two versions of modified reverse gear relay lever

heard to drop into engagement with the threads in the hole in the lever.
21 Now turn the bolt in a clockwise direction and tighten it to 25 lbf ft (3.5 kgf m).
22 Where difficulty is experienced in selecting reverse gear, the modified arrangement can be altered yet again by the purchase of a kit containing a detent plunger and plug of different length.
23 After a short period of production, the jaw type relay lever reverted to the original shift segment type.

8 Automatic transmission

General description

1 The type 089 automatic transmission superseded the earlier version from October 1975. The main differences between it and the type 003 transmission are as follows:

(a) A redesigned gearshift, moving the detents for the driving range from the gearshift to the gearbox
(b) The kickdown is operated mechanically by a second accelerator cable and a lever system in the gearbox instead of by an electrical solenoid
(c) Inside the geargox 1st and reverse gear trains are braked by discs instead of a brake band, and one forward/one reverse gearset is installed instead of a combined set
(d) The shift speeds are altered (see Specifications) and the speeds in Chapter 7, Section 2, are altered in consequence
(e) The construction of the final drive remains almost the same except that:

(i) The final drive housing flange has been altered to suit the gearbox
(ii) The drive pinion is modified and the shape of the pinion reversed so that the pinion head now meshes with the front edge of the crownwheel, see Fig. 14.185. The S3 and S4 shims have changed places.
(iii) Two seals are fitted to the pinion shaft cover on the new model as opposed to one on the old model
(iv) The one-way clutch housing and the final drive housing cover are now integral in one casting
(v) On the old box the ATF return flow was through the centre of the pump driveshaft. This is discontinued and the flow is now routed through drillings in the cover to the governor and the hydraulic control system

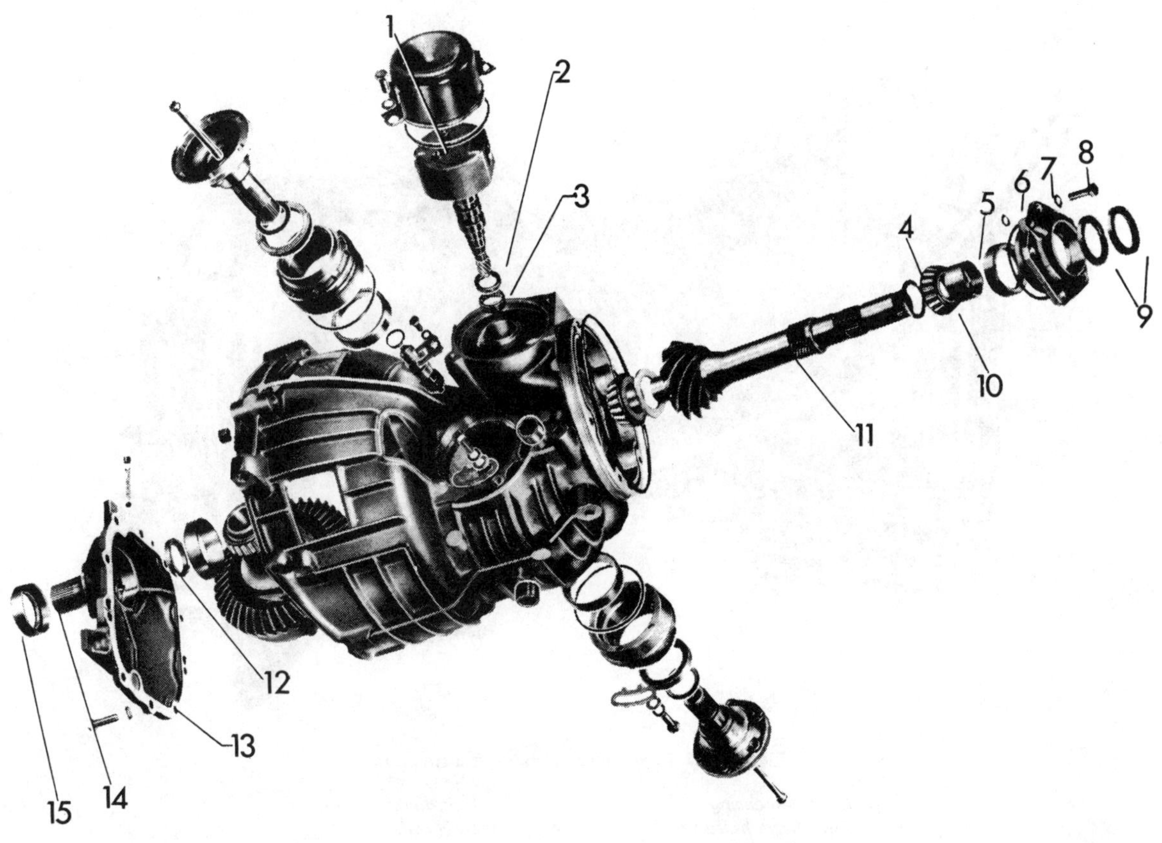

Fig. 14.185 Type 089 automatic transmission

1 Governor
2 Governor seal
3 Governor seal
4 Pinion shaft bearing and shim S4
5 Oil seal bush
6 O-ring
7 Pinion cover plate
8 Bolt
9 Pinion oil seals
10 Bearing - inner race
11 Pinion
12 Pinion oil seal
13 Final drive housing cover
14 One-way clutch support
15 Converter oil seal

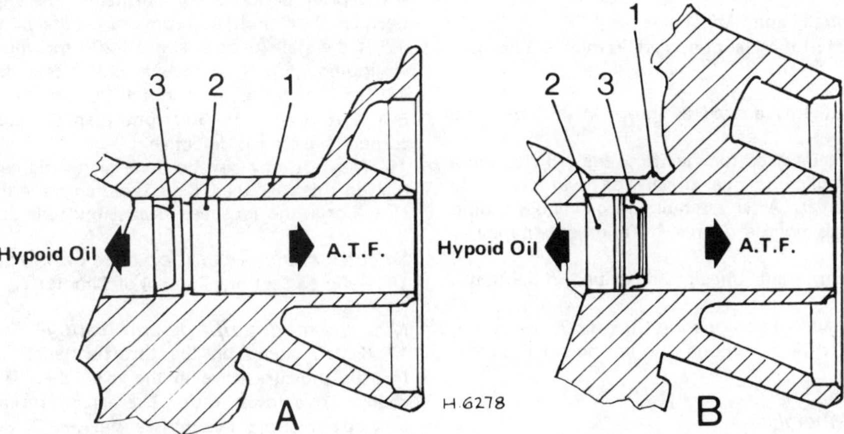

Fig. 14.186 Automatic transmission governor shaft bearing and oil seal

A Early (up to transmission ET 27015)
B Later (from transmission ET 27016)
1 Final drive housing
2 Bearing
3 Oil seal

(f) The throttle pressure valve is now operated by the second accelerator cable and makes the transmission directly responsive to load and engine speed variations

(g) The ATF filter in the oil pan is not washable. If it is clogged by carbon from brake bands it must be renewed.

(h) The governor bearings are modified. In the early models lubrication was by ATF. In the later models the lubrication is by hypoid oil from the final drive. The position of the oil seal has been changed and it now seals the ATF side of the bearing whereas before it was on the final drive side of the bearing. The actual positions of the seal and bearing have been interchanged. Fig. 14.186 refers.

Fig. 14.187 Type 089 automatic transmission

1 *Geartrain casing*
2 *Final drive housing*
3 *Fluid filter/dipstick guide tube*
4 *Kickdown valve lever*
5 *Governor*
6 *Transmission number*

2 The description in Chapter 7, Section 1 should be read in conjunction with the modifications given above, to understand the operation of the box.

Operation

3 Operation is as described in Section 2 of Chapter 7.
4 For 68 mph in paragraph 6 of that Section, read 60 mph (96 kph).

Maintenance and lubrication

5 Lubricant capacities are slightly altered as shown in the Specifications.
6 The oil in the final drive is installed for the life of the vehicle, unless it has been necessary to rebuild the final drive. The level should be checked at the specified intervals. After a rebuild an oil change should be done when the vehicle has done a further 1 000 miles. Thereafter top-up as required.
7 The ATF level is most important. Check as described in Section 4 of Chapter 7.
8 The changing of ATF is also as described in Chapter 7, Section 4, *but* the filter must be replaced by a new one. It is not possible to clean the old one.

Tests and adjustments - general

9 Before any accurate adjustments to the automatic transmission may be carried out the engine must be running correctly. Ignition and fuel supply adjustments must be within specified limits. If these are in order then, after checking the transmission for leaks and external damage and correcting such problems, run the engine up to operating temperature and proceed with the tests to the transmission.

Stall speed test

10 The engine must be warm and the ATF lukewarm. **Do not carry out this test for more than 20 seconds** or the transmission will overheat.
11 The object is to check whether the torque converter is functioning correctly, and the running symptoms are poor acceleration and low maximum speed. A tachometer to measure engine speed is necessary. Unfortunately the tachometer fitted to the dashboard is not considered accurate enough for this test so a more accurate one should be installed according to the instrument maker's instructions.
12 Put all the brakes hard on and with the lever at 'D' run the engine for a brief period at full throttle. The engine speed should drop to between 2200 and 1900 rpm immediately and remain constant.
13 If the stall speed is above 2200 rpm then either the forward clutch is slipping, or 1st gear one-way clutch is slipping.
14 If the stall speed is about 1700 rpm then the engine needs overhaul, but if it drops to 1500 rpm then the stator one-way clutch in the torque converter is defective.
15 The test may also be done in reverse gear. If the stall speed is too high in this gear then there is clutch slip either in the direct and reverse clutch or in the 1st speed/reverse multiple disc brake.

Selector cable - operation check and road test

16 Refer to Sections 7 and 9 of Chapter 7.

Kickdown - description and testing

17 If you stamp on the throttle pedal suddenly while driving, the throttle pressure valve in the valve chest is operated and the gear will change to a lower ratio. The effect is exactly the same as with the previous solenoid switch (see Chapter 7, Section 3) but the tests and adjustments are done on the accelerator cable linkages as described below.

Accelerator and kickdown switch cables - description

18 The accelerator cable arrangement is shown in Fig. 14.188. At the bottom of the accelerator at 'A' is an adjustable stop.
19 The inner cable is attached by a plastic connector to the top of the pedal and passes through a locating bracket which houses the securing bush for the outer cable. The cable then goes to an adjuster mounted on a bracket on the gearbox. The inner cable is attached to the operating lever of the throttle (kickdown) valve shaft of the transmission.
20 Refer again to Fig. 14.188. The operating lever is shaped like a bellcrank and on the other end a second cable is arranged to go to the

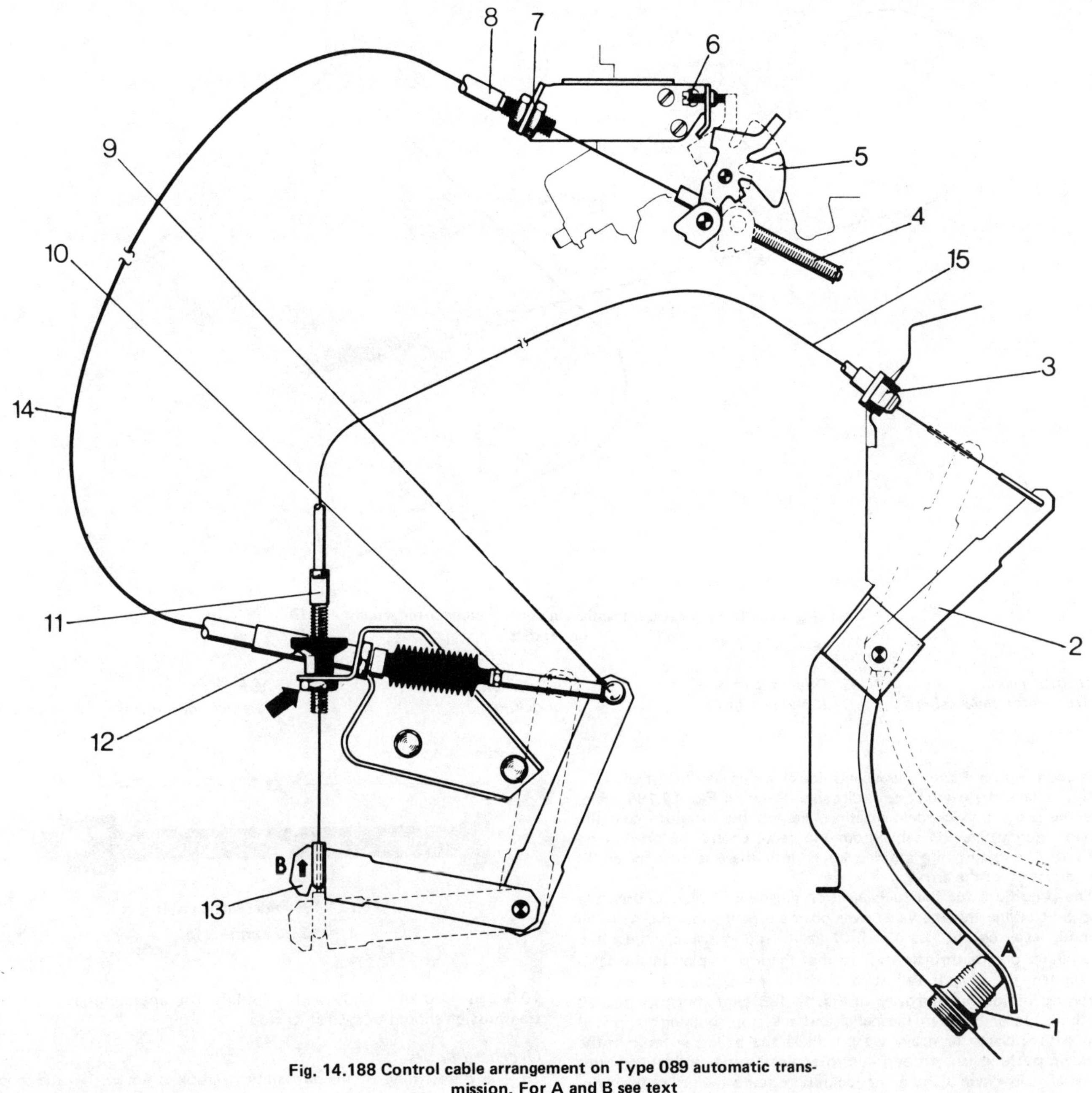

Fig. 14.188 Control cable arrangement on Type 089 automatic transmission. For A and B see text

1 Kickdown stop
2 Accelerator pedal
3 Outer cable anchorage
4 Spring
5 Linkage
6 Stop screw
7 Adjusting locknuts
8 Outer cable
9 Balljoint
10 Locknut
11 Cable anchorage
12 Adjusting nut and locknut (arrowed)
13 Gearbox lever
14 Cable
15 Cable

throttle valve lever of either the carburettor or the fuel injection throttle valves.

Accelerator and kickdown switch cables - adjustment

Models up to 1979

21 Refer to Fig. 14.188. Pull the cable balljoint away from the lever at 'B' and screw the ball socket off the cable. Remove the boot and take the cable off the retaining bracket. Disconnect the cable from the throttle lever and remove the cable from the bracket on the carburettor or throttle valve housing.

22 Hold the cable outer at one end and lift it horizontally. If the cable droops down the steel strip the cover is in the wrong plane. Turn the outer cable until the cable droops in an 'S' position. This is the correct refitting position. Attach the cable to the bracket on the gearbox, push the outer cable in and fit the securing clip. Turn the ball socket to screw it onto the cable as far as it will go and then turn it back a little to fit it on the ball-stud. Tighten the locknut and clamp the outer cable.

23 Push the throttle cable into position through the hole in the bracket and fasten it to the throttle lever. Squeeze the spring together with pliers and adjust the nuts on the bracket so that there is no strain on the cable.

24 To adjust the cable correctly first move the throttle lever on the carburettor to the end position so that the choke is open, the cam out of action, and the throttle closed. Now press the lever on the gearbox towards the accelerator cable as far as it will go and push the cable ball socket onto the ball-stud. Turn the nut on the carburettor bracket until all play in the cable is eliminated. The lever on the gearbox must still be

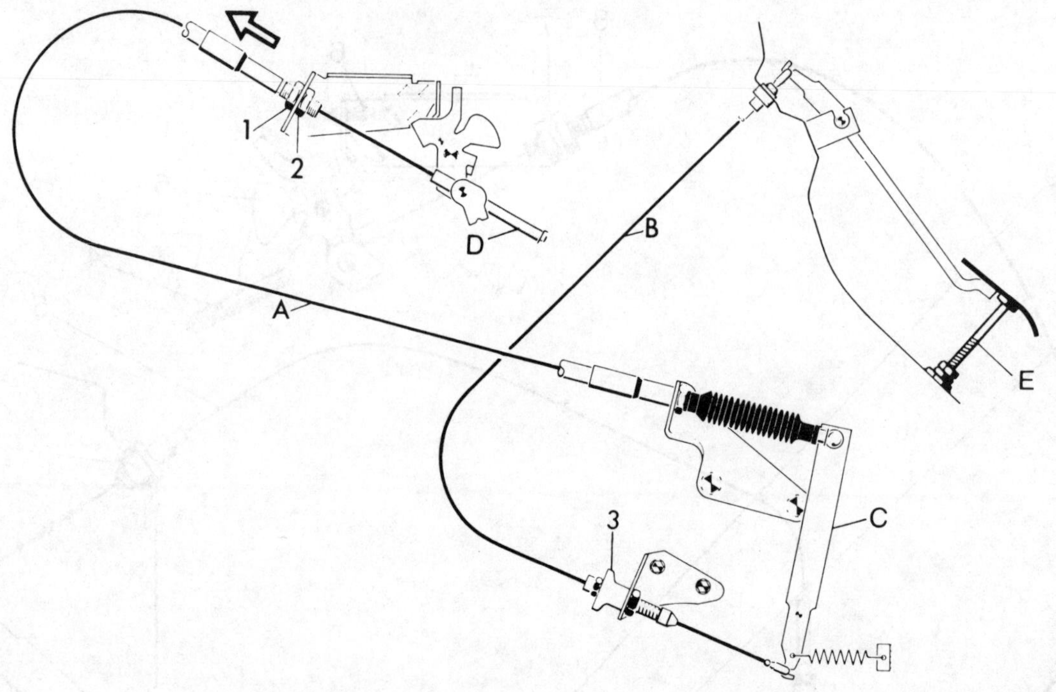

Fig. 14.189 Automatic transmission control cable arrangement - 1979 on models

A Throttle cable
B Accelerator pedal cable
C Operating lever
D Kickdown spring
E Pedal setting bolt
1 Locknut
2 Locknut
3 Adjustment nut at transmission bracket

in the end position. Fasten the second (lock) nut against the bracket.

25 Now check the gearbox control cable. Refer to Fig. 14.188 again. Move the pedal to kickdown position, slacken the locknut under the knurled knob where the cable from the pedal enters the bracket on the gearbox and turn the knurled knob until there is no play at 'B' in the direction of the arrow.

26 The procedure for the fuel injection engine is similar. Loosen the clamp bolt or the throttle valve lever on the throttle housing. With the bellcrank lever on the gearbox held at its end position, adjust the cable clamp on the throttle lever so that there is no play in the cable and tighten the clamp. Adjustment of the pedal cable is done by slackening the locknut (arrowed in Fig. 14.188) and after placing a 10 mm thick spacer between the pedal and the stop, holding the pedal down with a clamp or heavy weight. Press the bellcrank lever to the kickdown position (shown by interrupted lines) and hold it there. With the pedal held down tighten the locknut to remove all play from the outer cable. Take out the spacer and press the pedal down to the stop. Check there is no play on the bellcrank lever.

1979 on models

27 On later models, the accelerator pedal cable is adjusted by means of a nut at the cable support bracket on the transmission.

28 To adjust, have the engine at normal operating temperature with the air cleaner removed. Loosen the adjusting nut (Fig. 14.189).

29 With the choke valve plate wide open, close the throttle (carburettor models).

30 Release the throttle cable locknuts at the carburettor and then pull the outer cable as far as is possible in the direction of the arrow to eliminate any slackness. Retighten the locknuts.

31 Remove the accelerator pedal stop and substitute a M8 x 135 mm bolt with nuts adjusted as shown in Fig. 14.190.

32 Adjust the accelerator pedal cable by means of the adjusting nut so that the accelerator pedal pad rests on the bolt. The operating lever on the transmission must be in the 'throttle released' position.

33 To check the adjustment, depress the accelerator pedal as far as it will go without passing through the kickdown position. Check that the lever on the throttle valve plate lever is against its stop.

34 If the accelerator pedal is now pushed fully to its stop, the kickdown spring should be compressed to an overall length of between 10.0 and 11.0 mm (0.39 and 0.43 in). The operating lever on the transmission should be against its stop.

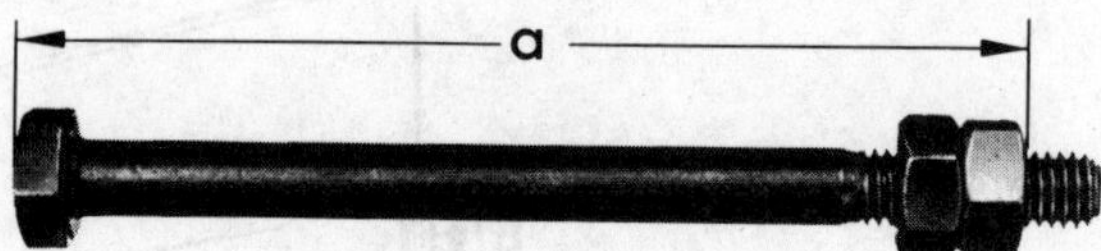

Fig. 14.190 Pedal setting bolt
a = 124.0 mm (4.9 in)

Overhaul limits

35 The dismantling of the automatic gearbox is not within the scope of the owner driver. A skilled mechanic could do the job if he had the necessary gauges and jigs but these are not available so if you dismantle the box you will not be able to assemble it correctly. If you are a skilled mechanic you will readily appreciate that point.

36 However, the transmission is easily removable from the car and it may be separated into its component parts. The box may then be taken for overhaul, with a considerable saving in labour charges. The fluid may be drained and the filter changed but there the repair stops. Some repairs may be done to the torque converter. These are discussed later.

37 Oil seals may be renewed in the final drive unit but the dismantling and reassembly of the gears again require jigs and measuring instruments which are not available to the d-i-y owner.

38 Some repairs may be made to the governor. These are discussed later.

39 The procedure for removing the transmission from the car is detailed below.

Automatic transmission (089) - removal and limited dismantling

40 Before doing anything else remove the earth strap from the battery.

41 Arrangements must be made to support the engine from above,

either with a hoist or an arrangement such as shown in Fig. 12.3. If you try to support it from below the support will get in the way. You must also be able to lift the left front wheel. It will be best to fit an axle stand under the left front side of the car.

42 Take off the air cleaner and detach the accelerator cable from the throttle lever. Disconnect the speedometer cable from the gearbox.

43 Disconnect and remove the exhaust pipe from the bracket on the gearbox, and then remove the upper engine/transmission bolts. Check that the engine is supported properly from above. Remove the torque converter cover plate.

44 Remove the starter and working through the hole left by the starter turn the torque converter so that you can see and remove the three bolts which hold the torque converter to the driveplate.

45 Undo the bolts holding the driveshafts to the final drive flanges and ease the driveshafts away. Cover the constant velocity joints with polythene bags and tie the joints out of the way (see Chapter 12, Section 10).

46 Disconnect the accelerator pedal cable from the gearbox.

47 Mark the position of the left balljoint on the left-hand wishbone and remove the balljoint from the wishbone (see Chapter 12, Section 6).

48 Slacken the bolts holding the mounting bracket of the gearbox to the body.

49 Make arrangements with a suitable jack to support the gearbox so that you will be able to lower it to the ground. Loosen the lower engine/transmission bolts, lift the box a little to take the weight and remove the bolts.

50 Pull the left wheel outwards as far as possible and lower the box gently to the ground. Watch that the converter does not fall out, and fit a retaining strap across the housing face as soon as possible.

51 When the box is down remove the throttle cable bracket from the gearbox and take the cable off the lever before it is damaged.

52 You may now take the box away, clean the outside carefully and dismantle it into its component parts.

53 The converter should be drawn off the shaft, taking great care not to damage the seals. Repairs to the converter are discussed in Chapter 7, Section 12.

54 Four studs hold the gearbox and final drive together. Three of them are short being secured with nuts to the rear flange of the drive housing. These should measure 1.24 in (31.5 mm) from the face of the gearbox flange to the top of the stud. The fourth stud goes right through the housing and should be 5.43 in (138 mm) long.

55 Remove the nuts and then holding the box firmly, remove the final drive from the studs. There is a gasket and an O-ring. These must be replaced with new ones when assembling the unit.

56 There is also a shim which limits the axial movement of the ring gear. If the box is dismantled the shim may need to be changed. This is determined by measuring the distance axially of the face of the centre bush from the face of the gearbox housing. To do this place a straight-edge over the housing and using a vernier depth gauge measure the distance from the top of the straight-edge to the housing face, this will give the thickness of the straight-edge. Using the gauge measure from the upper face of the straight-edge to the face of the bush. Subtract the thickness of the straight-edge and the answer gives the thickness of shim required. Two only shims are available, 0.4 mm and 1.2 mm. Using a combination of these build a shim of the correct thickness. If the dimension is below 0.84 mm do not fit a shim, this is allowable play for a running fit. Thereafter fit shims as under:

mm	*shim*
0.85 to 1.24	*1 x 0.4*
1.25 to 1.64	*2 x 0.4*
1.65 to 2.04	*1 x 1.2*
2.05 to 2.44	*1 x 0.4 + 1 x 1.2*
2.45 to 2.84	*2 x 0.4 + 1 x 1.2*
2.85 to 3.24	*2 x 1.2*
3.25 to 3.64	*1 x 0.4 + 2 x 1.2*
3.65 to 3.88	*2 x 0.4 + 2 x 1.2*

55 If the agent has overhauled the box it would be as well to ask him to supply the correct shim thickness.

Final drive - repairs

57 If the final drive is noisy then the unit should be taken to the VW agent for overhaul. Drain the oil from it but do not open it. If the oil seals are leaking renew them as detailed in Chapter 6, Section 11.

Governor - dismantling and reassembly

58 Overhaul of the governor is described in Chapter 7, Section 14, but from transmission No ET 27016 the location of the oil seal and bearing have been reversed, see Fig. 14.186. The transfer plate has also been modified and a small strainer fitted in it to deal with carbon particles. The valve and governor may now be exchanged separately.

60 When assembling the units there are a number of points to observe. If the shafts have been removed, and new ones fitted, the lengths must be checked. The pump shaft is 17.83 in (453.1 mm) and the turbine shaft 15.8 in (401.7 mm). The rings on the turbine shaft must be in good condition, lubricate them with ATF before installing the shaft.

61 When the shafts are assembled to the units and the box is joined to the final drive housing, the pump shaft must be engaged fully in the pump splines (Fig. 14.191).

62 Installing the torque converter on the shafts needs care. Ease it on, gently rotating it backwards and forwards so that it picks up the splines on the turbine shaft and then the pump shaft. Do not tilt it or ATF may spill out.

63 The transmission unit is now ready to go back in the car.

Automatic transmission (089) - refitting

64 Refitting is a reversal of removal. Fit the cable to the lever and install the bracket on the box. Pull the left-hand wheel out as far as possible and raise the box into position. Before tightening the engine/transmission bolts check that the converter turns freely, it can slip and get jammed, and will be damaged if you tighten the bolts with it incorrectly placed.

65 The correct torque wrench settings on assembly are given in the Specifications at the beginning of this Supplement. When the transmission is back in place with all the controls connected check the adjustment of the gearshift and accelerator cables.

Speed selector mechanism - removal, refitting and adjustment

66 Refer to Figs. 7.9 and 14.192. It will be seen that the main differences are the removal of the detent segments from the gearlever and the detent lever and spring from the bottom bracket.

67 To remove the selector lever follow the procedure below.

68 Disconnect the battery earth strap, undo the setscrew in the selector lever knob and remove the knob. The indicator plate is pressed into the console. Prise this out and remove the two screws holding the console in position. Remove the console.

69 It will be seen that four studs hold the selector assembly to the floor of the car. Remove the nuts and washers from the studs.

70 The cable is connected to the bottom of the lever by a bolt and

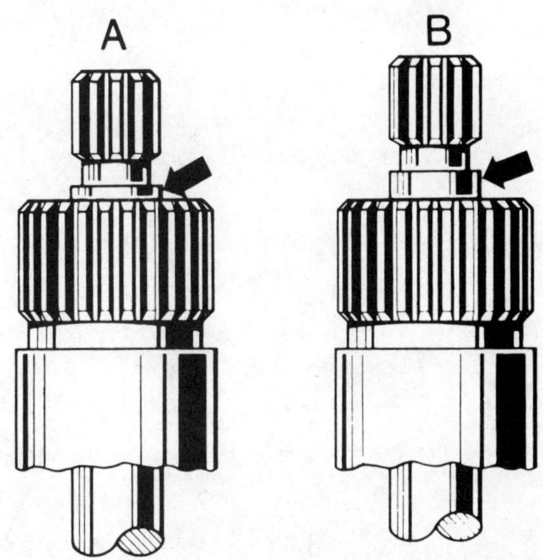

Fig. 14.191 Fluid pump shaft engagement on automatic transmission. Protrusion (arrowed) must be correct

A Correct *B Incorrect*

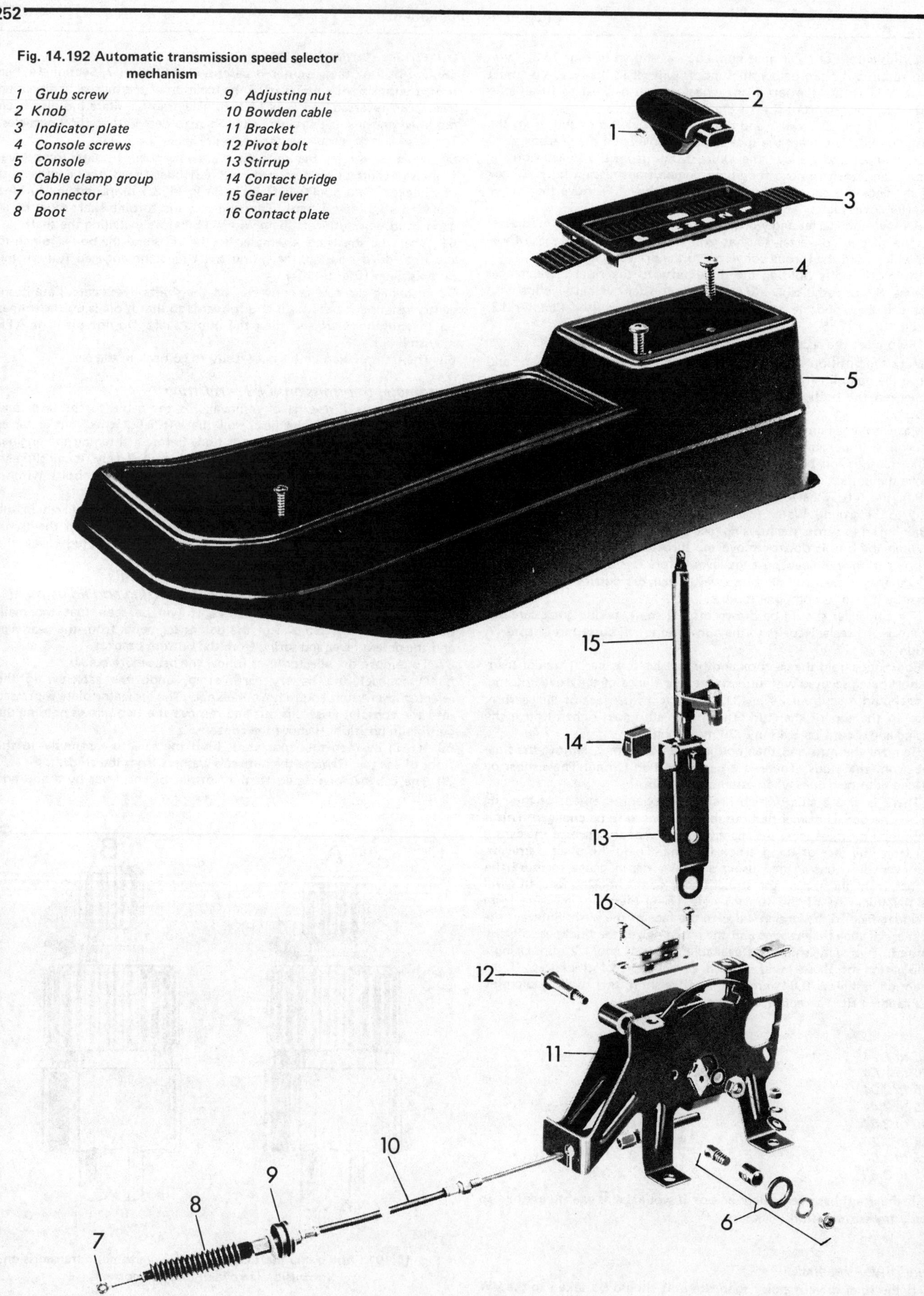

Fig. 14.192 Automatic transmission speed selector mechanism

1 Grub screw
2 Knob
3 Indicator plate
4 Console screws
5 Console
6 Cable clamp group
7 Connector
8 Boot
9 Adjusting nut
10 Bowden cable
11 Bracket
12 Pivot bolt
13 Stirrup
14 Contact bridge
15 Gear lever
16 Contact plate

clamp. Undo the bolt and pull the cable away from the lever.
71 Disconnect the wires from the neutral safety switch and the indicator light. Tag them for easy refitment.
72 To remove the selector cable, remove the selector lever as described above, and free the cable from the lever. It is necessary to pull the cable out from underneath the car.
73 Remove the clip which locks the cable to the lever on the gearbox housing. Undo the locknuts holding the outer cable to the bracket under the car and take the cable away from the bracket. Now pull the complete cable away under the car.
74 Refitting is the reverse of removal.

Selector cable adjustment

75 The cable must be adjusted if the correct letter or number is not illuminated when the gear is selected. The following procedure covers full adjustment on installation.
76 Select 'P' by setting the actuating lever on the gearbox under the car. Make sure the parking pawl has engaged by trying to push the car back and forward. If the car will move it is not engaged.
77 Remove the gearlever knob, prise out the indicator plate and remove the console. Slacken the nut on the cable clamp bolt so that the cable will move in the clamp at the base of the selector lever.
78 Refit the console and indicator plate and move the selector lever so that 'P' is illuminated on the indicator plate. Carefully remove the console and plate taking care not to move the lever. Tighten the cable clamp unit. Refit the console and indicator plate and check all the gears. The detents must engage when the corresponding letter or figure is illuminated. Readjust if necessary. When you are satisfied that all is in order refit the console, plate and knob permanently.

9 Braking system

Rear brakes with wedge type automatic adjuster

Description

1 On later models, the self-adjusting rear brakes incorporate a variable length pushbar and wedge. Wear in the linings is automatically taken up by normal action of the brake pedal. Use of the brakes allows the shoe adjusting wedge to move downwards under spring tension to fill the increased space between the pushbar and the leading brake shoe, and so position the shoe linings at the correct distance from the internal surface of the drum.
2 Lining wear can be checked on this type of brake by prising the plug from the brake backplate.

Shoe renewal

3 To remove the brake shoes, remove one roadwheel bolt, raise the rear of the vehicle and support it securely.
4 Insert a screwdriver into the vacant bolt hole in the wheel and engage the screwdriver with the automatic adjuster wedge. Rotate the wheel as necessary to do this. Lever the wedge upwards until it contacts its stop.
5 Remove the brake drum as described in Chapter 9.
6 Remove the shoe steady pins and springs by gripping the cupped washer, depressing it and turning it through 90°.
7 Pull the bottom ends of the shoes outwards and over the anchor block. Disconnect the lower return spring.
8 Move the handbrake lever that is attached to the rear shoe so that the cable can be disconnected from it.
9 Using pliers, unhook the spring from the adjusting wedge.
10 Unhook the upper return spring and remove the shoes from the vehicle.
11 Clamp the pushbar in the jaws of a vice and unhook its tensioning spring.
12 Set the new shoes out on the bench in the same relative position as the original.
13 With the pushbar again clamped in a vice connect the shoe, pushbar and spring.
14 Insert the adjusting wedge so that its lug is towards the brake backplate. Lightly grease the contact areas of the pushbar with brake expander grease, then connect the shoe with the handbrake lever as shown in Fig. 14.196.
15 Connect the shoe upper return spring, take the shoes to the backplate and reconnect the handbrake cable.
16 Locate the ends of the shoes on the wheel cylinder pistons, connect the lower return spring and then lever the lower ends of the shoes over and into the anchor block.

Fig. 14.193 Releasing the wedge type automatic adjuster

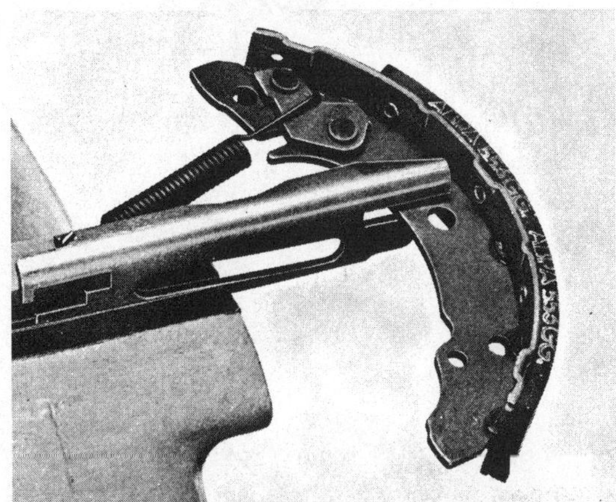

Fig. 14.194 Brake pushbar adjuster gripped ready for tension spring removal

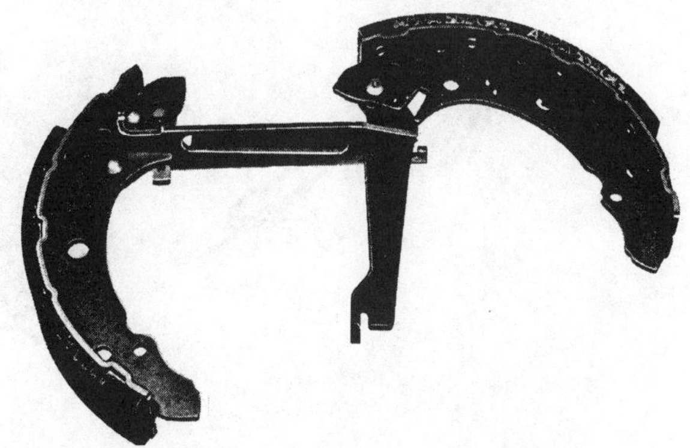

Fig. 14.195 Attaching handbrake lever to pushbar

17 Reconnect the adjusting wedge spring between the wedge and the brake shoe.
18 Fit the shoe steady pins and springs.
19 Fit the brake drum.
20 Apply the brake pedal hard to set the self-adjusting mechanism.
21 Renew the shoes on the opposite brake with the same type and grade of friction lining.

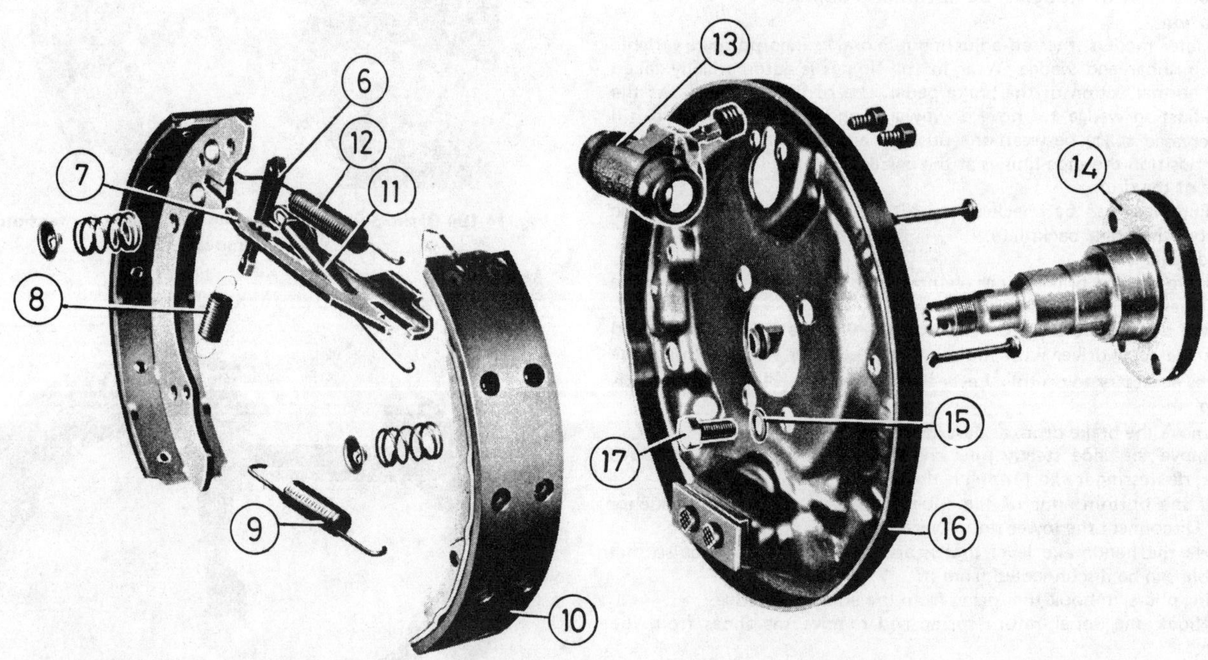

Fig. 14.196 Later type drum brake with pushbar and wedge automatic adjuster

1 Brake drum
2 Thrust washer
3 Nut
4 Split pin
5 Hub cap
6 Wedge
7 Pushbar
8 Wedge spring
9 Lower return spring
10 Brake shoe
11 Upper return spring
12 Tension spring
13 Wheel cylinder
14 Stub axle
15 Lockwasher
16 Backplate
17 Bolt

Pedal and pushrod - adjustment

22 Refer to Fig. 14.197 and 14.198, and the table which follows. There is considerable variation in the details of pedal arrangement. This means that the limits for adjustment vary, and so you must identify the type of pedal fitted to your car and then select the correct measurement. The dimension to be measured is 'A', the distance between the centres of the holes in the pedal lever for the pivot pin and the pin connecting the pushrod stirrup to the pedal lever. There are different settings for RH and LH drive, and for manual gearboxes with and without servo. There is also a setting for LH and RH drive vehicles with automatic gearboxes.

23 The method of adjustment is the same as that described in Chapter 9, Section 22, by adjustment of the total length of the pushrod. This is effected by undoing the locknut and screwing the pushrod in or out of the stirrup until the correct adjustment is obtained. For manual transmission without servo, first make sure that the pedal is held against the stop by the spring, slacken the locknut and turn the pushrod until there is 0.15 to 0.27 in (4 to 7 mm) play at the pedal plate. Tighten the locknut and check. Readjust if necessary.

24 For vehicles with servo, the critical measurement is as shown in Fig. 14.198, distance 'B' between the centre of the pedal tip and the underside of the steering wheel. Consult the table. The adjustment is done the same way. One method to measure dimension 'B' is to cut a piece of ¼ in (6.35 mm) dowel rod to the right length and use it as a gauge.

25 Identification of pedal and adjustment 'B':

	Dimension 'A' (mm)	Dimension 'B' (mm)
Manual gearbox with servo:		
LHD	55.5	608
LHD	47	600
LHD	50	600
RHD	55.5	580
Automatic gearbox:		
LHD RHD	55.5	580

Later type front disc brakes

Ventilated disc type

26 As from June 1979, a new Girling caliper is fitted which has a larger pad area.

27 The thickness of the pad friction material can be checked by shining a torch through one of the cut-outs in the roadwheel. If the total thickness of either pad, including backing plate, is down to the specified minimum, then they must be renewed as an axle set (four pads).

28 To renew the pads, raise the car, remove the roadwheel and take out the pad retaining springs.

29 Unscrew and remove the upper and lower guide bolts. Take off the cylinder assembly.

30 Withdraw the pads from the pad carrier.

31 Brush away any dust or dirt, taking care not to inhale it.

32 The caliper piston must now be depressed fully into the cylinder. This can usually be done using a wide-bladed tool such as a tyre lever. As the piston is pushed in, it will cause the brake fluid level in the master cylinder reservoir to rise. Anticipate this by syphoning off some fluid using an old but clean battery hydrometer or poultry baster.

33 Fit the new pads and the cylinder assembly. Tighten the guide bolts to the specified torque.

34 Fit the pad upper and lower springs.

35 Apply the brake pedal two or three times hard to position the pads against the disc.

36 Repeat the operations on the opposite brake and then top up the master cylinder fluid reservoir.

Non-ventilated disc type

37 Check the pad wear as described in paragraph 31.

38 To renew the pads, raise the car and remove the roadwheel.

39 Press the caliper cylinder assembly in the direction of the arrow (Fig. 14.204). This will push the piston back into the cylinder to accommodate the thicker pads. This action will cause the fluid level in the master cylinder to rise, so anticipate this by syphoning out some fluid using an old (clean) battery hydrometer or poultry baster.

40 Unscrew the lower guide pin bolt, holding the guide pin with an open-ended spanner.

41 Swivel the cylinder assembly upwards and remove the brake pads.

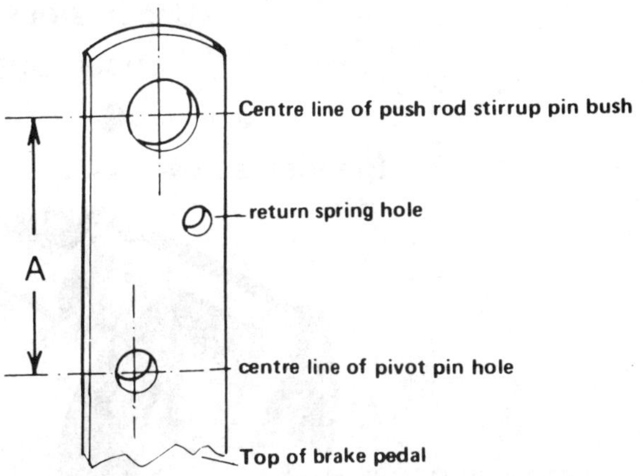

Fig. 14.197 Brake pedal arm detail. For A see text

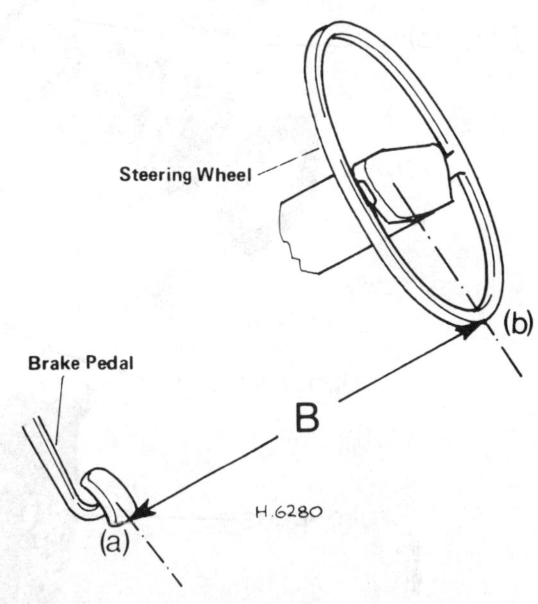

Fig. 14.198 Brake pedal setting diagram (with servo). Measure between points (a) and (b)

B Refer to table in text

Fig. 14.199 Checking disc pad wear (a)

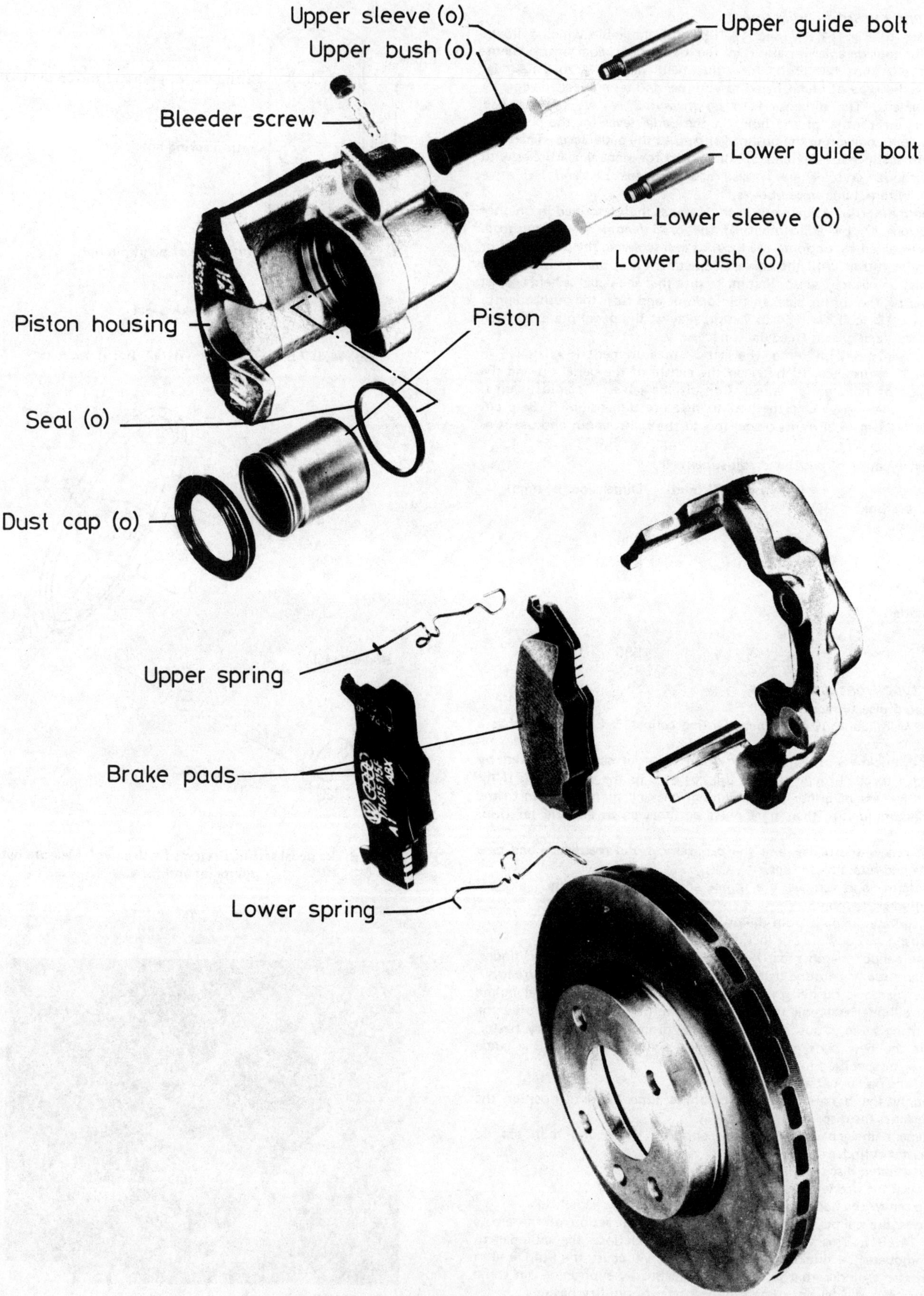

Fig. 14.200 Later type ventilated disc brake. Items marked (o) are included in repair kit

Fig. 14.201 Later type caliper guide bolts (arrowed) (ventilated disc brake)

Fig. 14.202 Later type disc pad springs (arrowed)

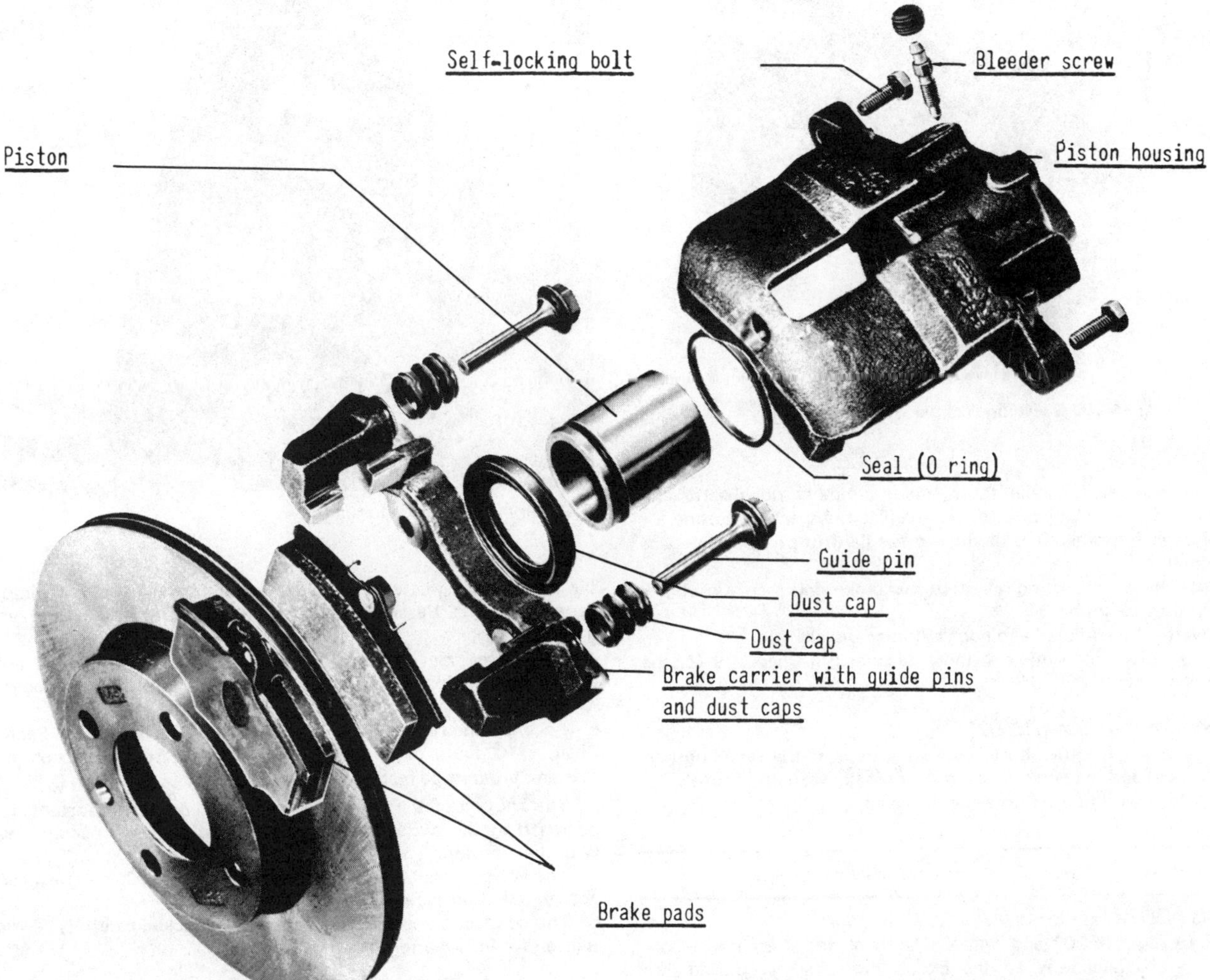

Self-locking bolt
Bleeder screw
Piston
Piston housing
Seal (O ring)
Guide pin
Dust cap
Dust cap
Brake carrier with guide pins and dust caps
Brake pads

Fog. 14.203 Later type non-ventilated disc brake

Fig. 14.204 Direction of movement for depressing piston

Fig. 14.205 Unscrewing a caliper guide bolt (non-ventilated disc)

Fig. 14.206 Swivelling caliper cylinder assembly

42 Fit the new pads, swivel the cylinder assembly downwards and screw in a new self-locking bolt, tightening it to the specified torque.
43 Apply the footbrake two or three times hard to position the pads against the disc.
44 Repeat the operation on the opposite brake and then top up the master cylinder reservoir.

Caliper overhaul (ventilated and non-ventilated discs)

45 The operations are similar to those described in Chapter 9 for the earlier type caliper.

Servo connecting hose (RHD)

46 It is possible for the short connecting hose at the servo unit to become kinked and in consequence to shut off the vacuum (photo).
47 Check for this condition at regular intervals.

10 Electrical system Part I: Generating and starting systems

Motorola alternator - description and overhaul

1 Refer to Figs. 14.207 and 14.208. Although the alternator is constructed in a similar way to the Bosch the detail is considerably changed. The cover, housing, and diode plate take a different form. The earth strap is bolted to the cover, not to the hinge as with the Bosch.
2 The brushgear may be removed as a unit and brush length checked (see Fig. 14.209).
3 The same principles apply for overhaul. The rotor should be checked for earth short circuit and continuity. The resistance between

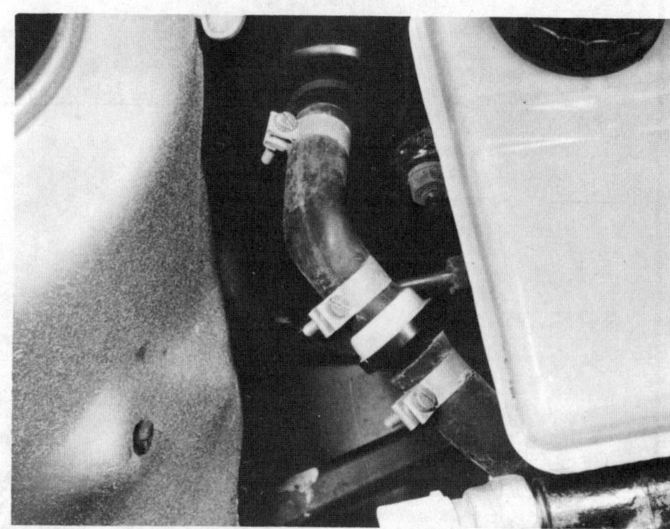
9.46 Servo elbow hose kinked

slip rings must agree with the Specifications, ovality of slip rings must be within limits. Bearings may be drawn off with a puller and renewed if necessary.
4 The stator may be disconnected from the diode plate and the winding tested for open and short-circuit. The resistance should agree with the Specifications.
5 Once isolated the diode plate may be tested, as in Section 9, Chapter 10, and a new one fitted if required. It is not recommended that any attempt be made to renew diodes.
6 The routing of the 'D+' wire inside the cover is important. It must be fitted in the two sets of clips provided or it will become involved with the armature.
7 The voltage regulator connections must be checked. The green wire goes to 'DF' and the red wire to 'D+'.
8 The connections on the cover must be checked carefully. A diagram is given for information (see Fig. 14.211).

11 Electrical system Part II: Lighting, instrument panel, electrical accessories and wiring

Rear lamps (Hatchback model)

1 The rear lamp bulb holder is accessible from the luggage compartment. Squeeze the bulb holder clips inwards and pull out the holder.

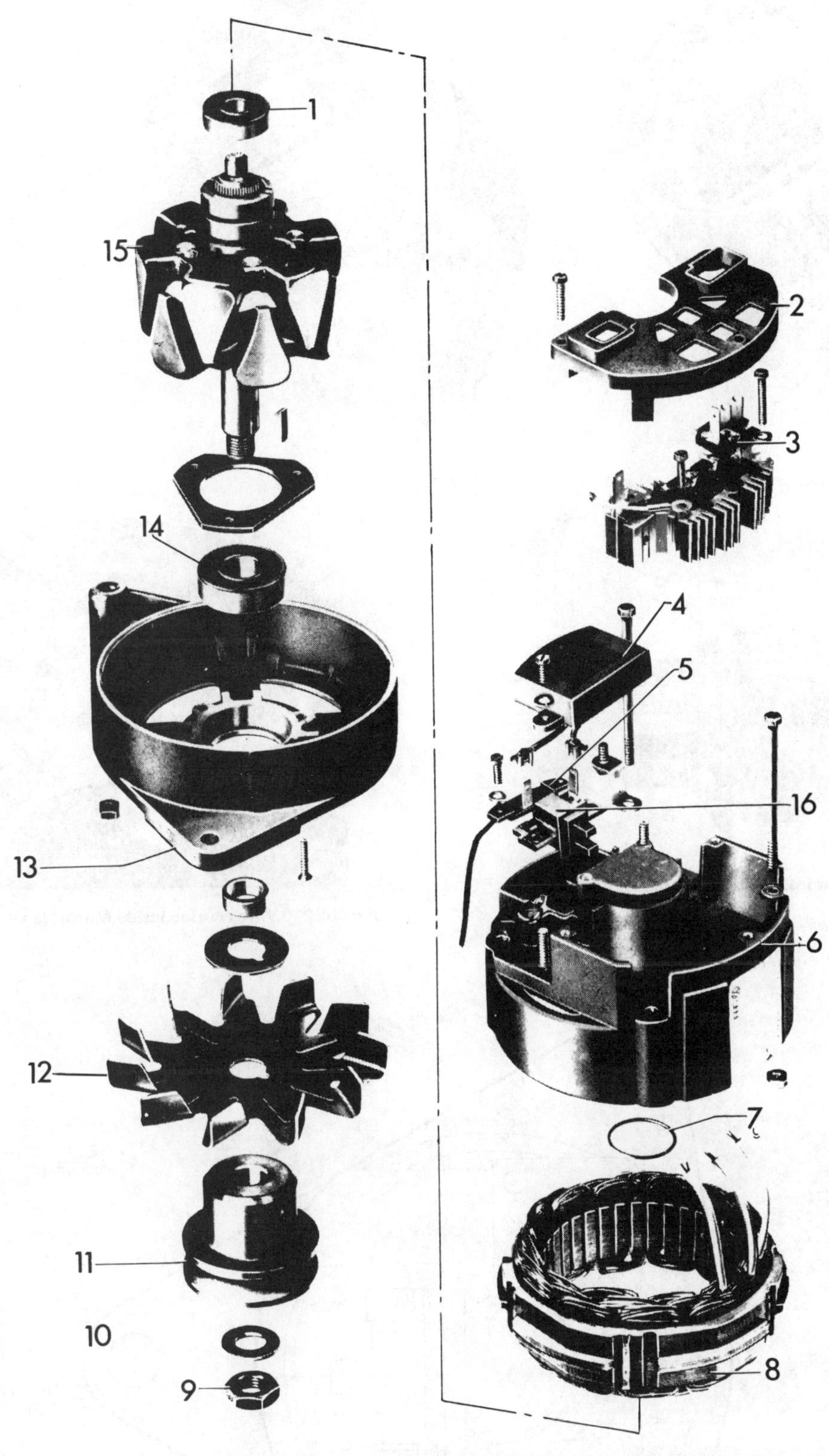

Fig. 14.207 Exploded view of Motorola alternator

1 Bearing race
2 Cover plate
3 Diode plate
4 Voltage regulator
5 Connector plate D+
6 Housing
7 O-ring
8 Stator
9 Nut
10 Thrust washer
11 Pulley
12 Fan
13 Endplate
14 Bearing
15 Rotor
16 Brushgear

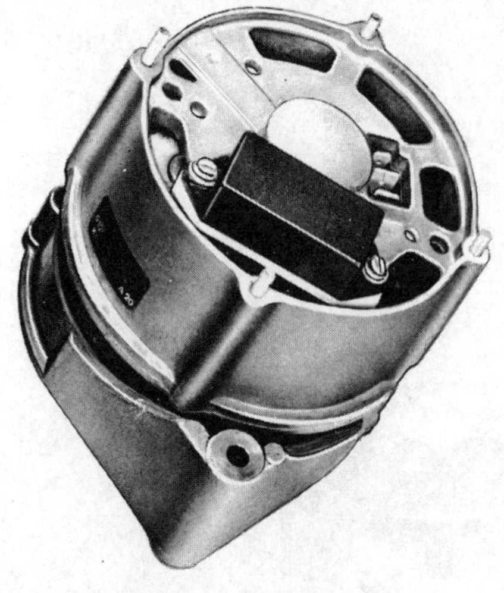

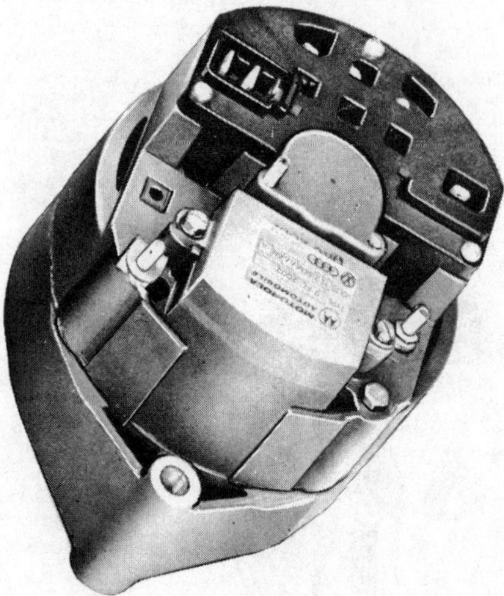

Fig. 14.208 Bosch (left) and Motorola (right) alternators

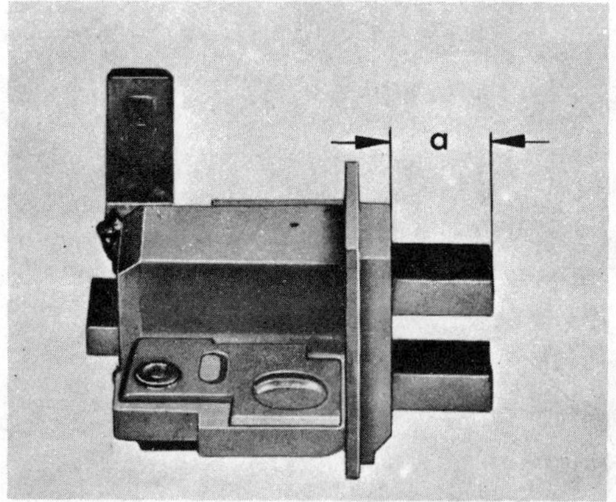

Fig. 14.209 Motorola alternator brush holder

a Brush length - wear limit 5 mm (0.2 in)

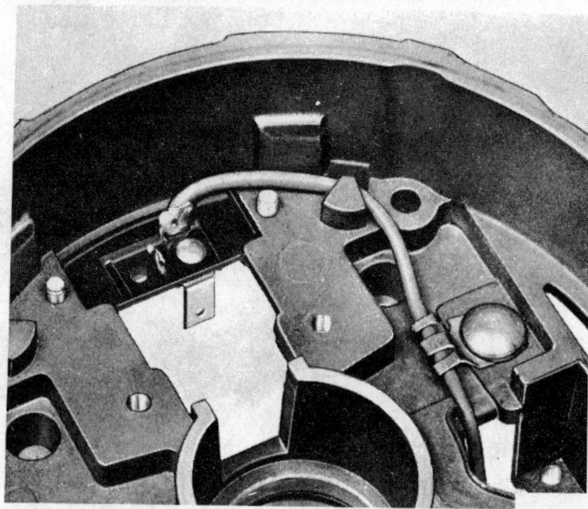

Fig. 14.210 Wire routing inside Motorola alternator cover plate

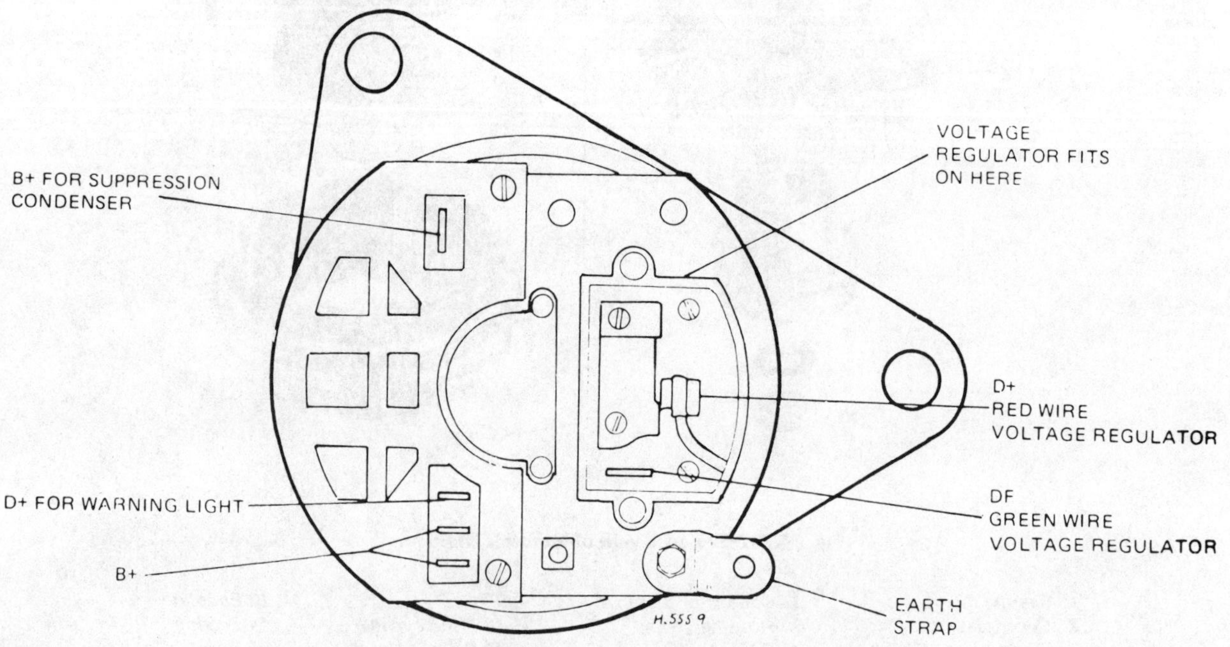

Fig. 14.211 Motorola endplate connections (voltage regulator removed to show D+ and DF wires)

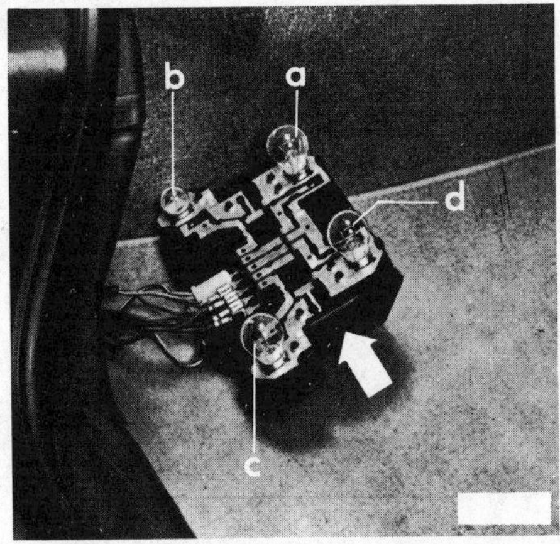

Fig. 14.212 Rear lamp bulb holder (Hatchback)

a Direction indicator   *c Stoplamp*
b Tail lamp   *d Reversing lamp*

Windscreen and tailgate washers

2 Various types of washer reservoir and pump may be encountered, depending on the date of production and whether a headlamp washer is fitted. On Estate models, the tailgate washer reservoir and pump are located behind a hinged flap at the side of the luggage area (photo).

Voltage stabilizers - modified for fitting radio

3 On vehicles without radio installed a simple bi-metal stabilizer is fitted. When fitting a new one the screws securing the fuel gauge should be masked with tape to prevent the stabilizer shorting the fuel gauge.

The voltage stabilizer for vehicles fitted with radio has a different part number from January 1977. The new one is an electronic type. The connections and voltage remain unaltered.

Instrument panel layout

4 Instrument panel layout varies considerably according to model. Refer to the appropriate current flow diagram for details of the wiring of supplementary instruments.

Modifications to 1976 on models, and additional circuits

5 On vehicles fitted with intermittent wash wipe a new relay is fitted to the relay/fuse plate. It is situated in an additional adapter located above socket 'M'. It may not be fitted to older vehicles.

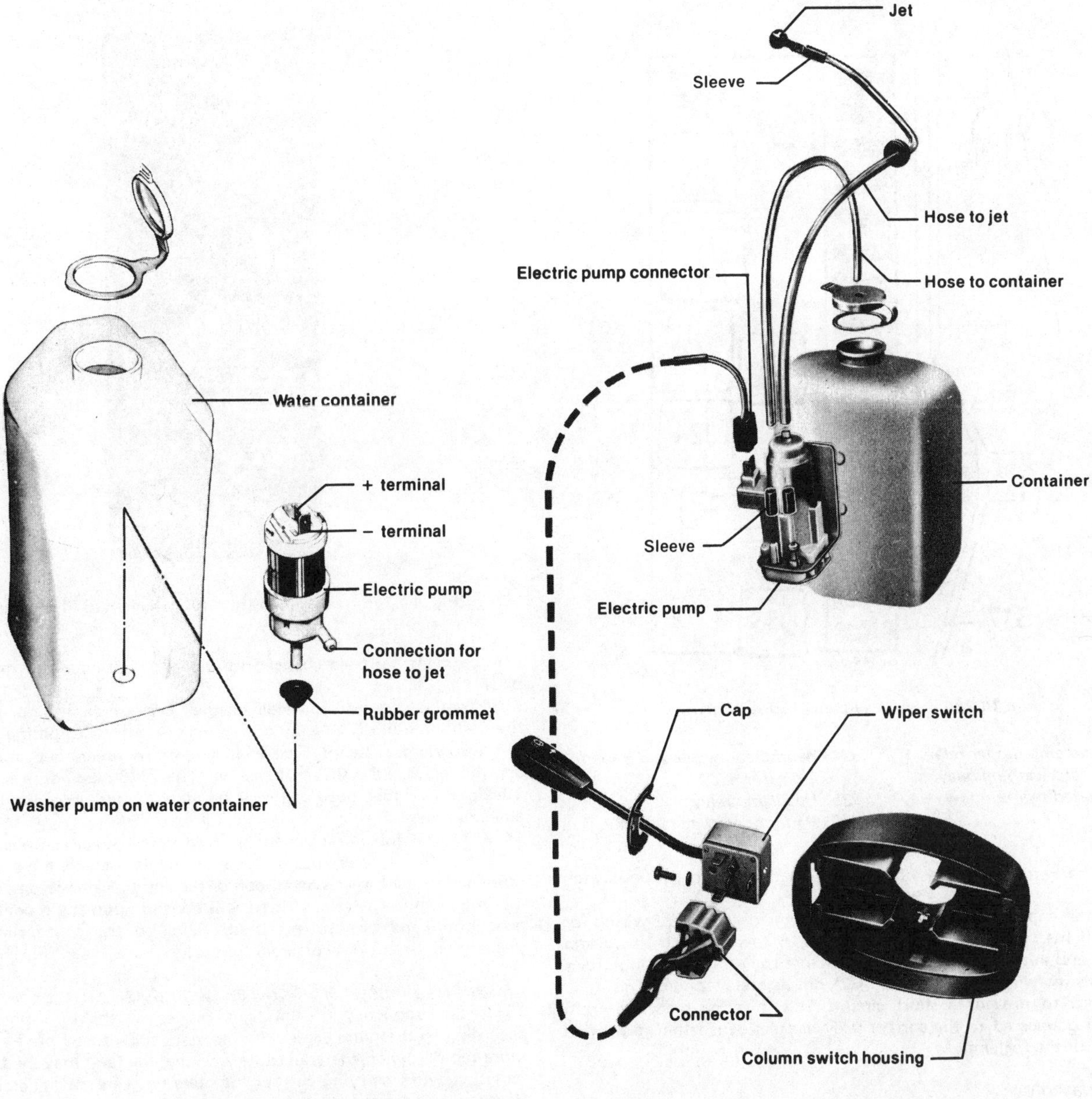

Fig. 14.213 Alternative types of windscreen washer assembly

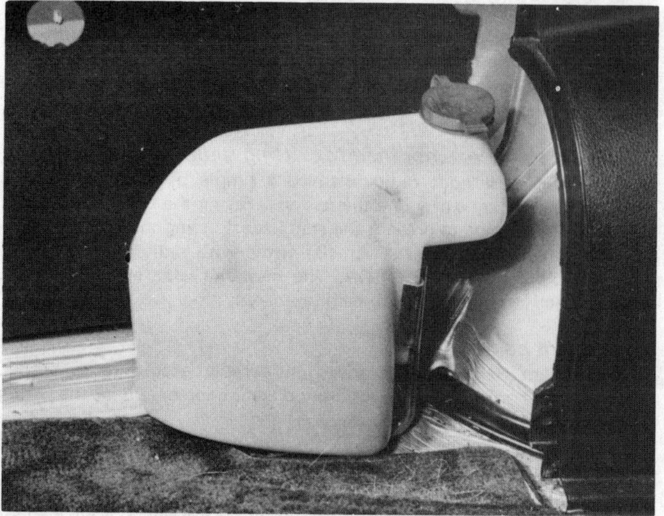

11.2 Tailgate washer reservoir and pump (Estate)

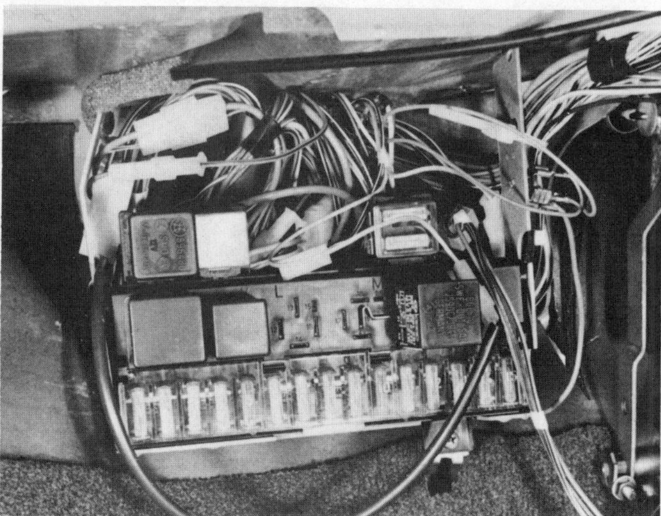

11.12 Typical fuse/relay panel

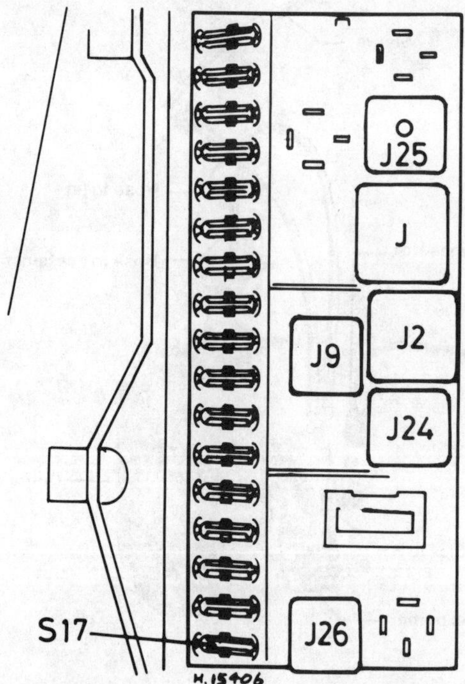

Fig. 14.214 Fuse/relay panel (1974 models)

J	*Headlamp dipper relay*	*J24*	*Windscreen wiper and direction indicator relay*
J2	*Hazard warning relay*	*J25*	*Headlamp relay*
J9	*Heated rear window relay*	*J26*	*Radiator cooling fan relay*

6 On the Passat N models the horn is operated by the wiper switch lever.

7 See the appropriate current flow diagram for details of wiring for the foglights, twin brake circuit indicator, towing hitch, headlamp washers and automatic transmission. When fitting a foglamp look for a yellow/white wire connected to 'G2' on the relay plate. This is so connected to prevent a short circuit. This must be detached from 'G2' and connected to the correct relay contact; it is fitted to provide current for the foglamps.

Fuse/relay block

8 The original location of the fuse/relay block within the engine

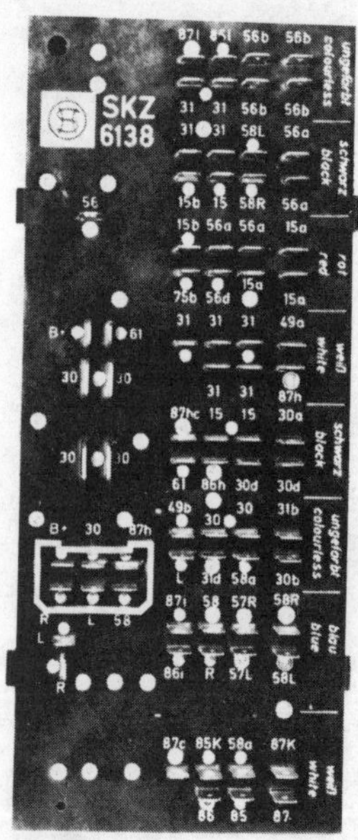

Fig. 14.215 Rear view of fuse/relay panel (1974 models)

compartment has been changed to under the left-hand side of the facia panel.

9 To get at it detach the shelf on the steering column side, or remove the dashboard bin (USA), by depressing the catch and folding the shelf/bin downwards. The 1975 cover is held on by a wire clip, remove this and the relays and fuses are accessible. The 1976 type has press-in clips.

10 Up to 17 fuse positions may be incorporated according to model and equipment.

11 A typical fuse arrangement is given in the Specifications, but it is suggested that the circuits for your particular vehicle are checked by reference to the owner's handbook or the appropriate wiring diagram.

12 The number of relays fitted will depend upon the model, year of production and accessories fitted. Refer to the appropriate wiring diagram or current flow diagram (photo).

Flasher frequency variation - early models

13 If the frequency of the light flashes of the turn signal varies according to the number of other accessories switched on, eg it flashes more rapidly when the wipers are working, the fault may be due to the fact that wires carrying current for these units are passing close to the flasher relay, and the magnetic field set up by these currents is affecting the operation of the relay.

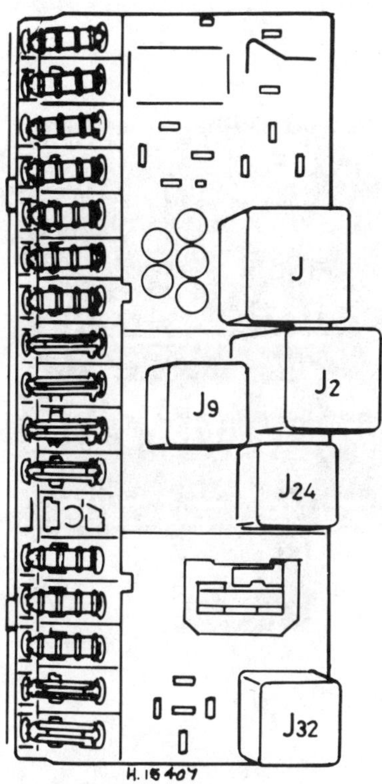

Fig. 14.216 Fuse/relay panel (1975 models)

J Headlamp dipper relay
J2 Hazard warning relay
J9 Heated rear window relay
J24 Windscreen wiper and direction indicator relay
J32 Air conditioner relay (where applicable)

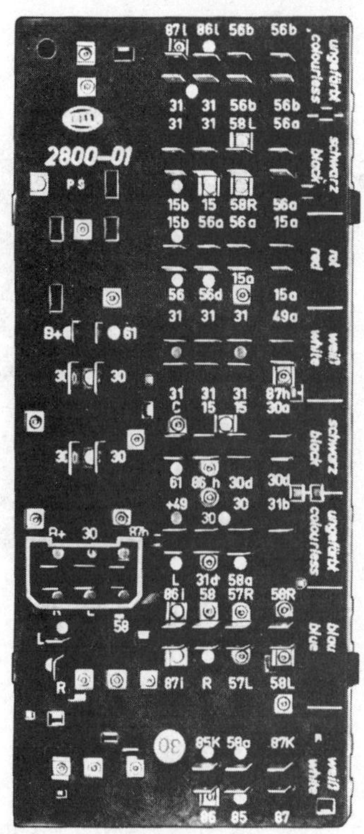

Fig. 14.217 Rear view of fuse/relay panel (1975 models)

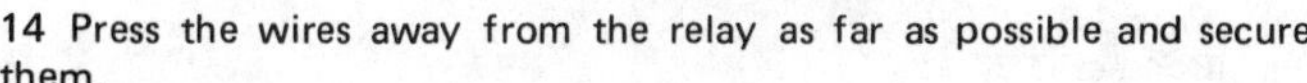

14 Press the wires away from the relay as far as possible and secure them.

15 Later models have a different type of relay which is not affected in this way and this can be used on earlier models.

Wiring diagrams and current flow diagrams

16 The earlier wiring diagrams for these models have been superseded by current flow diagrams.

17 The current flow diagram is generally accepted as being easier to follow than a wiring diagram. For those not familiar with this type of diagram, the following information should be of assistance when tracing wiring.

18 VW have produced an excellent system. Most vehicle mechanics dislike tracing wiring, so the way current flow diagrams work is to show each wire separately in an easily recognisable form. Turn to Fig. 14.231 which is the current flow diagram for the 1977 Passat range.

19 The thin lined section at the top represents the relay/fuse board with lines '15', '30' and '31' running through it' They are built in and so are all the other thin lines above the thick lined part. Refer to the key for the diagram, item 'J' is the headlight dip relay referred to with a conventional symbol. Turn to Fig. 14.220. This shows all the conventional symbols. Note that all junctions are marked with an 'O', solid for fixed (soldered), open for separable. Where wires just cross they are not joined but insulated from one another. Study the symbol synopsis and when you have a good understanding of it go back to the current flow diagram. At the bottom of the diagram is a straight line with a lot of numbers on it. This represents earth (ground) and the numbers refer to the current tracks.

20 In between the earth line and the relay plate are a number of these tracks each representing the wiring of one or more items. Start with an easy one, number 80. This is the wiring for 'M7'. Look at the key, 'M7' is 'Turn signal, front, right'. The circle with a cross in it according to the symbol chart is a bulb, which we would expect. The heavy line from the bulb to earth indicates that there is an earth wire. If it had been a thin line as in track 51 then earth contact is made by screwing the component to the frame, or as in track 58, 'G2', which is the coolant temperature sender unit, screwing the unit into the engine coolant union. Note that most of the units have earth wires.

21 Follow track 80 upwards, it goes to 'T1a', which the key says is a single connector in the engine compartment front right. The wire now joins the loom but just before the fusebox it joins a 4-pin connector by the fusebox. At the fuse/relay plate it has a number, 'C18'. Inside the plate 'C18' joins 'F16'. 'F' is the plug socket for the rear harness, and 'F16' is from the rear turn signal right. It also joins 'B19' which goes to a blob with a number on it, number 11. 'B' is the computer diagnosis harness plug and 'B11' is the connection for testing the right flasher circuit. Follow the line along the board and it comes out at 'E22'. 'E' is one of the plugs for the dash harness and 'E22' goes to 'E2' which, oddly enough, is the turn signal switch. It also gets mixed up with 'E3' which is the emergency flasher switch. Follow it back up track 68 and it goes back into the board at 'E3' (dash harness) where it goes to 'J2', the emergency light relay and thence to the supply. There is a side line to 'D1' which is connected to 'K5', the turn signal warning light. Actually your investigations will mainly stop at the board. If there is something wrong in the board go to the agent, because you can't repair the board, but you can trace faults outside the board and renew switches, lamps, earth wires or even just push connectors together where they have come apart.

22 There are a number of other small pieces of information on the chart. At the end of each wire is a number which indicates the terminal number. Between current tracks 82 and 83 is a wire apparently going nowhere from 'G2' and 'E7'. It ends in a black connector 'Tlg' and is labelled 'L22'. This is the spare wire for the foglights if you want to fit them. There are small breaks in the wire with figures 1.0 or 1.5. These are the wire sizes. A number of circles with numbers in them (at the bottom of the diagram) indicate earth points, and the key says where they are.

Fig. 14.218 Fuse/relay panel (1976 on)

	Contact	Relay terminal	Connected with
J			
Headlamp low beam flasher relay	1	56	Contact G 10, D 17, J 2
	2	56	Contact J 1
	3	56 b	Contact J 5, Fuse S 1, S 2
	4	56 a	Contact G 8, Fuse S 3, S 4
	5	56 b	Contact J 3
	6	30	Contact H 1 to H 7 (terminal 30)
	7	S	Contact E 8
K			
Rear window heater relay	8	86	Contact D 10, L 15, M 18, N 23 (terminal 31)
	9	30	Contact H 1 to H 7 (terminal 30)
	10	87	Fuse S 5
	11	85	Contact D 7
L	12	86	Contact A 3
	13	30	Contact H 1 to H 7 (terminal 30)
	14	87	Contact A 8
	15	31	Contact D 10, K 8, M 18, N 23 (terminal 31)
	16	15	Fuse S 8, S 9
M	17	15	Bridge for windscreen wiper motor from M 19 to M 21. Also on vehicles with intermittent wiper control.
	18	31	
	19	53 S	
	20	S 1	
	21	53 M	
N			
Turn signal/ emergency signal relay	22	49 a	Contact D 1, E 3
	23	31	Contact D 10, L 15, K 8, M 18 (terminal 31)
	24	+49	Contact D 12
	25	C	Contact D 6

Fig. 14.219 Rear view of fuse/relay panel (1976 on)

A Connection for front harness
B Connection for diagnosis harness
C Connection for front harness
D Connection for dash harness
E Connection for dash harness
F Connection for rear harness
G 1 Connected to G 6 via fuse S 15
G 2 Connected to contact E 7 and M 20
G 3 Connected to ignition switch, terminal 15
G 4 Connected to fuse S 12
G 5 Connected to generator, terminal D+
G 6 Connected to G 1 via fuse S 15
G 7 Connected to ignition switch, terminal X
G 8 Connected to dipper and headlight flasher relay, terminal 56a
G 9 Connected to oil pressure switch
G 10 Connected to lighting switch, terminal 56
H1 to H7 are connected to terminal 30

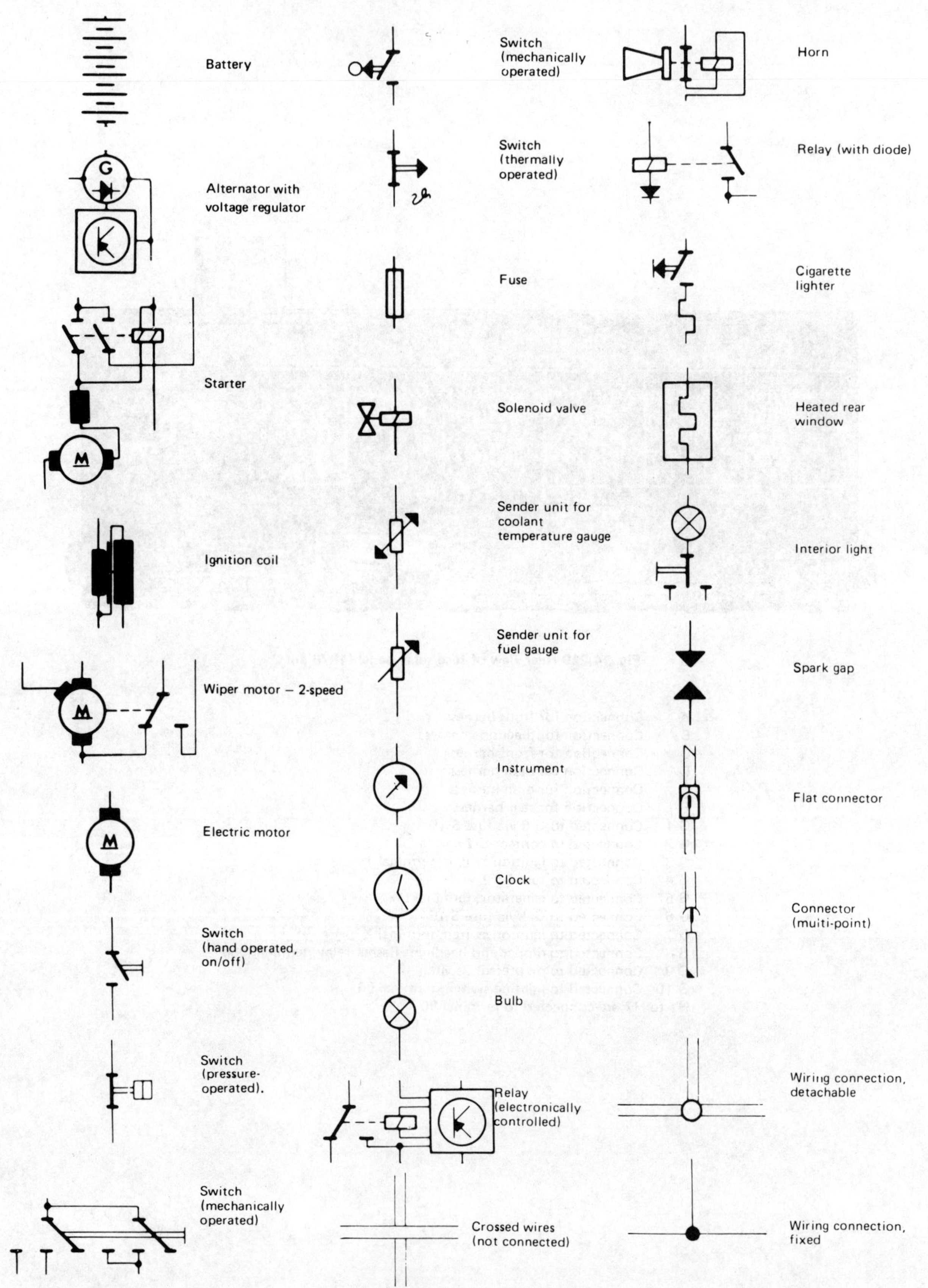
Battery
Switch (mechanically operated)
Horn
Alternator with voltage regulator
Switch (thermally operated)
Relay (with diode)
Fuse
Cigarette lighter
Starter
Solenoid valve
Heated rear window
Sender unit for coolant temperature gauge
Ignition coil
Interior light
Sender unit for fuel gauge
Spark gap
Wiper motor – 2-speed
Instrument
Flat connector
Electric motor
Clock
Connector (multi-point)
Switch (hand operated, on/off)
Bulb
Switch (pressure-operated).
Relay (electronically controlled)
Wiring connection, detachable
Switch (mechanically operated)
Crossed wires (not connected)
Wiring connection, fixed

Fig. 14.220 Key to symbols used in wiring diagrams

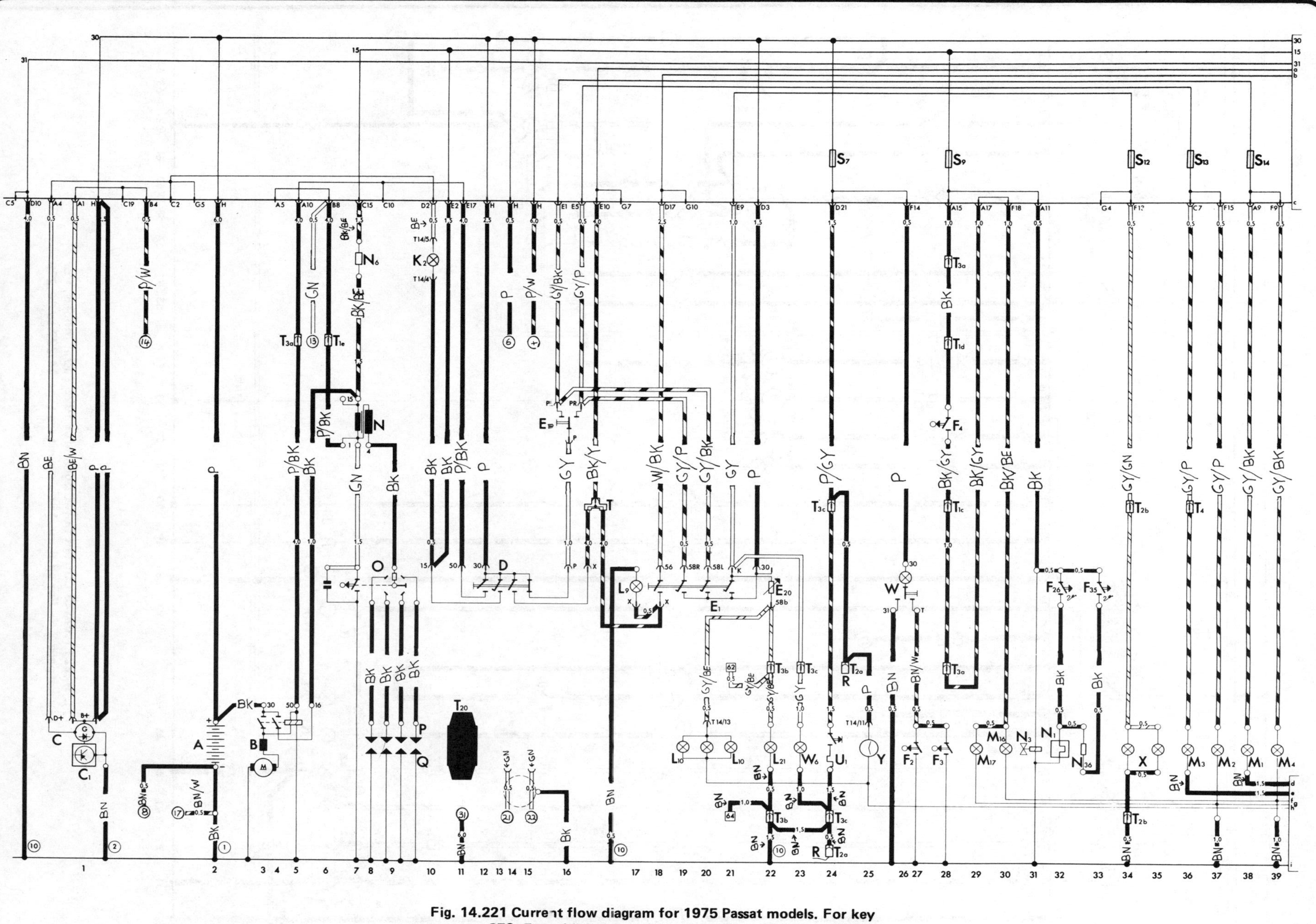

Fig. 14.221 Current flow diagram for 1975 Passat models. For key see page 270. For additional equipment see Figs. 14.222 to 14.229

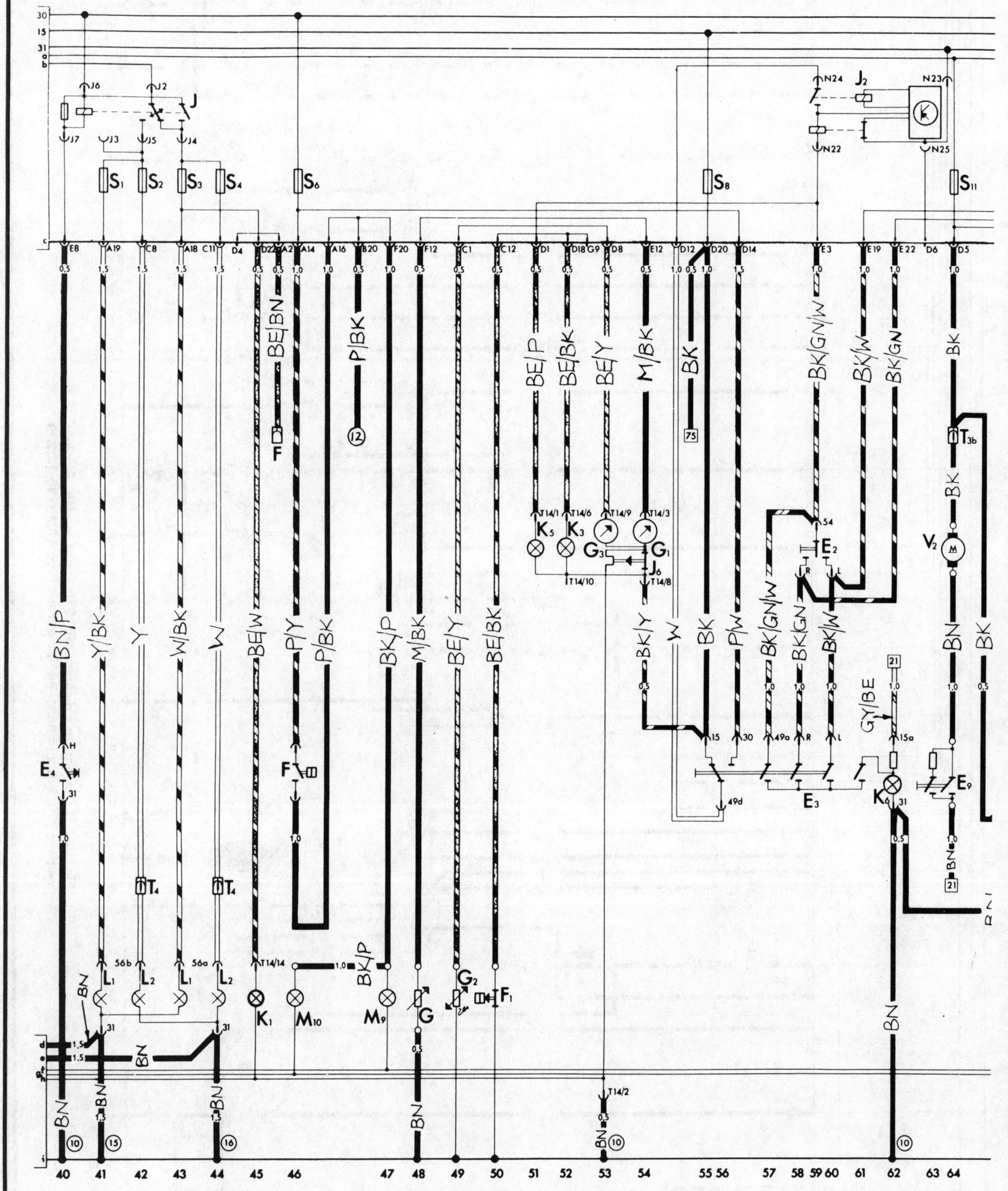

Fig. 14.221 (cont'd) Current flow diagram for 1975 Passat models. For key see page 270. For additional equipment see Figs. 14.222 to 14.229

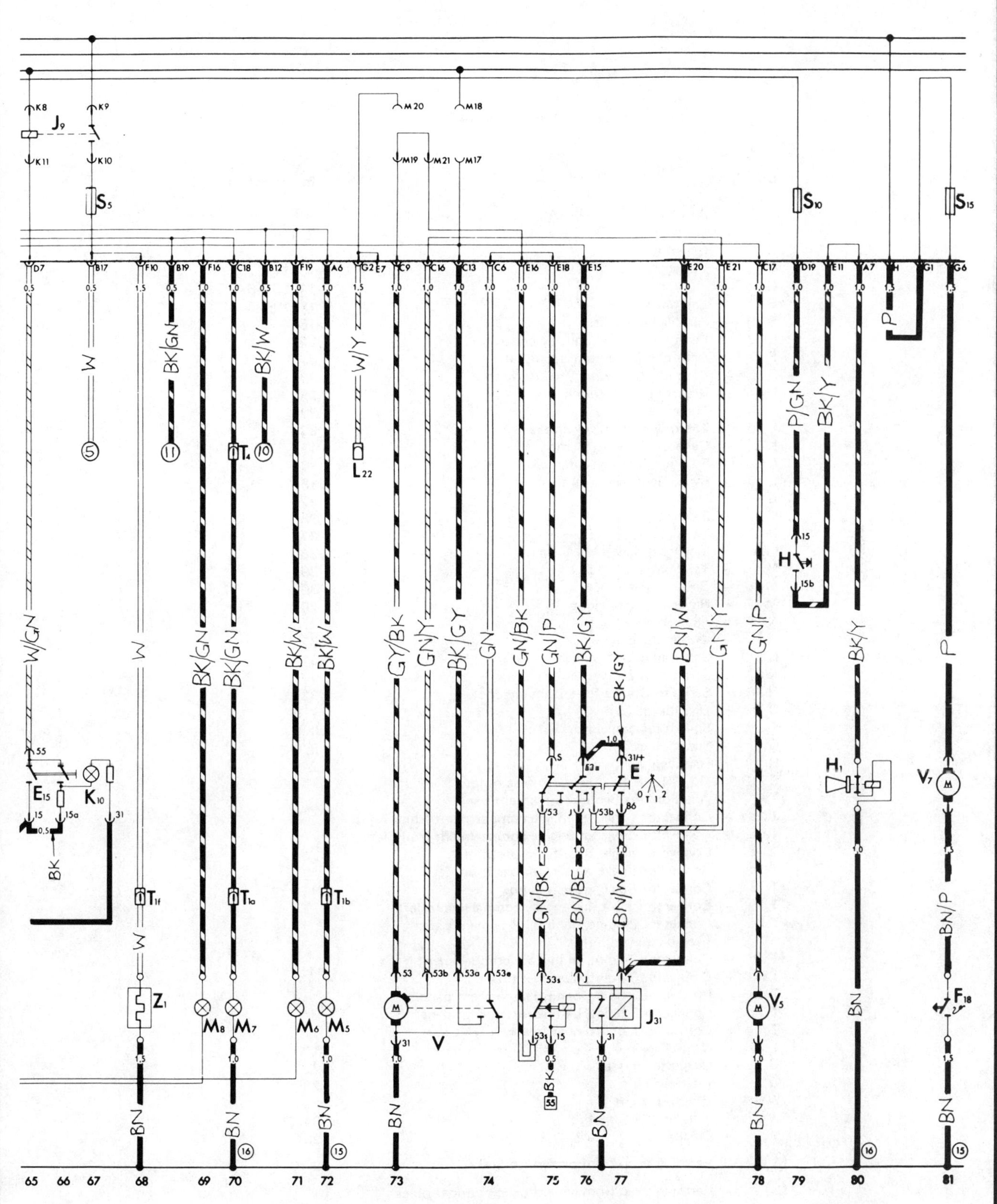

Fig. 14.221 (cont'd) Current flow diagram for 1975 Passat models. For key see page 270. For additional equipment see Figs. 14.222 to 14.229

Key to Fig. 14.221

Description			In current track
A	–	Battery	2
B	–	Starter	2, 4, 5
C	–	Generator	1
C 1	–	Voltage regulator	10, 11, 12, 13 14. 15. 16
E 1	–	Lighting switch	18, 19, 20, 21
E 19	–	Parking light switch	16
E 20	–	Instrument panel lighting control	22
F 2	–	Door contact switch, front, left	27
F 3	–	Door contact switch, front, right	28
F 4	–	Reversing light switch	28
F 26	–	Thermoswitch for choke	32
F 35	–	Thermoswitch II for choke	33
K 2	–	Generator warning lamp	10
L 9	–	Bulb for lighting switch illumination	17
L 10	–	Instrument panel light	19, 20, 21
L 21	–	Heater lever light	22
M 1	–	Sidelight, left	38
M 2	–	Tail light, right	37
M 3	–	Sidelight, right	36
M 4	–	Tail light, left	39
M 16	–	Reversing light, left	30
M 17	–	Reversing light, right	29
N	–	Ignition coil	7, 8
N 1	–	Automatic choke	32
N 3	–	Solenoid cut-off valve	31
N 6	–	Series resistance wire for coil	7
N 36	–	Series resistance for automatic choke	33
O	–	Distributor	7, 9
P	–	Spark plug connector	8, 9
Q	–	Spark plugs	8, 9
R	–	Radio connection	24
S 7, S 9, S 12, S 13, S 14	–	Fuses in fuse holder	
T	–	Junction box behind instrument panel	
T 1a	–	Connector single, in engine compartment front, right	
T 1b	–	Connector single, in engine compartment front, left	
T 1c	–	Connector single, near front partition	
T 1d	–	Connector single, near front partition	
T 1e	–	Connector single, near fuse box	
T 1f	–	Connector single, in luggage compartment, left	
T 2a	–	Connector 2-point, behind instrument panel (Radio connection)	
T 2b	–	Connector 2-point, in luggage compartment	
T3a	–	Connector 3-point, near fuse box	
T 3b	–	Connector 3-point, behind instrument panel	
T 3c	–	Connector 3-point, behind instrument panel	
T 4	–	Connector 4-point, near fuse box	
T 20	–	Central socket	11
U 1	–	Cigarette lighter	24
W	–	Interior lights	26
W 6	–	Glovebox light	23
X	–	Number plate light	34, 35
Y	–	Clock	25
(1)	–	Earthing strap from battery to body	2
(2)	–	Earthing strap from generator to cylinder block	1
(10)	–	Earthing point on body	

Key to Fig. 14.221 (cont'd)

Description			In current track
E	–	Windscreen wiper, intermittent switch	75, 76, 77
E 2	–	Turn signal switch	59, 60
E 3	–	Emergency light switch	55, 56, 57, 58 59, 60, 61
E 4	–	Dip and headlight flasher switch	40
E 9	–	Blower motor switch	63, 64
E 15	–	Heated rear window switch	65, 66
F	–	Brake light switch	46
F 1	–	Oil pressure switch	50
F 18	–	Thermoswitch for radiator fan motor	81
G	–	Fuel gauge sender unit	48
G 1	–	Fuel gauge	54
G 2	–	Coolant temperature gauge sender unit	49
G 3	–	Coolant temperature gauge	53
H	–	Horn plate	79
H 1	–	Horn	80
J	–	Dipper and headlight flasher relay	40, 42, 43
J 2	–	Emergency warning light relay	59, 61, 63
J 6	–	Voltage stabilizer	53, 54
J 9	–	Heated rear window relay	65, 67
J 31	–	Intermittent wash/wipe relay	75, 76, 77
K 1	–	High beam warning lamp	45
K 3	–	Oil pressure warning lamp	52
K 5	–	Turn signal warning lamp	51
K 6	–	Emergency light system warning lamp	62
K 10	–	Heated rear window warning lamp	67
L 1	–	Twin filament bulb for left headlight	41, 43
L 2	–	Twin filament bulb for right headlight	42, 44
L 22	–	To left and right hand foglights (pull wire off G 2)	72
M 5	–	Turn signal, front, left	72
M 6	–	Turn signal, rear, left	71
M 7	–	Turn signal, front, right	70
M 8	–	Turn signal, rear, right	69
M 9	–	Brake light left	47
M 10	–	Brake light right	46
S 1, S 2, S 3, S 4, S 5, S 6, S 8, S 10 S 11, S 15		Fuses in fuse box	
T	–	Adaptor behind instrument panel	
T 1a	–	Connector single, in engine compartment, front right	
T 1b	–	Connector single, in engine compartment, front left	
T 1c	–	Connector single, near front partition	
T 1d	–	Connector single, near front partition	
T 1e	–	Connector single, near fuse box	
T 1f	–	Connector single, in luggage compartment left	
T 2a	–	Connector 2 points, behind instrument panel	
T 2b	–	Connector 2 point, in luggage compartment	
T 3a	–	Connector 3 points, near fuse box	
T 3b	–	Connector 3 point, behind instrument panel	
T 3c	–	Connector 3 point, behind instrument panel	
T 4	–	Connector 4 point, near fuse box	
V	–	Windscreen wiper motor	73, 74
V 2	–	Blower motor	64
V 5	–	Washer pump motor	78
V 7	–	Radiator fan motor	81
Z 1	–	Heated rear window	68
(10)	–	Earthing point on body	
(15)	–	Earthing point in engine compartment, front, left	
(16)	–	Earthing point in engine compartment front, right	

The circles are the connections in the test network which are wired directly to the central socket (T 20). The numbers in the circles correspond to the terminals in the socket.

Wire colours

BN	Brown	BK	Black
BE	Blue	M	Mauve
W	White	Y	Yellow
P	Pink	GY	Grey
GN	Green		

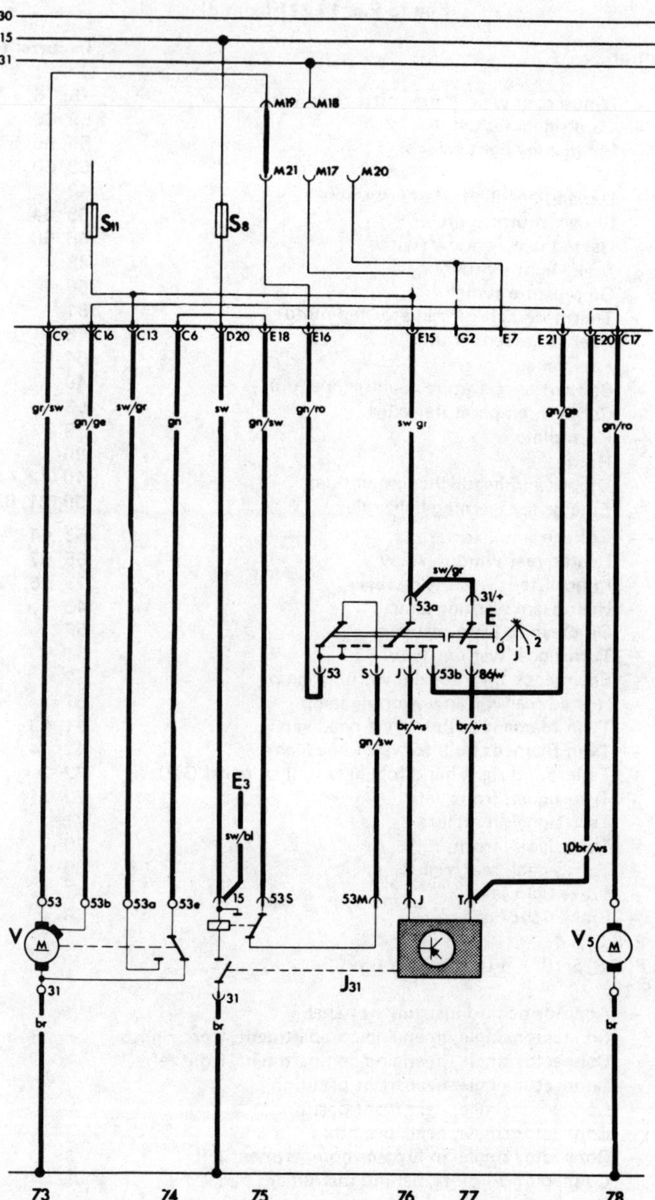

Fig. 14.222 Current flow diagram - intermittent wipers. Use in conjunction with Fig. 14.221

Description			In current track
E	–	Wiper switch for intermittent operation	76, 77
E 3	–	to emergency light switch terminal 15	75
J 31	–	Wash-wipe, intermittent wiper relay	75-77
S 8	–	Fuse No 8 in fuse holder	74
S 11	–	Fuse No 11 in fuse holder	73
V	–	Wiper motor fuse holder	73
V 5	–	Windscreen washer pump motor	78

Wire colours

gr	Grey	ro	Red
gn	Green	ws	White
sw	Black	br	Brown

The two black wires connected to contact D20 on relay plate (in current track 55) have been discontinued

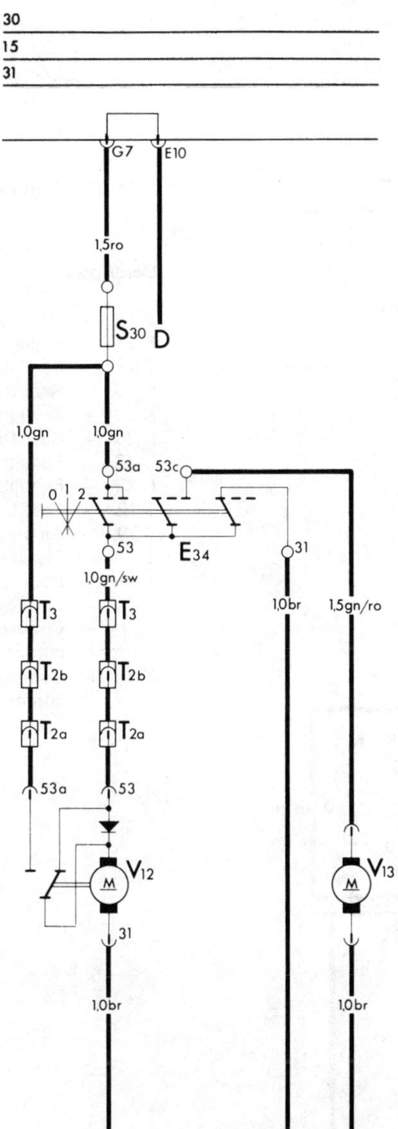

Fig. 14.223 Current flow diagram for rear wash/wipe. Use in conjunction with Fig. 14.221

Description		In current track
E 34	– Rear wiper and washer pump switch	1 - 4
D	– to ignition/starter switch, terminal X	
S 30	– Rear wiper separate fuse	2
T 2a	– Connector, 2 point in luggage compartment flap	1, 2
T 2b	– Connector, 2 point in luggage compartment, on left	1, 2
T 3	– Connector 3 point	1, 2
V 12	– Wiper motor	2
V 13	– Washer pump motor	5

Wire colours

ro	red
sw	Black
br	Brown
gn	Green

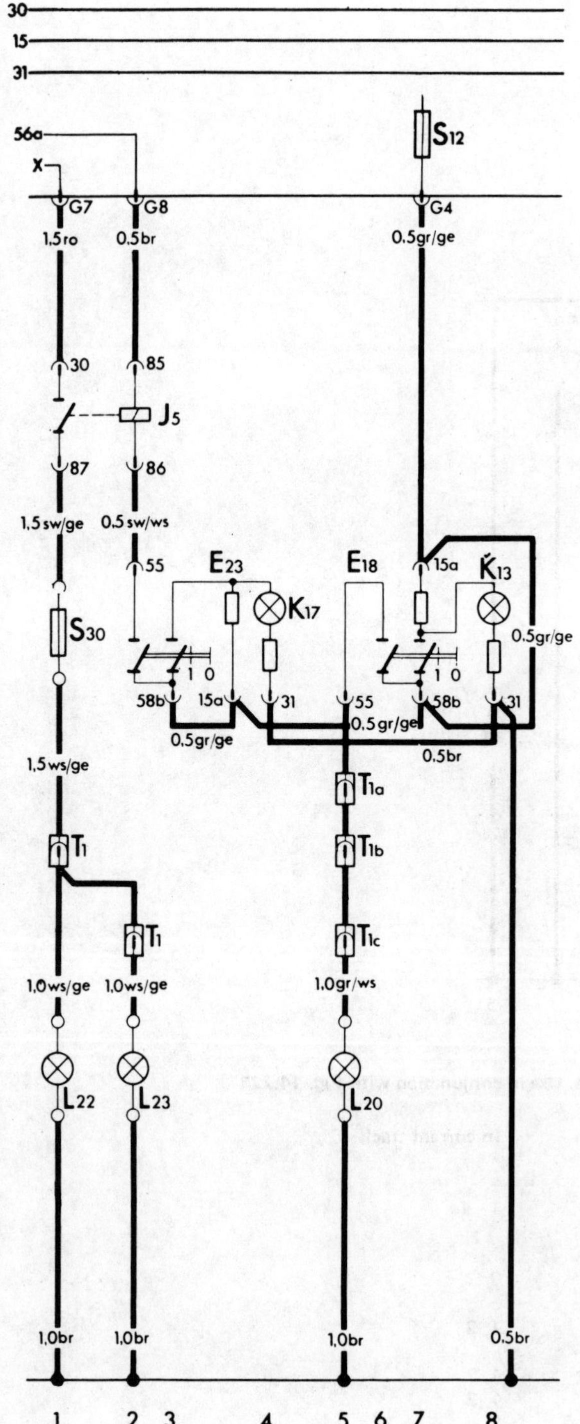

Fig. 14.224 Current flow diagram for front and rear foglamps. Use in conjunction with Fig. 14.221

Description			In current track
E 18	–	Rear foglight switch	5 - 8
E 23	–	Foglight switch	2 - 4
J 5	–	Foglight relay	1, 2
K 13	–	Rear foglight warning lamp	8
K 17	–	Foglight warning lamp	4
L 20	–	Rear foglight	5
L 22	–	Foglight, left	1
L 23	–	Foglight, right	2
S 12	–	Fuse in fuse holder	7
S 30	–	Separate fuse for foglights	1
T 1	–	Flat connector	1 - 2
T 1a	–	Connector behind dash	5
T 1a	–	Connector behind dash	5
T 1b	–	Connector in luggage compartment	5
T 1c	–	Connector in luggage compartment	5

Wire colours

br	Brown
ge	Yellow
gr	Grey
ro	Red
sw	Black
ws	White

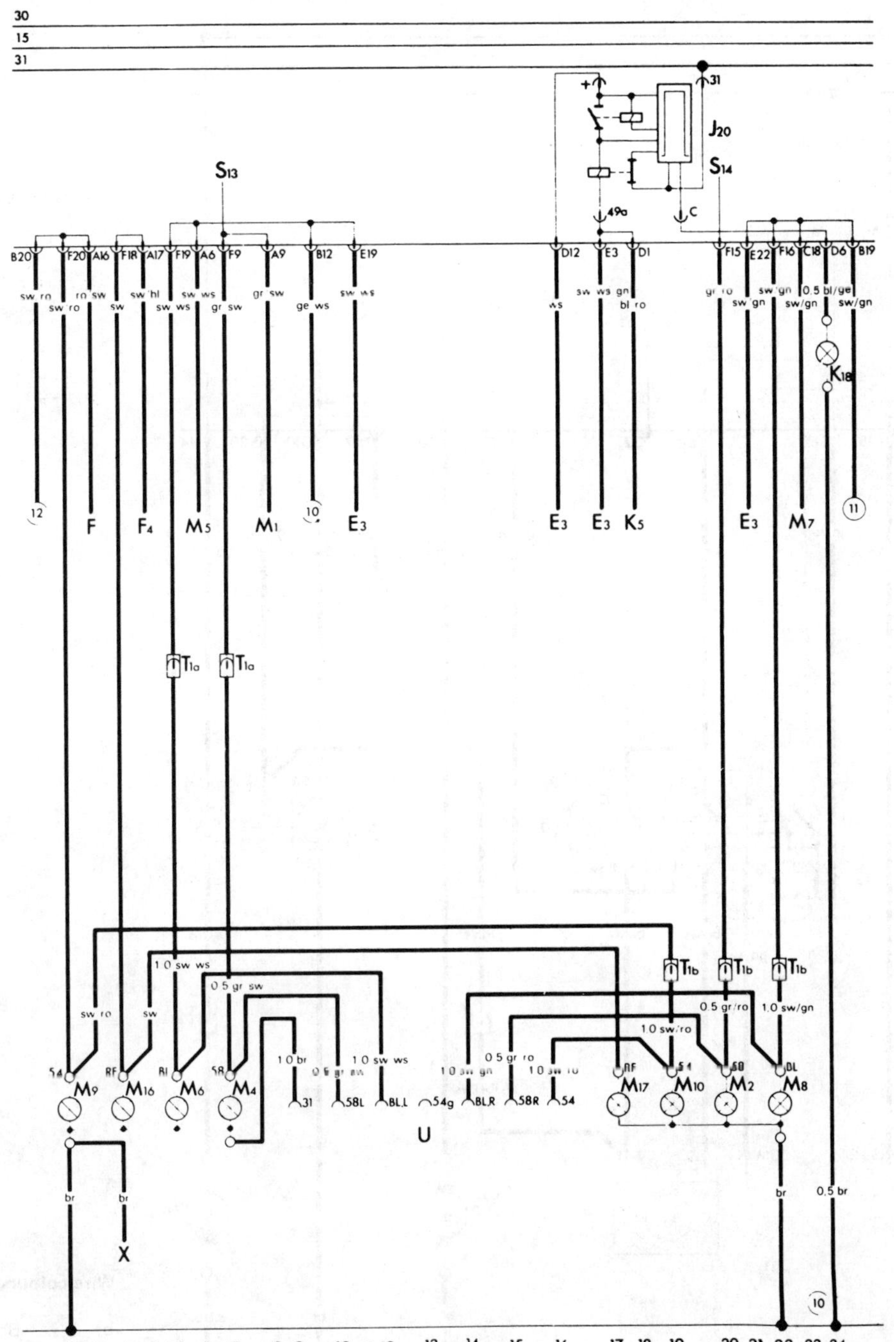

Fig. 14.225 Current flow diagram for trailer lamps. Use in conjunction with Fig. 14.221

Wire colours

bl	Blue
br	Brown
ge	Yellow
gn	Green
gr	Grey
ro	Red
sw	Black
ws	White

Description		In current track
E 3	– to emergency light switch	11, 16, 17, 21
F	– to brake light switch	2
F 4	– to reversing light switch	4
J 20	– Turn signal/emergency light relay for trailer towing	16, 17, 19
K 5	– to turn signal warning lamp	18
K 10	– to trailer warning lamp	24
M 1	– Parking light, left	8
M 2	– Tail light, right	20
M 4	– Tail light, left	7
M 5	– Turn signal, front left	6
M 6	– Turn signal, rear left	5
M 7	– Turn signal, front right	23
M 8	– Turn signal, rear right	22
M 9	– Brake light, left	1

Description		In current track
M 10	– Brake light, right	19
M 16	– Reversing light, left	3
M 17	– Reversing light, right	17
S 13	– Fuses in fuse holder	7, 20
S 14		
T 1a	– Flat connector, single in luggage compartment rear left	5, 7
T 1b	– Flat connector, single in luggage compartment rear right	19, 20, 22
U	– Trailer socket	9, 10
		12 - 16
X	– to licence plate light	3
(10)	– Earth point, dash	

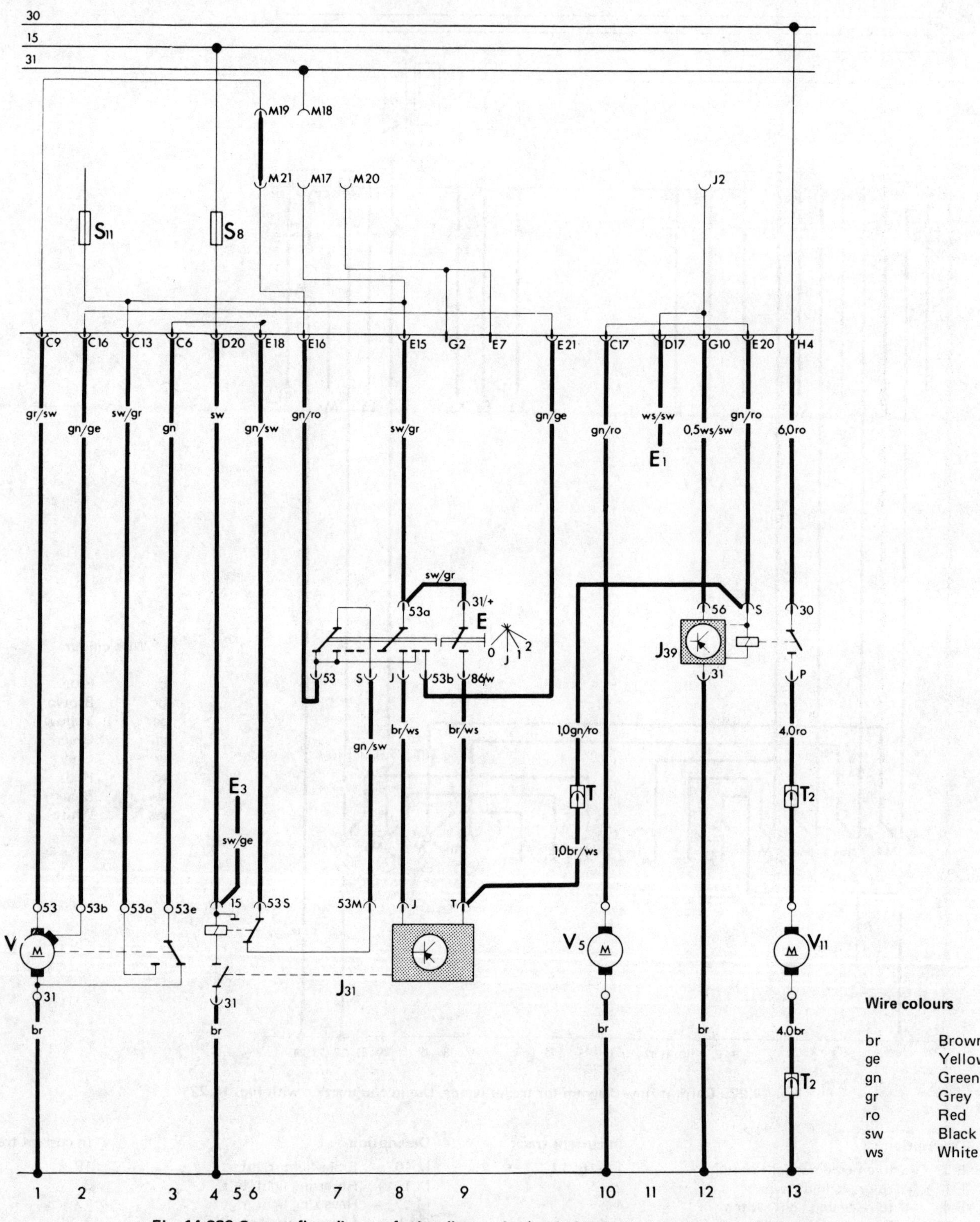

Fig. 14.226 Current flow diagram for headlamp wipe/wash. Use in conjunction with Fig. 14.221

Description		In current track
E	– Wiper switch for intermittent operation	6 - 9
E 1	– to lighting switch, terminal 56	11
J 31	– Wash-wipe intermittent wiper relay	6 - 9
J 39	– Headlight washer relay	12, 13
S 8	– Fuse in fuse holder	4
S 11	– Fuse in fuse holder	2
T	– Connector single	10
T 2	– Connector 2-point	13
V	– Wiper motor	1 - 3
V 5	– Windscreen washer pump motor	10
V 11	– Headlight washer pump	13

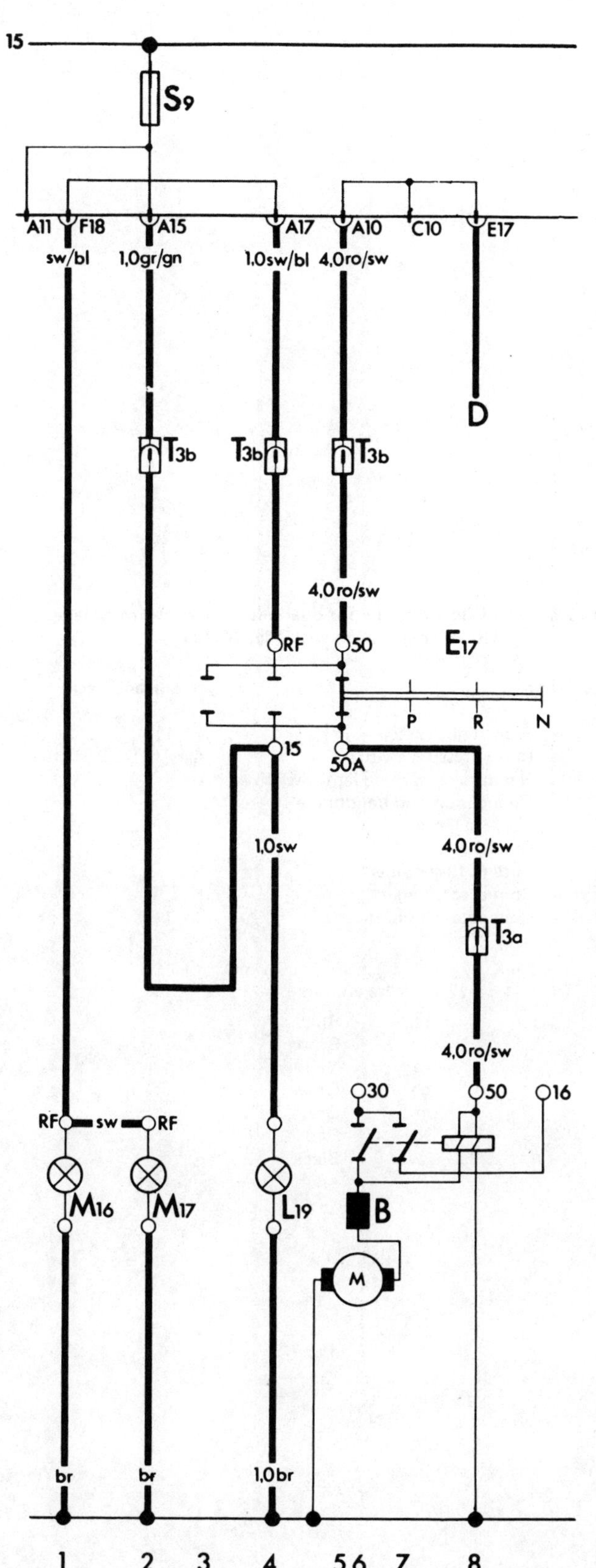

Fig. 14.227 Current flow diagram for automatic transmission. Use in conjunction with Fig. 14.221

Description			In current track
B	–	Starter	5 - 8
D	–	to ignition/starter switch, terminal 50	8
E 17	–	Starter inhibitor and reversing light switch	3 - 8
L 19	–	Shift lever light	4
M 16	–	Reversing light, left	1
M 17	–	Reversing light, right	2
T 3a	–	Connector in engine compartment, on right	8
T 3b	–	Connector under dash	2 - 5

Wire colours

bl	Blue
br	Brown
gn	Green
gr	Grey
ro	Red
sw	Black

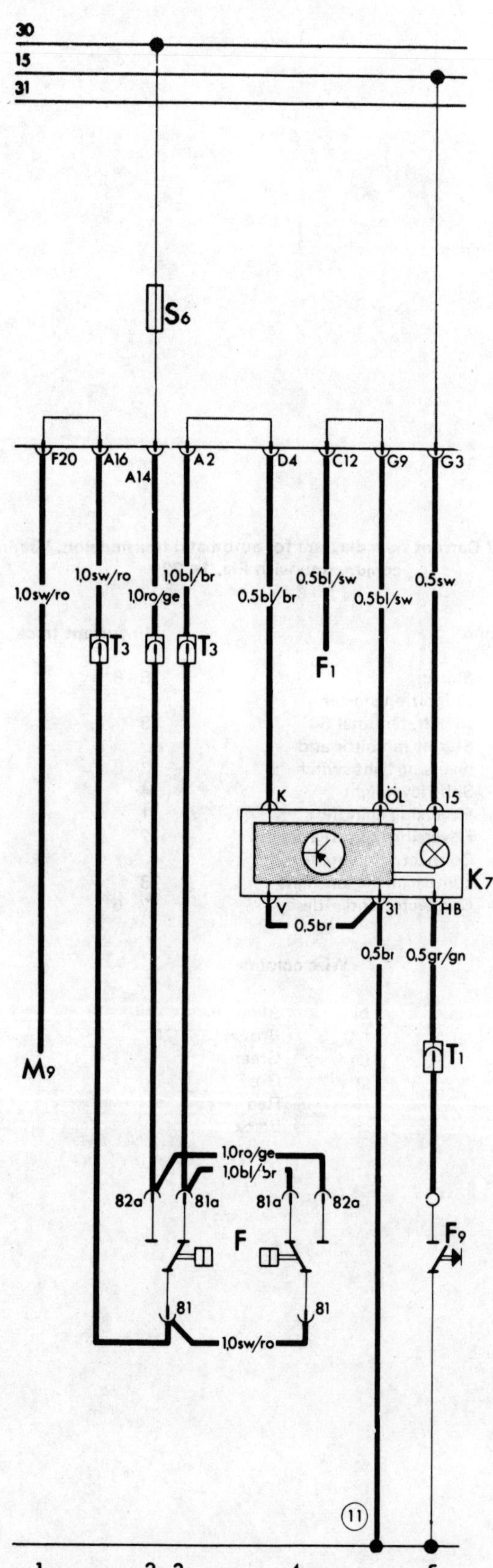

Fig. 14.228 Current flow diagram for dual brake circuit warning lamp. Use in conjunction with Fig. 14.221

Description			In current track
F	—	Brake light switch	2 - 4
F 1	—	to oil pressure switch	4
F 9	—	Handbrake warning lamp switch	5
K 7	—	Dual circuit and handbrake warning lamp	5
M 9	—	Brake light, left	1
S 6	—	Fuse in fuse holder	2
T 1	—	Connector, single	5
T 3	—	Connector, 3-point	1 - 3

Wire colours

bl	Blue
br	Brown
ge	Yellow
gn	Green
gr	Grey
ro	Red
sw	Black

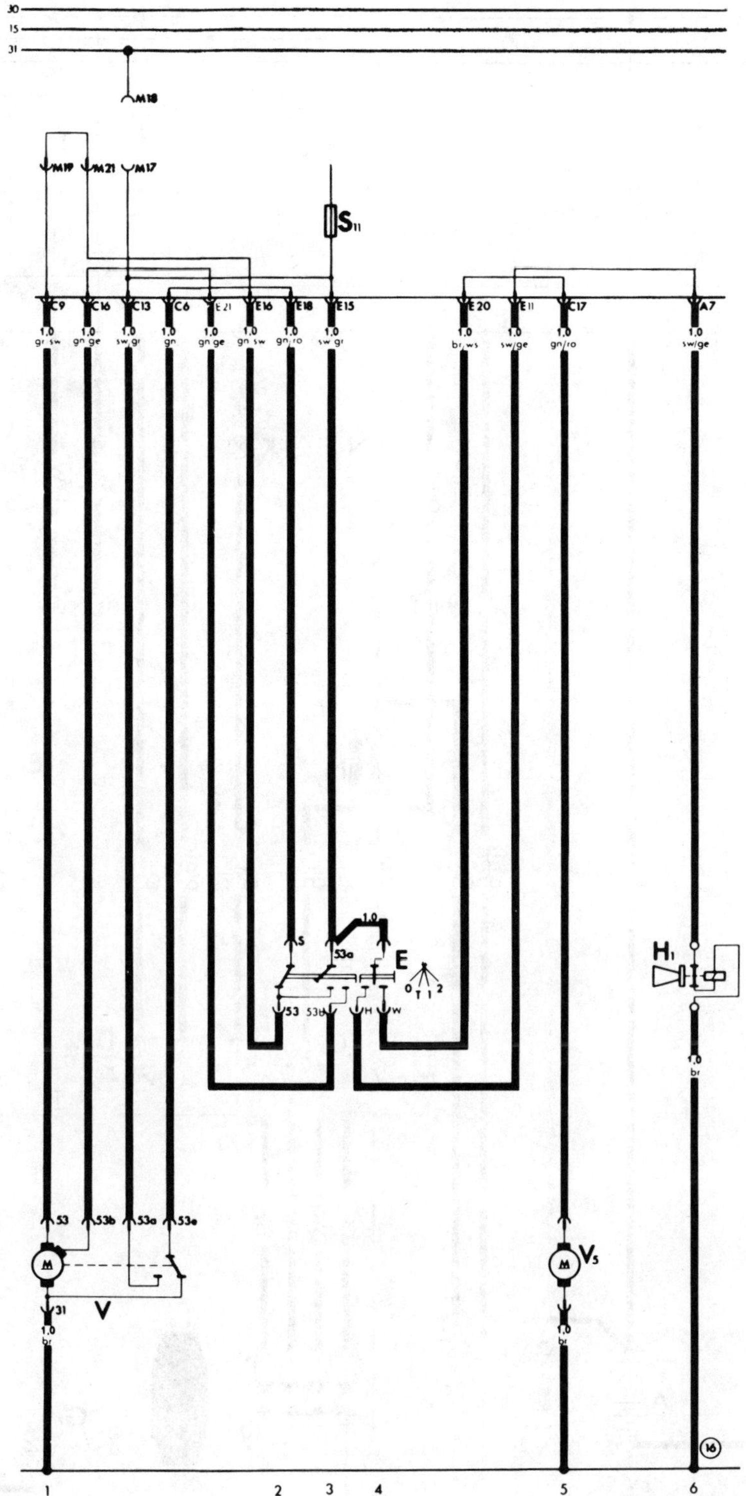

Fig. 14.229 Current flow diagram for horn on Passat N models. Use in conjunction with Fig. 14.221

Description			In current track
E	–	Wiper switch (with horn contact)	2 - 4
H1	–	Horn	6
V	–	Wiper motor	1
V 5	–	Washer pump	5

Wire colours

br	Brown
ge	Yellow
gn	Green
gr	Grey
ro	Red
sw	Black
ws	White

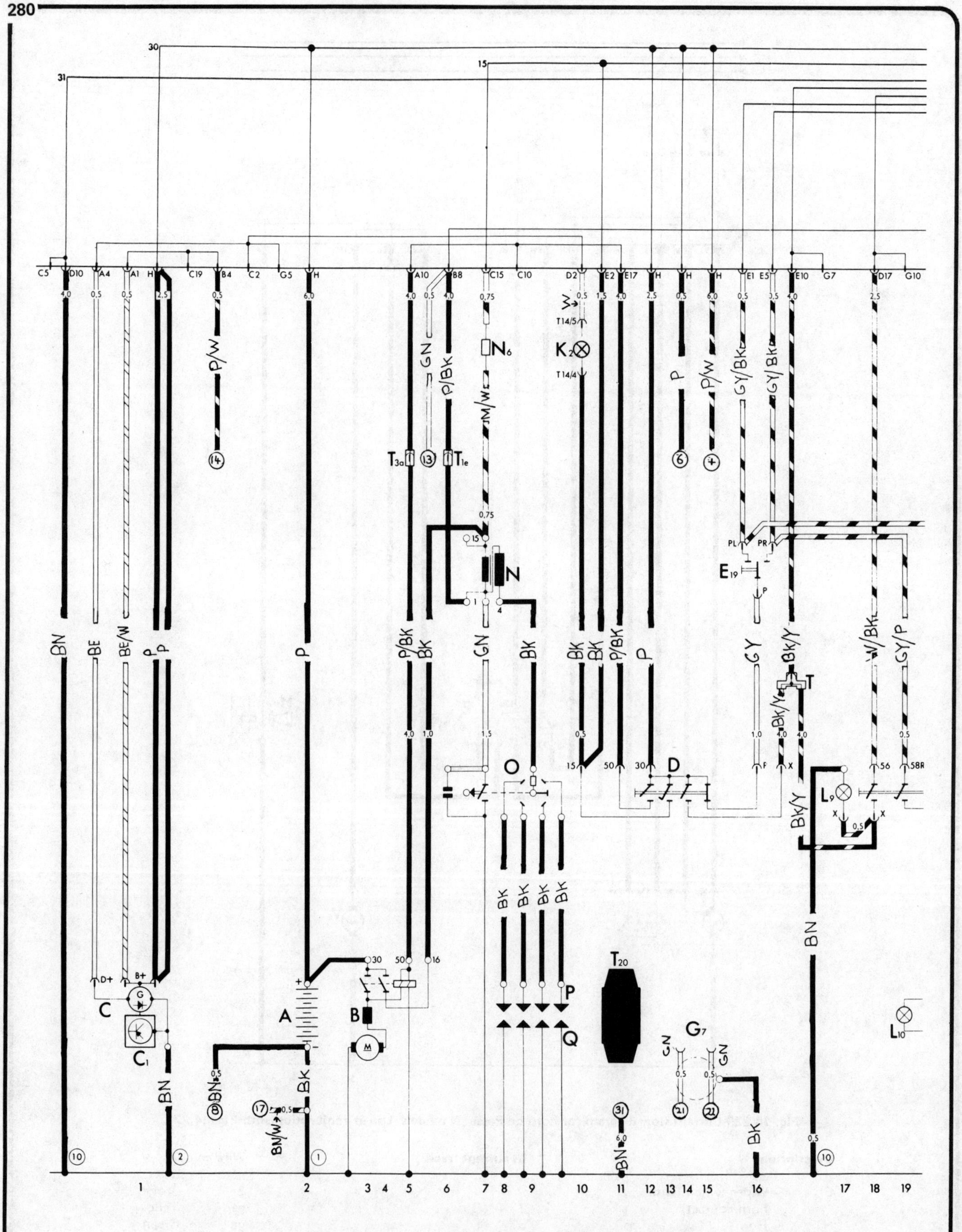

Fig. 14.230 Current flow diagram for 1976 Passat models. Not all items are fitted to all models. For key see page 284

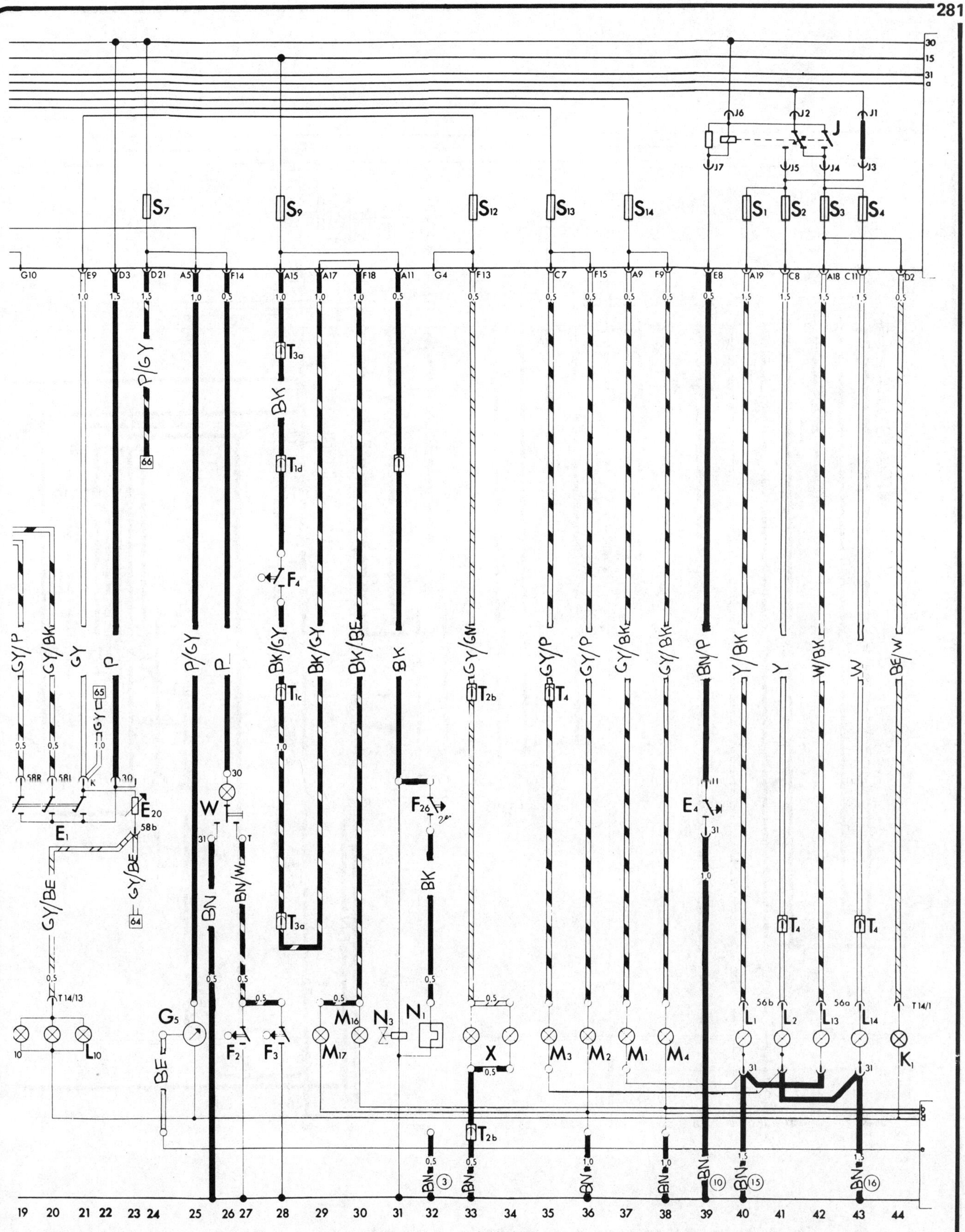

30 15 31 a

J6 J2 J1 J J7 J5 J4 J3

S7 S9 S12 S13 S14 S1 S2 S3 S4

G10 E9 D3 D21 A5 F14 A15 A17 F18 A11 G4 F13 C7 F15 A9 F9 E8 A19 C8 A18 C11 D2

P/GY 66 T3a BK T1d F4 T1c T3a F26 T2b T4 E4 T4 T4

GY/P GY/BK GY P P/GY P BK/GY BK/GY BK/BE BK GY/GN GY/P GY/P GY/BK GY/BK BN/P Y/BK Y W/BK W BE/W

65 GY 58R 58L K 30 E20 E1 58b GY/BE 64 W 31 T BN BN/W 30

GY/BE T 14/13 L10 G5 BE F2 F3 M17 M16 N3 N1 X M3 M2 M1 M4 L1 L2 L13 L14 K1 56b 56a T 14/1 T2b

BN 3 BN BN BN BN 10 BN 15 BN 16

19 20 21 22 23 24 25 26 27 28 29 30 31 32 33 34 35 36 37 38 39 40 41 42 43 44

Fig. 14.230 (cont'd) Current flow diagram for 1976 Passat models. Not all items are fitted to all models.
For key see page 284

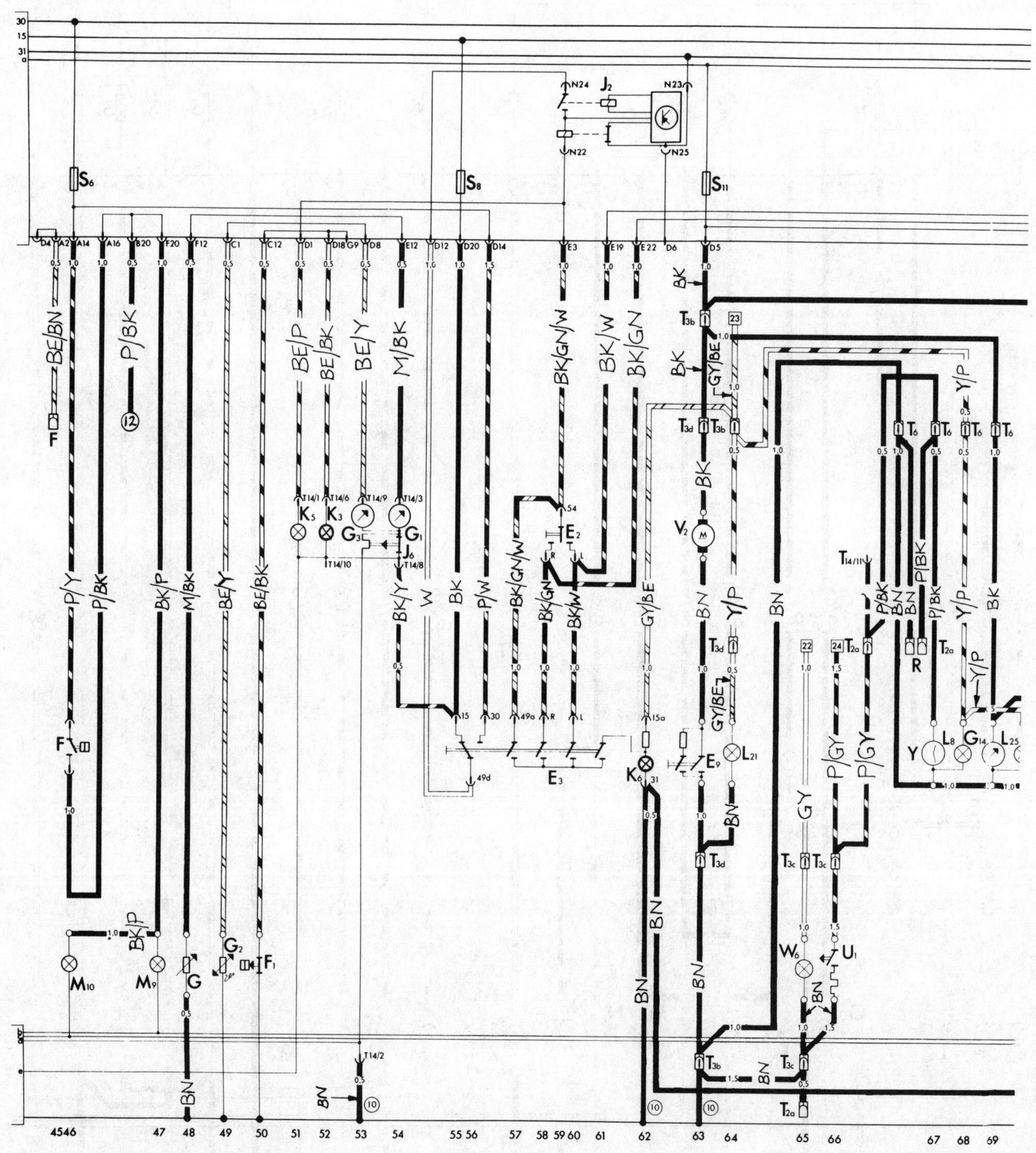

Fig. 14.230 (cont'd) Current flow diagram for 1976 Passat models. Not all items are fitted to all models.
For key see page 284

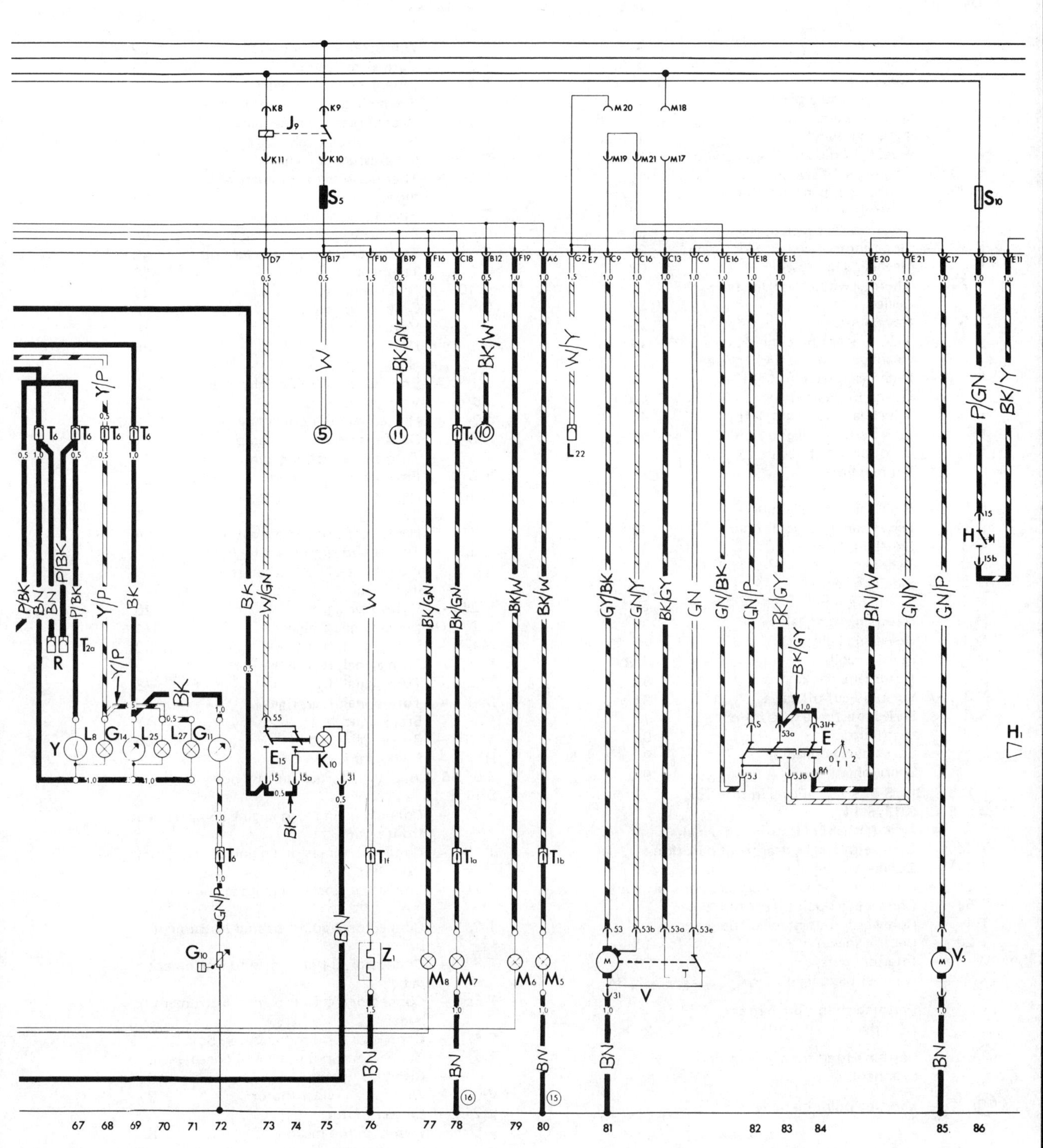

Fig. 14.230 (cont'd) Current flow diagram for 1976 Passat models. Not all items are fitted to all models.
For key see page 284

Key to Fig. 14.230

Description			In current track
A	–	Battery	2
B	–	Starter	3, 4, 5
C	–	Generator	1
C 1	–	Voltage regulator	1
D	–	Ignition/starter switch	10 - 16
E 1	–	Lighting switch	17 - 23
E 4	–	Headlight dip and flasher switch	39
E 19	–	Parking light switch	16
E 20	–	Instrument panel lighting control/switch	23
F 2	–	Door contact switch, front, left	27
F 3	–	Door contact switch, front, right	28
F 4	–	Reversing light switch	28
F 26	–	Thermoswitch for cold start device	32
G 5	–	Rev counter	25
G 7	–	TDC sender unit connection	14 - 16
J	–	Headlight dip and flasher relay	39 - 43
K 1	–	High beam warning light	44
K 2	–	Generator warning lamp	10
L 1	–	Low beam headlight, left	40
L 2	–	Low beam headlight, right	41
L 9	–	Bulb for lighting switch illumination	17
L 10	–	Instrument panel light	19 - 21
L 13	–	High beam headlight, left	42
L 14	–	High beam headlight, right	43
M 1	–	Sidelight, left	37
M 2	–	Taillight, right	36
M 3	–	Sidelight, right	35
M 4	–	Tail light, left	38
M 16	–	Reversing light, left	30
M 17	–	Reversing light, right	29
N	–	Ignition coil	7, 8
N 1	–	Automatic choke	32
N 3	–	Solenoid cut-off valve	31
N 6	–	Series resistance wire for coil	7
O	–	Distributor	9
P	–	Spark plug connector	9
Q	–	Spark plugs	9
S 1, S 2, S 3, S 4, S 7, S 9, S 12, S 13, S 14		Fuses in fuse box	
T	–	Adaptor behind instrument panel	
T 1c	–	Connector single, near front partition	
T 1e	–	Connector single, near fuse box	
T 2b	–	Connector 2-point, in luggage compartment	
T 3a	–	Connector 3-point, near fuse box	
T 4	–	Connector 4-point, near fuse box	
T 20	–	Central socket	11
W	–	Interior lights	26
X	–	Number plate light	33, 34
(1)	–	Earthing strap from battery to body	2
(2)	–	Earthing strap from generator to cylinder block	1
(10)	–	Earthing point on body	

Wire colours(

BN	Brown
BE	Blue
W	White
P	Pink
GN	Green
BK	Black
M	Mauve
Y	Yellow
GY	Grey

Description			In current track
E	–	Windscreen wiper switch	82 - 84
E 2	–	Turn signal switch	58 - 60
E 3	–	Emergency light switch	56 - 62
E 9	–	Fresh air blower motor switch	63
E 15	–	Heated rear window switch	73 - 75
F	–	Brake light switch	46
F 1	–	Oil pressure switch	50
F 18	–	Thermoswitch for radiator fan motor	88
G	–	Fuel gauge sender unit	48
G 1	–	Fuel gauge	54
G 2	–	Temperature gauge sender unit	49
G 3	–	Temperature gauge	53
G 10	–	Oil pressure sender unit	72
G 11	–	Oil pressure gauge	72
G 14	–	Voltmeter	68
H	–	Horn plate	86
H 1	–	Horn	87
J 2	–	Emergency warning light relay	59
J 6	–	Voltage stabilizer	53, 54
J 9	–	Heated rear window relay	73, 75
K 3	–	Oil pressure warning lamp	52
K 5	–	Turn signal warning lamp	51
K 6	–	Emergency light warning lamp	62
K 10	–	Heated rear window, warning lamp	75
L 8	–	Clock light	68
L 21	–	Heater control levers light	64
L 22	–	To left and right-hand foglights (pull wires off G 2 when service installing)	
L 25	–	Voltmeter light	70
L 27		Oil pressure gauge light	71
M 5	–	Turn signal, front, left	80
M 6	–	Turn signal, rear, left	79
M 7	–	Turn signal, front, right	78
M 8	–	Turn signal, rear, right	77
M 9	–	Brake light, left	47
M 10	–	Brake light, right	46
R	–	Radio connection	
S 5, S 6, S 8, S 10, S 11, S 15		Fuses in fuse box	
T 1a	–	Connector single, in engine compartment front right	
T 1b	–	Connector single, in engine compartment front left	
T 1f	–	Connector single, in luggage compartment left	
T 2a	–	Connector 2-point, behind instrument panel	
T 3b	–	Connector, 3-point, behind instrument panel	
T 3c	–	Connector 3-point, behind instrument panel	
T 4	–	Connector 4-point, near fuse box	
T 6	–	Connector 6-point, behind console	
U 1	–	Cigarette lighter	66
V	–	Windscreen wiper motor	81
V 2	–	Blower motor	63
V 5	–	Washer pump motor	85
V 7	–	Radiator fan motor	88
W 6	–	Glovebox light	65
Y	–	Clock	67
Z 1	–	Heated rear window	76
(10)	–	Earthing point in engine compartment, right	
(15)	–	Earthing point in engine compartment, front, left	
(18)	–	Earthing point on body	

The circles are the connections in the network which are wired directly to the central socket (T 20). The numbers in the circles correspond to the terminals in the socket.

Key to Fig. 14.231

	Description	In current track
A	– Battery	2
B	– Starter	3 - 5
C	– AC generator	1
C 1	– Voltage regulator	1
D	– Ignition/starter switch	10 - 16
E 1	– Lighting switch	18 - 20
E 19	– Parking light switch (in turn signal switch)	16
E 20	– Instrument panel lighting control	21
F 2	– Door contact switch, left	31
F 3	– Door contact switch, right	32
F 4	– Reversing light switch	32
F 26	– Thermoswitch (11° C) for choke (not on 75 bhp automatic and 85 bhp automatic and manual)	36
F 35	– Thermoswitch (25° C) for choke (not on 75 bhp automatic and 85 bhp automatic and manual)	37
G 7	– TDC sender connection	13 - 16
G 14	– Voltmeter	23
K 2	– Generator warning lamp	10
L 9	– Bulb for lighting switch illumination	17
L 10	– Instrument panel light	19 - 20
L 19	– Gearshift pattern light	21
L 21	– Heater lever lamp	24
L 25	– Voltmeter lamp	22
L 28	– Cigarette lighter lamp	27
M 1	– Side light, left	42
M 2	– Tail light, right	41
M 3	– Side light, right	40
M 4	– Tail light, left	43
M 16	– Reversing light, left	34
M 17	– Reversing light, right	33
N	– Ignition coil 1	7, 8
N 1	– Automatic choke	36
N 3	– Solenoid cut-off valve	35
N 6	– Series resistance wire for coil	7
N 36	– Series resistance for automatic choke (not on 75 bhp automatic and 85 bhp automatic and manual)	36
O	– Distributor	7 - 9
P	– Spark plug connector	7 - 9
Q	– Spark plugs	7 - 9
R	– Radio connection	29
S 1 – S 15	– Fuses in fusebox	
T 1c	– Connector single, in engine compartment	
T 1d	– Connector single, in engine compartment	
T 1e	– Connector single, near front partition	
T 1f	– Connector single, near front partition	
T 1h	– Connector single, near fuse box	
T 1i	– Connector single, behind instrument panel	
T 1k	– Connector single, below instrument panel	
T 2a	– Flat connector, 2-pin, behind instrument panel (Radio connection)	
T 2b	– Connector, 2-pin, behind instrument panel	
T 2c	– Connector, 2-pin, in luggage compartment	
T 3b	– Connector, 3-pin, near fusebox	
T 3c	– Connector, 3-pin, behind instrument panel	
T 3d	– Connector, 3-pin, behind instrument panel	
T 3e	– Connector, 3-pin, behind instrument panel	
T 4	– Connector, 4-pin, near fusebox 1	
T 6	– Connector, 6-pin, behind instrument panel (centre)	
T 14	– Connector, 14-pin, on instrument panel insert	
T 20	– Central socket	
U 1	– Cigarette lighter	28
W	– Interior lights	30
W 6	– Glovebox light	26
X	– Number plate light	38
Y	– Clock	29
(1)	– Earthing strap from battery via body to gearbox	
(2)	– Earthing strap from generator to engine	
(3)	– Earthing point near relay plate and fusebox	

	Description	In current track
E 2	– Turn signal switch	67 - 69
E 3	– Emergency warning light switch	63 - 71
E 4	– Headlight dimmer/flasher switch (in turn signal switch)	44
E 9	– Blower motor switch	72 - 74
E 15	– Heated rear window switch	75, 76
E 22	– Wiper switch for intermittent operation	87 - 89
F	– Brake light switch	53, 55
F 1	– Oil pressure switch	59
F 9	– Handbrake warning lamp switch	51
F 18	– Thermoswitch for radiator fan motor	53
G	– Fuel gauge sender unit	57
G 1	– Fuel gauge	64
G 2	– Coolant temperature gauge sender unit	58
G 3	– Coolant temperature gauge	62
H	– Horn plate	91
H 1	– Horn	92
J	– Headlight dimmer/flasher relay	44 - 47
J 2	– Emergency warning light relay	67 - 72
J 6	– Voltage stabilizer	62 - 64
J 9	– Heated rear window relay	75 - 77
J 31	– Intermittent wash/wipe relay	85 - 89
K 1	– High beam warning lamp	49
K 3	– Oil pressure warning lamp	61
K 5	– Turn signal warning lamp	60
K 6	– Emergency light system warning lamp	71
K 7	– Dual brake circuit warning lamp	50, 51
K 10	– Heated rear window warning lamp	77
L 1	– Twin filament headlight bulb, left	45, 47
L 2	– Twin filament headlight bulb, right	46, 48
L 22	– To left and right hand foglights	82 - 83
M 5	Turn signal, front, left	82
M 6	– Turn signal, rear, left	81
M 7	– Turn signal, front, right	80
M 8	– Turn signal, rear, right	79
M 9	– Brake light, left	56
M 10	– Brake light, right	54
N 23	– Series resistance, fresh air blower	72, 73
S 1 to S 15	– Fuses and fusebox	
T 1a	– Connector, single, in engine compartment, front right	
T 1b	– Connector, single, in engine compartment, front left	
T 1g	– Connector, single, in engine compartment	
T 1l	– Connector, single, behind instrument panel	
T 3a	– Connector, 3-pin, in engine compartment	
T 3c	– Connector, 3-pin, behind instrument panel	
T 3d	– Connector, 3-pin, behind instrument panel	
T 3e	– Connector, 3-pin, behind instrument panel	
T 4	– Connector, 4-pin, near fusebox	
T 14	– Connector, 14-pin, on instrument panel insert	
V	– Windscreen washer pump	83, 84
V 2	– Fresh air blower motor	74
V 5	– Washer pump motor	90
V 7	– Radiator fan motor	93
Z 1	– Heated rear window	78
(10)	– Earth point near relay plate and fusebox	
(15)	– Earth point in engine compartment front, left	
(16)	– Earth point in engine compartment front, right	

The circles are the connections in the test network which are wired directly to the central test socket (S 20) when fitted. The numbers in the circles correspond to the terminals in the socket.

Wire Colours

BN	Brown
BE	Blue
W	White
P	Pink
GN	Green
BK	Black
M	Mauve
Y	Yellow
GY	Grey

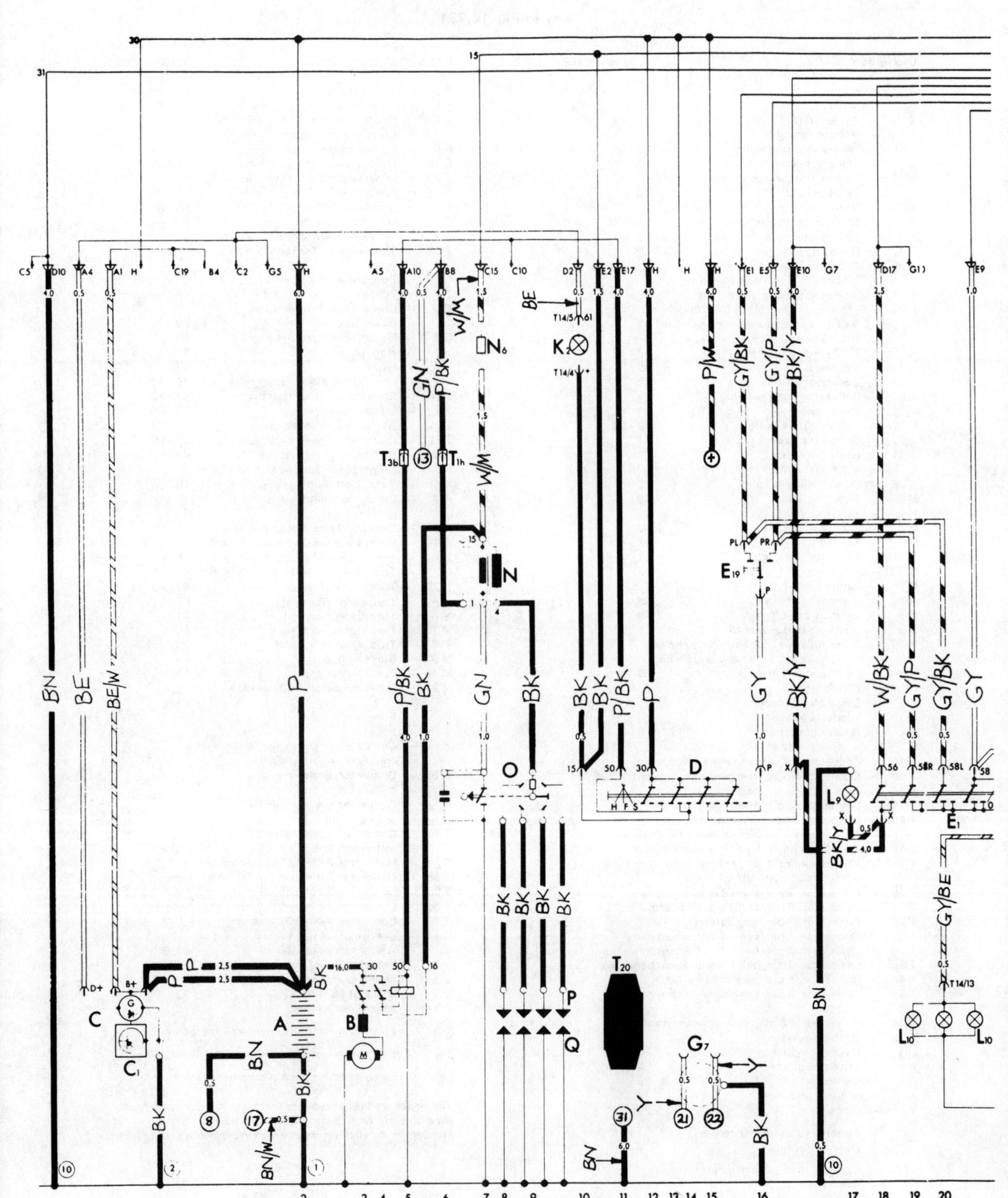

Fig. 14.231 Current flow diagram for 1977 to 1979 Passat models. Not all items are fitted to all models. For key see page 285

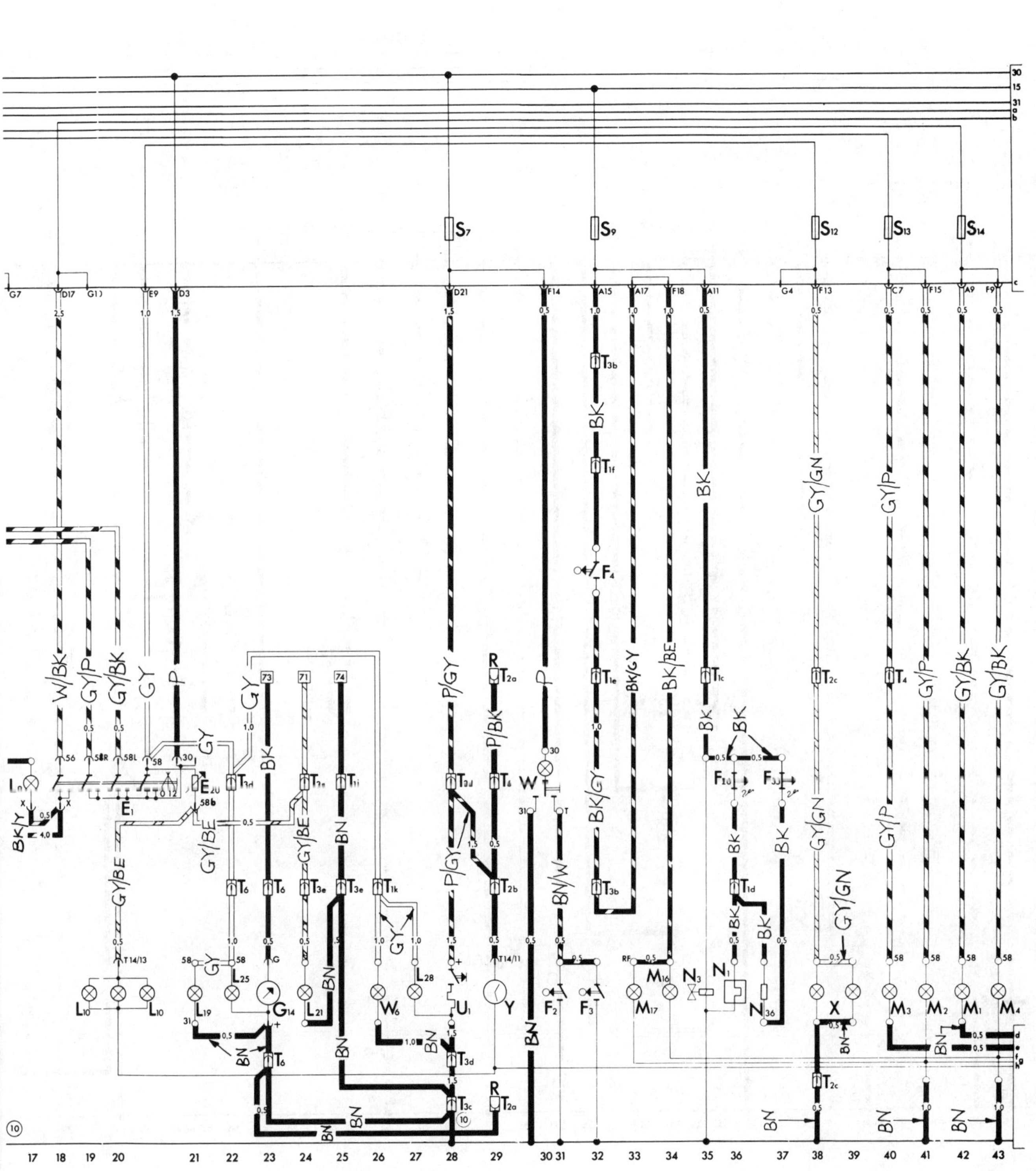

Fig. 14.231 (cont'd) Current flow diagram for 1977 to 1979 Passat models. Not all items are fitted to all models. For key see page 285

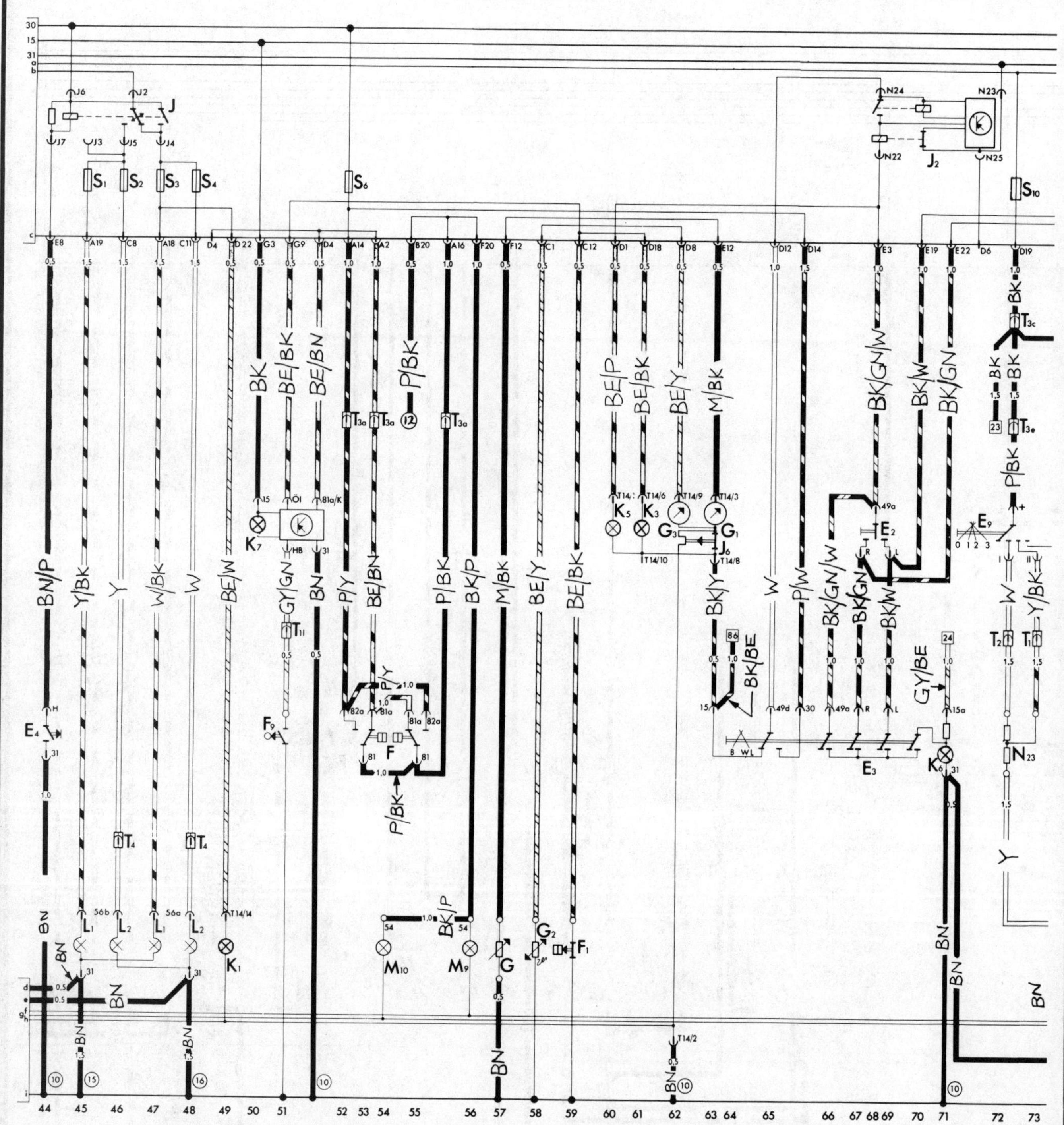

Fig. 14.231 (cont'd) Current flow diagram for 1977 to 1979 Passat models. Not all items are fitted to all models. For key see page 285

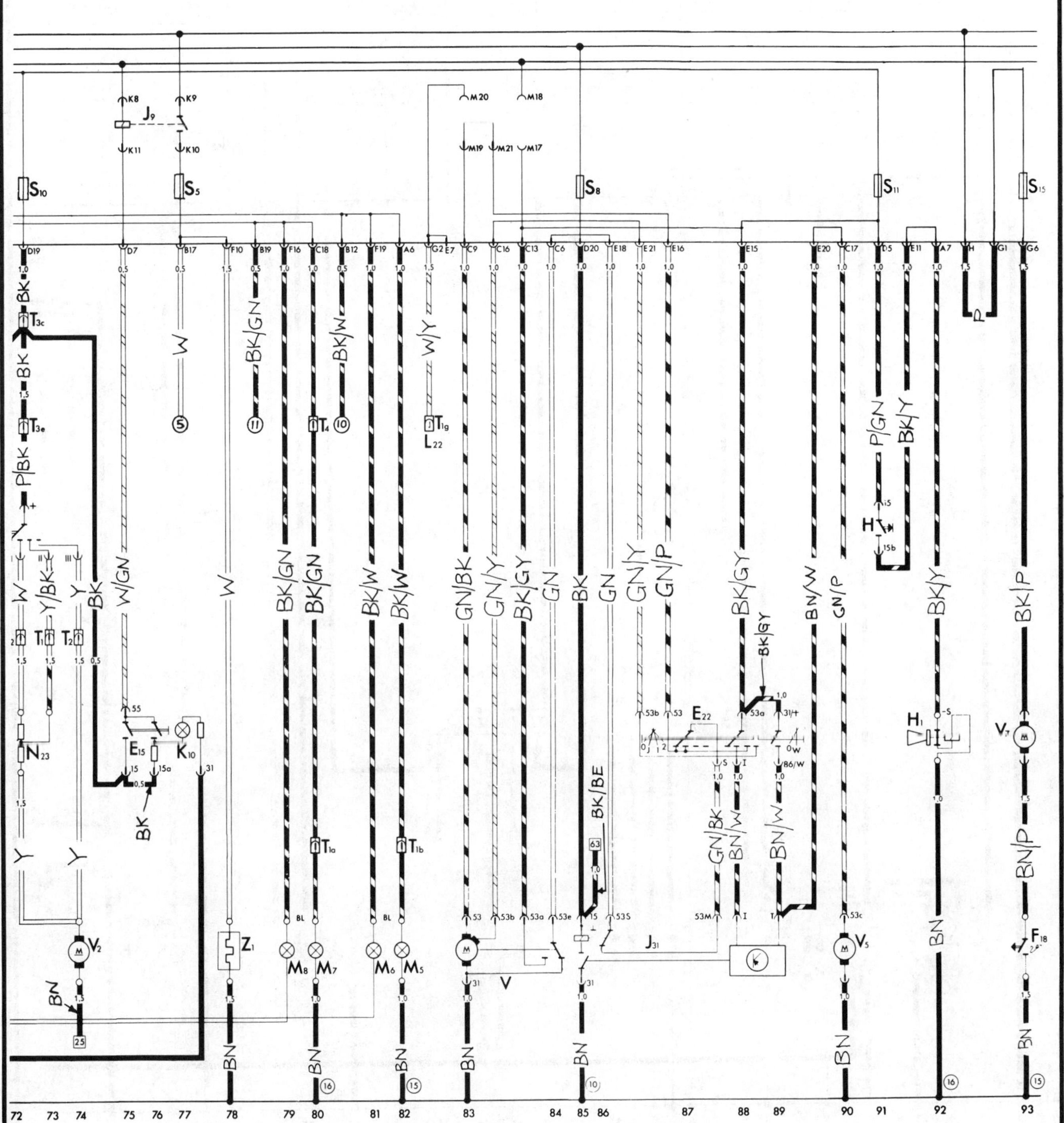

Fig. 14.231 (cont'd) Current flow diagram for 1977 to 1979 Passat models. Not all items are fitted to all models. For key see page 285

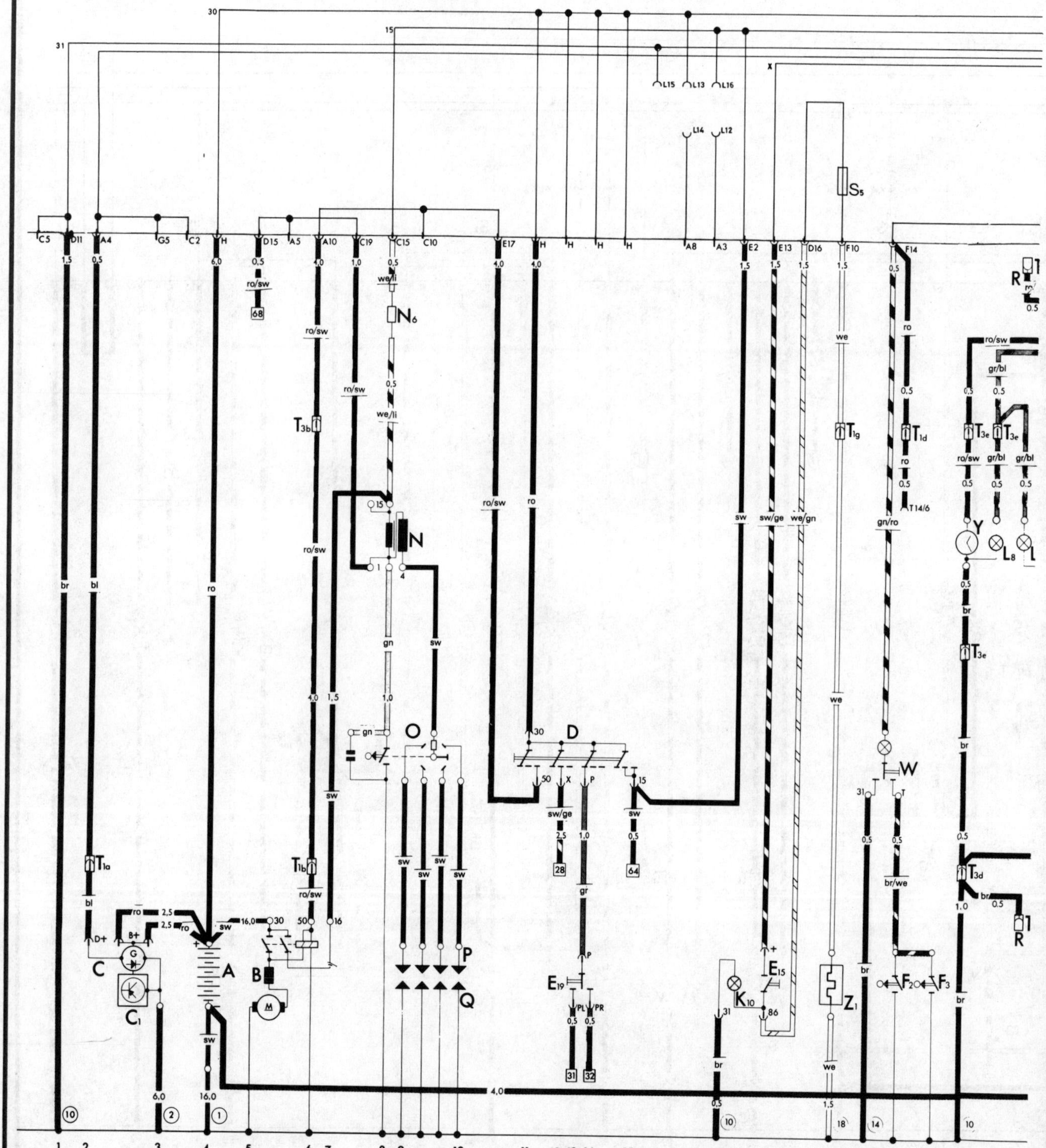

Fig. 14.232 Current flow diagram for 1980 onwards Passat models. Not all items are fitted to all models. For key see page 294

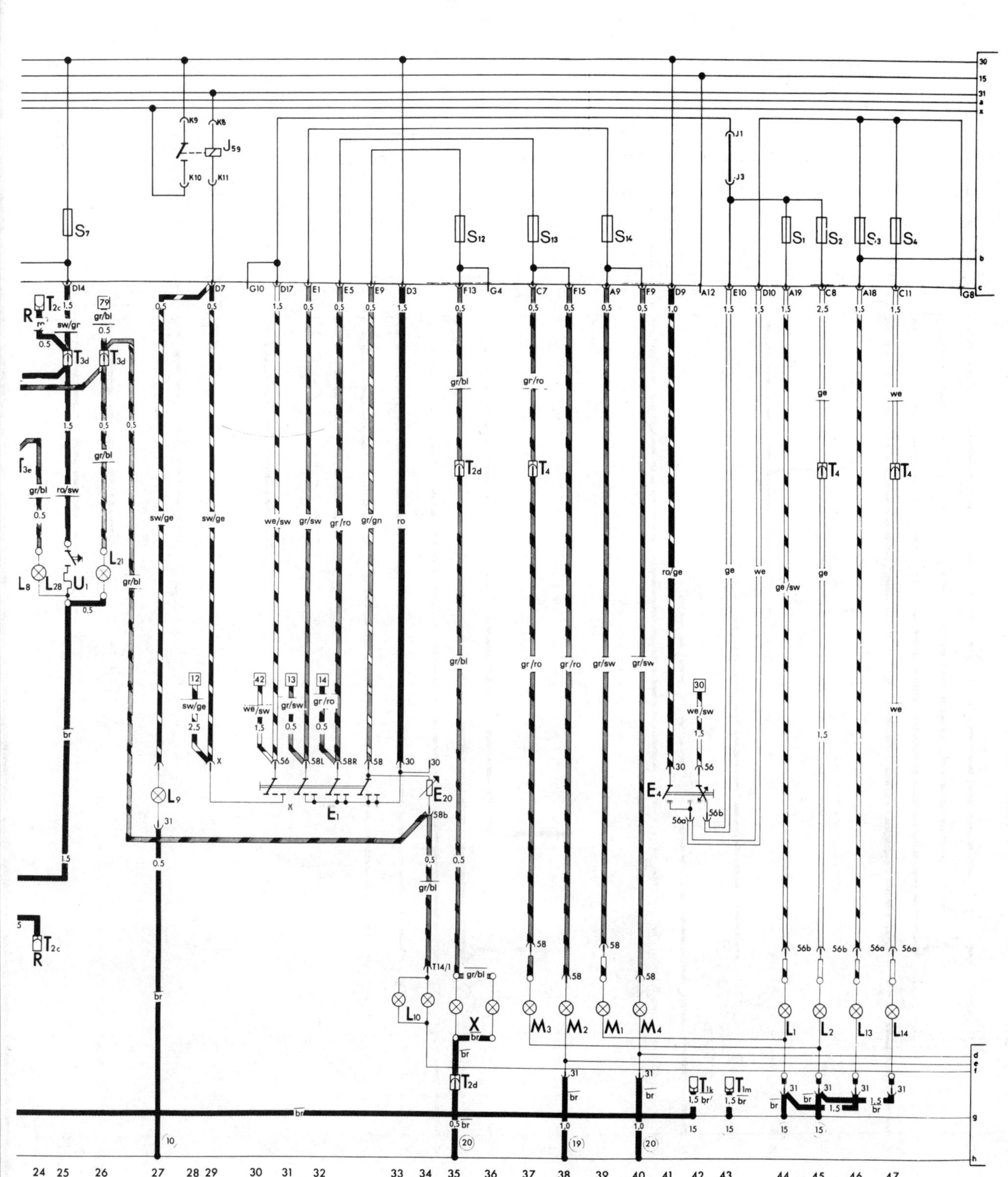

Fig. 14.232 (cont'd) Current flow diagram for 1980 onwards Passat models. Not all items are fitted to all models. For key see page 294

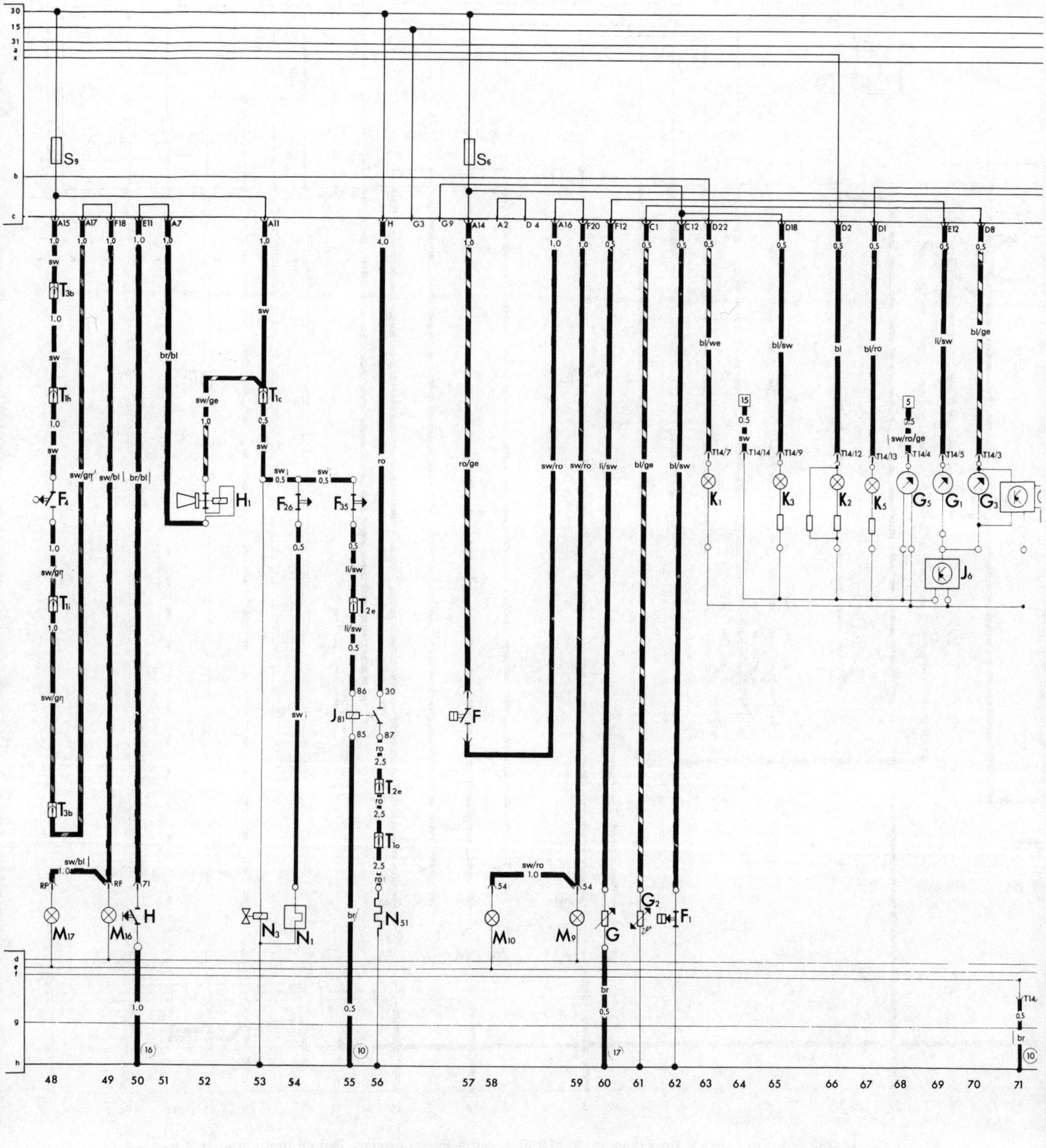

Fig. 14.232 (cont'd) Current flow diagrams for 1980 onwards Passat models. Not all items are fitted to all models.
For key see page 294

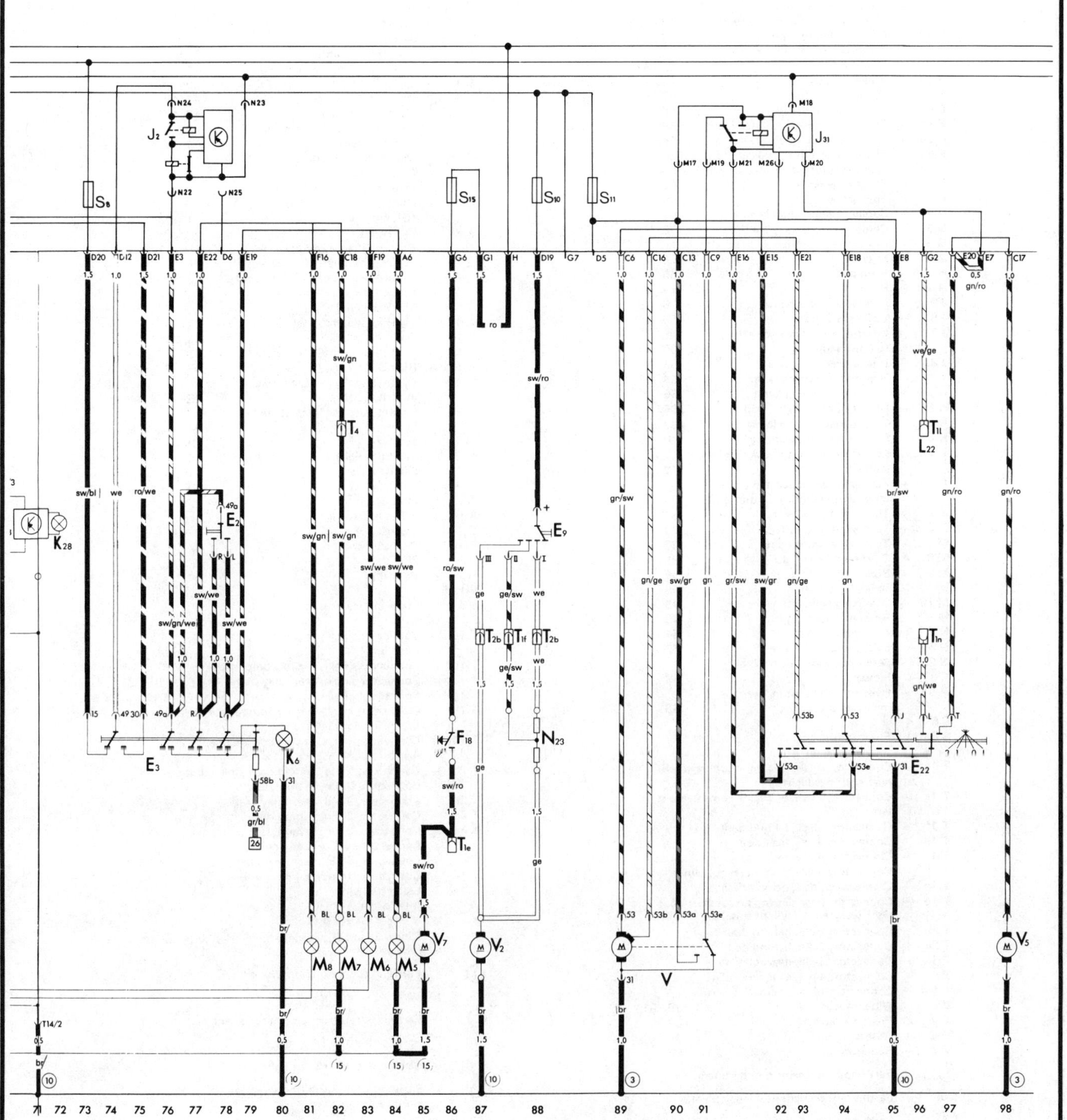

Fig. 14.232 (cont'd) Current flow diagrams for 1980 onwards Passat models. Not all items are fitted to all models.
For key see page 294

Key to Fig. 14.232

Designation			In current track
E 2	–	Turn signal switch	78
E 3	–	Emergency warning light switch	73 - 80
E 9	–	Fresh air blower switch	87 - 88
E 22	–	Wiper switch for intermittent operation	92 - 97
F	–	Brake light switch	57
F 1	–	Oil pressure switch	62
F 4	–	Reversing light switch	48
F 18	–	Thermoswitch for radiator fan	86
F 26	–	Thermoswitch for choke	54
F 35	–	Thermoswitch for intake manifold preheating	55
G	–	Fuel gauge sender unit	60
G 1	–	Fuel gauge	69
G 2	–	Coolant temperature sender	61
G 3	–	Coolant temperature gauge	70
G 5	–	Rev counter (models with 63 kW engine)	68
H	–	Horn pad	50
H 1	–	Horn	52
J 2	–	Emergency light relay	76 - 79
J 6	–	Voltage stabilizer	69
J 31	–	Intermittent wash/wipe relay (GL models)	90 - 93
J 81	–	Intake preheating relay	55, 56
K 1	–	High beam warning lamp	63
K 2	–	Generator warning lamp	66
K 3	–	Oil pressure warning lamp	65
K 5	–	Turn signal warning lamp	67
K 6	–	Emergency light warning lamp	80
K 28	–	Coolant temperature warning lamp (too hot, red)	72
L 22	–	Fog light connection (to service install wire as shown in diagram)	96
M 5	–	Turn signal front left	84
M 6	–	Turn signal rear left	83
M 7	–	Turn signal front right	82
M 8	–	Turn signal rear right	81
M 9	–	Brake light, left	59
M 10	–	Brake light, right	58
M 16	–	Reversing light, left	49
M 17	–	Reversing light, right	48
N 1	–	Automatic choke	54
N 3	–	Solenoid cut-off valve	53
N 23	–	Series resistance for fresh air blower	88
N 51	–	Heater element for intake manifold preheating	56
S 6 S 8 - 11 S 15		Fuses in fuse box	
T 1c	–	Connector, single, in engine compartment, near right headlight	
T 1e	–	Connector, single, in engine compartment, left	
T 1f	–	Connector, single, behind dash	
T 1h	–	Connector, single, near coil	
T 1j	–	Connector, single, near coil	
T 1l	–	Connector, single, near water container	
T 1n	–	Connector, single, behind dash	
T 1o	–	Connector, single, in engine compartment right (secured to coolant hose)	
T 2b	–	Connector, 2-pin, behind dash	
T 2e	–	Connector, 2-pin, behind dash	
T 3b	–	Connector, 3-pin, near relay plate	
T 4	–	Connector, 4-pin, near relay plate	
T 14/	–	Connector, 14-pin, on dash insert	
V	–	Wiper motor	89 - 91
V 2	–	Fresh air blower	87
V 5	–	Washer pump	98
V 7	–	Radiator fan	85
(3)	–	Earth point in engine compartment	
(10)	–	Earth point on right near relay plate	
(15)	–	Earth point in insulation sleeve of front loom	
(16)	–	Earth wire – steering box	
(17)	–	Earth point in boot near sender	

Designation			In current track
A	–	Battery	4
B	–	Starter	5 - 7
C	–	Alternator	2, 3
C 1	–	Voltage regulator	2, 3
D	–	Ignition/starter switch	11 - 15
E 1	–	Lighting switch	29 - 34
E 4	–	Dip and flasher switch	41, 42
E 15	–	Rear window switch	16, 17
E 19	–	Parking light switch (in turn signal switch)	13, 14
E 20	–	Dash lighting rheostat (GL models)	34
F 2	–	Door contact switch, left	20
F 3	–	Door contact switch, right (GL models)	21
J 59	–	Relief relay for X contact	28, 29
K 10	–	Rear window warning lamp	16
L 1	–	Dipped beam left (GL models)	44
L 2	–	Dipped beam right (GL models)	45
L 8	–	Clock light (models with 63 kW engine)	23
L 9	–	Lighting switch lamp	27
L 10	–	Dash insert lamp	33, 34
L 13	–	High beam left (GL models)	46
L 14	–	High beam right (GL models)	47
L 21	–	Heater lever lamp (L and GL models)	26
L 28	–	Cigarette lighter lamp (L and GL models)	24
M 1	–	Sidelight left	39
M 2	–	Tail light right	38
M 3	–	Sidelight right	37
M 4	–	Tail light left	40
N	–	Ignition coil	8, 9
N 6	–	Series resistance	8
O	–	Distributor	8 - 10
P	–	Plug connector	9, 10
Q	–	Plug	9, 10
R	–	For radio	24
S 1 - 5 S 7 S 12 - 14		Fuses in fuse box	
T 1a	–	Connector single, engine compartment, front left	
T 1b	–	Connector single, engine compartment	
T 1d	–	Connector single, near relay plate	
T 1g	–	Connector, single, in boot, left	
T 1k	–	Connector, single, engine compartment (earth fog light left)	
T 1m	–	Connector, single, engine compartment (earth fog light right)	
T 2c	–	Connector, 2-pin, behind dash (for radio)	
T 2d	–	Connector, 2-pin, in boot, left	
T 3b	–	Connector, 3-pin, near relay plate	
T 3d	–	Connector, 3-pin, behind dash	
T 3e	–	Connector, 3-pin, behind dash (models with 63 kW engine)	
T 4	–	Connector, 4-pin, near relay plate	
T 14/	–	Connector, 14-pin, on dash insert	
U 1	–	Cigarette lighter	25
W	–	Interior light	19, 20
X	–	Number plate light	35, 36
Y	-	Clock (L and GL models)*	22
Z 1	–	Rear window	18
(1)	–	Earthing strap from battery via body to gearbox	
(2)	–	Earthing strap from alternator to engine	
(10)	–	Earth point near relay plate	
(14)	–	Earth point on interior light	
(15)	–	Earth point in insulation sleeve of front loom	
(18)	–	Earth point in boot right	
(19)	–	Earth point in boot rear right	
(20)	–	Earth point in boot rear left	

** Models with 63 kW engine, clock in console*

Wire colours

bl	Blue
br	Brown
ge	Yellow
gn	Green
gr	Grey
ro	Red
sw	Black
ws	White

Key to Fig. 14.233

Description		In current track
A	– Battery	10
B	– Starter	11, 12
C	– Alternator	2
C 1	– Regulator	2
D	– Ignition/starter switch	13, 14, 15, 17, 18
E 1	– Light switch	22, 23, 24, 25
E 9	– Fresh air fan	32, 33
E 20	– Instrument panel lighting control switch	28
E 24	– Safety belt lock, left	20
E 25	– Safety belt lock, right	18
E 31	– Contact strip in driver seat	20
E 32	– Contact strip in passenger seat	18
F 2	– Door contact and buzzer alarm switch, left	16, 17
F 3	– Door contact switch, right	14
F 9	– Parking brake control light switch	21, 22
F 25	– Throttle valve switch	7
G 5	– to tachometer terminal 1	3
G 7	– TDC sensor	38
H	– Horn button	31
H 1	– Horn	39
J 34	– Safety belt warning system relay	13, 14, 17, 18, 19 20, 21, 22, 23
K 2	– Alternator charging warning light	1
K 7	– Dual circuit brake warning and safety belt warning system control light	24, 25, 26, 27
L 9	– Light switch illumination	27
L 10	– Instrument panel light	28, 29
L 21	– Heater lever illumination	30
M 1	– Parking light, left	46
M 2.	– Tail light, right	42
M 3	– Parking light, right	41
M 4	– Tail light, left	44
M 11	– Sidemarker lights, front	40, 47
M 12	– Sidemarker lights, rear	43, 45
N	– Ignition coil	4
N 1	– Automatic choke	8
N 3	– Solenoid cut-off valve	9
N 6	– Series resistance	4
N 13	– EGR valve	7
O	– Ignition distributor	4, 6
P	– Spark plug connectors	5, 6
Q	– Spark plugs	5, 6
R	– Radio	33, 34
S 1 to S 15	Fuses in fuse box	
T 1a	– Wire connector, single; behind dashboard	
T 1b	– Wire connector, single; in engine compartment	
T 1c	– Wire connector, single; in engine compartment right	
T 1d	– Wire connector, single; in engine compartment right	
T 1e	– Wire connector, single; in engine compartment left	
T 1f	– Wire connector, single; in engine compartment left	
T 1g	– Wire connector, single; in luggage compartment left	
T 1h	– Wire connector, single; in luggage compartment	
T 1i	– Wire connector, single; behind dashboard	
T 1k	– Wire connector, single; behind dashboard	
T 2a	– Wire connector, double; behind dashboard	
T 2b	– Wire connector, double; in engine compartment	
T 2c	– Wire connector, double; next to radiator	
T 2d	– Wire connector, double; in luggage compartment	
T 2e	– Wire connector, double; in body bottom	
T 2f	– Wire connector, double; below passenger seat	
T 2g	– Wire connector, double; below driver seat	
T 2h	– Wire connector, double; on body bottom	
T 3a	– Wire connector, 3-point; in engine compartment left front	
T 3b	– Wire connector, 3-point; in engine compartment, right front	
T 3c	– Wire connector, 3-point; behind dashboard	
T 3d	– Wire connector, 3-point; behind dashboard	
T 3e	– Wire connector, 3 point; behind dashboard	
T 3f	– Wire connector, 3-point; behind dashboard	
T 6a	– Wire connector, 6-point; behind dashboard	
T 6c	– Wire connector, 6-point; behind dashboard	
T 6d	– Wire connector, 6-point; behind dashboard	
T 6e	– Wire connector, 6-point; behind dashboard	
T 14	– Wire connector, 14-point; on dashboard cluster	
T 20	– Test network/test socket	24
U	– Cigarette lighter	34
V 2	– Fresh air fan	33
W 6	– Glove compartment light	35
X	– Licence plate light	36
(1)	– Ground strap – battery/body/engine	10
(10)	– Ground connector, dashboard cluster	25

Description		In current track
E	– Windscreen wiper switch	81, 83, 84
E 2	– Turn signal switch	60, 61
E 3	– Emergency flasher switch	59, 60, 61, 62 63, 64
E 4	– Headlight dimmer switch	48
E 15	– Rear window defogger switch	55, 56
F	– Brake light switch	88, 89, 90
F 1	– Engine oil pressure switch	70
F 4	– Back-up light switch	79
F 18	– Radiator cooling fan thermo switch	91
F 24	– Elapsed mileage odometer (CAT)	75
F 27	– Elapsed mileage odometer (EGR)	74
G	– Fuel gauge sending unit	73
G 1	– Fuel gauge	73
G 2	– Coolant temperature sending unit	72
G 3	– Coolant temperature gauge	72
G 20	– Catalytic converter temperature sensor	77
J	– Headlight dimmer relay	48, 49, 50, 51, 52
J 2	– Emergency flasher relay	63, 64
J 6	– Voltage stabilizer	71
J 9	– Rear window defogger relay	54, 55
J 24	– Relay activating emergency flasher relay	59, 60
J 31	– Windshield washer/wiper intermittent relay (optional)	80, 81, 83, 85
J 42	– Catalytic converter relay	76, 77
K 1	– Headlight beam warning light	53
K 3	– Engine oil pressure light	70
K 5	– Turn signal warning light	69
K 6	– Emergency flasher warning light	58
K 10	– Rear window demister warning light	57
K 21	– Catalytic converter warning light	75
K 22	– EGR warning light	74
L 1	– Sealed beam unit, left	49, 51
L 2	– Sealed beam unit, right	50, 52
M 5	– Turn signal, front left	67
M 6	– Turn signal, rear left	65
M 7	– Turn signal, front right	68
M 8	– Turn signal, rear right	66
M 9	– Brake light, left	89
M 10	– Brake light, left	90
M 16	– Backup light left	79
M 17	– Backup light, right	80
S	– Fuses S1, S2, S3, S4, S6, S7, S8, S9, S11 in fuse box	
T 1a	– Wire connector, single; behind dashboard	
T 1b	– Wire connector, single; in engine compartment	
T 1c	– Wire connector, single; in engine compartment right	
T 1d	– Wire connector, single; in engine compartment right	
T 1e	– Wire connector, single; in engine compartment left	
T 1f	– Wire connector, single; in engine compartment left	
T 1g	– Wire connector, single; in luggage compartment left	
T 1h	– Wire connector, single; in luggage compartment right	
T 1i	– Wire connector, single; behind dashboard	
T 1k	– Wire connector, single; behind dashboard	
T 2a	– Wire connector, double; behind dashboard	
T 2b	– Wire connector, double; in engine compartment	
T 2c	– Wire connector, double; next to radiator	
T 2d	– Wire connector, double; in luggage compartment	
T 2e	– Wire connector, double; on body bottom	
T 2f	– Wire connector, double; below passenger seat	
T 2g	– Wire connector, double; below driver seat	
T 2h	– Wire connector, double; on body bottom	
T 3a	– Wire connector, 3-point; in engine compartment, left front	
T 3b	– Wire connector, 3-point; in engine compartment, right front	
T 3c	– Wire connector, 3-point; behind dashboard	
T 3d	– Wire connector, 3-point; behind dashboard	
T 3e	– Wire connector, 3-point; behind dashboard	
T 3f	– Wire connector, 3-point; behind dashboard	
T 6a	– Wire connector, 6-point; behind dashboard	
T 6c	– Wire connector, 6-point; behind dashboard	
T 6d	– Wire connector, 6-point; behind dashboard	
T 6e	– Wire connector, 6-point; behind dashboard	
T 14	– Wire connector, 14-point; on dashboard cluster	
V	– Windscreen wiper motor	83 - 85
V 5	– Windscreen washer pump	82
V 7	– Radiator cooling fan	91
W	– Interior light	87, 88
Y	– Clock	86
Z 1	– Rear window defogger heating element	54

The circles are the connections in the test network which are wired to the central test socket (T 20). The numbers in the circles correspond with the terminals in the socket.

Wire colours

BN	Brown
BE	Blue
W	White
P	Pink
GN	Green
BK	Black
M	Mauve
Y	Yellow
GY	Grey

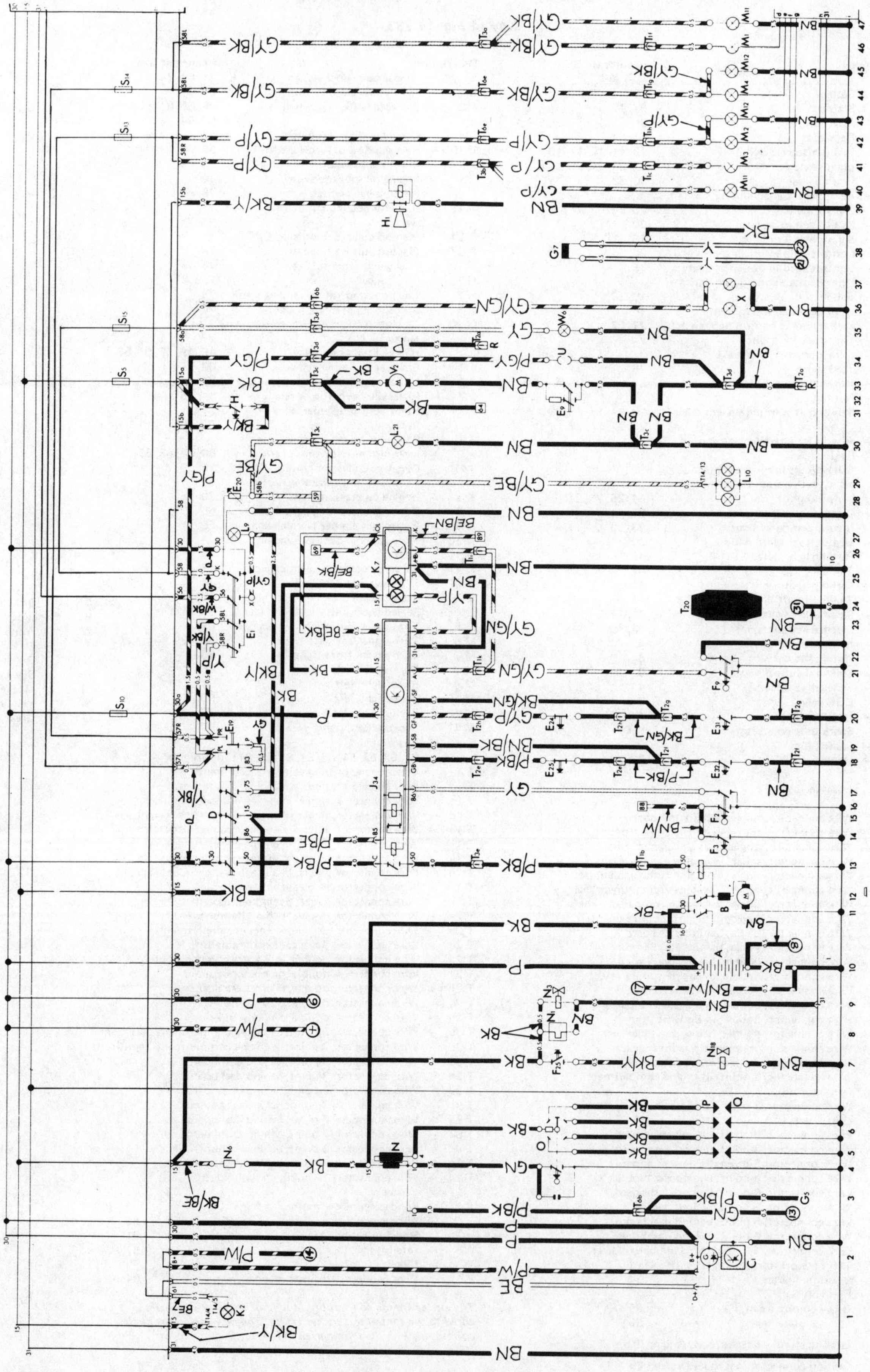

Fig. 14.233 Current flow diagram for 1975 Dasher models. For key see page 295

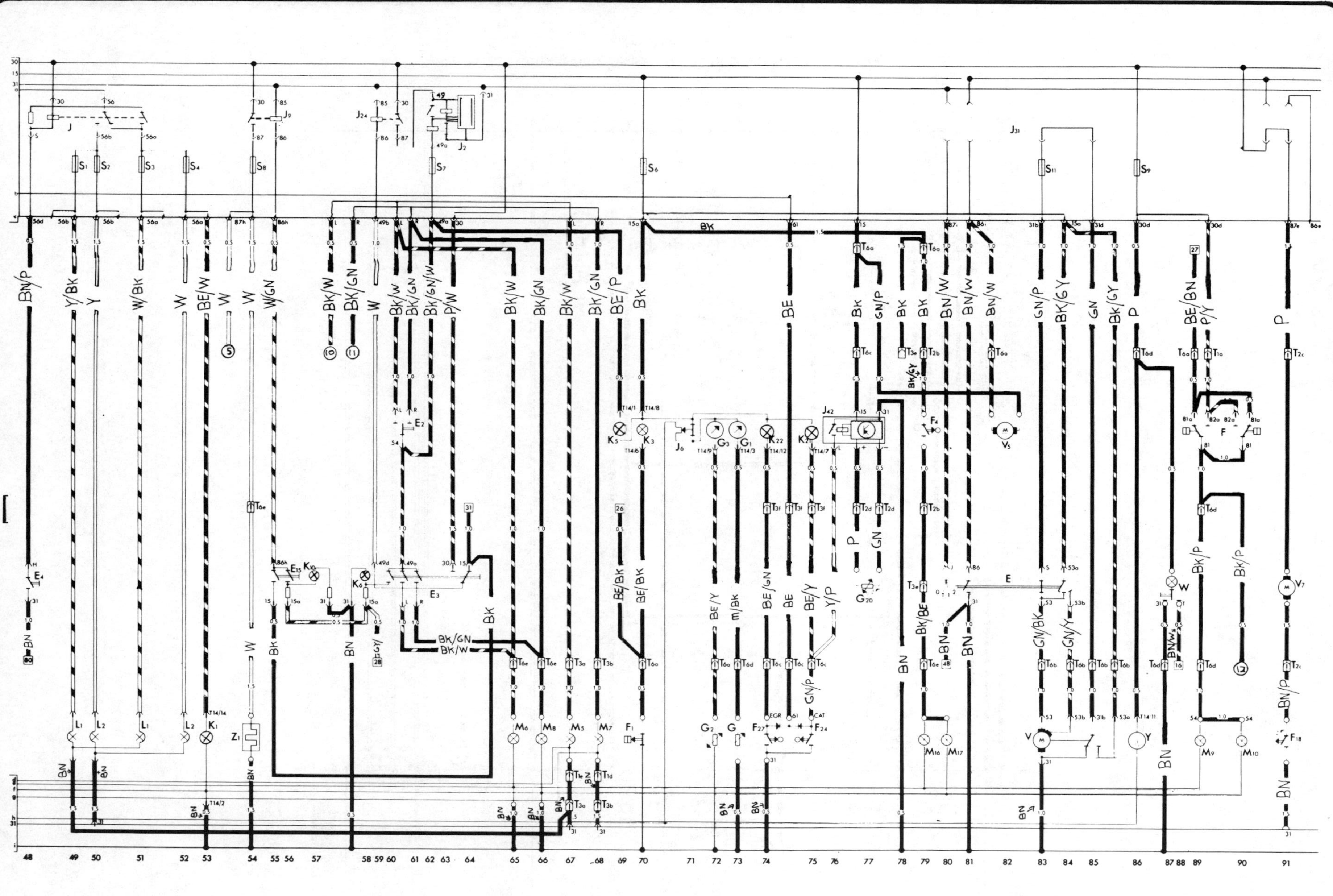

Fig. 14.233 (cont'd) Current flow diagram for 1975 Dasher models. For key see page 295

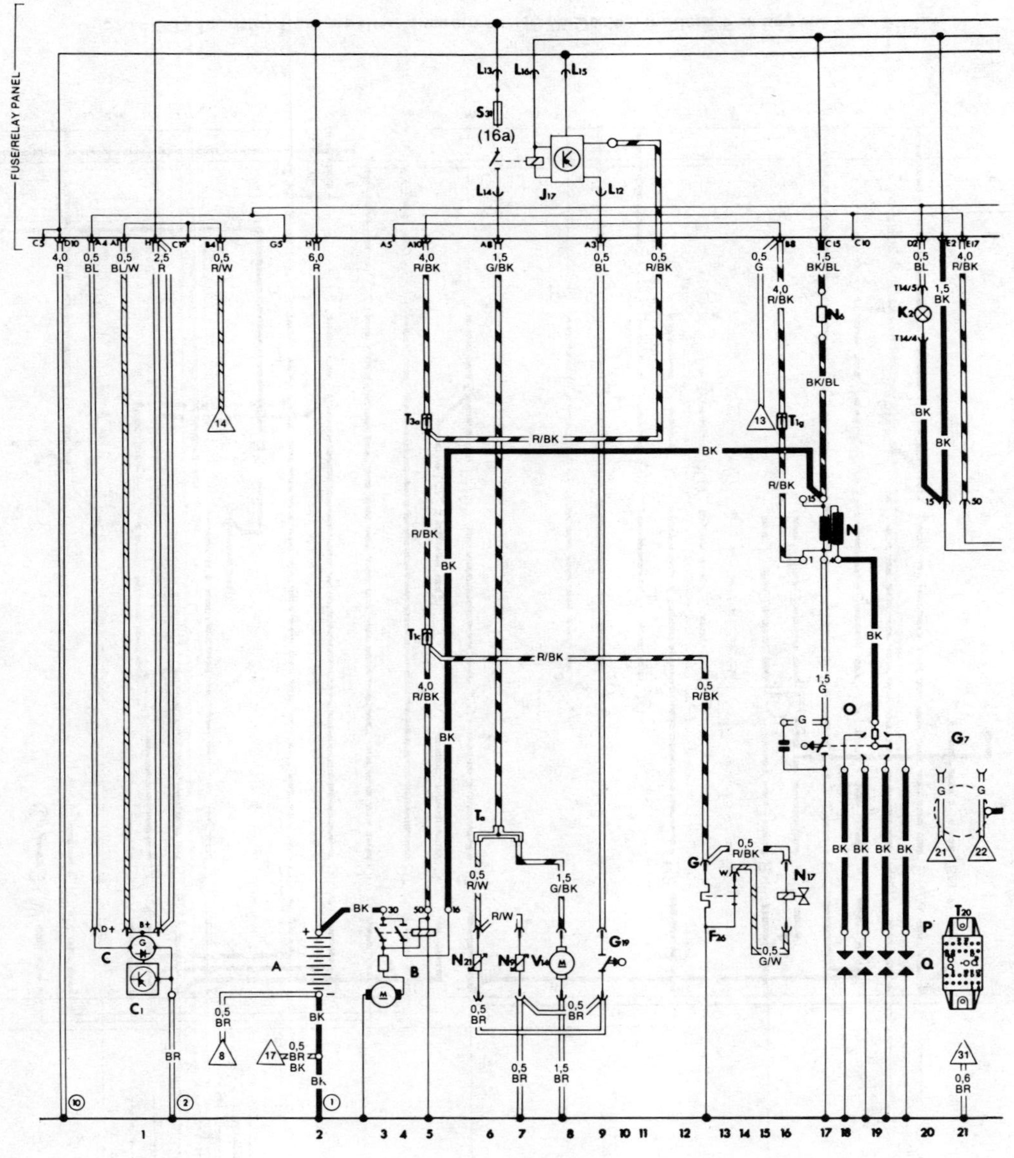

Fig. 14.234 Current flow diagram for 1976 Dasher models. For key see page 302

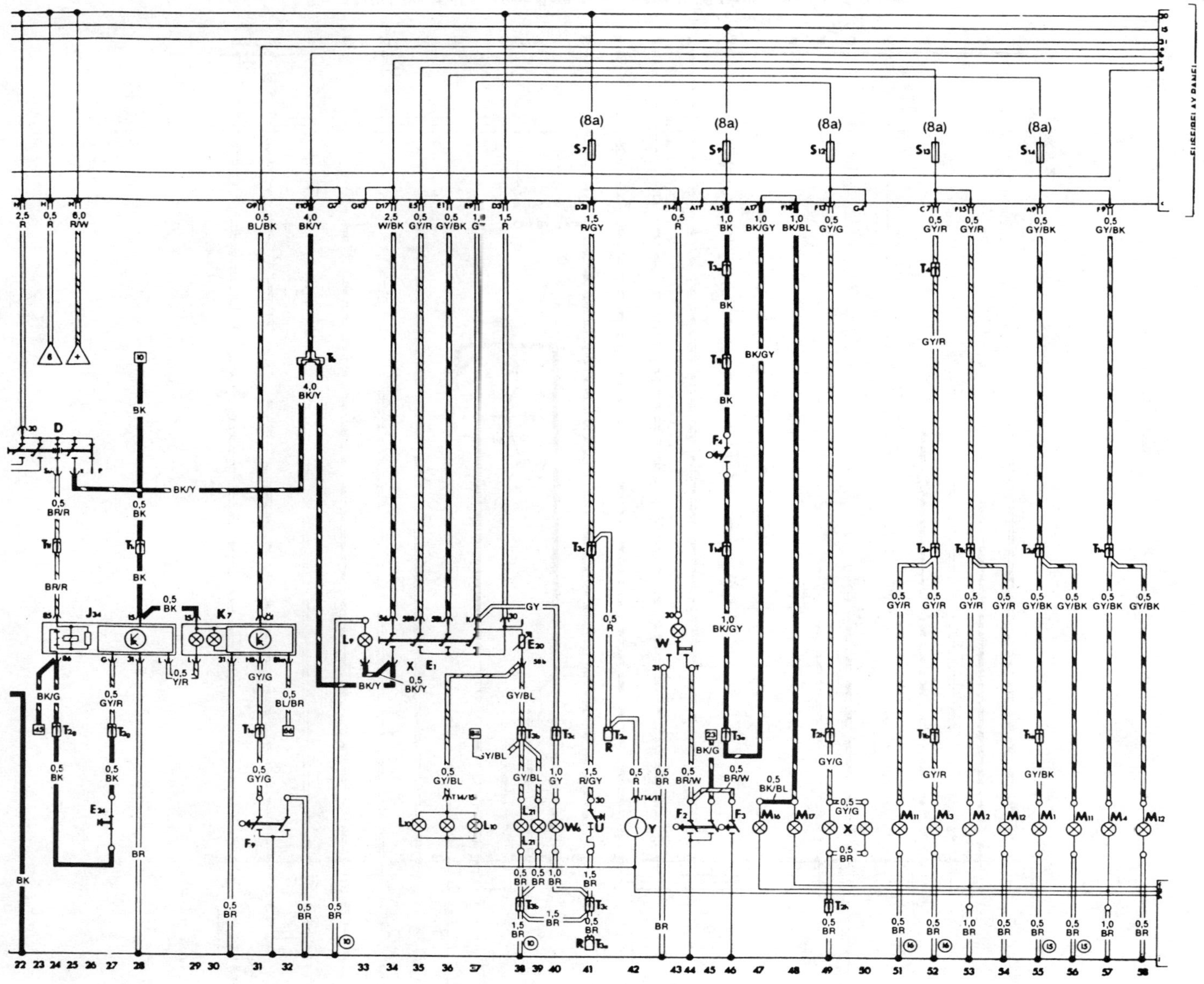

Fig. 14.234 (cont'd) Current flow diagram for 1976 Dasher models.
For key see page 302

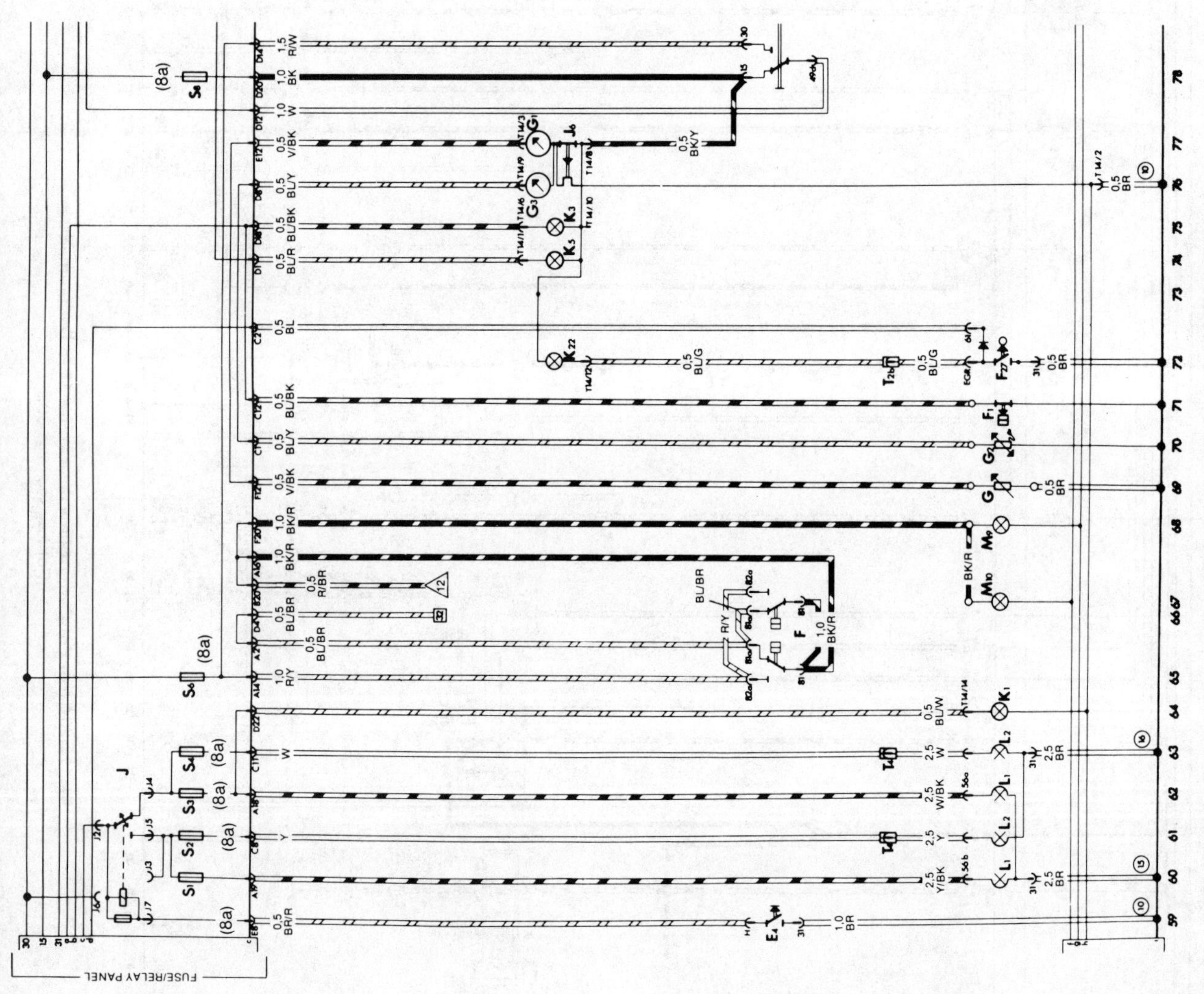

Fig. 14.234 (cont'd) Current flow diagram for 1976 Dasher models. For key see page 302

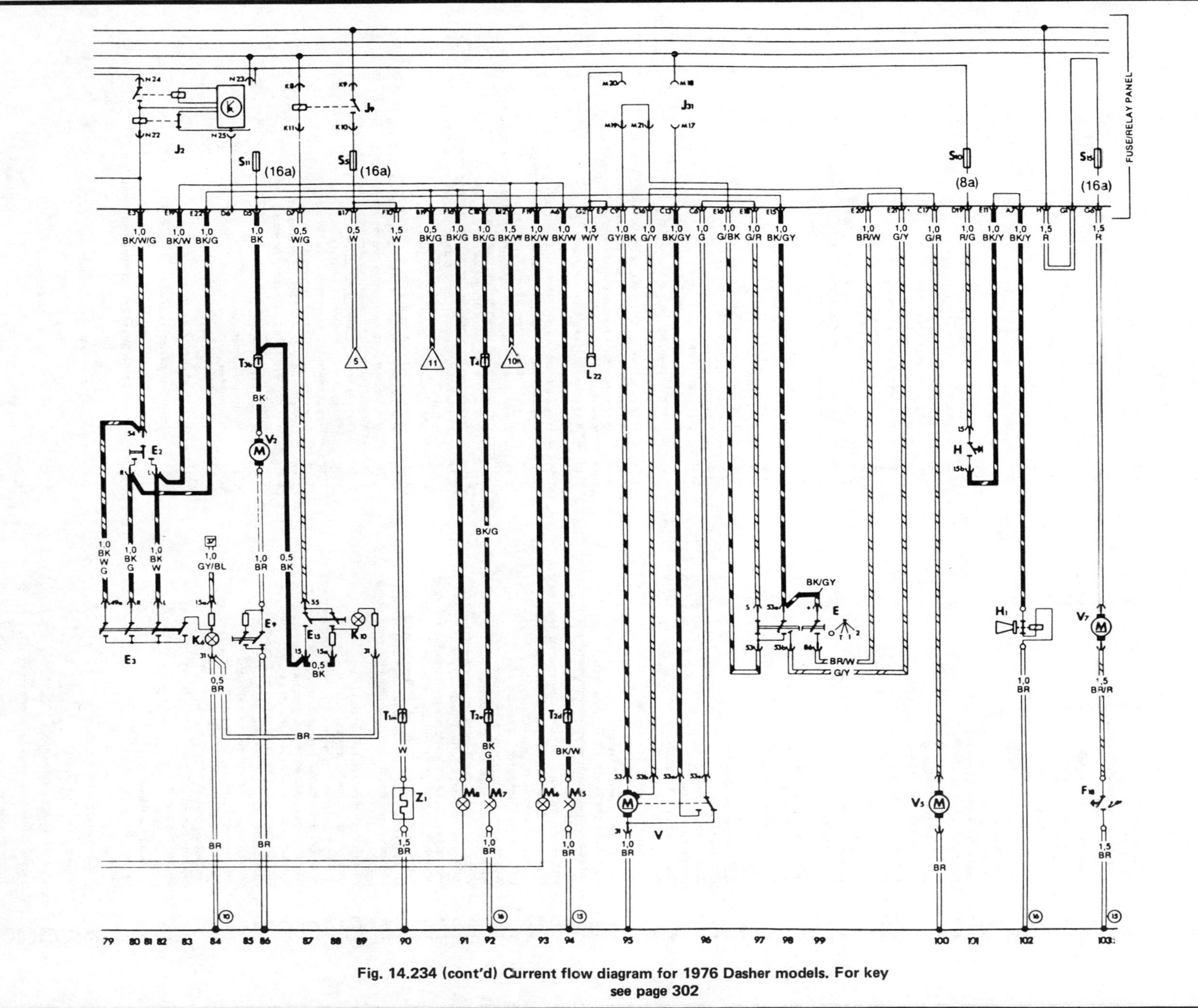

Fig. 14.234 (cont'd) Current flow diagram for 1976 Dasher models. For key see page 302

Key to Fig. 14.234

Description			In current track
A	–	Battery	2
B	–	Starter	3, 4, 5
C	–	Alternator	1
C 1	–	Regulator	1
D	–	Ignition/starter switch	21 - 26
E 1	–	Light switch	34 - 38
E 20	–	Instrument panel light/regulator	38
E 24	–	Seat belt lock, left	27
F 2	–	Door contact switch, left	44, 45
F 3	–	Door contact switch, right	46
F 4	–	Backup light switch	46
F 9	–	Parking brake indicator light	31, 32
F 26	–	Thermotime switch	13
G 7	–	To TDC indicator sensor	21
G 19	–	Intake air sensor	9
J 17	–	Electric fuel pump relay	6 - 10
J 34	–	Seat belt warning system relay	24, 27, 28
K 2	–	Alternator charging warning light	20
K 7	–	Dual circuit brake warning/parking brake and safety belt warning light	29 - 32
L 9	–	Light switch warning light	33
L 10	–	Instrument panel light	35 - 37
L 21	–	Heater lever illumination	38
M 1	–	Parking light, left	55
M 2	–	Tail light, right	53
M 3	–	Parking light right	52
M 4	–	Tail light, left	57
M 11	–	Sidemarker lights, front	51, 56
M 12	–	Sidemarker lights, rear	54, 58
M 16	–	Back-up light, left	47
M 17	–	Back-up light, right	48
N	–	Ignition coil	17, 18
N 6	–	Ballast resistor	17
N 9	–	Control pressure regulator	7
N 17	–	Cold start valve	16
N 21	–	Auxiliary air regulator	6
O	–	Ignition distributor	17, 19
P	–	Spark plug connectors	18, 19
Q	–	Spark plugs	18, 19
R	–	Connector for radio	41, 42
S	–	Fuses S 7, S 9, S 12, S 13, S 14 in fuse box	
S 31	–	Fuse for fuel injection system	6
T a	–	Wire connector, multiple; behind dashboard	
T b	–	Wire connector, multiple; next to light switch	
T 1a	–	Wire connector, single; in engine compartment, front left	
T 1b	–	Wire connector, single; in engine compartment, front right	
T 1c	–	Wire connector, single; in engine compartment, right	
T 1d	–	Wire connector, single; on bulkhead	
T 1e	–	Wire connector, single; on bulkhead	
T 1f	–	Wire connector, single; behind dashboard	
T 1g	–	Wire connector, single; behind fuse/relay panel	
T 1h	–	Wire connector, single; in engine compartment, front left	
T 1i	–	Wire connector, single; behind fuse/relay panel	
T 1k	–	Wire connector, single; in luggage compartment, rear right	
T 1l	–	Wire connector, single; behind dashboard	
T 1m	–	Wire connector, single; in luggage compartment left	
T 1n	–	Wire connector, single; in luggage compartment, rear left	
T 2a	–	Wire connector, double; behind dashboard (connection for radio)	
T 2b	–	Wire connector, double; behind dashboard	
T 2c	–	Wire connector, double; next to fuse/relay panel	
T 2d	–	Wire connector, double; in engine compartment, front left	
T 2e	–	Wire connector, double; in engine compartment, front right	
T 2f	–	Wire connector, double; in luggage compartment, rear right	
T 2g	–	Wire connector, double; under driver's seat	
T 2h	–	Wire connector, double; in luggage compartment	
T 3a	–	Wire connector, 3-point; behind dashboard	
T 3b	–	Wire connector, 3-point; behind dashboard	
T 3c	–	Wire connector, 3-point; behind dashboard	
T 4	–	Wire connector, 4-point; next to fuse/relay panel	
T 20	–	Test socket (not on 1976 models)	
U	–	Cigarette lighter	41
V 14	–	Electric fuel pump	8
W	–	Interior light	43
W 6	–	Glove compartment light	40
X	–	License plate light	49, 50
Y	–	Clock	42
(1)	–	Ground strap, battery/body/engine	2
(2)	–	Ground strap, alternator	1
(10)	–	Ground connector, dashboard	1, 33, 38
(15)	–	Ground connector, engine compartment front left	55, 56
(16)	–	Ground connector, engine compartment front right	51, 52

Description			In current track
E	–	Windshield wiper switch	97 - 99
E 2	–	Turn signal switch	80 - 82
E 3	–	Emergency flasher (hazard) switch	78 - 80, 82, 83
E 4	–	Headlight dimmer switch	59
E 9	–	Fresh air fan switch	85, 86
E 15	–	Rear window defogger switch	87, 88
F	–	Brake light switch	65, 67
F 1	–	Engine oil pressure switch	71
F 18	–	Radiator fan thermoswitch	103
F 27	–	EGR elapsed mileage odometer	72
G	–	Fuel gauge sender	69
G 1	–	Fuel gauge	77
G 2	–	Coolant temperature sender	70
G 3	–	Coolant temperature gauge	76
H	–	Horn button	101
H 1	–	Horn	102
J	–	Headlight dimmer relay	59 - 63
J 2	–	Emergency flasher (hazard) relay	81, 83, 85
J 6	–	Voltage stabilizer	77
J 9	–	Rear window defogger relay	87, 89
J 31	–	Windshield washer/wiper intermittent relay	95, 96
K 1	–	Headlight high beam warning light	64
K 3	–	Engine oil pressure warning light	75
K 5	–	Turn signal warning light	74
K 6	–	Emergency flasher (hazard) warning light	84
K 10	–	Rear window defogger warning light	89
K 22	–	EGR warning light	72
L 1	–	Headlight, left	60, 62
L 2	–	Headlight, right	61, 63
L 22	–	Connection for foglights (optional)	95
M 5	–	Turn signal, front left	94
M 6	–	Turn signal, rear left	93
M 7	–	Turn signal, front right	92
M 8	–	Turn signal, rear right	91
M 9	–	Brake light, left	68
M 10	–	Brake light, right	67
S	–	Fuses S 1 - S6, S 8, S 10, S 11, S 15 in fuse box	
T a	–	Wire connector, behind dashboard	
T b	–	Wire connector, next to light switch	
T 1a	–	Wire connector, single; in engine compartment, front left	
T 1b	–	Wire connector, single; in engine compartment, front right	
T 1c	–	Wire connector, single; in engine compartment, right	
T 1d	–	Wire connector, single; on bulkhead	
T 1e	–	Wire connector, single; on bulkhead	
T 1f	–	Wire connector, single; behind dashboard	
T 1g	–	Wire connector, single; behind fuse/relay panel	
T 1h	–	Wire connector, single; in engine compartment, front left	
T 1i	–	Wire connector, single; behind fuse/relay panel	
T 1k	–	Wire connector, single; in luggage compartment, rear right	
T 1l	–	Wire connector, single; behind dashboard	
T 1m	–	Wire connector, single; in luggage compartment, left	
T 1n	–	Wire connector, single; in luggage compartment, rear left	
T 2a	–	Wire connector, double; behind dashboard (connection for radio)	
T 2b	–	Wire connector, double; behind dashboard	
T 2c	–	Wire connector, double; next to fuse/relay panel	
T 2d	–	Wire connector, double; in engine compartment, front left	
T 2e	–	Wire connector, double; in engine compartment, front right	
T 2f	–	Wire connector, double; in luggage compartment, rear right	
T 2g	–	Wire connector, double; under driver's seat	
T 2h	–	Wire connector, double; in luggage compartment	
T 3a	–	Wire connector, 3-point; behind dashboard	
T 3b	–	Wire connector, 3-point; behind dashboard	
T 3c	–	Wire connector, 3-point; behind dashboard	
T 4	–	Wire connector, 4-point; next to fuse/relay panel	
V	–	Windshield wiper motor	95, 96
V 2	–	Fresh air fan	86
V 5	–	Windshield washer pump	100
V 7	–	Radiator fan	103
Z 1	–	Rear window defogger element	90
(10)	–	Ground connector, dashboard	59, 76, 84
(15)	–	Ground connector, engine compartment, front left	60, 94, 103
(16)	–	Ground connector, engine compartment, front right	63, 92, 102

Numbers in triangles relate to diagnostic test socket T20

Wire colours

BK	Black	O	Orange
BL	Blue	R	Red
BR	Brown	V	Violet
G	Green	W	White
GY	Grey	Y	Yellow

Key to Fig. 14.235

Description			In current track
A	–	Battery	2
B	–	Starter	3 - 5
C	–	Alternator	1
C 1	–	Regulator	1
D	–	Ignition/starter switch	16 - 21
E 1	–	Light switch	27 - 33
E 20	–	Instrument panel lighting control switch	33
E 24	–	Safety belt switch, left	21
F 2	–	Door contact switch, interior light/buzzer, left	38 - 40
F 3	–	Door contact switch, interior light, right	41
F 4	–	Back-up light switch	41
F 9	–	Parking brake light switch	24, 25
F 26	–	Thermotime switch for cold start valve	10, 11
G 6	–	Electric fuel pump	8
J 17	–	Electric fuel pump relay	6 - 9
J 34	–	Safety belt warning system relay	19 - 21
K 2	–	Alternator charging warning light	15
K 7	–	Dual circuit brake warning light	22 - 25
L 9	–	Light switch warning light	26
L 10	–	Instrument panel light	31 - 33
L 21	–	Heater lever warning light	29
L 28	–	Cigarette lighter light	34
M 1	–	Parking light, left	50
M 2	–	Tail light, right	48
M 3	–	Parking light, right	47
M 4	–	Tail light, left	52
M 11	–	Side marker lights, front	46, 51
M 12	–	Side marker lights, rear	49, 53
M 16	–	Back-up light, left	43
M 17	–	Back-up light, right	42
N	–	Ignition coil	13 - 14
N 6	–	Ballast resistor	13
N 9	–	Control pressure regulator	7
N 17	–	Cold start valve	11
N 21	–	Auxiliary air regulator	5
O	–	Ignition distributor	14 - 15
P	–	Spark plug connectors	14 - 15
Q	–	Spark plugs	13 - 15
R	–	Connectors for radio, on console	36
S	–	Fuses S 1 - S 15 in fuse box	
S 1	–	Fuse for fuel injection system	7
T 1a	–	Wire connector, single; in engine compartment, front left	50
T 1b	–	Wire connector, single; in engine compartment, front right	47
T 1c	–	Wire connector, single; in engine compartment	47
T 1d	–	Wire connector, single; in engine compartment	47
T 1e	–	Wire connector, single; in engine compartment	4
T 1i	–	Wire connector, single; behind relay plate	11
T 1k	–	Wire connector, single; behind dashboard	12
T 1l	–	Wire connector, single; in engine compartment	7
T 1m	–	Wire connector, single; behind dashboard	24
T 1n	–	Wire connector, single; in luggage compartment	52
T 1o	–	Wire connector, single; in engine compartment	48
T 2a	–	Wire connector, double; in engine compartment. left	50
T 2b	–	Wire connector, double, in engine compartment, right	47
T 2c	–	Wire connector, double; in luggage compartment	8
T 2d	–	Wire connector, double; behind dashboard for radio	36
T 2e	–	Wire connector, double; below driver's seat	19, 21
T 2f	–	Wire connector, double; in luggage compartment, left	44
T 3a	–	Wire connector, 3-point; behind dashboard, left	4, 41
T 3b	–	Wire connector, 3-point; behind dashboard, centre	34, 35
T 3c	–	Wire connector, 3-point; behind dashboard, centre	29, 87
T £	–	Wire connector, 4-point; behind dashboard	47
T 14	–	Wire connector, 14-point; on dashboard cluster	15
T 20	–	Diagnosis system/diagnosis socket	16
U 1	–	Cigarette lighter	35
W	–	– Interior light	38, 39
X		Number plate light	44
Y		– Clock	37
(1)		– Ground strap, battery to body	
(2)	–	Ground strap, transmission to body	
(3)	–	Ground connectors, on bulkhead	
(10)	–	Ground connectors, on dashboard	
(15)	–	Ground connectors, engine compartment, left	
(16)	–	Ground connectors, engine compartment, right	

Description			In current track
E	–	Windshield wiper switch	90 - 93
E 2	–	Turn signal switch	74, 75
E +	–	Emergency flasher switch	71 - 77
E 4	–	Headlight dimmer switch	54
E 9	–	Fresh air fan switch	86 - 88
E 15	–	Rear window defogger switch	82 - 84
F	–	Brake light switch	60 - 62
F !	–	Engine oil pressure switch	66
F 18	–	Radiator cooling fan thermoswitch	97
F 27	–	Elapsed mileage switch (EGR)	67
G	–	Fuel gauge sending unit	64
G !	–	Fuel gauge	70
G †	–	Coolant temperature sending unit	65
G 3	–	Coolant temperature gauge	69
H	–	Horn button	95
H 1	–	Horn	95
J	–	Headlight dimmer relay	54 - 57
J 2	–	Emergency flasher relay	75 - 77
J 6	–	Voltage stabilizer	69, 70
J 9	–	Rear window defogger relay	84, 85
K 1	–	Headlight light beam warning light	59
K 3	–	Engine oil pressure warning light	68
K 5	–	Turn signal warning light	67
K 6	–	Emergency flasher warning light	77
K 10	–	Rear window defogger warning light	82
K 22	–	EGR warning light	87
L 1	–	Sealed beam unit, left	55, 57
L 2	–	Sealed beam unit, right	56, 58
L 22	–	Connection for foglights	88
M 5	–	Turn signal, front left	81M 6
M 6	–	Turn signal, rear left	80
M 7	-	Turn signal, front right	79
M 8	–	Turn signal, rear right	78
M 9	–	Brake light, left	63
M 10	–	Brake light, right	62
N 23	–	Speed control resistors for fresh air fan	87
S	–	Fuses S 1 - S 15 in fuse box	
T 1	–	Wire connector, single; behind dashboard	86, 87
T 1g	–	Wire connector, single; in luggage compartment left	85
T 1h	–	Wire connector, single, behind dashboard	67T 2
T 2	–	Wire connector, double; behind dashboard	86, 87
T 2a	–	Wire connector, double; in engine compartment	81
T 2b	–	Wire connector, double; in engine compartment	79
T 3c	–	Wire connector, 3-point, behind dashboard centre	87
T 4	–	Wire connector, 4-point; behind dashboard	56, 58, 79
T 14	–	Wire connector, 14-point; on dashboard cluster	67 - 70
V	–	Windshield wiper motor	89 - 90
V 2	–	Fresh air fan	86
V 5	–	Windshield washer pump	94
V 7	–	Radiator cooling fan	97
Z 1	–	Rear window defogger element	85
(10)	–	Ground connectors, dashboard	
(15)	–	Ground connectors, engine compartment, left	
(16)	–	Ground connectors, engine compartment, right	

Numbers in triangles relate to diagnostic test socket T20

Wire colours

BK	Black
bl	Blue
BR	Brown
G	Green
GY	Grey
O	Orange
R	Red
V	Violet
W	White
Y	Yellow

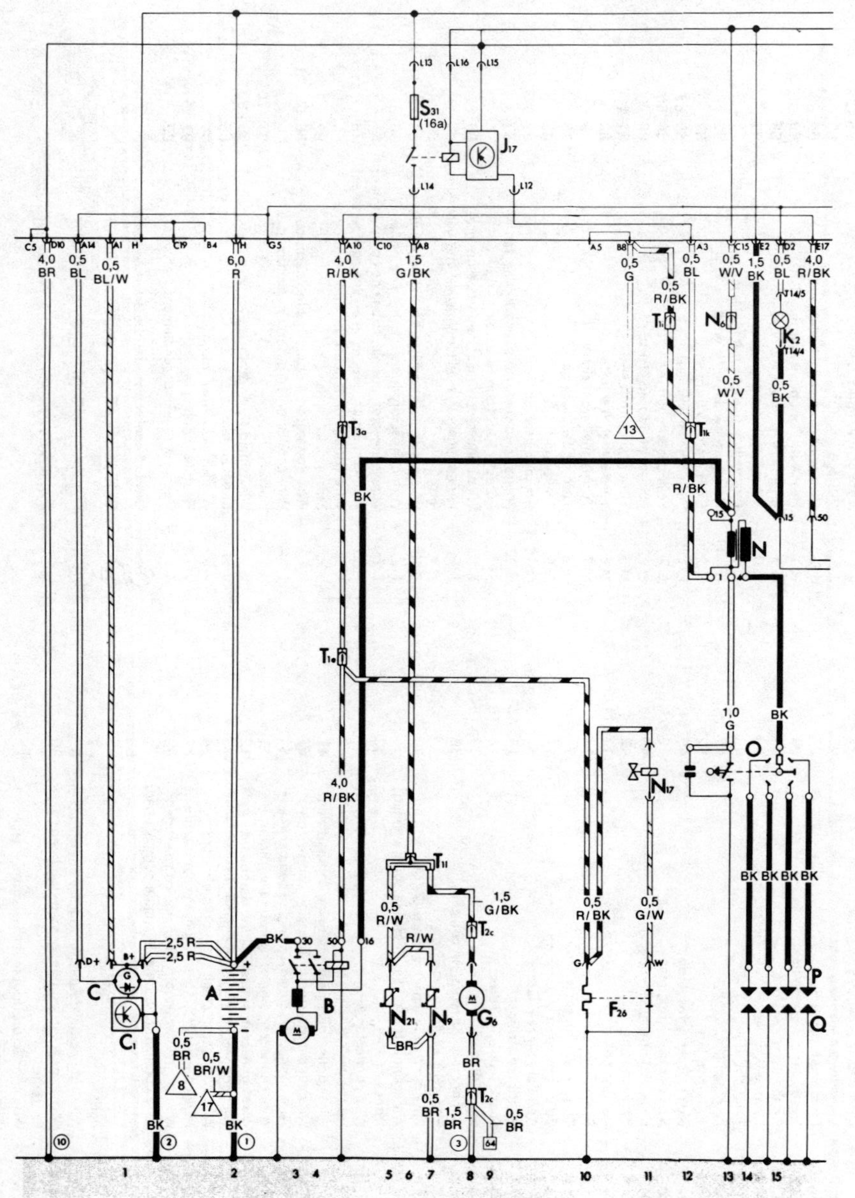

Fig. 14.235 Current flow diagram for 1977 Dasher models. For key see page 303

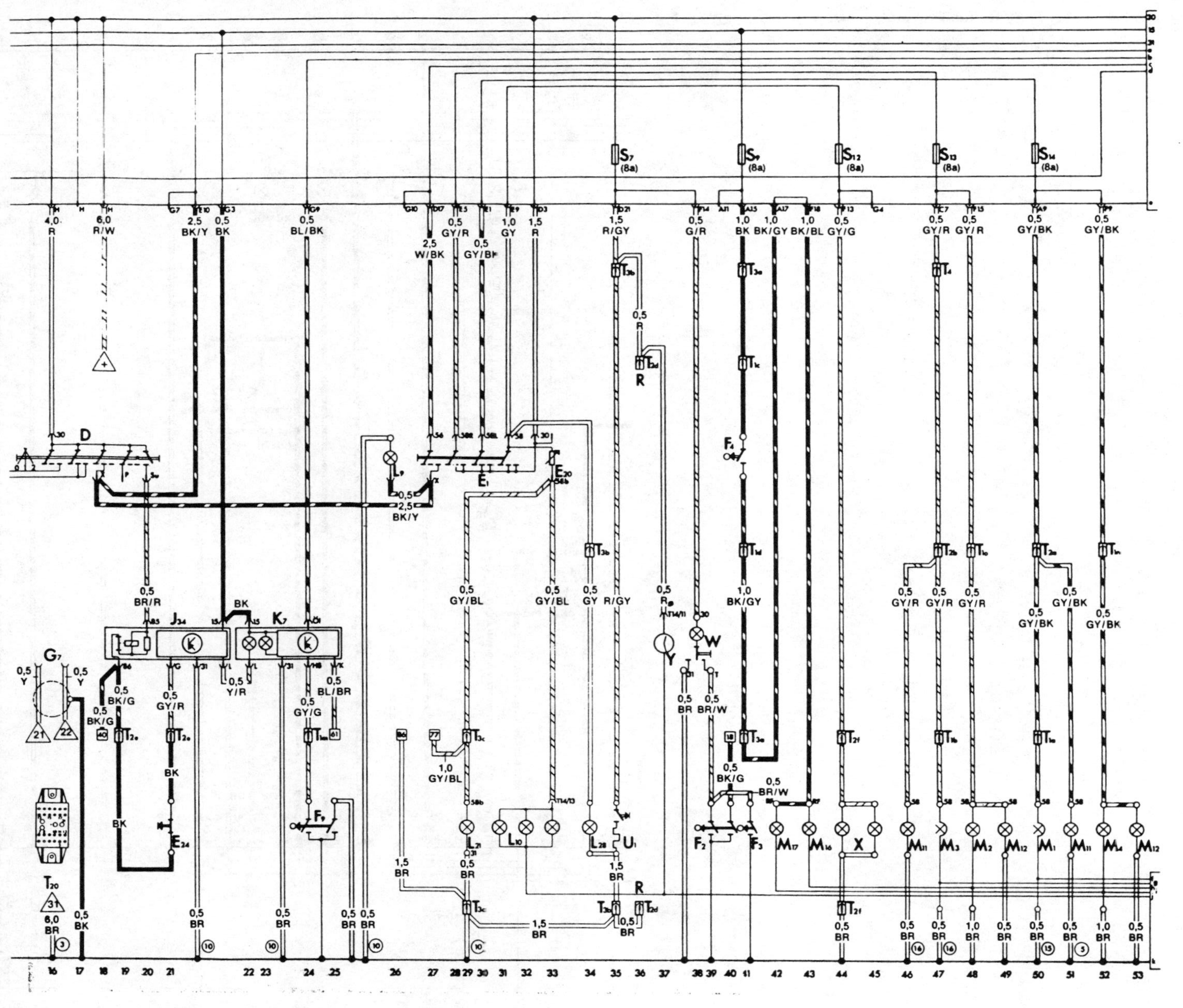

Fig. 14.235 (cont'd) Current flow diagram for 1977 Dasher models. For key see page 303

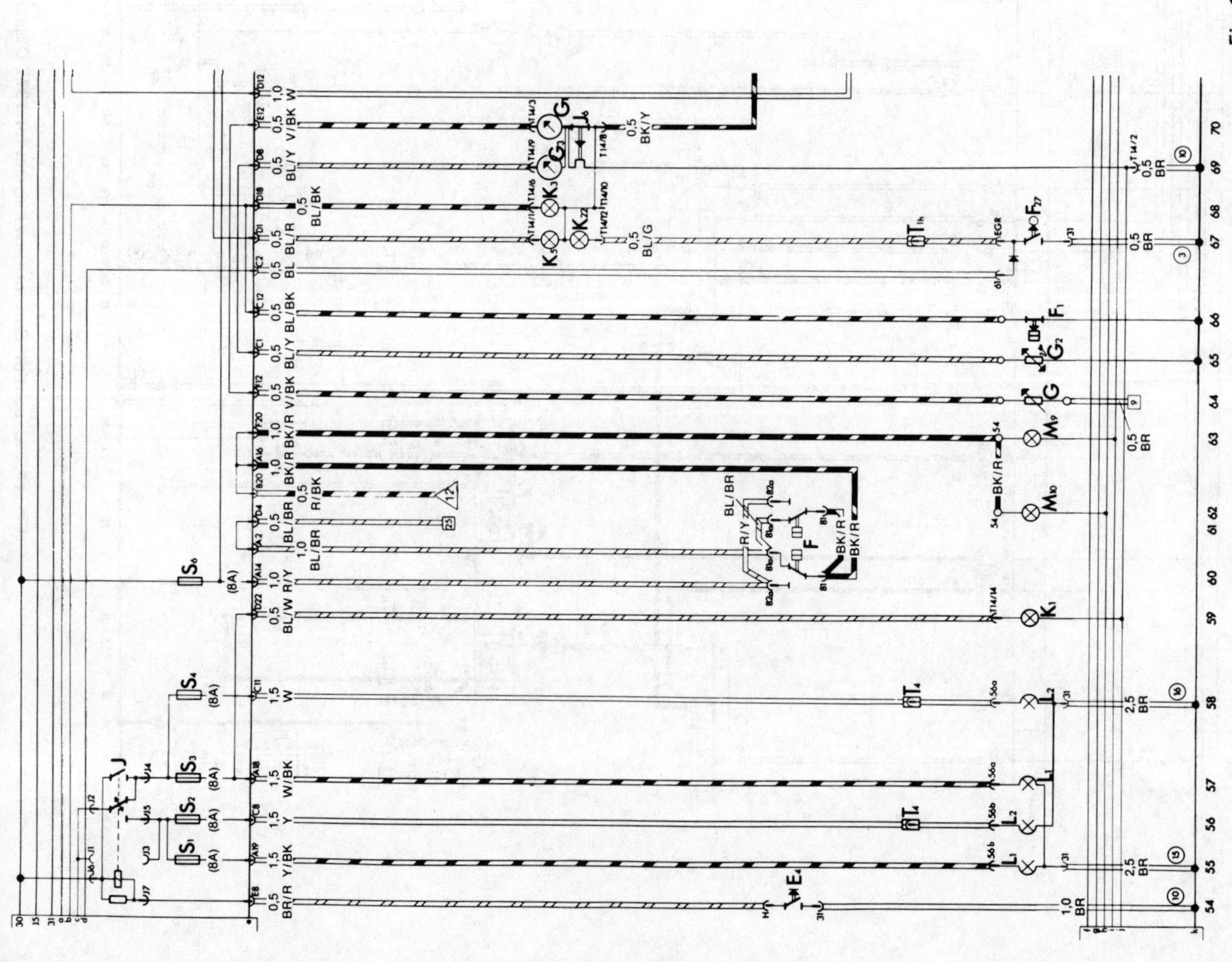

Fig. 14.235 (cont'd) Current flow diagram for 1977 Dasher models. For key see page 303

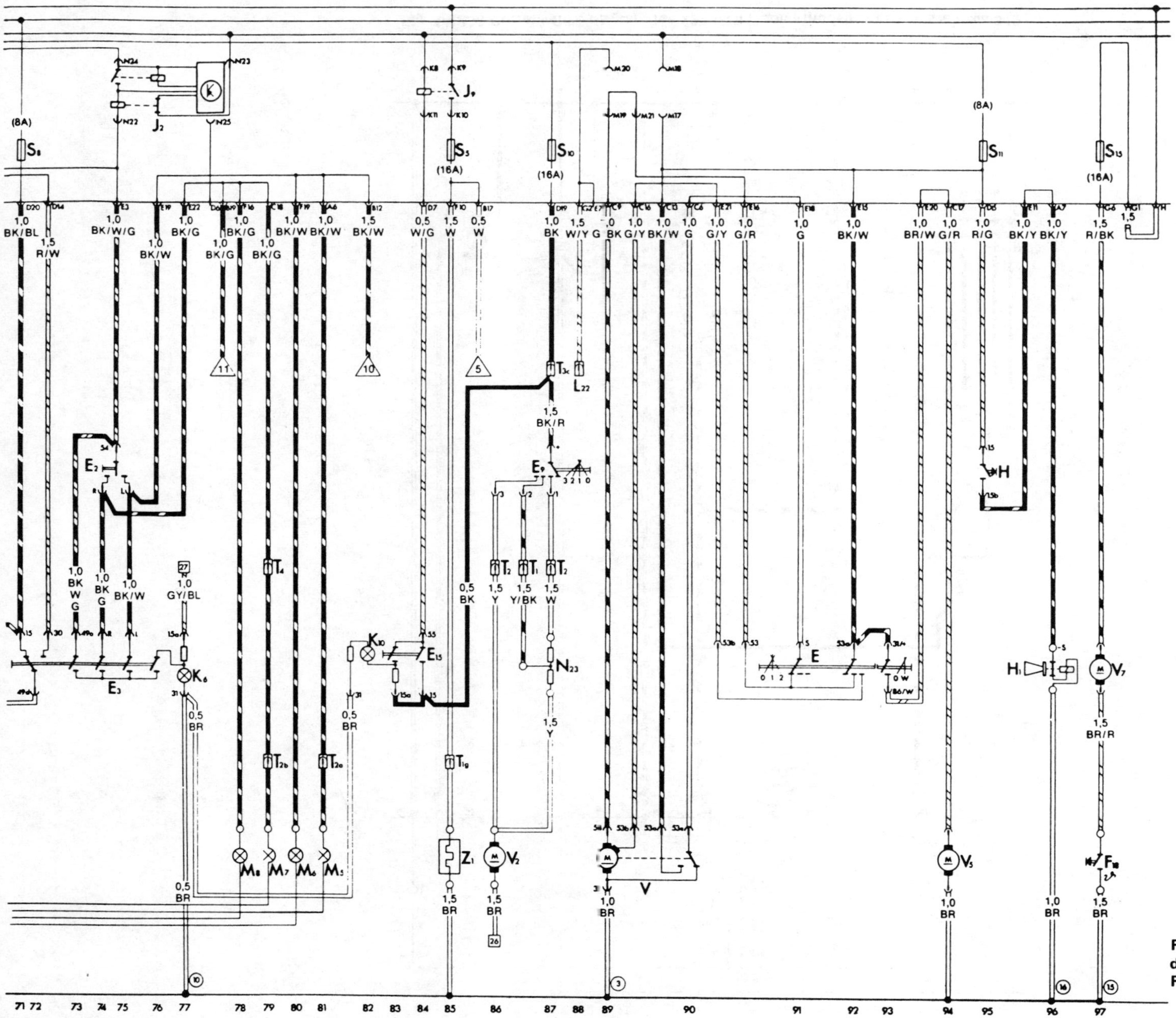

Fig. 14.235 (cont'd) Current flow diagram for 1977 Dasher models. For key see page 303

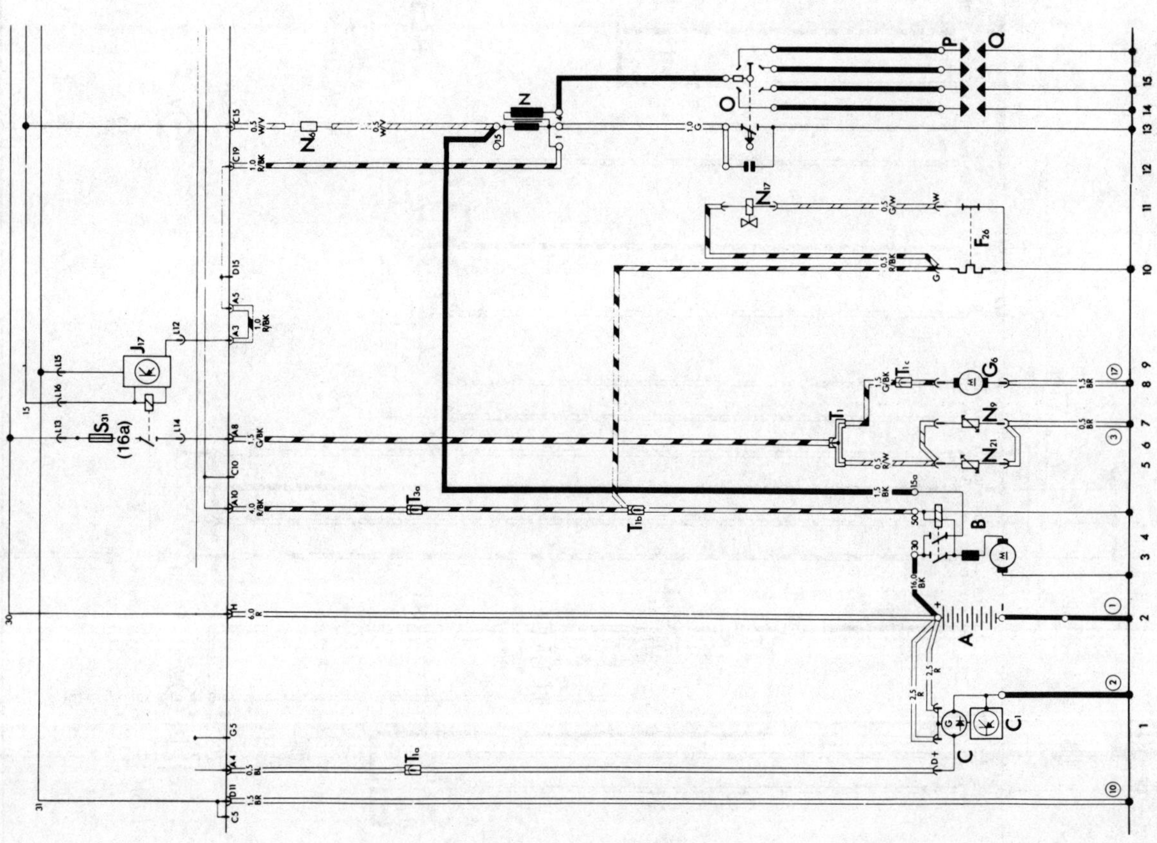

Fig. 14.236 Current flow diagram for 1978/79 Dasher models. For key see page 312

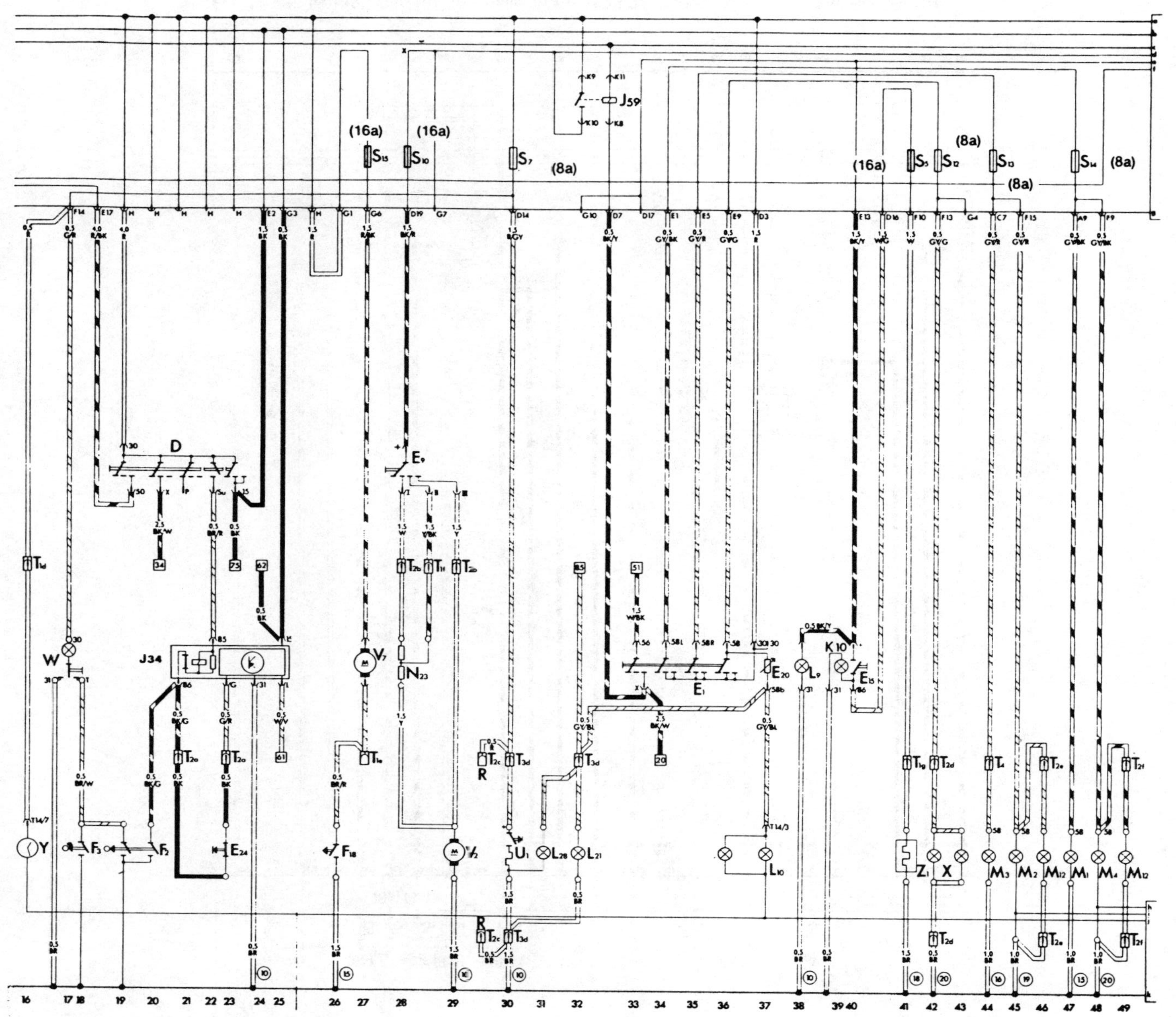

Fig. 14.236 (cont'd) Current flow diagram for 1978/79 Dasher models. For key see page 312

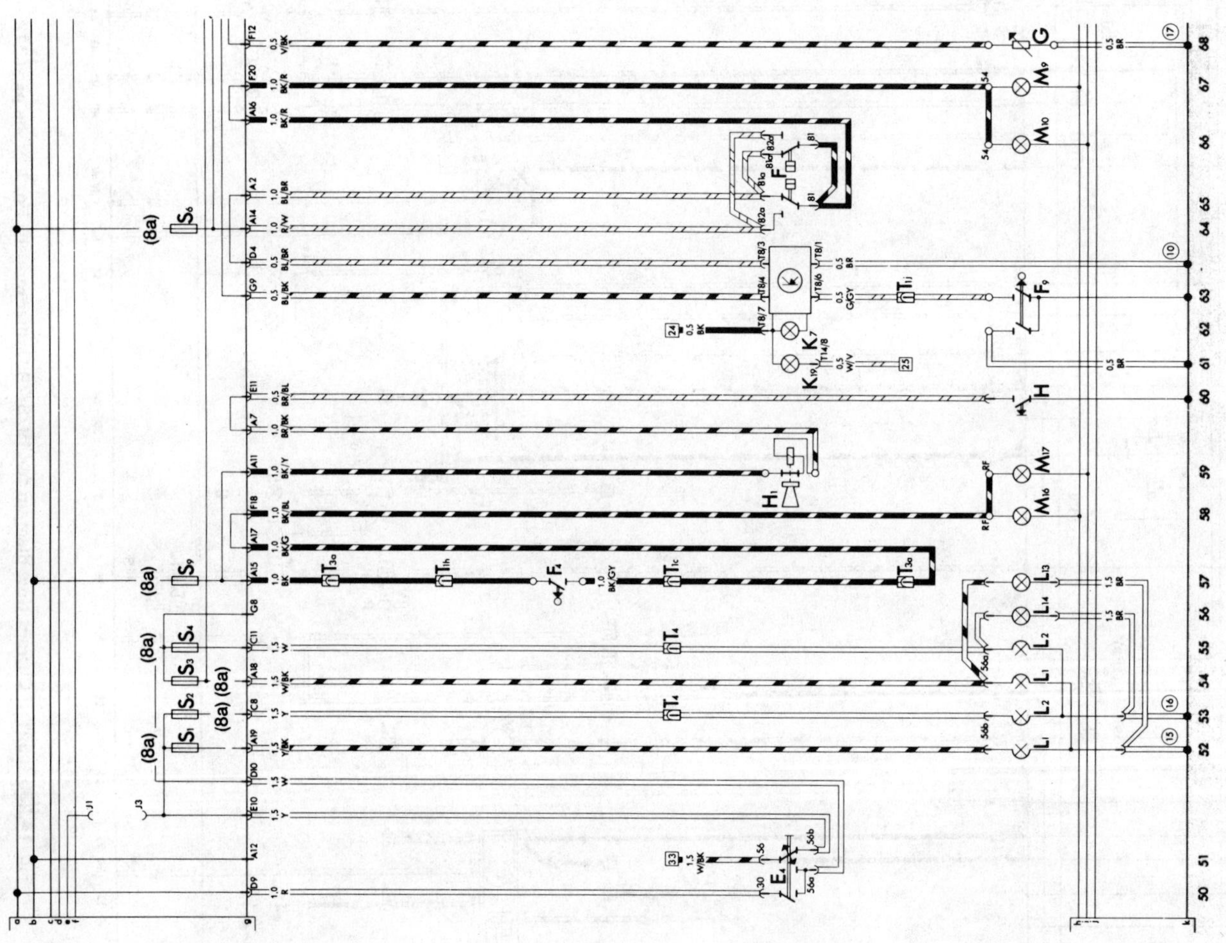

Fig. 14.236 (cont'd) Current flow diagram for 1978/79 Dasher models. For key see page 312

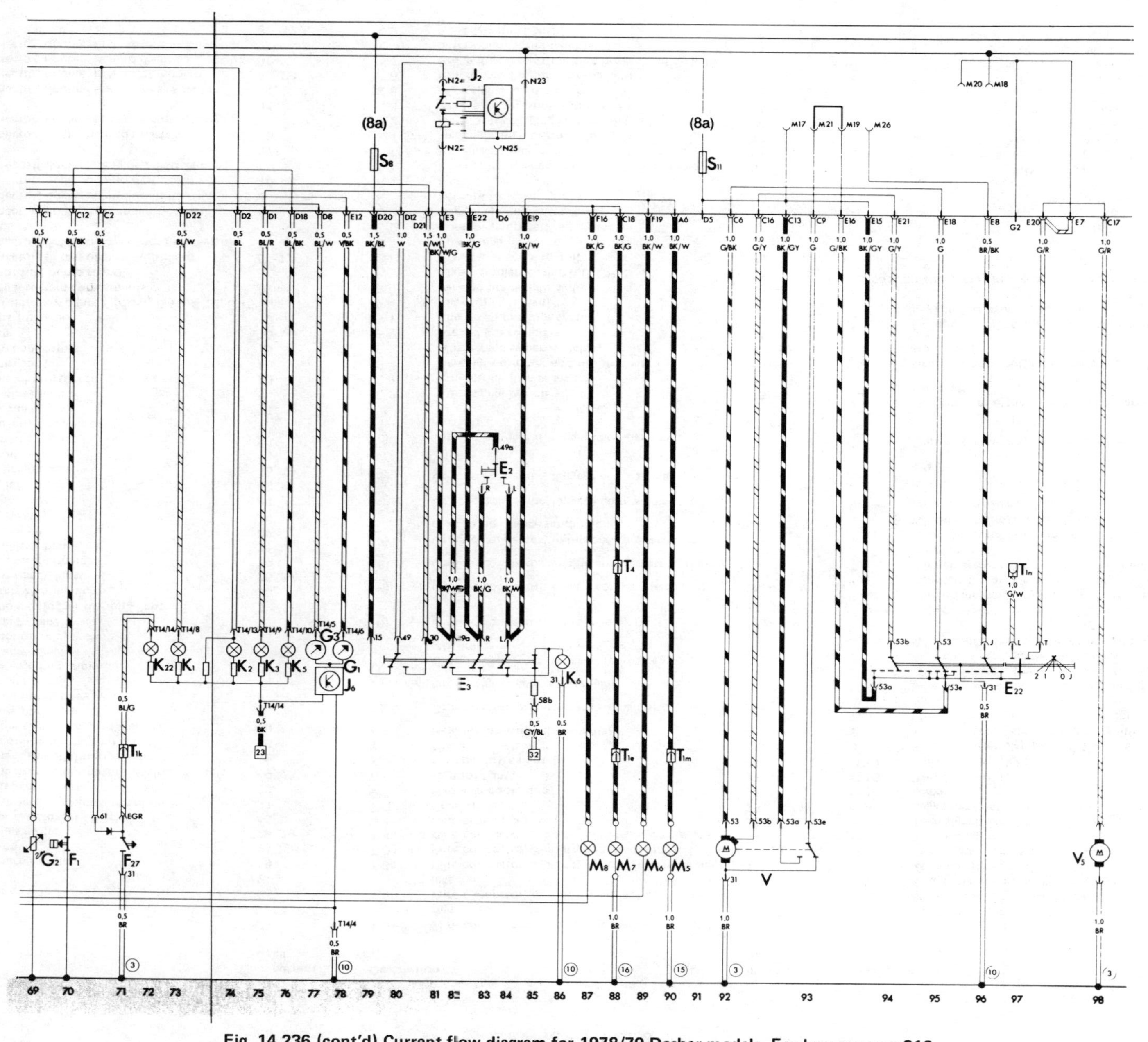

Fig. 14.236 (cont'd) Current flow diagram for 1978/79 Dasher models. For key see page 312

Key to Fig. 14.236

Description		In current track
A	Battery	2
B	Starter	3, 4
C	Alternator	1
C 1	Regulator	1
D	Ignition/starter switch	19 - 23
E 1	Light switch	33 - 36
E 9	Fresh air fan switch	28, 29
E 15	Rear window defogger switch	40
E 20	Instrument panel lighting control switch	37
E 24	Safety belt switch, left	23
F 2	Door contact switch, interior light/buzzer, left	19, 20
F 3	Door contact switch, interior light, right	18
F 18	Radiator cooling fan thermoswitch	26
F 26	Thermotime switch for cold start valve	10, 11
G 6	Electric fuel pump	8
J 17	Electric fuel pump relay (on fuse/relay panel)	6 - 9
J 34	Safety belt warning relay (on fuse/relay panel)	21 - 25
J 59	Load reduction relay (on fuse/relay panel)	32
K 10	Rear window defogger warning light	39
L 9	Light switch warning light	38
L 10	Instrument panel lights	36, 37
L 21	Heater lever warning light	32
L 28	Cigarette lighter light	31
M 1	Parking light, left	47
M 2	Tail light, right	45
M 3	Parking light, right	44
M 4	Tail light, left	48
M 12	Side marker lights, rear	46, 49
N	Ignition coil	13
N 6	Ballast resistor	13
N 9	Control pressure regulator	7
N 17	Cold start valve	11
N 21	Auxiliary air regulator	5
N 23	Speed control resistors for fresh air fan	28
O	Ignition distributor	15
P	Spark plug connectors	15
Q	Spark plugs	15
R	Connectors for radio	30
S	Fuses on fuse/relay panel S 5, S 7, S 10, S 12, S 15	
S 31	Fuse for fuel system components (on front of fuel pump relay)	6
T 1	Wire connector, single; behind dashboard	5 - 7
T 1a	Wire connector, single; below windscreen washer fluid container	1
T 1b	Wire connector, single; next to ignition coil	4
T 1c	Wire connector, single; behind dashboard	8
T 1d	Wire connector, single; behind dashboard	16
T 1e	Wire connector, single; in engine compartment, left	27
T 1f	Wire connector, single; behind dashboard	28
T 1g	Wire connector, single; in luggage compartment, left	41
T 2a	Wire connector, double; under driver's seat	21, 23
T 2b	Wire connector, double; behind dashboard	28, 29
T 2c	Wire connector, double; behind dashboard	30
T 2d	Wire connector, double; in luggage compartment, left	30, 42

Description		In current track
T 2e	Wire connector, double; in luggage compartment, right	46
T 2f	Wire connector, double; in luggage compartment, left	49
T 3a	Wire connector, 3-point; next to fuse/relay panel	4
T 3d	Wire connector, 3-point; behind dashboard	30, 32
T 4	Wire connector, 4-point; next to fuse/relay panel	44
U 1	Cigarette lighter	30
V 2	Fresh air fan	29
V 7	Radiator cooling fan	27
W	Interior light	17, 18
X	Number plate light	42
Y	Clock	16
Z 1	Rear window defogger element	41
(1)	Ground strap battery/body/transmission	2
(2)	Ground strap generator/engine	1
(3)	Ground connector, on cowl reinforcement, left side	7
(10)	Ground connector, on fuse/relay panel	1, 24, 29, 30, 38
(15)	Ground connector, engine compartment, left	26, 47
(16)	Ground connector, engine compartment, right	44
(17)	Ground connector, in luggage compartment next to fuel gauge sending unit	8
(18)	Ground connector, luggage compartment, right	41
(19)	Ground connector, luggage compartment, rear right	45
(20)	Ground connector, luggage compartment, rear left	42, 48
E 2	Turn signal switch	83, 84
E 3	Emergency flasher switch	79 - 85
E 4	Headlight dimmer and flasher switch	50, 51
E 22	Windscreen wiper switch	94 - 97
F	Brake light switch	64 - 66
F 1	Engine oil pressure switch	70
F 4	Back-up light switch	57
F 9	Parking brake light switch	62, 63
F 27	Elapsed mileage switch (EGR)	71
G	Fuel gauge sending unit	68
G 1	Fuel gauge	78
G 2	Coolant temperature sending unit	69
G 3	Coolant temperature gauge	77
H	Horn button	60
H 1	Horn	59
J 2	Emergency flasher relay	81 - 84
J 6	Voltage stabilizer	78
K 1	Headlight high beam warning light	73
K 2	Generator charging warning light	74
K 3	Engine oil pressure warning light	75
K 5	Turn signal warning light	76
K 6	Emergency flasher warning light	86
K 7	Brake dual circuit/parking brake warning light	62
K 19	Safety belt warning light	61
K 22	EGR warning light	72

Description		In current track
L 1	Sealed beam unit, left	52
L 2	Sealed beam unit, right	53, 55
L 13	Sealed beam unit, high beam, left	57
L 14	Sealed beam unit, high beam, right	56
M 5	Turn signal, front left	90
M 6	Turn signal, rear left	89
M 7	Turn signal, front right	88
M 8	Turn signal, rear right	87
M 9	Brake light, left	67
M 10	Brake light, right	66
M 16	Back-up light, left	58
M 17	Back-up light, right	59
S	Fuses on fuse/relay panel S 1, S 4, S 8, S 9, S 11	
T 1c	Wire connector, single; next to ignition coil	57
T 1e	Wire connector, single; in engine compartment, right	88
T 1h	Wire connector, single; next to ignition coil	57
T 1j	Wire connector, single; behind dashboard	63
T 1k	Wire connector, single; behind dashboard	71
T 1m	Wire connector, single; in engine compartment, left	90
T 1n	Wire connector, single; behind dashboard	97
T 3a	Wire connector, 3-point; next to fuse/relay panel	57
T 4	Wire connector, 4-point; next to fuse/relay panel	53, 55, 88
T 8	Wire connector, 8-point; on brake dual circuit warning light	62 - 64
T 14	Wire connector, 14-point; on instrument cluster	61, 72 - 78
V	Windscreen wiper motor	92, 93
V 5	Windscreen washer pump	98
(3)	Ground connector, on cowl reinforcement, left side	71, 92, 98
(10)	Ground connector, next to fuse/relay panel	63, 78, 86, 96
(15)	Ground connector, in engine compartment, front left	52, 90
(16)	Ground connector, in engine compartment, front right	53, 88
(17)	Ground connector, in luggage compartment next to fuel gauge sending unit	68

Numbers in triangles relate to diagnostic test socket T20

Wire colours

BK	Black
BL	Blue
BR	Brown
G	Green
GY	Grey
O	Orange
R	Red
V	Violet
W	White
Y	Yellow

Key to Fig. 14.237

Description	In current track
Alternator	2, 3
Alternator charging light	82
Auxiliary air regulator	11
Back-up light, left	67
Back-up light, right	68
Back-up light switch	66
Ballast resistor	17
Battery	4
Brake light, left	77
Brake light, right	76
Brake light switch (Dual system)	74, 75
Brake fluid level warning light	73
Cigar lighter	36
Cigar lighter light	37
Clock	20
Cold starting valve	9
Coolant temperature warning light	87
Coolant temperature indicator	86
Coolant temperature sender	90
Coolant thermotime switch	8, 9
Distributor	16 - 19
Door switch/buzzer, front left	23, 24
Door switch, front right	22
Electric fuel pump	13
Engine temperature sensor	7
Emergency flasher relay	93 - 95
Emergency flasher switch	97, 98
EGR warning light	88
Elapsed mileage switch (EGR)	89
Emergency flasher warning light	98
Fresh air fan	34
Fresh air switch	32 - 34
Fresh air fan speed control resistors	32
Fuel gauge sender	91
Fuel pump fuse (fuel pump relay)	
Fuel pump relay	12 - 14
Fuel indicator	34
Fuses S 1 - S 15, (fuse box) S 31 (fuel pump relay)	
Headlight dimmer/flasher switch	58, 59
Headlight high beam indicator light	79
Headlights	61 - 65
Heater lever light	38
Horn	68
Horn button	69
Ignition coil	17
Ignition/starter switch	23 - 26
Instrument lighting control switch	45
Instrument panel light	44, 45
Internal lighting	44, 45
Number plate lights	50, 51
Light switch	42 - 45
Light switch light	39
Load reduction relay (X contact)	40, 41
Oil pressure switch	78
Oil pressure warning light	81
Parking brake light switch	71, 72
Parking light, left	55
Parking light, right	52
Radiator fan	30
Radiator fan thermoswitch	31
Radio connector	35
Rear side marker lights	54 - 57
Rear window defogger switch	46, 47
Rear window defogger	49
Rear window defogger indicator light	46
Seat belt switch, left	26
Seat belt warning light	70
Seat belt warning relay	24, 28
Starter	5, 6
Spark plug connector	18, 19
Spark plugs	18 - 19
Tail light, left	56
Tail light, right	53
Turn signal, front left	102
Turn signal, front right	100
Turn signal, rear left	101
Turn signal, rear right	99
Turn signal indicator light	83
Turn signal switch	94 - 96
Voltage regulator	2 - 3
Voltage stabilizer	85
Warm air regulator	10
Windscreen wiper motor	104 - 106
Windscreen washer pump	111
Windscreen wiper relay	105 - 108
Windscreen wiper switch	107 - 110

Wire connectors

T – Cable distributor behind instrument panel
T 1 – Adjacent to ignition coil
T 1a – Front left engine compartment
T 1b – Behind instrument panel
T 1c – Behind instrument panel
T 1d – Left engine compartment
T 1e – Behind dashboard
T 1f – Rear left luggage compartment
T 1g – Adjacent to ignition distributor
T 1h – Adjacent to ignition distributor
T 1i – Behind dashboard
T 1j – Engine compartment right
T 1k – Engine compartment left
T 1l – Engine compartment right
T 1m – Engine compartment left
T 1n – Rear of dashboard
T 2a – Behind instrument panel
T 2b – Behind dashboard
T 2c – Behind dashboard (incl. radio connector)
T 2d – Rear left luggage compartment
T 2e – Right rear luggage compartment
T 2f – Left rear luggage compartment
T 3a – Adjacent to fuse/relay panel
T 3d – Behind dashboard
T 4 – Adjacent to fuse/relay panel
T 14 – On dashboard cluster

Ground Connectors

(1) – Battery/body/gearbox
(2) – Alternator/engine
(3) – Left engine compartment
(10) – Right of fuse/relay panel
(11) – Steering column
(15) – Engine compartment left reinforcement
(16) – Adjacent to parking switch
(17) – Rear luggage compartment to fuel sender

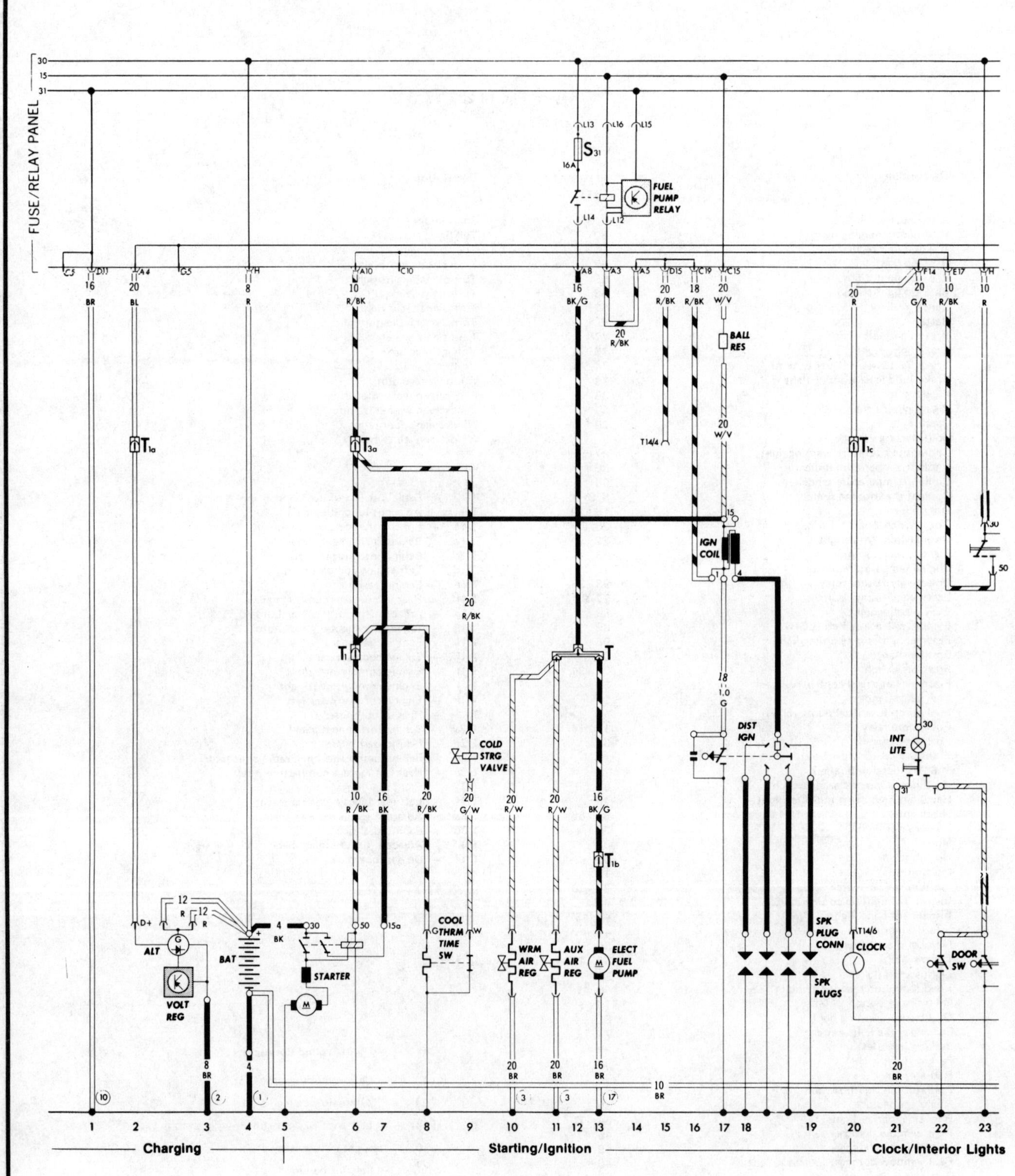

Fig. 14.237 Current flow diagram for 1980 on Dasher models. For key see page 313

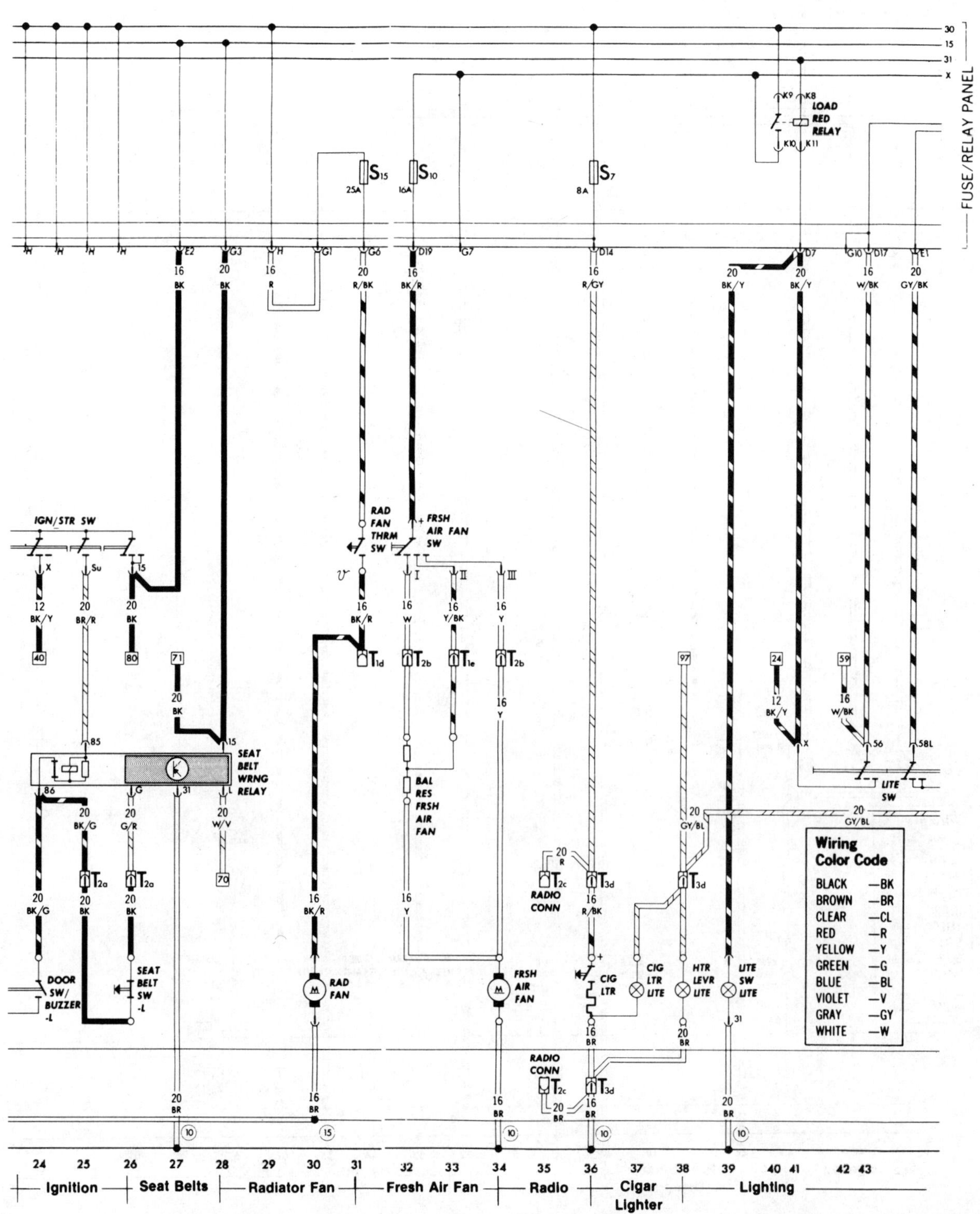

Fig. 14.237 (cont'd) Current flow diagram for 1980 on Dasher models. For key see page 313

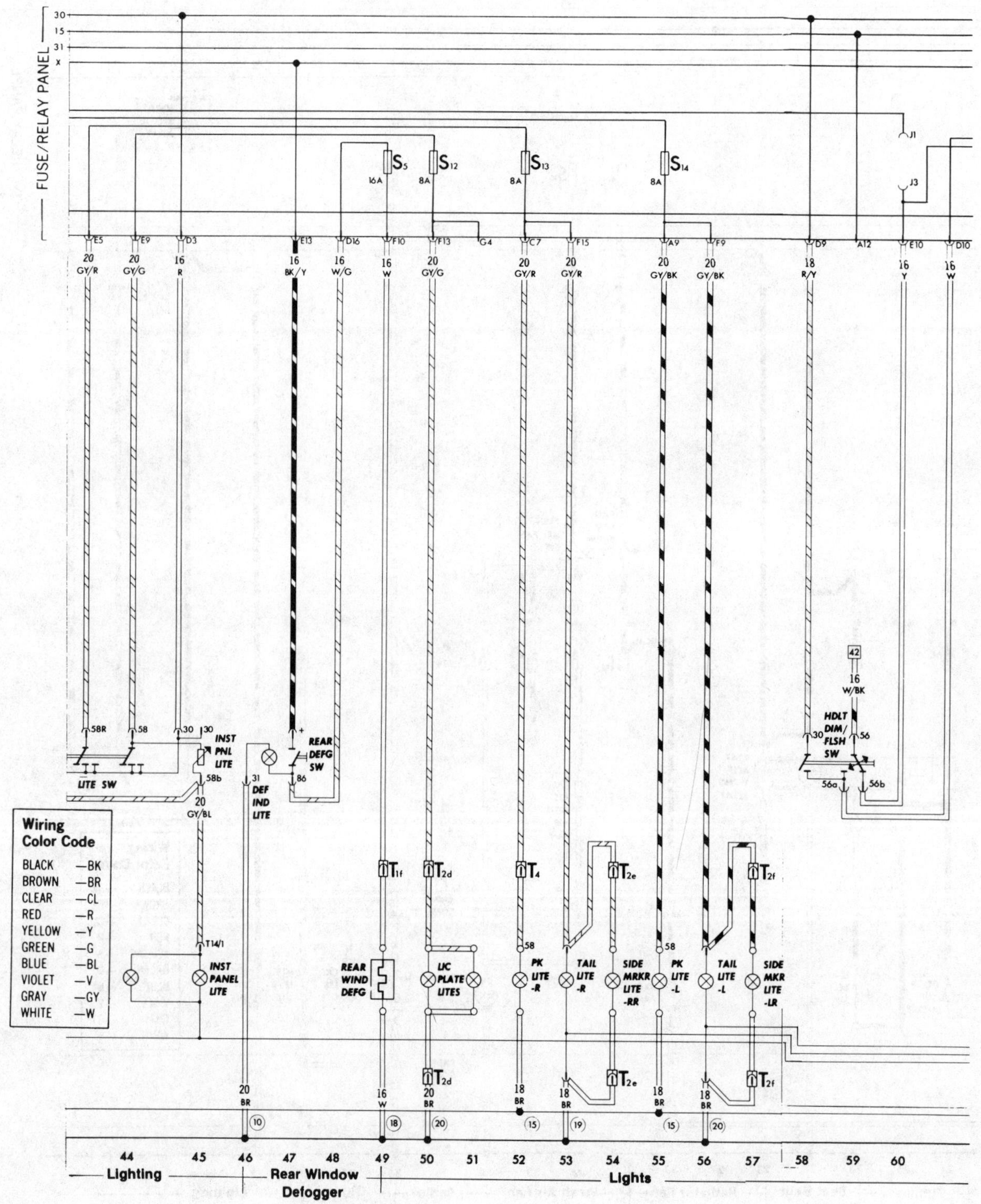

Fig. 14.237 (cont'd) Current flow diagram for 1980 on Dasher models. For key see page 313

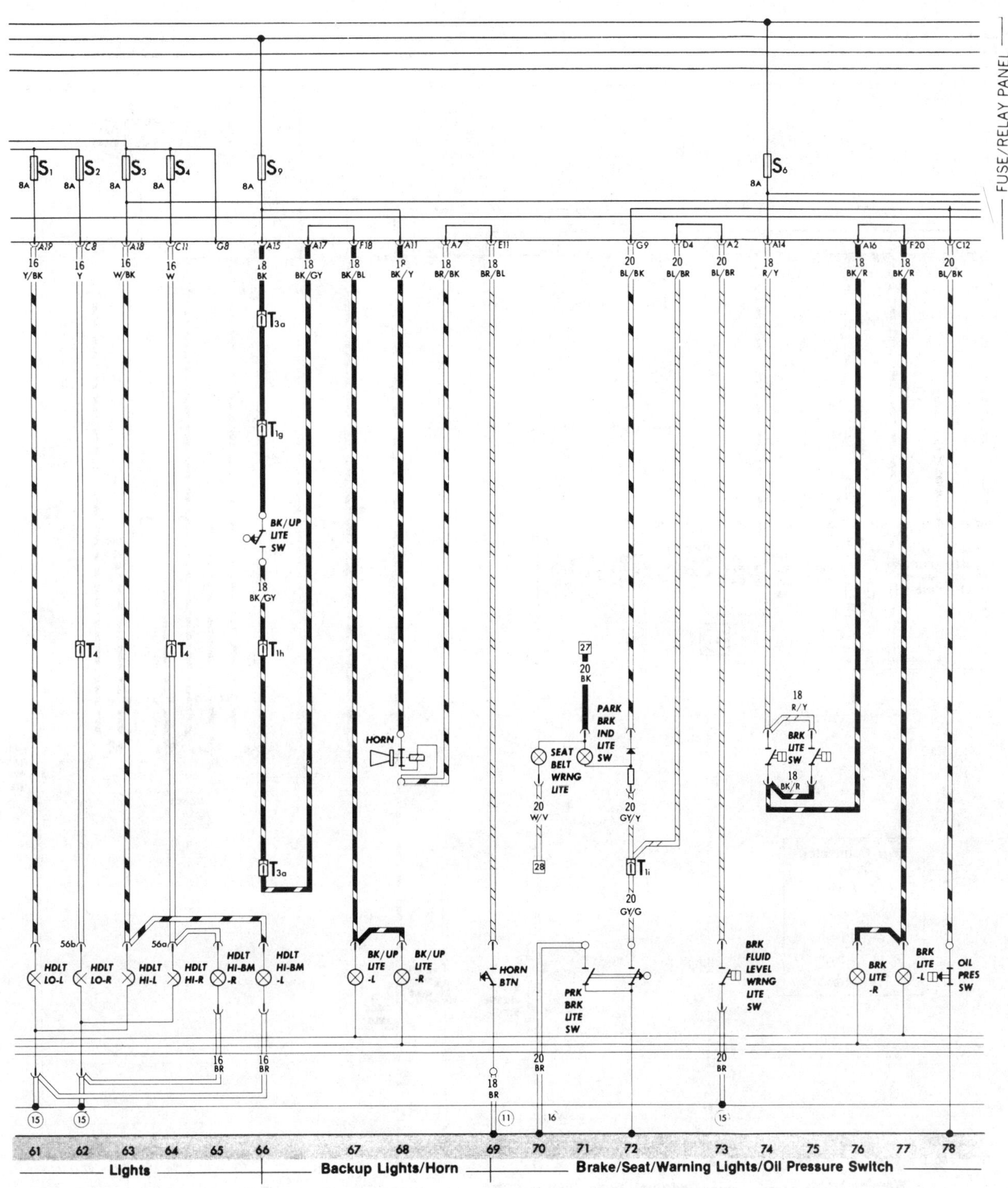

Fig. 14.237 (cont'd) Current flow diagram for 1980 on Dasher models. For key see page 313

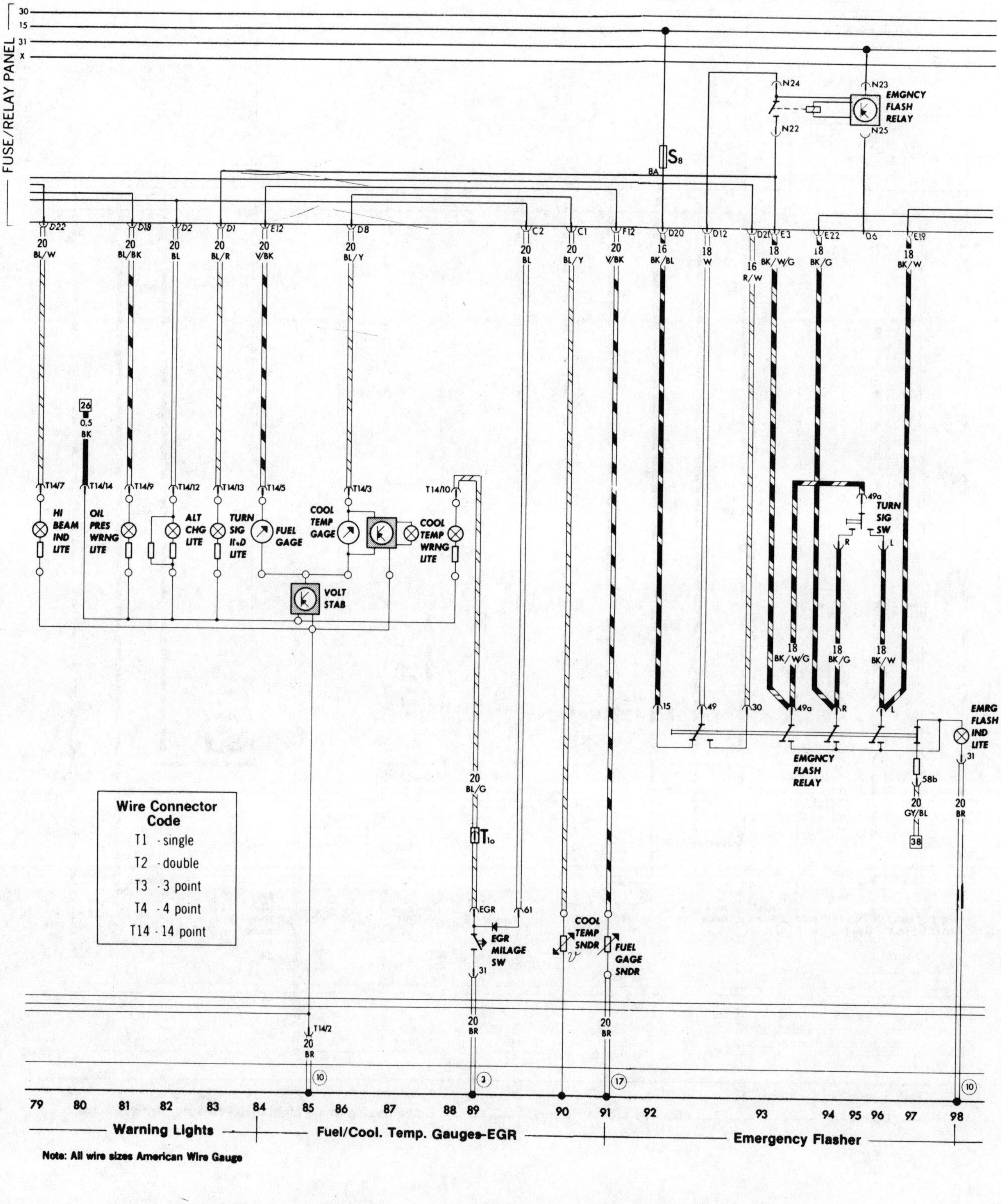

Wire Connector Code	
T1	- single
T2	- double
T3	- 3 point
T4	- 4 point
T14	- 14 point

Note: All wire sizes American Wire Gauge

Fig. 14.237 (cont'd) Current flow diagram for 1980 on Dasher models. For key see page 313

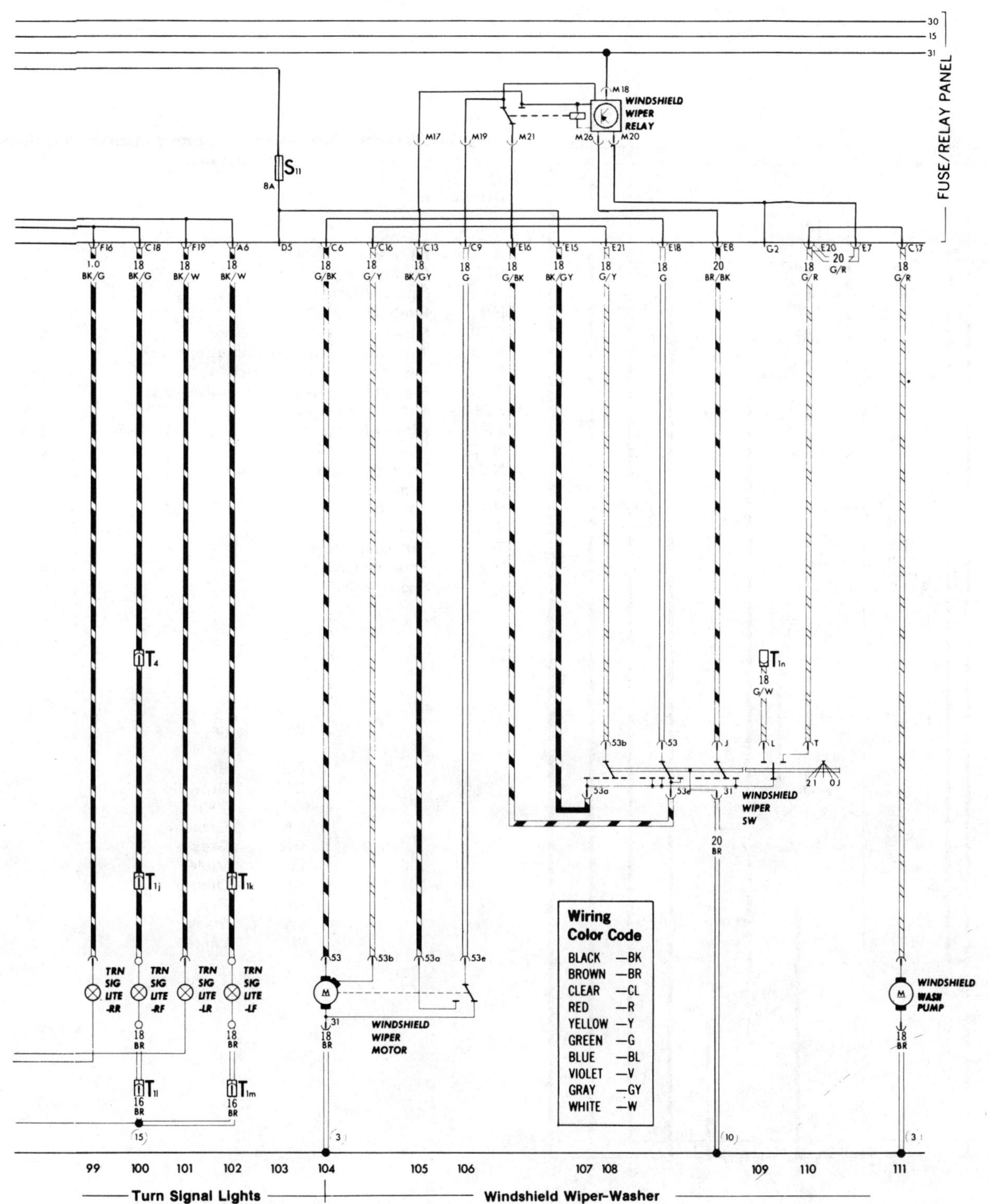

Fig. 14.237 (cont'd) Current flow diagram for 1980 on Dasher models. For key see page 313

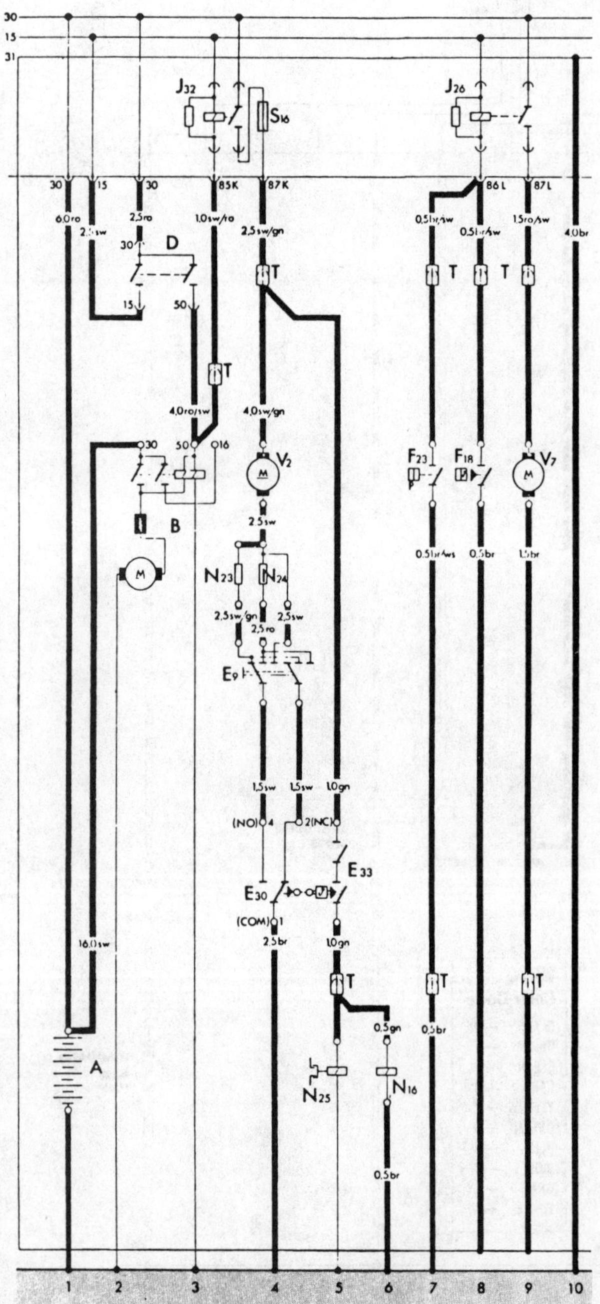

Fig. 14.238 Current flow diagram for factory fitted air conditioner, 1975 models

Description			In current track
A	—	Battery	1
B	—	Starter	2, 3
D	—	Ignition/starter switch	3
E 9	—	Fresh air fan switch	4
E 30	—	Microswitch	4
E 33	—	Thermostatic switch compressor clutch	5
F 18	—	Radiator fan thermoswitch	8
F 23	—	High pressure switch (on receiver-drier)	7
J 26	—	Radiator fan relay	7, 8
J 32	—	Air conditioner relay	3, 4
N 16	—	Idle control valve	6
N 23	—	Fresh air fan motor resistor	4
N 24	—	Fresh air fan motor resistor	4
N 25	—	Compressor clutch	5
S 16	—	Fuse 25 A	4
T	—	Wire connectors	
V 2	—	Fresh air fan	4
V 7	—	Radiator fan	9

Wire colours

BL	Blue
BR	Brown
GE	Yellow
GN	Green
GR	Grey
Li	Violet
OR	Orange
RO	Red
SW	Black
WS	White

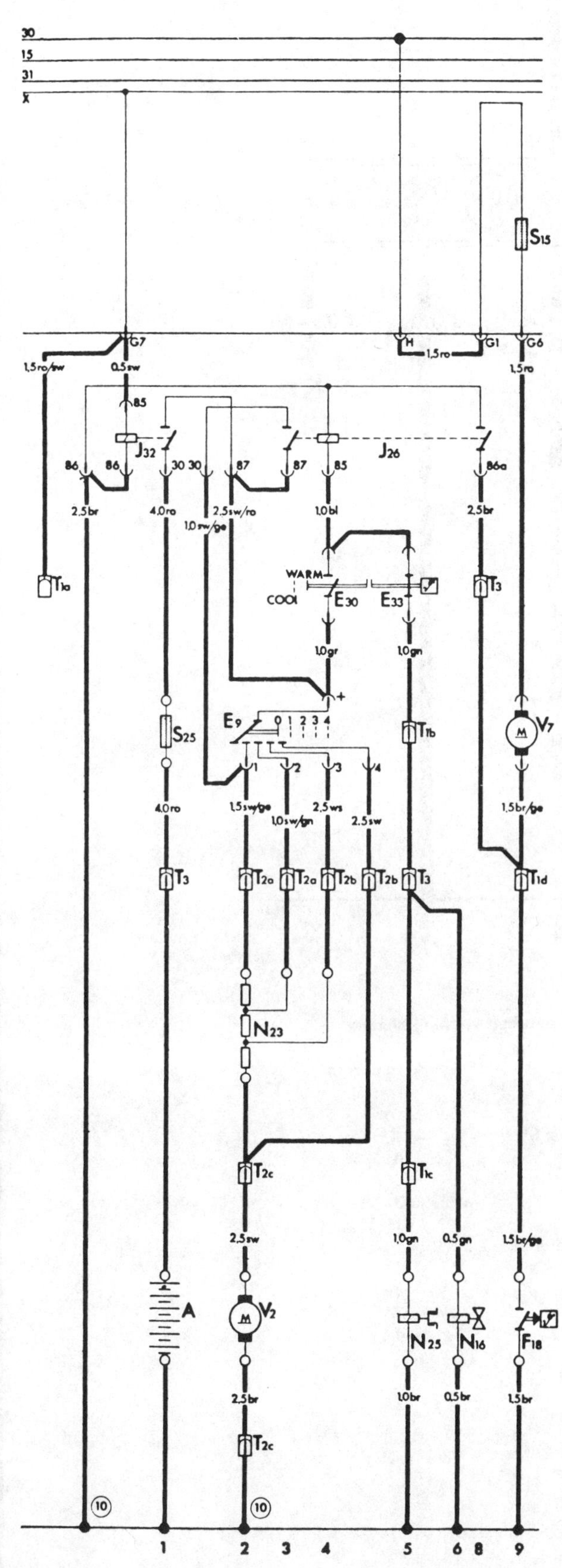

Fig. 14.239 Current flow diagram for factory fitted air conditioner. 1978/79 models

Description			In current track
A	–	Battery	1
E 9	–	Fresh air fan switch	2, 3
E 30	–	Microswitch	4
E 33	–	Temperature switch	5
F 18	–	Radiator cooling fan sending unit	9
J 26	–	Radiator fooling fan relay	1 - 8
J 32	–	Air conditioner relay	1, 2
N 16	–	Idle speed control valve	6
N 23	–	Fresh air fan resistor	2
N 25	–	Compressor clutch	5
S 15	–	Fuse in fuse panel (16 A)	9
S 25	–	Fuse, single (25 A)	1
T 1a	–	Wire connector, single; on fuse/relay panel	0
T 1b	–	Wire connector, single; behind dashboard	5
T 1c	–	Wire connector, single; next to compressor	5
T 1d	–	Wire connector, single	9
T 2a	–	Wire connector, double; behind dashboard	2, 3
T 2b	–	Wire connector, double; behind dashboard	4
T 2c	–	Wire connector, double; next to fresh air fan	2
T 3	–	Wire connector, 3-point; behind dashboard	1, 5, 8
V 2	–	Fresh air fan	2
V 7	–	Radiator cooling fan	9
10	–	Ground connector	0, 2

Wire colours

BL	Blue
BR	Brown
GE	Yellow
GN	Green
GR	Grey
LI	Violet
OR	Orange
RO	Red
SW	Black
WS	White

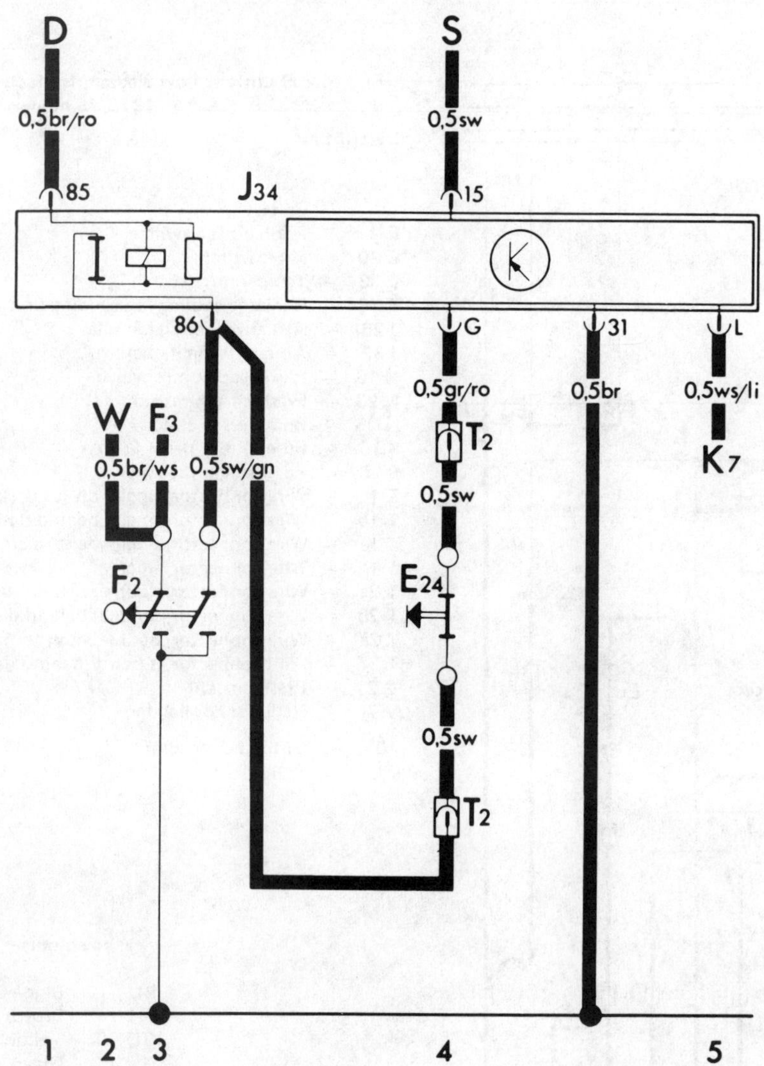

Fig. 14.240 Current flow diagram for seat belt warning system

Description			In current track
D	—	to ignition/starter switch, terminal SU	1
E 24	—	contact in seat belt lock, right	4
F 2	—	door contact switch, for buzzer, left	3
F 3	—	door contact switch, right	3
J 34	—	seat belt warning system relay	1 - 5
K 7	—	to seat belt warning system and dual brake circuit warning light, terminal L	5
T 2	—	wire connector, double; on frame	4
W	—	interior light	2
S	—	to fuse/relay panel terminal 15	4

Wire colours

BR	Brown
GN	Green
GR	Grey
LI	Violet
RO	Red
SW	Black
WS	White

Wiper blades - removal and refitting

23 The wiper blades are retained by plastic U-clips in the hooked ends of the wiper arms.
24 To remove a blade, pull it from the windscreen glass, swivel the blade, pinch the ends of the plastic clip together and then slide the blade and clip from the hooked end of the wiper arm (photo).
25 Refitting is a reversal of removal.

Courtesy lamp switch - removal and refitting

26 These switches are located in the door pillars and are of plunger type, retained by a screw (photo).
27 To remove a switch, extract the screw.
28 If the leads are being disconnected, take care that they do not slip back into the body cavity.
29 To reduce corrosion of the switch terminals, apply a little petroleum jelly to them.

Rear lamp cluster - Estate

30 Access to the bulbs on this type of vehicle is obtained by extracting the lens fixing screws and removing the lens.
31 All bulbs are of bayonet fixing type.
32 The rear number plate lamps are recessed into the bottom edge of the tailgate (photos).

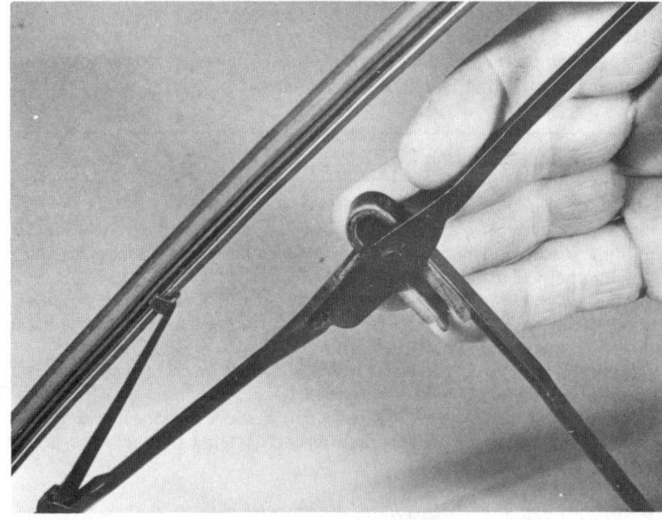
11.24 Wiper blade removal

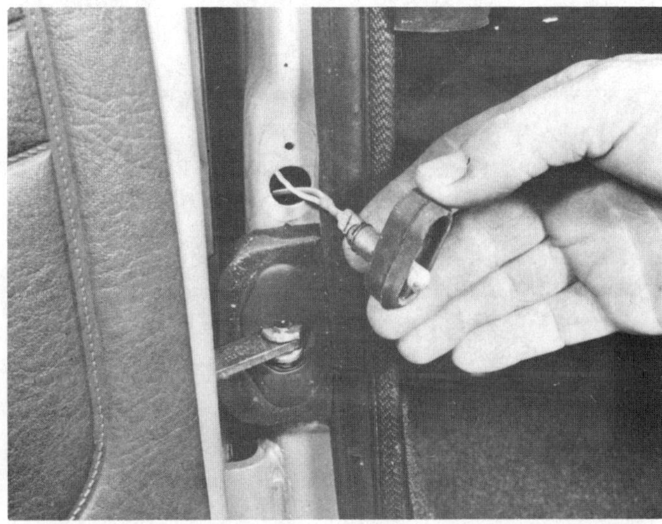
11.26 Courtesy lamp switch

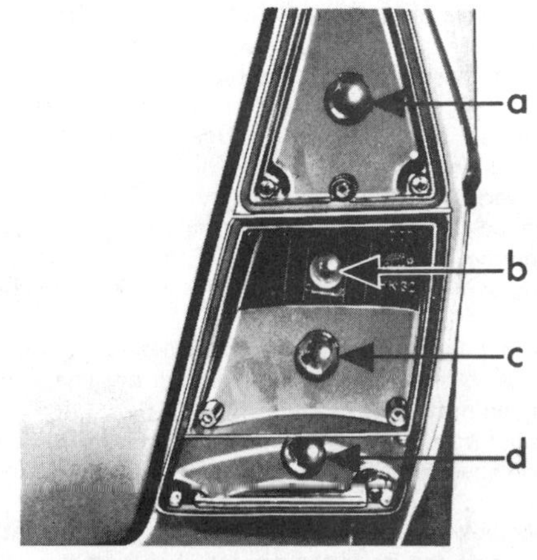

Fig. 14.241 Rear lamp (Estate)

a *Direction indicator* *c* *Stop-lamp*
b *Tail lamp* *d* *Reversing lamp*

11.32a Rear number plate lens screw

11.32b Rear number plate bulb and holder and lens

Direction indicator (flasher) relay

33 This unit is plugged into the fuse board.

34 It should be possible to remove or refit it by reaching up behind the glove compartment. If better access is required, remove the glove compartment after unscrewing the fixing screws.

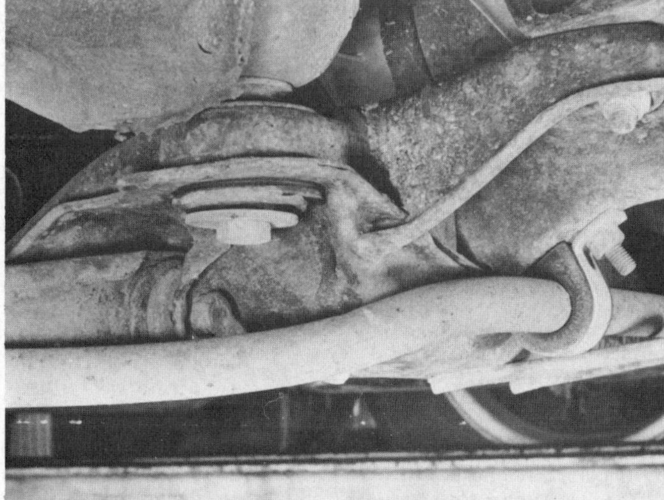

12.2 Front anti-roll bar correctly fitted

12 Steering and suspension

Front anti-roll bar - fitting precautions

1 It is possible to fit the front anti-roll bar the wrong way round. If the front suspension has been dismantled, take care to adhere to the following method of refitting.

2 Offer up the anti-roll bar and loosely fit the clips and flexible bushes. When viewed from the front, the curved end section of the bar should be deflected downwards (photo).

3 If the bar has been correctly fitted, then the bush clamps will be hard to locate around the flexible bushes.

4 Operate the vehicle on the road for a short distance and then tighten the clamp bolts to a torque wrench setting of 18 lbf ft (2.5 kgf m).

Steering angles and front wheel alignment

5 Accurate front wheel alignment is essential to provide good steering and road holding characteristics and to ensure slow and even tyre wear. Before considering the steering angles, check that the tyres are correctly inflated, that the front wheels are not buckled, the hub bearings are not worn or incorrectly adjusted and that the steering linkage is in good order, without slackness or wear at the joints.

6 Wheel alignment consists of four factors:

Camber is the angle at which the roadwheels are set from the vertical when viewed from the front or rear of the vehicle. Positive camber is the angle (in degrees) that the wheels are tilted outwards at the top from the vertical.

Castor is the angle between the steering axis and a vertical line when viewed from each side of the vehicle. Positive castor is indicated when the steering axis is inclined towards the rear of the vehicle at its upper end.

Steering axis inclination is the angle, when viewed from the front or rear of the vehicle, between the vertical and an imaginary line drawn between the top and bottom strut mountings.

Toe is the amount by which the distance between the front inside edges of the roadwheel rims differs from that between the rear inside edges.

If the distance between the front edges is less than that at the rear, the wheels are said to toe in. If the distance between the front inside edges is greater than that at the rear, the wheels toe out.

12.11a Tie-rod clamp and pinchbolt

7 Due to the need for precision gauges to measure the small angle of the steering and suspension settings, it is preferable that adjustment of camber be left to a service station having the necessary equipment. For information purposes, adjustment of the camber angle is carried out in the following way. Release the bolts which secure the balljoint to the suspension lower wishbone. Do not raise the vehicle off the ground. By inserting a tool in the hole in the wishbone, the balljoint/strut can be levered as necessary to obtain the specified camber angle.

Toe adjustment

8 To check and adjust the front wheel alignment, have the vehicle standing on its roadwheels on level ground, unladen with the steering in the straight-ahead position.

9 Obtain a tracking gauge. These are available in various forms from accessory stores, or one can be fabricated from a length of steel tubing suitably cranked to clear the sump and bellhousing and having a setscrew and locknut at one end.

10 With the gauge, measure the distance between the front wheel inner rims (at hub height) at the rear of the wheels. Push the vehicle forward to rotate the wheels through 180° (half a turn) and measure the distance between the wheel inner rims, again at hub height, at the front of the wheels. This last measurement should differ from the first by the appropriate toe-in/toe-out (see Specifications).

11 Where the toe-in/toe-out is found to be incorrect, release the pinch-bolt at the clamp on the left-hand tie-rod and the locknut at the outboard end of the rod (photos). Rotate the tie-rod to alter the toe. If a mark is made on the top of the tie-rod, then if the mark moves towards the front of the vehicle, the toe-in will be increased, if towards the rear, decreased. When the alignment is correct, set the tie-rod balljoint in the centre of its arc of travel so that it is not angled.

12.11b Tie-rod and ballpoint locknut. Grip flats on tie-rod when loosening or tightening

Tighten the clamp pinch-bolt and the tie-rod locknut to their respective specified torques.

Rear wheel alignment

12 Rear wheel alignment is not adjustable. If the angles are found to differ from those specified, suspect a distorted rear axle beam caused by collision damage.

Front suspension strut modifications

13 From February 1975, the replaceable cartridge type struts have been changed to a composite design. Renewal with the later type will mean a new or factory exchange unit.
14 From 1980, the strut coil springs have tapered ends with modified spring seats.

Steering gear modifications

15 With reference to Chapter 12, Section 17 (Rack and pinion unit - repair and adjustment), a kit may now be obtained to convert the old type to the later, adjustable type:

Part number with steering damper 321498061A
Part number without steering damper 321498061

An illustration of the conversion kit is given at Fig. 14.242. After conversion the shims between the cover and housing must not be reinstalled.
16 From August 1975 a modified steering wheel with a smaller hub is fitted. The four screws securing the combination switch are covered with an adhesive foil. Before removing the switch this must be pulled off to get at the screws. A new foil must be fitted, part No 321419681. When refitting make sure the cut outs in the foil are over the lower screws.

Alloy roadwheels

17 On vehicles with light alloy 5J x 13 wheels, on full left lock the wheel rim can touch the anti-roll bar. The right-hand tie-rod (non-adjustable) has therefore been shortened from 546 mm to 542 mm. If a replacement rod is required for the non-adjustable right-hand rod fit an adjustable rod set at 542 $\pm$ 1 mm. Vehicles with these wheels and automatic gearboxes have a cranked, non-adjustable tie-rod (part No 827419802C). If alloy wheels are installed the cranked tie-rod must be installed too. Consult the VW storeman if you are changing over to alloy wheels.

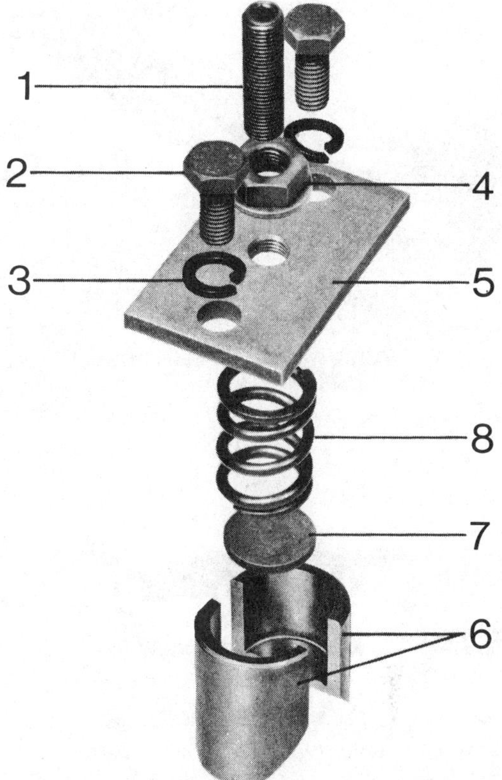

Fig. 14.242 Steering gear conversion kit

1	*Adjustment screw*	*5*	*Cover*
2	*Bolt*	*6*	*Thrust bush*
3	*Spring washer*	*7*	*Thrust washer*
4	*Locknut*	*8*	*Spring*

13 Bodywork and fittings

Bonnet lock

1 From 1978, only one bonnet lock is used instead of the two previously fitted (photo).

Door lock

2 From 1977, the door lock is mounted on the outside of the door instead of internally as was the case with earlier versions (photo).

Window regulators

3 A modified design of window regulator mechanism is fitted to 1976 and later models (photo).
4 If replacing an early type assembly with the later type, the glass lift channel must also be changed.
5 On rear doors, the regulator mounting holes must be elongated as shown in Fig. 14.245 to accept the new type regulator.

Facia panel - removal and refitting

6 Disconnect the battery earth lead.
7 Working under the centre of the facia panel, extract the four

13.1 Later type bonnet lock striker and safety catch

13.2 Using an Allen key to remove fixing screw from externally mounted door lock

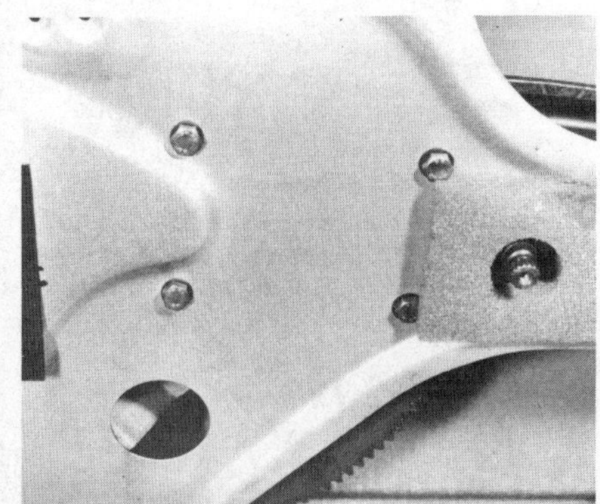

13.3 Window regulator mounting screws on front door

screws from the centre cover.
8 Disconnect the cigar lighter.
9 Open the glovebox lid and remove the fixing nuts.
10 Extract the screw from the right-hand under cover panel.
11 Remove the cover panel from under the opposite end of the facia.
12 Remove the parcels shelf from under the facia panel.
13 Extract the mounting screw from each end of the facia panel.
14 Remove the screw from under the front edge of the facia panel. Also remove the two fixing nuts.
15 Remove the flexible hoses which run to the two fresh air grilles on the facia panel.
16 Disconnect the speedometer cable (see Chapter 11, Section 16).
17 Disconnect all electrical plugs and wires from the rear of the instrument panel.

Fig. 14.243 Window regulator (1976 on)

Fig. 14.244 Glass lift channel

A Up to 1975 B 1976 on

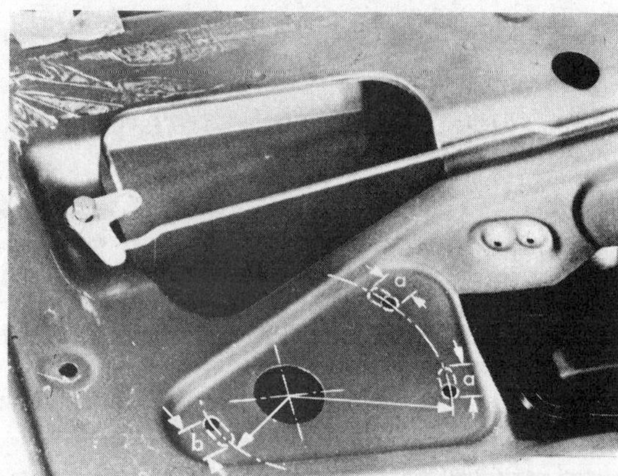

Fig. 14.245 Mounting hole modification diagram for new type window regulator (rear door)

a 15.0 mm (0.59 in) b 12.0 mm (0.47 in)

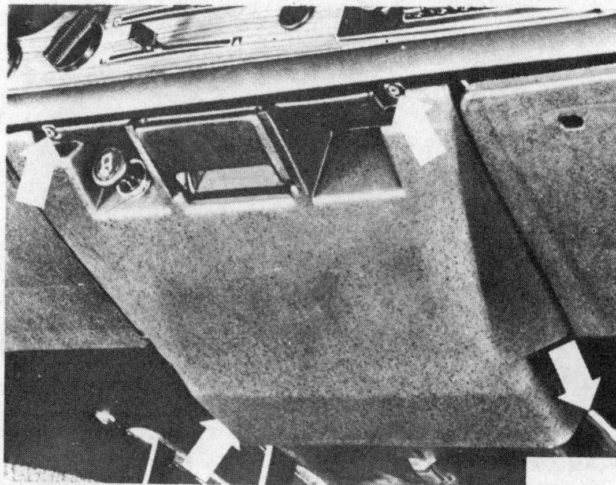

Fig. 14.246 Facia panel centre cover and screws (arrowed)

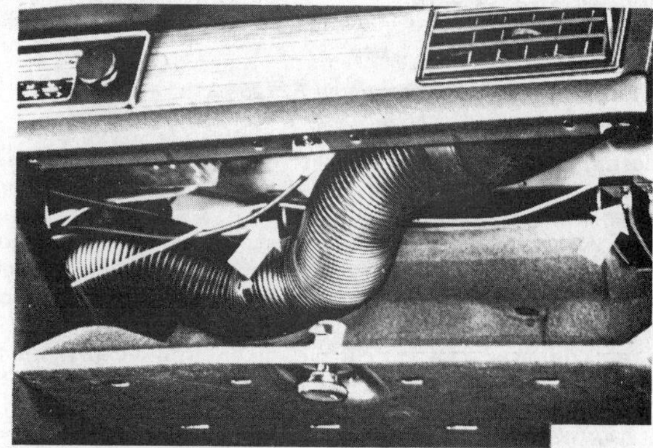

Fig. 14.247 Glovebox fixing nuts (arrowed)

Fig. 14.248 Right-hand under cover screw (arrowed)

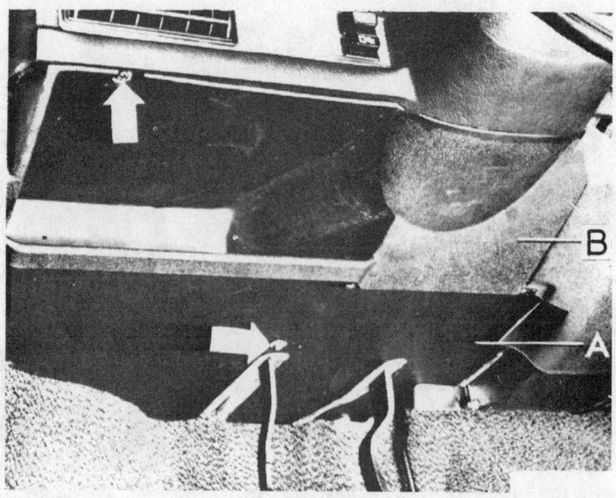

Fig. 14.249 Parcels shelf (A) and cover screws (B) (arrowed)

Fig. 14.250 Facia panel end screw (arrowed left)

Fig. 14.251 Facia panel end screw (right) and lower screw (arrowed)

Fig. 14.252 Water drain channel (arrowed) from sunroof

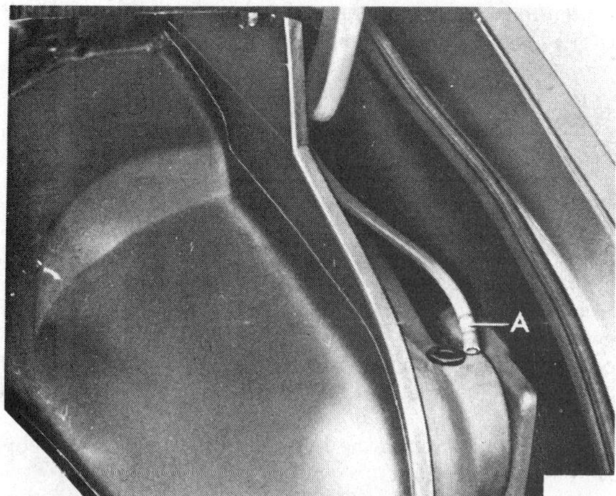

Fig. 14.253 Sunroof water drain pipe and valve (A)

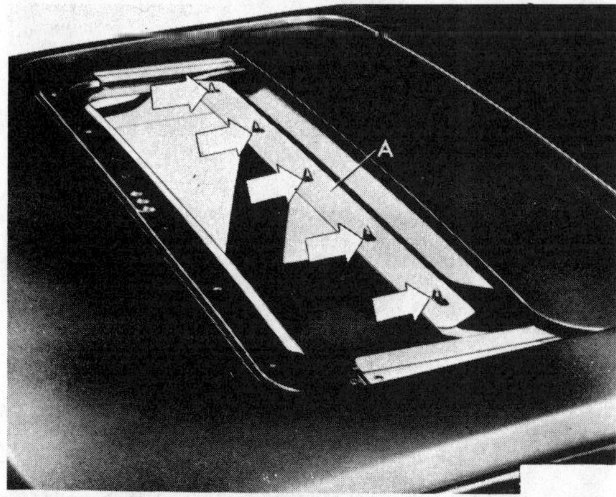

Fig. 14.254 Trim panel clips (arrowed) on sunroof (A)

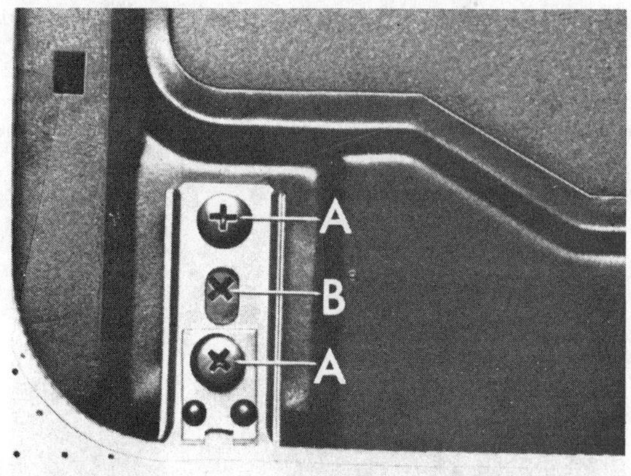

Fig. 14.255 Sunroof front height adjustment

A Fixing screws B Adjustment screw

18 Pull the facia panel forward and remove it.
19 Refitting is a reversal of removal.

Sunroof - maintenance and adjustment

20 On models equipped with a sunroof, periodically clean the drain channels by probing with a length of wire, cable or flexible curtain wire.
21 Working within the luggage area, pull the valve from the drain hose and then push the clearing wire up the drain hose.
22 Should the sunroof not operate smoothly or positively, check the following.

Front height adjustment

23 Remove the trim panel from the sunroof. Do this by opening the sunroof to the halfway position and detaching the trim panel clips.
24 Open the sunroof panel fully, slide the trim panel forwards until it stops and then bend it upwards and remove it.
25 Return the sunroof to the halfway position.
26 Slacken the screws (A) (Fig. 14.255) and then turn screw (B) until

the panel is flush with the roof surface. Tighten screws (A).

Rear height adjustment

27 Slacken the screw (B) (Fig. 14.256) and align the sunroof panel by moving the drivegear. Tighten the screw on completion.

Parallelism adjustment

28 Lower the sunroof panel by turning the lever through ½ a turn.

29 Remove the lever and loosen the drivegear by turning the screws (Fig. 14.257).

30 Pull the drivegear down off the cables.

31 Push the sunroof panel open and closed several times. Finally push it forward until the edge of the panel makes contact all along its edge.

32 Refit the drivegear and engage the cables. Tighten the screws and check that the sunroof operates without sticking.

Seat belts

33 Check the seat belts at regular intervals for fraying or cuts and renew if necessary.

34 Use only water and detergent for cleaning.

35 Never attempt to alter the original anchorage points, and note carefully the sequence of fitting of bolts, washers and spacers (photos).

36 On North American versions, a seat belt warning system is fitted which is interconnected with the ignition switch. The action of turning on the ignition without having first fastened the driver's safety belt will cause an audio-visual warning to operate for a short period.

Rear seat (Estate) - removal and refitting

37 To remove the seat cushion, fold it forward and unbolt the hinges (photo).

38 To remove the seat back, release the catches, fold the back down and remove the pivot bolt from each side (photo).

38 Refitting is a reversal of removal.

Door trim panel (Estate) - removal and refitting

40 Some minor modifications have been made to the door interior components.

41 To remove the trim panel, peel the flexible cover from the window regulator handle, extract the fixing screw and remove the handle (photo).

42 Remove the screw from the lock remote control escutcheon plate. Remove the plate (photos).

43 Remove the armrest screws and take off the armrest (photo).

44 Pull the trim panel from the door by jerking the fixing clips from their holes (photo).

Doors - removal and refitting

45 The door hinges are welded to the bodywork but are bolted to the door. Access to these bolts is obtained after removal of the trim panel as described in Chapter 13 (photo).

46 Always mark the position of the hinges in relation to the door before unscrewing the bolts. Support the bottom edge of the door on a jack or block with a pad of cloth to prevent damage to the paintwork.

Fig. 14.256 Sunroof rear height adjustment screw (B)

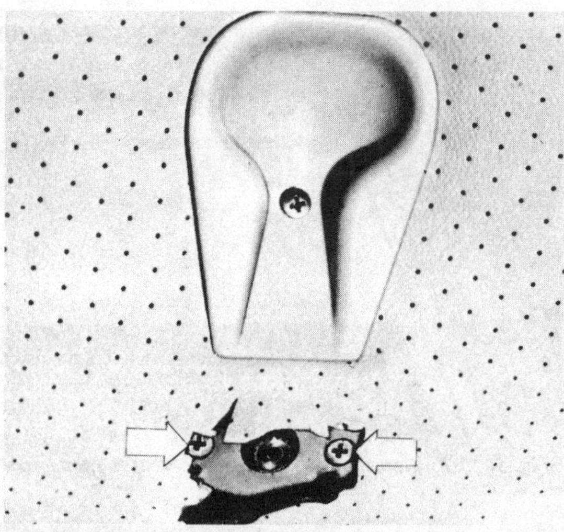

Fig. 14.257 Sunroof drivegear fixing screws (arrowed)

47 Refitting is a reversal of removal, but check the door alignment before finally tightening the hinge bolts.

Tailgate lock (Estate)

48 The tailgate lock is held by three screws. After removal of the screws, the lock button and cylinder are accessible for removal (photo).

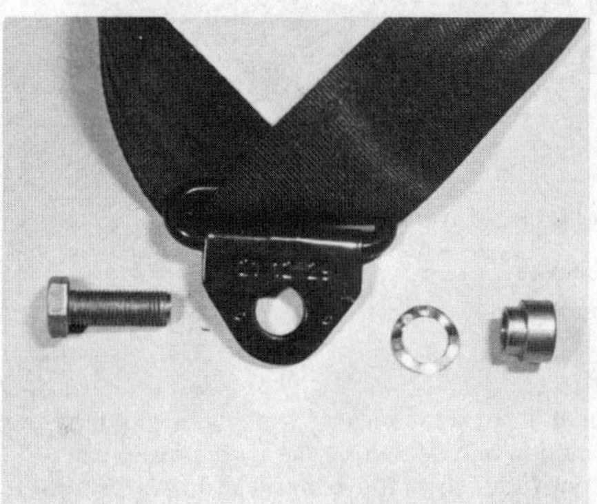

13.35a Seat belt anchor plate components

13.35b Tighten seat belt anchor bolt. Note position of wave washer

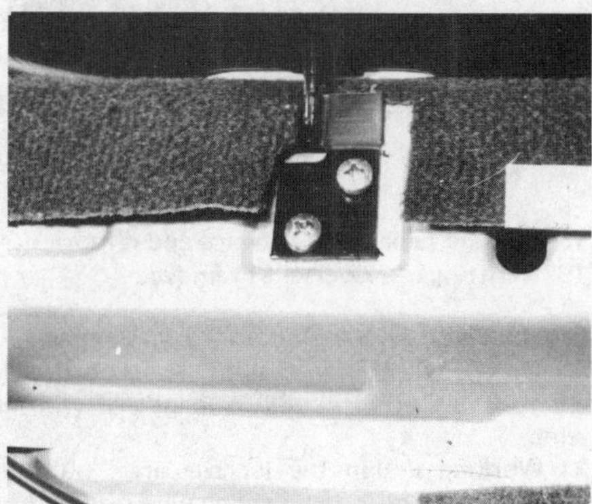

13.37 Seat cushion hinge (Estate)

13.38 Seat back pivot bolt (Estate)

13.41 Extracting window regulator handle screw

13.42a Extracting screw from lock remote control escutcheon plate

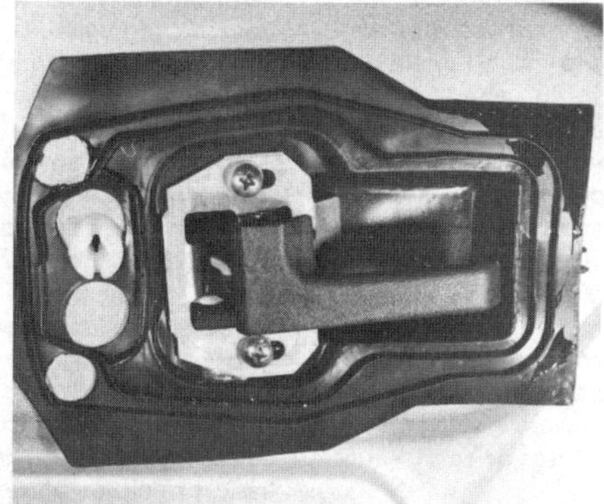
13.42b Door remote control handle

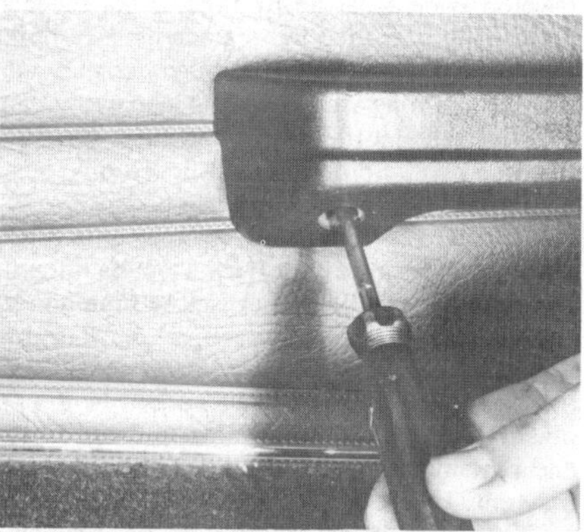
13.43 Extracting door armrest screw

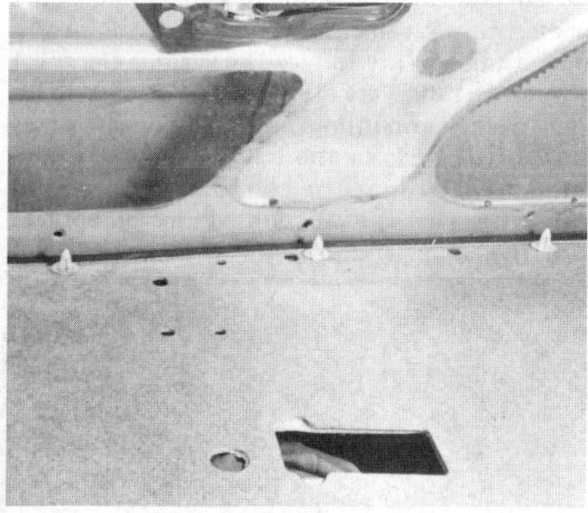
13.44 Door trim panel clips

13.45 Unscrewing door hinge bolts

13.48 Tailgate lock

Fault diagnosis

Introduction

The vehicle owner who does his or her own maintenance according to the recommended schedules should not have to use this section of the manual very often. Modern component reliability is such that, provided those items subject to wear or deterioration are inspected or renewed at the specified intervals, sudden failure is comparatively rare. Faults do not usually just happen as a result of sudden failure, but develop over a period of time. Major mechanical failures in particular are usually preceded by characteristic symptoms over hundreds or even thousands of miles. Those components which do occasionally fail without warning are often small and easily carried in the vehicle.

With any fault finding, the first step is to decide where to begin investigations. Sometimes this is obvious, but on other occasions a little detective work will be necessary. The owner who makes half a dozen haphazard adjustments or replacements may be successful in curing a fault (or its symptoms), but he will be none the wiser if the fault recurs and he may well have spent more time and money than was necessary. A calm and logical approach will be found to be more satisfactory in the long run. Always take into account any warning signs or abnormalities that may have been noticed in the period preceding the fault - power loss, high or low gauge readings, unusual noises or smells, etc - and remember that failure of components such as fuses or spark plugs may only be pointers to some underlying fault.

The pages which follow here are intended to help in cases of failure to start or breakdown on the road. There is also a Fault Diagnosis Section at the end of each Chapter which should be consulted if the preliminary checks prove unfruitful. Whatever the fault, certain basic principles apply. These are as follows:

Verify the fault. This is simply a matter of being sure that you know what the symptoms are before starting work. This is particularly important if you are investigating a fault for someone else who may not have described it very accurately.

Don't overlook the obvious. For example, if the vehicle won't start, is there petrol in the tank? (Don't take anyone else's word on this particular point, and don't trust the fuel gauge either!) If an electrical fault is indicated, look for loose or broken wires before digging out the test gear.

Cure the disease, not the symptom. Substituting a flat battery with a fully charged one will get you off the hard shoulder, but if the underlying cause is not attended to, the new battery will go the same way. Similarly, changing oil-fouled spark plugs for a new set will get you moving again, but remember that the reason for the fouling (if it wasn't simply an incorrect grade of plug) will have to be established and corrected.

Don't take anything for granted. Particularly, don't forget that a 'new' component may itself be defective (especially if it's been rattling round in the boot for months), and don't leave components out of a fault diagnosis sequence just because they are new or recently fitted. When you do finally diagnose a difficult fault, you'll probably realise that all the evidence was there from the start.

Electrical faults

Electrical faults can be more puzzling than straightforward mechanical failures, but they are no less susceptible to logical analysis if the basic principles of operation are understood. Vehicle electrical wiring exists in extremely unfavourable conditions - heat, vibration and chemical attack - and the first things to look for are loose or corroded connections and broken or chafed wires, especially where the wires pass through holes in the bodywork or are subject to vibration.

All metal-bodied vehicles in current production have one pole of the battery 'earthed', ie connected to the vehicle bodywork, and in nearly all modern vehicles it is the negative (–) terminal. The various electrical components - motors, bulb holders etc - are also connected to earth by means of a lead or directly by their mountings. Electric current flows through the component and then back to the battery via the bodywork. If the component mounting is loose or corroded, or if a good path back to the battery is not available, the circuit will be incomplete and malfunction will result. The engine and/or gearbox are also earthed

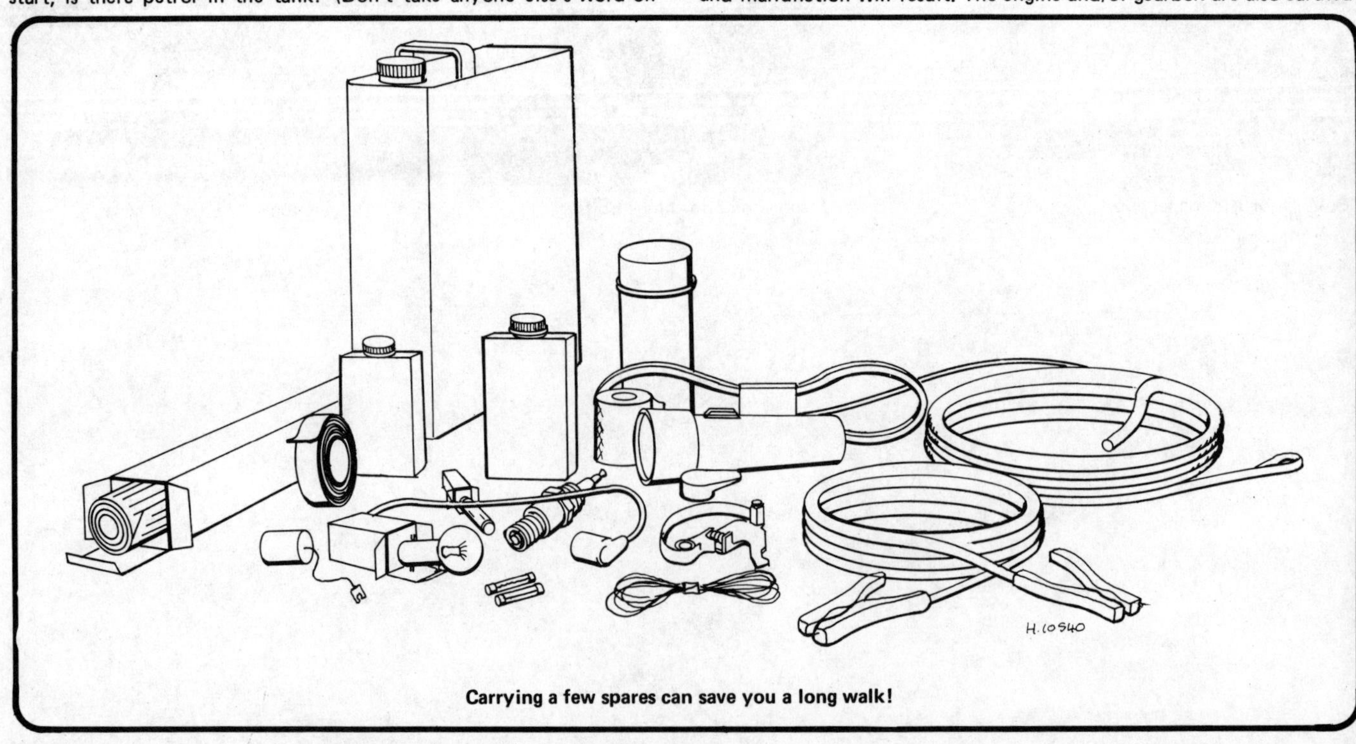

Carrying a few spares can save you a long walk!

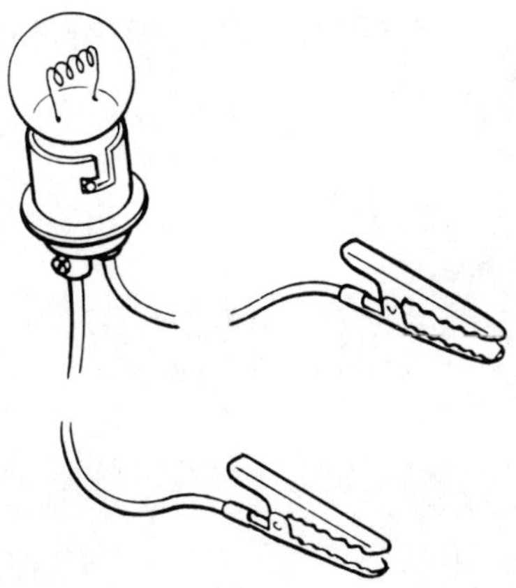

A simple test lamp is useful for tracing electrical faults

by means of flexible metal straps to the body or subframe; if these straps are loose or missing, starter motor, generator and ignition trouble may result.

Assuming the earth return to be satisfactory, electrical faults will be due either to component malfunction or to defects in the current supply. Individual components are dealt with in Chapters 10 and 11. If supply wires are broken or cracked internally this results in an open-circuit, and the easiest way to check for this is to bypass the suspect wire temporarily with a length of wire having a crocodile clip or suitable connector at each end. Alternatively, a 12V test lamp can be used to verify the presence of supply voltage at various points along the wire and the break can be thus isolated.

If a bare portion of a live wire touches the bodywork or other earthed metal part, the electricity will take the low-resistance path thus formed back to the battery: this is known as a short-circuit. Hopefully a short-circuit will blow a fuse, but otherwise it may cause burning of the insulation (and possibly further short-circuits) or even a fire. This is why it is inadvisable to bypass persistently blowing fuses with silver foil or wire.

Spares and tool kit

Most vehicles are supplied only with sufficient tools for wheel changing; the *Maintenance and minor repair* tool kit detailed in *Tools and working facilities*, with the addition of a hammer, is probably sufficient for those repairs that most motorists would consider attempting at the roadside. In addition a few items which can be fitted without too much trouble in the event of a breakdown should be carried. Experience and available space will modify the list below, but the following may save having to call on professional assistance:

Spark plugs, clean and correctly gapped
HT lead and plug cap - long enough to reach the plug furthest from the distributor
Distributor rotor, condenser and contact breaker points (as applicable)
Drivebelt(s) - emergency type may suffice
Spare fuses
Set of principal light bulbs
Tin of radiator sealer and hose bandage
Exhaust bandage
Roll of insulating tape
Length of soft iron wire
Length of electrical flex
Torch or inspection lamp (can double as test lamp)
Battery jump leads
Tow-rope
Ignition waterproofing aerosol
Litre of engine oil
Sealed can of hydraulic fluid
Emergency windscreen
'Jubilee' clips
Tube of filler paste

If spare fuel is carried, a can designed for the purpose should be used to minimise risks of leakage and collision damage. A first aid kit and a warning triangle, whilst not at present compulsory in the UK, are obviously sensible items to carry in addition to the above.

When touring abroad it may be advisable to carry additional spares which, even if you cannot fit them yourself, could save having to wait while parts are obtained. The items below may be worth considering:

Clutch and throttle cables
Cylinder head gasket
Alternator brushes
Tyre valve core

One of the motoring organisations will be able to advise on availability of fuel etc in foreign countries.

Engine will not start

Engine fails to turn when starter operated

Flat battery (recharge, use jump leads, or push start)
Battery terminals loose or corroded
Battery earth to body defective
Engine earth strap loose or broken
Starter motor (or solenoid) wiring loose or broken
Automatic transmission selector in wrong position, or inhibitor switch faulty
Ignition/starter switch faulty
Major mechanical failure (seizure)
Starter or solenoid internal fault (see Chapter 10)

Starter motor turns engine slowly

Partially discharged battery (recharge, use jump leads, or push start)
Battery terminals loose or corroded
Battery earth to body defective
Engine earth strap loose
Starter motor (or solenoid) wiring loose
Starter motor internal fault (see Chapter 10)

Starter motor spins without turning engine

Flat battery
Starter motor pinion sticking on sleeve
Flywheel gear teeth damaged or worn
Starter motor mounting bolts loose

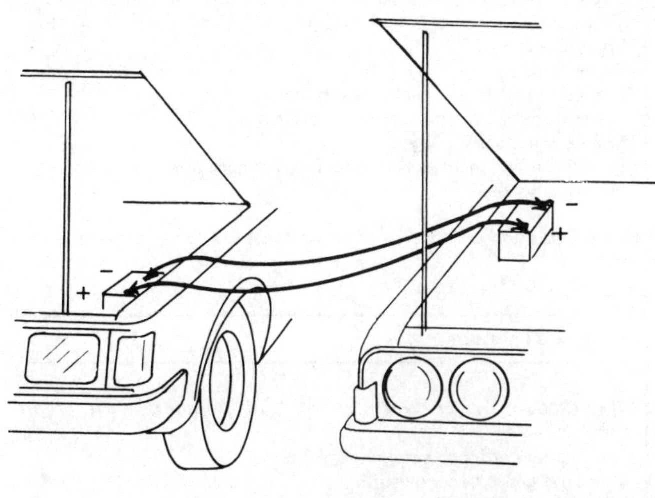

Correct way to connect jump leads. Do not allow car bodies to touch!

Engine turns normally but fails to start

Damp or dirty HT leads and distributor cap (crank engine and check for spark) (photo)
Dirty or incorrectly gapped distributor points (if applicable)
No fuel in tank (check for delivery) (photos)
Excessive choke (hot engine) or insufficient choke (cold engine)
Fouled or incorrectly gapped spark plugs (remove, clean and regap)
Other ignition system fault (see Chapter 4)
Other fuel system fault (see Chapter 3)
Poor compression (see Chapter 1)
Major mechanical failure (eg camshaft drive)

Engine fires but will not run

Insufficient choke (cold engine)
Air leaks at carburettor or inlet manifold
Fuel starvation (see Chapter 3)
Ballast resistor defective, or other ignition fault (see Chapter 4)

Engine cuts out and will not restart

Engine cuts out suddenly - ignition fault

Loose or disconnected LT wires
Wet HT leads or distributor cap (after traversing water splash)
Coil or condenser failure (check for spark)
Other ignition fault (see Chapter 4)

Engine misfires before cutting out - fuel fault

Fuel tank empty
Fuel pump defective or filter blocked (check for delivery)
Fuel tank filler vent blocked (suction will be evident on releasing cap)
Carburettor needle valve sticking
Carburettor jets blocked (fuel contaminated)
Other fuel system fault (see Chapter 3)

Engine cuts out - other causes

Serious overheating
Major mechanical failure (eg camshaft drive)

Engine overheats

Ignition (no-charge) warning light illuminated

Slack or broken drivebelt - retension or renew (Chapter 10)

Ignition warning light not illuminated

Coolant loss due to internal or external leakage (see Chapter 2)
Thermostat defective
Low oil level
Brakes binding
Radiator clogged externally or internally
Electric cooling fan not operating correctly
Engine waterways clogged
Ignition timing incorrect or automatic advance malfunctioning
Mixture too weak

Note: *Do not add cold water to an overheated engine or damage may result*

Low engine oil pressure

Gauge reads low or warning light illuminated with engine running

Oil level low or incorrect grade
Defective gauge or sender unit
Wire to sender unit earthed
Engine overheating
Oil filter clogged or bypass valve defective
Oil pressure relief valve defective
Oil pick-up strainer clogged

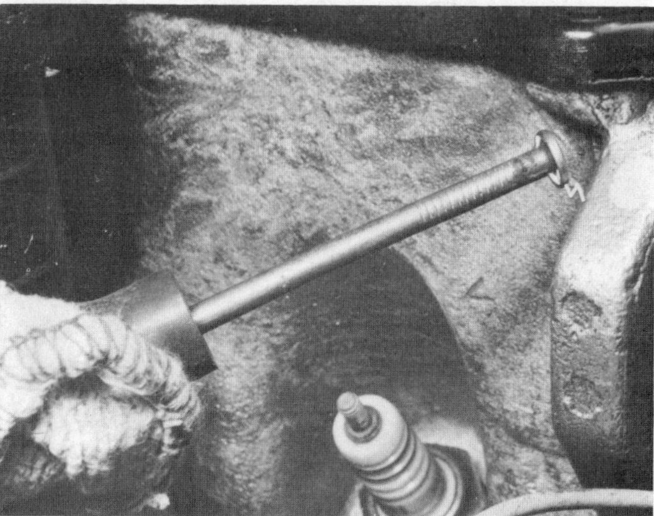

Crank engine and check for a spark. Use insulated pliers – dry cloth or a rubber glove will suffice. Do not carry out this check with electronic ignition

Remove fuel pipe from carburettor and check that fuel is being delivered (crank engine on starter). Disable ignition and take precautions against fire

Slacken fuel distributor (CIS) supply on return unions and check for fuel delivery (ignition switched on). Take precautions against fire

Oil pump worn or mountings loose
Worn main or big-end bearings

Note: *Low oil pressure in a high-mileage engine at tickover is not necessarily a cause for concern. Sudden pressure loss at speed is far more significant. In any event, check the gauge or warning light sender before condemning the engine.*

Engine noises

Pre-ignition (pinking) on acceleration

Incorrect grade of fuel
Ignition timing incorrect
Distributor faulty or worn
Worn or maladjusted carburettor
Excessive carbon build-up in engine

Whistling or wheezing noises

Leaking vacuum hose
Leaking carburettor or manifold gasket
Blowing head gasket

Tapping or rattling

Incorrect valve clearances
Worn valve gear
Worn timing belt
Broken piston ring (ticking noise)

Knocking or thumping

Unintentional mechanical contact
Worn fanbelt
Peripheral component fault (generator, water pump etc)
Worn big-end bearings (regular heavy knocking, perhaps less under load)
Worn main bearings (rumbling and knocking, perhaps worsening under load)
Piston slap (most noticeable when cold)

Tools and working facilities

Introduction

A selection of good tools is a fundamental requirement for anyone contemplating the maintenance and repair of a motor vehicle. For the owner who does not possess any, their purchase will prove a considerable expense, offsetting some of the savings made by doing-it-yourself. However, provided that the tools purchased meet the relevant national safety standards and are of good quality, they will last for many years and prove an extremely worthwhile investment.

To help the average owner to decide which tools are needed to carry out the various tasks detailed in this manual, we have compiled three lists of tools under the following headings: *Maintenance and minor repair, Repair and overhaul,* and *Special.* The newcomer to practical mechanics should start off with the *Maintenance and minor repair* tool kit and confine himself to the simple jobs around the vehicle. Then, as his confidence and experience grow, he can undertake more difficult tasks, buying extra tools as, and when, they are needed. In this way, a *Maintenance and minor repair* tool kit can be built-up into a *Repair and overhaul* tool kit over a considerable period of time without any major cash outlays. The experienced do-it-yourselfer will have a tool kit good enough for most repair and overhaul procedures and will add tools from the *Special* category when he feels the expense is justified by the amount of use to which these tools will be put.

It is obviously not possible to cover the subject of tools fully here. For those who wish to learn more about tools and their use there is a book entitled *How to Choose and Use Car Tools* available from the publishers of this manual.

Maintenance and minor repair tool kit

The tools given in this list should be considered as a minimum requirement if routine maintenance, servicing and minor repair operations are to be undertaken. We recommend the purchase of combination spanners (ring one end, open-sided the other); although more expensive than open-ended ones, they do give the advantages of both types of spanner.

Combination spanners - 10, 11, 12, 13, 14 & 17 mm
Adjustable spanner - 9 inch
Engine sump/gearbox drain plug key
Spark plug spanner (with rubber insert)
Spark plug gap adjustment tool
Set of feeler gauges
Brake adjuster spanner (if applicable)
Brake bleed nipple spanner
Screwdriver - 4 in long x ¼ in dia (flat blade)
Screwdriver - 4 in long x ¼ in dia (cross blade)
Combination pliers - 6 inch
Hacksaw (junior)
Tyre pump
Tyre pressure gauge
Oil can
Fine emery cloth (1 sheet)
Wire brush (small)
Funnel (medium size)

Repair and overhaul tool kit

These tools are virtually essential for anyone undertaking any major repairs to a motor vehicle, and are additional to those given in the *Maintenance and minor repair* list. Included in this list is a comprehensive set of sockets. Although these are expensive they will be found invaluable as they are so versatile - particularly if various drives are included in the set. We recommend the ½ in square-drive type, as this can be used with most proprietary torque wrenches. If you cannot afford a socket set, even bought piecemeal, then inexpensive tubular box spanners are a useful alternative

The tools in this list will occasionally need to be supplemented by tools from the *Special* list.

Sockets (or box spanners) to cover range in previous list
Reversible ratchet drive (for use with sockets)
Extension piece, 10 inch (for use with sockets)
Universal joint (for use with sockets)
Torque wrench (for use with sockets)
'Mole' wrench - 8 inch
Ball pein hammer
Soft-faced hammer, plastic or rubber
Screwdriver - 6 in long x 5/16 in dia (flat blade)
Screwdriver - 2 in long x 5/16 in square (flat blade)
Screwdriver - 1½ in long x ¼ in dia (cross blade)
Screwdriver - 3 in long x 1/8 in dia (electricians)
Pliers - electricians side cutters
Pliers - needle nosed
Pliers - circlip (internal and external)
Cold chisel - ½ inch
Scriber
Scraper
Centre punch
Pin punch
Hacksaw
Valve grinding tool
Steel rule/straight-edge
Allen keys and/or splined bolt keys
Selection of files
Wire brush (large)
Axle-stands
Jack (strong scissor or hydraulic type)

Special tools

The tools in this list are those which are not used regularly, are expensive to buy, or which need to be used in accordance with their manufacturers' instructions. Unless relatively difficult mechanical jobs are undertaken frequently, it will not be economic to buy many of these tools. Where this is the case, you could consider clubbing together with friends (or joining a motorists' club) to make a joint purchase, or borrowing the tools against a deposit from a local garage or tool hire specialist.

The following list contains only those tools and instruments freely available to the public, and not those special tools produced by the vehicle manufacturer specifically for its dealer network. You will find occasional references to these manufacturers' special tools in the text of this manual. Generally, an alternative method of doing the job without the vehicle manufacturers' special tool is given. However, sometimes, there is no alternative to using them. Where this is the case and the relevant tool cannot be bought or borrowed, you will have to entrust the work to a franchised garage.

Valve spring compressor
Piston ring compressor
Balljoint separator
Universal hub/bearing puller
Impact screwdriver
Micrometer and/or vernier gauge
Dial gauge

Stroboscopic timing light
Dwell angle meter/tachometer
Universal electrical multi-meter
Cylinder compression gauge
Lifting tackle (photo)
Trolley jack
Light with extension lead

Buying tools

For practically all tools, a tool factor is the best source since he will have a very comprehensive range compared with the average garage or accessory shop. Having said that, accessory shops often offer excellent quality tools at discount prices, so it pays to shop around.

There are plenty of good tools around at reasonable prices, but always aim to purchase items which meet the relevant national safety standards. If in doubt, ask the proprietor or manager of the shop for advice before making a purchase.

Care and maintenance of tools

Having purchased a reasonable tool kit, it is necessary to keep the tools in a clean, serviceable condition. After use, always wipe off any dirt, grease and metal particles using a clean, dry cloth, before putting the tools away. Never leave them lying around after they have been used. A simple tool rack on the garage or workshop wall, for items such as screwdrivers and pliers is a good idea. Store all normal wrenches and sockets in a metal box. Any measuring instruments, gauges, meters, etc, must be carefully stored where they cannot be damaged or become rusty.

Take a little care when tools are used. Hammer heads inevitably become marked and screwdrivers lose the keen edge on their blades from time to time. A little timely attention with emery cloth or a file will soon restore items like this to a good serviceable finish.

Working facilities

Not to be forgotten when discussing tools, is the workshop itself. If anything more than routine maintenance is to be carried out, some form of suitable working area becomes essential.

It is appreciated that many an owner mechanic is forced by circumstances to remove an engine or similar item, without the benefit of a garage or workshop. Having done this, any repairs should always be done under the cover of a roof.

Wherever possible, any dismantling should be done on a clean, flat workbench or table at a suitable working height.

Any workbench needs a vice: one with a jaw opening of 4 in (100 mm) is suitable for most jobs. As mentioned previously, some clean dry storage space is also required for tools, as well as for lubricants, cleaning fluids, touch-up paints and so on, which become necessary.

Another item which may be required, and which has a much more general usage, is an electric drill with a chuck capacity of at least 5/16 in (8 mm). This, together with a good range of twist drills, is virtually essential for fitting accessories such as mirrors and reversing lights.

Last, but not least, always keep a supply of old newspapers and clean, lint-free rags available and try to keep any working area as clean as possible.

Spanner jaw gap comparison table

Jaw gap (in)	Spanner size
0.250	$\frac{1}{4}$ in AF
0.276	7 mm
0.313	$\frac{5}{16}$ in AF
0.315	8 mm
0.344	$\frac{11}{32}$ in AF; $\frac{1}{8}$ in Whitworth
0.354	9 mm
0.375	$\frac{3}{8}$ in AF
0.394	10 mm
0.433	11 mm
0.438	$\frac{7}{16}$ in AF
0.445	$\frac{3}{16}$ in Whitworth; $\frac{1}{4}$ in BSF
0.472	12 mm
0.500	$\frac{1}{2}$ in AF
0.512	13 mm
0.525	$\frac{1}{4}$ in Whitworth; $\frac{5}{16}$ in BSF
0.551	14 mm
0.563	$\frac{9}{16}$ in AF
0.591	15 mm
0.600	$\frac{5}{16}$ in Whitworth; $\frac{3}{8}$ in BSF
0.625	$\frac{5}{8}$ in AF
0.630	16 mm
0.669	17 mm
0.686	$\frac{11}{16}$ in AF
0.709	18 mm
0.710	$\frac{3}{8}$ in Whitworth; $\frac{7}{16}$ in BSF
0.748	19 mm
0.750	$\frac{3}{4}$ in AF
0.813	$\frac{13}{16}$ in AF
0.820	$\frac{7}{16}$ in Whitworth; $\frac{1}{2}$ in BSF
0.866	22 mm
0.875	$\frac{7}{8}$ in AF
0.920	$\frac{1}{2}$ in Whitworth; $\frac{9}{16}$ in BSF
0.938	$\frac{15}{16}$ in AF
0.945	24 mm
1.000	1 in AF
1.010	$\frac{9}{16}$ in Whitworth; $\frac{5}{8}$ in BSF
1.024	26 mm
1.063	$1\frac{1}{16}$ in AF; 27 mm
1.100	$\frac{5}{8}$ in Whitworth; $\frac{11}{16}$ in BSF
1.125	$1\frac{1}{8}$ in AF
1.181	30 mm
1.200	$\frac{11}{16}$ in Whitworth; $\frac{3}{4}$ in BSF
1.250	$1\frac{1}{4}$ in AF
1.260	32 mm
1.300	$\frac{3}{4}$ in Whitworth; $\frac{7}{8}$ in BSF
1.313	$1\frac{5}{16}$ in AF
1.390	$\frac{13}{16}$ in Whitworth; $\frac{15}{16}$ in BSF
1.417	36 mm
1.438	$1\frac{7}{16}$ in AF
1.480	$\frac{7}{8}$ in Whitworth; 1 in BSF
1.500	$1\frac{1}{2}$ in AF
1.575	40 mm; $\frac{15}{16}$ in Whitworth
1.614	41 mm
1.625	$1\frac{5}{8}$ in AF
1.670	1 in Whitworth; $1\frac{1}{8}$ in BSF
1.688	$1\frac{11}{16}$ in AF
1.811	46 mm
1.813	$1\frac{13}{16}$ in AF
1.860	$1\frac{1}{8}$ in Whitworth; $1\frac{1}{4}$ in BSF
1.875	$1\frac{7}{8}$ in AF
1.969	50 mm
2.000	2 in AF
2.050	$1\frac{1}{4}$ in Whitworth; $1\frac{3}{8}$ in BSF
2.165	55 mm
2.362	60 mm

Use of English

As this book has been written in England, it uses the appropriate English component names, phrases, and spelling. Some of these differ from those used in America. Normally, these cause no difficulty, but to make sure, a glossary is printed below. In ordering spare parts remember the parts list may use some of these words:

English	American	English	American
Accelerator	Gas pedal	Locks	Latches
Aerial	Antenna	Methylated spirit	Denatured alcohol
Anti-roll bar	Stabiliser or sway bar	Motorway	Freeway, turnpike etc
Big-end bearing	Rod bearing	Number plate	License plate
Bonnet (engine cover)	Hood	Paraffin	Kerosene
Boot (luggage compartment)	Trunk	Petrol	Gasoline (gas)
Bulkhead	Firewall	Petrol tank	Gas tank
Bush	Bushing	'Pinking'	'Pinging'
Cam follower or tappet	Valve lifter or tappet	Prise (force apart)	Pry
Carburettor	Carburetor	Propeller shaft	Driveshaft
Catch	Latch	Quarterlight	Quarter window
Choke/venturi	Barrel	Retread	Recap
Circlip	Snap-ring	Reverse	Back-up
Clearance	Lash	Rocker cover	Valve cover
Crownwheel	Ring gear (of differential)	Saloon	Sedan
Damper	Shock absorber, shock	Seized	Frozen
Disc (brake)	Rotor/disk	Sidelight	Parking light
Distance piece	Spacer	Silencer	Muffler
Drop arm	Pitman arm	Sill panel (beneath doors)	Rocker panel
Drop head coupe	Convertible	Small end, little end	Piston pin or wrist pin
Dynamo	Generator (DC)	Spanner	Wrench
Earth (electrical)	Ground	Split cotter (for valve spring cap)	Lock (for valve spring retainer)
Engineer's blue	Prussian blue	Split pin	Cotter pin
Estate car	Station wagon	Steering arm	Spindle arm
Exhaust manifold	Header	Sump	Oil pan
Fault finding/diagnosis	Troubleshooting	Swarf	Metal chips or debris
Float chamber	Float bowl	Tab washer	Tang or lock
Free-play	Lash	Tappet	Valve lifter
Freewheel	Coast	Thrust bearing	Throw-out bearing
Gearbox	Transmission	Top gear	High
Gearchange	Shift	Torch	Flashlight
Grub screw	Setscrew, Allen screw	Trackrod (of steering)	Tie-rod (or connecting rod)
Gudgeon pin	Piston pin or wrist pin	Trailing shoe (of brake)	Secondary shoe
Halfshaft	Axleshaft	Transmission	Whole drive line
Handbrake	Parking brake	Tyre	Tire
Hood	Soft top	Van	Panel wagon/van
Hot spot	Heat riser	Vice	Vise
Indicator	Turn signal	Wheel nut	Lug nut
Interior light	Dome lamp	Windscreen	Windshield
Layshaft (of gearbox)	Countershaft	Wing/mudguard	Fender
Leading shoe (of brake)	Primary shoe		

Conversion factors

Length (distance)					
Inches (in)	X 25.4	= Millimetres (mm)	X 0.0394	= Inches (in)
Feet (ft)	X 0.305	= Metres (m)	X 3.281	= Feet (ft)
Miles	X 1.609	= Kilometres (km)	X 0.621	= Miles

Volume (capacity)				
Cubic inches (cu in; in^3)	X 16.387	= Cubic centimetres (cc; cm^3)	X 0.061	= Cubic inches (cu in; in^3)
Imperial pints (Imp pt)	X 0.568	= Litres (l)	X 1.76	= Imperial pints (Imp pt)
Imperial quarts (Imp qt)	X 1.137	= Litres (l)	X 0.88	= Imperial quarts (Imp qt)
Imperial quarts (Imp qt)	X 1.201	= US quarts (US qt)	X 0.833	= Imperial quarts (Imp qt)
US quarts (US qt)	X 0.946	= Litres (l)	X 1.057	= US quarts (US qt)
Imperial gallons (Imp gal)	X 4.546	= Litres (l)	X 0.22	= Imperial gallons (Imp gal)
Imperial gallons (Imp gal)	X 1.201	= US gallons (US gal)	X 0.833	= Imperial gallons (Imp gal)
US gallons (US gal)	X 3.785	= Litres (l)	X 0.264	= US gallons (US gal)

Mass (weight)				
Ounces (oz)	X 28.35	= Grams (g)	X 0.035	= Ounces (oz)
Pounds (lb)	X 0.454	= Kilograms (kg)	X 2.205	= Pounds (lb)

Force				
Ounces-force (ozf; oz)	X 0.278	= Newtons (N)	X 3.6	= Ounces-force (ozf; oz)
Pounds-force (lbf; lb)	X 4.448	= Newtons (N)	X 0.225	= Pounds-force (lbf; lb)
Newtons (N)	X 0.1	= Kilograms-force (kgf; kg)	X 9.81	= Newtons (N)

Pressure				
Pounds-force per square inch (psi; lbf/in^2; lb/in^2)	X 0.070	= Kilograms-force per square centimetre (kgf/cm^2; kg/cm^2)	X 14.223	= Pounds-force per square inch (psi; lbf/in^2; lb/in^2)
Pounds-force per square inch (psi; lbf/in^2; lb/in^2)	X 0.068	= Atmospheres (atm)	X 14.696	= Pounds-force per square inch (psi; lbf/in^2; lb/in^2)
Pounds-force per square inch (psi; lbf/in^2; lb/in^2)	X 0.069	= Bars	X 14.5	= Pounds-force per square inch (psi; lbf/in^2; lb/in^2)
Pounds-force per square inch (psi; lbf/in^2; lb/in^2)	X 6.895	= Kilopascals (kPa)	X 0.145	= Pounds-force per square inch (psi; lbf/in^2; lb/in^2)
Kilopascals (kPa)	X 0.01	= Kilograms-force per square centimetre (kgf/cm^2; kg/cm^2)	X 98.1	= Kilopascals (kPa)
Millibar (mbar)	X 100	= Pascals (Pa)	X 0.01	= Millibar (mbar)
Millibar (mbar)	X 0.0145	= Pounds-force per square inch (psi; lbf/in^2; lb/in^2)	X 68.947	= Millibar (mbar)
Millibar (mbar)	X 0.75	= Millimetres of mercury (mmHg)	X 1.333	= Millibar (mbar)
Millibar (mbar)	X 0.401	= Inches of water (inH_2O)	X 2.491	= Millibar (mbar)
Millimetres of mercury (mmHg)	X 0.535	= Inches of water (inH_2O)	X 1.868	= Millimetres of mercury (mmHg)
Inches of water (inH_2O)	X 0.036	= Pounds-force per square inch (psi; lbf/in^2; lb/in^2)	X 27.68	= Inches of water (inH_2O)

Torque (moment of force)				
Pounds-force inches (lbf in; lb in)	X 1.152	= Kilograms-force centimetre (kgf cm; kg cm)	X 0.868	= Pounds-force inches (lbf in; lb in)
Pounds-force inches (lbf in; lb in)	X 0.113	= Newton metres (Nm)	X 8.85	= Pounds-force inches (lbf in; lb in)
Pounds-force inches (lbf in; lb in)	X 0.083	= Pounds-force feet (lbf ft; lb ft)	X 12	= Pounds-force inches (lbf in; lb in)
Pounds-force feet (lbf ft; lb ft)	X 0.138	= Kilograms-force metres (kgf m; kg m)	X 7.233	= Pounds-force feet (lbf ft; lb ft)
Pounds-force feet (lbf ft; lb ft)	X 1.356	= Newton metres (Nm)	X 0.738	= Pounds-force feet (lbf ft; lb ft)
Newton metres (Nm)	X 0.102	= Kilograms-force metres (kgf m; kg m)	X 9.804	= Newton metres (Nm)

Power				
Horsepower (hp)	X 745.7	= Watts (W)	X 0.0013	= Horsepower (hp)

Velocity (speed)				
Miles per hour (miles/hr; mph)	X 1.609	= Kilometres per hour (km/hr; kph)	X 0.621	= Miles per hour (miles/hr; mph)

*Fuel consumption**				
Miles per gallon, Imperial (mpg)	X 0.354	= Kilometres per litre (km/l)	X 2.825	= Miles per gallon, Imperial (mpg)
Miles per gallon, US (mpg)	X 0.425	= Kilometres per litre (km/l)	X 2.352	= Miles per gallon, US (mpg)

Temperature

Degrees Fahrenheit = (°C x 1.8) + 32

Degrees Celsius (Degrees Centigrade; °C) = (°F - 32) x 0.56

**It is common practice to convert from miles per gallon (mpg) to litres/100 kilometres (l/100km), where mpg (Imperial) x l/100 km = 282 and mpg (US) x l/100 km = 235*

Index

A

B

C

T

V

W

HAYNES AUTOMOTIVE MANUALS

NOTE: New manuals are added to this list on a periodic basis. If you do not see a listing for your vehicle, consult your local Haynes dealer for the latest product information.

ALFA-ROMEO
531 **Alfa Romeo Sedan & Coupe** '73 thru '80

AMC
Jeep CJ – *see JEEP (412)*
694 **Mid-size models,** Concord, Hornet, Gremlin & Spirit '70 thru '83
934 **(Renault) Alliance & Encore** all models '83 thru '87

AUDI
615 **4000** all models '80 thru '87
428 **5000** all models '77 thru '83
1117 **5000** all models '84 thru '88
207 **Fox** all models '73 thru '79

AUSTIN
049 **Healey 100/6 & 3000** Roadster '56 thru '68
Healey Sprite – *see MG Midget Roadster (265)*

BLMC
260 **1100, 1300 & Austin America** '62 thru '74
527 **Mini** all models '59 thru '69
*646 **Mini** all models '69 thru '88

BMW
276 **320i** all 4 cyl models '75 thru '83
632 **528i & 530i** all models '75 thru '80
240 **1500 thru 2002** all models except Turbo '59 thru '77
348 **2500, 2800, 3.0 & Bavaria** '69 thru '76

BUICK
Century (front wheel drive) – *see GENERAL MOTORS A-Cars (829)*
*1627 **Buick, Oldsmobile & Pontiac Full-size (Front wheel drive)** all models '85 thru '90 **Buick** Electra, LeSabre and Park Avenue; **Oldsmobile** Delta 88 Royale, Ninety Eight and Regency; **Pontiac** Bonneville
*1551 **Buick Oldsmobile & Pontiac Full-size (Rear wheel drive)** **Buick** Electra '70 thru '84, Estate '70 thru '90, LeSabre '70 thru '79 **Oldsmobile** Custom Cruiser '70 thru '90, Delta 88 '70 thru '85, Ninety-eight '70 thru '84 **Pontiac** Bonneville '70 thru '86, Catalina '70 thru '81, Grandville '70 thru '75, Parisienne '84 thu '86
627 **Mid-size** all rear-drive **Regal & Century** models with V6, V8 and Turbo '74 thru '87
Regal – *see GENERAL MOTORS (1671)*
Skyhawk – *see GENERAL MOTORS J-Cars (766)*
552 **Skylark** all X-car models '80 thru '85

CADILLAC
*751 **Cadillac Rear Wheel Drive** all gasoline models '70 thru '90
Cimarron – *see GENERAL MOTORS J-Cars (766)*

CAPRI
296 **2000 MK I Coupe** all models '71 thru '75
283 **2300 MK II Coupe** all models '74 thru '78
205 **2600 & 2800** V6 Coupe '71 thru '75
375 **2800 Mk II** V6 Coupe '75 thru '78
Mercury Capri – *see FORD Mustang (654)*

CHEVROLET
*1477 **Astro & GMC Safari Mini-vans** all models '85 thru '90
554 **Camaro** V8 all models '70 thru '81
*866 **Camaro** all models '82 thru '90
Cavalier – *see GENERAL MOTORS J-Cars (766)*
Celebrity – *see GENERAL MOTORS A-Cars (829)*
625 **Chevelle, Malibu & El Camino** all V6 & V8 models '69 thru '87
449 **Chevette & Pontiac T1000** all models '76 thru '87
550 **Citation** all models '80 thru '85
*1628 **Corsica/Beretta** all models '87 thru '90
274 **Corvette** all V8 models '68 thru '82
*1336 **Corvette** all models '84 thru '89
704 **Full-size Sedans** Caprice, Impala, Biscayne, Bel Air & Wagons, all V6 & V8 models '69 thru '90
Lumina – *see GENERAL MOTORS (1671)*
319 **Luv Pick-up** all 2WD & 4WD models '72 thru '82
626 **Monte Carlo** all V6, V8 & Turbo models '70 thru '88
241 **Nova** all V8 models '69 thru '79
*1642 **Nova and Geo Prizm** all front wheel drive models, '85 thru '90
*420 **Pick-ups '67 thru '87 – Chevrolet & GMC,** all V8 & in-line 6 cyl 2WD & 4WD models '67 thru '87
*1664 **Pick-ups '88 thru '90 – Chevrolet & GMC** all full-size (C and K) models, '88 thru '90
*1727 **Sprint & Geo Metro** '85 thru '91
*831 **S-10 & GMC S-15 Pick-ups** all models '82 thru '90
*345 **Vans – Chevrolet & GMC,** V8 & in-line 6 cyl models '68 thru '89
208 **Vega** all models except Cosworth '70 thru '77

CHRYSLER
*1337 **Chrysler & Plymouth Mid-size** front wheel drive '82 thru '89
K-Cars – *see DODGE Aries (723)*
Laser – *see DODGE Daytona (1140)*

DATSUN
402 **200SX** all models '77 thru '79
647 **200SX** all models '80 thru '83
228 **B-210** all models '73 thru '78
525 **210** all models '78 thru '82
206 **240Z, 260Z & 280Z** Coupe & 2+2 '70 thru '78
563 **280ZX** Coupe & 2+2 '79 thru '83
300ZX – *see NISSAN (1137)*
679 **310** all models '78 thru '82
123 **510 & PL521 Pick-up** '68 thru '73
430 **510** all models '78 thru '81
372 **610** all models '72 thru '76
277 **620 Series Pick-up** all models '73 thru '79
720 Series Pick-up – *see NISSAN Pick-ups (771)*
376 **810/Maxima** all gasoline models '77 thru '84
124 **1200** all models '70 thru '73
368 **F10** all models '76 thru '79
Pulsar – *see NISSAN (876)*
Sentra – *see NISSAN (982)*
Stanza – *see NISSAN (981)*

DODGE
*723 **Aries & Plymouth Reliant** all models '81 thru '89
*1231 **Caravan & Plymouth Voyager Mini-Vans** all models '84 thru '89
699 **Challenger & Plymouth Saporro** all models '78 thru '83
236 **Colt** all models '71 thru '77
419 **Colt (rear wheel drive)** all models '77 thru '80
610 **Colt & Plymouth Champ (front wheel drive)** all models '78 thru '87
*556 **D50 & Plymouth Arrow Pick-ups** '79 thru '88
*1668 **Dakota Pick-up** all models '87 thru '90
234 **Dart & Plymouth Valiant** all 6 cyl models '67 thru '76
*1140 **Daytona & Chrysler Laser** all models '84 thru '89
*545 **Omni & Plymouth Horizon** all models '78 thru '90
*912 **Pick-ups** all full-size models '74 thru '90
*349 **Vans – Dodge & Plymouth** V8 & 6 cyl models '71 thru '89

FIAT
080 **124 Sedan & Wagon** all ohv & dohc models '66 thru '75
094 **124 Sport Coupe & Spider** '68 thru '78
310 **131 & Brava** all models '75 thru '81
479 **Strada** all models '79 thru '82
273 **X1/9** all models '74 thru '80

FORD
*1476 **Aerostar Mini-vans** all models '86 thru '90
788 **Bronco and Pick-ups** '73 thru '79
*880 **Bronco and Pick-ups** '80 thru '90
014 **Cortina MK II** all models except Lotus '66 thru '70
295 **Cortina MK III** 1600 & 2000 ohc '70 thru '76
268 **Courier Pick-up** all models '72 thru '82
789 **Escort & Mercury Lynx** all models '81 thru '90
560 **Fairmont & Mercury Zephyr** all in-line & V8 models '78 thru '83
334 **Fiesta** all models '77 thru '80
754 **Ford & Mercury Full-size,** Ford LTD & Mercury Marquis ('75 thru '82); Ford Custom 500, Country Squire, Crown Victoria & Mercury Colony Park ('75 thru '87); Ford LTD Crown Victoria & Mercury Gran Marquis ('83 thru '87)
359 **Granada & Mercury Monarch** all in-line, 6 cyl & V8 models '75 thru '80
773 **Ford & Mercury Mid-size,** Ford Thunderbird & Mercury Cougar ('75 thru '82); Ford LTD & Mercury Marquis ('83 thru '86); Ford Torino, Gran Torino, Elite, Ranchero pick-up, LTD II, Mercury Montego, Comet, XR-7 & Lincoln Versailles ('75 thru '86)
*654 **Mustang & Mercury Capri** all models including Turbo '79 thru '90
357 **Mustang V8** all models '64-1/2 thru '73
231 **Mustang II** all 4 cyl, V6 & V8 models '74 thru '78
204 **Pinto** all models '70 thru '74
649 **Pinto & Mercury Bobcat** all models '75 thru '80
*1026 **Ranger & Bronco II** all gasoline models '83 thru '89
*1421 **Taurus & Mercury Sable** '86 thru '90
*1418 **Tempo & Mercury Topaz** all gasoline models '84 thru '89
1338 **Thunderbird & Mercury Cougar/XR7** '83 thru '88
*1725 **Thunderbird & Mercury Cougar** '89 and '90
*344 **Vans** all V8 Econoline models '69 thru '90

GENERAL MOTORS
*829 **A-Cars** – Chevrolet Celebrity, Buick Century, Pontiac 6000 & Oldsmobile Cutlass Ciera all models '82 thru '89
*766 **J-Cars** – Chevrolet Cavalier, Pontiac J-2000, Oldsmobile Firenza, Buick Skyhawk & Cadillac Cimarron all models '82 thru '90
*1420 **N-Cars** – Buick Somerset '85 thru '87; Pontiac Grand Am and Oldsmobile Calais '85 thru '90; Buick Skylark '86 thru '90
*1671 **GM: Buick** Regal, **Chevrolet** Lumina, **Oldsmobile** Cutlass Supreme, **Pontiac** Grand Prix, all front wheel drive models '88 thru '90

GEO
Metro – *see CHEVROLET Sprint (1727)*
Tracker – *see SUZUKI Samurai (1626)*
Prizm – *see CHEVROLET Nova (1642)*

GMC
Safari – *see CHEVROLET ASTRO (1477)*
Vans & Pick-ups – *see CHEVROLET (420, 831, 345, 1664)*

(continued on next page)

** Listings shown with an asterisk (*) indicate model coverage as of this printing. These titles will be periodically updated to include later model years — consult your Haynes dealer for more information.*

HAYNES AUTOMOTIVE MANUALS

(continued from previous page)

NOTE: New manuals are added to this list on a periodic basis. If you do not see a listing for your vehicle, consult your local Haynes dealer for the latest product information.

HONDA
138 **360, 600 & Z** Coupe all models '67 thru '75
351 **Accord CVCC** all models '76 thru '83
*1221 **Accord** all models '84 thru '89
160 **Civic 1200** all models '73 thru '79
633 **Civic 1300 & 1500 CVCC** all models '80 thru '83
297 **Civic 1500 CVCC** all models '75 thru '79
*1227 **Civic** all models '84 thru '90
*601 **Prelude CVCC** all models '79 thru '89

HYUNDAI
*1552 **Excel** all models '86 thru '89

ISUZU
*1641 **Trooper & Pick-up**, all gasoline models '81 thru '90

JAGUAR
098 **MK I & II**, 240 & 340 Sedans '55 thru '69
*242 **XJ6** all 6 cyl models '68 thru '86
*478 **XJ12 & XJS** all 12 cyl models '72 thru '85
140 **XK-E** 3.8 & 4.2 all 6 cyl models '61 thru '72

JEEP
*1553 **Cherokee, Comanche & Wagoneer Limited** all models '84 thru '89
412 **CJ** all models '49 thru '86

LADA
*413 **1200, 1300. 1500 & 1600** all models including Riva '74 thru '86

LAND ROVER
314 **Series II, IIA, & III** all 4 cyl gasoline models '58 thru '86
529 **Diesel** all models '58 thru '80

MAZDA
648 **626** Sedan & Coupe (rear wheel drive) all models '79 thru '82
*1082 **626 & MX-6 (front wheel drive)** all models '83 thru '90
*267 **B1600, B1800 & B2000 Pick-ups** '72 thru '90
370 **GLC Hatchback (rear wheel drive)** all models '77 thru '83
757 **GLC (front wheel drive)** all models '81 thru '86
109 **RX2** all models '71 thru '75
096 **RX3** all models '72 thru '76
460 **RX-7** all models '79 thru '85
*1419 **RX-7** all models '86 thru '89

MERCEDES-BENZ
*1643 **190 Series** all four-cylinder gasoline models, '84 thru '88
346 **230, 250 & 280** Sedan, Coupe & Roadster all 6 cyl sohc models '68 thru '72
983 **280 123 Series** all gasoline models '77 thru '81
698 **350 & 450** Sedan, Coupe & Roadster all models '71 thru '80
697 **Diesel 123 Series** 200D, 220D, 240D, 240TD, 300D, 300CD, 300TD, 4- & 5-cyl incl. Turbo '76 thru '85

MERCURY
See FORD Listing

MG
475 **MGA** all models '56 thru '62
111 **MGB** Roadster & GT Coupe all models '62 thru '80
265 **MG Midget & Austin Healey Sprite Roadster** '58 thru '80

MITSUBISHI
*1669 **Cordia, Tredia, Galant, Precis & Mirage** '83 thru '90
Pick-up – *see Dodge D-50 (556)*

MORRIS
074 **(Austin) Marina 1.8** all models '71 thru '80
024 **Minor 1000** sedan & wagon '56 thru '71

NISSAN
1137 **300ZX** all Turbo & non-Turbo models '84 thru '89
*1341 **Maxima** all models '85 thru '89
*771 **Pick-ups/Pathfinder** gas models '80 thru '88
*876 **Pulsar** all models '83 thru '86
*982 **Sentra** all models '82 thru '90
*981 **Stanza** all models '82 thru '90

OLDSMOBILE
Custom Cruiser – *see BUICK Full-size (1551)*
658 **Cutlass** all standard gasoline V6 & V8 models '74 thru '88
Cutlass Ciera – *see GENERAL MOTORS A-Cars (829)*
Cutlass Supreme – *see GENERAL MOTORS (1671)*
Firenza – *see GENERAL MOTORS J-Cars (766)*
Ninety-eight – *see BUICK Full-size (1551)*
Omega – *see PONTIAC Phoenix & Omega (551)*

PEUGEOT
161 **504** all gasoline models '68 thru '79
663 **504** all diesel models '74 thru '83

PLYMOUTH
425 **Arrow** all models '76 thru '80
For all other PLYMOUTH titles, see DODGE listing.

PONTIAC
T1000 – *see CHEVROLET Chevette (449)*
J-2000 – *see GENERAL MOTORS J-Cars (766)*
6000 – *see GENERAL MOTORS A-Cars (829)*
1232 **Fiero** all models '84 thru '88
555 **Firebird** all V8 models except Turbo '70 thru '81
*867 **Firebird** all models '82 thru '89
Full-size Rear Wheel Drive – *see Buick, Oldsmobile, Pontiac Full-size (1551)*
Grand Prix – *see GENERAL MOTORS (1671)*
551 **Phoenix & Oldsmobile Omega** all X-car models '80 thru '84

PORSCHE
*264 **911** all Coupe & Targa models except Turbo & Carrera 4 '65 thru '89
239 **914** all 4 cyl models '69 thru '76
397 **924** all models including Turbo '76 thru '82
*1027 **944** all models including Turbo '83 thru '89

RENAULT
141 **5 Le Car** all models '76 thru '83
079 **8 & 10** all models with 58.4 cu in engines '62 thru '72
097 **12 Saloon & Estate** all models 1289 cc engines '70 thru '80
768 **15 & 17** all models '73 thru '79
081 **16** all models 89.7 cu in & 95.5 cu in engines '65 thru '72
598 **18i & Sportwagon** all models '81 thru '86
Alliance & Encore – *see AMC (934)*
984 **Fuego** all models '82 thru '85

ROVER
085 **3500 & 3500S Sedan** 215 cu in engines '68 thru '76
*365 **3500 SDI V8** all models '76 thru '85

SAAB
198 **95 & 96** V4 all models '66 thru '75
247 **99** all models including Turbo '69 thru '80
*980 **900** all models including Turbo '79 thru '88

SUBARU
237 **1100, 1300, 1400 & 1600** all models '71 thru '79
*681 **1600 & 1800** 2WD & 4WD all models '80 thru '89

SUZUKI
*1626 **Samurai/Sidekick and Geo Tracker** all models '86 thru '89

TOYOTA
*1023 **Camry** all models '83 thru '90
150 **Carina Sedan** all models '71 thru '74
229 **Celica ST, GT & liftback** all models '71 thru '77
437 **Celica** all models '78 thru '81
*935 **Celica** all models except front-wheel drive and Supra '82 thru '85
680 **Celica Supra** all models '79 thru '81
1139 **Celica Supra** all in-line 6-cylinder models '82 thru '86
361 **Corolla** all models '75 thru '79
961 **Corolla** all models (rear wheel drive) '80 thru '87
*1025 **Corolla** all models (front wheel drive) '84 thru '91
*636 **Corolla Tercel** all models '80 thru '82
230 **Corona & MK II** all 4 cyl sohc models '69 thru '74
360 **Corona** all models '74 thru '82
*532 **Cressida** all models '78 thru '82
313 **Land Cruiser** all models '68 thru '82
200 **MK II** all 6 cyl models '72 thru '76
*1339 **MR2** all models '85 thru '87
304 **Pick-up** all models '69 thru '78
*656 **Pick-up** all models '79 thru '90

TRIUMPH
112 **GT6 & Vitesse** all models '62 thru '74
113 **Spitfire** all models '62 thru '81
028 **TR2, 3, 3A, & 4A** Roadsters '52 thru '67
031 **TR250 & 6** Roadsters '67 thru '76
322 **TR7** all models '75 thru '81

VW
091 **411 & 412** all 103 cu in models '68 thru '73
159 **Beetle & Karmann Ghia** all models '54 thru '79
238 **Dasher** all gasoline models '74 thru '81
*884 **Rabbit, Jetta, Scirocco, & Pick-up** all gasoline models '74 thru '89 & **Convertible** '80 thru '89
451 **Rabbit, Jetta & Pick-up** all diesel models '77 thru '84
082 **Transporter 1600** all models '68 thru '79
226 **Transporter 1700, 1800 & 2000** all models '72 thru '79
084 **Type 3 1500 & 1600** all models '63 thru '73
1029 **Vanagon** all air-cooled models '80 thru '83

VOLVO
203 **120, 130 Series & 1800 Sports** '61 thru '73
129 **140 Series** all models '66 thru '74
244 **164** all models '68 thru '75
*270 **240 Series** all models '74 thru '90
400 **260 Series** all models '75 thru '82
*1550 **740 & 760 Series** all models '82 thru '88

SPECIAL MANUALS
1479 **Automotive Body Repair & Painting Manual**
1654 **Automotive Electrical Manual**
1480 **Automotive Heating & Air Conditioning Manual**
1763 **Ford Engine Overhaul Manual**
482 **Fuel Injection Manual**
1666 **Small Engine Repair Manual**
299 **SU Carburetors** thru '88
393 **Weber Carburetors** thru '79
300 **Zenith/Stromberg CD Carburetors** thru '76

See your dealer for other available titles

4-1-91

* *Listings shown with an asterisk (*) indicate model coverage as of this printing. These titles will be periodically updated to include later model years — consult your Haynes dealer for more information.*

Over 100 Haynes motorcycle manuals also available

Haynes Publications Inc., P.O. Box 978, Newbury Park, CA 91320 • (818) 889-5400 • (805) 498-6703